FRANK J. LAUSCHE

FRANK J. LAUSCHE
Ohio's Great Political Maverick

A Biography by
James E. Odenkirk

ORANGE FRAZER *PRESS*
Wilmington, Ohio

ISBN 1-882203-49-6
Copyright 2005 James E. Odenkirk

Additional copies of *Frank J. Lausche: Ohio's Great Political Maverick* may be ordered directly from:

Orange Frazer Press
P.O. Box 214
Wilmington OH 45177

Telephone 1.800.852.9332 for price and shipping information.
Website: www.orangefrazer.com

Layout: Tim Fauley
Jacket & Page Design: Jeff Fulwiler
On the cover: Re-elect Lausche pin courtesy of the Western Reserve Historical Society, Cleveland, Ohio and the Roosevelt-Lausche pin courtesy of the Ohio Historical Society.

Library of Congress Cataloging-in-Publication Data

Odenkirk, James E. (James Ellis), 1928-
    Frank J. Lausche : Ohio's great political maverick : a biography / by James E. Odenkirk.
       p. cm.
    Includes bibliographical references and index.
    ISBN 1-882203-49-6
       1. Lausche, Frank John, b. 1895. 2. Legislators--United States--Biography. 3. United States. Congress. Senate--Biography. 4. Governors--Ohio--Biography. 5. Ohio--Politics and government--1865-1950. 6. Ohio--Politics and government--1951- 7. Slovenian Americans--Ohio--Biography. I. Title.

E840.8.L35O34 2005
977.1'843'092--dc22
[B]
                                                    2005048769

For Benita

What is the use of being
elected or re-elected
unless you stand for something?

—Grover Cleveland

Table of Contents

Foreword

THE FOLLOWING ARE EXCERPTS FROM A SPEECH given by Senator George V. Voinovich in Cleveland in commemoration of Frank J. Lausche's 100th birthday. The Senator gave this presentation on November 12, 1995, two days before Lausche's birthday.

One can't help but be impressed when you consider Frank Lausche's achievements in light of his humble beginnings. Often I've had to pinch myself when I realize how far my own family has come, and how the grandson of immigrants grew up to become governor—yet how much further was Frank Lausche's journey, the third child born to Slovenian parents just four years after they arrived in America.

I remember a story my Dad told me about an older architect who had been his boss when he started out in his profession. Later in his career, he wanted very much to work for Dad. This was an exceptionally talented architect, and after he was hired, my Dad asked him why—when he could have joined just about any firm of his choosing—he wanted to work for him. " Mr. Voinovich," he said, "others started their businesses at a point well ahead of where you began, yet you've equaled their success. I wanted to work with someone who has gone the distance."

People like my mother and father—and Frank Lausche—cleared many paths for those of Central and Eastern European descent. They taught us that we could accomplish whatever our abilities, our determination, and our best efforts would allow, and that we could succeed if we worked hard. I remember many years ago sharing with my Mother how proud I was of my Slovenian heritage. She turned to me and said, "you know, it's good to be proud of who you are. But you should also be proud because of what you went through." She told me how, after she graduated from college, she couldn't get a teaching job because she was Slovenian and Catholic, and how my father faced a great deal of discrimination when he was looking for work because his name was Voinovich.

Frank Lausche was truly a trailblazer. He was the first ethnic, Catholic Democrat to become Governor of Ohio [and United States Senator] and I'm the first ethnic and the first Catholic Republican to become Governor of Ohio. When I first went to the Legislature, I was asked, "are you a Republican?" My response was, "I'm a Lausche Republican!" Frank Lausche never forgot the language, the culture, and the people of his Slovenian heritage. During his public service career, he mingled with presidents and princes, with kings and commoners, yet he always came back to his old neighborhood—to his home.

As an American of Slovenian descent, Frank Lausche kept a watchful eye on events and conditions in his parents' homeland. I wish he could have witnessed the dramatic transformation that has taken place in Slovenia (1995). I know Frank Lausche would be as impressed as we are with the progress Slovenia has made in such a short time. He would have been just as optimistic about how a thriving Slovenian economy can provide a model to Eastern Europe and the rest of what was once Yugoslavia for how peace, political stability and free enterprise can improve the quality of life for a nation's people.

Eastern Europe was another topic Frank Lausche and I agreed upon and discussed. My first research paper in graduate school was about how Yugoslavia was sold out at the Yalta Conference when the Tito regime was installed. Lausche was strongly in favor of the self-determination Eastern Europe had been promised, but had been denied. And, he believed in free enterprise rather than socialism. Those were the beliefs he had in common with Ronald Reagan, and they influenced his later support for Reagan's presidential bid.

Frank Lausche was truly an inspiration—he was Mayor of Cleveland during my early years. Dad got to know him through the Yugoslav University Club. After Mom and Dad were married, Dad's first architectural office was on Carnegie—not too far from where Frank and Jane lived—and their friendship continued. In fact, Dad stayed close to him throughout Frank Lausche's political career.

As I look back to that time, one of the worst disasters Cleveland ever suffered through was the East Ohio Gas Explosion in June (sic) of 1944 (The explosion was October 11, 1944). As Mayor, when Frank Lausche walked among the rubble and ashes, he wept for the lost lives and the destroyed households. Yet he acted swiftly to coordinate the community's resources and commence the healing process. I remember as a little boy how much I was moved by the depth of Frank Lausche's concern for his community.

Frank Lausche's most profound influence on me, on Ohio, and for that matter, on America—was described in November 2, 1995 article in *Ameriška Domovina*: "...the consistent theme that ran through his life is very basic to his origins and love of his Slovenian heritage: integrity; honesty; diligence to the task at hand; respect for faith, culture, and other people; and the belief that education is the best preparation for life and the primary means to eliminate ignorance. His brief personal motto summarized his Slovenian principles: "Mati, Domovina, Bog." Mother (family), Country (service), and God (religion)."

Frank Lausche was often called the Lincoln of Ohio. In a letter to Frank Lausche on his 90th birthday in 1985, then-President Ronald Reagan acknowledged this when he wrote, "People readily see how much you resemble Lincoln in homespun good sense and rugged honesty."

Frank Lausche's bedrock values anchored him throughout his career in public service as a Cleveland Municipal Judge (1932–1936), Cuyahoga County Common

Pleas Judge (1937–1940), Mayor of Cleveland (1941–44), Ohio's only five-term Governor (1945–1947; 1949–1957), and U.S. Senator from Ohio (1957–1968).

Frank Lausche was intensely patriotic. He served in World War I, and he achieved the rank of second lieutenant. He was also fiercely independent in his thinking. Although he ran for office as a Democrat, he was respected—and sought after—by both parties because he served with vigor, energy, and unwavering integrity. He would not accept undue influence from individuals or groups that had patently partisan agendas. "When I go home," he said, "I want to lay my head on my pillow and feel that I have acted honestly, in accordance with my own judgment, without dictation from outsiders." This was Frank J. Lausche's legacy.

(George V. Voinovich, a native of Cleveland, led the Cleveland comeback, serving as Mayor and setting a record for longevity (1979–1989). He was elected Governor of Ohio for two terms (1991–1999). Voinovich was elected to the United States Senate in 1998 (forty years after Lausche entered the hallowed halls of the Senate) and is currently serving his second term. His mother was Slovenian and his father of Serbian heritage.)

Preface

Shortly after Frank J. Lausche died in 1990 at the age of ninety-four, Dr. Rudolph M. Susel, editor of *American Home* (*Ameriška Domovina*) made a pertinent observation. He wrote that although much had been written about the venerable politician, a scholarly study of Lausche's political career was long overdue. Excellent biographies have been written about several of Lausche's Ohio contemporaries, notably Robert Taft, John W. Bricker, William B. Saxbe, and Michael DiSalle. No doubt a biography about James A. Rhodes will be forthcoming. It is my hope that this biography of Lausche may fill a literary void on the Ohio political scene.

During his long life, Lausche saw many changes in America and in the world. He witnessed the transition from horse drawn buggies on dirt roads to paved highways with fast moving automobiles. He saw his hometown of Cleveland become a melting pot for many ethnic families. Expanding suburbs encircled his early neighborhood near St. Clair Avenue and 60th Street. The Forest City grew to become one of the largest and most productive cities in the country, only to slide into an abyss. Critics identified Cleveland with the moniker *rust city*. Mark Winegardner, in his excellent novel entitled *Crooked River Burning*, vividly describes the scene in the rust city during the last half of the twentieth century.

The son of Slovenian immigrants, Lausche's epic began ten years after his father, a steel worker, came to America in 1885. He settled on Cleveland's east side and became part of the largest Slovenian settlement in the United States. Frank Lausche was born November 14, 1895 (four years to the day prior to my father's birth). During his youth Lausche received practical experience from his dad who became a saloon keeper, language interpreter for immigrants from Slovenia and a community leader. When Frank was age twelve, his father died, and Frank's brother, Louis, Jr., succumbed three years later of tuberculosis. The six remaining siblings and especially Frank—now 15 and titular head of the family—helped Ma Lausche, their revered mother, provide for the family.

Lausche found time to enjoy his love of baseball, and he became a crack infielder on the Cleveland sandlots. The young athlete was so good he believed he had a chance to play in the major leagues. He played minor league ball in Duluth, Minnesota and Lawrence, Massachusetts. Unfortunately Lausche's inability to hit a curve ball led to his downfall. The 22 year old joined the army in 1918, a few months prior to the end of World War I. When he was discharged in 1919 as a 2nd lieutenant, his mother convinced him that pursuing a law degree would provide more financial security than an unpredictable career in professional baseball. Lausche reluctantly agreed and received a law degree from John Marshall Law School in his hometown, placing near the top of his class in the state law exams. After two defeats as a candidate for Ohio state legislature, Lausche began a successful political career that lasted over 35 years. In 1928 Lausche married Jane Sheal, also from Cleveland, who became the ideal partner for her sometimes-aloof husband. They were married for 53 years.

Lausche's illustrious political career gained momentum when he was appointed to fill a vacancy on Cleveland's municipal bench in 1932. Voters elected him to this same post the following year. In 1937 Lausche was elected to the Cuyahoga County Court of Common Pleas, where he became known for his efforts to assist the so-called less fortunate. He accepted labor cases other judges were apparently reluctant to handle, fearing their decisions would foment repercussions from labor unions and the electorate. His work as a judge was not limited to making decisions on the bench. Lausche became known as Fearless Frank, Crime-Busting Judge in the late 1930s. He and safety director Eliot Ness took the initiative by closing three large gambling houses in outlying sections of Cleveland.

Lausche's success in routing the gamblers out of the suburbs of Cleveland won for him much public notoriety and praise. In 1941 and 1943 he campaigned for and won election as Mayor of Cleveland with large voting majorities. The attack on Pearl Harbor occurred one month after Lausche's first election. He faced a myriad of problems during his wartime tenure. More than half of the city's population of nine hundred thousand was foreign born or first- or second-generation Americans, and their loyalties during wartime were divided. Strikes were frequent due to low wages.

Avowing to a principle of being on the level with everybody, Lausche steered clear of major trouble, building a solid record as Mayor and catching the attention of state and national Democratic leaders. Concurrently, Lausche began to drift away from local and state Democratic organizations. The terms *independent* and *the man who walks alone* began to fit Lausche's mystique.

Lausche's star continued to shine in the 1940s, and he was encouraged to seek the governorship of Ohio. With the support of local newspapers, Lausche was elected to the state's highest office in 1944 where he had waged his campaign independent of party help. He initiated his personal style of courting voters by visiting county fairs, attending small town meetings and capturing the interest of rural voters. Lausche's election represented a victory over tradition. It was the first time in Ohio history a Catholic had been elected to the Governor's office.

This triumph marked the beginning of five two-year terms Lausche served as Ohio's chief executive. (Thomas J. Herbert defeated Lausche in 1946 by a narrow plurality of thirty-eight thousand votes.) Lausche, tall, handsome, and bushy haired retained a figure befitting a former baseball player. The attractive Jane Lausche provided the perfect touch as First Lady. Lausche's tenure in office was marked by frugal fiscal policies, which pleased the mostly GOP-controlled General Assemblies. His management of the Governor's office was not unlike that of Republican John W. Bricker, his predecessor. The Governor fought off lobbyists and pressure groups of all kinds. The popular Lausche attempted to run the state office based upon four principles: law and order, economy, equality of treatment among conflicting economic groups, and the pursuit of unity between city and rural interests. Inevitably Lausche's style of governance offended certain groups. Labor scorned him. Regular Democrats disliked him for his open and successful wooing of Republican voters. The crafty Lausche offered little or no assistance to running mates on the Democratic ticket and dodged all discussions of campaign issues.

After five terms as Governor, Lausche realized he should pursue a new challenge—the United States Senate. This he did for two terms from 1957–1969. Lausche found the Senate to be a different challenge where one matched wits with 95 different personalities (99 members after 1959 when Alaska and Hawaii gained admission to the Union). Lausche's tenure in the Senate proved to be his least satisfying experience in the political arena. He found himself on the losing side of domestic issues the majority of the time. Increasingly taciturn and rebellious, Lausche became known as the northern Harry Byrd. He crossed the aisle regularly to vote against spending bills advocated by John Kennedy during the New Frontier era and by Lyndon Johnson in his efforts to build a so-called Great Society.

Lausche was a true patriot who abhorred Communism with vehemence, nearly fanatical in nature. He served on the Foreign Relations Committee and, for the most part, supported Johnson's policies regarding Vietnam. Lausche was definitely in the camp with the hawks. He began to mollify his stance on Vietnam in early 1968. Lausche finally fell victim in the 1968 primary election to a powerful labor union campaign augmented by a well-organized Democratic state party who shunned the maverick ways of the incumbent. John J. Gilligan, a young liberal from Cincinnati carried the fight to Lausche and won convincingly. The 72-year-old warhorse was shunted to the sidelines. Estranged from his party, the non-conformist maverick voted for Republican presidential nominees until his death.

In retrospect, Lausche's political career left behind no impressive compilation of enduring achievements. He was a reactive politician, seldom one to seek notoriety by pushing for new legislation. Such behavior would have forced the statesman to go against his posture of frugality and balanced budgets. Ohio's most successful politicians, including Lausche, were able to move skillfully among the state's power blocs, creating a public image of rectitude and incorruptibility. Political opponents found it difficult to link Lausche with any scandals.

Lausche, the great vote getter, was a man of the people. He believed in the spirit of individual responsibility and the ideals that to him made America great: notably hard work, perseverance and readiness to face the next challenge, no matter the hardship.

Friends and relatives often ask me why I decided to write a biography of Frank J. Lausche, particularly in the twilight of my residence on this planet. The answer is associated with a late career venture into the study of American history. History is a subject that I find exhilarating. I had already earned a doctorate degree, but for credibility as a historian, I chose to pursue advanced degrees in history. Under the expert tutelage of Professor James R. Kearney, I received a master's degree in history at Arizona State University. My intellectual appetite whetted, I continued my studies at Northern Arizona University in Flagstaff. My mentor, Professor Monte Poen, a Truman scholar, pointed me in the right direction. After I completed forty semester hours of course work, only comprehensive exams and a dissertation remained to earn my doctorate in American history. In 1997 Benita, my wife, and I chose to move to Boise, Idaho. Dr. Poen retired at the same time and gave me sage advice: "Just write the book."

Being an obedient student, I accepted his advice. A native Ohioan from Mansfield, I had known of Frank Lausche. He served as Governor in the late 1940s and early 1950s when I attended The Ohio State University, my alma mater. I knew of his place in Ohio's political history. Research for this biography began in 1996. This literary accomplishment became a labor of love. The motivating force negated a need for faculty promotion or merit pay.

I did not collect my research materials on the backs of graduate students, then take personal credit for the final product, a disturbing practice prevalent in graduate programs. With rare exceptions, the collection and assemblage of research materials was a one-person undertaking. I followed an adage actor John Housman made popular in a television commercial, "We do it the old-fashioned way." A Luddite in my use of a computer, I wrote my rough copy of the biography in longhand (many pens and pencils). Benita transposed my often-illegible penmanship into a six hundred page typewritten manuscript.

Few biographies are collaborative efforts, but it is unlikely any such enterprise is completed without support from many people. This is certainly true with this publication. A variety of individuals have assisted in important ways. I wish to acknowledge the assistance and encouragement of the following people who contributed in a myriad of ways: William Meyers and the professional staff at the Ohio Historical Society. Cliff Eckle and Duryea Kemp were helpful in making available Lausche's artifacts donated to the special collections section of the Ohio Historical Society. Ann Sindelar and her assistants were particularly cooperative in helping me with my research at Western Reserve Historical Society; the staff at the Cleveland Public Library and the Cleveland *Plain Dealer*; Linda Deitch of the Columbus *Dispatch*; Gerri Hopkins, office manager of The Slovenian National Home located nearby Lausche's childhood home; Paul Hribar; Terry Demchak of the Catholic Cemeteries Association in Cleveland; Gerry Soule and Guen Johnson.

Fred Schuld and Joe Simenic were my "Cleveland connections" and verified the accuracy of important research materials when I was unable to travel to Ohio.

Behind the scenes the following were indeed helpful: Glenn Metzdorff, Don Demkee, Thomas Vail, Warren Van Tine, Lee Lowenfish and Senator George Voinovich. Lausche's Slovenian friends in Washington DC were most gracious, namely Cyril and Conrad Mejac and Stanley Sustersic. Also in Washington DC Virginia Wells, daughter of Ralph Locher, provided insightful information about Lausche's personal and professional life in the Capitol. Bishop Edward A. Pevec, a close friend of the Lausches, was generous in sharing anecdotes about a fellow Slovenian.

James V. and Madeline Debevec, long-time friends of the Lausche family and publishers of *American Home* directed me to important resources in my quest for pertinent information. Rudolph Susel, editor of *American Home* took time to provide answers to critical issues in the life of Mr. Lausche. He contributed excellent photographs to supplement the text. Only a few relatives of the Lausche family are still living. Two nieces, Gloria Rado and, in particular Sally Jones, daughter of August and Francis Lausche Uranker, were most hospitable and never seemed to tire of my incessant questions about their aunt and uncle. Sally generously gave me several photographs. I am indebted to both of Lausche's nieces.

In addition to Professors Kearney and Poen, the staff at Hayden Library, Arizona State University assisted me when needed. Fellow historians and friends Steve Gietescher, Bill Kirwin and Larry Gerlach would not allow me to give up on this project. I am grateful to the following individuals from the "heart of it all" who consented to write a few lines for the dust jacket: Richard O. Davies, John J. Gilligan, Brent Larkin, William B. Saxbe, James V. Stanton and my good friend Gary Krahenbuhl (who wishes he were from the Buckeye State). I would be remiss if I did not acknowledge my sister and brother-in-law, Barbara and Albert Wadley, who always gave me assistance with logistics when needed.

Like many historians, I yearn for writing skills that might approximate those of authors like David McCullough and Richard Dalleck. Short of that likelihood, the next best strategy was to recruit an editor whose competence helped smooth out the rough edges in my literary efforts. Jude Anson, my editor, affirmed her skill in converting my research into what I hope is enjoyable and meaningful reading. She has my sincere appreciation for going the extra mile. Any errors of fact or interpretation are entirely my responsibility. If I have failed to recognize any individuals who gave me assistance, accept my apology and chalk this miscue to my advanced age.

The dedication of this book to my wife and chief critic is a sincere expression of love and appreciation for her patience and untold hours of typing the manuscript. Her thoughtful editorial suggestions were most always accepted as an improvement over my initial draft. She has remained unusually quiet when I mention the possibility of writing another book.

(Early family photo) Frank J. Lausche's parents and three oldest children. From left to right: Louis, Jr., Frank and Josephine (shown above). (Courtesy of Dr. Rudolph Susel)

one

Early Cleveland
and the Arrival of Slovenes

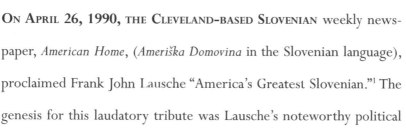

ON APRIL 26, 1990, THE CLEVELAND-BASED SLOVENIAN weekly newspaper, *American Home*, (*Ameriška Domovina* in the Slovenian language), proclaimed Frank John Lausche "America's Greatest Slovenian."[1] The genesis for this laudatory tribute was Lausche's noteworthy political career. Lausche, son of immigrant parents, climbed the political ladder to serve as a judge for the Cleveland Municipal Court, judge for the Cuyahoga County Common Pleas Court, Mayor of Cleveland, Governor of Ohio (a record five terms), and United States Senator (two terms). The judgment for whether any individual is the *greatest* based upon his accomplishments and ethnic background is a perilous task at best. Witness the debate that ensues when so-called experts are asked to name the greatest President, the greatest professional baseball player, the greatest orchestra, or the greatest fictional author. Definitions of greatness vary widely. No criterion is objective. In characterizing Lausche as the greatest, it seems pertinent to explain why this word is applicable to him and in what context.

Lausche was extremely proud of his Slovenian heritage, as well as of his achievements. He made reference to his ethnic background in speech after speech. His political career in the Buckeye State is best exemplified by his own words on his 80th birthday at St. Vitus Catholic Church located literally next door to his childhood home. "I was born less than 500 feet from here. I think of the Slovenian songs we sang then...and which I carry in my heart all the time.... The governorship, the senatorship all sink into insignificance.... Standing out most... are the friendships of my youth and the people of the neighborhood where I was reared. Forgotten is the fame of the offices I held." Without boasting Lausche believed he was the forerunner in giving many representatives of ethnic groups in Ohio an opportunity to achieve high public offices. His name Lausche was foreign and provoked many devious interpretations. "In southern Ohio, I was accused of being a slave of the Vatican of Rome, prepared to convert the Capital of Ohio into a branch of the Roman hierarchy. In northern Ohio, I was accused of being a renegade of the Catholic Church because I married my wife Jane, a member of the Methodist church."[2]

Lausche was one of the common people, who drove an old car, wore wrinkled suits, and seemingly didn't bother to comb his hair. His bushy, uncombed mane was his trademark.

Unless one watched him campaign, it was difficult to understand how this young descendent of Catholic immigrants appealed to white Anglo-Saxon, Protestant farmers of central and southern Ohio—decidedly a deeply conservative and prejudiced lot. Yet he did appeal to them. Lausche had them believing he was another Abraham Lincoln, a rugged, independent individual who could not be intimidated. He was representative of all the good old American verities, beholden to no one. To the ethnic groups in Cleveland he was simply one of their own. To the downstate small-townsmen he was for economy in government, against unions and bosses, in favor of home, mother, and the American flag. Lausche was one of the common people, who drove an old car, wore wrinkled suits, and seemingly didn't bother to comb his hair. His bushy, uncombed mane was his trademark.

One fact remained true throughout Lausche's political career: He was a strict conservative when it came to American foreign policy. He believed one could not sacrifice principle for expediency in foreign policy decisions. A rabid anti-communist, Lausche believed that as long as people were under the yoke of Communism or other totalitarian forms of government, liberty and freedom were in jeopardy.

One can be certain that Frank J. Lausche, then United States Senator, was not visiting his hometown on January 7, 1959. For it was then that Anastas Mikoyan, an Armenian who made good in politics by becoming Deputy Premier of the Union of Soviet Socialist Republics (USSR), visited Cleveland, and reportedly was visibly moved by his first glimpse of the Lake Erie metropolis. Those who stood near him when he looked at the downtown skyline swear the old Communist's mustache twitched and his eyes became misty as he raised an arm in comrade approbation and said, "Now you're talking. This is my kind of town!"[3]

This quotation may or may not be completely accurate, because even the best encomiums occasionally lose their meaning in translation. Something good must have piqued President Mikoyan's interest. Periodically local chamber of commerce members have expounded on Cleveland's virtues with the attention-getting slogan "The Best Location in the Nation." At one time, the lake front city was the largest city in population in Ohio and fifth largest in the nation. Like many large cities in the United States, however, Cleveland experienced long-term economic slumps after World War II and even bankruptcy in 1978, prompting pundits to disparagingly label the city as *the mistake by the lake*. Certainly this epitaph was less applicable in 1982 when, under the leadership of Mayor George Voinovich, Cleveland gained recognition as an All-American City. The city was no longer *the best kept secret* as once aptly termed by George E. Condon, Jr.. A long-time columnist for the Cleveland *Plain Dealer* and author of a popular history of the largest small town in America, he made Cleveland his beat five days a week.

⤳

SITUATED ON A PARCEL OF LAND KNOWN AS WESTERN RESERVE, Cleveland was founded in 1796 by a company led by Moses Cleaveland. Seven years later Ohio became the 17th state to join the union. Cleaveland was a member of the newly formed Connecticut Land Company, which negotiated the purchase of the Reserve from the Mohawk and Seneca representatives of two tribes of the mighty Six Nations. Although the town was named after him, Cleaveland in actuality spent less than a month there. (The spelling of the city of Cleveland differs from its namesake as a result of a surveyor's spelling error when recording the name on the first maps.) Stagnant waters and marshes in nearby areas along the meandering Cuyahoga River bred malaria, fevers, and other diseases at such a rapid pace, that nearly all development was slowed.[4]

By the turn of the nineteenth century the U.S. Census reported fifteen hundred residents in the entire Reserve, citing the only full-time resident of Cleveland as Lorenzo Carter, a member of the original survey party. Soon the village took hold, and by the 1830s, Cleveland became a center of frontier commerce, with the Erie Canal to the east and roadways being built to the west. The celebrated English author Charles Dickens visited America in 1842. His travels took him to Northern Ohio and Cleveland, "We lay all Sunday night at a town (and a beautiful town, too) called Cleveland...on Lake Erie. I found [Cleveland] a pretty town."[5] The town's early growth from a middle-ranked Western Reserve village to a dominant city in northeastern Ohio resulted from canal construction in the 1830s and 1840s, which connected Cleveland to southern and eastern Ohio grain farmers. In peak years until the mid 1850s, an estimated 43 percent of Ohio's wheat crop passed through Cleveland, stimulating the city's population to increase from 1,075 in 1830 to 43,417 in 1860.[6]

Strategically located between the Great Lakes and the Ohio Canal system, Cleveland became a natural center for the collection and dispersal of goods. Commercial activity expanded steadily throughout the second quarter of the nineteenth century. The completion of the Erie Canal in 1825 connected Cleveland to the Ohio-Missouri-Mississippi watershed. This waterway, in addition to connecting the Pennsylvania and Ohio Canal (in 1839) to Pittsburgh, initiated a vigorous economic interaction, which expanded mightily as the iron and steel industry gained momentum and importance.[7]

By the time of the Civil War, the railroad inevitably transformed Cleveland into a major industrial and rail center. In the 1840s advocates for railroad transportation constantly pointed out that Clevelanders were active only two-thirds of the year; for the other four months they burrow like animals. The iron horse, they argued, would stimulate year-round economic growth. After several ill-organized attempts, the most promising rail line, the Cleveland, Columbus and Cincinnati (CC&C) was funded. Construction proceeded quickly, and by early 1851, plans for a celebration marking the arrival of the first train were quickly completed. By year's end Cleveland was also connected with Painsville and Pittsburgh, and by 1853 with New York City, Chicago, and St. Louis. The lake front city was on its way to industrial greatness. Cleveland's frontier growth expanded, with ships filling the harbor Lorenzo Carter had bleakly predicted to early settlers would never become a commercial port.[8]

The CC&C rail line linked Cleveland with the South, finally making the city's commercial economy a twelve-month venture. At this time, iron ore mined in Ohio was refined in Cleveland. Cleveland's once limited activity expanded greatly with the opening of the Soo Canal between Lakes Michigan and Superior, where large amounts of high-grade ore had been discovered. As the nation agonizingly drifted toward the Civil War, Cleveland was poised to play an important role as a new center of production and distribution of iron, hardware and a vast array of consumer goods.

⁀

ON THE EVE OF THE CIVIL WAR, CLEVELAND—a fully developed city participating in national trends—stood ready to benefit from the spreading Industrial Revolution. Sufficiently isolated from the battlegrounds of the Civil War, yet connected by rail with the rest of the North, Cleveland emerged as a significant production center for war *materiel*. As a result of the Mississippi River being closed to commerce, the war stimulated trade on the Great Lakes. In 1860 five hundred men worked in this city's nascent iron industry; by 1866, three thousand did so. Cleveland's annexation process began in 1854 when smaller Ohio City on the west bank of the Cuyahoga River merged with a growing city. Annexation continued as portions of Brooklyn and Newburgh townships, East Cleveland, West Cleveland and parts of

Glenville were all added to the Mother City. Six railroads now operated in and out of Cleveland, and the Flats teemed with roundhouses, warehouses, oil tanks, and factories. The one-time residential neighborhood north and west of Public Square gave way to a rapidly developing commercial district. Hardware, furniture, grocery and clothing wholesalers built new and more substantial structures.[9]

A third tier of Cleveland's economy emerged—that is, the consumption of raw materials and the manufacture and production of finished goods for export to national and international markets. (The first two economic tiers, existing for some time already, were food consumption from surrounding agricultural counties and, secondly, development as a commercial and service hub for these rural neighborhoods). This third tier evolved—not so much by the slow demise of the canal system—but, rather, because of the rapid advent of a labyrinth of railroad lines connecting hamlets throughout the Midwest. These railroads, in addition to Great Lakes shipping and pipelines from the Pennsylvania oil fields, began to impact Cleveland's incipient manufacturing order and general economic state. Industrial barons were about to discover what was later touted the Best Location in the Nation.

Strategically positioned for dramatic growth Cleveland—the Forest City—was one of several Ohio cities to benefit from the Industrial Revolution. Cleveland's long-time nickname, Forest City, has murky origins. Credit for inspiring the name is generally given to William Case, secretary of the Cleveland Horticultural Society in the 1840s and Mayor 1850–51. He encouraged the planting of fruit and shade trees in the area. A count in 1940 found 221,198 trees in the city, in addition to 100,000 others in the parks. The Forest City was still the name of some 35 large and small firms in Greater Cleveland in 1985.[10]

The Buckeye State covers 44,803 square miles in what is commonly referred to as the Midwest. Located *in the heart of it all*, Ohio is bordered by the Ohio River on the south and southwest; the farmlands of the Hoosier State (Indiana) on the west; the industrial areas of Michigan and Lake Erie on the north; and Pennsylvania, the Keystone state, on the East. Ohio emerged as a great corridor for east-west transportation and migration, and a principal thoroughfare for shipping between the coalfields of the south and the iron ore deposits of the north. The state was to become a leader in transportation, especially by canal and rail for steel making, coal hauling, and manufacturing of all kinds.

The discovery of huge iron-ore deposits in the Lake Superior region and on the Mesabi Range in northern Minnesota in the 1850s sparked the growth of the iron and steel industry. With the completion of a canal at Sault Ste. Marie, Cleveland emerged as arguably the most important port on the Great Lakes in the nineteenth century. The canal, which opened a water route to the lower lakes, irrevocably changed the city's economy. Vast treasures of iron ore were shipped to this lake front city. The ore—along with limestone from Michigan and coking coal from the Appalachians—created a broad industrial band, which stretched from Buffalo to Pittsburgh and from Wheeling to Gary and Chicago. Positioned in the midst of such a landscape Cleveland soon became known as the industrial Ruhr of America, dwarfing its European counterpart.

In describing industrial growth of the late 1800s, William Ganson Rose, author of *Cleveland: The Making of a City*, vividly captured the smells and sounds of this Gilded Age: "The smoke of prosperity mingled with the odor of hemp and canvas, oil, and grease.... The air was filled with hoarse blasts from steamship whistles, the dong of ships' bells, and the hoot of tugs and locomotives. Industry was making men rich."[11] Cleveland attracted wealth beyond dreams as factories expanded to meet increasing demands for their products. An aura of recklessness and romance prevailed; opportunity abounded in cities like Cleveland, Toledo, and Youngstown and the new enterprises they spawned. However, prosperity often creates a darker side of the human condition. Immigrants, the critical human resource fuel for the industrial machine, had come seeking a better life; instead, many found themselves trapped by poverty and dehumanizing work.

The city fathers and industrial leaders faced the challenge of providing electricity for new industries, better means of transportation, and improved water and sewerage systems. Labor unrest resulted from conflicting attitudes about the rights and obligations of employer and employee. Rapid urbanization and a burgeoning influx of immigrants strained social problems of the ghetto, such as inadequate housing, care of orphans, unwed mothers and the aged, and poverty's root in economic and social inequality.

The end of the Civil War transformed Cleveland from a rural outpost of Connecticut's Western Reserve into a primary commercial city. The city's population and industry exploded during this internecine conflict between the North and the South. From 1860 to 1865 Cleveland's population increased by 50 percent, a greater proportional increase than was recorded in any urban area in the United States.[12] The city's favorable location along major rail and water routes augmented this rapid growth. Industry and commerce within the city busily supplied Union armies, constructed railroads, and manufactured commercial and industrial products. Coal, iron, and oil were key to Cleveland's emergence as an important industrial center.

John D. Rockefeller, one of the so-called robber barons, dramatically influenced Cleveland's economy and growth. Son of a snake-oil salesman, Rockefeller migrated with his family from New York to Cleveland in 1853. In the 1860s and 1870s oil flowed from wells in Pennsylvania and eastern Ohio, and this daring transplant made Cleveland the chief refinery city in the nation. The young entrepreneur established a crude oil refinery at the junction of Kingsbury Run and the Cuyahoga River. By 1865, the city claimed thirty oil refineries (Standard Oil Company), and the Board of Trade reported the excellence of fourteen rolling mills two years later, producing 400 tons of finished iron daily. The oil titan became one of the wealthiest men in the United States. Rockefeller induced pioneer chemist Eugene Grasselli to move from Cincinnati to Cleveland in the late 1860s. His talent was key in the production of massive quantities of sulfuric acid, a component vital in meeting the needs of oil refineries, particularly Rockefeller's Standard Oil Empire.

Cleveland's refining business probably climbed to its peak in 1886 when it attained the production of an average of 12,000 barrels of petroleum a day in thirteen refineries, turning out products valued at $12 million. The 1890 census, however, listed only seven refineries with products worth $10 million, and by 1900, the refining business had decreased significantly to only four refineries turning out less than $3 million in products. Thereafter, petroleum refining ceased to be a major industry in Cleveland.[13]

This massive industrial development of the 1860s and 1870s spurred tremendous economic growth. Unfortunately, it had deleterious effects upon the bowels of the community, effects which festered for several decades and later led to the term Rust City. Industrial wastes and untreated sewage runoff emptied into the waters of the Cuyahoga River, which flowed through the heart of Cleveland. Parts of the city became badly blighted. In sensational style, a local newspaper described one of the worst areas in the following way: "The hill leading out of the Flats on the West Side, [was inundated] with straggling half-whitewashed houses, filthy rags, dirty faced, half-naked, white-headed children, poorly clad women...the hundreds of cats and dogs, and...millions of flies."[14]

Some visitors (such as the individual who penned this 1883 glorification of the industrial scene) took notice of the change in Cleveland's landscape, "Since 1860 the city has rapidly developed in the direction of manufacturing industries...old pasture grounds of the cows of 1850 are now completely occupied by oil refineries and manufacturing...[including] copper smelting, iron rolling and iron manufacturing works, lumber yards, paper mills, breweries, flour mills.... The scene at night...[is] lit up with a thousand points of light from factories, foundries and steamboats...[and] are reflected in the waters of the Cuyahoga, which looks like a silver ribbon flowing through the blackness."[15]

☞

IN 1889 A RECENT IMMIGRANT DESCRIBED HIS FIRST IMPRESSIONS of the Cuyahoga River: "The water was yellowish, thick, full of clay, stinking of oil and sewage. The water heaped rotting wood on both banks of the river; everything was dirty and neglected." Still the Cleveland *Leader* typified the prevailing attitude toward industrial pollution when it warned that Cleveland would be ridiculed by rival cities if it "indicts her rolling mills because they smoke, and prohibits coal oil refineries because they smell badly."[16]

Were a prodigal son, who may have left Cleveland in 1870 to seek his fortune elsewhere, to return in 1900, he would not have recognized the city. Cleveland's vast size stretched for miles eastward and westward along the lakeshore. The metropolis had become one of the largest cities in the nation, the home of 381,000 people. This number included thousands only recently transplanted from peasant villages of southern and eastern Europe. They worked in a multitude of small shops and great smoke-belching factories in this huge American city. A great movement was astir about the community, a surge of struggling humanity. The city emitted a loud roar, the metallic-electric hum of power in action. The immigrants observed the thrill, the life, the movement, and the strength of the city—how they stood for the most representative Americanism! Cleveland had become the nexus of the worlds of finance, art, sport, journalism, and politics.[17]

Growth of this magnitude meant that Cleveland's industries and commercial businesses sought an ever-expanding labor force. Neither the native stock nor earlier immigrants from northern Europe equaled the demand for workers. During the late 1880s, colorfully named immigrant ghettos evolved: Cabbage Patch, Warszawa, Dutch Hill, Little Italy, Cuba, Chicken Village, Vinegar Hill, Whiskey Island, Goosetown, The Angle and The Haymarket.[18] These neighborhoods represented a multitude of ethnic groups who provided the labor to transform this growing city into an industrial metropolis. This burgeoning work force was represented by new immigrants migrating from eastern and southern Europe. They came from non-English speaking territories.

⌒

IN 1870, FORTY-TWO PERCENT OF CLEVELAND'S 92,000 RESIDENTS were foreign born. In 1890, the percentage of foreign born had declined slightly to 37 percent of Cleveland's total population of 261,353. This dramatic impact of immigration is emphasized by the fact that fully three-quarters of the city's population were now either foreign born or the children of foreign-born parents. Whereas the earliest immigrants to Cleveland had come primarily from Germany and Ireland, those arriving after 1870 included large numbers of Poles, Russians, Jews, Hungarians, Czechs, Slovaks, Slovenes, Croats, Serbs, Italians, Greeks and others. Another distinction is that the majority of these new arrivals came as workers, not as settlers. They were part of a massive and complex migration of labor to the United States and Canada, and simultaneously to the industrialized countries of Western Europe. Many more immigrants remained.

In addition to the availability of work, reasons for coming to Cleveland included relatives and friends already settled in the Forest City and the city's location on the national arteries of transportation—the railroads. By 1872, the influx of immigrants was so great the city posted special emigrant police at railroad stations to assist these newcomers and protect them from swindlers. The new arrivals came largely from agricultural societies and filled the void for the need of unskilled and semi-skilled laborers.[19]

There were no homogeneous Slavic neighborhoods in Cleveland. A number of separate ethnic conclaves composed of members of the same nationality group shared a similar language and heritage, and often a regional affiliation. They were in the majority Roman Catholic. Though often under the control of other nations, the Slavs had retained their national identities. An appreciation of America's religious and political freedoms, combined with opportunities to earn money in a growing industrial city, were factors that attracted large complements of foreign laborers. In some instances, Slavs who had settled in other areas of the country, particularly the Pennsylvania coalfields, came to Cleveland to escape harsher working conditions.[20]

Czechs, the first of the Slavic nationalities to immigrate to America, came to Cleveland as early as 1850. By 1890, their population equaled 10,000-plus. Cleveland became one of the largest Czech cities in the world, ranking fourth behind Prague, Vienna, and Chicago. Unlike many immigrant groups these new Czech immigrants worked largely at skilled trades—masons, carpenters, tailors, shoemakers, coopers, bakers, and brewers.[21]

Cleveland's Yugoslavs—the Slovenes, Croats, and Serbs—began arriving in significant numbers in the 1890s. The Slovenes settled in nearly every American state, although few lived in the South, Southwest, or New England. As a result of the fragmentary nature of census and immigration records with respect to the Slovenes, many were frequently listed as Austrians, Germans, Yugoslavs, or were grouped with the Croats. A reasonable estimate suggests that between 250,000 and 300,000 Slovenes crossed the Atlantic Ocean to the United States and remained there.[22]

These new eastern European immigrants (Slovenians) came from peasant stock. Large numbers settled in the Chicago-Joliet region, in Milwaukee, and West Allis, Wisconsin, and to a lesser extent in Michigan, Pennsylvania, and Minnesota. The largest segment settled in Cleveland, reaching approximately 40,000 in the 1920s.[23] They were overwhelmingly unskilled and semi-skilled laborers who took their places in Cleveland's growing industries. A number of early Slovenian immigrants resided in the Newburgh area near the American Fleet and Wire factory on the south side of the city. The largest contingent settled along St. Clair Avenue from East 30th Street to East 79th Street and south to Superior Avenue. The heart of this settlement was located near St. Vitus Catholic Church at 1114 Norwood Road, originally constructed in 1893. At the turn of the twentieth century, large numbers of Slovenes began to settle in Collinwood, directly east of the St. Clair settlement. In the 1920s, Edward Land Company sold property for housing in the then little village of Euclid eight miles east of the Slovene settlements on St. Clair Avenue, which especially attracted second-generation Slovene-Americans. Scattered pockets of Slovenes migrated to the west side of Cleveland and the suburbs.

$\frown$

WHO WERE THESE SLOVENES FROM WHICH THE LAUSCHE family emigrated, and what was their legacy? The Slovenes, or Slovenians, are a South Slav national group who once comprised a republic in the federation of Yugoslavia and formerly occupied the northwestern part of that country. This small country—20,296 square kilometers, or slightly less than 8,000 square miles—is approximately the size of Massachusetts, Wales, or Israel. Present day Slovenia borders Austria on the north, Italy to the west, and Hungary and Croatia to the east and south. The population of Slovenia was around 2,000,000 as of year 2000, approximately the same population as West Virginia. Described by journalists and tourists as "Europe neatly packaged," verdant Slovenia is blessed with a succinct swath of mountains, lakes, and the Adriatic coastline. This countryside envelops the gorgeous and entirely cosmopolitan capital of Ljubljana, which is latticed with stone bridges. Slovenian architecture includes Renaissance, Secessionist, and Art Noveau masterpieces. The religious background of approximately 95 percent Slovenes was at least nominally Roman Catholic. The country is adorned with numerous ornate churches. In the northeast section, wine vineyards are plentiful. The western band of the country is mountainous terrain, which extends south to the Adriatic Sea. Only a thirty-mile stretch of this sea borders Slovenia where the town Piron, with its labyrinth-like alleys, has much Old World charm. Hundreds of castles dot the Slovenian landscape, including Prodjama Castle, near Postojna, southwest of Ljubljana. The politically controversial seaport of Trieste is located only a few kilometers from Slovenia on the Italian border of the Adriatic Sea.

The world read and heard about the shattering of the federation in Yugoslavia during the 1980s and 1990s. The shards of that fragmentation drawing notice were Kosovo, Bosnia, Serbia, and Macedonia, and of course, Slovenia. A peaceful and prosperous entity, Slovenia was a part of the Yugoslav federation. Since the Middle Ages, neighboring multi-lingual, multi-ethnic empires had subsumed the Slovenes. Finally, following a ten-day war in 1991, Slovenia won its independence from Yugoslavia. On May 22, 1992, Slovenia was inducted as a permanent member of the United Nations.[24] This small country became one of seven former Communist countries officially to become accepted into the North Atlantic Treaty Organization (NATO) on March 29, 2004.

Prior to their drive for autonomy in the nineteenth century, the Slovenian people cherished their heritage, so dear to any ethnic entity. An example is the Slovene language. An extremely archaic Slavic language, it includes thirty-six dialects and twenty-nine sub dialects. Slovenian is the language of the oldest preserved written documents of any Slavic people. The Slovenes tenaciously retained their dialects while attending the Catholic Church, or participating in singing societies and drama groups.

The Slovenian culture emphasized the value of good health. The populace adopted the ancient Roman guideline "*Mens sana in corpore sana*," "A healthy mind in a healthy body." These values began at a young age and continued through the elderly years. Influential social organizations were the Eagles (*Orli*) and the Falcons (*Sokoli*). And there was always the favored ethnic cuisine. Popular dishes include potatoes (*krompirs*), dumplings (*comoki* and *struklji*), and Carniolan sausage (*kranjske klobase*). Slovenians had long established an international reputation for their excellent wines. In spite of political upheaval and geographical fragmentation, the Slovenians maintained their rich traditions for many centuries.[25]

Several factors contributed to the development of a national consciousness and, subsequently, to political nationalism. For Slovenes, as with most European nationalities, what is national in contemporary political terms was not evident before the 18th century. For many centuries Slovenes lived as part of medieval Europe whose institutions, political structure, and culture lingered on until the eve of the French Revolution.[26] Slovenia was not an independent state during the post Renaissance period. In the 15th century, the Hapsburg dynasty took possession of the Slovenian territory, where it remained until the collapse of Austria-Hungary in 1918. By the time they became Hapsburg subjects the Slovenes had long since become dependent people. Without a ruling class, they were serfs subjugated to feudal nobles, both secular and clerical, and mostly German.[27]

Slovene national awakening occurred during the second half of the eighteenth century amid the intellectual revolution known as Enlightenment, which had mesmerized Europe in the previous century. The development of capitalism resulted in the growth of larger towns with 3,000 to 7,000 inhabitants in the Slovene ethnic territory. These towns provided the origins of the Slovene culture, even though the predominant languages in this territory were German and Italian.[28]

During the first half of the nineteenth century, intellectuals and clergy primarily shaped Slovenian identity. Accordingly they assumed unofficial leadership of these peasant people. As was true with their European contemporaries, romanticism and idealism influenced these Slovenian leaders. Believing in the uniqueness of national cultures, they sought to explore and develop their Slovene spirit by studying language, history, and folklore. The writings of Jernej Kopitar, a linguist employed by Vienna as an imperial censor, defined Slovene as a distinct south Slavic language. Two other individuals critical to this period of cultural identity were Anton Slomšek and Janez Bleiweis. Slomšek, bishop of the province of Maribor, was responsible for introducing the Slovene language into schools, while Janez Bleiweis began publishing a successful newspaper for farmers and craftsmen in 1843.[29] Frank J. Lausche, the central figure of this biography and a lover of poetry, held special affection for France Preseren, Slovenia's most preeminent literary figure. A Romantic poet of the mid 1800s, Preseren established the basis for contemporary secular literature, which espoused a form of political liberalism. Preseren's poem "*Zdravljica*" (a toast) is now independent Slovenia's national anthem. This folk hero urged development of a separate Slovene language and literature, one suitable for a modern age. A large statue of Preseren is located in the heart of central Ljubljana.[30] Slovenia's small size and its long period of political subjugation denied the Western world the significance of these literary achievements. Bernard Newman, noted British author, wrote: "Slovenia's master ranged from Charlemagne to Napoleon but the people clung to their own culture and language.... It was a miracle of survival, almost without parallel.... The Slovenes used to share with the Scandinavians the reputation of being the best read people in the world—the number of books read per head of the population were four times the British figure.... In almost every village cottage I found a little library of high literary value."[31]

Slovenia's relatively small size and the country's century-long political subjugation (nineteenth century) meant that the Slovenians were relatively little known in America or in many other countries. Ignorance and prejudice against them have often been rampant. By contrast, when they've become better known, they have often enjoyed a solid reputation, as is illustrated by American writer, Reuben Henry Markham, who called the Slovenians, "one of the most advanced nationality groups or nations in the world...[whose]...coffee houses...were as reading rooms in American libraries."[32]

⤳

THE YEAR **1848** BROUGHT DRAMATIC UPHEAVAL ACROSS continental Europe. Economic strife caused the toppling of most European governments including Austria, where absolutism, clericalism, censorship, repression, and vestiges of serfdom had reigned since 1815. The Slovenes' first political program was formulated in 1848, the work of small groups of intellectuals, mostly notables of the cultural awakening. The objective was clear and simple: a United Slovenia. Their intent was for a United Slovenia to remain within Austria, although as a revolutionized federal, constitutional state. Unlike the nearby Magyors, who declared independence in those revolutionary times, the Slovenes were not then, nor would they soon become, separatists.[33] The intellectual and political climates of the pre- and post-1848 period differed radically; romanticism dominated the first half of the century, whereas realism became prominent the last half of the nineteenth century. Romanticism regarded nations as unique creations, whose cultural expression harmonized with that of others. Peace was considered a desirable goal. Realism judged nations in a Darwinian way, a biological confrontation striving for power and survival. The Franco-Prussian war of 1870 is generally cited as the first example of a conflict of rural cultures supported by a nationalistic sentiment. With such a view taking over in Europe, several territories were destined to lose. These empires became multinational, including the Hapsburg Empire and smaller and less developed territories like Slovenia.

Following several short wars during the 1850s and 1860s, Austria conceded power over certain territories or provinces to Italy, Prussia, and Hungary. These states were using their nationalistic appeals to enlarge their domains. Vienna gave up two valuable provinces (Lombardy and Venetia) to the newly created Kingdom of Italy and forfeited to Prussia/Germany its role as a dominant power in central Europe. Austria further agreed to the Austro-Hungarian Compromise of 1867, which created a Dual Monarchy (Austria-Hungary). This Compromise enabled the Hungarians to assume legal authority over the southeastern parts of the Hapsburg Empire. The Slovenes, one of Europe's lesser-developed nations, were divided territorially by these developments. Most remained in the Austrian half of the Hapsburg state, but 27,000 found themselves in Italy after 1866 and 45,000 in Hungary after the Compromise of 1867.[34]

The reorganization of the Hapsburg monarchy gave equal status to Austria and Hungary within the monarchy, but caused severe consequences for Slovenes. Predominance of the German bourgeois in the Austrian area of the monarchy became a reality. By the 1860s economic pressures in rural areas forced the Slovene population (then approximately 1.1 million) to seek employment in urban areas or to consider emigration. In most cases new industries employed from their own native populous rather than hire Slovenes scattered throughout the landscape. From the end of the 19th century until 1918, most Slovene lands were in the Austrian region of the monarchy. The Austrian Hapsburg dynasty did not permit the formation of a single geopolitical unit known as Slovenia. Instead, it distributed the Slovenian regions of the monarchy among several provinces, in only two of which—Carniola and Gorizia—did Slovenes constitute a majority.[35]

This disposition of a growing number of Slovenes forced young liberal Slovenes to take a leading role in effecting political changes. The liberals supported a more determined national policy, particularly in political and cultural issues. The liberals gained much of their strength from Slovene peasants. Between 1868 and 1871 these peasants formed massive people's assemblies. The liberal element used these assemblies to promote their political platform. A philosophical split between conservatives and liberals came to a climax in the late 1860s about whether or not to favor a concord with Rome, the seat of Catholic power. However, there was little discernible difference between the two groups regarding a national program.[36]

By the turn of the twentieth century Slovene society differed considerably from what it had been in 1848. Most Slovenes still remained in rural areas and worked the land. Legally all were free, for during the 1848 revolution the Austrian regime had abolished all remnants of serfdom. However, economic insecurity often accompanied newly established freedom, particularly given the sizable population growth during the second half of the nineteenth century. Land-holding patterns in Slovenia consisted of small family farms, some with as little as two or three acres of arable land. Few had more than 25 acres. Families were large, which resulted in rural overpopulation. The increasing population could not be absorbed by the still limited industrial development of this region. Many farm owners and their eldest sons, who were projected to inherit land, found it necessary to spend a few years working abroad in efforts to earn additional income. Many never returned to their homelands.[37]

Accordingly, a great majority of Slovene immigrants who migrated to the United States were poor peasants. Most of these newcomers were literate, although few had more than a basic elementary education. They departed their homeland, either because they had no choice or because they were ambitious and enterprising. The first coherent Slovene migration to the United States was that of Roman Catholic priests who came in the nineteenth century to serve as missionaries to the Indian tribes of northern Michigan, Minnesota, and the Dakotas. The most prominent of these missionary priests was Reverend Frederick Baraga (1797–1868). Later to become a candidate for beatification as a saint of the Roman Catholic Church, Baraga arrived in 1831. The Slovenian-born scholar, missionary and bishop labored on a vast 80,000 square mile piece of virgin territory including parts of Michigan, Wisconsin, Minnesota, and Canada. He and his followers built some of the first churches and schools in this territory. Father Andreas Skopec (Skopez) reached Fryburg, Pennsylvania, in 1846 and was joined by several of his Slovenian patriots. His example induced scores of fellow Slovene priests to follow him. A number of them ministered to the needs of lay Slovenes who began arriving in significant numbers in the 1880s to work in copper and iron mines of Michigan's Upper Peninsula and in the local lumber industry. One of the most active priests of this era was Reverend Joseph Buh (1833–1922), who sponsored the first Slovene-language newspaper in the United States, *Amerikanski Slovenec* (*American Slovenes*), which first appeared in Chicago in 1891 and was later published in Cleveland.[38]

Although a few Slovenian immigrants drifted intermittently to the New World by the late 1700s and early 1800s, the total number probably did not exceed 1,000 new citizens until the early 1880s. Early family groups of Slovenes settled mostly in California and Minnesota. Many who came in the 1880s were chiefly farmers. From 1900 forward, immigrants settled in the East and Middle West where laborers, coal miners, steelworkers, and railroad builders were in demand.

During the three decades prior to World War I, the trickle became a flood, particularly in Cleveland and in the Chicago-Joliet areas. By the mid-1890s, according to Rudolph Susel, Cleveland became the most significant center of Slovene settlement in the United States, a position it still retains.[39] Widening horizons in American cities amidst the awareness of untenable change in homelands prompted Slovenians and other southern Europeans to search for a means to survive and prosper. One immigrant remembered, "America appealed to me very much. The whole country seemed to be at the roof of the world."[40] With their promise of money and jobs cities beckoned not only to rural Americans, but also to Europeans. The commercial revolution of the eighteenth and nineteenth centuries, the transition through merchant capitalism, and the Industrial Revolution charged cities with magnetism. These metropolitan entities generated labor opportunities. In the second half of the nineteenth century and the first decade of the twentieth century, major cities constructed new or enlarged their municipal facilities. Public funds became available, and unskilled immigrants were a major part of the labor force. These working-men helped build streets, bridges, water and gas systems, sewers, schools, and government buildings for burgeoning cities.[41]

Reportedly, the first Slovene to settle in Cleveland was John Pintar. He came from the village of Andol in lower Carniola in 1879, but after only five months returned to his homeland. He stayed in Europe for four years and returned to the United States permanently. Fluctuating industrial conditions drove him from city to city in search of employment. The New World did not prove to be the end of the rainbow for this immigrant. He eventually died in a nearby Warrensville infirmary.[42] Joseph Turk is considered the first Slovene to settle permanently in Cleveland. He moved to East Cleveland on October 25, 1881, settling on Marble Avenue (East 74th to East 83rd Street) near the Newburgh Street iron and steel plant. By 1885, a dozen or so other Slovenes joined Turk, renting shacks on Marble Avenue. This area was called *Chicken Yard*, named after their landlord, Ciken, owner of a nearby saloon. Turk became a leader in his community. He saved as much of his earnings as possible, and by 1892 the budding entrepreneur acquired a combined grocery/general store, saloon, restaurant, and two apartments. A large Slovenian community soon developed around his buildings.

Frank Joseph Turk remembered his baptism in his new country, "The first night in America I spent with hundreds of other recently arrived immigrants, in an immense hall with tiers of narrow iron-and-canvas bunks, four deep.... The bunk immediately beneath mine was occupied by a Turk.... I thought how curious it was that I should be spending a night in such proximity to a Turk, for Turks were traditional enemies of Balkan people, including my own nation.... Now here I was trying to sleep directly above a Turk, with only a sheet of canvas between us."[43] Turk's oldest daughter (Mrs. Rose Skebe) was the first Slovenian woman in the city; she came to Cleveland in 1885. Mrs. Skebe recalled that there were only fourteen Slovenians in Cleveland at that time.

The oldest Slovenian settlement was near East 81st Street between Union Avenue and Aetna Road. Other Slovenes settled in the Collinwood and Nottingham neighborhoods, near the brickyards in the Brooklyn area, and in the industrial suburbs of South Euclid and Euclid. The largest and most influential Slovene settlement was along St. Clair Avenue between East 30th and East 79th Streets. Here Turk and other early Slovenian settlers began to pick themselves up by their bootstraps, so to speak. The boardinghouse became a source of income as the result of an influx of unskilled and semiskilled workers. Many worked at companies like American Steel and Wire, Otis Steel, and Collinwood Shale and Brick. Earning perhaps two dollars for a ten-hour working day, these new arrivals sought other venues for securing additional income. It was an uphill struggle for these basically uneducated newcomers. The nation was out of balance relative to the distribution of the gross national product. More and more wealth became concentrated in the hands of a relatively small urban elite, and the gulf between them and rural Americans and the urban poor—both native-born and immigrant—grew even wider. In 1900 a scant .35 percent of the population possessed three-fifths of the nation's wealth, and 25,000 to 40,000 families controlled $31 billion, or half of the nation's total financial resources. It was the age of the corporation, the trust, the holding company, and the plutocrat, of men who accumulated vast personal fortunes with little or no regard for their fellow citizens.[44]

Aside from a boardinghouse, the first Slovene business likely to appear in a settlement was the *gostilna*, a tavern. The tavern was important, both economically and socially. On Saturday nights, men might go from saloon to saloon. Each saloon had an accordionist who played Slovenian songs. It was not hard to start a saloon because the potential owner made an agreement with a brewery to sell only its product, and of course, breweries were quite prepared to handle many of the practical details in return for a commitment from the proprietor. Tavern owners often augmented their brewery product with the sale of homemade wine concocted from local vineyards. Some tavern owners assumed the role of banker and received interest on their loans, as there was an increasingly successful movement toward home ownership. By 1910 the business community along St. Clair Avenue included seventy Slovene-owned establishments: restaurants, saloons, clothing stores, furniture stores, funeral parlors, grocery stores specializing in Slovene food, stores selling Slovene merchandise and Slovene-language publications from Slovenia and the United States.[45]

Turk's saloon and associated enterprises were an example of how a local business might prosper within the immigrant community. For several years Turk was the only businessman in the East Cleveland settlement. His saloon was so prosperous he was able to give it to his daughter as a wedding gift. The beneficent father bought saloons for his five sons. Turk became so well known police directed Slovenes arriving at the railroad terminal immediately to his establishments. He lent money to his new-found countrymen, pooled bond for them, and acted as a character witness when they were in trouble with the law. Turk provided food and clothing for his fellow Slovenes in hard times (America was in the midst of a Depression in 1893).

⌒

THE ECONOMIC HARD TIMES IN THE **1890s** strained even Turk's considerable resources. He lost his property and had to rely on the earnings of his teenage sons. Eventually Turk overcame his financial problems, bought property in suburban Euclid where he grew grapes, sold the wine made from them, and then established a new saloon in the Nottingham section of Cleveland. The hardy Slovenian represented the spirit of the Slav pioneer who challenged, with some measure of success, the industrial city for himself, his children, and his fellow countrymen. Turk was also concerned about his fellow Slovenes' allegiance to the Catholic Church.

By all accounts prior to the building of their own church, the first Slovenian immigrants to Cleveland found a warm welcome in the Slovak parish of Our Lady of Lourdes on East 55th Street and Broadway Avenue and by the pastor, Reverend Stefan Furdek. Father Furdek ministered to the early Slovenians and later was instrumental in the founding of St. Vitus Catholic Church, the first Slovenian Church in northeast Ohio.

In 1890 Father Furdek visited Ljubljana on a recruitment trip for candidates for priesthood in the Diocese of Cleveland, and returned with a seminary student named Vitus Hribar. After a three-year stint at the local diocesan seminary, the twenty-three-year-old Hribar became the first pastor of St. Vitus Church in 1893. The parishioners purchased several vacant lots on the corner of Norwood Road and Glass Avenue (present location of the Church) for $6,000. A small wooden church and parish house were constructed, and on November 4, 1894, the new church opened its doors. Eventually St. Vitus Church grew to be the largest Slovenian Catholic Church in the United States.[46]

The saga of the Lausche family followed closely on the heels of Turk's path-finding achievements in Cleveland. Their story began in Slovenia. Lausche's grand-father and father were known as the Gottschee Germans who inhabited a small community, approximately 55 kilometers southwest of Ljubljana in the village of Hinje, near the town of Kočevje. This small tribe of 15,000 people surrounded by Slovenes was comparatively unknown, even in Yugoslavia. Even under Austrian rule for centuries, they had little or no connection with other German-speaking people. This region maintained an exclusive German culture and strict use of the German language for a time, and then intermarriage began to occur. The heritage of Gottschee that the Lausche family represented was aptly described in the following quote and helps explain why Frank Lausche often referred to his parents' homeland, "[they] have a fine appetite for meaty, sauce-laden food; they like to drink, to saunter across meadows blanketed with flowers, to climb mountains in the spring; they are passionately fond of music and hand embroidered costumes; they have vitality, a love for healthy indolence, and a gift of happiness."[47]

This excerpt might be appropriately credited to a scene from the well-known production *Sound of Music*. In the 1880s, this small territory of Gottschee, allotted to the settlers by ancient law, became too crowded with a population of approximately 30,000. Fifteen thousand emigrated to the United States and Canada in the next few months and years.[48] The Lausche brothers were one of such families to migrate from their homeland to the New World. Lausche's grandfather, Frank Lovše and grandmother Mary, whose maiden name was Jaklitsch, lived in Gottschee and were parents to five children—four sons and one daughter. All five children immigrated to Cleveland, but only Lojze Lovše remained in Cleveland. Lausche's aunt Josephine moved to California where she married a Joseph Velikovija. The three brothers—Jacob, George, and Charles—moved to northern Minnesota in the area of Cass Lake, fifteen miles east of Bemidji.[49]

Lojze Lovše arrived in Cleveland in 1889 at the age of 23. He soon changed his name to Louis Lausche. Lausche's mother Francka Milavec was born in Dvorska Vas, a small village between Ribnica and Velike Lascé, not far from the home of Louis. Francka Milavec was only sixteen when she arrived in Cleveland in 1891.[50] Lausche's mother worked as a hired girl in the home of the Turk family for a year or so, and there met Louis. She had a lovely voice and a determination to become a dressmaker. Francka changed her first name to Frances. After a brief period of courtship, Louis and Frances Lausche married in 1893. Louis worked in a local steel mill for several years. What little job choice Lausche and other immigrants had was determined by the nearby locality of heavy manufacturing industries or, in some cases, slaughter-houses. This heavy work was one of the great contributions of these pioneer Slavic immigrants in helping to build a modern industrial America. One of Lausche's con-temporaries, a Slovene immigrant, recalled after many years of hard work "how we helped build these buildings—we Slovenians and Croatians and Slovaks and other people who went to work. We helped to build many other cities, cities of which you never heard, and railroads, and bridges all made of steel, which people make in the mills. Our men from the Balkans are the best steelworkers in America."[51]

Although the home they purchased in the St. Clair area in the 1890s was small, the Lausche family "always had a spare bed and an extra meal for the often fright-ened and bewildered newcomer from their native land."[52] Soon after settling in Cleveland, the senior Lausche began to learn English. Combining hard work and thriftiness, he saved his money, and in a few years opened a saloon in the house of his uncle, Joe Jaklic, at the corner of East 61st Street and St. Clair Ave. By 1900 the hard-working family built a home of their own, which remained a landmark in the neighborhood for seventy-five years.[53] On St. Clair Avenue, in the heart of a solid workingman's district, Louis Lausche built the Lausche Building, a two-story frame structure with storefronts below and flats above. "At various times the Lausche Building housed a bowling alley, a shop selling Catholic religious articles, the presses of *Ameriška Domovina*, a Slovenian language weekly, a restau-rant, and until Prohibition, a wine shop where the Lausches pressed their own wine from Ohio grapes and sold it to an eager Middle European clientele. The Lausche Building was the hub of neighborhood society, the local political forum, and a sanctuary for new arrivals from the old country."[54]

The large family and boarders forced the Lausches to scramble for sustenance. Every harvest season the parents bought a wagonload of cabbage to be made into kraut. Bushels of potatoes filled their bins. The family bought whole hogs, and not even the ears were wasted. Certainly, Frank Lausche's penchant for personal and governmental frugality had its origin in his youth. "Any man or nation that does not practice economy cannot help but get into trouble" was Lausche's cry throughout his life.[55] The Lausche family grew rapidly, but not without tragedy. Of the ten children reared by the Lausches, two twin girls died in infancy, and Albert died at the age of five. Louis, Jr., the oldest son, died at the age of seventeen. Frank J. Lausche, the third of ten children was born on November 14, 1895. The other five siblings, three brothers (William, Charles, and Harold) and two sisters (Josephine and Frances), went on to distinguish themselves in professional and social circles in Cleveland. In this atmosphere of love, friendship, and hard work, Frank J. Lausche and his siblings were nurtured in the heart of the old Slovenian neighborhood.

THE ELDER LAUSCHES WERE PASSIONATELY PATRIOTIC, helping thousands of newly arrived Slovenians and other immigrants to put down roots in the U.S., giving them room and board until they were settled, and haranguing them with patriotic speeches to obtain their citizenship papers. Frances mothered the new arrivals, and Louis helped them with their legal and naturalization problems, and as an official interpreter, making good use of his knowledge of English, German, Croatian, and Slovenian. The senior Lausche often took Frank to court with him when his services as an interpreter were needed.[56]

This was a part of the Lausche family story known only to immigrants—whether Slovene or not—who spent their first night under an American roof, warming up on Mother Lausche's wonderful soup and homemade bread. Lausche's older sister (Josephine Welf) reminisced of their father frequently heading out in the snow at night for the railroad station, then located on the lake front. There he would meet "Slovenians coming in a train from New York. He would walk from East 61st Street and St. Clair Avenue where we lived, down to East 55th Street. I don't know how he picked out our young people—but he'd finally arrive home with what seemed like a mob, and mother would have a big pot of soup going." Josephine would continue, "When the visitors got down to some of Mother Lausche's 'strudel,' Father Lausche would say, 'Now the first thing you must do is to apply for your citizenship. This is a very fine country—and he would start with George Washington and come down to the current mayor of Cleveland." [Likely the renowned Progressive Tom L. Johnson] Welf concluded, "We had one room which we could use when there was a large number. We didn't have enough beds—after all there were eight children in our family...and so mother would improvise beds on the floor of this big room. Most of the immigrants brought addresses of relatives or friends to whom they were going. So mother would send out messages and the people would start arriving."[57]

As soon after their arrival as possible, the senior Lausche took the new immigrants to the courthouse for their first step toward citizenship. He served as a witness for the prospective citizens' good character, and took them out to dinner following the successful passing of their citizenship exam. When election time rolled around, Louis Lausche made sure *his* new Slovenian citizens knew the candidates, especially the Democrats, and that they voted. Wishing to have been a lawyer himself, the elder Lausche was on hand to help the immigrants with legal matters, translations, and real estate transactions. By the hundreds the new arrivals wanted to buy a business, a house, get married—and they had trouble with English. So back to the Lausche house they went. Father Lausche would put on his fine suit, Mother Lausche would tie his black silk tie, and he would be off to the lawyers' offices and the courts to translate.[58] For more than a decade, thousands of newly arrived Slovenians realized their start in America through the generosity of this family. None of the Lausches revealed the names of their temporary boarders from Europe.

In addition to all of these responsibilities, the Lausches operated their own winery. "Father used to buy 80 to 100 tons of grapes at a time and made excellent wine that was stored in huge barrels," recalled Frank's sister Josephine. "We received orders of wine from all over America. I especially recall various towns in Minnesota where we had many regular customers (and where many Slovenians had settled).... You know, my father always wanted to go a step further—to buy a large farm in Bay Village, with acres of vineyards of his own, where he would make wine from his own grapes."[59]

The activities at the Lausche building served as a hub for a political forum. Many local Slovenians and immigrants from other European countries were indebted to the Lausche family for their assistance in a new and strange environment. Lausche was fortunate indeed to inherit a ready-made base of support consisting of those people who were indebted to his family. It was in this tavern setting that the young Lausche boys and their friends became adept in bowling and billiards.

All seemed to be going well for the Lausches when tragedy struck the young family. In 1908, Louis Lausche, Sr. underwent surgery for gallstones—a relatively simple procedure in modern-day medicine. However, complications set in, and he died unexpectedly on July 6, 1908, at the age of thirty-nine. The hard-working Slovenian had endeavored to provide his large Catholic family with a better way of life. Politically active and patriotic, the senior Lausche had helped establish a strong Democratic Party foundation in the twenty-third ward. Different from boss-ridden cities like Boston, New York, and Chicago, Cleveland by 1900 had discarded old-style machine politics. Father Lausche's impact upon so-called new immigrants indirectly built the foundation, which later provided strength for young Frank when he entered the political arena. Frances was left to raise seven children (the youngest six weeks old; the eldest, 15). Two years later the eldest son Louis Jr. contracted tuberculosis. His mother rushed him to California and then to Denver in an effort to save the youngster's life. Unfortunately the medical world had not yet discovered a cure for this disease, and he died on September 5, 1911, at the age of seventeen, leaving Frank the titular head of the family at the tender age of fifteen.

In spite of these gut-wrenching tragedies, Mrs. Lausche rallied her family together. Frances *Ma* Lausche was a gentle, but strong matriarch. She was determined that her children gain a meaningful education and develop into worthy American citizens. No job was too hard or too irksome for Mother Lausche as she worked to send her children to school. In the ensuing years until the children became older, Frances Lausche had little time for Slovenian lodges, singing groups, or societies. This would all come later. She was too busy with her own family and with helping other young people over the rough bumps in life.

It was from Mother Lausche that young Frank developed his strong sense of duty. "Be a good citizen," she frequently admonished him, "You must put back in America what America gave to you." Frank developed great love and appreciation for his mother. "My greatest debt in life is to my mother," Lausche fervently stated. "She was a good, charitable person, wanting to help everyone, avoiding any acts or words that might hurt...other people."[60] During Lausche's formative years and early adulthood, his mother became the youngster's guiding light. Frank Lausche, like most children his age in the Progressive Era, had aspirations for a better life than their immigrant parents had experienced. But for now Lausche was consumed with his responsibility of helping his mother care for the younger children, maintaining a boardinghouse, and caring for the expanding wine business. The young man learned the hard lessons about how to survive economically. It was not long before he was confronted with decisions as to what to make of his future life. It would not be an easy task.

The Joe Gornik Tailors, an early Slovenian sandlot team in 1911. Lausche, second row, far right at age 15. (Courtesy of Dr. Rudolph Susel)

two

Young Frank Lausche—
Baseball or Law?

THE BEST LOCATION IN THE NATION AND CROSSROADS of American industry were two monikers deservedly describing Cleveland at the turn of the twentieth century. More than half the population of the United States and Canada lived within five hundred miles of this lake front city. Seventy-one percent of Cleveland's wage earners produced seventy-one percent of the nation's manufactured products.[1] Cleveland was one of the world's foremost manufacturing centers. Iron and steel mills, foundries and machine shops, meatpacking and auto-making plants, clothing, paint, and varnish factories provided sustenance to a growing population.[2] The population of Cleveland quadrupled from 1870 to 1900. This rapid growth accelerated between 1900 and 1910, almost doubling again from 381,768 to 560,663. The Forest City moved up a notch in the cities ranked by population, and proudly bore the title of *Sixth City*. Cleveland was a boomtown energized by its rapidly expanding population and industries.

Its work force grew because of the influx of new immigrants, particularly from Italy, Poland, and Hungary.[3] The proliferation of towering buildings encircling Public Square, downtown iron furnaces, and ore docks along the Cuyahoga River, along with nearby factories transformed the city into an industrial giant. The alchemy of coal and iron ore being transformed into steel created the ingredients for America's greatest industry of the twentieth century—auto making.

In the early 1900s Cleveland boasted of nine different made-in-Cleveland automobiles. Turn of the century residents were familiar with the names: Winton, Peerless, Chandler, Baker-Raulang, Stearns, Jordan, Rollin, the White Steamer, and Lozier. By 1914, an estimated 30 cents of every dollar invested in automobiles in the United States came into Cleveland.[4] The city's primacy in auto manufacturing encountered an overwhelming challenge from Detroit across Lake Erie. Detroit became the number one automobile production center by the conclusion of World War I. The Motor City also jumped ahead of Cleveland in population. Detroit showed greater initiative in securing new plants and in encouraging the enlargement of pioneer factories. The production of Henry Ford's Model T cannot be minimized. For years afterward, Cleveland moguls intermittently expressed regret that the motorcar business had been lost. Conversely, several city fathers believed that, had Cleveland retained the car-manufacturing industry along with that of automotive parts, it undoubtedly would have become predominantly a one-industry center. The city spread its wings embracing a well-balanced diversification of economic interests.[5]

When the automobile industry moved into high gear, the oil industry grew into a thriving eminence under the aegis of John D. Rockefeller. The titan retired from active management of his oil cartel in 1895 at the age of 55. His organization controlled 90 percent of the oil manufacturing trade. At one point, Cleveland rightfully claimed the title of oil capital of the world, even though the city was located many miles from the nearest oil field.

Rockefeller's Standard Oil Company suffered a blow in 1911. The United States Supreme Court ruled the oil trust was a monopoly. The trust dissolved and split into 34 separate companies. An important event took place in the oil refining business in 1911. Gasoline surpassed kerosene as Standard of Ohio's chief product. Thus, the auto and oil industries were joined. Sohio headquarters (as it was known in the Buckeye State) remained in the lake front city. Standard Oil expanded through mass marketing. No longer an oil capital, Cleveland remained a key production center of lubricants for automobiles.[6]

Cleveland—spurred by industrial and population growth—was a buoyant and prosperous city during the Progressive Era. The Cleveland Industrial Exposition of 1909 portrayed the city as one of the outstanding manufacturing centers in the world. A remarkable collection of vaudeville and motion picture palaces at Playhouse Square downtown vied for business with a lively uptown district at

Euclid Avenue and East 105th Street. The new Detroit-Superior Bridge—with its lower streetcar deck—opened in 1917, thus providing the city's first truly high-level connection across the industrial Flats. A bountiful era of culture and philanthropy flourished when the city's leading families endowed the Cleveland Orchestra, the Cleveland Museum of Art, the Cleveland Play House, the Cleveland Institute of Music, and a host of other institutions. The Cleveland Metropolitan Park District, formed in 1917, preserved some of the country's most scenic real estate for public enjoyment and established the foundation for a greenbelt of parks encircling Cuyahoga County.[7] The capitalistic aristocracy who had prospered during the rise of industry controlled the destiny of their hometown. The big names—Mather, Sherwin, Severance, Hanna, Feiss, Halle, Blossom, to name a few—were the power bloc of the early 1900s. These nabobs lost their tremendous influence as they died off, and many of their fortunes were left in trusts.

Cleveland faced a myriad of urban problems in spite of great economic development, unprecedented increase in population growth, and an air of prosperity and cultural development during the first two decades of the twentieth century. The city in the late 1800s survived as a low-tax, fiscally prudent municipality. Power in the executive branch of the local government operated *de facto* by the bureaucracy, because by choice and design the Mayor was a caretaker figure. Political power rested in the hands of the often-unscrupulous ward leaders who exerted considerable power and survived on local ethnic patronage.

PHILIP W. PORTER, LONGTIME JOURNALIST FOR the Cleveland *Plain Dealer*, wrote that Cleveland's Twentieth Century history of ups and downs demanded a unique explanation. When the city displayed elements of decay, pundits quickly spread their vitriolic rhetoric. This same civic rot eroded other big cities of considerable size—in particular St. Louis, Pittsburgh, Milwaukee, Boston, Baltimore, and Buffalo. Cleveland became a special target for critics. This periodic criticism emanated because of the city's rapidly expanding wealth, industrial diversity, civic leadership and their gung-ho willingness to take a chance. These elements are the principal ingredients which make a metropolis grow, yet still remain a desirable place to live.

Porter believed the seeds for Cleveland's stockmarket-like behavior were sown at the turn of the twentieth century. One might ask how. Porter explained, "Cleveland has for generations possessed two qualities that made it different from other big cities of slightly less than one million population...[Namely] political volatility and fragmentation." The journalist defended his thesis thusly, "Cleveland since the beginning of [the twentieth century] has been known for its mavericks and pop-off guys, the refusal to stay hitched long to one political party or novelty in government, its continuous battles over public transportation and the best way to develop downtown and the suburbs. Volatility, independence, and fragmentation seemed to be bred into Clevelanders year after year."[8] The first issue alluded to by Porter, namely volatility, erupted in Cleveland at the turn of the twentieth century. It came in the personage of Tom L. Johnson, recognized as one of the great reform mayors in America's urban city history.

Republicans generally controlled Ohio state and local governments in the late 1800s. Elections were hard fought, and in spite of massive voter turnouts, the margin of victory was close. Campaigns centered on cultural issues such as public education and temperance. Midwest Republicans modified their strategy in the 1890s after several defeats, promising to promote economic prosperity for all citizens regardless of ethnicity, religion or class. Several regional politicians went even further with their political agendas. Reform-minded Mayors like Hazen Pingree of Detroit, Samuel *Golden Rule* Jones of Toledo, and Mayor-elect Johnson took urban amenities like water, lighting, and streetcars out of the hands of private corporations, and gave the municipal government responsibility for their management. These actions rested on a reconstructed conception of the public good and a new sense of the role of local government in nurturing that conception. Within the tower of Babel, there was one language that everyone spoke. Not surprisingly, it was the language of material development.[9] This philosophy inspired Tom Johnson and other like-minded reform politicians.

At the turn of the twentieth century Cleveland residents were just beginning to focus their growing awareness on the need for efficient and progressive government. The citizenry cried out for effective actions to meet the multitude of problems that plagued their city. Many of Cleveland's needs were elementary ones: efficient sewerage systems; fast and cheap mass transportation; clean, safe streets and roads; housing codes and sanitary measures.[10] Although Cleveland ended the nineteenth century as one of the nation's great industrial and commercial centers, there was a negative side to this success. For many the city was bleak and inhospitable. The Women's Department of the city's centennial commission acknowledged the contrast in a time capsule deposited at the local historical society which read in part, "We bequeath to you a city of a century, prosperous and beautiful, and yet far from our ideal.... Many of the people are poor and some are vainly seeking work at living wages.... Some of our children are robbed of their childhood. Vice parades our streets and disease lurks in many places that men and women call their homes."[11]

Skillful manipulation of the ward system undermined the legislative arm of Cleveland's municipal government, specifically city council elections. The key to this maneuver was to retain a high ratio of wards in relation to the total population of the city. In 1900 Cleveland had 42 wards for a population of 381,000. With voting rights limited to male citizens over 21, these wards rarely generated over a thousand votes on Election Day. Ward-level politicians easily controlled such a small number of votes. In key elections, according to Cleveland historian John Grabowski, fraud was transparently clear when *bona fide* registrants voted early and often. Transients appeared at polling places sporting gift bottles of spirits, and the deceased rose Lazarus-like to claim their rights of franchise. These machinations elected a councilman who was powerful in his ward. As a public servant he faithfully represented the interests of those who elected him, including native- and foreign-born immigrants, the elite and businessmen seeking contracts and franchises from the municipality. Cleveland was never dominated by a single boss, as was true in New York, Chicago, Philadelphia, Boston or Cincinnati. Instead the city's ethnic, cultural and class divisions produced a ward-level sachem affiliated with either political party. By 1900, Cleveland's city council was highly representative of the city's ethnic and class composition.[12] It was this political environment which Tom Johnson and later Frank J. Lausche encountered in pursuing their political agendas.

Cleveland's political volatility became evident around the 1900s when the local Republicans, then the dominant force, split between Mayor Robert E. McKisson, a key member of the city machine politico (He was Mayor from 1895–1899; John Farley served as Mayor from 1899–1901) and Mark Hanna, business tycoon and campaign manager for President William McKinley. In 1901 the city faithful turned to Tom L. Johnson to give the city leadership it needed to meet these aforementioned problems. Here was a man to match and master the sprawling city. Johnson idealistically foresaw a future in which cities boasted broad boulevards, great public buildings, extensive public parks and government by, of and for the people. The Mayor was a typical product of the Gilded Age or as often described by historians, the Age of Robber Barons. He was a tough-minded entrepreneur who built a streetcar and steel plant empire in the hard-driving fashion of his day.[13]

Johnson read Henry George's *Progress and Poverty* and explored the belief that a single tax plan might eliminate poverty and unemployment that bred slums, disease and crime. This spirit of reform prompted the rotund Johnson to run for Mayor of Cleveland. From 1901 to 1909 this successful millionaire fought privilege, corruption and his friends of former years. He clashed with members of the exclusive Union Club. He made new friends with the city's young liberal zealots like the irascible William Stinchcomb, Peter Witt, Burr Gongwer and Carl D. Friebolin. His four terms in office were as spectacular as his famous tent meetings. There was a touch of the circus about Johnson's administration and its peculiar mixture of adherents—rabble-rousers like Witt, humanitarian clerics like the Reverend Harris R. Cooley, the egghead contingent, including Doctor Edward W. Bemis, Newton D. Baker and the political whip, Charles P. Salem.[14]

During his campaigns, Johnson brought the immigrant groups into the broad stream of American politics. Their level of participation demanded more than appearance at the polls to vote as directed by the political bosses. The carnival atmosphere of the Mayor's tent meetings attracted many immigrants who would have felt left out in a more formal setting. During the Democratic give-and-take of these meetings a brawl was always a possibility or at least a verbal clash over the political issues of the day. Johnson with his superb talent for leadership fashioned a means of communication that had been missing in the community for forty years. In a sense he restored the town meeting atmosphere of the pre-Civil War era.[15]

Life in Cleveland changed when the stout (260 pounds) curly-haired Mayor took office. While Cleveland voters had sown the wind, they reaped a whirlwind. Not many of the people in the street understood Johnson during his campaign. He inveighed against *Privilege* (industrialists and monopolists) and hammered words of criticism at monopolistic practices, especially the utility companies that provided the city's electricity, artificial gas, and street railway service.[16]

When he became mayor, Johnson did not fight the Democratic machine, recalled New Dealer Raymond Moley, "He took it over, controlled, directed it and measurably kept it clean."

The ebullient Mayor espoused a commitment with other reform politicians of the time, which promoted the idea that the history of the Buckeye state, like the history of the world, was a ceaseless struggle between the people and *Privilege*. Progress occurred only through victories of the former over the latter. Johnson pledged to end the corrupt relationship between businessman franchise holders and city councilmen. He wanted to eradicate the city of corrupt franchise alliances and replace them with public ownership of utilities and transportation.

Johnson set out to bring about low fares for transportation on the street railways. First he purged the city council of Mark Hanna and pro-traction representatives. Unable to push through municipal ownership of street railways because of a state disabling law, Mayor Johnson brought in a low-cost competitor and forced through an ordinance providing for three-cent fares. The traction interests secured an injunction against this low-cost line during its last important phase of track laying, which would have connected a new people line to the downtown terminus. Johnson struck back by ordering the new company's section crews to work at night, and under the cover of darkness they laid the last segment of the track.

The three-cent line began operating the following morning, and Johnson's long-sought working men's fare was then in effect on a portion of Cleveland's streets. The final rail settlement covering the entire city did not come until after Johnson's defeat for re-election in 1909. Without doubt the subsequent settlement was of Johnson's doing and clearly belonged to him. This new franchise, which covered the city, provided for sliding fares, a 6 percent return to the company on actual worth of the physical plant and the franchise without issuance of watered stock. A three-cent fare prevailed from 1910 to 1917. Johnson's dream of municipal ownership was finally realized in 1942.[17]

The city delighted in the spectacle of the new Mayor at work. People chuckled and applauded when he ordered the park department to pull up the Don't-Walk-on-the-Grass signs and invited the citizens to go out of their way to walk on the public greens wherever they found them. The city folk watched approvingly as he ordered new playgrounds, instituted reforms in the city's penal policy, bought farmlands for rehabilitation of juvenile delinquents, ordered the city to take over garbage collection and disposal, began a new policy of law enforcement, waged war against billboards and cleaned up the city streets.[18]

When he became Mayor, Johnson did not fight the Democratic machine, recalled New Dealer Raymond Moley, "He took it over, controlled, directed it and measurably kept it clean."[19] Johnson used money, influence, ward healers and all the classical techniques of the city boss to defeat those he perceived as his enemies and to help elect his own people to office.

It is difficult to overstate Tom Johnson's impact on his city and on the reform movement of his times. His mayoralty became a benchmark by which future mayors would be measured. "His greatest triumph has been that he aroused in Cleveland a civic sense," wrote Paul W. Haworth, his contemporary and a government authority, "He has made people realize that the affairs of the city are their affairs."[20]

There was a mystique to this Mayor, as seems evident among all great men. Those who fell under his spell lived dreamily and fanatically for his cause. Reflecting upon Cleveland's generally good government up to 1949, Moley asserted, "Behind Cleveland's government is an educated public whose basic training goes back to the still revered golden age of Johnson."[21] Even the skeptical muckraker Lincoln Steffens, who was not given to throwing around accolades, declared in 1905, "Tom Johnson is the best mayor of the best governed city in the United States."[22] Johnson's real importance lay in the fact that he acted as a catalyst in the political life of the city. His presence lifted both major political parties above petty maneuvering for office and spoils. The parties became vehicles for reform that made Cleveland nationally known as a city neither contented nor corrupted during the Progressive era.

The fragmentation Porter alluded to prior to and beyond Tom Johnson's tenure as Mayor festered with the influx of a large number of immigrants, particularly from mid and southern Europe. The social and cultural diversity of these new immigrant neighborhoods amalgamated with the city's transition into an industrial metropolis. Many nativist Clevelanders viewed these newcomers with suspicion and distrust. The newcomer's speech, dress, and customs were different, and many experienced difficulty providing for their large families. Ethnic groups received chastisement for their tendency to settle in autonomous groups. The task of assimilation of these new arrivals fell largely to the public schools, which offered classes in English, citizenship and housekeeping. Some of the city's branch libraries aided the foreign born. Eleanor E. Ledbetter, librarian of the Broadway branch for thirty years, attempted to ease the plight of these immigrants. Her library offered books in fourteen languages. To criticism that foreign-language texts discouraged the learning of English, Ledbetter responded, "To find books in one's own language is next to finding living friends, and only the exile can appreciate what it means."[23]

Two prominent American politicians lent credence to Porter's hypothesis of the importance of accepting and assimilating these new citizens into America's mainstream. In 1908, the year the senior Lausche died, President Theodore Roosevelt enthusiastically embraced Israel Zangwill's Broadway Play, *The Melting Pot*. In the plot, protagonist David Quixans belongs to a Russian Jewish family. Described as a new immigrant, Quixans flees to New York to escape the Russian pogroms. He seizes the opportunity America gives him, writes his American symphony, marries the gentile girl of his dreams, and becomes a proud American.[24] Roosevelt endorsed Zangwill's depiction of America as a land of unlimited opportunity. The bespectacled President applauded the playwright's insistence that even immigrants who came from allegedly less developed countries in Eastern Europe could become the most successful and best of Americans. It mattered too that Quixans succeeded in America, not unnecessarily by hiding his Jewish heritage, rather by assimilating into his new American culture. Zangwill's words expressed by the character David Quixans might well have come from Roosevelt's own pen: "America is God's Crucible, the great Melting Pot, where all the races of Europe are melting and reforming! Germans and Frenchmen, Irishmen and Englishmen, Jews and Russians—into the Crucible with all! God is making the American."[25] Roosevelt could have added Slovenians and other European nationalities to his list. His words and their meaning applied to young Frank J. Lausche, an up-and-coming son of immigrant parents.

Fiorello H. La Guardia, fellow New York politician and a second-generation immigrant, reiterated Roosevelt's rhetoric with his own words and deeds. La Guardia, U.S. Congressman and later mayor of New York, grew up amidst prejudice against immigrants. "Despite their own insistence that they were exuberant Westerners (the La Guardia family lived for several years in Prescott, Arizona), not immigrants, the La Guardias were thought of as an Italian family.... New York dockworkers denounced Italian longshoremen as racially inferior to 'white men.'... La Guardia remembered the cries years later, 'Hey, Fiorello, you're a dago too.' To a vulnerable child whose tough exterior never hardened against rejection, 'it hurts.'"[26] When La Guardia entered the political arena, his motivation in large measure was idealism in which he pursued the *good* in life as he saw it. He knew the life of the poor, the immigrant, and the laborer first hand. The rotund politician helped immigrants seek the full promise of American liberty and opportunity. La Guardia wanted to make government fair and honest. Young Frank Lausche observed his father treat immigrants in a like fashion. Lausche planned to establish this same reputation for himself.

Although these two political giants—Teddy Roosevelt and La Guardia—cried out for assimilation of the newly arrived foreign-born immigrants, their words often fell upon deaf ears. Prejudice has existed in the world for centuries regardless of color or ethnic background. Strange languages tend to restrict assimilation. Cleveland was no different from other large metropolitan cities. Porter's definition of fragmentation took an interesting turn in Cleveland's demographic development, bringing about the residential separations of the native-born and the foreign-born.

Cleveland, in effect, was two separate cities. With the exception of the western lakeshore wards, the heaviest concentration of native-born Clevelanders located on the east side. Native-born migrants clustered in wards around the central business district, the eastern lakeshore industrial district, and the eastern railroad beltline industrial district. The residential concentrations of foreign-born were almost an exact reversal of those of the native-born. These newcomers located in the urbanized outer ring of the westside settlement and the westside industrial district, most prominently in the Flats–area industrial district. A minority spilled over into the east side.

BY WORLD WAR I CLEVELAND, A MATURE INDUSTRIAL CITY, with its segregated allotments of space to specific human activities, resembled a doughnut. The center contained the bulk of business enterprises, and the most recently arrived, least urbanized, and least affluent of its citizens were surrounded by a ring of relative comfort and affluence.[27]

This backdrop of a city on the move could not help but make an impression on young Frank Lausche. The fatherless family was caught up in the excitement of many changes taking place in a vibrant and growing industrial city. Ethnic minorities were destined to play a major role in the political happenings in Cleveland. Lausche captured the machinations of back room political wheeling and dealing in the 23rd Ward where his family resided. This ward along St. Clair Avenue was only sixty short blocks from Public Square and the infrastructure of downtown Cleveland.

The most important task for the young Lausche was to help his mother hold their family together and provide the economic resources to rear a large family. Ma Lausche was a catalyst, and the children rallied around their beloved mother. From her Slovenian parents and her *Dvorska Vas* schooling, this mother inherited a rich common sense and unselfishness toward others. A gentle and tolerant woman, she loved America and had no patience with immigrants who came to America only to save a bankroll and later return to their homeland.[28] Under different circumstances Ma Lausche could no doubt have pursued a professional career in singing. She had a beautiful voice and loved to sing. Before the completion of the Slovenian St. Vitus Church in 1894, Mrs. Lausche was a member of the first local Slovenian Church choir. They sang at St. Peter's Church at East 17th Street and Superior Avenue in downtown Cleveland.[29] Her melodic voice and talents in music filtered down to all of her children who either played musical instruments or sang professionally in their adult years. Ma Lausche, as she was reverently called, was perpetually busy, yet she carried the burdens of life with a smile, a joke and a song on her lips. On a typical Sunday after 9 o'clock mass was over "Ma Lausche always had a regiment-sized buffet of breaded chicken, veal and pork chops, with a Slovenian side dish of sauerkraut and Roman beans on her dining room table. All day long the relatives, friends and neighbors came visiting—to eat, drink, gossip and talk politics. In the evenings, the family circle tightened around the upright piano in the parlor. Every member of the family played a musical instrument or sang. Ma Lausche assigned the voices and instruments and led the singing. Almost always, the finale was her favorite "My Country Tis of Thee."[30]

Young Frank was nurtured in this atmosphere of love, friendship, and hard work. Anton Grdina, long-time friend and neighbor, remembered, "Frank inherited from his Slovenian parents all those qualities [that would be so important in his political career]. Among other things, his parents transmitted to him and his siblings a knowledge of [their] Slovenian heritage, together with a genuine American patriotism. [They understood the meaning] of hard work, personal honesty, and love of poetry and music, especially Slovenian songs."[31] Lausche said of his parents, "They came with a vision. My father worked long and hard for little pay in the steel mills. He raised ten kids, but even with them to feed he was eventually able to go into business for himself. He believed in the old tried-and-true American virtue of honesty, thrift and opportunity."[32]

Frederick Tisdale, writing in the *Saturday Evening Post* in 1945, gave credence to Ma Lausche's vow that her sons would make something of themselves in life. "Frank Lausche is a product of the neighborhood devastated...by exploding gas tanks [1944].... His parents came to the United States from Slovenia. Their home was typical of the district. By day it was darkened by the soot of the steel mills and by night it was lighted by furnace fires. Most of the grimy kids lived a boisterous life and expected to sweat out their maturity at the fires and forges. 'Not my boys,' said Mom Lausche."[33]

In correspondence with Scott Lucas, former U.S. Senator from Illinois and good friend, Lausche recalled how as a youngster "barefooted, bareheaded, dressed only in bloomer knee pants and a blouse made by my Mother on her sewing machine, I would leave my home, go down toward Lake Erie—about a quarter of a mile away (the lake was more like three-quarters of a mile away) to play in the open and to fish off the piers that jutted into the lake."[34]

Frances Lausche insisted that her children take advantage of the opportunities this new country had to offer. Ma Lausche was robust and initially commanded attention because of her physical stature. She was definitely a leader in the Slovenian neighborhood where her family resided. Her children developed a love for sports, music, their Slovenian roots and what the Slovenians affectionately call culture. The

Lausche building housed two bowling alleys, and all the children, especially Charles, became excellent bowlers. Baseball fields near their home provided the neighborhood children with an opportunity to hone their skills. The local Slovenians built a beautiful church (St. Vitus Church) adjacent to a Catholic school. A few blocks away a large Slovenian National Home became the social center for many Slovenian activities. The Slovenians loved their music, whether it be ethnic, classical, or contemporary. Singing societies, of which Ma Lausche was a member, presented concerts, operettas and operas directed by prominent musicians. Notable musicians were John Ivanush, the father of Slovenian opera in Cleveland, and Anton Schubel, a former opera singer and talent scout for Carnegie Hall. Ivan Zorman, the gentle Slovenian poet and composer, and one of Lausche's cherished friends whetted the young man's love for and appreciation of poetry. There were Slovenian and English language libraries, lectures, music and ballet opportunities, and subsequently, a Slovenian art school directed by H. Gregory Prusheck,

Young Frank was nurtured in this atmosphere of love, friendship, and hard work. Anton Grdina, long-time friend and neighbor, remembered, "Frank inherited from his Slovenian parents all those qualities [that would be so important in his political career]...

internationally prominent Slovenian immigrant.[35] Many of Lausche's neighbors, as well as the Lausche children, rose to prominence in various fields of endeavor.[36] Unbeknownst to this Slovenian neighborhood, one of their own was destined to scale the political wall to national prominence.

In the early 1900s Lausche attended St. Vitus grade school for his first four years. The church school housed only those four grades, so Lausche attended nearby St. Francis grade school at 71st Street and Superior Avenue for his fifth grade. The next three years the young student spent his school time at the Madison Grammar School on Addison Street. After school hours when not playing on the playground or working, Lausche helped out as a stagehand for the Slovenian Dramatic Club at the Slovenian National Home. This responsibility helped him develop stage presence and was good preparation for Lausche's later efforts to capture his audience's attention with his political oratory. Lausche's church activities included his first communion at the age of ten in St. Vitus Church. He continued his schooling at Central Institute Preparatory school, which once occupied a corner at East 55th Street and Woodland Avenue. The young man worked in a print shop next door after school. He dropped out of school in 1911 when his older brother, Louis, Jr., died. He completed his high school education by correspondence while in the Army.

After Louis Lausche's death young Frank, particularly out of love and reverence for his mother, assumed the manly chores of the household. He helped out financially in his own way. The New York Central freight trains raced through Cleveland depositing and picking up scrap iron and brass. The tracks ran near by St. Clair Avenue. Lausche picked up scraps of iron and brass which fell off the boxcars and sold these materials to nearby brass and steel companies. He helped fold papers and fed the printing press in the small Slovenian newspaper office owned by his father. The obedient and well-behaved Frank, now a teenager, helped his mother by washing dishes for the many meals prepared for immigrant guests and friends.

Frank, husky and active, was a student with a quick apperception, and he mastered his subjects with little effort. He was not a particularly willing student. Sports fascinated Lausche, and he began to exhibit prowess in baseball. He much preferred playing marbles, pitching horseshoes, or playing on the baseball diamond to attending school. The wavy-haired, good-looking young man devoted little time to the fair sex or to his studies. He was always there to help his mother when needed. Lausche's first significant job was to light gas street lamps for the city. The job took less than an hour a day and paid $104 a year. It provided him with the opportunity to meet many neighborhood friends who became supportive in subsequent political endeavors. In his teen years, Lausche accepted a job as court interpreter for newly arrived Slovenian immigrants. This responsibility stimulated Lausche's interest in law and politics. The Slovenian newspaper, *Ameriška Domovina* (*American Home*) was printed next door to the Lausche saloon. Mike Kolar, a friend of the Lausche family, remembered that Louis J. Pirc, editor of the paper, "often talked to Frank and the other children,...especially to Frank, and got him interested in politics."[37]

⌒

IT WAS BASEBALL, AMERICA'S NATIONAL PASTIME, not politics, which really commanded Lausche's time and enthusiasm in his adolescent years. The youthful baseball star attended Central Institute Preparatory School during his early middle school years. His performance on the cinder lots near the New York Central tracks began to attract flattering notices from local sports writers. "The whole neighborhood used to go to the playground at E. 62nd Street to watch the ball games and he was one of the best."[38] The young phenom, having the time of his life, earned extra dollars playing for local semi-professional teams.

John Nielsen, a resident of the St. Clair Avenue neighborhood recalled delivering the Cleveland *Press* to the Lausche's *gostilna*. On Saturdays this newspaper boy collected the weekly charge of twelve cents for the paper. The daily at that time cost only two cents. He noted golf clubs and a couple of golf bags near the entrance of the second floor of the Lausche saloon. "To be playing golf in those days was a symbol of a sports-minded family or of a prestigious membership in the country club set." The Lausche boys were not members of a country club, but they were sports-minded and good athletes.

Nielsen possessed a copy of an early booklet entitled *Slovenska Baseball Liga* (*The Slovenian Baseball League*). A short article detailed the evolution of Slovenian baseball teams in Cleveland. Two local teams, *Ribnica* and *Zuzembeck*, were named after two towns in Slovenia from which many of the Slovenian-Clevelanders emigrated. Other Slovenian teams followed. Some 20 or 30 years later these leagues helped develop prominent players of Slovenian heritage [Al Milnar, Frank Doljack, and Joe Kuhel] who played in the major leagues. Lausche only played for these local teams sporadically because of his exceptional skill. His unusual talents evoked considerable attention among the more highly organized city amateur teams. Fast-paced Class A teams eagerly sought the services of the young infielder. Lausche began to receive inquiries about playing professional baseball.[39]

In the summer of 1914 Lausche was eighteen years old and faced a world about to enter into a global war. The rapidly maturing young man played third base for a neighborhood team grandiloquently called the Epicureans. The *Plain Dealer* reported that in a game against the Corbett Tailors third baseman Lausche had fourteen assists and one putout, statistics believed to be a record at that time. Lausche recalled that their pitcher Fred Dodd "had a sore arm and a slow curve. The result was that ball after ball was hit down the third base line. I got two for three at the plate that day too."[40]

The following year in 1915 the lanky nineteen-year-old signed a contract as guardian of the hot corner for the Stinchcomb Engineers. He thrilled the local fans from East 61st Street and St. Clair. The well-organized and competitive amateur baseball program in Cleveland gained nationwide notice for their high quality of play and sportsmanship. As an outgrowth of this amateur program, local sports writers triggered formation of the Cleveland Baseball Federation which was founded in 1921 and became a model for amateur baseball in the United States. Lausche reportedly set a fielding record by handling nineteen chances in one game.[41] Later in the summer the White Motor team recruited the young third baseman for playoff competition. He helped this team win a national championship for Class A teams.

Baseball scouts urged Lausche to try professional baseball. Minor league baseball in the early 1900s was a popular but precarious business. Teams were not part of a farm system and survived on their own financial capabilities or failed due to bankruptcy. One of these teams was Duluth, Minnesota, in the Class D Northern League. Lausche reported to this small town near the Canadian border to play in the spring of 1916. The league included teams from Minnesota, Wisconsin, North Dakota and Canada.[42] Lausche did not need much encouragement to go to Duluth, although he hated leaving his mother and her many family responsibilities. "I always felt in my adolescent years that baseball was the field in which I ought to devote myself. I vigorously and sincerely believed that I had the potential of playing big league baseball."[43] Playing professional baseball was a dream come true for the enthusiastic and excited youngster. Lausche began in spectacular fashion, hitting a home run, triple, and single in his first game.

Unfortunately the slick fielding third baseman soon had trouble hitting a curve ball and reminisced about his first weeks as a professional player, "In...spring training I fielded everything that came towards me and hit hard everything...the pitcher threw at me. When the season began I continued playing in the same form—hitting hard, fielding well, and winning games for the Duluth team. This continued for two months, then something happened which threw into reverse all the good I had done. My fielding became bad as well as my batting. When I look back, while it is hard to believe, I attributed my batting failure to the fact that in some way my favorite bat was lost."[44]

Prior to this slump the Duluth paper paid Lausche compliments about his play. The Clevelander was hitting .422, and a local sportswriter noted that he swallowed up every ball that hit toward third base. But after 31 games, Lausche's batting average dropped to .269. This slump forced the Duluth team to release the disappointed young athlete. A nearby semi-pro team in Virginia, Minnesota, quickly signed Lausche to their roster. After about two weeks of continued poor performance, he was sent back to Cleveland. Lausche played amateur ball in his hometown for the remainder of the 1916 season.

Rejuvenated during the winter of 1916–17, Lausche moved up the minor league ladder, reporting to a Class B team in Lawrence, Massachusetts, in the spring of 1917. He performed reasonably well, then again went into a severe batting slump and was released after 27 games. His batting average was only .155.[45] Like many American youngsters at this time, his mind was distracted from baseball. On April 2, 1917, President Woodrow Wilson announced America's entry into World War I. Life turned topsy-turvy, and for the moment, Lausche forgot baseball. He enlisted as an infantryman in the army in the summer of 1917. The twenty-one-year-old joined other recruits at Camp Gordon near Atlanta, Georgia. The young recruit completed basic training in the rust-colored clay of the Peach State. By spring of 1918, 60,000 men stationed at Camp Gordon made preparations for embarkment to the front lines in Europe. Lausche had been playing baseball whenever possible especially on the weekends. His talents did not go unnoticed. Of the plethora of quality players, Lausche was one of several chosen to be a member of the camp baseball team. Simultaneously while a member of the Camp Gordon nine, Lausche received a promotion to corporal the first week, to sergeant the second week, and to second lieutenant after eight months. Now assigned to officers' training school Lausche recalled his rapid rise in rank was more due to his baseball aptitude than to his soldiering capabilities. Lausche's high batting average spared the twenty-two-year-old from a trip across the Atlantic Ocean to the front lines.

During Lausche's stay at Camp Gordon, cadres of outstanding U.S. boxers came to the military base. They were assigned there to receive special training which would enable each boxer to set up a boxing program in the other camps. The group reminded one of a Who's Who in Boxing. They included Clevelanders Johnny Kilbane, feather-weight champion; Benny Leonard, lightweight champion; and Tommy Gibbons who would take Jack Dempsey to a 15-round decision in Shelby, Montana, in 1923. Several other notable pugilists received assignments to the camp. Lausche, athletically inclined and in good condition, received an inquiry if he would like to become a boxer. After observing this group of boxing elites Lausche quickly decided that discretion was the better part of valor and graciously declined this offer.[46]

Charles Frank, manager of the camp baseball team, in peacetime served as principal stockholder and manager of the Atlanta Crackers in the Double A Southern League. During the war, play in this league—as in most minor leagues—was suspended. Frank was impressed with Lausche's playing ability. After the war ended on November 11, 1918, but before Lausche received his discharge in January 1919, Frank made Lausche a tempting offer. The Atlanta manager asked Lausche to report to the Crackers team for spring training in 1919 and to sign a contract for a six-month season at $225 a month. After Lausche's discharge, the young officer returned to wintry Cleveland to discuss this offer with his family. While pondering his decision, Lausche enrolled in law school without having any prior college education, which was not uncommon in the early years of the twentieth century. He attended classes at night. Years later Lausche reminisced about his dilemma, "I faced the first important decision and maybe the most important decision of my life. I pondered profoundly which of the two courses I should take. I decided not to report to Atlanta but to continue my attendance at Cleveland's John Marshall Law School. How I did it I do not understand...my love for baseball was intense. I wanted to continue playing; I wanted to break into the big leagues."[47]

⌒

Ma Lausche undoubtedly influenced Frank to pursue a legal career. His mother insisted that he should pursue his education and a more worthy profession than playing baseball. Lausche had heard of ex-players who were sweeping streets and digging ditches. Such tales about players falling upon hard times made an impact on Lausche's decision. "I was baseball crazy but I had sense enough to know that baseball isn't much good as a life profession."[48] Years later Lausche reminisced about the success of several members of the Cleveland Indians baseball club who came from immigrant families. He referred specifically to Joe Vosmik (Bohemian), Al Milnar (Slovenian), and Hal Trosky (Bohemian). Lausche's dilemma about pursuing a baseball career was not unlike that of many other immigrant families in the early 1900s. Dozens of immigrants' sons scaled the ladder to reach the major leagues. There were many more examples of men like Lausche who fell by the wayside for one reason or another. They spent the remainder of their productive years in semi-skilled or unskilled occupations. Lausche resigned himself to playing sandlot baseball for several years in Cleveland, earning $15 to $25 a game.

Lausche's talents often earned him a position on a Cleveland All-Stars team. This team played a series of games with town teams in southern Ohio. On one trip to a small town in southeastern Ohio Lausche observed a sight that became a major environmental issue in his future political career, "I came into Belmont County, and there...I looked at those hills; and the ravages of strip mining were apparent. They struck me deeply. I could not believe that an ethical human being would...do to the land what was being done there. It left an indelible impression upon me."[49] Lausche did not forget this blighted landscape. He carried the torch to restore those desecrated hills and valleys of southern Ohio throughout his tenure in office, both as Ohio Governor and as U.S. Senator.

On another baseball trip to southeastern Ohio, Lausche, now playing in the outfield, was manager of a Cleveland All-Star team. They played the Dillonvale (in Jefferson County) town team who embarrassingly thrashed the All-Stars. The game had been billed as a match-up between the city boys and the local favorites. The manager of the Dillonvale team confronted Lausche after the game. He told the Cleveland manager "to take his guarantee money ($150) and not to show his damn face in Dillonvale again." It was not one of Lausche's more pleasurable experiences on the diamond. For several years during the 1920s Lausche could not bring himself to attend games of the Cleveland Indians, his favorite team. The Tribe played at quaint League Park on Lexington Avenue and 66th Street. Why could he not attend these games? "I would have seen myself out there at third base, and I couldn't have stood that," Lausche lamented many years later, "I still can't believe that I turned down that big chance to play professional baseball. Baseball has been my life. It was all I wanted through my adolescent years. Yet, when the opportunity presented itself, I chose...law. It's unbelievable." [50]

Decades later Lausche reminisced about his baseball career in a congratulatory note to Jack Edchert, who umpired in the Cleveland sandlot program for fifty-one years. The local umpire had worked some of Lausche's early games, and now the U.S. Senator mischievously wrote, "Strangely, I have a most unfavorable opinion of all the umpires in the league. Although I was firm in my belief that when I was batting they were always in error in the calling of the strikes and balls...in the advanced years of my life I am convinced that in all probability in the majority of instances these umpires were right." [51]

In 1920 and 1921 Lausche put professional baseball in the back of his mind and concentrated on his law studies. John Marshall Law School's night program, located in downtown Cleveland, allowed Lausche to work part-time. He continued to play amateur baseball in the Cleveland Baseball Federation.[52] The Federation gave support to the game on the sandlots, and Cleveland continued its leading role in amateur baseball. Lausche played on several teams in the 1920s. By 1946 the Cleveland Baseball Federation boasted a membership of 800 teams in its program.

While a law student, the hard-driving young Lausche gained valuable legal experience working as a clerk in the daytime for the reputable law firm of Locher, Green, and Woods. Cyrus Locher, of Lithuanian heritage, was one of the city's leading attorneys, and he proved to be an important influence upon Lausche's political future. After two and one-half years of study, Lausche graduated from John Marshall Law School, finishing second in his class. Soon thereafter the fledgling lawyer—as well as 159 other applicants—took the Ohio state bar exam. He ranked second among this group with a mark of 91.7.[53] Ma Lausche had reason to be proud of her good-looking twenty-five-year-old son. The neophyte lawyer then began to test his wings in the legal profession. The political itch came soon thereafter.

THE TWENTIES MARKED A DECADE OF INDUSTRIAL EXPANSION and overall prosperity in Cleveland. A city's progress depends in large measure upon the faith, resourcefulness, and hard work of its citizenship. Enterprising and diligent Clevelanders in the previous decade had advanced the industrial, commercial, and cultural standing of their city. Wartime prosperity carried into the post-war era, with the exception of a brief downturn in 1921. Second only to Detroit, Cleveland's strong position as a center of automobile production continued during the twenties. Consumerism reached an all-time high, especially with the purchase of electrical merchandise. The city's strong industrial growth provoked development of a labor movement, particularly within the larger contingents of immigrants who made up a major portion of the working force. In order to replenish this labor supply reduced by World War I casualties and the tightening of immigration laws, city leaders recruited blacks to come to Cleveland. Union organizations grew in numbers. The Brotherhood of Locomotive Engineers was the largest of these labor organizations. In all there were 150 unions in the city, and most of their members belonged to the American Federation of Labor. Unions lobbied for better hours, higher wages, and improved working conditions.[54]

A number of self-contained communities on the outskirts of the city were growing at a more rapid pace than was Cleveland.[55] Two shy and reclusive brothers changed the face of Cleveland. Entrepreneurial Mantis J. and Oris P. Van Sweringen, as part of their railway empire, built a rapid-transit system connecting their beautiful Shaker Heights suburb with downtown Cleveland. Other outlying areas sprung up, notably Lakewood, Cleveland Heights, Garfield Heights and Parma. Suburban voters, content with their residential environment and municipal independence, resisted annexation. In 1932 Cleveland was territorially arrested at seventy-six square miles.[56] The Van Sweringens were not finished. Under the aegis of these two brothers, the $150 million Cleveland Union Terminal opened on June 28, 1930. This complex included the Terminal Tower, (tallest building in Ohio at that time), an underground railroad station, the Builders Exchange, Medical Arts, Midland Building, and the Higbee Department Store. This impressive real estate development created a tremendous impact upon downtown Cleveland. The building complex eliminated a large area of squalor, and Public Square, the traditional center of business and civic life, re-emerged as the focal point in the heart of the city.[57]

A distinctive rhythm and air of optimism and modernity prevailed in the 1920s. Women won the right to vote and gained new independence with the flapper look (short hair and even shorter skirts). The city's first radio station—WHK—went on the air in 1922, and despite Prohibition, liquor was readily available at the city's many private clubs. A remarkable string of vaudeville and motion picture theatres rose in the new Playhouse Square District at East 14th Street and Euclid Avenue. The Palace and Lake theaters formed the core of the city's cinematic nightlife. The Hanna Theatre, also on Playhouse Square, succeeded the Euclid Avenue Opera House in 1921 presenting popular road shows. At Euclid Avenue and East 105th Street, Keith's 105th, the Circle, the University, the Alhambra and the Park Theaters mixed with the Elysium Ice Palace, nightclubs, and restaurants to form a vibrant uptown district. Nearby crowds filled League Park to watch their beloved Cleveland Indians compete in the American League. The town went giddy in 1920 when the team, led by player-manager Tris Speaker, won their first World Championship over the Brooklyn Dodgers.

Cleveland continued its heady industrial expansion and maintained a strong position in automobile manufacturing. The city advanced to fourth place in the nation relative to the percentage of home ownership.[58] Conversely the political scene in Cleveland characterized gloom and disenchantment in the immediate post-World War I years. Part of this feeling emanated from national disillusionment that World War I had not *made* the world safe for democracy. This wave of disappointment brought about a political change and so-called return to normalcy in 1920 when voters elected Ohio Republican Senator Warren G. Harding to the presidency in a landslide vote over fellow Ohioan James F. Cox. Locally, a feeling of despair descended both upon Republicans and Democrats and their political machines. The Cleveland Democrats had not produced a leader since Peter Witt lost the mayoral election in 1915. Newton D. Baker, who took over the Cuyahoga County Democratic reins after Johnson died, served as mayor from 1912–1916. In 1916, Baker departed for Washington DC to become President Wilson's Secretary of War. The county office holders were typical old-style politicians. The administrations of Republican Mayors Harry L. Davis and William S. Fitzgerald (1916–1921) were corrupt and inefficient. Although reform was in abeyance during the war, by 1921 the cumulative effect of several ineffective administrations persuaded city fathers to pursue charter reform and installation of a city manager plan.[59]

An additional factor prompted this push for a change in the municipal government in Cleveland. Distrust of ward politicians, who were supported by immigrants, was one of the motivating forces behind the demand for a city manager plan. This fact was especially true in Lausche's 23rd ward. This ward and neighboring wards accounted for one-fourth of the city's foreign-born population.

A drive for a city manager plan represented city leaders' efforts to dominate the governmental structure of the city, at a time when there was great concern about immigrant commitment to traditional American values. Simultaneously the local chamber of commerce (headed by former Mayor Newton D. Baker) led a major drive to cripple a union movement by advocating an open shop as an alternative to organized labor unions.[60] Locals would not have to worry about Frank Lausche's stance on these two issues. His position on his country's values and open shops became quite clear during his political career.

In 1921 the volatility of Cleveland politics raised its ugly head. The citizens said no to ward politics and voted for a city manager form of government. Cleveland became the first large city in the country to experiment with this innovative type of city management. The new charter abolished the traditional ward system and provided for a professional manager selected by a city council. The city was divided into four districts, from each of which five to seven council members were elected at large. The rationale for this new method of electing councilmen was based on the proposition that a more respectable class of citizens would be attracted to public office once the pernicious ward system with all its petty politics disappeared. Hopefully this new plan would promote the election of councilmen based on their qualifications, rather than on their ethnic background. However it happened that proportional representation and the district concept encouraged greater bloc voting instead of reducing it.[61] In 1923 the year before the city manager plan went into effect, the twenty-five members of city council included eleven persons who were of native stock. By 1929 there were only four members of native stock. The black population, composed of slightly over 71,000 residents, elected three councilmen. Of the remaining eighteen councilmen, sixteen were of German, eastern or southern European origins.[62]

Prior to the installation of a city manager plan in 1924, voter turnout created another of those paradoxes well known in the city's political history. They had elected the handsome maverick Fred Kohler as Mayor in 1922. Kohler served as police chief of Cleveland during the Tom Johnson era. He was thrown out of this office in 1913 after two sensational trials dealing with his amours. Kohler's mayoralty was a spectacular change from the usual political timeservers, whom he removed from office in an economy wave.[63] After two years Kohler departed to become Cuyahoga county sheriff. The potentially chaotic and turbulent city manager era descended upon the citizenry before they realized it. The city fathers were immensely proud of themselves for having solved their municipal ills by taking this new cure in one big dose. Party moguls Republican Maurice Maschke and Democrat Burr Gongwer controlled the majority of votes in the newly elected city council. These two politicians agreed on the respected and able William R. Hopkins for the city manager post. The two leaders kept a wary eye upon Hopkins during his noteworthy six-year tenure in office.[64]

City politicians realized that to be successful they must court the favor of local media, particularly the three newspapers. Although station WHK had opened its doors in 1922, radio was in an experimental stage during much of the 1920s. Political campaigning over the airways was uncommon. An avenue for exchanging political dialogue emerged through the City Club of Cleveland. Founded in 1912, the City Club, often referred to as Cleveland's Citadel of Free Speech, provided opportunities for political candidates to speak, debate, and receive inquiries from the membership.

The local newspapers gave these forums big play, and during any given year, practically every variety of opinion was heard from office holders, eggheads, reformers, capitalists, kooks, and even Communists.[65] Three local newspapers—The Cleveland *News*, Cleveland *Press* and Cleveland *Plain Dealer*—for the most part provided independent news and editorials about the city's political scene. The Cleveland *Call & Post* was founded in 1927 after the merger to two struggling weeklies, the *Call* and the *Post*, which dated from the beginning of the decade. This paper, more sensational than newsworthy in political coverage, provided support for local black Democrats. Equally important to the large ethnic population were foreign language dailies. Many of the new immigrants could not read English. The prominent Slovenian paper is *Ameriška Domovina* (*American Home*), still located adjacent to what at one time had been the Lausche residence on St. Clair Avenue. This paper filled an important void for the heavily populated neighborhood of Slovenian dwellers. Louis Pirc, a prominent early Slovenian immigrant, owned and edited this paper in the early 1900s. The bi-weekly grew to a daily paper in the late 1920s and became an influential political tool for local ethnic candidates. In the 1920s Cleveland claimed more successful foreign language dailies than any city in the country.[66]

⌒

THE POLITICAL ATMOSPHERE IN CLEVELAND and in the state of Ohio became more vibrant and exciting in the mid 1920s. Local government issues intrigued Lausche. He was politically active while working for Cyrus W. Locher's law firm. Locher, a well-known Cleveland Democrat, served as Commerce Director under Democratic Governor Vic Donahey. The Governor (1923–1929) appointed him to the U.S. Senate in 1928 (he served only a few months) to replace Republican Frank B. Willis, who resigned for health reasons. Locher gave Lausche sage advice about the state political scene. Lausche's baseball exploits and legal responsibilities made him well known in his 23rd Ward. Many neighbors remembered him from his youthful lamp-lighting days. The 23rd was Cleveland's strongest Democratic ward. Because of his personal popularity and growing reputation as a trial lawyer, Lausche soon became one of the most influential Democrats in East Cleveland. He demonstrated an unquestioned talent as an orator.

In 1922 when only twenty-seven years old, the youthful lawyer ran for the Ohio state assembly. Ohio Democrats were in the minority during the twenties, and Lausche was anxious to garner support wherever possible. Former Judge William C. Keough, a member of the Cuyahoga County Democratic committee, told the young political aspirant, "Go out to a Women's Christian Temperance Union meeting (in nearby Chagrin Falls) and make your pitch." Prohibition was in effect nationwide. Lausche accepted this advice and garnered a speaking engagement. The candidate spoke well and received a tremendous ovation. He was hopeful of gaining votes from this local gathering. As Lausche was about to leave the platform, a little old lady rose and called out, "You haven't said anything about light wine and beer. How do you stand on them?" Lausche, innocent and honest in his response to questions, replied, "I'm for 'em," clearing his throat, "I could use a cold glass of beer right now."[67] Anyone who had observed Lausche drink a bar-glass full of whiskey in one gulp and follow it with a beer chaser can well believe he meant it.

> *"You haven't said anything about light wine and beer. How do you stand on them?" Lausche, innocent and honest in his response to questions, replied, "I'm for 'em," clearing his throat, "I could use a cold glass of beer right now."*

Needless to say, as a result of his *faux pas*, Lausche lost what few supporters he may have impressed at this gathering. His error in judgment probably didn't make that much difference in losing the election. Lausche sought a state senate seat in 1924 and again went down to defeat, "The defeats left me embittered, but by 1931 I had recovered sufficiently to actively and enthusiastically support Ray Miller [a rising star in the Democratic Party] in his race for mayor of Cleveland. Upon his election I was twice offered places in his cabinet but because of my ignorance of the fields I refused."[68]

Lausche's defeats (two of only four defeats in his long political career) resulted mainly as a consequence of his Democratic label in a Republican dominated political era rather than as a reflection on his political astuteness. Later in his political career when voters knew him better, Lausche won victories in election years dominated by the Republican Party. The aspiring politician learned several valuable lessons from his early political ventures. Initially it was imperative for Lausche, given his lack of prominence, to confine his political aspirations to a friendlier constituency. That meant the 23rd ward with its large foreign-born population. By 1926 Lausche, now firmly entrenched in Locher's law firm, felt secure to take on new responsibilities. He taught a law class at John Marshall School of Law.

Lausche received one of his first big cases when Cyrus Locher was appointed United States Senator in 1928. Lausche's adversary was Harry Payer, a flamboyant and unforgettable figure in Cleveland legal circles. As manager of Tom L. Johnson's first mayoral campaign, Payer earned a reputation as the dean of Cuyahoga county's criminal lawyers. He was nicknamed Demosthenes because of his acknowledged oratorical skills. Payer wore a mane of white hair and snowy mutton-chop whiskers. He dressed in a Prince Albert coat, striped pants, patent leather shoes, flowing cravat, stiff wing collar and flowered waistcoat. When Payer addressed a jury, they swayed in the wind.

The point at issue was a plot of land confiscated by the Cleveland City Park Board from an exclusive country club. Payer represented the country club, which was demanding $130,000 for the property. Lausche, representing the taxpayers, was trying to prove that $65,000 was a more reasonable figure. "I was young and callow," recalled Lausche, "unwise in the ways of the courtroom. Payer was the picture of a great lawyer. Frankly, he frightened me to death."

Lausche's fright did not last long. With shrewd insight into human behavior that was the germ of his character, he soon saw that Payer was overplaying his hand. The senior lawyer arrived late every day, keeping the judge and the jury waiting. He was condescending to the jury, and he ignored young Lausche altogether. Lausche made a great point of arriving to the court early. When the jury filed in to wait for Payer, they found Lausche—wearing his most threadbare suit and his most earnest manner—studying his papers at the counsel table. Payer dismissed witnesses with a flick of sarcasm. Lausche was kind, patient and respectful. Payer orated thunderously. Lausche spoke simply, in a calm voice. Payer was cavalier with the jury. Lausche was bashful. "I began to sense," Lausche remembered, "a certain sentiment in the jury against Harry Payer." The jury returned a verdict of $65,000—the amount Lausche had asked for, to the penny. The courtroom battle with Payer set the pattern for Lausche's career as a lawyer. He was promoted to junior partnership with the Locher, Green and Woods legal office. In 1933 President Franklin Roosevelt appointed Payer, known as Mr. Pickwick, as assistant U.S. Secretary of State.[69]

Lausche continued to play baseball as time permitted. For relaxation in the winter months he honed his already excellent skills as a bowler and a billiard player. He was also ready to take an important step in his personal life. In 1925 Lausche served as best man at the wedding of John J. Prince, Sr., a Slovenian colleague. Several years earlier Prince and his fellow Slovenian friend Louis Petrash had introduced Lausche to a young and vivacious lady named Jane Sheal.

The somewhat shy and conservative Lausche courted Jane for two years, and their engagement carried on for five additional years. Finally on May 17, 1928, Lausche now thirty-three, took the important step into matrimony. It was one of the most fortuitous decisions of Lausche's long life. Jane Sheal would have a profound effect upon Lausche's political career. There were bumps along the road as in any marriage, but for the most part observers concluded this union was a marriage made in heaven. As the future politician entered more and more into the public limelight, Jane Lausche became the stabilizing force so necessary to balance Lausche's sometimes-tempestuous personality. She became his number one asset, whose mission in life was to see that her preoccupied and absent-minded husband always had a few dollars in his pocket, a clean shirt in his valise, and was transported to the airport on time. Her innocent lamb role became as effective as Lausche's growing political mystique.

Second lieutenant Lausche sent this picture to his mother from Camp Gordon, Georgia, July 1918.. (Courtesy of Dr. Rudolph Susel)

three

Here Comes the Judge

AN ATTITUDE OF EUPHORIA SETTLED ACROSS the United States during the Roaring Twenties. In spite of prohibition the country basked in an aura of unprecedented prosperity and speculation. Everyone believed the good times would continue to roll. At the same time second-generation immigrants in Cleveland's inner urban settlements reached new levels of maturity and self-assurance. Monetary pursuit often began with a pushcart from which an immigrant hawked vegetables on city streets. New citizens achieved economic stability, entered the political arena at local and state levels, and gained sporadic acceptance from the native-born. An immigrant's pursuit of success often demonstrated noble and decent efforts. But the newcomer's success did not come without a price. Nativist apprehensions swelled as new ethnic groups adapted to the American environment.

Fearful of being displaced by foreign elements, nativists fought back by propagating and coercing a sense of oneness. Extremists lashed out against the hyphenated newcomers by joining organizations like the Ku Klux Klan. In spite of periodic setbacks, intolerance, and restrictive immigration policies (Congress drastically reduced immigration quotas in 1924), an exceptional national identity became more evident. In 1880, 3,500 Jews resided in Cleveland. This number increased to 75,000 in 1920, representing nine percent of the city's population. Large numbers of Italians, Poles, and Hungarians also arrived during this period. The city's Italian-born population rose from 3,000 in 1900 to nearly 19,000 in 1920. Poles began arriving in Cleveland in 1870, and by 1920, 35,000 Polish immigrants inhabited Cleveland. Many settled along Fleet Avenue (at East 65th Street) and worked in nearby steel mills. The largest Polish colony came to be called *Warszawa*. The Hungarian community settled along Buckeye Road, expanding eastward to Shaker Square.[1]

Slovenians experienced comparable numerical growth when word drifted back to the motherland about job opportunities and life in general in the New World. This industrious and active nationality group began to move outward from

William played the piano, and she gave the pitch, saying, "You, Josephine, sing soprano. Louis, you sing first tenor. Charlie, your part will be second tenor. Harold, you sing bass. And you, Frank, you keep quiet."

Lausche's St. Clair neighborhood. Pockets of Slovenians settled in the Collinwood area near St. Mary's Church on Holmes Avenue, the Newburgh neighborhood around St. Lawrence Church near 81st Street, and in Euclid near 222nd Street where locals attended St. Christian Church. Each pocket of Slovenian immigrants worked diligently to provide funds for national halls where social events could be held. The opening of a national home was a seminal event for the Cleveland Slovene community. Concerts, plays, dances, and banquets filled the social calendar and never more so than in the 1920s and 1930s. Slovenians organized a number of singing societies, and these groups became permanent fixtures in the community.

The largest and most notable of the eight national homes in Cleveland, the Slovenian National Home, is located near Lausche's childhood home on St. Clair Avenue. This hall was constructed in 1924 and seated over 1000 patrons. Financed through the sale of shares to Slovene organizations and individuals, and managed by a board of trustees elected by the shareholders, these national homes acted as anchors in the Slovenian settlements in concert with the Roman Catholic national parishes.[2] The sociable and music-loving Slovenians congregated to hear one of many singing groups perform. They also enjoyed dancing to the music of local orchestras in which the accordion was the primary instrument.

The radio and phonograph created an unprecedented boom in popular music in the 1920s. Frankie Yankovic became the polka king in Cleveland, if not in the country. Music buffs often identified Cleveland as America's Polka Capital. A gathering would include refreshments, perhaps *klobase* (sausage) or *poticas* (nut rolls). The *Kres* dancers, one of the best-known Slovenian folk dance groups in Cleveland, often performed at the St. Clair National Home with Frank Lausche in attendance. *Kres* means bonfire in Slovenian and commemorates those dreadful occasions when the ancestors of the dancers received warnings of approaching Turkish raids by way of a network of bonfires on the peaks of Slovenian mountains.[3] *Glasbena Matica* (the Music Society), one of America's premier Slovenian choruses, entertained the Lausches at the Slovenian National Home, presenting operas and classical works. Two of Lausche's close friends, Anton Schubel of the Metropolitan Opera Chorus, and local poet and composer Ivan Zorman directed this chorus in the 1940s.[4] The cultural life in Cleveland's Slovenian community reached a peak prior to the Great Depression.

This Slovenian cultural boom and love of music was not lost on Lausche and his new wife. The newlyweds captured the spirit and mood of the Jazz Age. Prior to their marriage Lausche had introduced Jane to his weekly family musical get-togethers. Jane no doubt endeared herself to the new family early in the courtship. She possessed a musical background and played the piano. In an effort to fit in, the young bride devoted many hours learning the rudiments of the Slovenian language. She became adept at conversing with Ma Lausche in Slovenian. Jane learned to cook Slovenian dishes, one being red beans and sauerkraut, her husband's favorite dish.

The Lausche clan, a tight-knit group, remained even more so through their musical gatherings nearly every Sunday in Ma Lausche's parlor. "The Slovenes, particularly the Lausches, are emotional and poetic people with strong tribal fibers. They like to get together and sing."[5] On New Year's Eve the Lausche siblings arranged their party schedules in order to return to Ma Lausche's home and sing in the New Year at their mother's side. This tradition continued until Ma Lausche's death in 1934.[6]

Frank was the least musically gifted of their exceptionally talented family. During Lausche's professional career, particularly when attending a play or musical event, he would receive an invitation to say a few words. He often related to his audience how his mother would select a Slovenian or American song and then delegate various members of the family to sing their respective parts. William played the piano, and she gave the pitch, and said, "You, Josephine, sing soprano. Louis, you sing first tenor. Charlie, your part will be second tenor. Harold, you sing bass. And you, Frank, you keep quiet."[7] The audience always responded with hearty laughter. In actuality Lausche was adequate both in his singing ability and his violin playing, but true to his self-deprecating manner, avoided laudatory comparison to his family members. Jane, who enjoyed the family musical get-togethers, added to the levity about her husband's musical talents, "Frank is wonderful on the violin, he plays just like Jack Benny."[8] Jane, playing the piano, often accompanied her husband's violin playing.

Some years later during Lausche's legal career, a story circulated that Lausche fervently desired to play with George P. Baer and Samuel H. Silbert, two noted violinists better known as Cuyahoga county judges. To put Lausche off, Baer and

Silbert contended he could not play with them because Lausche was not a member of the local musician's union. Lausche countered that the two violinists were looking for a place to practice because their less than melodic efforts forced their spouses to prohibit practicing in their respective homes. Jane Lausche received word of their ploy and forbade the two judges to enter her father's home (where the Lausches were living). This whimsical story always brought a chuckle.[9] Lausche's musical skills no doubt suffered because he preferred to play baseball.

Although the entire Lausche family exhibited musical ability two siblings excelled with their talents, namely Josephine and William. Josephine, who was two years older than Frank, was married to lawyer Oliver Welf, and developed into one of the finest ethnic singers in Cleveland. She performed as soloist or in duets with her Slovenian friend Mary Udovich at numerous concerts, cultural and social events. Dr. William Lausche, one of Frank's younger brothers, became musically best known of the Lausche's children. A dentist by profession, William Americanized Slovenian tunes with contemporary dance-band arrangements and pioneered the polka sound that became associated with Cleveland. Lausche's original compositions, such as "Cleveland, The Polka Town," became polka classics. Several of his compositions were reminiscent of Dixieland Jazz.

Dr. Lausche organized an orchestra in the 1920s, and the group played live on John Grdina's Slovenian radio programs on WJAY, a local independent Cleveland station. In 1937 the *Plain Dealer* purchased the station and revised program selections. William, his sister Josephine, and Mary recorded for Columbia Records (known as Columbia Gramophone Company in its early years). Some sixty selections eventually hit the airways. This triumvirate, described as the sweethearts of Slovenian Columbia Records, earlier recorded briefly for Victor Talking Machine Company of Camden, New Jersey. After 1937, Dr. Lausche's combo performed on station WGAR. This group featured two outstanding accordionists, Lou Trebar and Johnny Pecon. In 1942 William and his trio recorded with Continental Records of New York. He subsequently played for local musical events in Cleveland and his brother Frank admired his talent, claiming that he was a "pioneer of Slovenian music in Cleveland."

One of his successors, Slovenian Frankie Yankovic, grew up in the Collinwood Slovenian neighborhood. The young bandleader signed a contract with Columbia Records in 1946. Dancers welcomed Yankovic's approach of fluid waltzes and slower polkas, which were simpler than the Chicago Polish style and less foreign than the Milwaukee German sound. The local Clevelander hit the recording charts in 1948 and 1949 with two million-selling arrangements of "Just Because" and "The Blue Skirt Waltz." Yankovic toured extensively, presenting as many as 300 performances a year. He received the title of America's Polka King in Milwaukee in 1948. Talented in their own right, several of his orchestra members went on to form their own orchestras and sign with major recording companies. Polka fever spread in the 1950s throughout Cleveland, and dances attracted the younger set to the Slovenian National Home on St. Clair Avenue.[10] The legacy of the musical talents of the Lausche family proved to be a major asset to Frank's political career. Political scientists have long established the thesis that name identification serves an important purpose when citizens enter the voting booth. The Lausche name became well known in Cleveland as Frank's brother and sister exploited their musical talents.[11]

⌒

SOON AFTER FRANK LAUSCHE AND JANE SHEAL took their marriage vows, Jane's father Robert invited the newlyweds to live with him. He and his wife Lillian resided in a large home. There was plenty of room for the Lausches, as Jane was their only child. The financially conservative Lausches agreed to this arrangement. With the Great Depression lurking on the horizon, the acceptance of this invitation turned out to be a prudent decision. The marriage had raised some eyebrows within Lausche's family, as well as among close friends. The Lausches and most of their friends were strong Catholics. Frank married a Protestant Methodist. This decision gave early evidence that Lausche did not plan to let religion obfuscate any potential political endeavors. Lausche did not wear his religion on his sleeve. He believed that one's religious preference was a personal matter. His view was evidence of Lausche's independent streak which became an integral part of his personality on the political trail.

The nationwide euphoria of the twenties—the feeling that prosperity and good times would continue—did not last beyond the decade. This same sentiment permeated metropolitan Cleveland. And then the Crash came. The stock market crash of 1929 and the subsequent Depression brought Cleveland to its knees. Industrialist Cyrus Eaton suggested that Cleveland was hurt more by the Depression than any other city in the United States. "That assertion," journalist George E. Condon, Jr. wrote in 1967, "is plausible enough to people who remember the exuberant, dynamic Cleveland of pre-Depression days and who can compare it with the somber, convalescent city that walked with a dragging gait and querulous expression..."[12]

Everything that could go wrong did. Unemployment quickly rose to 25 percent. Soup kitchens became commonplace, apple sellers set up at street corners, and blue chip stocks sold for under $5 a share. Few signs of improvement seemed imminent.[13] The desire to succeed seemed non-existent. Spirits sagged as banks closed. Economically, the bottom dropped out, and the future looked bleak. Conversely citizens noted some good happenings in Cleveland. The primary landmark in Cleveland, the Van Sweringen brothers' Union Terminal, had been dedicated in 1930. The Municipal Airport had opened, and the new Cleveland Municipal Stadium, under construction for several years, officially opened on July 1, 1931. The first major sporting event at the stadium took place, a boxing match between reigning world heavyweight champion Max Schmeling and W.L. Young Stribling, before a crowd of 36,936. With a population of over 900,000, Cleveland in 1930 ranked as the nation's sixth largest city after New York, Chicago, Philadelphia, Detroit and Los Angeles.[14]

Prior to the Great Depression the overall climate in Cleveland during the 1920s reeked of political upheaval. The Grand Old Party held a near monopoly of political power in the nation. With the exception of Democratic Vic Donahey's reign as Governor of Ohio (1923–1928), the same circumstances applied to Ohio. In 1928 for the first time in Ohio political annals, the Republicans held every seat in the Senate, and the Democrats filled only eleven seats in the 133 member lower house.[15]

Meanwhile Cleveland's city manager plan, in effect since 1923, fell out of favor, in spite of the laudatory tenures of city managers William R. Hopkins and Daniel E. Morgan. Political adversaries Republican Maurice Maschke and Democrat chief Burr Gongwer kept the political pot boiling during much of the 1920s. After early support for the city manager plan, confidence in Hopkins abated by 1928, particularly on the part of Maschke. Former three-time Mayor Harry Davis exacerbated the situation. He had completed a two-year term as Governor (1921–23), and in 1927 circulated petitions to dismiss the city manager plan and to provide for a special election for mayor. He nearly pulled off his scheme, but the opposition of Maschke and Gongwer and the local papers, the *Plain Dealer* and *Press*, thwarted the Davis plan by only six thousand votes.

Lausche's 23rd Ward became a major player in the local political arena during the 1920s. One of the strongest Democratic wards in Ohio, the 23rd Ward played a key role in the future success of Democratic aspirants seeking election, including those seeking statewide offices. Two major ward leaders—Louis Pirc and Adam Damm—developed a serious rivalry in a struggle for political power. Details of this rivalry are blurred and only known by insiders of their respective cliques.

Nearly every Tuesday, a group of prominent local Slovenians close to the Lausche family met at a different home to discuss political issues. This group played a Slovenian card game *Kenne Krufin* ("Call the King"). The group included James Debevic, Sr., publisher of the *American Home* newspaper, John Kovacic, John Mihelich, and Pirc, editor of *American Home*, and influential local businessmen. Pirc carried a lot of weight in political discussions. He and Mihelich were close to Lausche and urged him to enter the political arena at the appropriate time.[16] Lausche's allegiance throughout the years rested with Pirc who early in Lausche's political career served as his mentor. Lausche, young and somewhat inexperienced in political strategy, took a cautious approach before making any decision. He avoided burning any bridges unnecessarily. His personal makeup would not allow him to act in such a way.

Lausche's political fortunes took a sharp turn upward in the 1928–32 period. How Lausche's career changed is a reflection of the often topsy-turvy world of politics. During the years between 1925 and 1930, local politicians attempted five times to dump the city manager form of government and to return to the council-Mayor framework. After his tenure in the Ohio State Senate, the city council had elected Republican Daniel Morgan to succeed William R. Hopkins as city manager. Through no fault of Morgan's the city council in November 1931 abandoned the city manager form of government, and the city manager was out of a job.[17] A mayoral election loomed ahead in February 1932. Enter the name of Raymond T. Miller. An Irish Catholic outsider, Miller was born in Defiance, Ohio. He matriculated to Notre Dame University and received his degree in 1914. Miller and his brothers migrated to Cleveland after World War I. Raymond's younger brother Don gained notoriety as one of the famous "Four Horsemen," who played football for Knute Rockne at Notre Dame. Raymond, a World War I veteran, possessed the ingredients for success in the political arena. He was young, handsome, broad-shouldered, and aggressive. Miller spoke vigorously and eloquently and was eager to enter politics.

Nearly every Tuesday a group of prominent local Slovenians close to the Lausche family met at a different home to discuss political issues.

Gongwer persuaded Miller to run for county prosecutor in 1926. Democrats continued to lose elections in the 1920s, and Miller was no exception. Stalwart Republican Edward C. Stanton, who had held the county prosecutor's office six years, retained his position.[18] Miller's time came two years later. He again ran for county prosecutor and defeated Maschke's candidate, Arthur H. Day. Miller ran again in 1930 and was reelected. During his four years, the young prosecutor cut a dashing figure by successfully prosecuting crooked politicians—mostly Republican councilmen—in dramatic courtroom appearances.

These indictments were harmful to the Republican cause, and the good times were running out for the Republican Party who monopolized the 1920s. The Democrats started winning state and county offices. In 1932 Franklin D. Roosevelt garnered the presidency in a landslide election. Could a Democrat be Mayor of Cleveland? Ray T. Miller thought so, and became a candidate of the Democratic regulars, including Burr Gongwer. His candidacy provided Lausche with his first good political break. Adam Damm, a fat, jolly, popular man and former city treasurer was ward leader in Lausche's Ward 23. Damm broke with Miller. He announced his support for Peter Witt, a former Tom Johnson clone and independent. Witt was not the old warhorse of Johnson days, but he agreed to run. The Democratic Party promptly removed Damm as ward leader, and Miller invited Lausche to take over direction of his campaign in Ward 23.

The demise of the city manager plan forced the need to hold a special election for mayor in early 1932. The Republicans chose the highly respected Daniel Morgan, the recently deposed city manager. Peter Witt became an early favorite to win the primary election. Twice he had easily won election to the city council. Witt was a rabble-rouser par excellence and made good copy for the newspapers.[19]

In this election the political soothsayers and press underestimated the power of the Catholic Church. While not necessarily anti-Catholic, Witt made no apologies about being an agnostic who never attended church. Miller was a practicing Catholic, high up in the hierarchy of the Knights of Columbus. The Sunday before the January election, priests in every Catholic parish warned against the possibility of an admitted agnostic becoming Mayor, and went as far as possible to support Miller without acting as shills. The message proved to have a devastating effect on the election. Witt's normally sizeable Democratic following dropped off, and he finished a poor third. Miller gained Witt's votes in a runoff election. In the general election, Miller now faced Morgan, who had garnered 10,000 more votes than his opponent in the primary runoff.

Miller mounted a barrage of accusations against the Republican Party organization. Playing the familiar role of prosecutor, he charged the opposition with responsibility for all the corruption and ineptitude of the past fifteen years. Using well-turned phrases and biting sarcasm Miller recited the list of Republicans he had helped put in jail. While allowing that Morgan was a fine fellow, the brash political newcomer asserted that his opponent was surrounded by political corruption, which Miller labeled Maschkeism. Most of the corruption to which Miller referred occurred before Morgan became city manager. Miller's cutting attacks forced Morgan to spend an increasing amount of time defending himself, his safety director and his chief of police.[20] In the last few days of this campaign, Miller managed to maintain the offensive. He received additional momentum when, in a front-page editorial, the Cleveland *Press*, came out in support of Miller for Mayor. On Election Day—with considerable interest from voters—Miller emerged victorious by a small margin of 7,703 votes out of a total of 198,824.[21] Had he waged an independent campaign of the sort that ensured repeated victories for Republican Harold H. Burton and Lausche, it is possible that Morgan might have won, but his commitment to party loyalty forbade such a move.

Lausche told of this political campaign, "I shall not forget that fight. Adam Damm, Democratic leader of the old 23rd, my ward, supported Peter Witt, a Republican for mayor. I directed the Ward campaign for Miller.... We carried the 23rd, and Miller won the election."[22] Lausche's memory betrayed him, for Witt ran as an independent Democrat. Lausche carried out his political responsibilities in grand style. His ward gave Miller a big vote in the primary election and an even bigger one at the general election. This victory gave Lausche his first substantial political triumph. In gratitude Miller offered Lausche any one of three positions in his cabinet: secretary to the Mayor, safety director, or utilities director in his cabinet. When told of this offer Louis Seltzer, now editor of the Cleveland *Press* and an important growing force in Cleveland politics, asked Lausche, "Where do you want to go in politics?" "I would like to be a judge," Lausche responded.[23] He declined

Miller's offer. This decision was an early example of Lausche's determination not to be beholden to anyone for political favors. In the eyes of party politicians, Lausche's refusal of an appointment made him not only unique but eccentric.[24]

City council and mayoral elections in Cleveland generated much interest among eastern and central European immigrants. Councilmen debated important issues that affected ethnic groups. These groups campaigned for neighborhood improvements such as street paving, better street lighting, regional libraries, cheaper housing and public baths. Councilmen of their own ethnicity meant a better possibility that these local issues would be approved. The Slovenians were no exception in their drive for community improvements.

The Slovenians, with the support of two local nationality papers, *Ameriška Domovina* and *Enakopravnost*, had vigorously pushed the election of Slovenian John L. Mihelich to the city council in the mid-1920s. This candidate was successful in his election bid for three terms (1925, 1927, and 1929). Lausche and Councilman Adam J. Damm enthusiastically supported Mihelich. Mihelich represented the third district that included Lausche's 23rd Ward. He became the first of several Slovenian-Americans elected to Cleveland's city council. Lausche remained on the sidelines, discreetly building his political power base, waiting for the appropriate time to seek a public office.

The two nationality newspapers were in constant ideological and political conflict. *Enakopravnost*, a liberal newspaper, clashed with the conservative and Catholic-oriented *Ameriška Domovina*. When the Democratic Party seemed unable or unwilling to serve Slovene interests, Vatroslav Grill, the editor of *Enakopravnost*, accepted the presidency of the Republican Party in the 23rd Ward in 1932. Serious disputes eroded the strength of the 23rd Ward until Frank Lausche accepted the Democratic leadership of his ward in 1932. In his memoirs Grill maintained that when he switched to the Republican Party greater cohesion resulted among the Democrats, and they closed ranks in the 23rd Ward.[25]

The Slovenes continued to win seats in the city council in the 1930s, including candidates from Lausche's ward. These political successes may be partially attributed to intense political education campaigns by the two divergent Slovenian nationality papers. Slovenes brought with them from their homeland an attitude both for political struggle and compromise. Political struggle in the Austrian Parliament and in provincial assemblies served as a historical reminder of what to expect in the American political arena. Slovenes were accustomed to fighting for political positions, and often played pivotal roles among the individual ethnic groups in Cleveland. A growing economic power base contributed to the political success of selected Slovenian politicians.[26]

By 1933, Cleveland—like the rest of the country—was in the throes of the Great Depression. Many workers in the 23rd Ward were unemployed. Lausche continued as titular head of his ward. Old-timers recall that as many as five hundred faithful at a time congregated outside Lausche's ward office to plead for work. Overwhelmed with job requests, Lausche often retreated out a back door and over a fence. In spite of the scarcity of work, Lausche lined up 600 city jobs, more than any other ward leader. At one point the young politician retained more than 10,000 applications on file. When a work crisis abated there were rumors that Lausche heated the office building for two weeks disposing of piles of applications.[27]

Anxious to enter the judicial field, in late 1932 Lausche accepted an opportunity that suited his professional background and interest. Judge Arthur Day, a well-known name in Cleveland political circles, won election to the common pleas court. An appointment was necessary to fill his remaining term on the municipal court bench. Cleveland Bar Association members and the Cuyahoga County Democratic organization recommended Lausche for the position to Democratic Governor George White. The Democratic brain trust believed a representative of the Slovenian people deserved the appointment, especially because former Slovenian councilman John L. Mihelich had suffered defeat for the municipal court judgeship in 1931. Mihelich was in fact the personal choice of Mayor-elect Ralph Miller. However the astute Miller proposed Lausche for the position on the assumption that he could win the forthcoming election in 1933, whereas Mihelich could not win. Miller's judgment would prove to be correct.[28]

The day after Lausche's appointment on December 20, 1932, the *Plain Dealer* commented, "The appointment of Lausche is regarded as recognition of the importance of the Slovenian group in the Democratic organization of Cleveland." A few days later, the Cleveland *Press* partially foresaw Lausche's political future. "He will be a hard working judge, and less political than some who have had less experience in politics. In fact, our guess is that Lausche on the bench will forget politics."[29]

Many in the community, given to be suspicious of political leaders, looked askance at the appointment of a ward leader as judge. But the appointee dispelled any fears of partisanship or political shenanigans. As a lawyer Lausche soon became known for his ability to try cases and for his careful, thorough, and efficient court work. While a firm believer in the nonpartisanship of the bench he nevertheless held that even a judge might keep his place in party councils. Lausche resigned as ward leader the day he became a judge, but he retained his place on the Democratic Executive Committee.

A portion of Judge Lausche's daily docket included cases associated with human derelicts and petty criminals. He took each case as if it were a personal problem. The young judge often remained in his office late at night worrying about whether he was actually dispensing justice.[30] To add to his stressful position, his political-wise colleagues on the bench shuffled controversial cases, those which contained potential political dynamite, into his courtroom. Disgusted at such political maneuvering, calloused newspaper reporters covering these cases tried to put Lausche wise. He thanked the reporters and kept right on taking cases as they came.[31]

One of Lausche's hardest decisions endeared him to the hearts of the laboring class. A finance company attempted to repossess a car from a buyer who hadn't kept up with his payments due to hidden charges in the contract. Finance companies informed buyers who used the installment plan that charges would be based only on the legal rate of interest. However a person who bought a car on time payments often found in the chattel mortgage authority to charge attorney's fees and garage repair expenses.

Lausche had no quarrel with legitimate financing of installment purchases, but he ruled that chattel mortgages were null and void if they gave the finance company authority to make extra charges and defraud the buyer. This ruling became the law in Ohio and put mortgage shacks out of business.[32] Another case proved Lausche had not lost his informal manner in the dignity of the courtroom. The judge presided over a sanity hearing in which one of the lawyers offered proof of mental irresponsibility because his defendant refused to wear shoes. There was a sudden shuffling sound under the bench as Judge Lausche hastily felt around, trying to find his own shoes.[33]

Although a novice in the political arena Lausche at times raised his voice against party follies. United States Democratic Senator Robert J. Bulkley forced former Common Pleas Judge Maurice Bernon off the Board of Elections. Bernon delivered a bitter tirade against the Senator before the Democratic executive committee. Lausche took the floor and castigated Bernon for his attack. It was a bold act for the audience, handpicked by Gongwer, was not friendly to the Senator, and Lausche's words fell on deaf ears.[34]

The young judge quickly asserted his independence from local political bosses. On one occasion when Lausche failed to yield to the demands of an influential politician, the politician threatened reprisal, but the judge refused to budge. After his short tenure in office Lausche did not hesitate to seek re-election in late 1933. The local newspapers, often critical of public officials, summarized the judge's early performance on the bench, "Many in the community, given to suspicion about political leaders, look askance at the appointment of a ward leader as a judge...[Lausche] dispelled any fears of partisanship or politics. In the ten months he served before the [1933 election] he made such a record that the bar, the newspaper and the whole community hailed him, and his election was assured long before the day of balloting."[35]

Although receiving only lukewarm support from the local Democratic Party, when Election Day arrived on November 6, 1933, Lausche led a field of ten candidates with 82,863 votes. He was clearly the choice of the electorate, and the proud second-generation Slovenian carefully moved toward greater accomplishments in his budding political career. The municipal judge eagerly continued to fulfill his responsibilities as the country continued to suffer through the Great Depression.

Shortly after Lausche's election, friends and relatives gathered at the Slovenian National Home for a surprise banquet in honor of his political triumph. The

Lausche Booster Club, under the aegis of President John E. Lokar, Jr., close friend and subsequent campaign manager for seven of Lausche's campaigns, organized the affair. The judge came expecting to address the club and was completely taken by surprise when he found two hundred supporters in the hall cheering him.[36] Nine days later on December 2, 1933, he took the oath of office from Appellate Judge Neil W. McGill using a Bible which had been in the Lausche family for four generations. The prominent radio station WHK carried a live broadcast of the swearing-in ceremony. Three of Lausche's siblings—William, Charles and Josephine Welf—formed a string trio to serenade the newly elected official.[37]

Physically a big man for his era, Lausche stood six feet tall with heavy shoulders, a slim waistline, and the easy grace of an athlete. His winning smile has been described as often grave, yet warm; his speech as slow, having measured his words carefully, and then he would likely burst into an erupting cloud of rhetoric. Mostly direct and simple, he waved his big hands, and with his dark, Indian-like face aglow, he captured an audience in rapt attention.[38] He developed into a skillful, convincing, and emotional speaker. Like a superb actor Lausche could project himself and his message to audiences both large and small.

LAUSCHE'S DECISION-MAKING AS A JUDGE CAME TO A HALT on July 4, 1934. His beloved mother Frances passed away on Independence Day at the age 62. For the past year she had been confined to her bed most of the time, suffering paralysis. When Anthony Grdina (the local Slovenian undertaker) was told of Mother Lausche's death, he spoke of a woman who was revered and respected for many years. Louis J. Pirc, editor of *American Home*, recalled that he was one of hundreds of boys whom she had boosted over a rough spot in life. A friend described how helping others led to her illness. When Ray T. Miller was elected mayor in 1932 during the Depression, people stormed her house all day asking Mother Lausche to use her influence to get them city jobs. The rush was so terrific she suffered a nervous breakdown.[39] Saddened and distraught over the loss of his mother, Frank Lausche returned to his courtroom duties with a heavy heart.

Lausche's court record from 1933 to 1936 did not deviate from the non-partisanship he practiced during his first few months as judge. Greatly respected for his fair decisions, no courtroom shysters whispered in his ears. During his tenure the judge wrote more decisions than any other member of the municipal court.[40] Lausche related how he arrived at his decisions, "A senior member of my law firm advised, study the evidence and in accordance with your best and honest judgment...let come what may. During my entire career as a judge, I did not deviate from that course."[41]

An idealist, the judge was an admirer of the New Deal President, and therefore, gave his support to the newly elected Franklin D. Roosevelt administration. He rebuked local Democratic Party leaders for being so critical of Roosevelt's admittedly radical efforts to bring the country out of the Depression. He kept his contacts with his alma mater, John Marshall School of Law. Lausche loved the law profession, and for eight years he taught a night course entitled "Judicial Equity" on a part-time basis. He discovered that the first thing a teacher must learn is to stay ahead of his students. Other lawyers sought him out for advice with their difficult cases. Most of his colleagues preferred simple personal injury cases and the like; however, as a judge, Lausche particularly liked laborious cases in equity. Lausche took on difficult cases for which, without the aid of a jury, he interpreted both facts and the application of the law. In 1933 the popularity and respect he held with his professional colleagues became evident at his alma mater. The judge was elected to the presidency of the John Marshall Law School Alumni Association, a group of jurists numbering more than 600 members.[42]

By 1935 fellow courtroom lawyers regarded Lausche as a first rate judge whose temperament on the bench was even and judicious. He was as knowledgeable of the law as were the more seasoned judges. Lausche played the courtroom scene in an honest and fair manner. Of course he continued to assert his independence from the political bosses. Early in his political career, Lausche learned to court the support of local newspaper editors. One of these editors, Louis B. Seltzer of the Cleveland *Press*, was a man both loved and loathed by his literary constituency. The slight, dapper Seltzer became extremely powerful and influential in his role as editor. Casually known as Little Bromo among his critics—of whom there were more than a few— and as Mr. Cleveland among those who admired him, Seltzer wielded a heavy hand.[43] One of those individuals who admired him, Frank Lausche, made an early acquaintance with Seltzer, and they became fast friends. In Lausche's accomplishments in his judicial position and in his personal demeanor, Seltzer observed the attributes for political leadership. The two *young Turks* occasionally lunched together and shared the trials and tribulations of their respective professions.

Seltzer told of an incident which shaped Lausche's attitude toward politics in much the same way Seltzer's experiences influenced him when he covered the old Cleveland Police Court as a cub reporter. Lausche had been invited to Gongwer's office, Democratic political boss in Cleveland from 1924 to 1940, at which time he lost his position to Ray Miller. He wanted to talk to Lausche about organizational realignments in the 23rd Ward and neighboring wards in the section of Cleveland with which Lausche was most familiar.

The telephone on Gongwer's desk rang, and when the Democratic boss answered, it was evident that what he heard irritated him. "I'll see to that right away and I'll call you back," Gongwer said. He told his secretary to put in a call to the city's safety director. "I thought you promised me that Smith's place would not be bothered by the police," Gongwer said, "The police are out there right now. This fellow is important to us. He contributed $6,000 to our campaign. I wish you'd get those cops away as soon as you can." Then he reported back to the gambling proprietor, "It's all okay."[44] Lausche observed an example of the political machine's reciprocal relationships to those who contributed to the organization's treasury. These shenanigans did not impress Lausche. He determined to either break away from boss-controlled politics or get out of the political arena altogether.

In 1935 Seltzer came out with a front-page editorial in the Cleveland *Press* urging Lausche to run for mayor. After careful thought, and likely for personal reasons, the sitting judge declined this gracious offer. He again refused Seltzer's invitations in 1937 and 1939. Lausche wished to remain in his bench position. Seltzer, who literally could make or break any local politician of his choosing, was a bit miffed at Lausche's decisions. He reluctantly tried to understand Lausche's reasons for declining these offers. In his retirement years, Seltzer, commented that his friend was "the most honest man I've met in politics. He could have been president."[45] Lausche and Seltzer would revisit this issue later.

⌒

ONE SHOULD NOT JUMP TO THE CONCLUSION THAT LAUSCHE'S DECLINATION of the mayoral candidacy was to be interpreted as his having reached the pinnacle of political achievement. The judge was ambitious. He enjoyed his court duties, and in February 1936 Lausche decided to seek a position to a higher court—a judgeship in the common pleas court. Lausche's decision prompted the first of many confrontations with Democratic Party moguls. Pundits labeled Lausche as "an independent thinking and outspoken critic of his party's methods."[46] Democratic Judge Alvin J. Pearson already held this bench seat, but he was vulnerable in the 1937 election. The judge was under a cloud of suspicion with a disclosure that he had speculated heavily with unsecured loans of more than $100,000 from the now defunct Standard Trust Bank. Originally organized as the Engineers National Bank, this bank had grown rapidly in the late 1920s. Supported by the Brotherhood of Locomotive Engineers, and under the leadership of C. Sterling Smith (Pearson's brother-in-law), the bank reorganized in 1930 and became the Standard Trust Bank. This institution was neither a member of the Cleveland Clearing House nor of the Federal Reserve Bank. On December 21, 1931, the State Banking Department in Columbus took over the bank for liquidation. Friends of President Smith had taken out large loans without adequate security. Found guilty of misapplication of funds, Pearson's brother-in-law served time in the Ohio penitentiary beginning in 1933.[47]

As a result of this indictment a representative group of local attorneys took the unusual action of public dissent by refusing to participate in a poll on judicial candidates sponsored by the Cleveland Bar Association. This cadre of lawyers urged Lausche's election. These dissident attorneys proclaimed Lausche a jurist of outstanding ability, industry, and integrity. The coalition cited the untenable position of the Cleveland Bar Association. Poll results gave a plurality to incumbent Judge Pearson, in spite of the fact that the Bar Association's executive committee had demanded the Judge's resignation three years earlier in 1933.[48]

This controversy spilled over into the Democratic Party organization. Gongwer called the 43 Ward leaders together in an attempt to sell them on supporting Judge Pearson for another term. In spite of his previous leadership in the powerful 23rd Ward, opposition to Lausche emanated due to the young judge's independent posture on political issues. After two hours of intense debate the wards voted 24 to 19 to oppose Lausche's candidacy.[49] Gongwer's and the ward leaders' efforts crumbled on Election Day. Lausche scored a resounding victory, accumulating 191,000 votes to his opponent's 97,000 votes. Pearson's refusal to resign as a result of the Standard Trust Bank scandal came back to haunt him. More importantly, in spite of his reluctance to embrace the political machinations of local Democratic leaders, the independent-minded Lausche continued to establish a growing base of voter support. Several weeks later on February 23, 1937, hundreds of influential citizens, including Republican Mayor Harold H. Burton and Democratic U.S. Senator Robert J. Bulkley attended a gala affair to honor Lausche. Held at the spacious Slovenian National Home on St. Clair Avenue, the dinner featured Lausche's good friend, noted Slovenian poet and composer Ivan Zorman, who presided as toastmaster. Lausche's sister Josephine, now a recording artist, entertained the guests with Slovenian songs.[50]

Now earning $12,000 a year, Lausche likely would have remained in his elected judgeship for the remainder of his professional career. At forty-one years of age he was the next to youngest judge on the common pleas bench in Cuyahoga County. Shortly after taking the oath of office in January of 1937, Lausche was sidelined with an emergency appendectomy operation, but within two weeks he was back on duty.

On this new bench Judge Lausche continued to take difficult cases, regardless of their political ramifications. He recalled years later, "I soon found that most of the other judges were loath to hear cases tried by a judge with a jury, the usual equity cases. I decided I would not follow the easy way and let myself be fixed in a rut."[51]

Cleveland was one of the greatest bastions of organized labor in the United States during the 1930s, and no one was more aware of this fact than were the county's judges. Many members of the common pleas court resorted to every conceivable maneuver to dodge trying labor cases, particularly those involving injunctions against unions. Lausche refused to avoid these cases, and eventually adjudicated a record number of labor controversies, including contentious jurisdictional disputes and bitter injunction battles. Time and again he cracked down on the unions, especially where violence occurred.

Lausche's adjudications garnered considerable publicity and became a legal test case. In 1937 a local restaurant named Crosbys employed non-union employees. These employees did not want to join a union. The Hotel and Restaurant

Employees International Alliance (a component of the American Federation of Labor) wanted the employees to join their union and picketed the restaurant. Judge Lausche granted an injunction against the union, declaring there was no legitimate trade dispute. No quarrel existed between the proprietor and his employees, and picketing by strangers was unlawful.[52] The AFL took the case to the local appellate court, who overturned Lausche's decision. Later the Ohio Supreme Court upheld the judge's decision, and the case eventually reached the United States Supreme Court. Lausche's decision was upheld again. Union officials savagely attacked this decision, and fought it through repeated appeals. The supreme court re-examined this case, then reversed itself and established a precedent which held that picketing by outsiders was lawful.[53] Then began a strained relationship between Lausche and organized labor which eventually flared into open political warfare. Such labor decisions brought the common pleas judge wide publicity. Reversal of a decision rarely occurred in Lausche's judicial career. The seasoned judge tackled every case as if his life depended upon it. He earned a reputation both as a lawyer's judge and as a judge's judge. As a people's judge, local observers described Lausche as a "dynamic force for the good of the bench."[54]

Lausche served as a judge of the domestic relations court from July through December in 1937. The judge was alarmed by the number of divorce cases which ended up in court. The popular Lausche believed that the right for divorced people to remarry should be restricted. "The present divorce laws," he declared in late 1937, "are inadequate...we need better marriage laws and I have a definite idea on the point. The divorce court should have the power to restrict his or her right to remarry."[55] Before Lausche accepted an assignment with the divorce court, few petitions for divorce received a denial. Of the 1,537 divorce cases handled by the judge, 508 were dismissed.

Throughout his political career Lausche maintained that divorce decrees came too easily. Although not a strong Catholic, likely his philosophy emerged somewhat from the papal viewpoint that divorce violated church edicts. While a member of the United States Senate, Lausche supported Senate Chaplain Reverend Frederick Brown Harris and his viewpoint on divorce. Harris wrote a weekly column for the Washington *Star* entitled "Spires of the Spirit." In a column questioning the marital impropriety of New York Governor Nelson Rockefeller, Harris commented, "What avails anything prominent men in state or national posts of public service may advocate regarding our society in general, if, in their personal lives they strike selfish blows at the foundation of home, the institution of marriage, the fountainhead of all in our common life which is high and holy...such men reveal instabilities of behavior, which scholars have found to be historically characteristic of advanced societies on their way down."[56] Lausche was so impressed with the Reverend's thoughts that he requested the entire column be printed in the *Congressional Record*.

LAUSCHE, WHO HAD A PROPENSITY FOR ATTRACTING PUBLICITY, likely was unaware of his impending rendezvous with political greatness. The focus of this notoriety centered on Lausche's attack on the ills of organized gambling and crime in Cleveland and neighboring suburbs in the late 1930s. The backdrop for this scenario had formulated several years earlier.

By 1933, the greater majority of Americans perceived prohibition to be a failed social experiment. Originally passed by Congress in 1918 as the 18th Amendment, the Volstead Act implemented in 1920 cost the nation more than one billion dollars a year in lost taxes and import duties in the twenties. Clandestine drinking became the norm. In February 1933, Congress approved the 21st Amendment repealing prohibition. By the end of the year President Franklin D. Roosevelt proclaimed that the necessary thirty-six states ratified this amendment, putting an end to the dry law. After thirteen years, urban resistance finally toppled the controversial 18th Amendment. In the intervening years, a profound disrespect for the law damaged American society. The flamboyant excesses of bootleggers were only one of the more obvious evils spawned by prohibition. In city after city, police openly tolerated the traffic of liquor. Judges and prosecutors agreed to let bootleggers pay mere token fines, creating almost a system of license. Prohibition satisfied the countryside's desire for retribution, yet rural and urban America alike suffered from this overzealous attempt to legislate morality.[57]

Cleveland experienced the same social pitfalls encountered by other large metropolitan entities in the 1930s. In the mid-Depression period, idealism incurred a terrible pounding from the grim reality of day-to-day existence. Deeply rooted in the heritage of New England past and the conservatism of thousands of Central Europeans who had taken up a new life in the city, Cleveland's old standards of morality collapsed as badly and as dramatically as did the stock market, the banks, and the general economy.

Prior to the end of prohibition news reporters considered the flow of illegal liquor trivial in comparison to Cleveland's problems with organized crime, the corruption of elected officials, gambling, youth gang violence, and prostitution. Traffic control faded into utter confusion. The air became so polluted that dark clouds hung over the city, occasionally obscuring any view of the massive Terminal Tower which protruded from the landscape like a lone candle. On the sidewalks, panhandlers, pimps, and prostitutes prowled among the passing pedestrians.[58]

The thirties were not as gay as they were hysterical and abandoned—except in the hastily filled-in lake front where for two years (1936 and 1937) the Great Lakes Exposition gave the city and its followers, seven million in all, a kind of downtown Coney Island and miniature World's Fair jumbled together. Clevelanders loved the Great Lakes Exposition because it offered the most marvelous diversion from the adversity of the Great Depression. Even the jobless could occasionally scrape up enough dimes and quarters to take in the Exposition. Attendees enjoyed many shows, including one called the Aquacade, where young Billy Rose teamed with starlet Esther Williams.[59] Another attraction prompted fans to root for the Cleveland Indians, their local heroes at League Park. There the team battled the indomitable New York Yankees, led by aging Lou Gehrig and young Joe DiMaggio, a worthy replacement to departed Babe Ruth, the Sultan of Swat.

Cleveland's political climate paralleled that of Chicago. The public had long lost faith in their city hall. Cleveland did not have a public enemy as identifiable as Al Capone, but the city's police department stood as an embarrassment. Corruption ran rampant, from the beat cop all the way to the judge's chambers. Young Frank Lausche was a notable exception to this aura of deceit and crime. His honesty and forthrightness eventually captured public attention.

In 1935 while Lausche was completing his four-year term as a municipal judge, Harold Hitz Burton decided to run for the position of mayor. A former Republican state representative and future U.S. Senator and Supreme Court Justice, Burton ran on an Independent Republican ticket. He combined independent ideals with Republican practical politics. Burton defeated incumbent Republican Mayor Harry Davis in the primary election and former Democratic Mayor Ray Miller in the general election.

Burton knew the political ropes. He played a cagey game. He kept in constant touch with the three local newspaper editors and carried his problems to their doors. Burton became the first of a succession of newspaper mayors in Cleveland. Lausche, who admired Burton, later adopted many of Burton's political tactics, and he too would be pegged as a newspaper mayor. Lausche's respect for Burton caused him to resist Seltzer's pleas to run for the office.

Burton vowed to clean up corruption, wage war on crime, and make city streets safe again. The new Mayor knew he must appoint a clean and competent director of public safety. City hall had suffered from mismanagement under Davis. City finances were in sad condition, and the police department suffered from dishonesty and poor morale.[60] Both during the Miller and the Davis administrations, the top police officer operated politically rather than on a professional level. Police Chief George Matowitz, a 31-year veteran of the department and an honest man himself, proved to be ineffective over his long tenure and was only anxious to remain in office. The chief contented himself with issuing numerous platitudinous orders to enforce the law, but his police force knew the words carried little clout. These corrupt police officers carefully avoided raids on gambling joints of owners who contributed to the Mayor's campaign fund, whether they be Republican or Democrat. The victorious Burton faced an ominous task.[61]

The safety director in city hall exercised supreme authority over municipal law enforcement, which included some 2,500 policemen and ancillary services.

Incumbent Martin J. Lavelle had made a mockery of the position and outraged many citizens in the process. Burton sought an individual of integrity and skill to command the entire system of crime prevention, fire fighting, and traffic control. The name of Eliot Ness appeared on the short list of candidates.

Wes Lawrence, federal reporter for the Cleveland *Plain Dealer*, thought of Ness for this position. He admired Ness's work while covering the federal beat, "Ness would be the kind of guy Burton needs," he confided to Philip W. Porter, city editor of the *Plain Dealer*.[62] United States Attorney Dwight W. Green, one of the federal prosecutors in the Al Capone case and future Governor of Illinois, gave Ness a solid endorsement. William Clegg, a politically-connected Chicago stockbroker, lent his support to Ness. He served as foreman of the federal grand jury which had indicted Capone on tax violations as a result of Ness's testimony.[63] Burton had never heard of Ness. Based on these and other recommendations, on December 21, 1935, the new Mayor offered the position to Ness for an annual salary of $7,500. Burton, a Harvard graduate and personable gentleman, did not make this appointment in the guise of extroverted showmanship. The appointment of Ness became a masterstroke for the incoming Mayor. Burton's legion of supporters felt encouraged by his action in choosing a safety director who was an outsider. He possessed professional law enforcement credentials and maintained no ties to Cleveland's political scene.[64]

☞

A REAL BOMBSHELL, THE APPOINTMENT OF NESS AMAZED local politicians. Most veteran policemen expressed cynicism and didn't believe Ness would change the deplorable situation. Local newspaper editorials supported this appointment. The *Plain Dealer* commented: "If any man knows the inside of the crime situation [in Cleveland] his name is Ness."[65] Ness was an individual who commanded attention in every way. In an era of loose standards for public officials, the new safety director served as a sharp contrast. Only thirty-two years old, the new safety director's appointment made him the youngest public safety director in the city's history. Ness, a baker's son, was born in Chicago where his Norwegian immigrant parents had settled. After graduating from high school, Ness earned a degree from the University of Chicago, majoring in commerce, law, and political science. Six feet tall and weighing 172 pounds, Ness epitomized the collegiate look, ready to battle crime with the best of them. He became nationally known for his leadership of the Untouchables in Chicago during prohibition.

The new safety director had enjoyed the lake front in Chicago, which held an aura of sacredness. Now he looked down upon an oily, yellow Cuyahoga River that flowed out to an increasingly polluted Lake Erie. Cuyahoga, an Indian name meaning crooked, aptly applied to crime-riddled Cleveland and neighboring suburbs. Ness demonstrated his commitment to his new job almost immediately.

In a remarkably short time, devastating police corruption became public knowledge. Two policemen lost their badges after being caught while drinking on duty. Captain Louis Cadek invested $100,000 in a cemetery lot venture that smacked of elements of a racket. Another captain, Michael Harwood, owned a bootleg joint, which the local gendarmes raided. A domino effect developed as one policeman told of payoffs that led to confessions by other officers. Saloonkeepers began to phone Ness with tips. Quickly, seven policemen received indictments for various forms of graft; they were convicted and sent to prison. These convictions created a cleansing effect needed by Mayor Burton and Ness. A half-dozen other policemen of high rank and considerable seniority who had not been indicted, instead decided to take their pensions and retire.[66] Ness's low-key manner belied the fact that he could be tough. The Cleveland Police Department began to believe him when he transferred 122 policemen, including a captain, and replaced the head of the detective department.[67] Ness succeeded in his objective to force officers to sever their cozy alliance with the criminal element. "It is this simple," Ness insisted, "Either we have a law-abiding community, or we don't."[68]

Concurrently, Judge Lausche became involved in cleaning up racketeering that maintained a vise-like hold upon the citizenry of Cuyahoga and neighboring counties. The scenario paralleled the findings exploited by the Estes Kefauver Senate Investigating Committee on crime and politics in the early 1950s. "The county of Cuyahoga was rife with gambling houses that were exploiting the monies of families and contributing to the delinquency of the community," Lausche lamented, "The real robbers and perpetrators of these crimes were the operators. I decided to do something about it."[69] The common pleas judge graphically related several instances of plaintiffs and their plights with gaming habits that ended up in his court. Lausche remembered a Polish butcher, "He was a man who had developed a habit of going to the Harvard Club, a large-scale gambling joint just outside Cleveland city limits in Newburgh Heights...he eventually lost all his life savings and two butcher shops. When he sued to recover his gambling losses, the club owners called on him in a large black sedan. They threatened his life and the lives of his wife and children if he did not drop his suit. Should he testify in court and have protection of his own body and his family? Or should he yield to the gang threat and stay away from court? Well, he yielded to the gangsters and dropped his lawsuit!"[70] Then the thought occurred to Lausche, "The individual who commits a crime isn't the man to fear in the American society. The threat and danger to one's society is from organized gangsters and racketeers. One man in particular, a school superintendent, was before me. When I sat back to pass sentence there was in the rear of the room a lady who began to sob, and children who began to weep. And there and then, says Lausche unabashed in his sentimentality, 'I said, What a travesty! This man I am sending to the penitentiary—but the racketeers who have his money, these kids' money, are free.'"[71]

It was not unusual for large cities in the thirties to have a few private gambling clubs on a small and furtive basis, but the situation in Cleveland defied description. For years, gambling establishments encircled the city proper, operating in the open in buildings the size of warehouses. The street railway company ran special buses to these mammoth clubs. Cleveland policemen did not intervene, knowing that the houses were run by gangsters and guarded by machine guns. Customers included all walks of life—tellers, clerks, housewives, teachers, and blue-collar workers. These players incurred losses, which resulted in broken homes. Many committed suicide. Others went to prison for theft or embezzlement. These clubs became breeding grounds for the city's organized crime and a sanctuary for killers. Although in clear violation of the law, these casinos flourished because only one official, John L. (Honest John) Sulzmann, the Cuyahoga County sheriff, had authority to close these casinos, but he declined to act. The sheriff gave the excuse that he didn't know about the gambling. When that feeble statement broke down, he fell back on the alibi that the gambling clubs operated in various suburbs, but that he could not interfere because of a home rule policy. Enforcement agencies found their hands tied because witnesses hesitated to testify. The threat of bodily harm or worse hung over informers' heads.[72] Enter Eliot Ness and Judge Frank J. Lausche. Neither Ness nor Lausche objected to casual gambling. "In the army, I used to shoot craps myself," Judge Lausche recalled, "and I don't object to a little gambling among friends, but this organized gambling must stop."[73]

Outside Cleveland's city limits, three large gambling houses flourished. One gambling house, the Mounds Club in neighboring Geauga County, catered to the fashionable residents of Cleveland Heights who drank booze, ate well, and gambled without hindrance, often for high stakes. A second joint, the Pettibone Club in nearby Bainbridge, carried on its gambling functions outside the jurisdiction of the Cleveland Police Department. The third and most notorious nightspot, the Harvard Club, which over the years was located at six different locations near Newburgh Heights, operated one of the largest casinos between New York and Chicago. This operation accommodated 500–1,000 gamblers a night, who came from all over the country to play crap games, roulette, and poker. Ness was shocked when he discovered that this full-scale casino with over 300 slot machines had operated openly and unmolested for more than five years. Chief operator James "Shimmy" Patton, one of three co-owners, directed the majority of gambling profits to the Cleveland syndicate. At the same time, the Mayfield Road mob, a vicious gang of Jewish and Italian criminals, controlled the lucrative alcohol business at the Harvard Club.[74] Early in his term as safety director, Ness estimated that organized crime robbed Cleveland's economy of more that $1 million from illegal gambling alone. Ness told the Cleveland Advertising Club that in any city where corruption continues, it follows that some officers are playing ball with the underworld. If town officials are committed to a program of protection, police work becomes exceedingly difficult, and the officer on the beat, discouraged from his duty, decides it's best to see as little crime as possible.[75]

Ness confounded many businessmen when he proclaimed support for legalized gambling—a position that ran counter to Mayor Burton's pronouncements. His rationale suggested that such a move would cut deeply into the mob's profits. Ness conceded that any attempt to make gambling legal invited political suicide. Subsequently the safety director changed his position and spoke out against the legalization of gambling, citing case studies verifying that criminal behavior became an albatross attached to gambling activity. Ness prepared to make his move on the Harvard Club as a private citizen. This notorious gambling joint was situated in a barn-like building which once served as a warehouse. A fancy New Orleans-style façade erected in the front of the warehouse did not shield the building's major function. Skepticism abounded in local dailies as to whether Ness would receive full cooperation from the Democratic county prosecutor's office. This fear soon evaporated. Frank T. Cullitan, fifty-five and an honest and courageous official, had already gained Ness's respect despite the difference in their party labels. He ran the same sort of aggressive operation that served as the hallmark of Ray T. Miller, his predecessor.

Cullitan and Ness became great teammates in their pursuit of underworld thugs. They shared contempt for gambling houses operating with apparently open immunity. The county prosecutor, a respected tactician with strong courtroom oratory, had sent seven murderers to the electric chair. Judge Lausche assisted this team.[76] He continually reaffirmed the gambling problem in his hometown. Several in-city gambling casinos closed within a few days of Mayor Burton's election. Upon Lausche's election in 1936 he quietly announced that gambling clubs must close. All judges espoused this perfunctory statement. Nobody seemed surprised, and local citizenry didn't take these comments too seriously. A man of his word, Lausche, along with Ness and Cullitan, decided to raid the Harvard Club one month after Ness took office. The Cleveland police technically had no jurisdiction over another municipality. With his keen sense of knowing what the voters would accept, along with an inborn tendency to be crusader, Lausche issued a search warrant he could legally implement. On January 10, 1936, Cullitan shocked the underworld by deputizing nearly two dozen private detectives, and they arrived at the Harvard Club. Shimmy Patton's bouncers greeted them with submachine guns and threatened Cullitan and his deputies. "If one of them trys to stick his God-damned neck in that door," shouted the rotund Patton, "we'll mow 'em down with machine guns. We've got them and we'll use them." Assistant Cuyahoga County prosecutor Frank Celebrezze replied that he didn't want bloodshed and tried to arrange a truce to permit patrons to leave the club in safety. "The hell with that," yelled Patton. "You aren't coming in here. If you do you'll get killed."[77] In consideration of the citizen's safety who comprised the club's customers, the detectives moved their siege line back a half block.

Cullitan called Ness, who was attending a city council meeting in Cleveland,

and explained the situation. Ness swung into action with the reluctant approval of Mayor Burton. The Mayor agreed to let city police officers serve as special deputies of the Cuyahoga county prosecutor's office, with the understanding that the deputies were acting independent of any affiliation with the city. A tip-off warned the Harvard Club proprietors that the police planned a raid. A steady stream of men departed from the club with filled overcoat pockets. Trucks and cars loaded with equipment pulled out amid cheers from the crowds who now lined the nearby streets. With sirens screaming police led by Ness pulled up at a nearby gas station where Cullitan and his frustrated raiders waited. After a standoff of several minutes, deputies and detectives in plain clothes rapped on the door, while Ness and his uniformed men waited. Soon the front door slowly opened and a husky character in a tuxedo invited the group to enter the casino.

Patton had disappeared and investigators later determined that Alvin "Creepy" Karpis, one of the FBI's most wanted criminals, had exited the premises during all of the commotion. This peaceful admission served as something of an anticlimax to tense hours of siege. The only flurry of action inside the club occurred when Byron Filkins, Cleveland *Press* photographer, who was approximately five feet tall, received a push to his chair by a gambler who did not want his picture taken. Big Webb Seeley of the rival Cleveland *News*, roaring with indignation at the mishandling of Filkins, promptly laid a mighty haymaker on the gambler's jaw, stretching him across a crap table.[78] Despite some of the more sensationalized accounts of the Harvard Club raid, the event remained relatively uneventful except for its symbolic value. A victory of the first magnitude emerged for law and order. Ness expressed pleasure that city police officers took an interest in the raid on a voluntary basis. Many members of the Cleveland Police Department exhibited less support. They knew too much, and may have been on the take.

The safety director's ire over this lack of cooperation only strengthened the conspiracy of silence within the department. Eventually the honest officers who had nothing to hide became the majority and respected Ness for his tenacity. The road ahead to clean up the gambling joints posed a real challenge for Ness and Lausche. The Harvard Club reopened on February 15, 1936, with expanded gambling operations, including a fleet of limousines for free customer pickup from downtown Cleveland. This club continued despite repeated scandals, many threatened lawsuits, police raids, grand jury investigations, ownership changes, and a succession of different locations.[79]

⌒

THE SYNDICATE OWNED VARIOUS GAMBLING CLUBS and expanded beyond the suburbs of Cleveland. Gambling had made major inroads along the Ohio River between Cincinnati and Newport, Kentucky. Ness continued his good work beyond sensationalized investigations. He modernized the police and fire departments and worked to provide better equipment of all sorts. The safety director retained his tremendous popularity through the beginning of World War II. "We all liked Eliot," remarked John Patrick Butler, who served as executive secretary to Mayor Burke, "and we all admired him as an honest, thoroughly competent expert in the field of law enforcement. There never was anything like him in Cleveland. He really captivated the imagination of the public in his early years, and he was given a hero worship unlike that given to any city official within my recollection." Butler concluded, "Eliot missed the boat. He should have run for mayor in 1941 against Frank Lausche, who was then a comparative unknown with a hard name to pronounce. He could have beat Lausche then because at that time Ness was the most famous man in the city and the most admired."[80] (Ness ran as a Republican candidate for mayor in 1947; however, he was unsuccessful.)

While Ness deserved many accolades for his administration of the police force, Lausche quietly went about his efforts to close local gambling operations. For many years Lausche knew of the problem gambling presented in Cleveland. Most of the casinos were outside Cleveland's city limits. County officials and local politicians in several small communities adjacent to Cleveland resisted efforts to remove the racketeers. Lausche spoke out publicly in his campaign to rid the metropolitan area of gambling houses. In 1938 while commenting on a gambling issue, Lausche observed that little progress could be made against gambling until the state legislature changed the laws to outlaw this illegal activity. Again in 1939 in an address to the Young Men's Business Club in Cleveland, the judge described a case of a young father who had lost his business by gambling at the Harvard Club and dropped his case against the club on the eve of his trial. The plaintiff admitted he received a threat of bodily harm and received $200 as a payoff to drop the case.[81]

Speaking at the dedication of neighboring Euclid's new city hall on June 8, 1939, Lausche blasted the often-heard suggestions for fattening public treasures through licensing of gambling machines. He praised local officials in living up to their Euclid—A Clean City motto. The judge insisted the residents of certain eastern suburbs could consider themselves fortunate to have public servants whose chief concern was making justice, law, and order a part of good administration.[82] With the cooperation of Ness, Lausche continued to put pressure on the gambling bosses, and by 1940 employed all his judicial powers—and at times—exceeded them.

The judge combed Cleveland until he found a fearless and energetic man to serve as grand jury foreman. He instructed the jury to break up the racketeers and any public officials who protected them. Previous grand juries had tried this strategy, but did not have a proper judge to back up the jury. The grand jury first ordered Cuyahoga County Sheriff Martin L. O'Donnell to raid the notorious Harvard Club. The grand jury discovered the sheriff's office had conducted a phony raid. The chief detective for Sheriff O'Donnell received a citation for contempt of court. The Cuyahoga Bar Association began proceedings to remove Sheriff O'Donnell.

The grand jury compiled lists of names of patrons at various gambling casinos who had sued the clubs for losses and damages. Other lists included those individuals placed on probation for offenses committed because of losses at these clubs. When these witnesses arrived in court to testify, they encountered a no-nonsense judge ready to cite them for contempt of court. After making all kinds of excuses not to appear, mayors and city officials of the suburbs where gambling houses flourished found Lausche did not accept excuses, and reluctantly came to court and faced the music.[83] Disregarding recalcitrant and corrupt sheriffs, local prosecutors, state highway patrolmen, and even mayors, Lausche issued secret, handwritten warrants to a Cleveland police officer in his confidence. Nearly all of the gambling spots in Cuyahoga County closed their doors. The Harvard Club defied the judge's warrant.

Butler concluded, "Eliot missed the boat. He should have run for mayor in 1941 against Frank Lausche, who was then a comparative unknown with a hard name to pronounce…"

Lausche constituted Detective Captain Michael Blackwell, an officer of the court, to shut down the club. In April 1941 the Harvard Club succumbed to Blackwell and his squad of Cleveland police officers and finally secured its doors.

Years later Lausche reflected, "Not for a moment have I directed my efforts against the weakness of human flesh and human mind. There have always been these human frailties. But I am against organized gambling racketeers, the dynasty whose powers with the law-enforcement officials and agencies can be greater than those of the citizenry itself, a government within a government which can be more powerful than the sovereign authority of the community."[84]

Gambling casinos consisted of only one phase of Lausche's cleanup campaign. In addition to gambling, he directed his legal guns toward corrupt labor unions. The late 1930s developed into a tumultuous period for America's laboring force. The passage of the Fair Labor Act of 1935 (Wagner Bill) gave unions much more power. The American Federation of Labor, Congress of Industrial Organization, United Auto Workers and United Mine Workers flexed their muscles with support from new federal guidelines. The corrupt Teamsters Union, especially in Cleveland, gained considerable strength in the latter decades of the twentieth century. Lausche held little quarrel with unions governed in proper fashion. Corruption and racketeering in local unions raised the hair on the back of his neck. In the fall of 1940, Lausche presided over the trial of labor racketeer Albert Ruddy for improprieties and sentenced him to the Ohio Penitentiary in Columbus.

Like a winning football coach at a major university, Lausche became one of the most recognized and well-respected public officials in Ohio. His successful, hard-hitting actions against racketeers and corrupt unions made newspaper headlines. His future as a bench judge became more secure. On December 18, 1940, Lausche received a request to serve a second term on the criminal bench. No criminal court judge in Cuyahoga County had served two consecutive terms.

Judge Frederick P. Walther, speaking for his associates, emphasized that in naming Judge Lausche, the nominating committee "yielded to the pressure of public demand."[85] The following day Lausche accepted the challenge of a second term commenting, "I did not seek or want the appointment. But I have been chosen and I accept the responsibility of the choice."[86] However Lausche's tenure as a common pleas judge did not survive a second term.

The local press and important politicos now realized that because of Lausche's commendable judicial record, he was ready for a new political challenge. Lausche loved his responsibilities as judge. He built an enviable record on the bench. He broke into his judicial career by way of an appointment to the municipal bench, partly as a reward for his accomplishments as Democratic leader of the 23rd ward, an inauspicious way to begin a political career. Within three years Lausche so distinguished himself that local civic leaders led by Editor Louis Seltzer of the Cleveland *Press* seriously began to beat the drum for Lausche to seek his hometown's office of mayor. Lausche cautiously plunged into deeper and more complex political waters.

Frank Lausche as mayor of Cleveland, 1941–44. (Courtesy of Dr. Rudolph Susel)

four

"Fearless Frank" Becomes
Mayor of Cleveland

THE DECADE-LONG DEPRESSION BROUGHT CLEVELAND to its knees. George E. Condon, Jr. decried that "the Cleveland the world knew from 1930 to 1955 was a hurt town and it showed in many ways." The popular columnist emphasized, "There was a disposition toward petty bickering among the civic leaders on petty issues, while the large issues of Cleveland's future went untended and the sprawling downtown area turned gray and shabby."[1] The Steel Belt became the Rust Belt. The relative decline of heavily ethnic, nineteenth-century industrial cities such as Milwaukee, St. Louis, and Cleveland continued. Schemes for their revitalization proved problematic, or met with intermittent success. An additional factor became critical to the changing landscape of large northern cities: the flattening of white ethnicity in this Midwestern regionality resulted from the mass migration of tens of thousands of African-Americans from the South, particularly in the decades following both World War I and World War II.

African-Americans came to these cities drawn by the promise of a location where economic and moral progress could be shared with a wide variety of people. Local political leaders vowed to promote a city in which black people could succeed economically and participate fully in the public realm as citizens. Like many earlier migrants settling in metropolitan cities, African-Americans soon discovered the limited resources these cities offered. Clustered by choice and by *de facto* segregation in often-impoverished urban neighborhoods (for example, east Cleveland), blacks deeply resented the gap between rhetoric and reality.[2]

Fortunately in the decades ahead, Cleveland righted the ship. Interestingly George V. Voinovich, an individual whose political credentials are strikingly similar to Frank Lausche's, spearheaded Cleveland's economic revival. Voinovich, part Slovenian by heritage, served as Mayor from 1981–1991 (longer than any other mayor in Cleveland history). By mobilizing the support of Cleveland business leaders and by enlisting professional managers to run the city, Voinovich led a Cleveland comeback, taking the so-called mistake on the lake from bankruptcy to national recognition. Following in Lausche's political footsteps, the former mayor also served as Ohio governor (1991–1999), and won election to the United States Senate in 1998 and 2004. When Voinovich completes his career, historians will note a fertile subject for research. Lausche and Voinovich served in almost parallel political offices: Voinovich, a Republican; Lausche, a Democrat with Republican leanings.

In retrospect, Lausche might well have accelerated his remarkable climb up the political ladder as early as 1935. A group of civic-minded citizens had urged him to run for mayor. The Scripps-Howard Cleveland *Press* and its aggressive editor Louis B. Seltzer published a front-page editorial imploring Lausche to seek this office. Seltzer outlined in his plea the reasons Cleveland needed Lausche, noting that his candidacy would offer Cleveland a clean break from the corrupt politico previously imposed on the city, "He would fight to preserve law and order...he would preserve the civil liberties of every citizen. The alliance between politics and the underworld would end...he would be independent of any party boss, any political machine. Lausche would bring to the office the viewpoint of the common people of Cleveland, where he was born and where he has lived all his life "[3]

The 40-year-old Lausche could not be persuaded to leave his judgeship. He had encountered similar pressure to run for office a year earlier in 1934. Party regulars had offered their support if Lausche agreed to run for a seat in Congress against Martin L. Sweeney, the irascible incumbent Democrat. Lausche also declined this offer. He enjoyed his position as bench judge. Lausche preferred the serenity of the judicial chamber—its *absorption and dignity*—to the turbulence and clamor of an intense municipal campaign.[4] A naturally prudent man with a jurist's studied detachment from the vagaries of public opinion, Lausche demonstrated fairness and caution before rendering his decisions.

Lausche's personal philosophy and political aspirations compared uniquely with former Ohio politician William Howard Taft, twenty-seventh President of the United States. Blessed with a strong legalistic mind, and best qualified to be a judge, the rotund Taft became Teddy Roosevelt's all-purpose troubleshooter and Secretary of War before his own election as President. After he took office in 1909, Taft questioned his personal political choice. "If I were now presiding in the Supreme Court," he wrote a friend from the White House, "I should feel entirely at home, but...I feel just like a fish out of water."[5] In 1921 fellow Ohioan President Warren G. Harding granted Taft his fondest wish: appointment as chief justice of the United States Supreme Court. Successfully clearing the courts overcrowded docket, the former President again proved himself an effective administrator and remained a respected justice until he resigned shortly before his death in 1931. He is the only person to hold both of the nation's most prestigious offices. There were numerous occasions in Lausche's political career when he wished he had pursued Taft's line of reasoning.

Lausche continued to resist pressure from friends and from the press to run for office, particularly from Seltzer. At the risk of offending the fourth estate in a letter to the Cleveland *Press*, Lausche defended his duties as judge as being at least as important, if not more so, than that of a mayor. The judge believed that if he ran for mayor, he "would be required virtually to abandon the profession for which I have been trained by experience and theory. My affection lies with the bench."[6] Seltzer believed Lausche chose not to run for personal reasons, whatever they might be. The Lausches still lived with Jane's father and mother, and had no children. At this juncture in his political career, insiders speculated that Lausche desired official Democratic Party support. A more realistic answer may rest with the fact that only one Democrat—Ray T. Miller—had been elected mayor of Cleveland in the previous twenty-five years. Competent Independent Republican Harold Burton won the mayoralty election in 1935 with Lausche's endorsement. He gained re-election in 1937 and in 1939 during the troubled times of the Great Depression. Burton's tenure as mayor did not negate the fact that the Republican Party regarded Lausche a formidable political opponent. After Lausche won election as Common Pleas Court judge in 1937 George Bender, chairman of the Republican Central Committee of Cuyahoga County, commented at a banquet, "I'm glad to be celebrating his [Lausche's] election as judge. We don't know how close he came to being mayor. We were wondering whether the Democrats would be smart enough to run him, but they ran true to form and didn't."[7] In spite of Lausche's reticence to run for the mayor's office and whether by accident or by design, his political stature and popularity grew in the late 1930s, particularly among ethnic populations in Cleveland.

In a practical sense, the judge in one way or another helped accomplish several of the mandates for a better Cleveland without running for mayor, mandates which Seltzer outlined in his plea in 1935. Between 1935 and 1941, Lausche served as a key figure in eradicating much of the gambling and underworld activities so prevalent in

Cuyahoga County. The alliance between politics and the gamblers began to dissipate. With the cooperation of Safety Director Eliot Ness, the police force regained a large measure of respectability and took pride in their law-enforcement duties. Lausche also fought labor racketeering at a time when organized labor began to reach its zenith in political and organizational strength. Labor racketeers found it necessary to be on guard and guilty culprits faced jail sentences. Lausche's political star rose in a dignified and resolute manner. While inevitably unpopular with certain segments of society, his decisions in the courtroom brought Lausche wide publicity.

Lausche, a fiercely independent individual, gave early indications that he fervently disliked party bossism with a passion. His break with leaders of the Democratic Party began to surface as early as 1937. For a second time, the Cleveland *Press* urged him to run for mayor. The Democratic organization wanted Ray Miller for its candidate, and Lausche did not run. Lausche resented the fact that party leaders used "boss methods" to force Miller's nomination.[8] These tactics increasingly caused Lausche to shun so-called party politics. The judge found Republican Mayor Burton to be a strong and worthy incumbent who easily won re-election. This tendency to ignore party bosses became much more evident as Lausche's popularity and stature grew.

The editor of the Youngstown *Vindicator* best described Lausche's reticence to affiliate with political organizations and—in particular—political machines, shortly after his first term election to the Ohio statehouse. He wrote, "Fearless Frank makes a distinction between political organizations and political machines... the principal purpose of a political organization should be to render service to the government, while a political machine is a body ostensibly organized for that purpose but in reality functioning to gain spoils and patronage for itself."[9]

Lausche's distaste for bossism in politics did not extend to newspaper editors. He learned early in his career that newspapers could often make or break a politician. In a 1939 front-page editorial, the loved, loathed, and all-powerful Seltzer, for the third time urged Lausche to run for mayor. "He *made* me buy his original request for me to run for mayor," Lausche often remarked. Again Lausche declined the invitation, which again miffed Seltzer. Nevertheless the persistent editor endorsed Lausche in the mayoral race two years later.[10] Whenever Lausche returned to Cleveland from trips political or otherwise, he made it a point to visit the editors of the Cleveland *Plain Dealer* and the Cleveland *Press*. The Cleveland *News*, a less influential third paper, normally supported Republican candidates, except with rare exceptions at the local level. The *News*, an evening paper and junior partner with the *Plain Dealer* after 1933, provided the *Plain Dealer* with a certain nuisance value against the *Press*, also an evening paper.

The two leading editors—Seltzer of the *Press* and Paul Bellamy of the *Plain Dealer*—were strong rivals for nearly twenty-five years. Much of their rivalry embraced politics and the concern over community affairs in greater metropolitan

Cleveland. Bellamy tended to keep a lower profile on local issues. A Harvard graduate originally from Massachusetts, Bellamy joined the *Plain Dealer* in 1907. This easterner became city editor at the age of twenty-five. Bellamy inherited his writing skills from his father, noted author Edward Bellamy. The elder Bellamy wrote a prophetic book, *Looking Backward, 2000–1888*, which accurately predicted the wonders of science in the next generation. He exerted considerable influence on his bright son. Young Bellamy assumed leadership of the *Plain Dealer* in 1933 and remained in this position until 1954, when Thomas Vail replaced him.

Seltzer was a prime example of an overwhelmingly ambitious street-smart youngster, a sharp contrast to Bellamy. The young Seltzer set out to get ahead in the newspaper business despite lack of a formal education. He quit school at age 16 to become an office boy for the Cleveland *Leader*. After marriage to Marion Elizabeth Champlin at the tender age of 18, he began his long career with the Cleveland *Press* at the age of 20. In a short time, the young man became city editor, and by 1928, the thirty-one-year-old Seltzer advanced to the prestigious and powerful position of editor. He held this position for 37 years until he retired in 1966. All the while Seltzer built himself up as an ever-present personage, his rival Bellamy, who was not an extrovert, avoided even the tedious task of giving talks to small groups. By the end of the Great Depression, Seltzer's ubiquitous personality and political savvy began to pay off when he emerged as a political kingmaker, and *Life* Magazine dubbed him Mr. Cleveland.[11]

Lausche, a fiercely independent individual, gave early indications that he fervently disliked party bossism with a passion.

Seltzer latched onto Lausche's star early in the Slovenian's political career. The editor first saw young Lausche in action in September 1928 at a neighborhood meeting of the 23rd Ward at the Slovenian National Hall on St. Clair Avenue. Seltzer's interest in this man resulted from conversations with several friends in Cleveland politics who suggested the editor take a look at this young politician. Having been editor of the *Press* for only a few months, Seltzer listened carefully as Lausche spoke to a packed hall. The young ward leader urged his neighbors and friends to band together to protect their neighborhood, located not far from the downtown district, from the adverse changes which were taking place in similar areas. The crowd repeatedly cheered Lausche as he spoke alternately in English and in Slovenian. The gathering enthusiastically accepted his proposal for a neighborhood organization. "I came out here especially to see you on your own ball diamond," Seltzer explained as he identified himself to Lausche.[12] Seltzer visited Lausche in his office several days later, and his favorable impression of the man grew. Lausche expressed himself on important current issues in the city in a straightforward manner. The neophyte editor became convinced—as others had suggested to him earlier—that Lausche bore watching. Seltzer became a strong ally in the coming political fortunes of the young Slovenian.

THROUGHOUT HIS CAREER, LAUSCHE CAN BEST be described politically as a Renaissance man. Certainly, he believed in honesty and his political adversaries searched far and wide to unearth meaningful scandals during his political career. He espoused the spirit of American institutions and patriotism, and maintained a strong loyalty to his country, right or wrong, throughout his life. Lausche believed that a public office is a trust. To abuse that trust violated one's basic tenets of right and wrong. His stubbornness ensured a down-the-middle approach on most issues.

During the early Roosevelt days (Franklin D.) Lausche leaned left of center, a position he found less compatible with his political posture as the years went by. He believed that, under Roosevelt, America had taken on a social vision unknown to the country in previous generations. "The problems of the aged, the blind, the healthy man who was unable to find work in Depression times, the problem of the farmer...losing his property because of falling food prices—all these were given greater recognition under [FDR] than ever before in history. Many of the things he did are bound to make for a better America."[13]

Lausche, who in contrast to Roosevelt came up from the other side of the railroad tracks, shared the president's political agenda. Social security laws received his approval even as he expected these laws in all probability to be further extended. He favored a soft pedal on government interference in the daily lives of American citizens. To Lausche, a free enterprise economy meant "free from compulsory labor, free from exploitation by employers, unregulated monopolies or arbitrary public authority."[14] Above all else, Thomas Jefferson's words best capture Lausche's political philosophy, "I am a Jeffersonian Democrat," he often proclaimed.[15] He believed in minimal federal government interference. Lausche maintained that the more distant government strays from the people, the more improvident that government is likely to be. He seemed convinced that America's finest type of government is administered by township trustees under which governmental decisions take place clearly in view of the public. To Lausche voters cannot become indifferent. If so, the controlling political party becomes subservient to the rule of a few self-serving persons.

As early as 1938 Lausche spoke like an aspiring office-seeker. Those supporters close to him knew that he evoked sincerity and honesty in his words. Yet Lausche's mystique seemed to touch all elements of society, a ploy that worked for him throughout his political career. He gave a speech over WHK radio station that emoted a Lincolnesque overtone. "Although we live in America, we are still inclined to look upon each other as racially distinct. We have forgotten that the strength of a Democracy depends mainly upon the will of the people. The policy, whether liberal or conservative, to be pursued by the government, is a product of the will of the electors...when the discords become bitter and when, within our boundaries, we begin to look upon each other with suspicion and when we begin to demand things that seem to be just to ourselves but are obviously unjust to others, we, at that moment, begin to mock the memory of those who fought to create and preserve this Republic."[16]

Lausche continued exploiting this theme, as the pressure for him to seek the mayor's office mounted. He warned nationality groups who made up the membership of the Democratic Cosmopolitan League that they must keep themselves separate from the dictation of mercenary political machines, "We can't live separately and live successfully," Lausche cautioned and added, "We must live as a unit unmindful of the race or religion from which we come. I recoil from the thought that any might be motivated in the choice of public officials by race or religion. That must not be."[17]

Already in Lausche's early political career, he sent the message that he abhorred the formal political pressure prevalent in New York's Tammany Hall and in boss-ridden cities like Boston, Chicago and Cincinnati.

Reflecting upon his own ethnic background and aware that his words carried weight among blacks and other hyphenated Americans, Judge Lausche exhorted, "You must remember that when you speak in the name of the Hungarians or the Poles or the Germans or any group and are following the dictates of persons operating on a commercial basis as a political machine as separate from a political party, you are not doing that group a service. Can the men of rural Ohio be separated from those of Cleveland because they have different backgrounds? When this country was established there was then considered the fact that this country would always be made up of divergent peoples."[18]

Already in Lausche's early political career, he sent the message that he abhorred the formal political pressure prevalent in New York's Tammany Hall and in boss-ridden cities like Boston, Chicago and Cincinnati. Lausche possessed a keen understanding of political machinery and how it operated at the ward level. He understood the you-scratch-my-back-and-I'll-scratch-yours interplay which often dominated political activities. His independent inclination led to many interesting political showdowns.

Lausche continued to talk like a political aspirant in early 1941, a mayoral election year in Cleveland. He railed against the penal system in Ohio, which lacked proper resources to rehabilitate young offenders who might end up in a reformatory or, worse yet, in the state penitentiary with hardened criminals. Although a defective-delinquent law existed, Lausche found the law useless. Truant delinquents needed appropriate facilities and psychiatric care. "In trying to prevent crime you must do a bit of airing. Punishment is not the answer to [certain] crimes. We [must] proceed, not on the basis of revenge, but on the basis of education and rehabilitation."[19] With great effort, state Senator James M. Metzenbaum (a fellow Clevelander) worked several years before provisions became available to build correctional facilities for juvenile offenders as recommended by Lausche.

When Mayor Burton won election to the United States Senate in the fall of 1940, Lausche received inquiries in early 1941 about his availability for the major's office. He pondered the question for weeks, which often became his *modus operandi* on important political decisions. In May 1941, he and Jane traveled to San Jose, California, on a vacation trip to visit Jane's cousin, Mary Wilcox. Lausche told his supporters he would give them his decision upon his return. Lausche wistfully remembers that one day he dropped into an old church near Monterey; he heard the chant of the liturgy and saw the warm rays of the sun pouring through the windows bound with ancient iron. He began to meditate, finally made up his mind and decided he would not run for mayor.[20] The pressure for the judge to run did not abate in the coming days.

He returned to Cleveland, and something "clicked," as he put it, when he saw his hometown again. What prompted this reaction, he did not know. For two weeks he huddled with Ray T. Miller, Cuyahoga County Democratic chairman, former U. S. Senator Robert J. Bulkley, elder statesman of the local Democratic Party, other Democratic leaders and influential citizens. Finally after much persuasion, on June 30, Lausche agreed to carry the Democratic colors in the primary election in September. He resigned from his $1,000-a-month post on the Common Pleas bench on August 20, giving up nearly 18 months of a judicial term to seek a 24-month term as mayor.[21]

☙

NOTED AUTHOR JOHN GUNTHER RECALLED his admiration for Lausche's honesty when the judge decided to run for mayor. "He felt that it would be morally wrong to run for one office while holding another, though the opposite example has been set by...a hundred thousand other politicians who hold on to whatever job they have as long as possible."[22] As an example, Congressman Martin L. Sweeney, an opponent of Lausche's, chose not to resign from his congressional seat to run in the primary election.

The time for a Democrat to run for the mayor's position seemed appropriate. The City Council and Burton, now a U.S. Senator, appointed Edward Blythin, a Welsh immigrant and the mayor's law director, to serve the remaining eleven months of Burton's term. With Burton's exit, the Democrats believed they had a good opportunity to win the mayor's office. Lausche had built an enviable record as judge.

President Franklin D. Roosevelt had swept Cuyahoga County in heavy landslides in 1932, 1936, and 1940. The powerful Miller favored Lausche. The odds looked good for the mayoral challenger. Some individuals in Democratic Party headquarters expressed concern that Miller entertained a political agenda in abeyance to what Lausche had in mind. Lausche remained cautious in responding to questions from the press, particularly in reference to whether he planned to dismiss Republican Safety Director Eliot Ness from his duties. Lausche deferred those questions to Miller and went so far as to state he would accept Democratic organizational support only if he were free to act as he pleased in office. Lausche's response was another early indication of his lifelong independence from party influence.

Lausche prepared to open his campaign. In addition to Blythin, Sweeney and Republican Judge Arthur H. Day opposed Lausche in the primary election. Sweeney had been a controversial political maverick of the Democratic Party for over a decade. He joined with Father Charles Coughlin, the contentious radio priest from Detroit, in continually denouncing President Roosevelt and in warning against the possibility of war. Lausche gave his campaign-opening speech at the annual steer roast of the Democratic Party held at Geauga Lake Park. Before nearly 50,000 supporters, Lausche proclaimed Cleveland needed a new deal, which included the need for a referendum by the voters to determine whether the city should pay the inflated price of $45 a share for Cleveland Railway Company stock that controlled transportation services in Cleveland.

He believed buses might better serve the city's future transportation needs. At every turn, Lausche stirred the cheering crowd with his oration. On the platform Lausche effortlessly achieved contact with his listeners. His oratory was flowery, somewhat in the 1910 Fourth-of-July tradition. Lausche later remembered that, at this inaugural campaign address, the populace warmly greeted him as he stepped to the rostrum. The candidate carefully laid his speech on the stand, and put on his glasses. Lausche had labored for weeks preparing this important message. He read the first paragraph, then, to emphasize a point, snatched off his glasses and waved them in the air. "I put the glasses back on," the future Mayor related, "looked at the manuscript, and I couldn't read a word of it! When I waved my glasses, one of the lenses had fallen out. The biggest moment in my life, the greatest speech I ever wrote—and damn—blast it, I couldn't make out the words! First I shut one eye and tried to read through the lens that remained—but folks in the front row saw me making faces and began to giggle. So in desperation I took off my glasses, swept the speech to the floor, and let 'em have it extemporaneously."[23]

The local Democratic organization jumped into line behind the judge in his quest for the mayor's office. However, several undercurrents of criticism permeated a party wing comprised of a county engineer's organization and those loyal to the late Sheriff Martin L. O'Donnell, who had dragged his feet about the gambling raids. Working with the Democratic organization Lausche asked voters directly, via a questionnaire, their views on important services provided by city government. These questions ranged from lowering the rental costs of Municipal Stadium and Public Hall to attracting more gatherings and conventions. The questionnaire asked whether city employees were courteous and willing to serve, and was city government making an honest effort to operate "on a sound, efficient and economic basis?"[24] The tabulated results would serve as a guide for Lausche if and when he won the election. As the election neared Lausche looked to be a *natural* in Cleveland. He came from the ranks of nationality groups who made up a large portion of the city's population. These groups became conscious of their voting power in the 1920s under the leadership of Democratic boss Burr Gongwer and his intricate system called the proportional representational (P.R.) scheme, another name for bloc voting. This technique played one ethnic group against another for votes. By 1940, Gongwer lost his political power to the heavy-handed, yet gifted Miller. The P. R. system fell by the wayside. Every nationality group swelled with pride when Lausche had to run. They forgot petty jealousies and differences in the belief that one of their own might occupy the mayor's chair.

Even though Lausche cracked down on the unions while on the bench, the Congress of Industrial Organization (CIO) supported him in this election, convinced he was an honest person. The American Federation of Labor (AFL) refrained from official endorsement for the Democratic candidate. Lausche, who learned well from former Mayor Harold Burton, campaigned vigorously. Regardless of the size of the gatherings, Lausche gave his political pitch. Campaign funds trickled in, mostly in small amounts. He received loyalty funds from his many friends and neighbors in the 23rd Ward. Lausche showed disdain for any large contributions, particularly from lobbyists, unions, or businesses. The mayoral aspirant chose to be politically beholden to no one.

Lausche moved along the campaign trail cautiously, raising concern about those issues appearing to be most pertinent to the city's well being. One issue—the exodus of inhabitants from Cleveland—alarmed the Cleveland native. In the 1930s, 2.4 percent of the residents (22,000) moved out of Cleveland. The metropolitan community failed to keep pace with growth experienced in the rest of the country. In typical campaign rhetoric, Lausche implored that "Our main objective...must be to make Cleveland a more advantageous place in which to earn a living, and a healthier more convenient, cleaner and more attractive town for living.... The major issue is that of "Progress[ion] vs. Regression."[25]

A valid criticism of Lausche throughout his political career focused on his uncanny ability to straddle the fence on key issues. Earlier in his campaign he had expressed his support for municipal ownership of the Cleveland Railway Company. In a qualified response to a questionnaire by the League of Women Voters, the Democratic candidate commented, "The issue...is not altogether a question of municipal or private ownership, but rather a question of provision for speedy transportation at a reasonable price expeditiously attained."[26]

Voters trekked to the polls on September 30, 1941, to vote in the non-partisan primary election. The results boded well for Lausche. He gained the most votes of any of the five competing candidates, including incumbent Mayor Edward Blythin. Lausche's 23rd Ward demonstrated loyalty and affection, giving him 255 out of 269 votes cast.[27] Lausche faced Blythin in the general election on November 4, 1941. All three newspapers jumped on the Lausche bandwagon in pre-election editorials. In sporting world parlance, the election resulted in a no contest. Lausche polled a record 61 percent of the vote, winning by 50,000 votes.

The following morning on November 5, the Cleveland *Plain Dealer* carried an article written by reporter Joseph Gambatese, a long-time Lausche friend, entitled "City Melting Pot Molds a Mayor." The main thesis of his column explained, "only two days before his election as a 'nationality' Mayor, a syndicated Washington columnist likened Lausche to New York's Mayor Fiorella La Guardia because of similar ethnic backgrounds and political independence."[28] Lausche's ethnicity and political success were linked together many times throughout his Horatio Alger-like career. The new Mayor set a precedent for future ethnic politicians who would be elected to the mayor's office for the next 28 years. Reverently titled *Lausche clones*, these names read like a Who's Who in Cleveland politics—Thomas A. Burke, Anthony J. Celebrezze, Ralph Locher, and Ralph Perk. Following the tenure of Carl Stokes, Cleveland's first black Mayor in the late 1960s, Ralph Perk, a Republican with Czech background, became Mayor in 1971 and frequently referred to himself as the last of the Lausche clones. Lausche publicly proclaimed his vote for Perk during his three campaigns for mayor.

⌒

ON NOVEMBER 10, 1941, LAUSCHE TOOK THE OATH of office with a "promise to administer the city's affairs efficiently and a plea to citizens of Cleveland and city employees to cooperate with him."[29] In the simplest of ceremonies, the inauguration drew the largest outpouring of friends, relatives, and political figures ever gathered for a mayor's inaugural in Cleveland. The proud Jane Lausche, resplendent in a new fur coat adorned with a bright orchid, stood by her husband's side after briefly addressing the crowd. An informal luncheon at Rohr's restaurant followed the ceremony, where city hall reporters and political analysts honored Lausche, his family, and selected friends.

Lausche faced a major challenge to bring cohesion to a fractured city. The ominous storm clouds of an impending war hovered above the city. Wages had remained sluggish for years. The inhabitants of this great industrial center did not want war. More than half of Cleveland's 900,000 citizens claimed another country as their birthplace or declared they were first- or second-generation Americans. Ethnic groups—many of whom supported Lausche—often divided their loyalties between the United States and their homeland.

Politically Lausche's election reverberated with national implications. He became only the second Democrat elected to the mayor's office in 26 years. With the exception of Cleveland, nearly every large American city was governed by a

Democratic mayor during the Roosevelt era. Cleveland finally joined the crowd. The Lausche victory reinvigorated the local Democratic Party and meant possible political gains for the party in coming local, state, and federal elections. An example of the euphoria produced by the Lausche (or Lausche-Miller) victory came in a letter from the inimitable James A. Farley, National Democratic Chairman, to Miller. Farley wrote, "I am sure that a real Democratic mayor will be able to strengthen the [Democratic] organization in Ohio and will be of material assistance in the next gubernatorial campaign. It must please you very much...to see the result of your efforts so successful."[30] Likely Lausche, with his independent bent, would not have reacted with great enthusiasm to the inference that Miller and the Democratic Party received so much credit for this victory. All would change in a matter of days.

With rare exceptions, Lausche avoided nepotism when making appointments. John Lokar became an exception. A close friend, he served as Lausche's right-hand man early in his political career. Lokar, a fellow Slovenian, was a son of a crony of Lausche's father and was younger than Lausche. The two youngsters played together when both were growing up near St. Vitus Church. Lokar resigned from his job with the Internal Revenue Service in 1937 and took the responsibility as Lausche's bailiff in Common Pleas Court. In 1941 he remained with his friend as campaign manager, and then assumed the role as secretary and executive assistant to the mayor's office, and throughout a portion of Lausche's tenure as governor. Any successful administrator is generally only as strong as his staff members. Lausche could count on Lokar to help him over the inevitable bumps that occur in high-level political offices.

All seemed well on the local political front. On July 24, 1941, the Cleveland *Press* had carried a headline "Frank Lausche and I [Miller] are in complete accord."[31] The headline implied that Lausche and Miller agreed on political strategy, city cabinet appointments and general management of the mayor's office. To start off on the right foot, Lasuche appointed three trusted allies to important city posts: Thomas A. Burke, law director; Joseph T. Sweeny, finance director; and Samuel David, service director. The rest of the cabinet members consisted of Democrats recommended by Miller. The situation changed dramatically two days after Lausche took his oath. One fly remained in the ointment. What to do with Republican Safety Director Eliot Ness? As a local icon, he had served in the two preceding administrations. The heavy handed, yet gifted Miller had summoned Lasuche to a meeting with party leaders and was told to sack Ness. According to Condon, Lausche at first expressed little enthusiasm for retaining the safety director. Lausche had worked with Ness on cleaning up gambling casinos and labor graft. He feared public reaction to the dismissal of a hero. On the other hand several labor leaders protested the retention of Ness in office, as did some of the spokesmen in the police and fire departments and Democratic Party headquarters. Each group had a grievance to settle. Miller dramatically offered to go to J. Edgar Hoover and get a real G-man if Lausche fired Ness.[32]

Two days after taking the oath of office, Lausche decided to retain Ness. A furious Miller charged that Lausche privately promised to remove the safety director. The Mayor denied this accusation. The Democratic old guard exploded. Long-time party professionals looked on Lausche with a wary eye. "I had a close relationship with Ness," Lausche said in defending his decision. "Ness was deeply in my consciousness as the best man to fill that post. So I kept him and that's when the split with Miller took place."[33]

Disappointed in Lausche's decision, Miller conferred with Congressman Stephen Young, also from Cleveland and a loyal member of the Democratic old guard. Young commented, "I'm afraid our friend [Lausche] went haywire in the appointment of Ness. It sort of closes the door on a lot of us."[34] From that point on Lausche and Young were not close and even crossed swords many times when both served in the United States Senate at the same time (1958–1968). It evolved into an issue of a liberal Democrat opposing a conservative Democrat, both from Cuyahoga County.

Understandably, Miller may have felt betrayed by Lausche, particularly after receiving the following laudatory letter from James W. Shocknessy, influential Democratic attorney from Toledo who practiced law in Columbus. "Now that you have come through a National and State Election and a Municipal Election as well so successfully, you can face down any critics you have heretofore had and your friends can be joyful that their judgement (sic) of you always was correct. It is a pleasure to us elsewhere in the State to see its greatest City in so capable hands as it now finds itself with its mayor and its Chairman."[35]

Shocknessy later served as commission chairman of the Ohio Turnpike during the Lausche gubernatorial reign in the 1950s. This rift with Miller never healed. Two strong personalities refused to bend on the Ness issue. In Lausche's mind Miller, who helped launch his political debut, demonstrated machine boss tactics of the old school. He accurately figured that if he could get away with defying Miller, he could move a long way toward achieving real political power himself.[36] Lausche was now identified as the man who walks alone, on the political highway. Both the *Press* and the *Plain Dealer* supported Lausche in this decision. The dailies contended that the safety director's position did not constitute a political issue, and maintained that Ness had cleaned up the city.

Fearless Frank had taken his first major step toward seeking political independence. The breach between Lausche and Miller widened, and they eventually became bitter political enemies. Cuyahoga County Democratic Party professionals looked upon Lausche with suspicion and disdain. Miller tried to cut Lausche down at every opportunity.

After a few months in the Lausche cabinet, personal incidents involving Ness took care of the volatile situation. In March 1942, Ness and his wife Evaline left a nightclub in downtown Cleveland. Driving on a slippery street, Ness slammed into another car injuring the driver of the other vehicle. Sensational headlines blackened the front pages of the afternoon papers of what was termed a hit-skip accident. No charges were filed, but the mishap damaged Ness's public image in Cleveland. The safety director made himself further vulnerable to attack by serving as consultant to the federal Social Protection Program, a campaign to curb social diseases. His absence from his office became more frequent and prolonged. These two negative factors forced Lausche's hand. On April 29, 1942, the Mayor summoned Ness to his office for a private meeting. Records do not provide the gist of the meeting, except that Lausche had made a decision. Ness tendered his resignation the next morning. Despite his personal problems (an earlier acrimonious divorce), Ness received accolades from the local press for his accomplishments in restoring a sense of dignity to a beleaguered community. From that point on Ness experienced a checkered career with many ups and downs and little financial security. He died in 1957 at the age of 54.

With Ness's departure Lausche appointed the competent and well-respected Democrat Frank Celebrezze to the vacated position of safety director. Celebrezze, brother of Anthony, the future Mayor of Cleveland previously served as assistant county prosecutor and municipal judge under Mayor Burton. He remained in this position until 1947, and then won election as judge of the municipal court. He died suddenly in 1953 at the age of 54, after many years of faithful service to the city.

⌒

LAUSCHE LOST LITTLE TIME IN ATTACKING CONTROVERSIAL issues germane to the well being of the city. He immediately moved to outlaw all types of pinball and coin-operated skill amusement devices in the city. This order reflected his continued battle against gambling and games of chance. Lausche carried out his pledge to end the marathon fight with the near-bankrupt Cleveland Railway Company. Mayor Burton originated a plan for municipal ownership, and Lausche supported this plan. He completed arrangements for the $14 million purchase of the Cleveland Railway Company in early 1942. In 1943 an ordinance directed the Mayor to appoint a three-man board to operate the new Cleveland Transit System (CTS). Cleveland's transportation system claimed one of the lowest streetcar fares in the country.

During his campaign Lausche promised Cleveland material improvements, including better garbage disposal, 300 new buses, lower taxes and a more beautiful lakefront. These promises went by the wayside within a month after taking office. On December 7, 1941, the Japanese bombed Pearl Harbor, and the United States declared war one day later. Like all mayors in the country, Lausche now organized his city to help fight this war. In a somewhat tragic way, (at the cost of many lives) Cleveland rebounded economically with the advent of war. The city's factories began producing planes, tanks, trucks, artillery, bombs, binoculars, and telescopes. The city enjoyed a diversified industrial base as a producer of machine tools, electrical goods, and metal products. War *materiels* moved off assembly lines, supported by a large supply of trained workers and abundant low-cost power and water. Cleveland prospered with its ideal location to receive necessary raw materials.

Industrial workers, including large numbers of Appalachian whites and southern blacks, swelled Cleveland's wartime population. To meet the demand for housing, builders subdivided single-family homes into several units, initiating a pattern of overuse and overcrowding, as well as laying the groundwork for a blighted city and exodus by many residents from the inner belt. Pent-up demand brought about large new housing projects in Brooklyn, Lyndhurst, Mayfield Heights, Maple Heights and South Euclid.[37] A Cleveland Chamber of Commerce report published in 1941 acknowledged the phenomenon of decentralization stating, "It is evident that most people who live in Cleveland are anxious to move to the suburbs.... Experience has shown that if their economic status permits, the majority of Clevelanders prefer to live outside of the central area."[38] At war's end the housing shortage worsened with the return of servicemen eager to start new families.

Not only did Lausche face the problem of a decreasing population, but he also faced a myriad of other issues as a wartime Mayor. Besides resolving the street railway fight, he pledged himself to initiate real city planning for the future development of the community, to maintain strict law enforcement, to establish economy of operations, to eliminate political influences in municipal affairs, and to revive political liberalism in city government (shades of Tom Johnson). In suppressing political cronyism, Lausche went to extreme lengths. Friends dared not ask for employment or special favors. Nor did staff members recommend anybody for employment in fear of a boomerang effect. In January 1942 a city employee inserted in the Mayor's budget an estimate of $2,000 to buy a rug for his office. The city hall building rocked from the explosion emitted by Lausche when he discovered this item. He gained considerable success in winning the support of all classes at a time when such cooperation was extremely important to the city and the nation. He steadfastly refused favors to or from special groups. Neither labor nor management claimed him as "our" man.

Lausche faced an awesome task uniting the city in an all-out war effort. Men hurried to join the army and navy by the thousands. Ration cards for gasoline, sugar, liquor, tires and other commodities became a reality. The government ordered prices and wages frozen. Lausche excelled as a wartime leader. No one could make a better patriotic speech. Naturally an emotional and sentimental man with a devotion to the United States that was more persuasive among ethnic groups than the sons of earlier settlers, his flag-waving oration nearly always brought his audience to tears.[39]

The Mayor spoke early and often to any sort of public meeting urging wholehearted support of the war. He regretted his age prohibited military duty.

Lausche no doubt expressed surprise at one source of support received in his office. In a letter dated December 8, 1941, Elmer Fehlhaber, Cuyahoga County Secretary of the Communist Party, pledged to Lausche "as the mayor of Cleveland our willingness and eagerness to participate in every effort for winning the war."[40] This correspondence included a three-page memorandum of support signed by William Z. Foster, Chairman of the National Committee of the Communist Party. Foster's memorandum concluded with a plea that "All honest Americans who have been misled by the Lindberghs, the Coughlins, the Norman Thomases, Wheelers, Nyes, by the America First Committee, must now see the treachery, the threat to the national existence of our country that lies in the intrigues of such organizations and must break with their influences."[41] Neither the Soviet Union, an ally of the United States during World War II, nor Communism received much encouragement from Lausche. A fervent anti-Communist, he might have been disposed to shuttle this letter into file thirteen.

Lausche exerted uncommon leadership early in his two-year term. He used plain common sense, yielding to no fanatics, social reformers, do-gooders, or pressure groups.

Lausche exerted uncommon leadership early in his two-year term. He used plain common sense, yielding to no fanatics, social reformers, do-gooders, or pressure groups. Long before any directives arrived from Washington, DC Lausche set up a 12-man Mayor's War Production Committee. The committee included Lausche and six representatives of management and six representatives of labor, which won wide acclaim. Every person ranked high in his field of endeavor. "The idea," the Mayor said in the first meeting, "is not to try to settle any disputes by compromise. Our sole purpose will be to induce striking men and women to return to work and continue to produce munitions of war while they submit their disputes to legal authorities."[42] In March 1942—with orders amounting to $4 billion worth of war *materiel* roaring into the city during the first two years of the war—Lausche realized that something must be done quickly to end strikes. With labor gains under the Roosevelt administration in the thirties, Cleveland workers developed the habit of striking whenever a grievance, no matter how insignificant, became apparent. The demands of the war had not broken the workers of that strategy.

During his first two years in office, Lausche's committee persuaded 45,000 striking workers in 55 walkouts to return to their jobs. In nearly every case, the appeal went out to men and women "to show America that labor is just as patriotic as the men in uniform."[43] Most importantly, the committee convinced the workers they would receive quick and fair settlement of their grievances. They generally returned to work in less than 24 hours.

"We aimed to keep the men working until regular machinery could handle the disputes," and Lausche added, "Until Russia became our ally, we had to deal with some recalcitrant, shortsighted—and in some instances, I'm sure, subversive—labor leaders who precipitated work stoppages for some pretty doubtful reasons."[44]

This committee also took the lead in staggering work hours and promoting ride sharing for greater wartime efficiency.

In 1943, the United States Chamber of Commerce sent a health plan to all cities and urged its adoption. "I couldn't restrain myself," the mayor exclaimed, "I wrote and told them it was a wonderful plan and I knew it was wonderful because we'd been using it for more than a year."[45] Activities ranged from backyard cleanups to safeguarding newborn babies, from fighting the common cold to promoting safety first.

With a keen understanding of juvenile delinquency problems from his court years, Lausche continually fought the delinquency issue. He led the fight statewide effort to subsidize in part his social programs from the state's idle surplus of $30 million. He successfully raised money to increase the number of playgrounds from 48 to 64 in the war-crowded city. A new juvenile squad joined the regular police force. A report by the Cleveland Welfare Federation showed that juvenile delinquency dropped two percent in Cleveland in 1942. The Mayor expressed disappointment that the delinquency rate rose 27 percent in the first six months of 1943. Lausche received little consolation from reports that, in two other great war-work areas, Los Angeles and Detroit, delinquency escalated 34 percent and 43 percent, respectively.[46] With the absence of so many fathers, juvenile delinquency continued to plague these cities during the war years.

After December 7, 1941, civilian defense readily became important on the home front. A large organization of volunteers under the direction of Civilian Defense Director William A. Stinchcomb developed and began rehearsing lighting blackouts by the summer of 1942. Lausche, like most mayors of industrial cities during the war, faced the inevitable issues of black market. He fought these problems with such tenacity the Office of Price Administration (OPA) reported that he had done the most thorough job of any big city mayor in prosecuting and eliminating black market operators. Lausche started price-gouging surveillance when rationing began and kept his inspectors busy cooperating with the OPA. Few Cleveland housewives knew the meaning of a black market.[47]

By the end of Lausche's first year in office, the public realized they had elected a man of great strength, character, and firmness. When the Mayor believed strongly about an issue he seldom compromised, and in some cases took no bread instead of a half loaf. A person or group who did not receive what they asked for came away from the encounter impressed that Lausche took himself quite seriously, determined to stick to his personal moral code. At one time or another during his first term, Lausche said "no" to nearly every group in Cleveland. Most organizations left his office reasonably satisfied because they realized no other group received favors. Lausche exhibited intensity and vigor when he spoke on a favorite subject. He would light a nickel cigar in the middle of his dissertation, sometimes puffing so vigorously that it bursts into flames. Suave, yet frank and honest, Lausche displayed the wisdom not to volunteer information his enemies could use against him. He played his cards close to his chest. Basically a private person, Lausche developed the traits of a master politician. He made himself available for public events, to the delight of his legion of supporters. Still fond of baseball, the mayor relished the tradition of throwing out the first ball for the opening day games in Cleveland.

Lausche often acted on or spoke out about issues, sometimes insignificant, that ensured the public he remained the people's choice and acted with their best interests at heart. In April 1943, Ben Goetz concessionaire for baseball games at Cleveland Stadium increased the price of hot dogs from 10 cents to 15 cents. This increase violated a contract agreement with the city of Cleveland. To the delight of fans, Lausche ordered the price reduced back to 10 cents. He supported President Roosevelt's decision to allow major league baseball to continue competition during the war years. Lausche gave his blessings to the national pastime as a morale builder and diversion from the trials and tribulations of wartime environment. He proposed morning baseball programs for the benefit of workers on the graveyard shift.[48]

Not all remained a bed of roses for the Mayor. A major issue for Lausche centered on keeping men and women on the job without the repercussions of strikes. Labor organizations in Cleveland, primarily bread-and-butter oriented, concentrated their energies on the relatively narrow objectives of higher wages, shorter hours, and improved working conditions. Lausche caught the brunt of numerous strikes that took place during the war years. The mayor, who disliked strong-arm methods in unions or union bossism, confronted these issues head-on. Increasingly in his career he moved farther away from union leadership for his political support. In turn, the union bosses and legislators loyal to the union cause looked upon Lausche as a nemesis. This animosity between unions and Lausche intensified during and after World War II.

Shortly after Lausche took office and the transit system became municipally owned and operated, the local transit workers union called a strike. The union's action occurred after the transit board granted a two and a half-cent per hour raise, plus a number of salient improvements in working conditions. This raise amounted to more than could have been granted under the Little Steel formula, had the public employees been subject to the War Labor Board's jurisdiction. To save face for the union officials, the Mayor's Labor Management Committee resolved the matter, recommending a one cent per hour raise. The transit workers cancelled their strike. One year later on April 29, 1943, the transit workers again asked for a pay raise and went on strike, crippling the city's capacity to produce war goods. Lausche expressed his frustration with the union. He lashed out in controlled anger. "Some of the leaders of the Street Car Men's Union...will not hesitate to effect another walk-out...if it will serve their selfish purpose...there will be no permanent solution on this constant threat and menace until the state of

Ohio and Congress deal fearlessly with the problem. Laws must be enacted which will make possible vigorous prosecution of every individual who willfully and defiantly disobeys orders of the United States Government."[49]

Lausche further put his political future with labor organizations in Cleveland and Ohio on the line, bluntly exhorting, "In the transit strike, the War Labor Board issued an order to the men to immediately return to work. Mr. Thomas P. Meaney, the President of the Street Car Men's Union, in respect to that order commented, 'To hell with the War Labor Board.' If statements of this character go unpunished, every indifferent union leader in the country will adopt a similar attitude toward orders issued by the Commander-in-Chief and the agencies acting in his behalf."[50]

Though seething inside, Lausche used tact and diplomacy to end the transit strike after an 18-hour transportation tie-up. Three members of the Mayor's War Production Committee representing the Cleveland Federation of Labor stepped up to the plate and stopped the wildcat strike almost as soon as it had started. The Cleveland *News*, although supportive of Lausche, believed the Mayor might have averted a strike by calling in his War Production Committee to take action before the car men went on strike.

For more than a year, during numerous strikes Lausche confided to close associates that, no matter how much conscientious employees and employers wanted to continue production, they would remain at the mercy of a dominant minority until the President and Congress took an unmistakable position on the labor problem.[51] No doubt these labor uprisings led by unscrupulous leaders only inflamed Lausche's antagonism toward labor unions. The public and local businessmen applauded his action. Vernon Stouffer, prominent Cleveland restaurateur and later owner of the Cleveland Indians, wrote to the mayor, "Praise the Lord for this kind of leadership! You have shown the backbone to follow through with your principles in the Cleveland Transit matter."[52]

A few months later the city council granted a pay increase to municipal craftsmen, and forwarded the proposal to Lausche for approval. Lausche carefully reviewed the recommendation for a broad band of city employees and with few exceptions vetoed the increases. Lausche defended his veto, "the Federal Government is actively rolling back the prices of commodities…the employees of the City of Cleveland are protected by Civil Service regulations. The City of Cleveland cannot begin competing with war industry in the payment of salaries to employees. It is my purpose to grant pay raises that are reasonable and conform to the policy laid down by the President of the United States, the Stabilization Director, Mr. [James] Byrnes, and the pronouncements of the War Labor Board of the United States."[53]

Because city-building workers toiled full-time, Lausche believed their wages need not be as high as private craftsmen's who suffered seasonal losses in their work. He supported wage increases for charwomen, janitors, and other low-paid employees. The city council eventually overrode Lausche's veto and granted pay raises. Pundits perceived Lausche to be a dead duck politically in view of his constant veto of pay raises and insistence upon extreme frugality with the city budget.

The Lausche's labor troubles continued into late summer of 1943, which was a mayoral election year for Cleveland. In August seven thousand workers making ball bearings for airplane engines at the Cleveland Graphite Bronze Company plant went on strike. Lausche and his War Production Committee went into action immediately. Lausche took to the airways imploring workers, with an eloquent plea to return to work. The determined Mayor ordered Cleveland's renowned mounted police to clear a way for those workers who responded to his request to return to work without outside interference. He asked the workers to show America that labor demonstrated the same kind of patriotism as the men in uniform. "The howls of local labor leaders reverberated throughout the city loud and strong," Lausche admitted, firmly reminded of circulars calling him strikebreaker.[54] The strikers went back to work, and Lausche survived further attacks from labor bosses.

In early 1943, the country suffered a nationwide coal workers strike. Lausche denounced the lawlessness of John L. Lewis, legendary labor leader. The mayor continually dashed any hope of future peace pacts with union leaders. Lausche's leadership during these trying times impressed the citizenry. His personal magnetism served as a tranquilizer to calm widespread wartime hysteria. He received credit for soothing tensions which could easily have resulted in full-scale riots. In this respect, the Mayor demonstrated qualities that compared him favorably with President Roosevelt. Indeed, journalists frequently identified Lausche with the President during the war years.

Lausche demonstrated his leadership abilities in various ways during this election year. He professed concern about Cleveland and community life after the war ended. At a luncheon at the Statler Hotel in mid-1943, the Mayor organized a Postwar Planning Council to begin recruiting contracts for peacetime production and to coordinate planning for all levels of community well being. Having gained financial support from business, industry, and labor, Mayor Lausche instructed this high-powered council, "not only to build the bridge from war to peacetime production but also to lay plans for making Cleveland's industrial advantages so patent that we can keep all of the industries we have and attract new ones...."[55] Lausche warned that Cleveland was in a race with other industrial cities, and that the days of rapid growth were over. The council demonstrated two outstanding features. First, it assumed that existing agencies possessed the capabilities to handle the community's postwar problems, insofar as they could be handled locally. Virtually all the city's many civic organizations embraced the council program, which conceived of its job as one of coordination. Second, labor as well as industry played an important part in the council's program. Both desired to maintain a high level of employment. The panel on the needs of returning service men received leadership from prominent industrialists and CIO officials. The postwar setup, as envisioned by Lausche, professed no easy answers. A grassroots organization, the council planned to use all the community's resources to anticipate and meet problems as they arose. The improvisation of large-scale public works entered the picture only as a last resort. Under the direction of S. Burns Weston, the council's executive director, five panels began to study transportation, public works, interracial relations, the needs of returning servicemen (160,000 Clevelanders answered the call to serve), and public finance.

Before Lausche could give this program his undivided attention, he surprised no one by announcing his plans to run for a second term in the fall of 1943. Few if any candidates, either Republican or Democrat, contemplated opposing the popular Mayor. Despite hurting the pocketbooks and feelings of certain pressure groups, Lausche brought back memories of Tom L. Johnson to old-timers. Republicans persuaded Edward C. Stanton, a longtime Cuyahoga County prosecutor to oppose the incumbent. Stanton, a steady and faithful party member, gave the campaign his best effort. Because of wartime conditions, both candidates ran low-key and lackluster campaigns. The worst accusation Stanton emitted during the campaign referred to Lausche as Cleveland's No. 1 Glamour Boy. Lausche naively campaigned on a slogan of *Vote for the Wholesome Influence*. In spite of Lausche's opposition to strikes and—in his judgment—unjustified pay increases, the mayor garnered considerable support from labor. Several pundits called him the CIO candidate, and to confuse the electorate, opponents also aligned him with the business community.[56] Industrial and business moguls, normally sources for financial support to Republican candidates, hesitated to give *carte blanche* support to Stanton. They held little hostility toward Lausche. Several powerful Republicans and businessmen made a *lion* of Lausche. Robert A. Weaver, president of Ferro Enamel Company who raised four hundred thousand dollars in Cuyahoga County in 1940 for Republican presidential candidate Wendell Wilkie, became one of Lausche's close confidants. Ben F. Hopkins, brother of the first city manager and president of the huge Cleveland Graphite Bronze Company, frequently visited the Lausche home. Robert F. Black, president of the White Motor Company, assisted Lausche as a member of the Mayor's War Advisory Committee, which handled all labor disputes in Cleveland during the war years.[57]

In addition to the business community, the Mayor solicited support from other traditional bastions of Republican votes. An example included the black wards that previously contributed to heavy Republican majorities. Lausche carried these wards by promising to continue his fight against discrimination. He supported a black candidate for judge and three black candidates for city council.[58]

The Lausche annihilated his opponent at the polls on November 4, 1943. Lausche garnered 112,864 votes in contrast to challenger Edward Stanton's 45,955 votes. Lausche's margin of victory represented 71 percent of the overall vote, an increase of eleven percent from his 1941 mayoral count. One individual expressed the view of many voters, commenting, "Maybe I can't explain exactly what democracy is, but I felt I voted for it when I dropped Lausche's name in the ballot box."[59] Lausche, who carried 32 of 33 wards, became the first Democratic mayor in Cleveland in thirty years to be returned to office.

Edwin A. Lahey of *The New Republic* concluded that Lausche's secret to success centered on "his honesty and simplicity which do not need exposition by a press agent to persuade voters."[60] Lausche loomed as the Democratic political sensation of the year. His overwhelming victory earned him a story in *Time* magazine entitled "Man to Watch." The *Union Leader*, a local labor organization paper, noted that Republicans swept in to power in New York State and in Philadelphia and defeated pro-labor mayors in Akron and Detroit. In contrast, the labor editor characterized Lausche as an outstanding New Dealer fighting for the victory policies of Commander-in-Chief Franklin D. Roosevelt. This union paper commended Lausche as chief executive of the country's sixth largest city "Who welds all diverse interests and all groups into unity behind the war effort. Apparently he received the votes of this coalition. He received support of the Democratic party and many Republicans...he was staunchly supported by the CIO, some AFL unions and some business groups, nationality organizations and others."[61]

Although Lausche gave tacit support to the liberal policies of President Roosevelt, particularly during wartime, he carefully gauged his political loyalties. On the mantelpiece in his mayor's office sat a picture of two Republicans, Abraham Lincoln and a bust of General Douglas MacArthur. Roosevelt's picture did not adorn the office walls. Lausche received support from a wide spectrum of political forces. This mix of political support became more convoluted in subsequent elections.

Lausche's mayoralty responsibilities received a major assist from Jane Lausche, the woman behind the man. Married for fifteen years, Jane contributed profoundly to Lausche's political success. A popular native of Cleveland, the winsome commercial artist managed her own home, designed and made her own clothes and hats, and worked hard at the local Red Cross chapter. During her husband's campaigns, she gave speeches to community women's organizations. An attractive lady, Jane dressed smartly and maintained a quietly clever demeanor. City hall reporters often questioned the mayor about whether he realized how much of an asset his wife lent to his public image.

Jane attended every city council meeting. Her husband often teasingly suggested she come downtown so she could ride home with him. This suggestion lacked merit because Frank Lausche had established a notorious reputation for his less than adequate driving skills. Mrs. Lausche, an excellent judge of character, understood city government and kept well informed on national affairs. In spite of her intuition, Jane seldom gave an opinion unless asked, nor did she jump on the bandwagon for particular civic causes.

The Lausches continued to live with Jane's father in an unfashionable section of Cleveland. They did not play bridge, and seldom entertained. Certain civic affairs dictated a mandatory appearance. Otherwise, the twosome seldom left the comfort of their fireplace unless they attended a symphony concert, occasional movie or sporting event. The Mayor's eating habits worried Jane, but since he avoided illness, she resisted comment. Lausche seldom ate lunch and enjoyed a sumptuous dinner. Prior to dinner, the mayor often imbibed in a drink of bourbon whiskey and possibly a chaser of beer. His favorite dish, Yugoslav in origin, included sauerkraut with red beans. Lausche enjoyed most ethnic dishes.[62] After dinner he often enjoyed a White Owl or Roi-Tan cigar. Lausche's official duties consumed most of his time and took priority in his daily regimen. An early riser, he dictated letters at home before arriving at his office. He made time while on duty to see visitors or to resolve particular problems, and seldom turned away guests, many of them foreign-born.

☞

LAUSCHE CHARGED INTO HIS SECOND-TERM mayoralty duties. The Allies approached a turn-around point in World War II. Military victories in Europe and the South Pacific came at a high cost of human lives. The United States readied itself for the D-Day invasion on June 6, 1944. The war *materiels* shipped out of Cleveland and other major industrial sites favorably impacted the war effort.

Due to the impetus for production of war goods, employment in Cleveland by September 1944 climbed 34 percent above its 1940 level. Nearly all of this increase took place in the manufacturing sector, where employment rose from 191,000 to 340,000. Thompson Aircraft Products Company (TAPCO), a small company in 1941, began building aircraft engines and fuel booster pumps. Federal government aid helped make TAPCO Cleveland's largest employer with a work force of 21,000 at the war's end. Two large facilities rose on the perimeters of Cleveland Municipal Airport. The Fisher Cleveland Aircraft plant, originally planned for production of Boeing B-29 parts, underwent successive postwar metamorphoses as the Cleveland Tank Plant and later as the International Exposition and Trade Center. On the other side of the airport, the National Advisory Committee for Aeronautics and Space Administration constructed the world's largest wind tunnel, which became part of NASA Lewis Research Center. "Cleveland is one of the nation's industrial centers which has expanded most since the beginning of the war," concluded the U.S. Bureau of Labor Statistics.[63] Lausche's continued foresight helped minimize labor problems and potential racial uprisings. Major racial threats began to surface as a result of wartime explosion in the labor force and concurrent expansion of the black population.

Increased labor demands saw the African-American population grow 50 percent during the 1940s from 85,000 to 148,000. Cleveland, with all the potential for trouble, faced postwar racial issues. In launching the Postwar Planning Council, Lausche noted slums existed with "living conditions unfit for human beings."[64] The city expanded carelessly, and the mansions that remained on Millionaires Row

(Euclid Avenue) intermingled with billboards, car wash lots, tourist homes, and factories. The pace of decentralization accelerated. The mayor knew the problem of interracial relations must be addressed.

Urged in part by antipathy to Nazi racial doctrines, the Cleveland Welfare Federation in 1943 began a two-year study of racial and economic conditions in Cleveland's black community. The purpose of this study focused on factors that underscored racial problems and proposed measures to cope with these conditions. The study never fulfilled its action-oriented promise to identify the real potentially organizable forces to implement programs of community welfare. Findings concluded that an artificial community had grown up in the mid-town area— artificial, in that its main criteria was color, and color implied difference.[65]

In the same year, Lausche established the Committee on Democratic Practice, comprised of the city's leading black and white civic activists. Serving on this committee were well-known blacks: Charles W. White, assistant city law director; Clarence W. Sharpe, president of the Cleveland NAACP; and William O. Walker, editor of the *Call & Post*. White community leaders included Charles McCrea, president of National Malleable Iron and Steel; Frederick C. Crawford, president of Thompson Products; and W.J. Holliday, president of the Cleveland Chamber of Commerce. This committee faced the task of developing a broad educational program against racial intolerance and working toward the eradication of specific problems related to discrimination in employment, housing, and public accommodations. Although their early work involved only public statements issued through the press, the committee's efforts symbolized the city's growing awareness of its black citizens.[66]

One panel of the Mayor's 150-member Postwar Planning Council chaired by Dr. Leonard Mayo of Western Reserve University investigated how the city should address these burgeoning problems. This panel looked at areas of greatest concern— housing, recreation, health, and employment practices. Recommendations by the panel urged the mayor to follow a policy of preventive action rather than to wait for problems to come to a head. As a result of the panel's work, Mayor Thomas A. Burke, Lausche's successor, appointed a Cleveland Community Relations Board in 1945 with a mission "to promote amicable relations among the racial and cultural groups within the community."[67] This Board developed a national reputation for instigating improvement in race relations.

Several practical issues faced Lausche during his second term. One factor of major importance concerned a reduction in specific coal shipments to Cleveland due to wartime demands. This decision emanated from the United States Department of Interior and the powerful Secretary Harold L. Ickes. Lausche addressed his concern directly to the secretary. The Mayor argued that Greater Cleveland systematically developed a smoke abatement program during the war, and its citizens spent millions of dollars for the installation of equipment to burn a cleaner grade of coal and, therefore, decrease pollution. Without an anticipated shipment of cleaner burning coal, Lausche feared the possibility of a coal shortage for the winter of 1944. He argued as Mayor that, "It will be rather difficult...to explain why other communities in the northern part of the State have been given a preference and Cleveland denied shipment. I do not want to imply that there has been any deliberate discrimination, but I am certain that many citizens of this community may draw that inference in as much as no reasonable explanation can be given..."[68]

Lausche fought a good battle, but lost his appeal when the government diverted 1,000 tons of coal from Cleveland to Wisconsin Electric Power Company.[69] This decision irked Lausche. Earlier in 1944 he established a Committee on Air Pollution to determine how best to combat increasing pollution that became a bane of large industrial cities during World War II. Lausche realized the city faced an age of decadence within the industrial inner belt of the city. Steam generating plants suffered deterioration to the point that the capacity to generate necessary steam could only be met by use of higher grades of coal. Cleveland's coal stockpile contained lower grades of fuel. Industrial breakdowns seemed imminent. For the bowels of this wartime city, the conditions of a Rust Belt moved closer to reality.

In an attempt to stave off the blight of the Rust Belt, Lausche used his highly publicized Postwar Planning Council to promote a large public works program (a remnant of Roosevelt's New Deal program in the thirties) to counter further deterioration in municipal facilities after World War II. If approved, these projects would provide employment for many returning servicemen. In a letter to Major General Philip B. Fleming, Administrator of the Federal Works Agency, Lausche detailed his request for $90 million to cover a six-year (1945–50) capital improvement program. Lausche also wrote to Congressman Walter Lynch (Dem-NY) arguing for need of federal financial aid to rehabilitate the city. He argued that "municipalities—at least in Ohio—look principally to real estate taxes for their revenues." The Mayor argued, "taxes, in a large degree, are preempted by State and Federal governments, and for that reason there is a limitation placed upon the local communities in the collection of revenues." He pleaded that, "Unless money is provided for the local communities either by federal or state governments, I feel quite positive in saying to you that the hope of municipalities in the postwar period making public improvements that are of a permanent utility and which will give some measure of work to the returning men will be practically nil."[70]

Lausche and Civilian Defense Director William A. Stinchcomb pushed hard for federal aid to improve arterial streets of metropolitan Cleveland. The widening and improvement of existing streets would not suffice. The construction of a metropolitan system of freeways became imperative, not only in Cleveland, but also in all large cities. Lausche argued for local responsibility where city planning and neighborhood development became of prime concern. Lausche's foresight paid dividends. In 1944, the Express Highway Subcommittee of the Regional Association of Cleveland completed a master freeway plan.

This plan followed on the heels of a freeway program endorsed by voters four years earlier, but was delayed by the war and the lack of a comprehensive plan. This plan, with state and federal assistance, called for a $240 million integrated freeway system as a solution to metropolitan Cleveland's traffic woes. Within two decades an interlocking system of freeways would provide a more expedient traffic flow through and around downtown Cleveland. Lausche's administration laid the foundation for Mayor Thomas A. Burke, his successor, to push forward with highway improvements and other municipal projects.

The specter of wartime strikes constantly loomed large during Lausche's second term. Increasing animosity developed between the Mayor and organized labor. Lausche consistently vetoed proposals for, in his judgment, unwarranted pay increases during wartime. On March 31, 1944, the Cleveland City Council inflicted the most resounding defeat of Lausche's city hall career, voting unanimously to give AFL steamfitters and plumbers a 10-cent an hour increase. Lausche's veto of this raise, supported by detailed research, fell upon deaf ears and deepened the alienation between Lausche and local labor organizations. The behavior of the union personnel at this particular city council meeting only aggravated the situation. Distressed at the impolite treatment from the back of the chamber, the Mayor said with emotion, "My interest in the city is just as great as yours, if not greater. If you were in my place, I would treat you differently than you have treated me."[71]

"My interest in the city is just as great as yours, if not greater. If you were in my place, I would treat you differently than you have treated me."

In reply, the union's assemblage burst into laughter. In defeat Lausche retained support of the local press on his labor stand.

Workers—both municipal and industrial—believed their wages lagged behind in the overall economy. Part of this reasoning festered from uncommonly low wages paid during the Great Depression. The Amalgamated Association of Street Railway and Motor Coach operators threatened to strike on May 20, 1944. Lausche arranged for a hearing with the union and the Regional War Labor Board located in Cleveland. Mediation took place, and the operators returned to work. Two months later the Office Workers Union threatened to place a picket line around city hall. In a memorandum to union members, Lausche appealed to the workers and their patriotic duty during wartime. After mediation with the Regional War Labor Board the workers voted to stay on the job.

In December of 1944, Lausche again encountered a major labor issue. The City Police and Firemen's Union sought a significant pay increase. Exhaustive research determined that the salaries of these units compared favorably with similar units in most large cities in the country. Using persuasive facts and figures to back his argument, Lausche asked the city council to veto the proposed ordinance for a pay raise. The council sustained him on this decision.[72]

$\frown$

AMIDST THE MANY RESPONSIBILITIES OF RUNNING the largest corporation in Ohio (Cleveland) and performing admirably in the view of his constituents, Lausche heard whispers and suggestions that he should run for governor. In April of 1944, the Mayor again consulted with Louis Seltzer. "What do I do about this Governorship," he asked, "Remember the time the Utilities Directorship had been offered to you," Seltzer responded. Lausche recalled the occasion. "I asked you on that occasion two questions, and I'm going to repeat them. The questions were—What do you want to do? Where do you want to go?" Lausche replied with, "But they say that the State's tradition is all against me." "Do you really think that should stop you?" queried Seltzer. "No," Lausche responded, "I want to be Governor. I would like to demonstrate, too, that this is really a democracy—that it can be done."[73]

Increasingly, Ohio began to read and hear good things about Cleveland's war mayor. His record setting political victories attracted attention from many national journalists who wrote stories of his popularity and accomplishments. Newspapers all over the state picked up the momentum and encouraged Lausche to enter the Democratic primary for his party's gubernatorial nomination. One day before the deadline for filing (Lausche always waited until the last moment to file) he told a couple of city hall reporters loyal to him that he thought he would run for Governor. Lausche filed and became one of five candidates.[74]

Late in his tenure as mayor, tragedy struck close to his heart and boyhood home. The skies, overcast in Cleveland on Friday morning October 20, 1944, cleared by afternoon, and the temperature climbed to the lower fifties. The *Plain Dealer* carried news of the war. In the Pacific, Douglas MacArthur's forces landed on Leyte in the Philippines, while in Europe American soldiers entered the German town of Aachen. Clevelanders worked hard to contribute nearly $6 million into a local war chest.[75]

Despite the fact that Lausche no longer lived at his original homestead, the heavily Democratic, mostly Catholic St. Clair-Norwood neighborhood still admired their favorite son. First- and second-generation immigrants, largely Slovenian, inhabited this community of small frame houses and neatly kept lawns. Many families took in boarders who worked in nearby factories. The neighborhood, on the downgrade as a pleasant residential section, shared the area with war-fed industries. One industrial neighborhood located a few blocks away included East Ohio Gas Company's Number Two Works. The residents could scarcely have suspected as they went about their daily routines on that crisp fall afternoon, that by day's end, their community would resemble the war zones they had been reading about in the morning paper.[76]

At approximately 2:30 p.m. Tank #4 of the East Ohio Gas Company, holding millions of gallons of liquid natural gas, exploded. The earth trembled, sending fragments of metal thousands of feet away. Houses on both sides of East 61st and

East 62nd Streets burst into flames. The fire ran for 20 blocks engulfing rows of homes while missing others. At 3 p.m. Tank #3 exploded. The ball of flame could be seen as far away as John Adams High School, seven miles in the distance. The intense heat scorched houses and factories a half-mile away. The liquid gas ran down the streets and into sewers, turned into vapor and seeped into basements. Houses exploded, and manhole covers flipped dozens of feet into the air. Birds, burned to death by heat waves estimated at 3,000 degrees Fahrenheit, fell from the sky. Employees of East Ohio Gas Company tried to escape by hiding in metal lockers. Only their bones and jewelry survived. The Red Cross tried to care for approximately 680 homeless victims.[77]

Mayor Lausche hurried back from a Bucyrus campaign stop to view what remained of his old neighborhood and to confer with a *coterie* of city officials who were leading the relief effort. These officials included Safety Director Frank D. Celebrezze, Law Director Thomas A. Burke, Councilman Edward Kovacic, and Coroner Samuel R. Gerber. Lausche stayed on duty throughout Friday night, visiting refugee centers and comforting the survivors. Early Saturday morning touring the destroyed area through tear-stained eyes, Lausche commented, "This is where I played when I was a boy…. And this," he said, pausing before the smoking ruins of a dwelling on East 61st Street and standing near the gaunt upright chimney, "is where my cousin Mrs. Josephine Lach lived."[78]

Pardonably nervous, the people with Mayor Lausche on his unusual inspection sighed with relief as he edged away from the yards of the burning gas company, where even firemen hesitated to venture. He stopped his inspection group once more, pointing to a heap of rubble off to one side. "That was a wire fence," he remarked, "and I used to go over there to practice sling shots." Lausche finally retreated to St. Clair Avenue, pointing to a pile of glass on the sidewalk that had been windows in a home. "I lived there for a long time," he reflected.[79] Many of Lausche's neighborhood friends took comfort that *their Mayor* who grew up in this neighborhood took time to be *in their corner* during this emergency. The following day Lausche ordered Police Chief George J. Matowitz to file a comprehensive damage report. One hundred sixty acres had been affected, with an area of twenty-nine acres completely gutted. The most disastrous fire in Cleveland's history destroyed 79 homes, two factories, 217 cars, seven trailers, and one tractor. The death toll reached 130 victims, 50 of whom worked for the gas company.

Irritated by reports that lawyers began signing victims to contracts guaranteeing themselves as much as 30 percent of any damages recovered from East Ohio Gas Company, Lausche asked the Cuyahoga County Bar Association to form a legal commission to represent claimants free of charge. East Ohio Gas Company opened up an office to receive claims, foregoing legal representation. The Mayor encouraged the formation of a Slovene Relief Commission to help victims prepare their claims. The gas company, though uninsured, made good on paying these claims.[80]

Mayor Lausche appointed a board of inquiry to ascertain the blame for these explosions. After several months the board released a report that divided responsibility among the company, the builder, and the city. A number of factors taken in combination or in accidental coincidence caused the disaster. Ironically, none of the inquiries pinpointed an exact cause of the fire that consumed a portion of Lausche's childhood neighborhood. A contemporary president of East Ohio Gas Company summarized the cause of the explosion by writing, "This was a case when pioneering technology developed by good people for the right reasons, failed. How or why this failure occurred will never be fully known."[81]

Recommendations for the future could not diminish the scope of what transpired in this holocaust. The Mayor's board found that "if all of the hydropower west of the Mississippi River were put to work destroying property for about two hours, it would accomplish the same destruction if similarly directed."[82] The St. Clair-Norwood neighborhood resembled a firebombed village transported from the European front.

On October 28, Mayor Lausche called together a newly appointed Mayor's Committee on Disaster even before the flames cooled. The committee, chaired by Anton Grdina, owner of Grdina-Faulhaber Funeral Home and former president of North American Bank, paved the way for survivors and newcomers to relocate in this blighted area. Lausche explained to the committee the procedures followed after the Los Angeles Dam disaster (March 12, 1928) where 385 persons died and destruction of property exceeded $15 million. The settlement of claims took place without a lawsuit.

Sixteen new single-family, colonial brick homes, designed by architect George Voinovich replaced several of the destroyed homes. Priced from $9,000 to $16,000, these homes allowed several homeless families to return to the St. Clair-Norwood neighborhood. East Ohio Gas Company returned to their site as well, donating part of their land for a playground, complete with a ball diamond. The gas company constructed a new facility on the remaining land that continues to operate to date.[83] After speaking at memorial services for the deceased the following week, a distraught Lausche returned to the campaign trail. Only a few days remained before Lausche would learn whether his political fortunes would take him to the Governor's office in Columbus, or whether he would remain in Cleveland.

The wartime Mayor served Cleveland for three years. The general consensus gave Lausche high marks. He accomplished a number of projects that his predecessor Harold Burton left undone—among them the purchase of the city street railway system. Lausche worked out an admirable postwar economic program and established a wartime labor-management commission that served as a model for other big industrial centers. Critics complained that he tried to run the whole city government by himself. His cabinet and city hall subordinates, some said, sat in the nickel seats in the balcony. If true, this shortcoming may have resulted from a lack of administrative experience. Historically, many high-ranking U.S. politicians have suffered this malady.

Lausche took pride in the universality of groups who formally supported him—organized labor, organized business, and other organized professions. He wasted little time with politicians, did as he pleased, always with his eyes on the newspaper columns. The war provided Lausche with a stage. Accused of being an actor, he brought tears to listeners with his flag-waving oratory. He spoke early and often to any sort of public meeting, urging wholehearted support for the United States in its war effort. In his campaign for governor, Lausche followed his conscience. His adoption of the Lausche method Embraced a simple philosophy: Be on the level with everybody. Work hard for the good of the whole, never for any special group. The gubernatorial candidate's style would be tested, if and when he moved to the governor's mansion.

Frank and Jane Lausche with his brothers and sisters. Back row from left to right: Harold, Mrs. Josephine Welf, Dr. William, Mrs. Frances Uranker, Charles, (1944). (Courtesy of Sally Jones)

five

Wartime Governor of Ohio

FRANK J. LAUSCHE'S POLITICAL STAR SHONE BRIGHTLY in election year 1944. His two lop-sided mayoral victories and his solid performance in the Mayor's office caught the eye of the national press and politicos. The fact that he espoused the Catholic religion and was the son of an immigrant family, who bore a truly foreign-sounding name (pronounced LOW-SHE and rhyming with NOW-SHE), attracted attention among the voting populace. Being of the Catholic faith was a political anathema, for Ohioans had never elected a Catholic Governor. Lausche's efforts to foster a citywide program for wholesome black-white relationships in Cleveland caught President Roosevelt's attention. The President appointed Lausche to a three-person Racial Discrimination Board to investigate charges of discrimination made against southern railroad unions.[1] The nation seriously began to agitate against the injustice of segregation and racial bias prevalent in many parts of the country. Lausche became an early trailblazer in addressing this national problem of discrimination.

In March 1944, *American Magazine* published an article about Lausche entitled "Everybody's Mayor," authored by staff writer Jerome Beatty, who extolled Lausche's virtues and foibles, many well known to local citizenry. Beatty wanted to find out how Lausche fared so well in the 1943 election, a year in which Republicans dominated the political scene. He discovered Lausche's personal strengths and, in particular, his love of poetry, an unusual trait for a politician. "Poetry," proclaimed the Mayor, "arouses qualities that I never knew I had." Beatty challenged Lausche's sincerity about poetry and asked him what authors he most enjoyed. "Well, I don't know exactly. I like Dryden's *Song for St. Cecilia's Day*—There's magnificent music in it—and Burns, *To a Mouse*, and *Othello*, and *Julius Caesar* and *Horatius at the Bridge*." So surely did Lausche convince Beatty of his honesty and integrity, he went home and read *St. Cecilia's Day*. Beatty concluded, "[Lausche's] got something there and wished for more like him in high political offices."[2]

When it came to political issues, Lausche seldom reached quick or decisive decisions concerning his intent. In January and early February of 1944, the Mayor deliberated on his political future. His reticence to announce his intentions for the gubernatorial office frustrated party regulars and, in fact, encouraged four other Democrats to announce their candidacy. The two most prominent challengers blocking Lausche's path included Frazier Reams, Jr. of Toledo and James Huffman of Columbus. Both men bore names easily recognizable among party faithful throughout the state. Reams, former collector of internal revenue and prosecutor for Lucas County, had been appointed by former Democratic Governor Martin L. Davey to head a special committee to investigate conditions at the Ohio penitentiary. Huffman, son-in-law of Vic Donahey former Democratic Governor, served as the Governor's executive secretary.[3] Lausche considered several important factors before making his decision to run for governor.

Many of his friends advised Lausche not to run. Pundits considered him a dark horse candidate. As the son of Slovenian immigrant parents, Lausche had often heard natives call Slovenians and other Eastern European ethnic groups Pollackers, Hunkies, Bohunks, Greiners, and worse. How would rural southern Ohioans respond to this big-city mayor with a foreign name? The Cleveland *News* entitled an editorial on February 1 1944, "Frank Lausche—Don't."[4] Although supportive of Lausche, the *News* editor criticized his intentions to run for governor on the premise that he was too valuable to be spared from his job as Mayor.

This tongue-in-cheek plea from the *News* brought a response from the Cleveland *Plain Dealer*, "This we believe is too provincial a point of view. If we are to have good state and federal administration, the officials of those governments must be experienced.... To rule out a candidate for higher office because he is doing a good job at a lower office would be to deprive ourselves of the very best material for state and federal government..."[5]

The Cuyahoga County Democratic organization attempted to draft federal judge Robert N. Wilkin for the governorship. Wilkin, appointed judge of a United States District Court in June 1939, chose to remain in his more secure position. The door opened wider for Lausche. Heeding the advice of Seltzer and other friends close to him, and in spite of gloomy predictions that he could never win a statewide election, Lausche declared his candidacy on February 28, 1944. The Mayor made his decision without an endorsement from the Cuyahoga County Democratic organization. John Lokar went into action. He rushed to have petitions printed, circulated through the mail, and signed by electors in each of the state's 88 counties. Lokar enclosed in each envelope a special delivery stamp to ensure timely return of the petitions. On March 9, the last day for filing, the executive assistant boarded a train for Columbus and deposited the petitions three hours before the deadline.

Lausche stayed in Cleveland during the early days of the primary election, campaigning in Cuyahoga and neighboring counties. With the support of all three local dailies, Lausche borrowed from the strategy he successfully employed in his mayoralty elections. In mid-April, with little if any financial backing, Lausche departed for southern Ohio and his only campaign trip during the primary election. Speaking in Springfield, Lausche exhibited an acute awareness of the major tasks facing the next governor of Ohio. While several remarks might be interpreted as political jargon, the *Plain Dealer* called his words those of a genuine progressive. Editor Paul Bellamy supported Lausche's plank to strengthen state and local government as a defense against steady concentration of federal power.[6] Lausche emphasized the need for rehabilitation and modernization of the state's welfare programs, a vigorous conservation plan and resistance to the trend against local government home rule. Conservation of natural resources became one of Lausche's trademark themes throughout his political career.

The primary election heated up in April. Frazier Reams, one of Lausche's chief opponents, charged that the Cleveland *Press* and Lausche's board of political strategy attempted to ram the Mayor of Cleveland down the throats of Ohio Democrats under the false inference that he was the choice of the White House and of the national Democratic Committee. Speaking with typical campaign flair, Reams contended that, "Through the last four years the Cleveland *Press* has been violently anti-Roosevelt and among the administration's most vehement critics. By what kind of political double talk can it now advise Democratic voters to choose...the Mayor of Cleveland, whom the *Press* claims to be the Roosevelt choice when the *Press* is a Roosevelt hater?"[7]

As Lausche was wont to do when opponents directed political attacks his way, he kept quiet. Rather than retaliating to Reams' attack, Lausche spoke benevolently about the President. He charged that attacks on the President bordered on "almost treasonous in their nature" and "nearly subversive, harmful to the war effort." While defending free speech as one of the tenets for which the country cherishes, Lausche expounded that attacks upon the President ignored his great service as commander-in-chief, "Under him America has taken on a social vision that it had never had before. The problems of the aged, the blind, the healthy man who was unable to find work in depression times, the problems of the farmer who was in danger at times of losing his property because of falling food prices—all these were given greater recognition under him than ever before in history."[8]

The Mayor's defense of Roosevelt's liberal government-sponsored programs projected an image of Lausche which would subsequently be an anathema to his political philosophy. He demonstrated a liberal attitude toward government spending in his early political days. With an independent bent, his philosophy grew more and more conservative when the national debt exceeded reasonable limits. Pundits claimed Lausche merely straddled the fence so that his constituency never knew where he truly stood on certain political issues. His utterances and personal behavior became more convoluted as Lausche climbed the political ladder. For the time, he set his sights on winning a primary election.

During his nine-day campaign trip throughout southern Ohio, Lausche took every opportunity to declare his independence from all interest groups, whether political or economic. The Mayor spoke before small groups of citizens, not merely politicians, and managed to convince them of his sincerity and integrity. He campaigned hard, shaking thousands of hands. Lausche found out that, in Ohio's southern rural areas, citizens responded to him enthusiastically. Although he did not seek the endorsements of various county Democratic Committees, he gladly accepted their support. The Democratic Party hopeful insisted that their support was not tantamount to political favors if he won the governorship. Gradually, several party leaders began to back the Mayor on his bid for nomination.

An incident in the primary campaign explained Lausche's course of action toward political independence. Having been invited to Columbus by the powerful Franklin County Democratic Central Committee, any candidate might have expected to be pressured into being known as a good party Democrat and to have heard some talk of the spoils of victory. Lausche told the committeemen his intentions, "As Governor my sole objective will be to render justice to all the people of Ohio. In this troublesome, perilous time we must be Americans first and Democrats second."[9] The committee waited for Lausche's bid for their support, but the candidate did not accommodate them. He promised no jobs. The candidate welcomed the committee's support, but they would have to accept him on his own terms. On April 13, Lausche received endorsement from the Franklin County Democratic Committee.

Lausche also received tacit endorsement from several southern counties, an unexpected development. Two days before the primary election Darrell S. Jones, the state Democratic chairman, gave his support to Lausche. Lausche's own Cuyahoga County did not provide needed support. Ray T. Miller continued to abstain from burying the hatchet with Lausche. The county Democratic organization voted to withhold endorsement of Lausche's candidacy. Miller gave the pious explanation that "The center of democracy is a free choice of candidates, especially in a primary." Chastising Miller for Democratic stupidity, the *Plain Dealer* reacted by reporting that, "it would do no violence to the Democratic tradition if an organization were to express its preferences for a hometown candidate particularly when the candidate... stood head and shoulders above other aspirants.... If Lausche should win handily without a local endorsement, the Miller organization would look pretty silly for its shortsightedness in not having climbed on the bandwagon."[10]

Except for several baseball-related excursions during his playing days, Lausche seldom visited the hill country of the southeastern part of Ohio. On one political sojourn he observed a sight greatly disturbing to him—the scarred and marred hillsides where steam shovels stripped both the topsoil and the underlying earth to reach coal beds. Lausche expressed his displeasure using words that sound much like those uttered by contemporary environmentalists. "The sight emphasizes the program that not only Ohio, but every state will have to institute, and that is conservation and rehabilitation of natural resources wherever possible. Something [must] be done legally to insure the replacement of denuded timberland and stripped lands so that the future may bring assurance of vegetation and restoration of this area to its normal agriculture richness."[11]

Lausche's repeated reiteration of this position would lead to a major reforestation program in Ohio during his tenure as Governor. As the gubernatorial candidate concluded his campaign trip outside Jackson (Jackson County), he suffered a not so uncommon occurrence during wartime with a shortage of rubber. The automobile in which he toured southern Ohio's rugged hillsides blew a tire. Soon thereafter the driver of the truck gave Lausche a ride into the county seat in the cab of the sand truck, to the amazement of the welcoming committee.

The Mayor returned to Cleveland and immediately sent tongues wagging by remitting a check in the amount of $416.12 to the City Treasurer of Cleveland for his period of absence from mayoral duties while campaigning (his annual salary amounted to $15,000). Opponents quickly attacked this gesture as a political gimmick. Local press convinced the Ohio electorate that this act merely demonstrated already well-known evidence of Lausche's honesty. Several writers suggested this ploy showed up out-going Governor John Bricker, who prior to the 1944 Republican convention in Chicago traveled considerably on taxpayers' time to keep alive his slender chances for an office at the national level.[12]

Evidently the pre-election banter did not inflict an adverse effect upon Lausche's campaign efforts. The voters spoke on May 9, 1944. Lausche won an overwhelming victory. In this particular election primary—which resulted in a disappointingly small voter turnout—Lausche garnered 179,000 of the 300,000 votes cast, considerably more than all the other candidates combined. Lausche's voter strength (greatest in Cuyahoga County) spread to many rural counties where voters had met Lausche for the first time in the few weeks preceding the election.

Lausche now faced a major challenge to win the governorship. For the most part, the state leaned toward the Republican Party. The popular and dapper John W. Bricker, white-thatched ex-farm boy from Madison County (Mt. Sterling), had served three terms in the Governor's office (1938–44). Rumors circulated Bricker's name about as a possible candidate for President in 1944. Republican Party leaders expressed confidence that Ohioans would cast their twenty-five electoral votes for the Republican candidate in opposition to President Roosevelt and his attempt to win an unprecedented fourth term. Ohio citizens had voted for Roosevelt in the three previous elections. In 1944, the Governor, both U.S. Senators and twenty of the state's representatives to Congress carried the Republican label. The prospects for Republicans retaining the governorship appeared bright. Lausche hoped to upset this political applecart.

Bricker considered himself a viable candidate for the presidency, but to hedge his bets, he also planned to pursue a fourth term as Governor. Ohio law permitted Bricker to enter both presidential and gubernatorial primaries. The ultra-conservative could become the first person in Ohio history to win a fourth term as Governor. Ed Schorr, state Republican chairman from Cincinnati, led opposition to this gambit. The state chairman's disagreement with Bricker over patronage issues had long provided a source of friction between the two men. After a protracted period of indecision, Bricker determined to enter both races. When word about Bricker's plans leaked out, Schorr declared political war. He and several county chairmen supported Cincinnati Mayor James Garfield Stewart for Governor. They opposed Bricker's dual candidacy. Senator Robert Taft agreed with Schorr and told Bricker that his plans indicated a lack of confidence in his presidential aspirations.[13] Bricker backed off, and in a contentious four-way battle, Stewart won the Republican primary election for Governor. During his four-year tenure as Mayor of Cincinnati, Stewart primed himself to become Ohio's next Governor. In Lausche's own words, "Stewart was a brilliant scholar and a tremendous debater."[14] The Republican nominee stepped into the political limelight at the party's national convention in Chicago in July 1944. He placed John Bricker's name in nomination for the presidency. Unsuccessful in his bid, Bricker accepted the vice presidential spot.[15] In the November 1944 presidential election, the Thomas E. Dewey–Bricker ticket proved unsuccessful in efforts to dethrone the Roosevelt juggernaut.

The campaign for Ohio's governorship got underway. The country sensed that victory in World War II was imminent. On D-Day—June 6, 1944—thousands of allied troops had invaded France at the Normandy beachhead. Heavy bombing raids on key German industrial centers and supply lines took their toll on Nazi military forces.

In the Pacific theatre, General Douglas MacArthur returned to the Philippine Islands and began the tedious task of island hopping toward the Japanese mainland.

Laborers in Cleveland and elsewhere produced a bountiful supply of war *materiels* despite the threat of strikes. Lausche continued to carry out his responsibilities as Mayor of Cleveland. The 1944 Ohio gubernatorial campaign began much more slowly than usual. In contrast to modern-day elections, candidates for state offices seldom campaigned for months on end prior to Election Day. Lausche campaigned sporadically on weekends until he officially opened his campaign in mid-October.

Lausche established a campaign precedent in 1944. For every day spent on the campaign trail he returned his earnings as Mayor of Cleveland to the city coffers. John Lokar—Lausche's campaign manager, who was affectionately nicknamed "Lindy"—removed himself from the city payroll on July 1, 1944, and traveled the state on his own savings, preaching the Lausche gospel. Lokar and three old-time friends and campaign helpers, Helen Erben, Mollie Toll, and Jack Hafey, all worked until Election Day without a cent of pay. Fifty to seventy-five volunteers gathered nightly in Lausche's old neighborhood at Knaus Hall at East 62nd Street and St. Clair to fold campaign literature and address envelopes. Leading up to the fall election, several Lausche volunteers unfortunately lost their lives in the East Ohio Gas Company explosion (October 20, 1944). Coroner Samuel R. Gerber, touring the ravaged homes, found several boxes of handbills supporting Lausche's campaign.[16]

With a full head of campaign steam, the city-bred Lausche stormed into country towns and county fairs. He noted that people responded to him enthusiastically in rural areas much the same as they had in his old 23rd Ward. On occasion the erstwhile Mayor traveled around Ohio by bus. Lausche's campaign reeked of unorthodox but effective tactics. For instance, whenever the Democratic candidate met voters at strawberry festivals or one of the innumerable county fairs held in late summer, he usually managed to slip in through a side entrance to avoid the official greeters. He mingled with the crowd, shaking all hands and admiring babies. His common touch of earnestly talking politics on a one-to-one basis made for excellent word-of-mouth publicity.[17]

The underdog candidate knew he must gain support from rural southern counties who tended to have a built-in bias against so-called city-slicker politicians. The upstate candidate faced the indomitable task of convincing these voters he actually represented what his campaign rhetoric professed. Many voters certainly believed Lausche's election would result in the Pope running the state. "One day at the Cleveland Athletic Club," Lausche recalled, "a down-state leader boldly, cruelly and realistically told me that, if nothing else did, my being a Catholic would defeat me." The determined candidate continued, "When I went down to Lawrence County (the southern-most county located adjacent to the Ohio River), I was met with a scurrilous attack...in the newspapers there. It was rough, but I threw away my speech, wrote another one borrowed from a friendly reporter, and sailed into bigotry with everything I had at my command."[18]

Lausche arrived in Hamilton County—location of Cincinnati, then Ohio's second largest city and home of his Republican opponent. He completely ignored the regulars and old-time politicians, but rather made just two talks. He addressed the Women's City Club, composed of influential ladies of Hamilton County. The good-looking and charismatic Lausche *wowed* the small audience of scarcely a hundred attendees. The Democratic candidate moved cross-town to speak to the Commercial Club, an equivalent to the historic Union Club in Cleveland, the Union League in Philadelphia, or the Somerset in Boston. Hardly a Democrat entered the portals of this organization. One pundit humorously joked members ate Democrats for breakfast. Lausche spoke for an hour, after which one member commented, "Before he came, it was a dead sure shot that 90 percent of the people would vote against him, when he left, 90 percent were on his side." [19] The guests included James Stewart, Lausche's opponent. Next Lausche called on the publishers of the Cincinnati *Enquirer* and Cincinnati *Post and Times Star*, both arch Republican publications. To each he said simply, "I know you're against me.... All I want is a fair deal." [20]

Lausche followed the same technique throughout his campaign. He would stay a day or two, and then move on. By the time he left, the town would be buzzing with his name. John Gunther enumerated some of the barriers Lausche needed to overcome, "People said he was too ambitious, too clever, too impetuous, and a 'narrow-horizon man.' They were aghast that he practically refused to speak to Al Horstman, the powerful Democratic state chairman; they asserted he was 'woolly minded,' a terrible administrator and all things to all men. Some people disliked him for being Catholic and many Catholics disliked him for having a non-Catholic wife. Some labor people said he should have done more for labor, anti-labor people said he did too much, and the AFL refused to take any stand at all. He was accused of being a parvenu (the snobs could not forget his foreign and plebian origin) and a slave to the Chamber of Commerce. In industrial cities he praised Roosevelt highly; in the rural communities he never...mentioned Roosevelt's name—particularly in the America First belt of Ohio, in the western tier of counties—so he was accused of opportunism and equivocation." [21]

⌒

LAUSCHE RAN WITH EVERY DEMOCRATIC ORGANIZATION LEADER in the state opposing him. Having no organization of his own, so to speak, it became necessary to create one from among a few independent people in the 88 counties of the state. Speaking to Seltzer some time during the mid point of the campaign, Lausche commented "It's awful rough, Louie, awful rough. What they're saying cuts right down into you." [22] Anyone who knew Lausche well learned that he lost all his campaigns before the election, only to win them on Election Day. The more discouraged, the harder he fought.

Somehow Lausche put together a winning combination: Republicans downstate and Democrats in Cleveland. He developed a lot of contacts with Vic Donahey supporters, whom Lausche emulated by following the former governor's pattern of conservative economics and down-with-the-bosses attitude. The Cleveland native paid little attention to his own hometown and neighboring communities. His small campaign committee displayed politeness to Ray Miller and the Cuyahoga County Democratic Committee. Ohio's largest bloc of votes existed in Cuyahoga County, home to a population of a million or more citizens. Lausche could afford this independence. The gubernatorial candidate knew he would carry this county simply by filing his petitions and occasionally showing up at a meeting. This maverick, who ran as a Democrat and acted like a Republican, commanded the solid support of foreign industrial workers in Cleveland, as well as in other lakefront industrial cities.

The plethora of campaign funds accumulated by contemporary politicians would have left Lausche in a state of shock and dismay. Establishing a precedent literally unheard of in modern-day politics, Lausche rejected campaign funds extended with strings attached. Even though funds were desperately needed, he never realized a significant amount of campaign money. For obvious reasons, party moguls showed little enthusiasm to support their standard-bearer. Lausche returned a two thousand dollar campaign contribution made by the political action committee of the otherwise standoffish CIO. Furthermore, reports circulated that the Democrat returned a campaign contribution from the Democratic National Committee. He supported President Roosevelt, but resisted any Washington-based effort to dictate his political agenda. [23] The national committee sent Lausche's campaign office $19.50 worth of Roosevelt posters with a curt note that read, "Please remit check to cover." [24] Lausche refused to accept what he considered improper contributions. The largest contributor to the Mayor's campaign organization, Marshall Field (whom Lausche never met) chipped in one thousand dollars. Several donors contributed $250 or $500, but by and large, a $100 limit remained in force. Lausche claimed a fairly sizable backing from Republicans, including several wealthy Ohioans who bought into his honesty. Occasionally the coffers at the Lausche headquarters did not contain enough money for stamps, a crisis that dissipated once a newspaper story brought forth a stream of small-change offerings. During his campaign Lausche made an astonishing announcement which took the electorate and press by surprise. "No contributions to campaign funds will be accepted, directly or indirectly, from anyone having business dealings with the state" [25] Campaign money ran out, and both Lausche and Lokar financed several down-state trips out of their own pockets.

Lausche officially opened his campaign on October 10, 1944, in Youngstown. Addressing a cheering crowd of approximately one thousand supporters, the candidate asked the rhetorical question whether Ohio wished to be governed by a Democratic candidate or by Ed Schorr, a prominent Cincinnati lawyer and state Republican boss, who wasn't running for anything. *Bossism* became his primary campaign theme. Lausche claimed his opponent served as a pawn for the powerful Schorr. He quoted three Republicans who opposed Schorr in previous elections. In 1940 Senator Harold H. Burton told the public "Ed Schorr is a baneful influence." Two Republican primary election candidates spoke out against Schorr. Attorney General Thomas J. Herbert commented, "Schorr is making improper use of his position as state chairman by employing the party machinery to nominate Stewart" and Lieutenant Governor Paul M. Herbert added, "Stewart is a tool of Ed Schorr." [26]

The general consensus strongly suggested that Stewart functioned as a pawn for Schorr. Schorr's manipulation of the Hamilton County Republican Party became a distinct liability to Stewart's political success. Most of the state's major newspapers supported Lausche's charge of bossism, making the Republican nominee the scapegoat of their opposition to Schorr. [27] Lausche pounded away at the bossism theme. "The methods of...political bosses in rendering public service," he challenged, "are not in accord with mine. They believe in the party first and the country second and...believe...they constitute the party." [28] In an editorial, the Youngstown *Vindicator* concluded, "Actually the choice is not between Lausche and Stewart, it is between Lausche and Boss Schorr." [29]

Stewart struck back with a vengeance. Speaking in Cleveland—Lausche's lair— the Cincinnati Mayor asserted, "The issue is one of conflicting philosophies. Your mayor is of the latter New Deal philosophy. He is the candidate of the president, and I believe the salvation rests on the rejection of a fourth term [FDR's]." [30]

Lausche campaigned on the timeworn theme of government frugality and a clean administration. He advocated retention of natural resources and proper care for the mentally ill. On the campaign trail in Ironton (Lawrence County), Lausche responded to charges that communists dominated the Democratic Party. Declaring these charges were an insult, the Democratic candidate lashed out stressing that the returning soldier finds he has been insulted as he prepares to exercise his right to vote, the heart of the Democratic process. The Cleveland Mayor contended that only President Roosevelt had the experience to represent America at the peace table. [31] Overall, historians and Ohio politicians considered Lausche an accomplished orator. His speeches were usually short and were almost always slightly ponderous. On his principal issue—bossism—voters believed what he said. [32] With Election Day approaching Lausche recalled, "The professional politicians began to send out bitter barbs, saying my wife [Jane] could scarcely speak English and that I was born in Europe, and that only foreign-born and communists were backing me. These canards kicked back and made many friends for me. In both parties the average voter is generally fair." [33] Several days before the election, the *Plain Dealer* summarized Lausche's supposedly inept campaign strategy by saying that Lausche had no campaign organization, and had only a rudimentary one in the closing days of the campaign. He faced the resistance, if not the enmity of many of the organization Democrats in the state. The challenger "had no money, no plan of campaign which extended beyond his own individual efforts and those of a handful of friends and associates and was faced with the state-wide belief that his popularity was a Cleveland oddity, largely the fiction of Cleveland newspapers and that he had... inherent handicaps which made it almost impossible...to get a single vote outside Cuyahoga County."[34]

The citizenry of Ohio soon learned whether Lausche's poor man efforts would propel him into the Governor's office. On Election Day, Tuesday, November 7, a record number of voters streamed to the voting booths in Ohio's 88 counties. Ohio voters encountered perfect voting weather. When all the ballots had been tallied Lausche emerged with a resounding triumph over Stewart to become Ohio's 55th governor. The newly-elected Governor collected 1,603,809 votes to Stewart's 1,491,450 total, a victorious margin of 112,000 votes. As expected, Lausche garnered a majority of over 200,000 votes in Cuyahoga County. He ran well in downstate, traditionally Republican counties, although he carried a winning vote in only 18 of 88 counties. Lausche's victory did not carry over for Roosevelt in the national election. Although successfully elected, President Roosevelt lost Ohio to challenger Thomas E. Dewey by a mere 12,000 votes. Lausche became one of only three governors from Cleveland to have been sent to the statehouse and the only Democrat. The other two governors elected from Cleveland were Harry L. Davis, a steel worker who became a true-blue Republican (1921–23) and George V. Voinovich, an ethnic Republican (1991–1999).

Commenting on Lausche's momentous victory, the *Plain Dealer* editorially extolled his virtues on the road to victory, "...Lausche plugged along making few major campaign speeches,...traveling quietly about the state getting acquainted with the people of small towns and farms.... What he had to offer them was a very intangible thing which might be called 'a wholesome influence'...[the voters] went to the polls and by the thousands crossed party lines to cast their ballots for this big city mayor who talked and acted like an unsophisticated son of the soil."[35]

LAUSCHE'S VICTORY DISAPPOINTED THE TWO LEADING REPUBLICANS in the state, Senator Robert Taft and departing Governor John W. Bricker. Taft could not understand the psychology of the newspapers, which refused to advocate a continuation of Republicans in office. He was confident that Stewart would have retained practically all the personnel appointed by Bricker. In a letter to Bricker, Taft commented that, "It is obvious...that a sectional prejudice and certain faults in Jim Stewart's campaign made it more difficult to elect him than some other, but that seems no excuse for the editors who swung to Lausche." Bricker replied, "I hate to quit in the midst of the war. I never felt worse than in turning the state government over to Democrats. Jim [Stewart] should have been elected. He was defeated on a phony issue."[36] Bricker had been selected to run as the Republican vice presidential nominee in 1944.

Taft continued his critical comments about Lausche prior to the 1944 election. In a letter to John S. Knight, influential publisher of four major newspapers including the Akron *Beacon Journal,* he solicited support for Stewart at the expense of Lausche. Taft believed Stewart would be an excellent successor to Bricker. As for Lausche, the Senator commented that, "Lausche is an attractive man, but from what I can learn, he is not a particularly good administrator, and his strongest point is his handshaking ability and the pleasant impression he makes when he [delivers] speeches. I cannot personally see in any respect in which he would make a better Governor than Stewart."[37]

Taft saved his most offhanded and inaccurate remarks about Lausche for Captain Ingalls of the U.S. Navy. He believed "The Cleveland papers greatly over estimate Lausche's vote-getting possibilities outside of Cleveland. He has a foreign name and looks foreign, which does not go well in rural Ohio. He is Catholic, but married a divorced woman, which leaves him rather weak with both religious groups."[38] If Taft had made these remarks in public, he likely would have ensured Lausche's victory. There's no evidence that Jane Lausche had ever been married before, much less divorced. In addition, Taft did not read Ohio voters very well, for Lasuche consistently garnered more votes than his opponent in rural Ohio, particularly near Taft's lair in the southern counties.

If Lasuche had seen or heard of these remarks from Mr. Republican, likely their budding friendship would have cooled off significantly. Lausche was extremely sensitive to any criticism directed toward him. He reacted sharply to anyone who challenged his integrity. Lausche would not have taken kindly to Taft's falsehood about Jane. The unknowing Lausche eventually nurtured a strong relationship with Taft until his untimely death.

Lausche could not have been elected governor without the overwhelming support of his fellow townsmen, the Cleveland *Press* and the *Plain Dealer.* Additionally, he could not have won the election without the votes of thousands upon thousands of people in other parts of Ohio, who never before had cast their votes for a big-city candidate. Somehow he put together a winning combination—Republicans downstate and Democrats in Cleveland. Lausche's strategy of frugal economics and anti-bossism proved successful, with two exceptions, for the next twenty-five years. William F. McDermott, highly respected columnist for the *Plain Dealer,* provided an erudite profile of Lausche. "Here was a man in politics who was wholly truthful and without guile. This man may make mistakes but he is a good man. He means what he says. He will not cheat or lie or dissemble. He has principles in which he passionately believes...and he will not betray them. His personality emits an aura of candor, warmth and simple goodness."[39] McDermott added an analogy,

"In the world's mind honesty is a rare attribute among the practitioner of politics. Shakespeare, in 'Hamlet' describes a politician as 'one who would circumvent God.' He also pays the tribe his respects in 'King Lear,' 'Get thee glass eyes; and like a scurvy politician seems to see the thing thou dost not.'"[40]

Traditionally, politics becomes a systematic pursuit of what seems expedient. What seems expedient is not always morally right. A successful politician is popularly supposed to scheme, connive, compromise, make allowances where he can, promise whatever he must to get votes, cater to groups at the expense of the public and to the injury of what proves to be just and proper. Lausche tried desperately not to fall into this trap. He believed that voters might overwhelmingly welcome a politician who refused to play the political game, who attempted to be absolutely frank, honest, and high-minded in all his dealings.

Whether by design or not, Lausche best demonstrated his creed of honesty in dealing with finances and party bosses. The day after the election his campaign quarters "literally didn't have a nickel left...and were in debt $3,700."[41] Impressed by the decisiveness of his victory, the Democratic National Headquarters telephoned the new Governor-elect from the Biltmore Hotel in New York and offered to let bygones be bygones. They volunteered to help pay the bills, *ex post facto*, insisting that any check their office sent should be payable to the local executive committee of the Democratic Party. Lausche had little, if anything, to do with this committee and refused the money. Lausche further gave evidence of his unorthodoxy in his campaign. He filed a statement with the Secretary of State verifying his campaign expenses amounted to the miniscule sum of $27,132. Lausche's warfare against bossism garnered the maximum number of votes for a minimum expenditure of campaign funds.[42] In contrast, James Stewart spent $988,000 in a losing cause. Lausche's opponent displayed messages on billboards, distributed tons of expensive literature, hired high-powered publicity and advertising agencies, purchased prime radio time, contracted subordinate speakers and services of organization workers in a losing effort.

Lausche's fiscal policies when campaigning compared favorably with the views of former President Gerald Ford. Commenting on campaign finance reform, the ex-Congressman noted that in his Grand Rapids (Michigan) district, congressional candidates [in 2000] would spend over half a million dollars. "I...hesitate to be a candidate if I had to go about and raise that much money. I always had a guilt complex when I raised $20,000."[43] Both Lausche and Ford would likely concede that finance reform is a sham, especially with reports that President George W. Bush and Republican strategists envisioned raising as much as $250 million for the 2004 presidential campaign.[44] Political scientist Dr. Wellington Fordyce summarized his assessment of Lausche's victory pointing out, "The election of...the American-born son of Slovenian immigrants to the governorship...must be regarded as a rebuke to those who have tried to make political capital of race, religion, and urban-rural factionalism within the state."[45]

Lausche completed his remaining two months as Mayor. Shortly after January 1, 1945, the Lausches departed from Robert Sheal's 80-year-old home to make the 150-mile journey to Columbus. They traveled in Lausche's tattered and torn 1939 Chevrolet to assume new responsibilities. The Governor's mansion located in Bexley, a wealthy suburb on the east side of Columbus, became the Lausches' residence for the next two years. The Governor-elect owned one extra suit and two pairs of shoes (outgoing Governor John Bricker reputedly departed from the mansion with 92 suits).

Unlike many lawyers and politicians, the penny-pinching Lausche lived with few material assets. He earned ten thousand dollars yearly as Governor, five thousand dollars less than he did as Mayor. The Governor rejected an unofficial effort during his first year in office to increase his salary. Two-sevenths of his salary helped pay for expenses at the mansion. Every two weeks Lausche received a check for $302.96. The rest of his salary went for taxes and mansion upkeep. Saving money was all but impossible. Gunther asked friends of Lausche about his finances. "Why, the guy don't have nothin!" Another friend interjected, "Whatever money you may have in your pocket at this moment, I will make a wager for any amount that Frank Lausche is carrying less."[46] Maintaining his bent for political honesty, Lausche returned $2,250 of his mayor's salary. Of this amount, $450 represented his salary during the time he was campaigning for the Democratic nomination and $1,800 represented those days missed during the general election. Critics charged Lausche with a cheap campaign tactic. This information did not reach the media until after the general election.[47]

Early guests at the Governor's mansion on Inauguration Day met Lausche, hatless and coatless, testing the frosty winter day on the front steps. "Just fortifying myself with a breath of fresh air,"[48] the Governor explained as he ushered his guests inside. Before the end of the day, Lausche discovered and worked out in the small gymnasium in the mansion's basement. He announced that he planned to eat breakfast in the kitchen, at least when no guests were staying at the mansion.

An acute and exasperating wartime housing shortage existed in Columbus. For the early months of his tenure, Lausche hastened to open an unused wing of the executive mansion to house a twenty-one-year-old veteran and his expectant wife rent-free.[49] He encouraged his wife Jane, now the First Lady of Ohio, to "make the soil [adjacent to the mansion] to produce food when food is needed. The trusties from the Ohio Penitentiary did the heavy work,... Mrs. Lausche was no mere superintendent. She planted, cultivated and harvested,"[50] thus reducing the expenses for food. The Governor retained John Lokar as his secretary in the Governor's office, which was augmented by a small staff.

Basking in national and statewide limelight, the 49-year-old Lausche took the oath of office on January 8, 1945. He exhibited a personality that remained sincere, folksy, unconventional, unpredictable, incorruptible, and as unorthodox as ever.[51] A somber and cautious man, the Governor exuded vitality. He retained his attractive mop of black hair, which he combed straight back. His eyes were black as coal. His oval face gave him a hint of the mongoloid family strain that surfaced when the Tartars dashed the gates of Vienna centuries earlier.

Lausche's theme of independence highlighted his inaugural address on January 13, 1945. His numerous siblings, along with their families, and Lausche's 23rd Ward friends attended this gala affair. He stood on the statehouse steps where once his hero Abraham Lincoln had spoken en route to Washington DC for his inauguration in 1861. The following day the Columbus *Dispatch* headline read "Gov. Lausche Spurns Partnership in Speech." The Cincinnati *Enquirer* reported "New Governor Works Hard, Defies Politicians." A wartime Governor, Lausche assured Ohioans that there must not be a relaxation in efforts to produce supplies for the military. His principal aim emphasized *unification* of every effort to bring the war to a prompt ending."[52] To aid the war effort the Governor planned to use his executive power when necessary. He had gained valuable experience as a wartime mayor. Whenever a strike threatened public welfare, Lausche acted with alacrity, taking all sanctions available. Several weeks after he took office, the Goodyear plant in Akron, which produced war materials, went on strike. The Governor directed the Selective Service Board of Akron to induct striking employees into the armed forces unless they returned to work immediately. In another war-related incident, Lausche strongly recommended renewal of the Ross Bill, which extended working hours for women during the war emergency. Of this proposal, he said, "It doesn't seem conceivable that we will permit, in this time of war, a revision to a peacetime formula of work."[53] These actions did not endear Lausche to labor organizations in Ohio, and actually eroded some of his political support. The Governor claimed not to be unfriendly to labor per se, but only that he was more interested in Ohio's war production and winning the war.

> "The election of…the American-born son of Slovenian immigrants to the governorship…must be regarded as a rebuke to those who have tried to make political capital of race, religion, and urban-rural factionalism within the state."

Lausche went against conventional political wisdom in several ways. Upon election he announced there would be no general removal of Republican jobholders to make way for Democrats. In a particularly painful application of this philosophy, [to Democrats], Lausche retained Herbert D. Defenbacher in the key position as Director of Finance. The Governor told shocked Democrats, "…I believe you get the best government if those in responsible posts act impartially."[54] The newly-elected Governor retained Republicans in several other high-ranking state offices. Another example of his unorthodox management concerned his two major opponents in the 1944 gubernatorial primary. Frazier Reams, Jr. of Toledo and James Huffman of Columbus both held a measure of esteem in the state Democratic Party. The Governor appointed Reams Director of Welfare, one of the most important positions in Ohio's state government. In the fall of 1945, President Harry S. Truman appointed 57-year-old Republican Senator Harold Burton to fill a Supreme Court position brought about by the retirement of Owen J. Roberts. Lausche appointed Huffman to fill this vacant senate seat, a position he held for only one year before John W. Bricker defeated him in the 1946 senatorial election. To forgive and forget fit well into Lausche's basic philosophy.[55] This attitude would be severely tested in subsequent political encounters.

Lausche's program as Governor evolved around four basic tenets: law and order, equality of treatment among conflicting economic blocs, fiscal responsibility, and unity between urban and rural interests.[56] Bricker's exit after his six-year tenure as Governor found the state with a $92 million surplus, replacing a $20 million debt when he entered the statehouse. This surplus accumulated partly as a result of a Bricker-initiated sales tax. The wartime boom exacerbated the state's surplus. Lausche attempted to build up a much more substantial financial reserve fund "to help provide jobs when the war boom bursts."[57] Jobs and housing for veterans ranked among his major concerns as World War II ended in the summer of 1945. Lokar accurately expressed Lausche's wartime hiring policy after receiving 3,500 job applications within two weeks after his inauguration. "Service men will get preference in state jobs.... And no one now working in a defense plant stands a chance of getting a [state] job. We have a war to win, and until that's won we aren't taking any men who can find their niche in war industry."[58]

⌐

THE NEW GOVERNOR ENCOUNTERED NUMEROUS EXAMPLES of miserly handling of state revenue, partly due to Bricker's hesitation to spend state funds. The State mental hospitals, described by one pundit as medieval entities, held high priority. The state welfare program had been woefully neglected for thirty years. Lausche secured approval from the Republican dominated legislature for nearly $17 million to construct state facilities. Because these new facilities could not be built overnight, existing facilities in Cleveland, Akron, Tiffin, Youngstown and Cambridge needed immediate renovations to alleviate the abominable conditions facing the overwhelming number of mentally ill citizens. The Lausche administration converted Mount Vernon Hospital into a facility for the desperately needy, the mentally ill, and those afflicted with tuberculosis. Among other projects, the Governor launched health programs to attack tuberculosis (a somewhat common and life-threatening disease at that time), and substantially reduced the incidence of cases. During his term of office, Lausche increased allowances for the aged, the blind and dependent children, as well as unemployment compensation.[59] The Governor received $6 million from the State Legislature for desperately needed veteran's housing. New officeholders often succeed with their political platform in a more positive manner than do incumbents. Lausche experienced his share of successes in a turbulent era of Ohio history. Compromise—an important tactic in the political arena—became a way of life for the Governor.

In spite of a large surplus in state coffers, Lausche practiced his well-established conservative economic strategy. One might question the well-meaning Lausche about why he didn't use these surpluses for critical needs within state welfare agencies. The war-weary state of Ohio found itself in dire need of federal support, particularly so because of Governor Bricker's parsimonious administration. Numerous state projects remained shelved during the war. Lausche's fiscal stance pleased Republicans. He sided with those who believed private initiative could more effectively address statewide economic issues. His philosophical bent harkened back to the days of Herbert Hoover and the former President's plea for volunteerism to stem an impending slide into a depression. In Condon's words, Lausche often used *Frank's fence* to straddle issues necessitating the expenditure of state funds. In addition Lausche ignored the demands of the Democratic State Committee that their leaders should have say in filling state jobs. The Governor insisted that lobbies at the statehouse remain *verboten*. Organized labor, normally connected with the Democratic Party, generally found Lausche unsympathetic to their demands.

> Lausche's program as governor evolved around four basic tenets: law and order, equality of treatment among conflicting economic blocs, fiscal responsibility, and unity between urban and rural interests.

Lausche's humane instincts drifted toward helping the underprivileged in the work force, but labor bossism rankled the Governor at every turn. Near the end of the war Lausche encountered a struggle with the CIO. The dispute concerned revision of the Unemployment Compensation Law, which as recorded in the books, provided sixteen dollars in weekly payments for eighteen weeks for qualified unemployed laborers. The CIO wanted this figure raised to twenty-five dollars for twenty-six weeks. Lausche fought for an exact mathematical compromise, twenty-one dollars for twenty-two weeks. He believed the CIO plan, which would have increased the cost of unemployment insurance by 140 percent, to be too expensive. "I believe in giving, but not to the point of exhausting the body that gives." Then he changed the metaphor, reiterating, "There can be such a thing as too much reform, if it takes the wheels off the wagon."[60]

The public school system backed by the Ohio Education Association—the most powerful lobby in the state in 1945—encountered similar reticence from the new governor. Under Lausche's education plan, schools would have been given a total of over $108 million for the next biennium, an increase of ten million dollars over 1943–44. Teachers and administrators demanded more, to which Lausche replied, "In my opinion, the figures recommended by me are reasonable and just."[61] The Dayton *News* surmised, "No other governor ever had openly opposed the school lobby, but Lausche refused to yield to political expediency."[62] He was, of course, at odds with the Republican-controlled State Assembly.[63] Legislators pushed for a retroactive wartime pay increase for state employees, including teachers. The Governor argued, "It smacked of pork and the taxpayers deserve better treatment."[64] The governor scored additional political points by vetoing a move to raise his own salary.

Lausche's continuous disregard for powerful pressure groups undoubtedly cost him many votes, but conversely his firm stands gained him many supporters. The not-always-so-friendly Cincinnati *Enquirer* noted, "...it is Lausche's personality that sells him.... That personality is in the way he shakes one's hand [often with dirty fingernails], the way he puts a person at ease, his youthful smile, his manner of conveying an immediate conviction that he is sincere in what he says and not just talking to public consumption while he deals through the backdoor with a group of bosses...."[65] Lausche's personal touch worked in other ways. During wartime, gasoline rationing restricted vehicular travel. Lausche often picked up passengers on his way to the statehouse from the governor's mansion to set an example for citizens to share the ride. Another unusual departure caused statehouse tongues to wag. He visited the offices of various department heads rather than having them come to his office. The Governor wanted to get around and see the offices and personnel firsthand.

The unleashing of atomic bombs by the United States on Hiroshima and Nagasaki in mid-August 1945 brought the long and tortuous World War II to a merciful conclusion. Now a peacetime Governor, Lausche faced a myriad of social and economic issues. Along with the rest of the nation, Ohioans anxiously moved forward amidst a desire to spend money saved during the war. Ohio became a microcosm of postwar America. The United States, including the Buckeye state, enjoyed an unprecedented period of prosperity in the two decades following the Second World War. Thousands of Ohio men and women, a portion of the twelve million Americans in uniform, wended their way back into the state's mainstream and the job market. The GI Bill, the Baby Boom, suburban growth and expanded peacetime industries impacted the ballot box and state government.[66] The flow of migrants to Ohio from the South, both white and black, continued after the war. By 1950 over one-half million African-Americans resided in the state, representing 6.5 percent of Ohio's population.

The Buckeye state's core industries thrived during this postwar period. The Big Three carmakers added production and assembly plants in the state, solidifying Ohio's rank as the second largest auto producing state, following Michigan. New industries such as aluminum moved into the Ohio River Valley to take advantage of cheap river transportation and publicly subsidized power generation.[67] During World War II, unemployment in Ohio fell to nearly zero, industrial wages rose by 65 percent, farm income grew by close to 200 percent, and defense contracts brought $18 billion into the state economy. The average weekly wage for laborers in manufacturing rose from $29.55 in 1940 to $52.52 in 1944; the average number of weekly work hours increased from thirty-eight to forty-seven. Union strength soared to an all-time high with some 36 percent of nonagricultural workers enlisted as union members. Unions became a powerful political entity.[68]

From the 1930s through the 1960s, Ohioans remained politically polarized. Many citizens embraced a more activist government and endorsed collective action in contrast to those who saw the solution to the Depression as a modified revival of what had become traditional values of self-discipline and civic responsibility. During and after World War II, this schism manifested itself in heightened debate over the power of unions, the role of the federal government, and charges of radicalism and anti-Americanism aimed at citizens who called for significant reform in political and economic structure in the United States. Increasingly comfortable with their lives as consumers, Ohioans showed little interest in prolonged political controversies.

However, neither citizens nor politicians could ignore postwar problems that plagued society. Segregation, strikes, Communism, the Cold War, and a host of other issues forced the public to act or react in a rapidly changing society. Noted author and native Ohioan Louis Bromfield may have expressed the situation best, "A return to the past can never be accomplished and the sense of fortified isolation and security is no longer possible in the world of automobiles, or radios,...telephones and airplanes. One must live with one's times and those who understand this and make the proper adjustments and concessions and compromises are the happy ones."[69] Lausche, a good friend to Bromfield who shared the gentleman farmer's views on conservation, found himself caught in this swirling cauldron of political, social, and economic issues during the remaining months of his term.

For the most part, political analysts gave Lausche positive marks during his first term. He provided leadership in improving housing and care for the mentally ill and those individuals receiving welfare benefits. The Governor pushed for veteran's housing with some success and managed to maintain a modicum of aid for cities. He kept the state budget in line and increased the already ample surplus. As always, Lausche continued his struggle against organized crime and gambling. The Governor's term did not bring evidence of any scandals or glaring sins of omission or commission.[70]

Lausche faced several obstacles over which he had little control in promoting his agenda. The heavily dominated Republican legislature pigeonholed several of the Governor's forward-looking measures. He faced resistance trying to make available better mental welfare, to establish a commission to ameliorate the sad state of Ohio employees' salaries, and to appoint a veterans' commission to set in place the machinery to aid veterans returning to civilian life. Republican opposition to the Governor lurked in the Rules Committee and other important assembly committees.[71] Lausche suffered an additional defeat on one issue vital to him. Vigorously promoting legislation to restrict strip-mining and to replenish the hills in southeastern Ohio with plants and trees, the Governor felt the wrath of Ed Schorr, his political nemesis from Cincinnati. With a heavy hand, the titular head of the state Republican Party solicited his southern Ohio legislators to successfully thwart passage of strip-mining legislation.[72]

Nineteen forty-six did not bode well for the Democratic Party, either at the national or the state level. In a mid-term election year, the party out of office tends to gain seats in Congress and political strength at the state level. This first peacetime election after World War II proved to be no exception. Voters reacted negatively to Roosevelt's four election victories and fourteen years of Democratic national rule. Republicans gained control of Congress. Labor unions threatened nationwide shutdowns, slowing the production of consumer goods desperately sought by the public.

Directly after the war's end, many Democratic office holders—including Lausche—suffered from a backlash against high meat prices and price controls. Growing public resentment spilled over against all wartime restrictions. Roosevelt's successor, President Harry S. Truman—and by inference the Democratic Party—received blame for a national meat shortage. An active black market took over in bootlegging meat, butter, liquor, and women's silk stockings. Returning veterans found they could not obtain places to live because of rent control restrictions. Wartime occupants simply refused to move out, though they occupied too much space. Soviet expansionism in Eastern Europe—including Lausche's family homeland of Slovenia—fueled the first stirrings of a Cold War, which prompted growing suspicions of *commies* in powerful positions in the United States.[73] John Bricker, campaigning for a U.S. Senate seat, captured the complex issues confronting the United States with what he considered flawed platitudes for the New Deal. "The American people are tired of promises and red tape and confusion. They are tired of red ink and deficit spending. They are tired of rubber-stamp congresses and brain trusts. They are tired of soap shortages, white shirt shortages, meat shortages, housing shortages and black markets...[The New Deal] has made government so big, so complex, so contradictory, and so expensive that it has become a dangerous monstrosity."[74]

An exceedingly well-managed Republican Party confronted the incumbent Governor in 1946. Ray Bliss, Ohio Republican state chairman who became national Republican chairman in 1965, was a symbol of good organization. He served as Robert Taft's campaign manager in 1950, when Taft startled the nation with his overwhelming victory for the U.S. Senate over Joseph R. Ferguson, the Democratic candidate. Bliss' stock continued to escalate when he received credit for Nixon's unexpected victory in Ohio in 1960. The badly fractionalized Democratic Party would never have selected an individual with Bliss' organizational skills for the chairmanship's responsibilities. In contrast, Democratic county chairmen regarded their organizations as totally independent entities with only a coincidental similarity of name to tie them with the state and national Democratic organizations.[75]

Though in no way responsible for national conditions, the freshman wartime Governor saw himself caught in a downdraft. Lausche took a political stance on several issues which cost him votes at the ballot box. He urged the public not to buy merchandise unless it was needed for health or welfare. With shortages in nearly all commodities, Lausche asked businessmen "to act justly and fairly with those who are compelled to buy and not ruthlessly and mercilessly take advantage of the opportunity that lies with him as a seller."[76] He implored President Truman to end all controls at once. Lausche's Catholicism did not inhibit his strong stand on principle concerning the controversial issue of direct financial aid to church-controlled educational institutions. He opposed aid because in his judgment such aid would be illegal.[77]

☞

LAUSCHE LEFT NO DOUBT THAT HE PLANNED TO RUN for re-election. The upcoming campaign became far more vitriolic than Lausche anticipated. Enemies can help to defeat you, as Lausche found out in his bid for re-election. Lausche analyzed the situation. "I have never had any entanglement with any economic group wanting state favors—business, labor, or what have you. You ask me what is my secret of success? Well, I'd say it has mostly been due to the enemies I have made."[78] The growing rift between Ray Miller and the Governor broke out into open warfare. Word spread through Lausche's old strongholds in Cleveland that "he had gone high-hat and preferred opera to the polka, (Slovenians also enjoyed opera) had forgotten his old friends, and spent too much time with the country club set."[79] Critics complained that the Governor, trapped in his statehouse duties, stopped attending marriages, wakes, christenings, and other ceremonial gatherings in the immigrant neighborhoods of Cleveland.

Many Democratic leaders in Ohio expressed unhappiness with Lausche's administration of state government, and especially with their loss of patronage jobs. In an effort to thwart Lausche's re-nomination, former state Senator William G. Pickrel and Miller endorsed William J. Kennedy for the Democratic gubernatorial nomination. A threatened split in the party failed to materialize because Kennedy failed to file the necessary petitions. The road became clear for Lausche's nomination in the primary election without any significant opposition. Angered over Lausche's nomination—as well as over a squabble regarding distribution of license plates in Cuyahoga County—Miller resigned his county chairmanship in July 1946. A special citizens committee, the Cosmopolitan Democratic League of Cuyahoga County, organized and endorsed the Governor and supported his campaign.[80]

The Republicans, sensing the possibility of victory over Lausche, nominated handsome and popular Attorney General Thomas J. Herbert to oppose the Governor. Herbert served in World War I as a pilot, shooting down one German plane, and he was shot down himself, receiving the U.S. and British Distinguished Service Cross and Purple Heart.[81] Returning to the United States, Herbert earned his law degree from Western Reserve University. He was appointed assistant law director in Cleveland in 1920, then served as assistant Cuyahoga County prosecutor in 1923–24. The aspiring Herbert entered private practice until 1928 when he received an appointment as assistant state attorney general. In 1932 he lost his bid for a congressional seat. The lawyer then gained recognition for his efforts as special counsel to the state attorney general in the liquidation of the Union Trust Company. Due to Roosevelt's landslide in 1936, Herbert lost his bid for the state attorney general's office. He rebounded in 1938 and won three consecutive terms as attorney general, before losing to Stewart in the Republican primary election for Governor in 1944.

Herbert proved to be a formidable opponent for Lausche. John Bricker, in spite of a close friendship with Lausche, provided trickle-down support for Lausche's opponent. Challenging James Huffman for a senate seat in 1946, following his unsuccessful effort to be elected vice president on the Dewey ticket in 1944, Bricker spent enormous sums of money in an effort to secure his election. He won the senate seat, and the spillover effect was beneficial to Herbert's campaign.

The Democratic Party struggled with the onset of the Cold War and many domestic problems in 1946. The public questioned the competence of Truman's administration. Herbert struck hard at Lausche during the campaign, charging the Governor with New Deal leanings. At every opportunity in his campaign, Governor Lausche refuted this New Deal accusation by isolating himself from the Truman Administration. The Governor seldom referred either to the President or the national party. The state Democratic Party platform drafted by Lausche's staff ignored the national political scene and gave high praise only to the management of state affairs.[82]

Herbert continued his political attack, in some cases making wild charges without substantial evidence. He contended that Lausche had espoused major campaign promises with few, if any, accomplishments. The challenger charged the Governor with political maneuvering in the state liquor department and corruption in campaign financing. The most ludicrous accusation implied that Lausche harbored communists in the state government who planned violent overthrow of the government.[83] An ardent American patriot, Lausche never courted favor with the communists and became well known during his political career for his strong anti-communist stand. Gobetz suggested that to a large extent the 1946 campaign against Lausche capitalized on fear and prejudice. Although Lausche was born and educated in America, on several occasions, opponents falsely portrayed him as being foreign-born and un-American.[84]

The Governor's press friends struck back in his behalf. Louis Seltzer of the Cleveland *Press* wrote in an editorial, "Lausche is being smeared...with fake issues— 'meat,' 'communism,' 'liquor control,' because the real issues of constructive achievement won't stand the test of Republican campaign argument."[85] C.J. Doyle of the Oberlin *Times* summarized Lausche's first term accomplishments. He pointed out that with little fanfare the Governor had succeeded in cleaning up most of the ills from the Bricker administration. More money was spent under

Lausche's administration, but at the same time, the surplus at the end of the year was the largest in the history of the state. "His Republican predecessor starved the local governments, schools, and hospitals for the mentally ill to build up a state surplus for political purposes. Under Governor Lausche the local governments are receiving nearly twice as much money from the state as they did under the Bricker administration."[86]

Lausche occasionally confounded newspaper journalists in the state, particularly those outside of Cleveland. He habitually reviewed and rewrote press releases for forthcoming speeches. This action prevented Ralph Kelly, his publicity agent (who had served as political columnist for the *Plain Dealer*) from releasing a speech until it became too late for accompanying reporters to file anything but a stopgap *early lead*. In spite of this behavior, Pulitzer Prize winning James "Hal" Donahey, longtime political cartoonist for the *Plain Dealer*, urged voters to recognize Lausche as "a governor of all the people."[87]

One political issue cost Lausche significant support for his re-election. A nationwide clamor for approval and distribution of a veteran's bonus forced the hand of politicians. One month before the election, Lausche stated he would lead the fight for a veteran's bonus. He qualified his pledge by opposing payment of the bonus immediately due to a high rate of inflation. Lausche argued, "If a bonus had been paid a year ago or even now, it is obvious that under inflation the dollar that would have been given to [the veteran] would have a negligible buying power."[88] The Governor's logic may have been sound, but the timing of his remarks proved damaging. Lausche's propensity for stubbornness gave the Republican state legislature leverage on this issue during the campaign.

Near the conclusion of his two-year term, the Governor proposed using some of the state surplus, which accumulated before and during World War II for public welfare projects. Concurrently, Republicans urged Lausche to call a special session of the legislature to pass a bill awarding bonuses to all returning veterans. Lausche balked, contending a special session enabled the GOP-controlled General Assembly to pass needless laws. Lausche agreed to sign a bonus bill when the legislature reconvened the following year. This decision proved politically unwise for Lausche, as there would not be a next year for Governor Lausche.

An oddity occurred on Election Day in early November. Both Lausche and Herbert lived in the same neighborhood, the same political ward, and even the same precinct. The two candidates voted side-by-side in the basement of the Euclid Avenue Christian Church, East 100th Street and Euclid Avenue.[89] In a somewhat stunning upset, the electorate failed to return Lausche to the governor's office. Thomas Herbert carried the state by a narrow plurality of 40,553 votes, ousting Lausche with 1,166,550 votes to the Governor's 1,125,997. Herbert garnered 50.8 percent of the total votes. Election analysis indicated that Lausche lost important voter strength in his home county (Cuyahoga) and in Mahoning County (home of populous industrial Youngstown). Although he carried nearly the same eighteen counties that he had in 1944, Lausche dropped 128,000 votes below his previous total in Cleveland alone. This decrease in voting strength may have been attributed to labor's disenchantment with Lausche's political stance and his failure to maintain close ties with his constituency. With the battle cry of *Had Enough,* the GOP swept to victory in both houses of Congress. To say the least, this defeat hurt Lausche's pride. "I was heartbroken," he lamented."[90] Lausche's loss marked the last time Lausche would lose an election until 1968.

It may be argued that Lausche took his opponent too lightly, particularly in a year when Republicans expected to do well. Tom Herbert, a white-haired fifty-two-year-old widower, proved to be an energetic campaigner with a hearty appetite for ice cream and corn on the cob. His reputation as a war hero enhanced his chances of election. He declared his candidacy from his bed in University Hospital in Columbus in October 1945, a full six months before the filing deadline. The candidate continued to recover from an operation on his leg due to complications from a wartime injury. He proceeded to campaign in all 88 counties and logged more than 30,000 miles. Herbert proved to be more successful at Lausche's own political strategy, that is, courting voters with handshakes and one-on-one interaction.[91]

Cut to the quick, Lausche did not help his political stature with his behavior after the election. He practically disappeared from the statehouse in mid-November and December. During that time his subordinates ran wild, granting last minute political favors through liquor permits and pardons.[92] These actions would never have taken place had Lausche been more attentive to his duties. Distraught over defeat, the deposed Governor retreated to his hometown to contemplate his professional future. In time the dark political clouds dissipated. In an unforeseen development, Ray Miller—Lausche's constant antagonist—helped catapult the now ex-governor back into the political arena.

Lausche, Al Horstman of Dayton, former Democratic state chairman and President Harry S. Truman on the campaign trail at Crestline, Ohio, June 4, 1948. (Courtesy of AP/Wide World Press)

six

Baseball Commissioner—No;
Back to the Statehouse—Yes

A DISTRAUGHT LAUSCHE AND WIFE JANE RETURNED to his revitalized
hometown in early 1947. Rather than succumb to ominous signs
that Cleveland would soon turn into a *rust city*, political leaders and
the business community set forth to give credence to a positive by-
line (first expounded in 1944) that Cleveland was the best location in the nation.[1] Thomas A. Burke, Lausche's successor and good
friend, provided quality municipal leadership. Burke served nine
years as Mayor (1945–1953), handily brushing aside his opposition in four consecutive elections. The Mayor manifested many traits similar to those of Lausche's, that
is a fair-haired boy to the newspapers, a personable charmer, an articulate speaker
with a keen sense of humor, and a person with a shrewd mind who made few if any
major political mistakes during his tenure in office.[2] Burke inherited leadership over a
city projected as a microcosm of postwar America. The Great Depression had nearly
brought the city of Cleveland to its knees.

The city recovered and provided men and *materiel* for the most expensive and destructive war to date. Post-World II predictions gave indications of a prosperous era to follow. One could argue that for several postwar years the Forest City enjoyed what is benevolently referred to as a golden era.

The G.I. Bill, increased birth rate, demands for domestic goods, suburban growth and expanded peacetime industries contributed to a postwar boom. Union power expanded through new memberships. Unfortunately, the return of war veterans caused minorities and women to face barriers in obtaining new jobs or even to maintain their present employment.[3] The underlying symptoms of racial tensions particularly in east Cleveland surfaced during the war, and initial steps were taken to ease the problem during Lausche's mayoral reign. Housing shortages worsened with the return of service men eager to start new families. A growing pattern of metropolitan decentralization intensified.

Although Mayor Burke seemed at times to coast while in office, important public works, with popular support, became a reality under his helm. During the late 1940s, the Mayor initiated the first municipal projects since the twenties, when the fabulous Van Sweringen brothers had remade the face of the city. Burke engineered the development of a downtown airport near Municipal Stadium to alleviate Cleveland Hopkins International Airport of the need to handle large numbers of smaller aircraft. The Mayor activated a dormant plan, first conceived by the Van Sweringens, for a system of rapid transit lines serving the inner belt of Cleveland. By the mid-1940s, the Cuyahoga River received a facelift in the form of widening, straightening and deepening the river channel to offset the deleterious blight associated with this mid-town waterway. The city's stock of public housing increased with over one thousand new units. Voter support approved construction of a comprehensive system of freeways for metropolitan Cleveland.

Superficially at least Cleveland became a revitalized city during the early postwar years. The Cleveland Convention and Visitors Bureau reported that conventions enticed over 150,000 visitors to Cleveland in 1946.[4] In the world of sports, Cleveland proudly accepted acclaim as a city of champions. The flamboyant and unpredictable Bill Veeck purchased the Cleveland Indians baseball club in 1946. His leadership produced a World Championship in 1948, the first in twenty-eight years. The Cleveland Buckeyes won the Negro World Series in 1945. The newly formed Cleveland Rams began playing in the All-American Football Conference in 1946, winning four consecutive league titles before joining the National Football League in 1950. The fledgling team continued its winning ways by claiming the NFL Championship in their first season. The popular Cleveland Barons, called the New York Yankees of minor league hockey, regularly drew over 10,000 fans to Cleveland Arena.

Throughout 1946 Clevelanders celebrated the city's 150th birthday with pageants, parades, and entertainment, drawing national attention. L. H. Robbins of the *New York Times Magazine* wrote profusely about the city and its people, "Clevelanders display an exuberant enthusiasm for their town and their way of life such as you don't recall ever noting in any city east of the Alleghenies…. It is really remarkable, their town boosting local pride and contentment…."[5] There was a sense of well-being, light spiritedness, and optimism now that the war had ended.

Lausche had not expected to lose the governor's election in 1946. He faced a decision as to what to do with his career. The deposed governor did not command much wealth, and so employment became imperative. Speculation that he and his good friend Mayor Thomas Burke would form a law partnership fell by the wayside when the Mayor won re-election in 1947. If the former Governor had realized that lean times were forthcoming after the 1946 election, he might well have more vigorously pursued the position of major league baseball commissioner in 1945. Twice during a six-year period (1945–1951), Lausche's name emerged as a viable candidate for the most powerful job in professional baseball. A moral zealot and autocratic in nature, Judge Kenesaw Mountain Landis died in November 1944, after a tumultuous 24-year tenure as baseball's first commissioner. Baseball hierarchy faced an important decision as World War II came to a bombastic conclusion. Sixteen major-league owners deliberated until mid-April 1945 before deciding on a newly elected commissioner.

Politically, Lausche was a hot item. A baseball aficionado and former professional player, he had served admirably as Mayor of Cleveland and had won election as Governor of Ohio in the fall of 1944. A four-man sub-committee of owners accepted the charge to screen the large slate of candidates. Alva Bradley, President of the Cleveland Indians, served as committee chairman. Other members were owners Philip K. Wrigley (Chicago Cubs), Sam Breadon (St. Louis Cardinals), and Don Barnes (St. Louis Browns).[6] It is unclear whether Lausche was aware that club owners seriously considered him for the commissionership. He undoubtedly received permission from Alva Bradley to allow his name to be placed in nomination. There was a question of whether Lausche could or would accept because of his position as Governor. The list of eleven potential candidates read like a Who's Who in America, and included the names Herbert Hoover, Thomas E. Dewey, J. Edgar Hoover, Fred Vinson, James A. Farley, Justice William O. Douglas, and John W. Bricker. A highly complimentary biographical summary on the Ohio Governor was read during deliberations.[7]

On April 24, 1945, at the Hotel Cleveland, the sub-committee put forward five names to club owners for consideration, including Frank J. Lausche, an eleventh-hour dark horse. The other candidates were Albert "Happy" Chandler, Democratic Senator from Kentucky, James A. Farley, former Postmaster General, Ford Frick, President of the National League, and Robert Hannegan, national chairman of the Democratic Party. Interestingly and certainly not intentionally, four of the five candidates held strong allegiance to the Democratic Party. On the first ballot Lausche received three first place votes (Branch Rickey, President of the Brooklyn Dodgers, believed Alva Bradley and Philip K. Wrigley voted for Lausche).[8] He had survived to the final three candidates. Serving as chair of the meeting, Bradley suggested a second ballot with only these top three candidates listed, namely Chandler, Hannegan, and Lausche. The results gave Chandler eight votes, Hannegan five votes and three votes for Lausche. The owners discussed what to do next. Comments from owners supported both Chandler and Hannegan. Rickey commented that, "Lausche had no open supporters but had great strength in the minds of everybody...."[9] Sam Breadon suggested a third ballot limited to the two leading candidates, Chandler and Hannegan.

In revisiting 1946 and his jobless circumstances, what was Lausche to do for gainful employment? For one of the few times in his political career, the former governor violated one of his timeworn political axioms.

The successful candidate must garner three-fourths of the votes. Chandler received the necessary twelve votes. He quickly accepted the offer to become commissioner for seven years at an annual salary of $50,000. Thus Lausche experienced his baptism in dealing with the political world of professional baseball.

Chandler conducted the affairs of major league baseball with flair, in contrast to the moralistic and conservative style of the late Judge Landis. In the next five years a mixture of new and old owners questioned Chandler's ability to continue as commissioner. After Landis's death, the owners had determined never to have another *czar*, and Happy Chandler did not prove sufficiently pliant. The Kentuckian encountered several serious issues during his tenure. One issue was integration of black players at the major league level, and Chandler took his stand, "If a black boy can make it in Okinawa and Guadalcanal," he told a black reporter, "hell, he can make it in baseball."[10] Other contentious issues for the owners and for Chandler surfaced with the exodus of seventeen major leaguers to play in the Mexican League in the postwar years. By 1950 professional baseball encountered attacks by the House Judiciary Committee on the study of monopoly power in professional baseball. The players were agitating for a pension plan, and talk about the formation of a player's association escalated. When Chandler began in 1949 to allocate $1 million annually from broadcast rights to the World Series and the All-Star games to the player's pensions in defiance of the owners, he sealed his own fate.[11]

Two years later (1951), the owners relieved Chandler of his duties. Again Lausche's name came to the forefront as a leading candidate for commissioner. Backroom politics over who would be chosen flourished. On February 10, 1951, the Columbus *Dispatch* reported that an important Washington official predicted flatly that Lausche would be the next baseball chieftain. "Lausche will be the next commissioner of baseball," the spokesman declared, "I'd bet my house on that."[12] When asked, Lausche feigned innocence about the issue, "Except for what has been told me by the newspapermen, I have no knowledge of what has been reported."[13]

The politicking continued through the summer months. In July, Branch Rickey, a native Ohioan and then vice president of operations for the Pittsburgh Pirates, wrote a letter concerning the commissionership to Del Webb, vice president and major stockholder of the New York Yankees. "My first name I care to submit...is George Trautman [President of the National Association of Professional Baseball Leagues, otherwise known as the Minor Leagues]. The second name is Governor Lausche of Ohio. I do not know him. I have never met him, but I think I know a lot about him. He is qualified." [14] Rickey knew that Trautman would not be considered because he was Jewish. Rickey's prestige and outward successes began to slip when he took over as vice president of operations for the Pittsburgh Pirates in 1950. Still his recommendations carried considerable clout.

Lausche could not disguise his interest in this opportunity. The Governor had now changed his reply to questioners about the position. Asked by newsmen if he had been approached officially, Lausche said, "In the past when the question has been asked, I have said 'No,' now I say, ' No comment.'" The position paid $65,000 yearly; he earned $20,000 as Governor. The so-called confirmed candidate traveled to New York in August to huddle with owners of several clubs, including the New York Yankees and New York Giants who, "just wanted to meet him." [15] The Governor's enthusiasm seemed to wane on his return to Columbus. Lausche knew he did not command the necessary twelve votes to win nomination.

In a somewhat surprise move on September 16, 1951, Governor Lausche withdrew his name from consideration for the commissionership. No doubt Ohio Republicans were sorely disappointed with his decision. As always, Lausche covered his tracks well. "In truth, I would like very much to take [the job], but I have a responsibility as governor which I cannot abandon with any moral justification." [16] The Governor's great pride was an important factor in his decision. Confidantes believed that Lausche would prefer to withdraw his name and believe in his own mind that he could have won the appointment rather than remain in the race and face defeat. In the fall of 1951, the owners appointed Ford Frick, a former sportswriter, one-time ghostwriter for Babe Ruth, and National League President since 1934, to the top spot in baseball. Lausche continued holding his abiding interest in baseball, but an opportunity to serve as baseball commissioner was now a thing of the past.

In revisiting 1946 and his jobless circumstances, what was Lausche to do for gainful employment? For one of the few times in his political career, the former Governor violated one of his timeworn political axioms. He accepted a position as counsel for a powerful lobby, the Association for Railway Progress, led by tycoon Robert R. Young, President of Allegheny Corporation and the Chesapeake and Ohio Railroad. This new organization had changed its name to the Association of American Railroads. Young's future plans envisioned a nationwide development of the railroad-transportation systems. The entrepreneur gained control of the New

York Central Railroad in 1954. Young's plans then went awry. Despondent over New York Central's financial difficulties Young committed suicide on January 25, 1958, in the billiard room of his Palm Beach residence.[17] In Lausche's 1953 message to the Ohio General Assembly, Lausche warned legislators to be aware of special-interest lobbyists. "There is no registered spokesman for the general public," he beseeched, and "unless you and I act as the people's spokesmen, the millions of Ohioans who placed their trust in us will be powerless and defenseless."[18] Lausche railed against the political influence of lobbyists throughout his political career. His affiliation with the railway lobby brought repercussions years later.

Likely Lausche would have remained in his position as lobbyist for the Association for Railway Progress had not fate turned his head in the personage of Ray T. Miller, his long-time political rival. The powerful Miller, still chairman of the Cuyahoga County Democratic Party, believed he possessed enough political clout to capture the Democratic primary election for governor. In early 1948 with the support of trusted local party hacks, he declared his candidacy. Naturally, this decision caught Lausche's attention. In no way could the former Governor allow his archrival's candidacy to proceed without a challenge. In a matter of days Lausche threw his hat in the ring. Now the battle began for party endorsements.

Miller lined up unions and numerous state party leaders in his behalf, taking advantage of Lausche's past difficulties with union leadership and so-called party bossism. Several behind-the-scene machinations took place in both political camps. Frazier Reams, former state welfare director during Lausche's administration, bowed out of the primary race. Divided opinion emerged among party regulars as to who made what deal in reference to Reams' departure. One theory suggested that, if there was a field of only two candidates, the stage was set for regular party support to line up behind Miller rather than to be split amongst several candidates. If this interpretation seemed valid, it was regarded as a direct blow to the former Governor who continued his attacks on machine politics in what Lausche hoped would be a popular appeal to the electorate. On the other side of the fence word leaked out that Lausche met with Reams several times in 1947. He may have convinced Reams that his own nomination could be enhanced if the field included only Miller and himself. Reams evidently concurred with this line of reasoning and yielded to Lausche's wishes.[19]

An additional factor added confusion to the coming election. The National Democratic Headquarters did not look kindly upon a prospective intra-party fracas in Ohio, in what political scientists believed would be a pivotal state in the 1948 election. President Truman, a likely bet to be nominated, and national Democratic chairman J. Howard McGrath both knew the President faced an up-hill battle (although several revisionist historians considered Truman the favorite) to win the 1948 election. McGrath expressed consternation over political upheaval and insisted that President Truman stay out of the fray until Miller and Lausche settled who would control the Democratic Party in Ohio.[20]

Lausche spent several months repairing his political fences in preparation for the primary election. Gene Hanhart, Tuscarawas County Democratic chairman who stood high in the Lausche administration, canvassed the eastern part of the state to ascertain the ex-Governor's political strength. Ray Augenbright from Mt. Sterling did the same politicking in the western part of Ohio. Hanhart later became state Democratic chairman with Lausche's blessings.

Thus began one of the most colorful elections in Ohio's political history. Lausche relaxed his iron hand over platform writers. He continued to assert that he would be a man free of any party dictates if elected for a second term. Newspapers published headlines like "Lone Wolf Lausche" and "Lausche Asserts Independence."[21] Still in control of the Cuyahoga County Democratic machine, Miller lined up nearly every Democratic leader in the state. The battle became reminiscent of the 1944 gubernatorial and presidential elections. Lausche, in one of his patented campaigns, hit the road covering county fairs and the picnic circuit. The primary election pitted Miller's organization with its army of doorbell ringers and bulging treasury against Lausche's personal charm.

The campaign denigrated into a smattering of mudslinging. Lausche fought off charges related to a state liquor scandal that erupted after his defeat in 1946. Allegations included the accusation that John Lokar (Lausche's secretary) and Charles J. Lausche (the ex-Governor's brother) received liquor permits at the last minute, ahead of hundreds of other applicants who had previously applied. Lausche was personally exonerated of any wrongdoing, but several of his associates flaunted the Governor's authority, casting his first-term administration under a cloud of suspicion in the waning weeks.[22] Seldom if ever was such questionable behavior leveled against Lausche during the remainder of his political career.

With the primary election rapidly approaching in May, Lausche charged Miller with boss control and party bossism. Miller retaliated, "When he [Lausche] ran for the mayor's office...he had full party backing. He had it again when he ran for governor and won the first time. He didn't have it when he ran a second time and was defeated. I guess it makes a lot of difference where you stand and [how] you look at something."[23] Miller declared that the party bosses who had backed Lausche before no longer joined the Lausche bandwagon because he publicly stated he didn't need their support. In Miller's opinion, Lausche deserted his party and claimed he was an independent.

Miller further responded to charges by Lausche that big gambling interests actively backed his campaign, "The only gamblers backing me," he laughed, "are the kind who play pinochle on Saturday nights in their own homes or in the homes of their friends.... I don't know a major gambler nor a major gambling interest in the state. Sure, I've heard of them, who hasn't?"[24]

The Cuyahoga County Democratic chieftain claimed that his opponent's gambling charge held about as much water as did his bossism. Miller insisted Lausche as Governor had only closed down one smalltime slot machine operation at Brady Lake, a small resort southeast of Cleveland. Public opinion had forced his hand on this closure. Lausche again countered with strong remarks about bossism insisting, "in the interest of democracy, it is essential that the members of our political parties be given the opportunity to select their standard-bearers without the compulsion that comes from the gaping shoguns held by political overlords."[25]

Republicans delighted at the verbal bashing by these two opponents, assuming it would be of great value to Herbert's chances for a second-term victory. Two other candidates filed for the Democrat primary: Joseph Terok of Youngstown and Robert Cox from Millersburg. Neither hopeful influenced the final vote count. Nor, in fact, did Miller make a viable challenge in the primary election. The former Cleveland mayor learned the harsh truth of Lausche's ability to appeal to grassroot voters over the heads of party leaders. The challenger carried 87 of 88 counties, including Cuyahoga County. Ray Miller relinquished his power in state politics. Lausche left no doubt who owned the Democratic Party in Ohio.

Having learned a lesson from his defeat in 1946, Lausche closed ranks with Democratic Party leaders, both at the state level and at the national level. Now the titular head of the statewide Democratic Party, Lausche urged delegates to select Eugene H. Hanhart as state Democratic chairman. The delegates acceded to Lausche's request with little dissent. Hanhart proved to be the balance wheel Lausche lacked during his first term in office. The smart, personable insurance agent from Dover, nicknamed *Cheese*, knew state politics intimately, and equally important, he understood Lausche's political philosophy. Although his personal staff never exceeded more than three people, he countered the well-oiled Republican organization with some semblance of party unity, at least as far as the race for governor was concerned. He later became Lausche's contact person concerning patronage in Washington, DC.

⌒

GOVERNOR TOM HERBERT EASILY WON THE BLESSINGS of the Republican Party to run unopposed for a second term. The two Clevelanders waged an intense battle for the top political job in Ohio. Lausche carried on a perpetual campaign in small Ohio towns, demonstrating he was a man of the people, fighting to save the taxpayer's money and preserve noble American virtues. He remained a political maverick, claiming at a rally in Youngstown, "A Democrat ought not to vote for a bad Democrat. Nor should a Republican vote for a bad Republican." He emphasized, "Your selection should be made only on the basis of what is best for your country and my country."[26] Lausche attacked Herbert's two-year administrative term claiming the Governor had lost $37 million in federal matching funds designated for highway construction in Ohio. The former governor further charged that Herbert spent $26 million more than Lausche had spent in his two years in office.

He criticized a strip-mining control law passed as a "shotgun acceptance of an honorable responsibility to preserve land."[27] Restoration of land mutilated by destructive mining techniques remained one of Lausche's prime targets throughout his political career. He initiated a major statewide program of planting trees that snowballed during his tenure as governor. Not easily swayed Lausche listened to the pleas for soil conservation from friends, particularly from author and conservationist Louis Bromfield and William Stinchcomb, the father and directing genius of the Cleveland Metroparks System.

Herbert fired back at Lausche's charges, describing eight specific pledges he carried out while in office, including for the first time in Ohio history legislation regulating strip mining. The Governor took credit for disbursement of a bonus to over 575,000 World War II veterans. This legislature provided for increased state aid to public schools. Lausche countered that his administration laid the foundation for passage of these bills.

A few days before the election, the Cleveland *Plain Dealer,* the largest newspaper in Ohio, endorsed Herbert for re-election. This endorsement came primarily because of Lausche's espousal of President Truman for re-election. The editorial asserted the President "represents the worst surviving aspects of the New Deal and who would extend the power of the federal government further into the lives of the American people." The editors maintained that in a realistic comparison, "We are convinced that Herbert is the superior of the two candidates in the management of the executive branch of the state government."[28] The Cleveland *News* and most southern Ohio dailies, including the Cincinnati *Enquirer,* came out in support of Herbert.

The majority of Ohio's small town papers donned the guise of independence, with a proclivity to support Republican candidates. This disturbing trend failed to bother Lausche, who over the years received the moniker of newspaper candidate because of his excellent press relations. He could always count on the support of the powerful Seltzer of the Cleveland *Press.* When Lausche remarked shortly before the general election that he believed President Truman would be elected, the Columbus *Citizen* defended the gubernatorial challenger's stance, "It's too late to pin any New Deal labels on Lausche now. His own record of independence and honest conviction...is too well known for the voters to be fooled."[29]

For all practical purposes, the gubernatorial campaign ended on Saturday, October 30 when the two candidates met, shook hands, and outlined their platforms at the Cleveland City Club forum. Lausche reiterated his pledge to political independence, "if elected I would be a free man, with no commitments to business or to labor, with no promises made to political bosses. I would give a square deal to the people according to the dictates of my intellect and conscience."[30]

The political battle between Lausche and Herbert presented Ohio voters with much food for thought. The gubernatorial contest served as an interesting contrast to the presidential foray. The public became caught up in one of the most exciting and thoroughly analyzed national elections in American political annals. What position would the politically independent Lausche adopt with President Harry S. Truman? He was well known for his reticence to be a party man or to align himself with regular Democratic Party members, particularly a strong party man like Truman. Nearly all political barometers predicted a Republican victory after sixteen years of Democratic leadership in the White House.

Several revisionist historians have argued that President Truman actually held the favored position prior to the 1948 election. Historian Harold I. Gullan argued that Truman had ample justification to point with pride when he delivered his third State of the Union address on January 7, 1948. The nation enjoyed virtually full employment. Fourteen million more people held jobs than in 1938. During a single decade (1938–48) the nation's output of goods and services increased by two-thirds, the average income by more than 50 percent. The gross national product rose ten percent in 1947 alone. Inflation declined to three percent in 1948, and the housing shortage appeared to ease off. The United States demonstrated more prosperity and power than at any time in its history.[31]

> *"We were told quite candidly by people close to him [Lausche], that he had bipartisan appeal, and he could see no point in linking his name with a sure loser like Harry S. Truman."*

Millions of veterans enjoyed the benefits of the GI Bill, especially the educational component and opportunity for low-cost loans. As measured by public opinion polls, fear of international Communism gradually replaced domestic problems as the primary concern of the majority of Americans. The administration's firm stand on foreign policy met with general approval. In particular, Truman gained approbation for his proposal to extend foreign aid to Turkey and Greece in 1947 and to thwart the possibility of Communist intrusion into those countries bordering the Iron Curtain.[32]

During Truman's first term, Lausche occasionally spoke critically of the President's *Fair Deal* programs, including *give-away* legislation and liberal policies toward labor. "The State," Lausche insisted, "can give no more than it receives through taxes. And if we complain, it is because we have been led [by Washington] to expect too much."[33] The Truman administration became wary of any political assistance from budget-conscious Lausche.

Republican standard-bearer Thomas E. Dewey carried Ohio in 1944 and seemed certain to carry the Buckeye State again. To his later regret, he did not actively campaign in Ohio. At one point while at a railway stop in Ohio, Dewey failed to bother stepping out onto the rear platform, but sat in his compartment with his window blind drawn. Even after having been told that a crowd outside hoped to catch a glimpse of him, the challenger did not bother to raise his blind.[34]

THE EVER-CAUTIOUS LAUSCHE EXTENDED LITTLE or no commitment to the national ticket early in the campaign. Truman accepted the Democratic nomination in mid-July in steamy Philadelphia. He began a series of whistle-stop treks across the country, attempting to jump-start what looked like an impossible task to unite a fractured Democratic Party. Thus he endeavored to avail himself of a chance to win the election. His last major jaunt, which began on September 14, lasted 33 days and covered over 21,000 miles by rail. Lausche's independent stance began to waver during the final month of the campaign. The Truman bandwagon began to pick up steam. Increasingly larger crowds cried out "Give 'em hell, Harry."[35] On a cold and rainy Monday, October 11, Truman continued his barnstorming trip beginning in Cincinnati and criss-crossing through Ohio. Spirits among the Truman entourage appeared subdued. The fight was uphill all the way. As formidable a Republican stronghold as any of the forty-eight states, Ohio posed a serious challenge. Twenty-five electoral votes rested in the balance. Nineteen of twenty-three Ohio Congressmen carried the Republican banner. Robert Taft (Mr. Republican) and John Bricker held Senate seats, and of course, Governor Herbert augmented the overwhelming Republican majority.

When the coy Lausche received word of the large crowds Truman attracted at every whistle stop, he reconsidered his campaign strategy. Margaret Truman, the President's daughter, recalled the scene, "We were told quite candidly by people close to him [Lausche], that he had bipartisan appeal, and he could see no point in linking his name with a sure loser like Harry S. Truman."[36] Only after considerable verbal arm-twisting did Lausche agree to board the *Ferdinand Magellan* at all. He joined the campaign train outside Dayton, but made it clear he was getting off as soon as the train reached the city. The entourage arrived at the first whistle stop of the day. The small town with 7,000 in attendance roared their approval of the President in the middle of the morning. Lausche could not believe his eyes. Then came Dayton. The crowd was practically standing on each other's shoulders at the station, and the overflow of people spilled out into the streets to stop traffic in all directions.

Margaret Truman continued in a lighter vein, "Is this the way all crowds have been?" Mr. Lausche asked cautiously. "Yes," Dad said, "but this is smaller than we had in most states." Mr. Lausche swallowed hard. "Well," he said, "this is the biggest crowd I ever saw in Ohio."[37] Miss Truman said that, when they pulled out of Dayton on the way to Akron, Lausche was still aboard the train.

Lausche continued to campaign with the President the rest of the trip to the mutual benefit of both candidates. However, in doing so he left himself vulnerable to attack from Herbert. The Governor charged Lausche with divorcing independence to marry the Fair Deal. In an obvious attempt to emphasize the need for ticket splitting, Dewey–Lausche buttons circulated.[38] Lausche admitted he had earlier joined the chorus of naysayers who believed Truman faced defeat. "I didn't think he had a chance," he recalled, "We took a train through the state near the end of the campaign and no one on the train thought he had a chance. Only Truman thought he had a chance."[39]

Regardless of what Lausche or the general public thought about Truman's chances, the President sensed he would pull a stunning upset. Speaking in Akron on October 11, after a daylong trip across Ohio giving speeches at eleven stops, Truman exhorted, "I have lived a long time—sixty-four years—and I have traveled a lot," he told the huge crowd, "but I have never seen such turnouts all over this great country of ours.... The Republicans have the propaganda and the money, but we have the people and the people have the votes. That's why we're going to win!"[40] While stopped in Willard prior to his visit in Akron, Truman said, "And I think you are going to elect Frank Lausche Governor of Ohio."[41]

By the end of a whirlwind day of campaigning, Lausche began to realize that a groundswell for Truman might result in a major upset victory. For one who seldom overtly backed any candidate, Lausche came forth with a ringing endorsement of the president in a near poetic statement, much to the surprise of many Ohio politicians, "Harry Truman possesses a soul that reflects the soul of America. He is a good man, a fearless man. He has tried to conduct the affairs of this country so as to bring the greatest good to the greatest number. I will cast my ballot for him in the belief that the nation will be secure by his guidance."[42]

The two men joined hands as the campaign came to an exciting climax. This statement of support represented the only time during the campaign that Lausche mentioned Truman's name.[43] Lausche's unexpected show of support for the incumbent President caused interesting reactions. One political foe later claimed that Lausche's backing came at a time when he mistakenly believed no reporters were present. Lausche expressed fear the next day that his support of Truman would hurt him politically. Another wit suggested, "People were so stunned to hear Lausche praising another Democrat in public that they went out and voted for Truman in a daze."[44] Years later Lausche—who often flipped the coin or straddled the fence—made no bones about his opinion of Truman, placing the former President at the head of the class as a person and as a President. "He was a remarkable individual. He is the outstanding president of our time, along with Reagan. Truman and Reagan were the only ones with the guts to take on the spendthrifts."[45] In contrast Lausche no doubt would not have appreciated a remark reputedly attributed to the former President in the 1950s, speaking of Lausche, "You just can't trust the b_ _ _ _ _ d."[46]

The President and Lausche would join together one more time before the election. This occasion brought on another clash between Lausche and his nemesis, Ray T. Miller. The situation developed when Truman's seventeen-car campaign train arrived in Cleveland on October 26. The President had ridden across northern Ohio and planned to give one of his last major speeches at Public Hall.

Miller, still supported by the old guard of the Democratic Party in parts of Ohio, claimed Lausche received an invitation to accompany the President's entourage from Toledo, but declined. Additional contentious political maneuvering occurred when Truman arrived in Cleveland. Lausche and his wife Jane avoided scheduled social events at the Hotel Cleveland. They subsequently joined the President in a motorcade to Public Hall. Miller argued that Lausche planned to ride to Public Hall in his own car, but when he saw the size of the crowd, decided to ride with President Truman. The stench of petty politics overshadowed this conclave.

Conflicting stories bewildered Alvin Silverman of the *Plain Dealer*. The popular political columnist claimed witnesses for Lausche insisted "their man" did not receive an invitation to ride on the presidential train. Neither did he have any opportunity to be in the spotlight, nor to deliver a few words at the biggest Democratic rally in Ohio. Miller wanted to show the president who ran the political show in Cleveland. Witnesses for Miller and he himself argued that Lausche received invitations to participate in the train excursion, reception, and rally. Miller contended that the fellow Clevelander gave no intention of joining festivities until it became too late to alter arrangements. The outcome of this latest imbroglio between two strong-willed politicians demonstrated that Miller still ran the Democratic organization in Cuyahoga County, but Lausche was the favorite of the galleries. In an effort to plead his case, Miller sent a letter to all county precinct committee members explaining the upshot of this political altercation.[47]

Silverman's poetic prose described the scene, "with a twist and flutter of his left hand, Harry S. Truman, the poor man's doctor...stitched a gash in the Cleveland Democratic body caused by another collision between Frank J. Lausche and Ray T. Miller."[48] While speaking before 15,000 supporters, the President motioned and whispered Lausche to his feet to acknowledge tremendous applause. He told the crowd, "Just consider the man who will be your next governor...a man of the people, who, like Cleveland's great mayors, Tom Johnson and Tom Burke, thinks with his heart and his head."[49] If Lausche felt shunned by the Democratic old guard in his hometown, the president's words echoed like music to his ears.

For decades, political prognosticators emitted the slogan, *As Maine goes, so goes the nation*. While Maine's peculiar election date in the northernmost New England state assisted political forecasters, actual results—particularly since 1900—indicate Ohio might better serve as an accurate political barometer for predicting presidential winners. During the twentieth century, Ohio voters delivered the electoral tallies to the winning candidate in twenty-five of twenty-seven presidential elections. Ironically, one notable exception occurred in 1944 when challenger Thomas E. Dewey with Ohioan John W. Bricker as his running mate carried Ohio, although losing the national election to Franklin D. Roosevelt. Overall, Ohio voters aligned with losing presidential candidates in only ten contests (out of 51 elections) since the first electoral votes were cast for Thomas Jefferson in 1804.[50]

Political scientists make a case for Ohio's pivotal position, noting, "Presidential campaigns for this century [twentieth] have all assumed Ohio as one of the battlegrounds where victories are significant and defeats costly.[51] The 2004 election results are a prime example. The historical evolution of a strong two-party system dominates state politics. This fact—coupled with a traditional disposition to split tickets and to independent voting—adds significance to the pivotal nature of Ohio politics.[52] Truman, a historian in his own right, knew that to win the election, he must do well in three key states: California, Illinois, and particularly Ohio who commanded 78 electoral votes.[53] In view of supposedly overwhelming odds facing Truman in Ohio, historian Richard Davies questioned why the President bothered to campaign in the Buckeye State. In 1944 Dewey captured the state against a formidable foe (Franklin D. Roosevelt) by twelve thousand votes. With a solid core of Dewey supporters theoretically lined up, Truman's chances seemed nil.[54]

Likely Dewey miscalculated his strength, or lack of it, in Ohio in his carefully structured campaign. He refused to campaign in Ohio, although he twice crossed the state in daylight hours, only making a solitary speech in Cleveland. He was firmly convinced that Ohio was a sure thing. Nearly all political analysts contended that, "Truman had his back to the wall in Ohio."[55] In spite of the dreary predictions, Truman worked harder for votes in Ohio than in any other state, with the possible exception of New York.[56]

The weather throughout the country, including Ohio, was generally fair and cool on Election Day, November 2, 1948. Truman returned to his home in Independence, Missouri, while Lausche and Herbert remained in Cleveland, several blocks from one another other. Neither Lausche nor Herbert received endorsements from the AFL or CIO, exacerbating the pollster's difficulty in determining who would be the recipient of a large bloc of labor votes. The Buckeye voters left little doubt as to their choice for governor. Lausche returned to the statehouse with a resounding victory. The former Governor garnered 1,619,775 votes to Herbert's 1,398,514 votes, a winning margin of over 221,000 votes. President Truman also captured the twenty-five electoral votes from Ohio, but in contrast to Lausche's large victorious margin, the President defeated Dewey by a narrow count of 7,000 votes. Lausche amassed a majority vote of 53.6 percent and carried 35 counties out of 88, his greatest show of geographical strength to date. The re-elected Governor carried all the heavily populated regions, with the exception of Hamilton County (Cincinnati). In industrialized Mahoning County (Youngstown), Lausche garnered a majority of over 65 percent. The native Clevelander failed to reestablish his large majority in Cuyahoga County, compensating for this decrease by picking up new support in rural areas, particularly southern agricultural counties.[57] The incidence of split ticket voting meant President Truman accumulated 167,000 fewer votes than Lausche. Part of this difference resulted from third-party candidate Henry Wallace, who captured 37,000 votes. Dixiecrat candidate Strom Thurmond did not appear on the Ohio ballot.

Political pundits have spent considerable time contemplating and writing thousands of words attempting to ascertain either why Truman won, or how Dewey lost, the election. A prime reason for the upset (and general consensus supports the thesis about Truman's upset, in spite of Gullan's revisionist assertion of the upset that wasn't) was the switch in the farm vote in the Midwestern states of Ohio, Illinois, Iowa and Wisconsin. Secondly, one may argue as Davies does that Truman's whistle-stop campaign, particularly in Ohio, became an important factor in the final victorious vote. An additional point showed up in an analysis of Ohio voters by the *New York Times*. Many Roosevelt haters, such as the Coughlinites and those opposed to a third- or fourth-term candidate, now switched to support Truman. Dewey received the harvest of Roosevelt haters in 1944, but not in 1948.[58] Finally, a strong case can be made, particularly in Lausche's case, for accepting the reverse—coattails thesis—that instead of the President pulling local candidates on his coattails, Truman rode to victory on the coattails of more popular statewide candidates. For example Lausche won the governorship by a 214,000 margin in votes over Truman's total. Adlai Stevenson won the governorship in Illinois by 560,000, and Paul Douglas gained a senate seat by 400,000 votes. However, Truman squeezed through with only a 33,000-vote margin. Similar scenarios occurred in Iowa, Colorado, and Tennessee.[59] It is impossible to completely establish the efficacy of Lausche's impact upon Truman's slight margin of victory in Ohio. Lausche rebounded with election results that amounted to a 260,000 vote turnaround (He lost by 40,000 votes in 1946). Logic suggests that the overwhelming surplus of Lausche's accumulated votes influenced several thousand voters to place their "X" by Truman's name, giving him a victorious margin. This election presented another niche of support in the claim of as Ohio goes, so goes the nation.

Many state Republican leaders attributed the Lausche victory to a highly successful whispering campaign against Herbert. Rumors circulated that Herbert suffered from a drinking problem. Although the merit of this claim seems dubious on the surface, Herbert insisted five years later that malicious gossip was the major cause of his defeat. He commented, "The most consistent lie was that I had been drinking heavily and was unfit to be reelected Governor."[60] One could argue that such a rumor could influence voters in pious, rural sections of the state. Herbert won election to the Ohio Supreme Court in 1956, but a severe stroke prevented his seeking re-election.

Lausche received overwhelming support from blue-collar workers, in spite of reticence from labor organizations to endorse him. This labor backing became a decisive factor in returning large industrial populations to the Lausche fold. Labor patronage became an enigma for the returning Governor in the next two years. For one of the few times in the second half of the twentieth century, Democrats captured all state offices except state treasurer, Don Ebright, winner of a sixth term. For the first time in a decade, Democrats gained control of the Ohio State Assembly.

Lausche ignored the rumors about Herbert and readied himself for his second term as Governor. He hoped to correct some shortcomings of his first term. Lausche inherited a more amenable general assembly to work with, although the Democrats held only a one-vote edge in the 33-member Senate. The Democrats gained a five-vote edge in the 135-member House of Representatives. Any number of possible circumstances could tip the scales. For instance in the case of a legislator's death, a replacement would not be made until the following election year. An ill-timed absence could mean a legislator or Senator might miss an opportunity to vote, or a caucus brawl might persuade some wounded member he could do better making a coalition deal with the more experienced and more regular Republican group—a vote in exchange for a choice committee job—could tip the scales.

Lausche's relations with his legislative body, both as Mayor and as Governor, had never been free of acrimony. He hesitated to crack the whip, allowing veteran legislators to go their own way and present roadblocks to Lausche's proposed legislative agenda. Lausche had received criticism during his first term as governor for administering a lax and less than professional office. Now more experienced, the comeback governor intended to change that image. He had the rarity of support of a state cabinet made up of nearly all Democrats. State Democratic Chairman Eugene Hanhart stood by on the sidelines with valuable counsel when requested. Lausche learned that running a state government required some delegation of authority and that yes-men do not necessarily make good department chiefs. Lausche appointed his good friend, Ralph Locher as his executive secretary. A notorious loner, the Governor resisted all political pressure and confided only with Hanhart and Mayor Thomas Burke on major appointments.

Like most previous Governors, Lausche presented a program of action to the Ohio General Assembly. His proposal contained several items taxpayers like to hear, such as no increase in taxes, an equitable system of taxation and distribution of tax revenues, and an attack upon commercialized gambling. Beyond these points in his inaugural address, Lausche spoke in generalities about prevailing social concerns with a New or Fair Deal flair. He made mention of the need for adequate protection against the hazards of unemployment, adequate provision for the disabled, financial aid for the aged, elimination of slum areas, an intelligent conservation program, a welfare and hospital building program, and a highway improvement program to counter an increasingly inadequate road system.[61]

Lausche encountered legislative troubles immediately after taking the oath of office. With apologies to former President George H.W. Bush, Governor Lausche—as was his bent—insisted the legislators watch his lips carefully when he proclaimed "no new taxes." Senator Margaret Mahoney, a three-time Democratic Senator from

Cleveland, became the first woman elected Senate President *pro tempore*. Lausche submitted to Senator Mahoney and her legislative colleagues a biennial budget of over $649 million, barely a fraction of the $30 billion budget submitted to the Senate in the early 1990s.[62]

Characteristically, Lausche's budget contained no request for new or increased taxes. Almost immediately the Governor and Senator Mahoney faced open rebellion in the legislative ranks on both sides of the aisle. A bipartisan group of Senators pushed through the Senate Rules Committee proposals that added $47 million to the budget and required no new taxes—proposals opposed both by Lausche and by Mahoney, who chaired the rebellious rules committee. One proposal increased teacher salaries by $25 a month, these funds coming from a special appropriation of $27 million. Another proposal called the Youngstown Plan directed the state tax on intangible personal property to the local government fund and increased receipts of the funds from the state sales tax by about $6 million annually.

Lausche met personally—and unsuccessfully—with the rebel Senators, and then went public with a stinging attack. "When I submitted my budget, the opposition in the Legislature labeled it as an extravagant one. Subsequently, we had the revealing spectacle of one of the very men who vigorously attacked me setting into motion the machinery for the passage of a bill that will spend $47.5 million of new tax money."[63] This vitriolic remark was directed mainly at Republican Senator Roscoe Walcott of Columbus (who received support in the bipartisan uprising in the rules committee by fellow Republican Senator Fred Adams of Bowling Green) and Democratic Senators Clinton Jackson of Youngstown and Emmett R. Guthrie of Coshocton. Lausche insisted that the legislators' package would disrupt his budget plans, unbalance the budget, and increase state taxes, and Walcott, Jackson, and Guthrie were aware of it.[64] Eventually the teachers received their pay increases, and the Youngstown plan of an intangible tax was earmarked for the local government fund. Lausche won over the reticent Senators and virtually set in stone the precedent of the executive branch initiating—or not initiating—major taxes in the Ohio budget process. Rarely would a future legislator initiate a major new tax bill, especially if the governor was calling for new or increased taxes. This practice was commonplace in subsequent administrations, including Lausche's remaining tenure.

Lausche actually requested the largest budget in the state's history. Three months after the request, the Governor launched a drastic reduction in his economic program. This rigid retrenchment occurred because of an anticipated shortfall of $40 million from projected revenue of nearly $560 million. Lausche refrained from sending the state into any deficit spending program. Nor did he wish to tap the $95 million in reserve funds. Early in his second term, approximately $75 million were forecast for projected capital improvements. By March 1, 1949, $54 million in contracts were awarded for university dormitories and classrooms, power plants, mental hospitals, general hospitals, tuberculosis hospitals, conservation projects, and state buildings. At this point fellow Democrat and State Treasurer, "Jumpin Joe" Ferguson, proved to be a thorn in Lausche's side. Late in 1949 he notified George B. Sowers, director of the department of public works, that payments for contracted work would not be forthcoming. Ferguson insisted that his office needed more funds to hire a large staff of inspectors to check and verify the quality of labor and materials being furnished to the state of Ohio for public works. This political ploy by the ludicrous state treasurer provided little comfort to Lausche and Sowers. The Governor expressed relief when the popular Ferguson chose to run for a U.S. Senate seat against Republican Robert Taft in 1950.

If the die had not already been cast, Lausche's conservative political philosophy became ever more transparent during his second term. He established himself as a reactive politician rather than a proactive one. His penchant for pinching the penny held favor with taxpayers. Unfortunately more and more public-financed state entities lost ground in facility renovation and in pursuit of a progressive agenda. The country's economy demonstrated strength after World War II, and money was available. Many state institutions cried out for rehabilitation and facility improvement because little or nothing had been accomplished prior to and during the war years. Enterprising innovations and new state programs met with resistance as part of Lausche's conservative *modus operandi*. Lausche knew how to play the political game, avoid deals, and maintain his political independence without losing the public's confidence.

⌒

THE GOVERNOR OFTEN PLAYED BOTH ENDS AGAINST THE MIDDLE. In March 1949 he wrote to Frank Pacy, director of the federal budget, complaining that a cut in the budget for internal state flood control constituted a major mistake and was a penny-pinching policy. Lausche referred specifically to the need for $1 million to complete the Mill Creek Valley flood control program near Cincinnati and the Rocky Fork Reservoir in Highland County, which directly affected Chillcothe and Portsmouth. He argued that, during the period from 1936 to 1949, Ohio had not received a fair share of the $3.7 million distributed during this time span. The Governor's plea also went to the subcommittee on appropriations in the U.S. House of Representatives. Funds were soon approved to complete the flood control portion of the reclamation project.

Demonstrating political savvy, Lausche seldom missed an opportunity to seek favorable publicity. However, sometimes his mission backfired. The Governor generated mixed responses when he questioned whether Ohioans receiving state unemployment benefits used these funds to travel to Florida or California during the winter months. His query resulted from a statistical report, which had reached his desk. His staff had not obtained factual reasons for the migration to warmer climates. The Toledo *Blade* chastised Lausche for a less-than-thorough analysis of the exodus of snowbirds (health or associated reasons). The *Blade* recommended that Lausche seek information about this issue through the fraud unit of the Ohio State Bureau of Unemployment. If infractions occurred, factual evidence enhanced Lausche's stance, rather than relying on a less-than-reliable statistical study.[65]

The Democratic-controlled General Assembly assisted Lausche with the approval of several legislative initiatives. Having failed in previous attempts, the Governor succeeded in steering through the assembly a bill to create an Ohio State Department of Natural Resources. To avoid duplication among several state agencies, this department absorbed agencies dealing with public parks, shore erosion, forestry, wildlife and conservation in general. The Ohio Natural Resources Act became a model for several other states.

With Lausche's approval in 1949, the state assembly authorized the establishment of the Ohio Turnpike Commission, one of the largest projects ever undertaken by the state government. This commission accepted responsibility for toll road construction, particularly a $336 million turnpike across northern Ohio. Legislation coordinated the municipal court system and administrative procedure under a single law, as well as establishing the fiscal year to begin on July first. The assembly rewrote the decadent mental institution commitment law and approved a badly needed mental hygiene program.

The Governor's relations with labor leaders remained strained during his second term. Although Lausche kept an arm's length from organized labor, he continued to receive support from average Joe workers in the factories. The general assembly threatened to pass a law to repeal an existing law prohibiting public employees from going on strike. The Governor vowed to veto the bill if it reached his desk. The bill died in the Ohio Senate.

⌒

FEW CRITICS ACCUSED THE PARSIMONIOUS AND HARD-WORKING Lausche of extravagance or of being a slacker in his gubernatorial responsibilities. He lacked well-organized administrative skills and made up for these shortcomings by working long hours. Ralph Locher called Lausche a working Governor. "He has no outside business or professional interests. Most important above all, though, is his unimpeachable honesty. He is honest in not only pecuniary matters but in the way he arrives at decisions. That is why people are willing to allow him to make decisions. They know he will call it as he sees it."[66] He relied on a small staff to cover for him when necessary (which sometimes meant a golf engagement).

A typical day at the Governor's mansion began at 5:30 or 6:00 a.m. when Lausche went through large stacks of mail himself and dictated replies into a Dictaphone until 8:00 a.m. He sipped coffee alone from a thermos bottle set out the night before. He finished dictating, and then went to his office, a short distance away at Broad and High Streets in the heart of Columbus. Oftentimes, he would retreat to a small room at the back of the mansion and play his violin for half an hour, if he was worried or had some particularly difficult problem.

Lausche often scheduled breakfast conferences with state officials. He remained in his office until 1:00–1:30 p.m., and then walked to a small out-of-the-way restaurant for lunch. Lunch normally included a sandwich, hamburgers or Limburger cheese with onions. Afternoons were filled with meetings or additional work in his office. He returned to the governor's mansion in late afternoon to walk one of his three family dogs. A story circulated, true or otherwise, that Lausche left his office lights on late in the evening to give taxpayers the impression that he was working late.

A low handicap golfer, Lausche primarily played golf at the Columbus Country Club or Scioto Country Club. Not opposed to drinking in the evening, the governor occasionally enjoyed a bit of bourbon, looked over more mail, dined with Jane, and went to bed by 8:30 p.m., where he studied more reports, read poetry, and was asleep by 9:30 p.m. There was seldom, if ever, social life at the mansion during the weekday evenings. Lausche slept until midnight, at which time he read newspapers or a book for an hour or so. Then he dropped off to sleep until daybreak.

Jane Lausche selected and purchased all of her husband's clothes, simply because he could not be bothered. He didn't try on the clothes she purchased, so Jane had the houseman try on the suits to be sure they fit properly. Jane related that she once bought the Governor a blue suit that fit him perfectly. She immediately bought another suit just like it, but did not tell him. She smilingly recalled, "He thought the one suit was holding up exceptionally well." She added he often did not even open his Christmas presents. "I gave him the same gift four years in succession."[67] The Governor sometimes took off on an out-of-town trip carrying only a toothbrush in his coat pocket. Many times he was observed walking with untied shoelaces.

Basically a shy person Lausche demonstrated joviality on those rare occasions when a party took place at the governor's mansion or when he accepted an invitation elsewhere. He liked a songfest and enjoyed telling stories—especially jokes on himself. Occasionally, though, his shyness backfired on him. He recalled going to a local hospital in Columbus to visit a sick friend. When he stopped at a reception desk for a visitor's card, the attendant said, "Oh, governor go right on up. Everyone knows you." He arrived at the elevator where a firm-jawed woman operator demanded his visitor's card. He replied weakly that he had been told he didn't need a card. "Are you a doctor?" asked the operator. "No" "Are you a patient" "No" "Then you gotta have a card. Who do you think you are anyway?" By now, the elevator was filled with impatient passengers, which forced the hesitant and embarrassed Lausche to reply softly, "I'm the governor." The operator gave him a frightened look, slammed the door and took him to the fifth floor without a single stop. Lausche squared his shoulders uncomfortably and stepped out, but as the door closed, he heard the operator apologize to other passengers whose floors had been missed. "Sorry, folks, but I didn't want to stall around with that guy. He's one of the nuts we got here—absolutely nuts!"[68]

Although Lausche loved to tell stories, he portrayed the behavior of a worrywart. In many respects a lonely man, he purposely avoided close personal relationships. "Sometimes he seems to trust no one," according to a long-time acquaintance. "He has a kind of phobia about the possibility of friendship influencing his decisions. If I recommended anybody for a job, he would refuse even to see the man—and might refuse even to speak to me again."[69] Whereas future Governor Republican James Rhodes was a gregarious, hand-slapping politician, Lausche was just his antithesis. Lausche maintained a reasonably close relationship with Seltzer of the Cleveland *Press* and Paul Bellamy and Tom Vail, editors of the Cleveland *Plain Dealer*. Jane occasionally arranged social get-togethers with the William Stinchcombs of Cleveland and the Louis Bromfields of Malabar Farm near Mansfield.

In researching five contemporary Ohio Governors, R. Dean Jachius uncovered additional information about Lausche's personal demeanor and views about personal finances. He viewed himself as "still in a low economic level. The fact is that when I became governor, I was on many notes and mortgages which were executed by me and my law partners back in the late 1920s in the purchase of land." Lausche realized that when he entered the Governor's office, "One is vested with tremendous power [and] there is a grave danger of that one becoming tyrannical and corrupt. I tried to guard myself from becoming a victim of power that corrupts. It brought my wife and I closer together. She was a great help to me in the management of the mansion."[70] Lausche added, "I did suffer the loss of support from many who wanted me to do things which I didn't believe I could morally and justifiably do, and I believe that was one of the reasons that I was eventually defeated in the [senatorial] primary [in 1968]."[71]

Two-year terms in the governor's office restricted efforts for long-range planning. In early 1950 Lausche and his fellow statehouse Democrats faced important issues in addition to promoting their own re-elections. Republican Senator Robert A. Taft also faced re-election. The senior Senator co-authored the controversial Taft-Hartley Bill, which among other things restricted the right for workers to strike. As a result Taft struck a nerve with organized labor. He had barely won election in 1944 against William G. Pickrel, a weak opponent from Dayton. Labor believed that with strong organization and a reputable candidate, Taft could be defeated. The AFL's International United Auto Workers believed they had an answer. At their regional meeting in November 1949 they started a Draft Lausche for Senator movement. A spokesman said, "If Ohio's Governor, Frank Lausche will run against Senator Robert Taft, we think we can win."[72]

Organized labor consented to smoke the political peace pipe with Lausche if he acquiesced to run against Taft. It was an unlikely marriage. Lausche had no intentions of becoming a labor candidate. Even before the Auto Workers plea, the Governor gave a hint of his intentions when he and Taft met on the speaker's platform at Ohio Wesleyan University after receiving honorary degrees. Lausche interjected into his prepared speech, "I might say, Senator Taft that I am deeply grateful to have this opportunity to be with you on this day.... It probably should be considered...that we ought not engage in any controversy in any way."[73]

This occasion and Lausche's comment did not deter national Democratic leaders from urging Lausche to forfeit desires for a third term, but rather to seek a United States Senate seat. Lausche declared for the last time via a telegram to the United Auto Workers that he would not be a senatorial candidate.[74] The connection between the *Down With Taft* campaign was not yet terminated. On the contrary, the Governor's comments would have far-reaching ramifications for the 1950 elections.

Governor Lausche opening the Ohio Turnpike, October 1, 1955. On right is James W. Shocknessy. (Courtesy of the Cleveland Plain Dealer. All rights reserved. Reprinted with permission.)

seven

Governor—Again,
and Again

"*He was not a bold man, the kind who would mount a quixotic campaign. Such had never been his style. If limited to one adjective to describe him, it might be 'calculated.' He did not take chances, which was one of the reasons he seemed reluctant to speak out on issues. He delayed decisions, perhaps more than he should have…he could be swift and decisive, but only when the odds were good.*

"*If Coolidge was known for anything, it was honesty, integrity, and incorruptibility. As far as the bosses were concerned, these hardly were the kinds of attributes they sought in a president. The bosses sought compliance from the candidate and Coolidge was too much of a loner.*"[1]

Historian Robert Sobel described Calvin Coolidge with this poignant characterization in his biography of the thirtieth President, *Coolidge, An American Enigma.* Sobel might well have been writing about Frank J. Lausche. The similarities in political style are stark. The Ohio Governor played his cards close to the vest. He repeatedly demonstrated that he did not require a cadre of advisors to give him direction in making political decisions. He became more taciturn with each passing year.

Despite his apparently strong position with voters, Lausche left little to chance when running for office. An experienced Ohio editor commented, "Why shouldn't he be successful? He works at making Frank Lausche successful 24 hours a day." Another observer who had for many years watched Lausche in action added, "He's a great actor. The public only sees him on the stage—the red-white-and blue patriot, the political maverick, independent, dedicated to the cause of humanity. What they do not see is Lausche shrewdly moving pieces of the political chessboard—self-centered, throwing over his party's faithful, a man of ruthless ambition."[2]

Lausche supporters countered this somewhat vitriolic portrayal of their man. In October 1950, Seltzer characterized the Governor as, "A man of deep, warm human sympathy and understanding. He likes people. He is eager to serve them and he has an independence of mind that makes him seek for any problem the solution that he conceives to be in the best interest of all the people, regardless of selfish or partisan pressures."[3]

The 1950, election provided another example whereby Lausche wouldn't necessarily act like a Democrat, and demonstrated his ability to work the political chessboard to his advantage. Although Lausche had declined an offer from organized labor to challenge Robert Taft for his Senate seat, Ohio labor leaders pursued other avenues to remove the co-author of the anti-labor Taft-Hartley law from office. The highly respected Murray T. Lincoln, from Taft's hometown of Cincinnati and head of the Ohio Farm Cooperative, appeared to be a likely candidate.

Lincoln agreed in principle to consider a run for the office, providing he received assurance from Lausche that the state Democratic organization would not interfere with his candidacy. This assurance was not to be. Every time the liberal Lincoln appeared ready to announce his candidacy, a spokesman from the Lausche camp hinted that the Governor might reconsider pursuing the Senate seat after all. Several years later a journalist reported that Lausche had met with Lincoln and Hulbert Taft (Robert Taft's cousin and publisher of the Cincinnati *Times-Star*) to persuade Lincoln not to run against Taft. Lausche replied immediately to this charge. In a letter to Hulbert Taft, Lausche claimed, "the statements which it contains are absolutely false. There never was a meeting in which Murray Lincoln, you and I were in attendance discussing whether Murray Lincoln should run for the Senate." Taft responded two days later, "I never had a meeting with Murray Lincoln to discuss the senatorial situation or for any other purpose. If you would like a statement backing up a denial from you, that would be all right with me."[4]

Lincoln determined that this in-fighting did not serve him well. He decided not to contest Joseph T. "Jumpin' Joe" Ferguson, a solidly entrenched party-man who had jumped into the senatorial contest. Shortly after Lincoln bowed out of the race, Lausche declared, "My petitions are being printed. I will be a candidate for the governorship."[5] The anti-Taft faction could not agree on anyone else. Finally, they chose Ferguson, the popular three-term state auditor.

Cries of *deal* emerged from labor forces. Taft denied such charges. Richard L. Maher, Cleveland journalist writing for *Nation*, pointed out, "Lausche could have done no more for Taft if the two men had a signed and sealed contract of mutual aid."[6] While not openly antagonistic toward Ferguson, Governor Lausche publicly refused to participate in any fund-raising campaigns for the state auditor.[7] He later refused to endorse Ferguson when officials at Democratic national headquarters offered to compensate handsomely the Lausche campaign treasury.[8]

For the most part the fifty-eight-year-old Ferguson carried on his campaign alone. The short and slight, sandy-haired politician became state auditor in 1937. Hard working, affable, careful with the state's money, a trait Lausche appreciated, the devout Catholic—he told voters in 1950 he had not missed a Sunday or holy day mass in 52 years—let few opportunities to publicize himself pass. He sponsored an outstanding softball team, the Ferguson State Auditors, which routinely won and brought him wide recognition. The state auditor sent out thousands of Christmas cards—100,000 by 1949—depicting his family and adding to his renown.[9] On the surface, Ferguson appeared to be a worthy opponent to the venerable Robert Taft. In reality, that was not the case. His crude and unsophisticated behavior and lack of knowledge about national and foreign affairs did not bode well in challenging the well-versed and powerful Taft. Syndicated columnist Stewart Alsop wrote, "As a representative of American liberal tradition, Ferguson is a joke."[10]

In June of 1950, Lausche further stirred the pot with a convoluted political utterance. He traveled to the Governor's conference at White Sulphur Spring, West Virginia, where a bipartisan group of Governors elected Lausche chairman. At the conference, the Ohio Governor's response to an interviewer's question dropped a bombshell of nationwide repercussions. He believed Ferguson had been a good and fearless auditor. Lausche felt the same way about Senator Taft as a public official, "My general predisposition would be to vote for the Democratic candidate.... I haven't heard if Mr. Ferguson or Senator Taft is going to vote for me. When I have determined the issue, I will vote for the candidate who will serve my nation best.... I will not allow party interests to overcome my interests in the country."[11]

Democrats nationwide expressed shock and anger over Lausche's endorsement of the Republican Senator. Sources believed that the Governor had a statement of endorsement for Taft in his pocket, but at the last minute switched to his more ambiguous remarks.[12] While in Ohio campaigning for Ferguson, Democratic National Chairman William Boyle curtly commented, "Any official has the right to vote for anyone he wants."[13] While speaking at a news conference a week after Lausche's statement, President Truman obviously directed his remarks at the Governor, commenting, "All real Democrats should support the Party's program and all duly selected nominees."[14]

Organized labor, as might be expected, voiced dismay and anger. Mathew Wall, second vice president of the AFL, accused the Governor of deserting his party, "I can only express regret that [Lausche] has not made up his mind. He's either for Taft or against him. He is for the workers or against them."[15] William Green, President of the AFL and Jack Kroll of the CIO's Political Action Committee threatened that labor would seek revenge at election time unless the Governor endorsed Ferguson outright.[16]

As the campaign wore on, Lausche assiduously avoided an open endorsement of fellow Democratic candidates. Insiders claimed it was an open secret that, in the privacy of his office, the Governor had more than once intimated that it would be *calamitous* if Senator Taft lost because "it would remove the strongest spokesman the minority party has in the Senate and thus would be a severe blow to the effective maintenance of the two-party system."[17] The unpredictable Lausche had committed political heresy. His overt expression of doubt about Ferguson's qualifications was bound to have an impact upon both Democratic and Republican voters. Lausche feared the mobilized 1.25 million union voters in Ohio might turn the tide against Taft. The strong-minded Governor deliberately risked these consequences. Added to the drama of this situation is the question of whether Lausche held a grudge against Ferguson. In 1945 (Lausche's first term as governor) he retained Herbert Defenbacher, former chief financial officer for Governor Bricker who had engineered the state surplus. The retention of the chief financial officer so irritated Ferguson that he refused to attend the Governor's inauguration.[18] Lausche respected Bricker for his management of state funds.

⤙

IN HIS TRY FOR A THIRD TERM, LAUSCHE CONDUCTED his usual campaign. He swept away token opposition in the primary election in the person of Clarence H. Knisley, former state treasurer, refusing even to campaign. In the general election he faced a much more formidable opponent. Donald Ebright, six-term treasurer, was the only Republican state official to survive the 1948 Democratic sweep. He had built a creditable record as state treasurer. Lausche campaigned in generalities, not promoting specific programs for the general assembly to consider. He seldom referred to his opponent, nor gave overt support to fellow Democrats, including Ferguson. The Governor preferred to criticize aberrant groups who brought "danger from within and without."[19] The cagey campaigner attacked his favorite target: bosses and racketeers. He had caustic comments to make about lobbyists.

The nation and its encounter with Korea provided Lausche with a platform to extol his patented patriotic themes. In reference to the Korean War, he might end a speech with these heart-warming words, "Good friends, I am not asking you to vote for me, but vote in a manner that best serves your country and state. When you go to the polls, listen to the voices of fallen Americans saying to you; 'We are young men who have died so that you might vote,' vote for the best interests of your country."[20] After such a speech he and the audience frequently ended up in tears. Philip W. Porter, long-time analyst of Ohio politics for the *Plain Dealer*, questioned how much of Lausche was phony and how much was real. "There is no question he believed everything he did was sincere and according to his conscience." The journalist surmised, "There is also no question that he knew what his every act, vote, or speech would mean in terms of public reaction and news coverage."[21] His personal demeanor added to the Lausche mystique. One questioned how much of his inattention to small personal details of dress or protocol was staged. How much was simply part of his odd-ball way of life is impossible to determine—his losing of hats, missing planes and keeping no fixed schedule. Reporters trying to cover him went out of their minds.

Lausche went about his business campaigning throughout October. He assiduously avoided any open statement endorsing the Ferguson candidacy. In a Toledo address, the Governor called for the election of the Democratic ticket, but did not mention the state auditor by name. Speaking before the State Democratic Convention, Lausche neither supported Ferguson, nor publicly subscribed to the party platform, which gave a blanket endorsement to the entire slate. The closest *Jumpin Joe* came to receiving a blessing from the incumbent governor occurred at a Cuyahoga County Democratic steer roast where Lausche, who unexpectedly appeared through the efforts of Mayor Burke, began his greeting with the statement, "Fellow candidates and especially Mr. Ferguson...."[22] Later in October, the Governor attended a Canton rally where Vice President Alben Barkley supported the Ferguson candidacy. Lausche still refused to comment, even though he received the vice president's endorsement for re-election. Aloof was the best term to describe his political behavior.

In addition to the Democrats, many Republicans voiced distress at the Lausche-Taft machinations. When Lausche expressed his inclination in White Sulphur Springs to vote for Taft, Ebright charged the Governor with double talk.[23] Ebright supporters complained of Taft's silence. Finally, Senator Taft publicly endorsed the Ebright candidacy on August 17, but he failed to participate in any effective joint campaign. A group of industrialists who overtly supported a Taft-Lausche ticket tried to arrange open meetings at which both men would be present. When the Senator made a tour of small industrial plants under the auspices of this group, he made no mention of Ebright.[24] Despite the fact that public interest largely concentrated on the senatorial contest, Ebright made a serious effort to raise issues in the gubernatorial race. The Republican contender challenged the Lausche administration in the contentious areas of school aid, highways, conservation, and public health.

Election Day November 7, 1950, dawned mild and pleasant throughout most of Ohio. United States military forces, under the command of General Douglas MacArthur, discovered Chinese Communist soldiers aligned with North Korean forces. The general remained confident. The Chinese soldiers were volunteers. With American troops racing toward the Yalu River, the war would soon be over. American boys might be home by Christmas. A larger than expected turnout of voters flocked to the Ohio polls. Split ticket voting was most obvious in this election. This normal Ohio tendency received a mandate when the general assembly passed a state constitutional amendment allowing for a Massachusetts office-type ballot. In this ballot the names of the candidates were grouped under the title of the office they sought and straight ticket voting under party emblems was impossible. This amendment was affirmed in the May 1950 primary and owed its existence to a petition circulated by Taft forces.[25] It was introduced to eliminate the possibility of GOP candidates losing to a tidal wave of straight Democratic votes in a state where registered Democrats usually outnumbered the Republicans.

Likely the amendment helped Governor Lausche overcome the 1950 Republican landslide.[26] In the same metropolitan areas where Senator Taft was victorious, Governor Lausche found his major sources of strength. When the dust settled, Lausche emerged the victor for a third term without much difficulty. He equaled the three-term records of Vic Donahey (1923–1929) and John W. Bricker (1939–1945). Lausche collected 1,552,000 votes to Ebright's 1,370,000, a margin of 182,000 votes or 52.6 percent of the total vote. Lausche's geographic strength was reduced by twenty counties. His majorities in all the cities except Cincinnati were sufficient to overcome a valiant run by Ebright. Lausche's home county, Cuyahoga, strongly supported him, giving the Governor his only majority of over 65 percent. Ebright ran well throughout the state, but only carried one county by more than 65 percent. With the exception of Cincinnati, Republican majorities were limited to the rural areas.

Robert Taft had little difficulty in winning his third senatorial term over Ferguson. He received a plurality of 431,000 votes—the second largest in Ohio history of senatorial elections (next to Republican Theodore Burton's 572,000 in the Hoover landslide of 1928).[27] Ferguson proved to be a weak candidate in opposition to the Taft juggernaut. Lausche's earlier kind words for Taft did nothing but help the Senator's cause. Of course this tactic did not set well with hard-line Democrats. "Taft could probably have beaten Ferguson anyway," one frustrated state Democrat commented, "but, goddamit (sic), would he have beaten him by 450,000 votes if Lausche hadn't kissed Taft on both cheeks on the steps of the Statehouse?"[28] On a *Meet the Press* program in 1956 Lausche allowed that, "If I would say I did not vote for Bob Taft, I would not be telling the truth."[29]

This verification of Lausche's voting choice could have been exploited on the day after the election had it not been for Seltzer. A Cleveland *Press* photographer took a picture of Governor Lausche casting his vote in a Cleveland voting booth. When developed the angle of the picture clearly showed that the governor had marked an *X* for Senator Taft. In newspaper parlance, this picture showing Ohio's Democratic Governor voting for Mr. Republican would be termed a scoop that would be sent by wire services to newspapers throughout the country. After some debate in the *Press* editorial offices the picture was shown to Seltzer. The editor-in-chief decided, "The *Press* has no right to publish the picture, newsworthy as it might be, because it represented a direct invasion of the privacy of an individual—whether a governor or a plain citizen—and of his right to cast his vote in absolute secrecy."[30]

The major factors in the Lausche victory appeared to have been his strong newspaper support and his ability to pose as a crusading independent. Many Republicans hoped that Democrats would scuttle Lausche because of his failure to endorse Ferguson. Likely Lausche's behavior as demonstrated in the senatorial race also proved beneficial to Taft. By refusing to endorse so obviously an inferior candidate as Ferguson, Lausche gained the respect and support of many Republicans and Independents who jumped on his bandwagon. In spite of Lausche's tacit support of the Senator, "The extraordinary popularity of Mr. Lausche," Taft grumbled privately a few days after the election, "is wholly undeserved...businessmen...can't seem to understand that the victory of a conservative Democrat can often do more harm in the long run than that of left-wingers."[31]

Governor Lausche took the oath for his third term on January 8, 1951. In contrast to the governor's first gubernatorial inauguration in 1945, this brief, private ceremony marked the quietest inauguration the State Capitol had witnessed in many years. Only Jane Lausche, relatives of the couple, and a few close friends witnessed the proceedings. The Governor had matured in the political arena, and had become vastly different from the first-term newcomer who walked into the Capitol in 1945. At that time he had no organization, nor staff, and few friends except taxpaying supporters from Cleveland. Those friends came to Columbus by the thousands to wish him well.

In political terms the inauguration left both parties with little desire to celebrate. The GOP controlled the assembly and the state offices, but their victory remained somewhat shallow without possession of the state's highest office. Apart from the independence of the Governor, whom they found infuriating as the figurehead of state government, Democrats discovered their hands were tied by the Republicans in the Assembly and in the lesser state offices.[32]

⌒

AS A RESULT OF HIS THIRD TERM VICTORY, LAUSCHE gained national political prominence. In January 1951, senate members invited him to Washington DC to testify on gambling before Senate hearings, chaired by Senator Estes Kefauver of Tennessee. In May of the same year, President Truman appointed Lausche to a National Civil

Defense Council. During this same year Lausche withdrew from consideration for the Major League baseball commissioner's position. The governor's rejection of this lucrative option boosted his esteem in the eyes of many of his constituents.

Following a visit with Harry Truman in August 1951, the Governor astounded the media with an announcement that he had urged the President to seek re-election in 1952. Those reporters who recalled Lausche's reluctant and lukewarm endorsement of the Truman candidacy in 1948 seemed confounded by the inconsistency of this pronouncement. To those journalists who knew him well, the statement seemed right in character. One confidante exclaimed, "I don't believe it!" Then, as an afterthought, he mused, "But you never can tell with Lausche."[33]

Some pundits saw Lausche's statement as a gesture to place himself in line for the Democratic vice presidential nomination in 1952. Others thought his objective might be directed toward a nomination for Senator in opposition to incumbent Republican John W. Bricker. One of Lausche's closest friends, however, envisioned the Governor as Ohio's favorite-son candidate at the 1952 Democratic National Convention. This line of reasoning did not seem plausible. Lausche's stand on the 1950 senatorial election did not make the Governor acceptable to the national party leaders as a favorite-son candidate. Others reasoned that his statement supporting Truman meant he was the best person to hold Ohio's electoral votes for the presidency.[34] Political analysts again found themselves perplexed in attempting to understand the actions and rhetoric of the incomprehensible Lausche.

Lausche's political ascension meant more invitations to give speeches at regional and national conventions. He addressed the Tenth General Assembly of the States in Chicago on November 7, 1950. His theme concentrated on the American will to work from within on an unselfish basis to withstand the threat of Communism and all it represented. Only five years after the conclusion of World War II, the country was now embroiled in police action in Korea. The Governor emphasized the need for better civil defense, a topic of vital concern to him. He had distinguished himself on this issue during World War II while Mayor of Cleveland. Lausche gave a stirring speech, as only he could deliver, and the audience left the conference with a greater appreciation of the Ohioan.

The following October 1951, Lausche—serving as chairman—gave the keynote address at the 43rd annual meeting of the Governor's Conference in Gatlinburg, Tennessee. He addressed social and economic problems that particularly faced state and local governments. The Governor urged that state and local officials adhere as closely as possibly to the philosophy of their constituents. Emphasizing his stringent fiscal policies, the governor stressed that those who wanted the supposed joy of spending also had the bitter responsibility of taxing themselves. The citizens would remedy this wrong if they noted that their state government was improperly rendering services, spending too much money or imposing excessive taxation.[35]

Lausche was now ready to move forward politically in the fifties, a term made popular by journalist David Halberstam's bestseller *The Fifties*. In retrospect, the fifties appeared to be an orderly era, one with a minimum of social dissent. In that decade of good will and expanding affluence, few Americans doubted the essential goodness of their society. Even if the specter of Communism lurked on the horizon, Americans trusted their leaders to tell the truth, to make sound decisions and to keep them out of war.

For a while this traditional system of authority held. The men (not men and women) who presided in politics, business, and media generally had been born in the previous century. The advent of so strong a society, in which the nation's wealth was shared by so many, represented prosperity beyond one's wildest dreams. Several social critics, irritated by the generally quiescent attitude and the incessant appetite for consumerism, described the fifties population as a silent generation. Many people began to question the purpose of their lives.[36] A vast and surprisingly broad degree of dissidence evolved, and social ferment bubbled below this placid surface. Lausche began to experience this political challenge during his first term of the fifties.

In March 1951, Lausche greeted the new Republican-dominated legislature with a record budget of over $729 million—about two percent of the 1993 level.[37] Almost every new state budget became a record. The Governor, politically supported in the state cabinet only by Democrat Lieutenant Governor George D. Nye, continued to expound his dictum of *no new taxes* and argued against needless expenditures, waste and extravagance.[38] The proposed increase in his budget resulted from population and economic growth within the state, and in Lausche's opinion, obviated any need for a state tax increase. The Governor continued his tirade against illegal gambling in the state, the desire to eliminate strip mining and a need for a plan of restoration of scarred mining land, the urgency for improved welfare and old-age programs and facilities, and the rebuilding of a now decadent statewide highway system.

Having been successful in Cleveland in closing gambling dens and fighting hoodlums, Lausche found this message played well on the statewide stage. He branded commercialized gambling a major menace to Ohio, and continued his campaign against this multi-million dollar racket. Because Lausche placed little trust with local law enforcement agencies, he worked with several state departments utilizing executive pressure in every possible way. He intended to apply this pressure—particularly on four gambling nests: the Mounds Club in Lake County (located just outside Cleveland and a long-time thorn in Lausche's side); the Benore Club in Toledo; the Jungle Inn in Trumbull County; and the Continental Club in Scioto County. In mid-summer of 1951, the Governor testified at Senate hearings in Cleveland on gambling, and proposed a federal ban against betting wires.[39]

THE SOCIAL FERMENT IN THE FIFTIES ALLUDED TO BY HALBERSTAM reached Lausche's desk in 1951. Increasingly, public pressure dictated that social issues fostering inequality between the black and white populations needed to be addressed. In 1948 President Truman engineered the integration of the armed forces. This action coincided with a strong civil rights platform adopted by the Democratic Party at the 1948 convention. An emotional speech given by Hubert Humphrey, Mayor of Minneapolis, triggered impetus for awakening the nation to racial unrest. In 1954 the ferment for equality provoked a crisis in Little Rock, Arkansas. President Dwight D. Eisenhower ordered federal troops to Little Rock Central High School to bring about tenuous integration of this public facility. These actions by Truman and Eisenhower slowly forced the doors of integration to open, amidst bloodshed, anger, and hatred. Overt signs of a peaceful co-existence came slowly in the years to follow.

Governor Lausche encountered his own issue of segregation during his third term, involving the esteemed Ohio State Highway Patrol. In November 1951, William H. Brooks, President of the Ohio State Conference of Branches, National Association for the Advancement of Colored People (NAACP), wrote to the governor charging that, in at least two instances, black trainees seeking to join the patrol, suffered abuse in physical endurance contests. Brooks added this unjustified treatment caused prospective trainees to hesitate making application to the State Highway Patrol.[40] An ethnic minority himself, Lausche had established a solid, if not enviable, record in his dealings with minorities, particularly the black population. The wheels of equality moved slowly, and in June 1952—an election year— the Ohio State *Journal* lashed out at the continuing refusal of the State Highway Patrol to enlist an African-American for employment and forced Lausche's hand by printing "Some place within the machinery of Ohio's government, there is a man who can weed out the traps set by the Highway Patrol to eliminate young Negro men who could easily qualify for the posts if treated fairly.... If the director refuses to do it, then it is the job of the governor TO SEE TO IT that he does. He owes that much to the citizens of the state who entrust him with the job as their chief executive."[41]

Always sensitive to public criticism, Lausche fired off a stinging memorandum four days later to Colonel George Mingle, Superintendent of the State Highway Patrol. The Governor alluded to an earlier memorandum (January 15, 1952) when he commented, "It does seem abnormal to me that in all of the examinations we have given for employment with the State Highway Patrol no Colored person has been found to be eligible." This observation followed another complaint, this one from the headquarters of the NAACP in Washington, DC. Lausche ended his directive, insisting, "that absolute equality and fairness of treatment be accorded to all persons applying to take the examination."[42] One week later Ted J. Kauer, Director of Ohio

Department of Highways and Mingle's boss, sent a letter to Mingle. He stated in no uncertain terms that "White and Colored persons shall have equal opportunity in all branches of the department and I want no person rejected for employment with the Patrol either in civilian or officer capacity because of race or creed."[43] Pressure remained on the State Highway Patrol and on Colonel Mingle.

Finally on November 4, 1955, after continued coercion, Louis B. Sharp became the first African-American to enter the ranks of the Ohio State Highway Patrol. One of 26 members of the 44th Academy Class (one other African-American dropped out of this class), Sharp previously excelled as a football player at Florida A & M College. He served in the State Patrol for a number of years. Sharp later won election as Mayor of Urbancrest, as small community in the southern part of Franklin County.[44] It seems reasonable to assume that Colonel Mingle had stone-walled efforts for black applicants to graduate from the Police Academy. While still in office in 1955, Governor Lausche had failed to apply enough pressure on Colonel Mingle to bring about an earlier change in policy as to who matriculated from the Highway Patrol's training program. Colonel Mingle retired from his position as superintendent in 1957.

Lausche continued to encounter run-ins with organized labor, which further alienated labor's rank and file from the Governor. An ugly situation developed in 1952 when a Cleveland Heights homeowner decided to do his own masonry work on his home. Unidentified individuals driving by his home at night splashed the masonry with stain and grease. At the insistence of Thomas E. McDonald, business manager of the AFL Building Trades Council, the homeowner, Ralph Patterson, Jr., had already signed an agreement to cease his masonry work. The public reacted in an uproar. Editorials denounced this act of vandalism and demanded action. Governor Lausche received letters of protest. "Can this be America where a man cannot work on his own house or is it Russia? We need strong state laws to combat this [behavior] with heavy penalties...."[45]

The Governor expressed indignation over this incident and ordered the State Highway Patrol to use all its resources in an investigation. Two more incidents of vandalism on homes occurred. Seltzer wrote in an editorial suggesting that although there was nothing but circumstantial evidence to implicate the unions, the leaders of the various Building Trade Unions and the Cleveland Federation of Labor needed to take action to clear the good name of labor. In the editor's judgment, local labor organizations had not done enough to clear up these underhanded attacks on citizens. Seltzer recommended the use of lie detectors to ferret out the truth and bring the perpetrators to trial.[46] Lausche realized the unions could easily cover up any association they may have had with hoodlums who steal away at night and cover their tracks. Although unsolved, these incidents only increased Lausche's disdain for organized labor and their strong-arm tactics.

ANOTHER POLITICAL ISSUE OF THE FIFTIES—the threat of Communism—began to make headlines. On February 9, 1950, Joseph R. McCarthy, Republican Senator from Wisconsin, grabbed nationwide attention with his accusation of Communists harbored in the State Department. Such accusations, commonly known as red baiting, had been going on for several years. On this date in Wheeling, West Virginia, McCarthy almost casually claimed that these Communists in the State Department controlled American foreign policy. To paraphrase journalist Richard Rovere, McCarthy was a political speculator who found his gusher.[47] This gusher became part of a witch-hunt that mesmerized American citizens for the next ten years, split the country apart, and reached as high as the presidency of the country.

A year later when the Governor's office faced a spin-off from this anticommunist frenzy, Governor Lausche might well have wished he had accepted the baseball commissioner's position. McCarthy's mother lode spilled over onto the Governor's desk in the guise of academic freedom and the invitation of off-campus academic speakers with Communist leanings. Specifically, this particular political bombshell became known as the Rugg controversy.

This issue took place on the Ohio State University (OSU) (now known as The Ohio State University) campus located only a few miles north of the state capitol. The problem concerned card-carrying Communists speaking on campus. The Cold War had settled in, and McCarthy's inflammatory remarks only intensified fear and suspicion of a Communist threat in the United States. After World War II the OSU Board of Trustees and President Howard Bevis passed a series of resolutions to regulate political discussions on the Ohio State campus, the appearance of outside speakers, and the right of faculty members to discuss controversial subjects in the classroom.

Given the board's composition, its accommodation to the Cold War ethos was hardly surprising. During the postwar period, the Board included Chairman Brigadier General Carlton Dargusch, a former Deputy Director of the Selective Service, and Senator John W. Bricker, a supporter of McCarthy. Other board members—all of whom were appointed by the governor's office but not necessarily by Lausche (he appointed only Robert Black, a friend and President of Cleveland's White Motor Corporation)—included Charles Kettering, research genius at General Motors; Forest Ketner, an agriculture association executive; and Black. Governor Lausche did not sit on the Board, but he maintained close contact with members, particularly Chairman Dargusch. As early as December 1946, Senator Bricker, an alumnus, accused the University of harboring Communists. This accusation led to a board-sanctioned university loyalty oath. The board forbade the use of campus facilities to all candidates for public office and their surrogates. In 1947 the trustees warned the teaching staff that, although it was their right to teach objectively in controversial areas, they were to maintain "complete impartiality of opinion in classroom discussion."[48] The board barred both Paul Robeson and Henry Wallace from speaking on campus during the 1948 presidential campaign, although Socialist Norman Thomas was allowed to speak, as were two Republicans, Senator Wayne Morse (Oregon) and Congressman John Vorys (Ohio). Only in 1950 did the board amend its rules to permit one campus meeting per party each year, an opportunity only the Republicans chose to utilize.[49]

This was the situation when in July 1951 the powerful Wolfe newspapers—the Columbus *Dispatch* and the Ohio State *Journal*—became enraged because a group of graduate students in the College of Education invited Dr. Harold Rugg, professor emeritus at Columbia University, to deliver the Sixth Annual Boyd H. Bode Memorial lecture. A nationally prominent, progressive educator and intellectual compatriot of philosopher John Dewey, Rugg wrote numerous social science textbooks. Subsequently, many of his textbooks were dropped by various school systems for being too leftist.

After a particularly bitter cycle of attacks in 1939–40, the Columbia professor finally wrote his book *That Men May Understand* to answer his critics, "I am not a Communist. I have never been a Communist. I have never been a member of or affiliated with the Communists, directly or indirectly, in any way whatsoever. I am not a Socialist. I have never been a Socialist. I have never been a member of or affiliated with the Socialist party. Nor have I taken part in the work of that party."[50]

Dr. Rugg's 1941 declaration failed to silence the opposition, at least not permanently. A consensus of non-biased observers contended that professional Rugg-baiters did not really believe he was a Communist sympathizer; rather they were offended by his basic belief in the possibility of a better society. The conference took place amidst much publicity by the three Columbus newspapers. In spite of great controversy and bitterness, Rugg's comments drew little attention. He seemed to focus on two points: first, the postwar world with its increasing complexities demanded a new effort from schools to use history to teach about current affairs. Secondly, that a new social order was possible through the application of advanced knowledge of human behavior.[51]

The well-respected University President Howard Bevis responded to these charges against Rugg and Ohio State by appealing to the tradition of academic freedom, asserting that the university must allow wide latitude of expression. In late July, Bevis further clarified his position and implicitly refuted the charge of conspiracy within the education faculty. Bevis suggested that he thought the invitation showed poor judgment and that he disagreed with much of what Rugg supposedly had said, but "within the bounds of loyalty to the Government, considerable latitude of expression must be allowed on a university campus."[52] If the attack upon Rugg's appearance had included nothing more than the virulent reactions published in the Columbus newspapers, President Bevis' public stand might well have ended the incident. Enter: the *big bad Wolfe* papers, the board of trustees, and Governor Lausche. The Wolfe newspapers demanded that Lausche call upon the university board for an investigation of Dr. Rugg's appearance on campus. The Governor complied immediately. In addition, he urged the board to go beyond the Rugg incident "and study the entire problem with a view of working out a plan which will assure proper screening of the different meetings...and the individuals who are invited to participate as principals."[53]

On controversial issues, Lausche took great care with his written responses and with how he answered questions in exclusive interviews.

The board of trustees gave the governor and the Wolfe papers everything they asked for. The board met secretly in a closed meeting at Gibraltar Island (Sept. 4, 1951) and after a scant hour of discussion approved the following statement (edited), "The Board of Trustees finds...the invitation extended to Dr. Harold Rugg [is] not in accord with the tradition and objectives of Ohio State University.... In order to avoid a recurrence of an unfortunate incident, the Board...has adopted a rule requiring that all speakers appearing on the campus shall be cleared through the president's office. The function of the university is teaching, not of indoctrination. The university must not be used as an agency of un-American propaganda."[54]

Immediately tagged as the Gag Rule, this policy set off a furor far surpassing the original uproar over Rugg's appearance. It soon became apparent that the speaker's rule was an administrative and intellectual nightmare. In the three weeks after the rule's adoption, Bevis had to evaluate 138 separate requests, each one in effect demanding its own security investigation. This process was not only a physical impossibility, but required the president to decide on the fitness of individuals about whom he often knew very little.[55]

Governor Lausche's office received a barrage of letters of protest. He answered a protester with one of his fence-straddling responses, "I can not subscribe to the rule that any or all persons, regardless of their advocacy of and their participation in programs for the overthrow of our government, ought to be given encouragement and rostrums at our state institutions. I do not mean by this that I believe that Dr. Rugg is advocating the overthrow of our government."[56] Letters and telegrams continued to pour in to Lausche's office, mostly challenging the need for a gag rule on the OSU campus. This uprising reminded Lausche of a comment he once made, "that the governor ought to keep out of the affairs of a state university."[57]

When asked whether any of the trustees had contacted him to obtain his ideas about the issue, the governor responded that he spoke to one member, but chose not to give his name. Information in Lausche's papers strongly suggests that General Dargusch, chairman of the board, had corresponded with him. Both Dargusch and Senator Bricker carried a torch for strong anti-communist legislation. In an October 11, 1951, letter to Lausche, Dargusch emphasized that, "In all matters affecting this issue,...it has been clear to me that the time has come when Americans must be willing to stand up and be counted. Those who believe in the principles upon which our nation was founded are going to have to go to work for there is not much time left."[58] There is no record of a response from Governor Lausche. On controversial issues, Lausche took great care with his written responses and with how he answered questions in exclusive interviews.

Under incessant pressure, the board of trustees met in Wooster four days later and proceeded to modify their speaker's rule. The only substantive change suspended the ten-day clearance provision for prospective speakers. The trustees issued a clarifying statement designed "to encourage the fullest academic freedom consistent with national security."[59]

Until this time the board, President Bevis and the Governor had stood firm on their position. Certain professional and conference groups cancelled their scheduled meetings on campus, which had a severely adverse effect on the city's hotel and restaurant trade. More importantly, according to historian Steven Gietschier, the board's perception was that they had over-reacted in September, and as a result, Ohio State was severely criticized in the national media, including the *New York Times*.[60] Still the board stood firm on the speaker's rule, and General Dargusch transferred the dirty work to the university administration asserting, "The President of Ohio State still has the final say about campus speakers."[61]

In an exclusive interview with the Columbus *Citizen* (the only non-Wolfe owned paper in Columbus) following the October 15 meeting, Lausche reiterated his position that the gag rule be left entirely up to the board of trustees and the university President, "I am not going to impose my judgment on the university trustees. They will work it out." Lausche added, "I would not for a moment feel I was serving my country if I felt I was offering speaking facilities at public institutions to a person advocating the overthrow of our government."[62]

Lausche admitted that the issue was complicated and for that reason controversial. The governor then composed a statement, which finally defined his position on this issue. He believed it was axiomatic that academic freedom be preserved, and those who wanted to overthrow our government should not be given rostrum in any of the state's public institutions. "By the simple exercise of common sense, the objective toward which we all strive can be maintained.... That objective is the one of protecting our government. We can maintain free speech and academic freedom."[63]

In another exclusive interview with the *Plain Dealer* ten days later, Lausche emphasized there must be a middle course of action without submitting to extremism on either side. The university President need not be charged with this responsibility alone, but ought to have power to delegate this administrative charge. He added that the media's misuse of the term gag rule gave the wrong connotation to the intent of the speaker's rule.[64]

Attorney Russell N. Chase, a Clevelander and close friend of Lausche's, chastised

Lausche with biting lines of protest. "I do not believe that our grand republic rests upon such a brittle foundation as to warrant public officials in a state of dither to attempt to prescribe nor proscribe what speakers are to say nor more importantly to prescribe or proscribe what the sovereign American people are to hear." Knowing Lausche's love of poetry, Chase added, "the bigoted, intolerant spirit of the times [the McCarthy Era] brings to mind...the following lines from Shakespeare:

> "Man, Proud man
> Drest in a little brief authority
> Plays such fantastic tricks
> Before High Heaven
> As make the angels weep (sic)."[65]

Whether Lausche responded to this letter of protest is unknown. What is known were Lausche's early public denouncements of Communism or any *ism* that might threaten the basic tenets of American democracy. The controversy surrounding the invitation and appearance of Harold Rugg at Ohio State University became an intense, protracted struggle, which divided the university community. Both sides realized they were arguing over those principles by which a university ought to be run. The failure of the 1951 compromise to resolve the dispute became apparent when political life revived on campus in the early 1960s. The administration invoked the speaker's rule to ban California radical William Marx Mandel in 1961, to prevent three opponents of the House Un-American Activities Committee (HUAC) from speaking in 1962, and to bar Communist Party theoretician Herbert Aptheker from addressing a campus audience three years later.[66] The speaker's rule was modified in 1987. The board of trustees and administration rewrote the guidelines in 1992, reducing the edict to one paragraph with a liberal interpretation of the governance of guest speakers on campus. This issue remains dormant, and free speech remains fettered at The Ohio State University.

The unpredictable Ohio Governor often turned the tables on an issue when least expected. At the height of the Cold War and Korean conflict during the early 1950s, red-baiting, McCarthyism and investigations by the HUAC continued.[67] Ohio had established its own Un-American Activities Commission, a joint House-Senate group created in 1951 by the 100th Ohio General Assembly. Samuel Devine, an attorney and Republican House member from Columbus, served as chair of this commission. A former FBI agent, he investigated subversives during World War II. During their first three years of existence, the commission investigated forty Ohioans, asking each of them the question, "Right now, are you an active member of the Communist Party?" All forty cited Fifth Amendment immunity from answering the question, and all were subsequently indicted by grand juries in counties where the hearings were held. At least fifteen were convicted.[68]

In 1953 Devine sponsored a package of bills extending the life and powers of the joint commission. Lausche signed three of these bills under tremendous Cold War-era pressure throughout Ohio and the country. Perhaps remembering his own troubles with red-baiting in his 1946 campaign for Governor, Lausche vetoed the main Devine anti-Communist bill, which created jail terms and stiff fines for targets of commission investigations. Lausche issued a blistering rebuke in his veto message on July 30, 1953, nearly a year before the highly charged Army-McCarthy hearings. The Governor ascertained he was in sympathy with the view that Communism is a menace to our country, but he warned against the besmirching of the reputations of interrogated citizens. "I can see nothing but grave danger to the reputation of innocent people against whom accusations can be made on the basis of rumor and frequently rooted in malice."[69]

Lausche also criticized the Devine bill's language that would make criminal any act that would constitute *a clear and present danger* to the security of the country. In Lausche's judgment, no judge or juror could clearly determine what constituted a clear and present danger. He clarified, "Criminal laws ought to be clear and certain in their definition...." [70] Devine and his legislative colleagues, who extended the life of the Commission for many years to come, over-rode Lausche's veto. The Governor's veto message was unexpected, in view of the Cold War and the demagogic upheaval perpetrated by Senator McCarthy and his ilk. Possibly Lausche remembered when he came under attack because of his ethnic background.

⌒

IN SPITE OF LAUSCHE'S PARSIMONIOUS APPROACH toward spending funds for state services, the history of his ten-year tenure as Governor records the completion of several important projects. Without doubt, the construction of the James W. Shocknessy Ohio Turnpike and highway construction in general topped the list of Lausche-led accomplishments. Regardless of modernization efforts, Ohio's highway system—woefully inadequate—could not keep up with economic development and population growth in the postwar era. Pennsylvania led the way with the first modern toll-road—the Pennsylvania Turnpike—which began to carry traffic in 1940. Toll roads were already under construction in New Jersey and New York by 1949. More and more semi-trucks transported raw materials and finished products on Ohio's antiquated highways to contiguous heavily populated states. Outside city limits Ohio's principal highways had been in place for nearly a half-century without significant improvement to match newer automotive technology.

During the first year of Lausche's third term, the 99th General Assembly appropriated $80 million in new highway construction. By 1950 the highway mileage in Ohio totaled 18,393 miles, of which 16,075 miles extended through rural areas, and 1,230 miles were located in villages. Ohio's state highway system ranked fourth in the country in miles, and was exceeded only by Texas, Pennsylvania, and South Carolina. In December 1950 Lausche called a meeting of fifteen regional states, to ascertain with factual information and road tests, the actual effect of large semi-trucks upon existing highways. This gathering of states led to a formation of the Inter-Regional Council on Highway Transportation. In 1951 Lausche called a special session of the legislature and appointed a highway commission to deal with the need to build a highway system to meet the postwar explosion in population, car and truck travel, and suburban growth.[71]

Under the direction of Director Ted J. Kauer, the state highway department proposed a super highway be located in northern Ohio so as to be more easily linked with the already constructed Pennsylvania Turnpike. The cross-state highways in northern Ohio had been pounded to pieces by wartime trucking from Youngstown to Toledo. The highway department had neither the time nor money to rebuild these roads. The proposed route began at Petersburg in Mahoning County, about 15 miles south of Youngstown. This route moved westward midway between Cleveland and Akron, then halfway between Norwalk and Sandusky, skirted Fremont on the south and Perrysburg on the north, about ten miles south of Toledo. The turnpike eventually hooked up with a proposed Indiana Turnpike, approximately five miles south of the Ohio-Michigan border. Minor adjustments slightly altered this route before the toll road was completed.

The building of the Ohio Turnpike encountered unexpected delays and legal complications. After months of wrangling in 1949, the General Assembly authorized the creation of an Ohio Turnpike Commission by a three-vote margin and empowered this body with authority to construct, operate, and maintain modern express highways. At this point Lausche, a staunch supporter of turnpike legislation, made one of his best appointments during his tenure as governor. The appointee was James W. Shocknessy of Columbus who assumed chairmanship of the Ohio Turnpike Commission. Shocknessy, born to a Catholic family in Springfield, Ohio, in 1906, graduated from Notre Dame University. He earned his law degree from Harvard in 1931. Politics ran strongly in the family, and young Shocknessy joined his mother in her campaign to repeal prohibition and help elect Clevelander Robert Bulkley to the United States Senate in the 1933. His long friendship with Bulkley brought him to Columbus. On the Senator's recommendation, he became assistant state counsel, and later state and regional counsel for the Home Owner's Loan Corporation, supervising loans totaling well over $300 million.

In 1939 Shocknessy established his law office in the Huntington Building overlooking the statehouse. Recruited into the Army Air Force during World War II, he would handle even larger sums of money. "The Air Force was buying materiel and [was in need of] lawyers. I remember signing one contract for $658 million."[72] He returned from the war to find an old Cleveland acquaintance [Lausche] about to take over as Governor. The Governor called Shocknessy, a dedicated

Democrat, and borrowed on his broader statewide acquaintances in making some key appointments. Thus began a long, sometimes difficult, but continuing association. Regarding Lausche as one of the great natural politicians of Ohio history, Shocknessy recalled, "He gets through to people. He has that quality the French call *spirituel*." Schocknessy's appointment gave Ohioans at large their first real look at his distinctive manner of getting things done. Big, brusque, bustling, prickly, proud and extremely vocal, the Ohio Turnpike chairman was not an *easy* man and relished not being so.[73]

Neither Lausche nor Shocknessy expected so many roadblocks during the first eighteen months of the construction of the Ohio Turnpike. The press received a constant political barrage from turnpike opponents. Farmers lamented the loss of prime agricultural land due to state condemnation, merchants located on existing highways worried about the loss of diverted traffic, and the petroleum industry feared increased gas taxes to help pay for the turnpike. A major interference in the commission's task emanated from a fellow Democrat and Lausche nemesis—state auditor Ferguson, who controlled the purse strings. The state auditor vehemently opposed toll super highways and put up a ferocious fight to prevent construction of the highway, known as Interstate 90. Initially, he refused to honor highway department vouchers for the turnpike commission. The highway department finally prevailed upon the state Supreme Court to force Ferguson to turn over the money. Again he held up an original $600,000 set up in the turnpike fund and finally released the money after he was threatened with a contempt of court action[74]

The state auditor continued his delaying tactics by refusing to pay two engineering firms for their surveying services ($27,500 each). The companies sued the auditor's office for non-payment. Finally, Attorney General Herbert Duffy stepped into the fray, submitting to the Ohio Supreme Court intervening petitions. The Supreme Court eventually cleared the way for payment of accrued bills and subsequent approval for the turnpike commission to proceed as directed by the general assembly. Other obstacles in building the turnpike were forthcoming in the ensuing months.[75]

Shocknessy had a private agreement with the Governor to resign from the commission on September 8, 1950. His relationship with commission members had been laudable, but understandably, he was frustrated with numerous delays perpetuated by Ferguson and subsequent Ohio Supreme Court delays on court appeals. After much persuasion by the governor, Shocknessy agreed to remain on the turnpike commission. It would be one of several times Shocknessy threatened to leave the trials and tribulations of a very difficult responsibility. Shocknessy was not alone with his turnpike frustrations. Lausche received letters from big hitters questioning the validity of the proposed turnpike. One such letter came from B.W. Bowden, President of the Bowden Oil Company, who opposed the building of the toll road. He was worried about the cost of the turnpike and the resultant increase in gas prices due to an additional tax to help support the maintenance of the highway. Lausche responded with aplomb and diplomacy. He cited the positive experience of various states that had already built toll roads. The Governor added, "the cost of the roads [is] amortized out of the revenues obtained mainly from commercial users of the road and in part from the passenger cars taking long distance journeys. The building of toll roads [makes] it possible to use gasoline taxes, automobile and drivers' license revenues in greater degree on the General Highway system of the road."[76]

Seltzer, Lausche's ally, got into the act by questioning the possibility of billboards being located along the turnpike or on right-of-ways and easements leading to the turnpike. Shocknessy reassured Seltzer that the turnpike commission was committed to rejecting the placement of billboards on the turnpike. On all right-of-ways in question, trees, shrubs, and other natural decorations were to be planted to obstruct the view of any defacement beyond the right-of-way.[77] Seltzer and Louis Bromfield, another concerned friend of Lausche's, seemed satisfied with Shocknessy 's proposal to beautify the turnpike.

⤢

HIGHWAY PROBLEMS ASIDE, THE GOVERNOR LEFT little doubt that he planned to run for an unprecedented fourth term. Lausche began to attract national attention, in spite of his maverick behavior in the political arena. Nineteen fifty-two was a presidential election year, and with Truman out of the presidential race, the Democratic nomination appeared wide open. Lausche's name occasionally came to the forefront as a possible presidential candidate. Lausche's support of Republican Robert Taft in the 1950 U.S. Senatorial election placed a stigma upon the independent politician. Still Lausche's friends believed that his endorsement of Truman for the 1952 Democratic campaign helped re-establish the Governor as a favorite-son candidate and the best person to hold Ohio's 25 electoral votes for the likely nominee.[78] Lausche, always the reticent candidate at the national level, stayed in the background when the Democratic National Convention convened in Chicago in July.

In the Democratic gubernatorial primary, the unopposed Lausche received 511,000 complimentary votes. Michael V. DiSalle, from Toledo, and former head of the Office of Price Stabilization for the Truman administration, won the Democratic nomination for United States Senate. The incumbent John W. Bricker opposed him. Lausche gave his open endorsement to DiSalle, somewhat of a rarity for the Governor. In this same primary Eugene Hanhart, state Democratic chairman and friend of Lausche's, lost in his attempt to win re-election to the party's state central committee. The Governor showed little remorse over his friend's defeat. "The state chairman has never meant anything to me. It has generally been proven to me that they can produce nothing. Some Governors may need state chairmen."[79] Lausche spoke from a position of great personal voter strength. The

Ohio Democratic Party soon realized that the Republicans had chosen a strong state chairman. Ray Bliss, always an astute operator behind the scenes and national Republican chairman under President Nixon, had considerable impact on the political fortunes of party candidates.

In the Republican primary a three-way battle developed for governor among former Governor Thomas J. Herbert, state Senator Roscoe Walcott, and Charles P. Taft, younger brother of Ohio's senior Senator. Herbert waged a vigorous campaign in an effort to seek vindication. Party regulars had long viewed the more unpredictable and liberal "Charlie" Taft as a maverick. An athletic extrovert, Charles established a distinguished niche for himself (besides having the magnetic name of Taft). He worked for the Federal Security Agency and the State Department during World War II. After the war the young Taft presided over the Federal Council of the Churches of Christ in America. Public spirited and idealistic, he seemed more appealing, if indeed not more able, of the two Taft brothers. Charles hoped to cap his political career by running for Governor.

The road to the nomination was not easy. Over the years, Charles had alienated many party regulars with his abrasiveness. Others opposed him because he had worked under Franklin D. Roosevelt in Washington, DC. He wrote a book in 1936 entitled *You and I and Roosevelt,* in which he commented, "I shall probably vote against Mr. Roosevelt, but I can't and I won't damn F.D.R. and all his works.... Some of the Republican orators who do give me a pain in the neck."[80] Charles even defended the CIO in a series of legal battles in Ohio. He alienated more party regulars when he helped establish the local Charterite movement in Cincinnati, which overthrew the Republican machine. He went on to serve on the city council for seven years.

To regulars in Cincinnati—and to long-time conservative Congressman Clarence Brown—the thought of Charles Taft heading the state Republican ticket in 1952 was repugnant. This internecine struggle within the party presented an embarrassing dilemma for his brother. Robert clearly desired the Republican nomination for President. Two Tafts on the ballot might result in an unpleasant reaction among voters. Robert tried to persuade his brother not to run, and Charles pressed for his brother's support. The difference of opinion precipitated the worst heated political argument the two men had since the 1920s.[81] (See endnote) Convinced of the futility of further discussion, Charles drafted a statement of neutrality for his brother to issue relative to the election. On the face of things this letter ended the matter. Robert remained impartial while his friends did their best to defeat his upstart brother. These episodes left Robert Taft somewhat bruised for his neutrality stand prior to the primary. His actions, or lack of same, pleased his friends and struck others as ungracious and selfish.[82]

Charles won the gubernatorial nomination by 70,000 votes. Immediately, he announced his statewide issues would be highways, welfare, and school problems.

The challenge made it clear he planned to blast the Lausche myth and win back Lausche Republicans. Some observers believed that the nomination of Eisenhower would hurt Charles. He likely would have benefited more so from money poured into the campaign for his brother, had Senator Taft been selected as the presidential standard-bearer.[83]

Charles moved forward with his campaign, insisting the highway system needed major revamping. The Republican advocated a permanent highway organization that remained stable in spite of changes in political administrations. Speaking to the Midwest Truckers Association, Taft claimed, "Lausche had no good explanation for the breakdown of the new road [Ohio Turnpike] or the execrable condition of U.S. Highway 42, the main highway artery from Cincinnati to Cleveland." Discussing a 20- to 30-year proposed highway program, Taft pointed out "we have the beginning of that in the work of the Ohio Program Commission. But I know from our Cincinnati experience that it takes more than a Master Plan in blueprint stage; it takes an iron determination to keep it moving forward. I did that in Cincinnati; I propose to do that for the state of Ohio."[84]

Taft kept the pressure on Lausche throughout the summer months. He charged, rightly so, that Ohio ranked near the bottom in mental health and vocational education. His major thrust was highway construction and the fact that the Ohio Turnpike lagged behind in construction.[85] Charles suffered a disappointing blow when his brother failed to gain the Republican nomination for President at the national convention in Chicago. The overwhelming popularity of Dwight Eisenhower was too much for Senator Taft to overcome. Hard core Republicans who disliked Charles because of his liberal bent on certain issues may have otherwise supported him out of loyalty to his brother. The only organizational support Charles could rely upon was from Bliss. The Republican hierarchy owed its first allegiance to the Presidential and Senatorial elections. Senator John Bricker carefully kept his distance from the Republican gubernatorial nominee throughout the campaign.[86]

The Democratic state convention met in Columbus in August, and Lausche strongly endorsed Democrat Adlai Stevenson, Governor of Illinois, for President. He had known and admired Stevenson for several years, claiming, "He will give the people of the United States good government.... He will be subservient to no one except his conscience and the people." [87] The Governor particularly appreciated Stevenson's strong stand against the gambling cartel in Illinois. Lausche continued to support the senatorial candidacy of Michael DiSalle, who faced an uphill battle against the venerable Bricker, "He is a fearless, untrammeled, hardworking, honest man. I will gladly vote for him."[88] Charles Taft seized upon these endorsements as proof that Lausche was not as independent as he professed to be. Taking an additional jab at the incumbent the Republican candidate emphasized the difference between the 1950 and 1952 elections, charging "there is no room in...1952 under the campaign hat of Bob Taft for this political hitchhiker [Lausche]."[89]

Lausche campaigned pretty much as he always had, that is as a loner and independent. Although on one occasion, he chose to travel with a group of touring Democratic aspirants. In Oxford, Hamilton and Middletown he failed conspicuously to mention his fellow platform candidates a single time. On the way to a final meeting in Dayton, a freshman candidate for Congress sat next to Lausche in his car, "Governor," he said, "I'm new to politics running for the first time. But it seems amazing the way you've been talking. I thought we were in this together." Lausche threw back his head and roared, "You're a fine fellow," he said. Then, still chuckling, he reached into his pocket and drawing out a Lausche button, pinned it on his companion's lapel. "Everybody for Lausche," he roared.[90] The Governor did not like to play a losing game or back a risky candidate.

On the campaign trail Lausche fooled some of his critics by amending his no new taxes position. He advocated a one-cent increase in the gasoline tax and higher taxes for racetrack operators. The Governor came out strong for a weight-distance tax on trucks, which caused a furor when he initially proposed this tax earlier in the year. He charged the truck lobbies with efforts to defeat him. Throughout the campaign the Democrat used the truckers as a whipping boy, charging that their lobbies had defeated his proposal in 1951. He maintained that Charles Taft received their support, politically and financially.[91] Lausche opened up another can of worms with organized labor when he proposed a Fair Employment Law. Organized labor, strongly objected to this proposal. At the annual convention of the Ohio Federation of Labor loud cheers greeted a demand for Lausche's defeat.[92]

Cleveland's two major newspapers, the *Press* and *Plain Dealer,* supported Lausche. The *Plain Dealer* crossed political lines and endorsed Eisenhower for President. This pattern of ticket splitting prevailed among many conservative dailies in Ohio. The *Press* challenged Taft's accusation that Lausche was a do-nothing Governor. Editorials claimed that, during Lausche's tenure, eight thousand additional patients were admitted to mental hospitals with larger staffs of better-paid employees. The *Press* conceded that the genesis for these improvements originated with Bricker and Herbert, using wartime surplus funds. Lausche continued to expand these mental programs, which for years suffered from lack of funds and qualified personnel. The *Press* gave the Governor high marks in his efforts, especially in working with Republican General Assemblies. He received praise in his efforts to stamp out large-scale commercial gambling, his missionary work to curb the ravages of strip mining, and his sincere devotion to what he considered to be best for the people of Ohio, ignoring the demands or threats of special-interest groups. "He has been a good governor and we see no reason for replacing him with another good man."[93]

The newspapers knew political mavericks made good copy, and Lausche was an excellent example. Throughout his political career, he courted favor with not only newspaper editors, but political writers as well, rather than party officials.

An example of Lausche's political acumen and unorthodox demeanor took place in late October, a few days before the election. Lausche suspected correctly that Eisenhower would carry Ohio by a large margin. He felt confident of his own chances, but one could not have too many votes, including those of independent voters who might split their ballot and vote for Eisenhower and Lausche.

Eisenhower stopped in Columbus to deliver a brief speech on the statehouse lawn. The general came up to the side entrance before ascending the capitol steps. Governor Lausche carefully inconspicuous (but making sure the reporters and photographers were watching) made a sudden appearance at the entrance, greeted the Republican candidate with great cordiality, then slipped back to his office to listen to the speech. This ploy gave the Governor as much notoriety as if he had taken part in the formal ceremonies. The Ohio press gave his overture considerable play. Lausche later remarked of Eisenhower, "He's a great American and it was a great speech."[94]

⌒

LAUSCHE ENCOUNTERED A MAJOR CRISIS AS THE CAMPAIGN entered its final days. On Friday, October 31, Halloween evening, while Lausche campaigned in Cleveland, inmates rioted at the 118-year-old Ohio Penitentiary. The antiquated facility in downtown Columbus was located only a few blocks from the state capitol. More than 4,700 convicts were incarcerated behind the brick walls of a facility designed to hold only 2,400. The riot began as a food strike about 5 p.m. and first abated at approximately 11 p.m. that evening. Lausche flew back to Columbus. With the election scheduled the following Tuesday, the Governor predictably hoped to announce an early end to the riot. But, it was not to be. The rioting resumed on Saturday and continued for five days. Lausche sent the Ohio National Guard in to restore order. Numerous official announcements reported the end of the riot, which were incorrect. On the morning of Wednesday, November 5, the day after the election, the 1,600 holdout rioters capitulated. The melee left one inmate dead, six more wounded, and one state trooper wounded. Six buildings suffered $500,000 in damage from fires. The rioting spurred renewed talks of removing the penitentiary from downtown Columbus.[95]

Crowding in the prison had become more acute, reaching an all-time record of 5,235 in 1955. A Cleveland judge described the prison as "a dungeon from the Middle Ages without a moat."[96] Lausche dismissed plans to relocate the prison, though he did support spending to increase the size of other state prisons. On June 24, 1968, the worst series of riots in the penitentiary's history spurred efforts to close the facility. The 1968 violence convinced civic officials that the old prison could no longer be a part of the downtown skyline in a developing and image-conscious city, particularly the capitol of the state.

Governor James A. Rhodes ordered a replacement maximum-security prison built in remote Lucasville in southern Ohio. Under the Lausche regime correctional institutions were built in Marion, Lebanon, and Louisville. In August 1984 the last prisoner left the Ohio Penitentiary. The historic facility, which has since been razed, was empty and calm for the first time in 150 years.[97]

In a last ditch effort to sway voters, Taft attacked this issue of penal facilities. He charged that the penitentiary uprising represented a bad situation that had festered for many years. The challenger pledged to build a reformatory-style prison to replace the ill-reputed facility. Governor Lausche answered this challenge, "It would be folly to entertain such a proposal which in effect would amount to the discarding of a $50 million plant on the basis of a $1 million return for the land."[98]

Election Day found Ohio enjoying the fruits of the land in spite of the Korean conflict. Veterans rejoined the civilian population. Pent-up consumer demands continued to stimulate the economy, augmented by the baby boom. These conditions, in addition to the economic stimulation of the Korean War, contributed to what economist John Kenneth Galbraith labeled the *affluent society*. Ohio's population continued to swell, adding 1.760 million persons in the fifties, a 22 percent increase, the state's largest of the twentieth century. Employment remained high. Throughout the 1950s, Ohio, with 5.3 percent of the nation's population, produced about 6 percent of the gross national product.[99]

All of these positive factors no doubt favored the incumbent Lausche. Certainly, Taft's spirited campaign and the general appeal of a Republican national sweep did not slow down the Lausche juggernaut. Amassing more than two million of the total of 3,605,000 votes recorded, the Governor swept to his fourth term with a plurality of 425,000 votes. Lausche demonstrated greater geographic strength, carrying 52 of the 88 counties. The incumbent captured every metropolitan city, including for the first time, Taft's hometown of Cincinnati.

In contrast to expected victories by Eisenhower and Bricker, Lausche's triumph demonstrated a classic example of split ticket voting. The 56-year-old Governor garnered a plurality of votes in many of the same areas won by the new president, but the shift in percentage of votes from the Republican side to Lausche was significant. One hundred thousand fewer voters marked the gubernatorial ballot, yet Lausche's plurality approached the Eisenhower margin of more than half a million votes.[100]

Political pundits offered various theories for Taft's overwhelming defeat. Several observers suggested that, although both candidates exhibited strong independent leanings, voters chose to stay with the incumbent.[101] The Republican Party's inattention to Taft's campaign seemed a more plausible explanation. The state organization concentrated on the Presidential and Senatorial candidates and "Taft did not have the hearty approval and help of all his fellow party workers."[102] To many old-line Republicans, Taft was a radical and a New Dealer, while Lausche's reputation remained conservative. Taft's great plans for highways, schools, and mental health sounded expensive and might have required new taxes. As the *Plain Dealer* explained, "people trusted Lausche," and Taft was an unknown entity.[103] The Taft name should have been an asset, but Robert gave little assistance to his brother's campaign. The split ticket allowed voters to make individual choices, regardless of their political affiliation, for all offices. Blaming the ballot for the large numbers of Republican fallout, the Dayton *Daily News* said, "Thanks to Senator Taft."[104]

Regardless of the split ticket, Lausche continued to exhibit a certain charisma that enhanced his attractiveness to voters, particularly common citizens without any vested interests. His folksy campaign style seemed contagious. The fact that he was a son of an immigrant family from Slovenia, adhered to the Catholic faith, and held no allegiance to party bosses did not deter his political success. The Governor's tremendous victory over a reputable opponent lent credence to the view that, by this time, many Ohio citizens considered Lausche tantamount to a permanent institution.

The Governor prepared for his fourth term. The Akron *Beacon Journal* believed he would be guided by a philosophy that "In any and all decisions, which he may be called upon...we believe he will ask himself, 'What is the best for the people of Ohio?'"[105] The incumbent Governor would prevail as a non-partisan political maverick.

Gubernatorial candidate Michael DiSalle, Senatorial candidate Lausche and Democratic presidential candidate. Adlai Stevenson, October 18, 1956, Courthouse Square in Toledo. (Courtesy of AP/Wide World Photos)

eight

Will Lausche Ever Leave the Statehouse? Yes

THE UNITED STATES ENJOYED AN UNPRECEDENTED period of prosperity in the two decades following the Second World War. Ohio was both a cause and a recipient of that prosperity. The state benefited from expansion of industrial plants, as well as high wages in the private sector that accompanied the postwar wave of growth. The state turned out a large share of the nation's supply of iron and steel, rubber products, automotive parts, industrial machinery, machine tools, and construction and mining equipment. Cleveland boasted a new Ford foundry and engine assembly plant—the largest in the world and immense General Motors plants. A new Chrysler plant took shape at Twinsburg, a suburb of Cleveland. Since the outbreak of the Second World War, Cincinnati experienced an orderly expansion. Automotive, aircraft and electrical plants moved into the Queen City to join the old, well-managed companies that made this city solvent. Columbus began to shed its moniker of town and country. Westinghouse and other industries moved to the capitol city.

Akron continued to thrive as the rubber capital of the world. A substantial chemical industry grew along Lake Erie near Ashtabula where a fruitful combination of fresh cold water, salt, and silica meshed with accessible limestone, electric power, and transportation facilities.

The Ohio waterways, particularly the Ohio River, served as important corridors for commerce and economic growth. River trade boomed after World War I when it took on much of the overload the railroads could not handle. This river trade convinced the federal government to develop the Ohio River much like a canal. The Army Corps of Engineers completed forty-six locks and dams by 1929. This engineering feat turned the river into a series of pools and a channel of a minimum of nine feet in depth. Since 1950 industrial expansion along the Ohio River moved forward headlong. New or expanded plants represented $8 billion of investment in the first seven years of the Fifties.[1]

An important factor encouraged industries to locate in Ohio in the two decades after World War II. The Congress of Industrial Organizations (CIO) had become a political force in other states. This was not the case in Ohio. Most of Ohio's major industrial cities had good and conventional government prior to the mid-century. For twenty years the state elected conservative governors, beginning with John W. Bricker in 1938. During his tenure Lausche gave viable evidence to all that the CIO would not capture state government as had befallen the state of Michigan.[2] Industry flowed into the Buckeye state with some assurance of immunity from class government and labor union domination. Ohioans prospered, both those who worked and those who invested.

In the 1950s Ohio existed within an intriguing balance of forces—economic, social, ethnic, and political—which tend to cancel each other out. Politics was a compromise. Ohio possessed so many qualities to compromise that its lowest common political denominator became very low indeed. The ethnic mix in the Buckeye state was unique. Political scientists infer this mixture was the single reason for Ohio's political stalemate. This hypothesis may be challenged. When traveling through the 88 counties, motorists could travel from a German Catholic village to an Amish community within a distance of few miles. A short distance down the road one might encounter a small town with racial friction because it happened once to be a depot for the Underground Railroad and later became populated with southern hill people. Outsiders have marveled at the state's compact, nearly European diversity.

The city-states in Ohio are legendary, and disparities among them were gargantuan. Youngstown's politics seemed at times almost Mafia-dominated. Toledo, surrounded by rich farmland, exemplified a blue-collar atmosphere influenced by the Motor City 75 miles north on Highway 75. Dayton was a business town of toolmakers and petty bourgeoisie. Cleveland's population consisted of an amalgam of southern Europeans and New Englanders.

The state presents a balance of people and a balance of interests. Buckeye citizens during the Lausche era kept the government on a short rope. Examples included the ten-mill tax limitation, a ban on state debt except through constitutional amendment, a double hurdle for home rule charters, annexation difficulties by cities, and the comparatively large number of school districts. School districts consolidated only after much anguish. An exception to this overall political compromise had occurred during Governor James M. Cox's first term (1913–1915) during the Progressive era. He mapped out a 56-point reform program in his first address to the Ohio Assembly. Ninety days later almost every point was successfully written into law.[3] Mayors Tom L. Johnson of Cleveland and Samuel M. *Golden Rule* Jones of Toledo had effected similar reforms.

In an 1899 article in the *Atlantic Monthly* entitled "The Ohioans," Rollin Hart best described the pulse of Ohio voters, suggesting the Buckeye citizens set about making Ohio one vast college of civics. The citizenry reduced the Governor's appointing power, allowing more officers elected by ballot. The inhabitants divided their territory into 88 counties, each a political centre or vortex. Residents determined that every public question should be ferociously debated in district schoolhouses. Hart emphasized that with such debates one felt the force of discordant ancestry. He wrote, "Cavalier joined issue with Puritan, Knickerbocker with Pennsylvania Dutchman, Quaker with Kentuckian; no two men had the same point of view. Never, I venture to propose did argument draw redder fire from keener steel. And although there are not wanting those philosophic cynics who urge that political excitement, like feminine loveliness, runs but skin-deep, there is no denying that common people get monstrously cross about it."[4]

In an 1899 article in the Atlantic Monthly entitled "The Ohioans," Rollin Hart best described the pulse of Ohio voters, suggesting the Buckeye citizens set about making Ohio one vast college of civics.

One wonders whether Lausche with his philosophic bent and the conservative tendency of Ohio citizens realized that he possessed the right formula to mesmerize the state's voter. The Buckeye political battle cry was a lot of emotion, not too much motion. Essentially the state seemed to be apolitical. Sound Democratic theory, according to the Ohio populace, advocated for less government. Charles F. Kettering, automotive genius from Dayton, would certainly have caught Lausche's ear with his oft-repeated statement that "It is a good thing we don't get all the government we pay for; we couldn't stand it." For Lausche, Abraham Lincoln (whom he dearly admired) said it best, "government exists to do for people what they can't do for themselves or only what it can do for them better than they can do for themselves."[5]

This political philosophy fit the Lausche mold like ham and eggs for breakfast. Historically, Ohio voters tended to distrust politics and politicians. Lausche was an exception. Plain living, plain speaking, with an honest-looking face, Lausche became the sort of politician Ohioans tended to trust.[6] Although considered flamboyant by some pundits Lausche took care to understate his campaigning efforts. He often showed up unexpectedly on county fair midways, or moved apologetically in bowling alleys to shake hands. The governor took pride in saying he formally campaigned for only ten days every two years, but seldom mentioned that he never missed an important church, school, fraternal or business function anywhere in Ohio at anytime.[7] He did not campaign in the orthodox fashion—party rallies, debates with his opponents, poster cards and gimmicks, motor caravans and publicity handouts every hour on the hour.

An example of the Governor's campaign technique took place in Youngstown in 1954 when he attended a large Negro Baptist convention in Youngstown. He gave a brief welcoming speech and then sat down for the remainder of the program. When the program ended the chairman expressed appreciation for the Governor's remarks and added that, of all the public officials who had attended this particular convention down through the years, Lausche was the only one who had remained until the end of the program. The Governor received an additional accolade when another delegate, one of the most influential pastors at the conference, pointed out that Negroes of Ohio never had a better friend in the State House. "This man not only ought be elected governor," he concluded, "He should be president of the United States."[8]

In spite of these kindly remarks, Lausche surprised his legion of supporters in December 1952. He planned to retire to the peace and dignity of private law practice at the end of his fourth term. Commenting that, because of his independence from party machines, he believed politically that he had done as much as feasible. "It has not been and will not be my intention to participate in politics on a national basis."[9] Lausche desired to serve on the bench again and hoped for an appointment to a federal court, possibly even the United States Supreme Court. Whether Lausche was laying down a smoke screen for some undetermined reason remains unknown. Newsmen learned to pay little attention to such remarks, for the record shows that public service has always had an irresistible pull on him. In the following months the Governor's increasing visibility as a national political figure and persuasion from friends induced the governor to change his mind.

His personal feelings did not keep *Curleytop*, (as Lausche was affectionately labeled by several journalists) from playing his bipartisan role. An extraordinary example occurred just prior to Eisenhower's inauguration in January 1953. The Ohio Republicans, flushed with triumph after 20 lean years of Roosevelt and Truman, staged a huge reception at the Sulgrave Club in Washington, DC. The leading Ohio Republicans were standing in the receiving line—Senators Taft and Bricker, George M. Humphrey, the Cleveland millionaire appointed secretary of the treasury, Congresswoman Frances Bolton, Congressman George Bender, Ohio Attorney General C. William O'Neill and a host of state legislators, councilmen and ward leaders. At least 500 Republican supporters moved through the receiving line when an interruption occurred at the rear of the room. Frank Lausche had slipped in the back door, and a commotion ensued. Many in the crowd paid more attention to the Governor than to the orthodox receiving line. Lausche, with great friendliness and mock modesty, was in his glory shaking hands.[10]

A few days later after taking his oath for a fourth term, the Governor faced a myriad of problems confronting one of the most populous and prosperous states in the Union. Ohio's population reached 9.7 million by the end of the decade. Lausche amended his timeworn no new taxes position to the Republican-dominated general assembly, by advocating higher existing taxes on gasoline and race-track operators.

Speaker of the House William Saxbe, the country squire from Mechanicsburg and a major Republican figure, held almost unlimited power to organize and run the House. Governor Lausche had little interest in or power with the legislature. The few times he tried to promote or defeat a measure, the Republican majority in both houses easily overrode his veto. The state was rich, but in trouble. The prisons, schools, public employees, and local governments all needed more money to bring them up to standard. Many teachers with seniority received less than one hundred dollars a month, and full-time judges received $8,000 a year. Lausche, determined to guard what he called his surplus, continued to do so.

Saxbe believed that Lausche's politically erratic behavior prevented legislators from depending on him. On one occasion Saxbe, along with Alvin "Bud" Silverman, Statehouse reporter for the Cleveland *Plain Dealer* and William C. Rhodes, executive director of the state highway department, played golf with Lausche. Silverman related a story about trotting-horse people. The thoroughbred races ran rain or shine, but the trotters could not race on rainy days, and the track lost business. Lausche said that was unfair and something ought to be done about it.

Saxbe recalled, "With [Lausche's] approval I volunteered to get a bill through and give the trotting track people relief, allowing the track to make up lost days and thus giving them parity with the thoroughbred tracks. We got a bill through...the House within a week, which was unheard of, and sent it to the Senate. It passed, but when it got to Lausche, he vetoed it."[11] In Saxbe's view, this behavior so typified Lausche. The Governor wanted to be all things to all people. Voters thought he was a great Governor, although many, like Saxbe, believed he didn't do anything.[12]

Lausche's fiscal stratagem resulted in minimal improvements in state services—mostly allowed by natural growth of state revenue in an expanding postwar economy. Public welfare spending for 1952–53 increased to a total of $97.4 million, a pittance by standards a decade later. Forty years later, in 1993, the Ohio House cut three times that amount from the Governor's $13.7 billion budget for the Human Services Department and still allowed for $2 billion growth in welfare spending.[13] The Governor continued to warn the legislators not to be snared by special-interest lobbyists, emphasizing there "will be no registered spokesmen for the general public" and "unless you and I act as the people's spokesmen, the millions of Ohioans who placed their trust in us will be powerless and defenseless."[14] Lausche continued to demonstrate that politically he was in no one's pocket.

The public put great pressure on Lausche for an improved statewide highway program. He threw his support to a Republican plan for an axle-mile tax on commercial trucks. The incumbent was kept busy with the construction of the Ohio Turnpike, restoration of existing highways and a proposed freeway (Route 71) between Cleveland and Cincinnati. Critics abounded among the press and in the private sector. Dissension existed within the Ohio Turnpike Commission. Dr. J. Gordon McKay, a turnpike commission member, denounced the commission for sloppy legislative procedures and too many off-the-cuff decisions.

Lausche responded to this attack, noting that road building had increased 150 percent during his tenure. The Governor worried whether monopolistic road builders cheated Ohio citizens. Lausche contended the public received the best deal when the road-building firms started fighting among themselves. In defense of his proposed axle-mile tax on trucks, Lausche asked, "Who is breaking down the state's roads and highways? Are the little passenger car operators and light farm truck drivers paying more than their share for maintaining our roads?"[15] Lausche received protests against increased taxation from trucking companies, highway building interests and engineering companies. Charges were leveled that Lausche was appeasing rural citizens. The Governor responded to one contractor with his standard rebuttal, inferring that, as a public official, he was committed to keep road builders at arm's length. He maintained that he owed "nothing to either the builders of cement, asphalt or hot mix roads except that I treat them on an equal basis. They have been kept away from me...to enable me to serve the interests of the public. The contractors tied to the use of special road materials make the charges of 'monopolistic control.' They charge each other with exploiting the public. It is they who in effect make this charge against themselves that the public is being gypped."[16]

Lausche came under additional attack by Republican leaders in March 1953 for an agreement with the Federal Bureau of Public Lands. The federal government planned to provide matching funds for road improvements on Highway 23 leading into Pike County to serve that area's new atomic energy plant. Under this agreement, the state and the federal government would split the costs ($6,655,000 each) and the federal agency would provide an additional $10 million for road improvements from Waverly to Chillicothe. Congressman J. Harry McGregor (Rep., West Lafayette) and Saxbe, to a lesser degree, believed Lausche had struck a bad deal. Saxbe questioned the wisdom of all the federal aid monies going to one county. Lausche defended his decision by arguing that Ohio received far more in special highway access funds to atomic energy plants than had Colorado, Kentucky, and South Carolina.

McGregor's public criticism of the state's highway deal with the federal government smacked of partisan politics and incensed Lausche. In a biting rebuttal, he questioned, "how loudly [McGregor] would protest...if you were a Congressman of Kentucky, or Colorado, or South Carolina and knew that Ohio was allocated 250 percent more than South Carolina, 700 percent more than Kentucky, and infinitely more than Colorado."[17] The Governor rested his case. After several months of delay, continued bickering from the Ohio Republicans, and downward adjustment of federal monies, the project moved forward to completion. Overall the financial stringency for highway construction eased in the fall of 1953 when voters approved a $5 hundred million highway bond providing for $125 million allotted yearly for the next four years.

Before the advent of railroads and highways, rivers served as a primary mode of travel for individuals and commerce alike. During the early development of Ohio, rivers and, in particular the Ohio River, became the great highways of the region. The Ohio River became the means whereby coal, a nearby resource, could be shipped to cities along the river routes. This very busy inland waterway in the United States tied in with man-made canals and the National Road (now Route 70). Ohio found itself in a strategic position for industrial growth in the latter half of the nineteenth century.

The growth of railroads pushed the canals to the sidelines. The mighty Ohio and Lake Erie vied with a rapidly developing rail system for low-cost transport of raw materials. By midpoint of the twentieth century, the locks and dams on the Ohio River had become antiquated. In 1951, the Army Corps of Engineers developed a plan approved by Congress, to reduce the number of locks and dams from 46 to 21 over a twenty-year period. Lausche vigorously backed this proposed renovation. He wrote to President Eisenhower in 1954 requesting support for the new lock and dam construction. The president approved the legislation, with the assistance of McGregor and Congressman Wayne L. Hays from Belmont County in Southeastern Ohio.[18] The first new lock and dam constructed along the Ohio border was the New Cumberland project, located 56 miles below Pittsburgh. Lausche received a jab from Thomas A. Jenkins, House Representative from Ironton on the Ohio River. The long-time Congressman informed Lausche he had been fighting for new dams for over twenty years without hearing from Lausche or the governors of Kentucky and Indiana.[19] Although Lausche generally resisted requests for federal funds, he believed these new dams would expedite movement of goods on the river and would reduce costs. The Ohio River served as a spinal artery for a rich and fast-growing industrial empire of steel, chemicals, aluminum, oil refining, atomic energy, electric power, and diversified manufacturing.[20] The river, stretching 423 miles along Ohio's eastern and southern borders, along with the installation of a massive atomic energy facility near Jackson, became major factors in Ohio's prosperity during Lausche's ten-year reign in the statehouse.

POLITICAL SCIENTISTS OFTEN ACCUSED OHIO POLITICIANS and the citizenry of ignoring statewide issues of importance. Democratic disorganization, honed by Lausche's political independence, exacerbated his party's unsuccessful efforts to promote issues during statewide campaigns. Lausche did take a proactive position on conservation of natural resources before this issue drew national attention. He was concerned about conservation of Ohio's natural resources. Soon after his first gubernatorial election, Lausche established a voluntary *Plant Ohio* campaign, urging special planting of trees on Arbor Day. The Governor made it a point each Arbor Day to visit a school, and with the children, plant several small trees on the school grounds. Seedlings were readily available from the U. S. National Forest Service at a small cost. He restructured the Ohio Department of Natural Resources, and an estimated 27 million trees were planted in Ohio during the Governor's tenure. Lausche expressed his fear that the loss of natural resources exceeded the gains. "The bulldozer is a mighty weapon when used to clear the land for artificial structures. Every time I see one of them operating or see the consequences of its past operation, I feel depressed."[21]

Opposition to strip mining in eastern Ohio became another issue in Lausche's conservation agenda. After a bitter struggle with the mining lobby, the governor pushed through a bill to force the mining companies to plant trees or grass on the denuded land left from mammoth earthmovers. It came as no surprise that Lausche contacted his friend Senator Taft in the spring of 1953 to ask for his support to preserve the Ohio forests. H.R. Bills 557 and 1864 would authorize the sale of state forests acquired under Title III of the Bankhead–Jones Farm Tenant Act, to private ownership. Should these bills have passed, in Lausche's words, "It would permit exploitation of the resources of these lands by unscrupulous timber butchers."[22] The Civilian Conservation Corps (CCC) had largely reforested these lands during the Great Depression. Since that time the lands had been administered by the Ohio State Division of Forestry, protected against fire and greatly improved by modern forestry methods. Lausche urged Taft to support H.R. Bill 981 which would transfer and provide title of these lands to the Forestry Divisions of the various states. Lausche was convinced the forests would help provide protection for strategic watersheds. Eventually this bill gained passage, to the satisfaction of the conservation Governor.

Lausche fought and succeeded in placing the Federal Soil Conservation program in Ohio under the jurisdiction of the newly formed Ohio Department of Natural Resources, as provided by Public Law 566. The primary reason for retaining state control of the soil conservation program was to avoid having watersheds selected on a political basis. Previously these watersheds were chosen and approved in Washington, DC without consultation with state or local agencies.[23] At every turn,

Lausche resisted federal intrusion into state government whenever he believed such an arrangement meant a duplication of responsibilities and expenses.

Lausche's request of Taft would be his last to Mr. Republican. The veteran Senator was diagnosed with terminal cancer in late May and died suddenly on July 31, 1953 at the age of 63 in New York Hospital. Ohio and the country had lost a political giant. Lausche faced the difficult task of appointing a successor to the Ohio Republican. This decision was critical. With Taft's death the Senate makeup included 48 Republicans, 47 Democrats and Wayne Morse of Oregon, a maverick Republican who often voted with the Democrats, necessitating Republican Vice President Richard Nixon to cast the deciding vote.

The Governor took an inordinately long time to make his decision. The Republican-controlled Ohio General Assembly decided not to aggravate Lausche on his appointment strategy or change the law whereby an immediate election could be held. Many Republicans thought Lausche would appoint someone to their liking. Lausche's only comment suggested he would "do nothing to destroy the organization of the Senate."[24] The Governor basked in the limelight of this situation. In reality Lausche wanted to be a U.S. Senator. Friends urged him to resign the governorship with the possible agreement that Republican Lieutenant Governor C. William O'Neill would appoint him in Taft's place. "If I were to do a thing like that," he told Seltzer, "the people would never forgive me, and they would be right. It's dishonest. If I become a senator, it will only be by election."[25] Lausche asked Seltzer to accept the senatorial appointment. Seltzer declined because his life was dedicated to journalism. The *Press* editor quoted a statement attributed to Colonel Henry Watterson, a famous Kentucky editor, made under a similar circumstance: "A journalist who a politician would be, never again a journalist can be."[26]

Lausche's continued delay in making an appointment irritated state Republicans. The pressure increased, and on October 9, 1953, Paul M. Herbert, Columbus attorney and former Lieutenant Governor, asked the Ohio Supreme Court to appoint a successor immediately.[27] On October 12, 1953, one day before the court was to meet, the Governor selected his good friend Thomas A. Burke. Burke served as director of law during Lausche's mayoralty of Cleveland and succeeded him as Mayor. Congressman George Bender immediately chastised the Governor for appointing a so-called New Deal Democrat and one not politically aligned with the late Robert Taft.[28]

Burke served a year in office before running for election in 1954 against Congressman-at-large George Bender to complete the final two years of Taft's six-year term. A six-term Congressman who represented the 23rd District (Cleveland), Bender was considered a political hack. Well known throughout the state, he was not particularly well liked by the state Republican hierarchy and Republican county chairmen. He was the pawn of big money in Cleveland (and on occasion the Teamster's Unions) because he did exactly as he was told. One of his biggest boosters included George Humphrey of Cleveland. Humphrey was important to the GOP and to Ray Bliss, still state party chairman.[29] With statewide help from newspapers (including the *Plain Dealer*, which decided that President Eisenhower needed Republican help in the Senate), Bender defeated Burke by the narrow margin of 2,870 out of approximately 2.5 million votes cast.

Whether inadvertently or otherwise, Lausche may have contributed to Burke's defeat. Early in the campaign the governor appeared in a one-minute television endorsement in which he praised Senator Burke. The Burke forces had purchased considerable time throughout Ohio to make the most of this quasi-endorsement from the best vote-getter in the state. Late in the campaign Lausche gave a video-taped address at a Democratic dinner in Cincinnati. He said nothing about his fellow Democrat running for the Senate. At the conclusion of his remarks, Lausche saw himself extolling the merits of Burke on a television monitor. Local Democrats had spliced the pre-recorded film short onto the end of Lausche's address. The next day the Governor forbade further use of the film.[30]

Again Lausche refused to associate himself with the rest of the Democratic ticket, even including his good friend. Burke supporters believed his inability to exploit this influential endorsement in the crucial last weeks of the campaign likely cost Burke the necessary votes for victory. Burke retired to private law practice, commenting that most politicians stay in office too long. Remaining friends with Lausche in spite of this ill-advised campaign snub, Burke recalled, "The boss—that is what we called Harry Truman—didn't like Lausche. Truman came through the party machine and he didn't like or understand Lausche's way of doing things."[31] The popular Burke died in 1971 at the age of 73.

BURKE'S APPOINTMENT TO THE U.S. SENATE HAD A RIPPLING effect on Lausche's political life. With strong support from Seltzer, Anthony "Tony" Celebrezze, a state Senator for two terms, became Cleveland's Mayor in 1953. A second-generation Italian, his brother Frank served as Lausche's safety director during his mayoral years. For the next ten years Celebrezze reigned as Mayor, becoming an extension of the Lausche-Burke mayoral dynasty. The press affectionately referred to Celebrezze as one of *Lausche's clones*. One of the new Mayor's appointments directly affected Lausche. Ralph S. Locher, Lausche's executive secretary since 1949, became the city's law director. Locher followed Celebrezze to the Mayor's office in 1962. Celebrezze subsequently became Secretary of Health, Education and Welfare in the Kennedy-Johnson administrations. After leaving his cabinet post in 1965, the Clevelander accepted an appointment as federal judge for the 6th Circuit Court of Appeals. Locher, succeeding Celebrezze, served two terms as Mayor (1962–1967) before the roof collapsed upon the dynasty of Lausche clones. Amidst the nationwide black uprisings of 1967, the local citizenry elected Carl B. Stokes, the first *elected* Black mayor of a major American city. (Walter Washington became the first black Mayor of a major U.S. city, when he was appointed by President Johnson to lead Washington, DC in 1967. Washington was actually elected to the same post seven years later.)

Ray M. White from Millersburg replaced Locher as executive secretary and served with Lausche for the remainder of his governorship, and then followed him in a similar capacity to the United States Senate. Although Lausche's name began to be bantered about as a potential presidential candidate, he gave no encouragement to this speculation. "I am content in my own domain in Ohio," he remarked, "My wings are not strong enough for me to fly to those lofty heights which others are speaking in my behalf. I cannot keep my eyes on the stars while stumbling in the mudholes of my present path."[32]

> *"My wings are not strong enough for me to fly to those lofty heights which others are speaking in my behalf. I cannot keep my eyes on the stars while stumbling in the mudholes of my present path."*

In May 1953 the press reported that the Governor discussed his fifth term possibilities with Democratic leaders at a meeting in his office. Lausche, who possessed a temper, expressed anger at speculative talk at this time.[33] In June 1953 the Governor gave a dinner for members of the press. Each member facetiously received a statement that the Governor would not seek another term, but the statement was dated January 10, 1955, which still allowed for the possibility of a fifth term.[34] As the year progressed, GOP officials delayed announcing who would oppose Lausche if he ran, because none of the hopefuls were anxious to face Lausche in the general election. Finally on December 8, 1953, the Governor announced he would seek an unprecedented fifth term.

Lausche had no desire to run for the Senate in place of his friend Tom Burke. He had resisted any consideration baseball ownership extended to him for the commissioner's job, and he had earlier declined an offer by the Eisenhower administration for a seat on the District of Columbia Circuit Court. Lausche's salary had now reached $20,000 a year (plus the governor's mansion, servants, food, and automobiles).

On September 23, 1953, State Auditor James A. Rhodes had written a letter to Governor Lausche proposing new methods of bookkeeping and streamlining the auditor's office. He had asked for Lausche's cooperation to create an accounting system that would be efficient and "one that will result in the savings of thousands and thousands of dollars belonging to the taxpayers of Ohio...."[35] This proposal, music to Lausche's ears when saving of state funds was involved, had received his hearty approval. Lausche likely did not realize Rhodes would soon be his political adversary.

Somewhat by default, Rhodes emerged as Lausche's opponent in the 1954 gubernatorial election. State GOP chairman Ray Bliss strongly urged Ohio House Speaker William Saxbe to run for Governor. Saxbe declined and subsequently acquiesced to challenge unpopular Congressman George Bender for Burke's Senate seat in the Republican primary. When Saxbe declined, Republican moguls—including Bliss—agreed that Attorney General C. William O'Neill had earned the opportunity to seek the state's highest office. Unfortunately, O'Neill was running for re-election as attorney general. Midway through a four-year term (only the auditor among state officials served a four-year term), Rhodes was not in jeopardy of losing his job. Rhodes agreed to be the party's guinea pig in challenging the nearly invincible Lausche. Rhodes later regretted this decision.

James Allen Rhodes, born on September 13,1909, in Coalton in Jackson County near the Ohio River, was one of five children, two of whom died in childhood. His early years paralleled those of Lausche's youth. His father, James, died in 1918 when Rhodes was nine. The impoverished family refused any help from government officials. With the threat that authorities were prepared to place the three children in a county home, Rhodes' mother moved the family to Springfield, fifty miles west of Columbus. Young Rhodes held his mother in high regard in the same way Lausche had held Frances Lausche in high regard. Rhodes helped his mother operate a restaurant and boarding house. He attended Springfield High School, and although he did not excel academically, he made a lasting impression on his classmates and teachers. Charles Fox, principal, recalled he was a "very popular, active school citizen...he was a real promoter, a pretty good [basketball] guard, booked bands, always hustling someway to make a buck." [36] Rhodes graduated from Springfield High School and moved to Columbus and the Ohio State University area. He attended the university, ultimately taking only a few classes, beginning his career climb up the political ladder. The ambitious Rhodes won election as a Republican ward committeeman in 1934, gained election to the Columbus Board of Education in 1937, and was twice elected city auditor, in 1939 and 1941. He reached the pinnacle of municipal government, being elected mayor of Columbus in 1943 at the age of 34, the youngest Mayor of any large U.S. city. He married Helen Rawlins, his childhood sweetheart from Jackson in December 1941.

In 1950 Rhodes tried for the GOP nomination for governor and lost to Don Ebright in the primary election. Rhodes reached the statehouse in 1952, defeating incumbent *Jumpin Joe* Ferguson for the state auditor's position. [37] Entering the Governor's race, Rhodes knew he was the underdog against Lausche. As one pundit quipped, "Who wanted to go against Big Frank?" [38] The unpolished state auditor had no opposition in the Republican primary election, so he began his vitriolic attack upon the incumbent early in his campaign. From the Republican standpoint, this campaign developed into one of the dirtiest in Ohio political annals.

Although rough around the edges, Rhodes had been through the political portals long enough to manifest the necessary savvy to be successful. Nineteen fifty-four would not prove to be one of those years. Much like Lausche, Rhodes never downplayed his untutored, proletarian background. He was proud of his Jackson County roots. A favorite Rhodes one-liner described a seven-course dinner in Jackson County as a possum and a six-pack.[39] He had learned the value of attending county fairs, enjoying a hot dog with the local citizenry and kibitzing with one and all. Rhodes' overall campaign strategy compared favorably with that of Lausche's.

If Lausche had worried about stumbling in the mud-holes of his political career, he needed to worry more about his opponent's mudslinging. From time to time Lausche had been rebuked by the press and opponents about political issues, but nothing compared to Rhodes' invective accusations. In 1952 Charles Taft had called Lausche a *do-nothing* Governor and blamed him for state-made license plates, which had become rusty in a hurry.[40] Voters shrugged off the naysayers and continued to support the incumbent. In an effort to win voters away from the Governor's juggernaut, Rhodes set out with a muckraking campaign that far surpassed any previous attacks on Lausche.

Early in 1954 Rhodes began his aggressive campaign which by his own admission was planned to explode "the myth that the Governor is above and beyond all things commonplace."[41] The state auditor challenged the Governor to make public the monies and gratuities he had received from the Federation of Railway Progress (FRP) while serving as Governor. Lausche had been on record as endorsing the St. Lawrence Seaway when Mayor of Cleveland. Rhodes charged the FRP opposed the seaway project and claimed Lausche's prior connection with the FRP as a lobbyist was another instance where the Governor attempted to serve two masters.[42]

The Republican nominee next charged Lausche with improper conduct regarding the State Liquor Department. He claimed the department had purchased spurious brands of whiskey from friends who merely furnished names and labels; the auditor called it *friendship whiskey*. One of Rhodes' favorite ploys, first used against Lausche in the case of the so-called liquor scandal, was to insist that his opponent look into this accusation. Speaking to about 600 citizens in a Painsville Park, Rhodes challenged Lausche to call in the attorney general or the state legislature to investigate a supposed half-million dollar liquor department scandal. The challenger added, "If Lausche doesn't know what's going on, he doesn't deserve a fifth term."[43] Liquor agents in Cincinnati and Cleveland received indictments in connection with an alleged shakedown of liquor-permit holders, but the case was later thrown out.

Rhodes continued his fallacious attack, directing his venom at Lausche's associates. He claimed that these faithful had been paid off, noting that Democratic State chairman Eugene Hanhart wrote millions of dollars of insurance for the state and that Shocknessy, vice-chairman of the state Democratic Party, headed the multi-million dollar turnpike commission. He added that scandals existed in the turnpike commission that called for criminal indictments. Obviously tipped off in advance, Shocknessy refuted these allegations with affidavits and official records almost before the charges reached the newspapers. The Cleveland *Plain Dealer* called these accusations "obviously ridiculous and unreal."[44] On one point the two opponents agreed. Conditions in the state mental hospitals were abominable and, as the Governor implied, indefensible, particularly at the Cleveland State Hospital. Lausche blamed the Republican dominated legislature for insufficient appropriations.

The most demeaning incident of the campaign occurred in July 1954. While attending a Governor's conference at Lake George, New York, a photographer asked to take a picture of Lausche with Governor John S. Fine of Pennsylvania. Lausche agreed, and they went to what was supposed to be Fine's room. When the door opened, there stood Governor Herman Talmadge of Georgia. The photographer looked surprised and said, "Oh, we've got the wrong room! But I'd like a picture of you anyway."[45] This ruse was an attempt to identify Lausche with the segregationist Governor. A pamphlet that included this picture, along with charges that several state departments specified *white only* in their personnel requests, reached the homes of thousands of black voters throughout Ohio. The photographer later confessed that he had been employed to smear Lausche and inject racism into the campaign. Rhodes denied any connection with this plot.[46] Dan T. Moore, a leading black activist from Cleveland, wrote a letter to syndicated columnist Drew Pearson setting the record straight, "Governor Lausche, both as mayor of Cleveland and in his job, has been the greatest friend of the Negro that we have had...in Ohio. Nevertheless, the picture which shows Governor Talmadge's arm around [Lausche's] neck, may do considerable damage unless the trick is widely publicized."[47]

Initially Governor Lausche chose to ignore Rhodes' charges. Eventually he became irritated at the flagrant attacks and began to defend himself with the help of allies in statewide newspapers. In contrast to the negative tone of Rhodes' crusade, Lausche campaigned in a more positive manner. His major proposals included a north-south turnpike linking the three Cs: Cleveland, Columbus, and Cincinnati (Route 71). He advocated a revision of the utility rate laws for more equity, waged war on obscene literature and horror comics, and supported legislation to help implement the St. Lawrence Seaway. The Governor promised to fight for more funds for mental institutions.

In late October 1954, Lausche took to television, a novice entity in many homes, employing his familiar technique of complaining he was under vicious attack. He insinuated that special interests such as the trucking industry, public utilities, and racketeers were bent on bringing about his defeat. At one point the Governor claimed that, "more abuse had been heaped on him in the past ten months than in the previous twenty years."[48]

Prior to Election Day, Rhodes made a last ditch effort to snatch victory. President Eisenhower campaigned with the challenger in Cleveland just prior to the election. Full-page advertisements in Ohio newspapers pictured Rhodes and the president together and stated, "The President Supports James A. Rhodes."[49]

The Republican struck at Lausche's record saying he would "exterminate rather than preach about gambling and vice" in Ohio—a clear shot at an issue Lausche felt he owned.[50] He made some inroads with voters when he attacked the concept of a fifth term, saying, "No man has squatter's rights to the governorship of the great state of Ohio."[51]

In a last minute thrust to add insult to injury, ministers received a letter implying that Lausche was a hard-drinking man. Lausche responded, pointing out that Ohio dailies, "through their editorials, are repudiating my opponent on account of the gutter-level campaign that he is conducting. During the past year I have probably made 500 public appearances. If there were any truths to the libelous mail that was sent to you, there would be no need of a hidden political campaign attack to establish the fact."[52]

Instead of exploiting a Lausche myth, the Rhodes' campaign left the populace, including many Republicans, with an odious reaction. Lausche received the majority of newspaper endorsements. The Cleveland *News*, a staunch Republican paper that had opposed the Governor in each of his previous gubernatorial contests, endorsed him "for the good of Ohio."[53] The Cincinnati *Enquirer*, another Republican paper, followed suit. The Akron *Beacon Journal* spoke for many citizens in an editorial claiming the Rhodes campaign seemed to indicate that he "had a low opinion of the intelligence and maturity of the Ohio voters."[54] The voters made their voices heard on Election Day.

ON NOVEMBER 2, 1954, VOTERS WOKE UP to encounter one of the worst snowstorms of the year. Many residents could not dig themselves out of the drifts to reach the polls, especially in the Lausche stronghold of northeastern Ohio. Nevertheless, Lausche maintained his winning ways for an unprecedented fifth term, garnering 1,405,262 votes to Rhodes' total of 1,192,528 (a majority of 53.8 percent of the total votes). The snowstorm and an off-presidential election year contributed to a one million-vote drop-off from 1952. Few political experts expected different results. Lausche carried all eight metropolitan areas to counter victory in only 26 of the 88 counties. He received over 65 percent of the vote in only Mahoning and Pike Counties. Rhodes carried only Fulton County by more than 65 percent. He did not carry his own Franklin County.

Political observers surmised that Lausche lost some voter strength because of the unprecedented fifth term issue. Balancing this loss he gained Republican voters turned off by Rhodes' mudslinging tactics. Researcher Joe Bindley intimates that Rhodes might have won had he concentrated on the fifth-term issue and reminded Republicans that Lausche appointed a Democrat to fill the Senate seat vacated by their beloved Robert Taft. Rhodes disregarded his advisors and blasted away at trivialities, ignoring the Burke appointment as a political issue. The estimable Bliss commented, "Lausche didn't defeat Rhodes—Jim beat himself."[55] For Rhodes, it was a campaign in which he learned a hard lesson in politics. "I really never thought I could win because Frank was and is a great American and a great humanitarian. He had more of a command of the English language on the platform.... He was a straight arrow who would never violate his own principles."[56] Rhodes later chastised himself, "I liked Frank Lausche, and I didn't like my campaign. It wasn't like me. The thing that people want is answers."[57] Seltzer, of the *Press,* jubilantly reflected after the election, "[Lausche] has restored the respect of Ohioans for the State House. People don't have to worry about state government as long as Lausche is there."[58]

Politics often make strange bedfellows. In spite of the hateful campaign Rhodes conducted, the two men eventually became good friends. They often partook of golf matches at Scioto Country Club. After a match, the two politicians retreated to the clubhouse for a bit of libation where several club members joined them. An employee noted the difference in their personal demeanor. "Lausche ordered buttermilk and Rhodes ordered a mixed drink. Lausche carried on a conversation with one and all at the table in such a way that made everyone feel they were important to him. He did not force attention upon himself. In contrast the state auditor in his blustery and braggadocio manner, sought attention to himself."[59]

Rhodes recalled that Lausche served as an exemplary role model for ethnic groups and as a positive force for the future Governor. During Rhodes' political tenure he often delivered a speech with Lausche flair. A member of the audience remarked that "he sounded like Lausche," and Rhodes shot back, "Is there anyone better?"[60] Rhodes defined Lausche as a populist without a political machine. To those who claimed Lausche always went with the wind, Rhodes responded that the wind was in the right direction. He commented that Lausche often had words with political enemies, men like State Senator Frank King who had strong ties with the Ohio AFL-CIO. However, according to Rhodes, Lausche never held a deep-seated animosity toward his adversaries.[61]

After his defeat in 1954 Rhodes regrouped and won election to the governorship four terms (1963–1971 and 1975–1983). Although the Governor is most frequently identified with the Kent State tragedy (May 1971), the general consensus gave Rhodes high marks for his tenure as governor, particularly his first two terms. According to Richard G. Zimmerman, Ohio political columnist, Rhodes was a Governor the likes of whom Ohio had not previously seen. He contended that Bricker, Lausche, Thomas Herbert, and O'Neill were essentially men of limited vision and skinflints. "This description did not apply to the former state auditor. Rhodes not only had the vision for the state he truly loved, he had both the skill and the tenacity to get most of what he wanted from Ohio for Ohio.... He left Ohio a very different and in many respects, a far, far better place than it had ever been."[62] With the exception of a handful of colonial Governors and George Clinton of New York, a post-Revolutionary Governor who had served twenty-one years, only George Wallace of Alabama held a Governor's seat as long as Rhodes (16 years). Rhodes likely had Lausche to thank in part for his longevity in office. After his defeat in 1954, the ambitious Rhodes analyzed the imperturbable Lausche's campaigning style and adopted many aspects of it. However, Rhodes never mastered the Lausche county fair technique—getting out of a car a half-mile from the entrance, paying his own admission, settling down on a bale of hay beside one of the natives and saying, "I hear the governor's at the fair today—have you seen him?"[63] Mr. Ohio, as Rhodes was reverently called, died in 2001 at the age of 91.

> "I liked Frank Lausche, and I didn't like my campaign. It wasn't like me. The thing that people want is answers."

In spite of Rhodes' subsequent illustrious career as governor of Ohio, Lausche remained king of the hill during the 1950s. With the retirement of Thomas E. Dewey in 1954, Lausche became the nation's senior governor. His success at the polls weighed heavily upon political thinking. He shaped his political course without regard to organization whims, often in defiance of them. His fifth-term election placed him in a unique niche in Ohio politics. The vast majority of the voters in his home state demonstrated unbounded faith in his judgment and integrity. Shortly after Lausche's victory, Jane Lausche received a note from Barry Wood, president of NBC, "Let me add my congratulations to those of the many you must have received. Can I just say that I hope this will be the governor's most successful term!"[64] Jane responded on Thanksgiving Day, "No wonder our hearts belong to NBC. Your Ohio candidate pulled through—with a comfortable margin—after a most uncomfortable campaign."[65] Whether this term would be Lausche's most successful was still to be determined, but there was little doubt it would be his last.

Lausche's uncanny and successful style of campaigning bewildered not only Rhodes but also state Republican chairman Ray Bliss. In 1954 in an attempt to find an answer to Lausche's campaign success, Bliss employed Attorney William F. Marsh of Maumee as an administrative assistant. The chairman charged Marsh with the task of tracking Lausche during the campaign, observing him at public gatherings and on television. Marsh reported back to Bliss that the Governor didn't address many issues of substance; rather he came across as a master orator who used emotionalism to gain public favor and support. Lausche was not above shedding a tear or two when making a poignant statement about his beliefs and value system.[66]

WHATEVER THE SECRET WAS TO LAUSCHE'S POLITICAL ACHIEVEMENT, Republican legislators ultimately put a halt to Lausche's continuous elections to the statehouse, with assistance from Ohio voters. In the 1954 election voters approved a constitutional amendment increasing the Governor's term of office to four years, effective January 1959. This new amendment restricted a Governor to serving two consecutive four-year terms. This Republican ploy, designed to derail Lausche, actually backfired somewhat against Rhodes. He served two terms and was ineligible to run for four years. He then ran successfully for two more terms, sat out for one term and suffered to defeat at the hands of incumbent Democrat Richard F. Celeste in 1986.

Before taking the oath for his fifth term, Lausche suffered a setback on the constitutionality of a film censorship law. A controversial campaign issue, Lausche fought for a censorship law. On December 1, 1954, the Ohio Supreme Court by a 5-2 vote nullified the censoring of films. This decision did not abolish the censorship board, but weakened its right to censor objectionable films. Lausche insisted Ohio must have a film censorship law. He commented, "The showing of films tending to debase morality and having a harmful influence in the performance of our ethical obligations cannot be left to the voluntary self-imposed restraints of the movie picture industry."[67]

Lausche commanded considerable support for his stance against obscenity in literature and movies, especially from conservative counties in the southern part of the state. One supporter, Charles H. Keating, Jr. of Cincinnati, wrote to Lausche several times praising the Governor for his stand on this issue.[68] Keating, a devout Catholic, incorporated an organization called Citizens for Decent Literature (CDL) in 1958. Soon the CDL had 300 chapters nationwide (eventually the organization claimed 100,000 members) and became the largest anti-pornography movement in the country. The press dubbed the Cincinnatian *Mr. Clean* for leading an anti-smut campaign in his hometown.

Keating moved to Phoenix in 1978. This sanctimonious builder of Continental Homes brought his anti-porn group to the Southwest with a new name, Citizens for Decency Through Law. Drawing assets from his parent company, Continental Corporation, he purchased Lincoln Savings and Loan bank located in Los Angeles. The so-called entrepreneur fulfilled his dream of being a merchant banker. Keating accumulated millions of dollars through the sale of junk bonds. Among many handouts he donated $900,000 to Mother Teresa over a five-year period. Newspapers carried headlines with disclosure of Keating's questionable contributions to five Senators identified as the Keating Five (Senators Alan Cranston, Dem-CA; John Glenn, Dem-OH; Don Riegle, Rep- MI; John McCain, Rep-AZ.; and Dennis DeConcini, Dem-AZ). These contributions were given with the expectation that Keating and his highly suspect operation of Lincoln Savings and Loan Bank would be shielded from federal investigation for financial improprieties. The Senators were reprimanded for their role in what was to become a major scandal.[69]

The roof caved in on Keating and his financial empire in the late 1980s when charges of racketeering, securities fraud and conspiracy were leveled against him. He was found guilty in 1993 and sentenced to twelve years in a federal prison in California. The deposed Keating served 4 ½ years of his sentence and gained release from prison on October 3, 1997. Mr. Clean returned to Phoenix still somewhat haughty, but a broken man.[70]

Lausche and Keating were on the same page in their campaign against obscenity in its multiple forms. Their efforts were laudable on an issue that continues to have much public support. There is always the question of how one distinguishes what is obscene and what is or is not in violation of the First Amendment. This issue likely will never be resolved to everyone's satisfaction in a Democratic society. Beyond this point Lausche—always careful to avoid cronyism—was no doubt thankful that his career did bring him into further political contact with Charles Keating. John Glenn, one of his senatorial successors, was less fortunate.

After the election, the Lausches' spent a quiet holiday in Columbus and Cleveland. On January 10, 1955, the Cleveland sandlot player who could only make the minor leagues in baseball stood at the pinnacle of state government. Always austere and unorthodox on such occasions, Lausche wore his twelve-year-old overcoat because "it's plenty good enough."[71] He took the oath upon a small flag-bedecked platform in the rotunda of the capitol. The Governor read from the Book of Micah, an Old Testament prophet who fought oppression and injustice. "He has showed you, O man, what is good; and what does the Lord require of you but to do justice, to love kindness, and to walks humbly with your God?"[72] Pomp and oratory were missing from the ceremony. The Governor made one concession to custom. He stood in a reception line in the Governor's executive offices and greeted hundreds of well-wishers. Lausche discouraged the Young Democratic Clubs of Ohio from having an unofficial inaugural ball, but he did not forbid it. He did not attend the ball, but Jane upheld the honor of the family with her presence. The Spartan Lone Wolf preferred to return to his governor's mansion where he smoked several of his nickel cigars (He was known to smoke part or all of as many as twenty cigars in a day). There alone he gave attention to his three dogs, Rod, an English setter; Demi, a half beagle; and Wong, a Pekingese.

In the solitude of the mansion Lausche made a valiant effort to play the violin. Coming from a musical family the Governor had inherited less than his share of a melodic gift. The mood often struck him to play a few selections in the evening or before breakfast. An incident connected with his violin practice convinced Lausche, once and for all, that he wasn't material for the concert stage. He recalled, "I played when no one was around. The only people who could hear me were some of the trusties from the state prison, who worked around the grounds of the Governor's mansion. One day, one of the trusties escaped. The police quickly caught him and asked why he spoiled his good record by trying to run away. 'It was the governor and his fiddle. I couldn't take another note.'"[73] Lausche was tempted to pardon the suffering inmate, but instead had him transferred out of earshot.

Lausche's long tenure as governor Prompted many such anecdotes. Colleagues recalled a local teacher telling a fifth grader, "You have a holiday tomorrow. It is Columbus Day." The youngster replied, "Who was Columbus?" The teacher answered, "Columbus discovered America." The schoolboy responded, "No Ma'am, America was discovered by Frank J. Lausche."[74]

⁀

THE OHIO GENERAL ASSEMBLY CONVENED IN late January. Lausche seemed comfortable with his fourth Republican-dominated legislature. For the most part the conservative Governor's frugal fiscal policies meshed with the tight-fisted demeanor of the GOP majority. Revenue had nearly trebled (from $396 million to $1,019,759,404) during the Lausche decade. Voters had not voted a general tax increase during this period.[75] Political analysts questioned if this conservative fiscal approach without provision for additional taxes would allow a growing Ohio to keep up with needed state supported services (highways, schools, prisons and correctional institutions, and mental health programs to name a few). A verdict would be forthcoming. Locher described his mentor as tightfisted and fiercely independent, "He was free as a bird. There were tough problems. He was more careful with the state's dollars than with his own. But he was extremely compassionate. He spent hours reading the record on all clemency matters."[76]

As he moved into his last two years in the statehouse, Lausche continued to push for certain legislation within the confines of budget restrictions. Following a bitter struggle with the mining lobby, the Governor pushed through a bill to force the strip miners of eastern Ohio to cover up their eroding handiwork when a mine became depleted.[77] As part of his "Plant Ohio" campaign, thousands of trees were planted on the denuded hills damaged by the wrack and ruin of coal mining. There was little doubt that author and conservationist Louis Bromfield influenced Lausche's conservation bent. Bromfields and Lausches had been friends for several years, and the Lausches occasionally visited the author and his wife at their well-known Malabar Farm southeast of Mansfield. (Humphrey Bogart and Lauren Bacall exchanged marriage vows at this home in 1945.) Bromfield died in 1956 at the age of 59.

In one of his last tributes to conservation and state park development, the Governor spoke to the Hocking County chapter of the Izaak Walton League. In 1946 during his first term in office, Lausche promised this chapter that Lake Logan State Park would be built. Ten years later the 341-acre man-made lake and state park became a reality. Lausche exclaimed, "It is a joy and an inspiration to see this placid mirror of water reflecting the lights of heaven."[78] The Governor reiterated his long-standing plea for soil conservation, intensification of efforts by state and local governments to protect streams from pollution, to increase the number of inland lakes, to provide more farm ponds, and to plant trees, grasses, shrubs and hedges. Lausche's stand on environmental issues placed him in the forefront among his fellow politicians.

Lausche proved successful in his efforts to persuade the legislature to acquire Cedar Point Beach near Sandusky, approximately 4,000 feet in length and receding gently into Lake Erie. Cedar Point, much better known for its commercial amusement park, was one of the finest beaches in the entire Great Lakes region. Lake Erie provided limited viable recreational beach frontage. Ohio's impressive state park system flourished under Lausche's leadership. The pace of this development accelerated due to population pressures, coupled with diminishing amounts of open land. It became imperative for the state to acquire available recreational lands. During the Lausche era, in addition to Lake Logan State Park, the state built beautiful rustic lodges at Punderson, Mohican, Salt Fork, Burr Oak, Lake Hope, Shawnee Forest, Deer Creek, Hueston Woods and Atwood Lake in the Muskingum Conservancy District. By 1997 Ohio managed seventy-two state parks, most of which offered camping, swimming, boating, hunting and hiking.[79] In the mid-1990s, Ohio ranked second in the nation in the number of visitors to its state parks—more than 61 million per year, trailing only California.

Lausche's long tenure as governor prompted many such anecdotes. Colleagues recalled a local Columbus teacher telling a fifth grader, "You have a holiday tomorrow. It is Columbus Day." The youngster replied, "Who was Columbus?" The teacher answered, "Columbus discovered America." The schoolboy responded, "No Ma'am, America was discovered by Frank J. Lausche."

During the 1955–57 biennium the Ohio Assembly approved legislative appropriations of $150 million for capital improvements (mainly for college and university buildings, mental hygiene institutions, and prisons). Over Lausche's objection, the assembly approved a state board of education composed of twenty-three members as dictated by an amendment to the Ohio Constitution approved by voters (one member from each congressional district). Prior to his departure from the statehouse, Lausche proposed elimination of three powerful state boards (Ohio Planning Commission, the Highway Construction Council, the Legislative Service Commission) and the reduction of the Ohio Board of Education down to a reasonable number, preferably one. He called the boards mongrel satellite governments and charged them with chipping away at the executive's duties and responsibilities. "The people on these boards are well-intentioned," he reflected, "but the Legislature has created boards having more power in the determination of state policy than the governor who is elected by all the people. Give the governor the responsibility and hold him accountable."[80] The approval of these boards by the general assembly pained the Governor, not only by thwarting him personally, but also in his view, hindering the execution of orderly government.

The historic *Brown vs Board of Education Supreme Court* decision in May 1954 declared segregated schools unconstitutional. President Dwight Eisenhower, lukewarm at best over the decision but faced with a constitutional imperative, ordered federal troops to Central High School in Little Rock, Arkansas. On September 24, 1954, under federal protection, nine black boys and girls entered the high school, and the tortuous process of integration moved forward with numerous setbacks and uprisings. Lausche generally frowned upon interference by the federal government upon state affairs. He viewed the civil rights issue differently. When the Democrats ruled the Ohio legislature in 1948–1950, Lausche nearly won passage of a fair employment practice act with enforcement procedures. In his state of state message in January 1955, Lausche asserted the Supreme Court decision met with his complete approval. "We simply cannot live as a free people if we...chip away from any member of our society the guarantees given to him by the Lord on the day that person was born and then reaffirmed with pen and ink in our Constitution."[81]

During Lausche's last term he pointed with pride to several statewide accomplishments. Only New York exceeded Ohio in manufacturing output and employment. The value of the Buckeye State's manufactured goods exceeded all of the New England states by thirteen percent. Ohio placed first in the nation in 1954 in gain of births over the previous year and recorded the largest decrease in the number of deaths. The average yearly income of $3,692 was exceeded only by Michigan and California.[82]

John Gunther called Lausche a man of charm, vitality, of absolute honesty, and sympathy for the underdog, whose only major defects stemmed from a lack of an academic education and a disinclination to think abstractly.

The mental health program, under the direction of Dr. John D. Porterfield, showed significant improvement over Lausche's ten-year tenure. Since 1945 capital expenditures for Ohio's mental health institutions had totaled more than $64 million. The Ohio Assembly appropriated an additional $2.5 million for the 1956–57 biennium. One-third of the voter-approved $150 million building bond issue was designated for mental health facilities. Daily per capita cost at these facilities increased from a woeful 87 cents in 1945 to $3.19 in 1956. Under Lausche's reign, the state became a pioneer in receiving hospitals. These hospitals were designed specifically for prompt and intensive treatment of individuals whose mental health seemed incipient or in an early stage. Prior to 1945 Ohio possessed no receiving hospitals. By 1955 a total of eight hospital units had opened in Youngstown, Cleveland, Athens, Cuyahoga Falls, Toledo, Columbus, Portsmouth and Cincinnati. Funds became available in 1955 for a new receiving unit in Dayton.

In 1955 for the first time, a decline occurred in the number of patients housed in Ohio's hospitals for the mentally ill. This decline happened in spite of a record admission figure of more than 10,000 a year as the state's population continued to grow. Because the death rate in Ohio's mental institutions had not risen, the decline in resident patient population resulted from an increased discharge figure. When Lausche left office in 1956, individual patient care for the mentally ill increased by more than 500 percent from 1945 when Lausche first took office in the Statehouse.[83]

226

Without doubt Lausche's proudest moment as Governor took place on October 1, 1955. He officially opened the remaining 219 miles of the Ohio Turnpike (later named the James W. Shocknessy Turnpike). The construction of this turnpike had been a long, arduous battle beginning in 1949 when the legislature voted to float a bond issue (approved by popular referendum in 1953) to finance long-term highway improvement programs in the state. The Ohio Turnpike stretched 241 miles across northern Ohio, linking up with the already completed 360 mile Pennsylvania Turnpike. Motorists and truck drivers traveled from just north of Philadelphia to the Ohio-Indiana line (601 miles), the longest contiguous superhighway then available in the United States. Constructed at a cost of $326 million, the toll-way generated so much income that its bonded indebtedness was retired early.

The interstate highway system expanded rapidly. The Federal Interstate Highway Act, passed in 1956, provided a national network of high-speed turnpikes. This act, the largest and most expensive public works project in the nation's history, provided for the construction of 41,000 miles of superhighways. By 1963 the Buckeye State was the leading contractor of interstate road construction in the nation.[84]

Lausche and the turnpike commission began preparing legislation to build a second major superhighway from Cleveland to Cincinnati (Route 71). None of these proposals came to fruition without considerable political in-fighting. Republican Senator David Ferguson from Cambridge, an outspoken critic of the turnpike commission, made no secret of his contempt for certain of its members and how the commission conducted its business.[85] In April 1955 verbal sparring created a wide split between the Governor and Joseph W. Bartunek (Democrat, Cuyahoga County), the party's Senate leader. Bartunek's bill proposed to establish a legislative committee with authorization to determine the routing of future toll roads and control over the sale of highway bonds. Another subcommittee of the senate highway committee recommended a bill that would strip the Ohio Turnpike Commission of the right to determine the route of future superhighways. Neither of these bills passed, but gave indication of the power struggle between the administration and the legislature.[86] Neither Lausche nor Shocknessy wavered in their efforts.

Often Lausche had to buck up the commission chairman who was under constant pressure from various constituencies for favors to hire friends. He had to fend off attacks from the press and taxpayers as to why delays occurred in completing the turnpike. Ethel Swanbeck, Republican representative from Erie County, provided Shocknessy with one such headache. She requested approval of four job applications for constituents from her county, which were accompanied with an endorsement from the Erie County Republican executive committee. These requests sent Shocknessy into orbit. He forwarded memos to the governor venting his frustrations and anger, always adding an acerbic comment or two.

Shocknessy diplomatically informed Swanbeck it was of no consequence what executive committee cleared the applications. The chairman referred to a guest column he wrote for the Cleveland *Press* soon after the commission was established. "There will be no political favoritism tolerated and there will be no political endorsements recognized by the Ohio Turnpike Commission as long as I am chairman or its membership remains as presently constituted."[87]

Criticism of the turnpike commission came from the press. Lowell Cridwell, staff writer for the Columbus *Citizen*, wrote a series of critical articles in 1955. He charged the highway-building program with confusion, red tape, over-cautiousness and an old-fashioned attitude about highway needs. The Governor came under attack for holding back highway monies until he was certain that adequate funds were available. Cridwell believed construction could be hastened because the money was indeed available. These attacks did not please the Governor or the turnpike commission chairman. Shocknessy threatened to resign his position several times, but each time the Governor coerced him to remain on the job.[88] Plans moved forward for the construction of superhighway No. 2, Route 71 from Cleveland to Cincinnati. This badly needed north-south highway opened for traffic in 1973.

After Lausche departed from the political arena in 1969, the Akron *Beacon-Journal* carried an article (March 9, 1969) detailing the origin, growth and present status of the Ohio Turnpike. Lausche wrote to James D. Hartshorne, former director of information and research for the Ohio Turnpike Commission. He affirmed that in his judgment there was not another turnpike in the whole country that was built with a breadth of vision, honesty, and efficiency, and subsequently managed equal to that of the Ohio Turnpike. He wrote, "I chuckle when I think of the editorial carried by the Cleveland *Plain Dealer* when I appointed the original members of the Commission.... It stated that none of the persons had particular experience in that field or operation. My objective was to appoint individuals who... were honest men possessed of reasonable business experience and who would abstain from allowing politics in the Governor's office to interfere with their work"[89] Lausche took pride in the fact that all of the highway projects under his direction did not suffer from a spectacle of fraud and special contract awards associated with similar projects in other states.

> The state's most successful politicians—men like [Mark] Hanna, John Bricker, Frank Lausche, James Rhodes are those able to move most skillfully among the state's power blocks...

When Frank J. Lausche first entered the statehouse in 1945, he bore all the marks of a true American folk hero. The first generation Slovenian, the son of an immigrant steelworker, became a self-made lawyer, and an outstanding city judge. The popular young man vaulted into the Mayor's office of his hometown and then to the governorship.[90] John Gunther called Lausche a man of charm, vitality, of absolute honesty, and sympathy for the underdog, whose only major defects stemmed from a lack of an academic education and a disinclination to think abstractly.[91]

With the passing of time, historians and political analysts present a *mixed bag* review of his tenure in the Governor's office. Lausche's success at winning elections, possibly unbeknownst to himself, was linked to a timeworn cliché: the right man at the right time. He read the Ohio political landscape beautifully. A generalized ignorance or an indifference to government and politics existed among a large majority of non-farming, low-income citizens. Pollster Louis Harris noted in "A Study of Issues and Candidates in Ohio" in 1958 that there was "an almost complete lack of associating economic self-interest and the real problems in people's lives with their vote for state-wide offices in Ohio."[92] Political scientist John H. Fenton defined voter apathy as a serious negative factor among Ohio voters. This indifference toward politics and government developed as a by-product of the history, culture, and power structure of the state.[93]

Lausche adopted Ray Bliss's prescription for Republican victories in Ohio politics. The prescription read: Keep issues out of campaigns.[94] Lausche seldom spoke of issues in his campaign speeches. He emphasized his dedication to honesty, integrity and fiscal responsibility. Coupled with his attacks on lobbyists and racketeers, the charismatic Governor captured voters with personal charm, outstanding oratorical skills and avoiding significant campaign promises. His political races developed into pointless contests of personalities devoid of meaningful issues. Hence the reason Ohioans did not connect their day-by-day problems with their votes was that seldom did they detect any visible association between the two variables.

Other political factors benefited Lausche. Farmers, particularly in the Corn Belt counties of central and southern Ohio, were relatively prosperous in the post-World War II years. Lausche did not propose to rock the boat. Many farmers of European heritage, related to Lausche's ethnic background and folksy, down-on-the-farm demeanor. Despite his big-city apprenticeship, Lausche garnered an increasing number of votes in these traditionally Republican counties. Secondly, in contrast to Michigan, the labor organizations in Ohio were not a strong political force. The leadership of the Ohio unions reflected the rather narrow intellectualism of their members. Lausche appealed to a laborer as an independent entity, not a *Stepford* member of a union. The laboring force responded with strong support (at least in the fifties). Thirdly, and possibly most importantly, Lausche's avowed independence from the Democratic Party transcended normal party lines. He attracted voters with strongly Republican leaning tendencies. Remarks like "Government should not become the property of the business tycoon or the labor leaders" or "If gambling racketeers aren't run out of business, they will drive the little businessman out of business" had wide appeal to a broad spectrum of voters.[95] Finally, Lausche developed a strong reputation for fairness. This boded well for voter support from the tightly knit enclave of nationalities, particularly in Cleveland, Lausche's home base. "He played on the nationalities like a guitar."[96]

In the final analysis, it is often difficult to appraise fairly a politician's accomplishments. Length of tenure in office does not necessarily equate unfavorably with quality of performance. Lausche's reputation for rugged honesty proved laudable. He practiced his brand of independent politics with the same single-minded devotion that his fellow Ohioan Senator Taft used to foster an all-embracing Republicanism.

Lausche loyalists pointed to a surplus of $36 million remaining in the state treasury when he left the governorship. He upgraded Ohio's once sorry highway system to rank second in the nation. The Governor imposed a special tax on trucks, obliging them to pay a fair share of highway repair and building costs. He pushed through a law requiring strip-miners to repair damaged land. The Governor strengthened workmen's compensation and fair employment practices laws, and hastened the integration of Ohio's few segregated schools. He cracked down on corrupt Teamsters Unions, which had been victimizing honest drivers—years before the McClellan committee addressed this issue in Congress. Lausche added more than 6,500 beds to Ohio's woefully overcrowded mental hospitals. Despite arguments to the contrary, he strengthened union security in the state by refusing to interject state power into labor disputes that could be settled by free collective bargaining.[97] These major accomplishments resulted in spite of four out of five Republican-controlled General Assemblies. Republicans labored futilely to find any significant scandals during the Lausche years.

This laudatory synopsis of Lausche's achievements in no way absolves him from valid criticism. Using a broad brush, reporter David Hess painted a harsh, but not wholly inaccurate summation of Ohio's special-interests-first politics. He argued that, for the first seventy-five years of the twentieth century, the state's politics had reeked of intrigue and manipulation. Hess wrote, "The state's most successful politicians—men like [Mark] Hanna, John Bricker, Frank Lausche, James Rhodes are those able to move most skillfully among the state's power blocks, wheeling and dealing for favors and concessions while deftly creating a public image or rectitude and incorruptibility. Such men are pragmatic, alert to opportunity, and only superficially committed to any ideology or grand design of government."[98]

Hess contended that these men accommodated themselves to the interests of big business, since great power resides in the directorates of Ohio's giant mills, banks and insurance companies. They also knew that the stolid and prosperous farmers in rural Ohio endorsed the conservative tone of the urban establishment. All of this, along with an increasing conservatism of Ohio's trade and industrial unionist, produced a milieu in which Progressivism as defined in the early 1900s could hardly flourish.

The frugal and conservative Governor imposed a strict pay-as-you-go philosophy, akin to the low-spending Byrd regime in Virginia. Ohio failed to retain its respectable position among other states services to people—in education, welfare, criminology, and mental health care, which the state held prior to Lausche's governorship. Benefiting first from a wartime-generation surplus in the state treasury, and later refusing adamantly to increase taxes, Lausche failed to inaugurate needed capital investments to adequately finance basic state services.

Ohio's five state universities combined received less money than the University of Illinois alone during his tenure. Ohio's allotment of public funds to elementary and secondary public education amounted to 1.9 percent of personal income. Ohio's tax effort (as a percent of personal income) ranked 41st in the nation in 1950 and 42nd when Lausche left office.

When Lausche entered the statehouse in 1948, Ohio's per capita expenditures for education, welfare, and highways compared favorably with the average for all states. The figures were less impressive when Lausche left office in 1956. During a prosperous decade, Ohio's per capita state expenditures for education were $22.48 compared with the all-state average of $34.75; $13.85 for welfare, compared with the all-state average of $16.35; and $42.16 for highways, compared with the all-state average of $32.74.[99]

Fenton pointed out professionals in finance, education and welfare insisted that a major share of the direct burden of Lausche's policies fell on children. According to Lausche's critics, the reason for spending so little on children's services was that they did not vote. For example, in Lausche's last year as Governor, some 1,000 boys resided in the Boys' Industrial School, which admitted to a rated capacity of about 600. In the sleeping quarters of the school, as many as seventy beds were jammed one against the other so that the only access to beds beyond the outer row was to step from bed to bed. Conversely, critics asserted that the Governor invested substantial sums in a highway program because, first, it was needed and, second, because money spent on highways provided the biggest political payoff in terms of jobs, potential campaign contributions from contractors and visible evidence of achievement.[100]

In the mind of Lausche critics the Governor's ten-year tenure was not a record of vigorous leadership or great accomplishment. But it was a record of parsimonious honesty. That seemed to be what the people of Ohio desired. One's evaluation of whether a public official has served his constituency well often depends upon what one expects from a state government. If voters anticipate a debt-free ledger with minimal tax-supported services Lausche scored high. For the citizen who prefers higher taxes and attendant improvements in social services, Lausche did not fare well.[101]

Lausche believed he had served his constituency well, "My strength grew throughout the years of my governorship. I was stronger when I left the governorship...than I was in 1944 when I first was elected. And many, who were my enemies originally, became my friends at the end of my incumbency."[102] Lausche enjoyed his years as Governor. "I did not regret it. There were experiences of joy and experiences of sorrow. The sorrow came when powerful political organizations and economic groups sought through the threat of defeating me at politics to cause me to change my views on what was right for the state."[103]

Lausche concluded that, while from a standpoint of esteem, the Governor occupies a much loftier position than that of U.S. Senator, it was time for him to step down. The Governor later affirmed that he could have been elected to a sixth term. His candidacy would have been legal despite the state's new constitutional amendment. "I want to tell you frankly, however, that I would have felt embarrassed to go to the voters and ask them to vote for me for the same office on six separate occasions."[104]

To the surprise of absolutely no one, Lausche, in keeping with his reticence to communicate his political intentions, finally declared his candidacy for a seat in the United States Senate on December 21, 1955. Fearless Frank would attempt to unseat Republican George Bender and join the most exclusive club in America. Lausche's intriguing persona and remarkable vote-getting ability had caught the public's attention. Syndicated columnists and political leaders, including President Eisenhower, speculated on his political future. The Governor's impressive performance on a *Meet the Press* program in January 1956 only served to showcase his well-established political savvy. Lausche had reached the pinnacle of his professional career. The dark horse presidential candidate awaited his political fortunes.

Governor Lausche with State Auditor James A. Rhodes (later governor of Ohio). (Courtesy of Columbus Dispatch).

nine

The Senator and Whisperings
of the Presidency

EIGHT U.S. PRESIDENTS HAVE ORIGINATED FROM Ohio, either by birth or as the state of their primary residence. The first—William Henry Harrison—lived in Ohio when he won the presidency in 1840, although he was born in Virginia. Affectionately known as "Old Tippecanoe," Harrison, a war hero and a Whig, served his country's highest office for only one month before dying of pneumonia. All the remaining seven native Ohioans who became President wore the Republican mantle: Ulysses S. Grant, Rutherford B. Hayes, James Garfield, Benjamin Harrison, William McKinley, William Howard Taft, and Warren G. Harding. Could Lausche break through to become the first Democrat from Ohio to enter the portals of the White House?

As early as 1947, Gunther prophesied that the 49-year-old Lausche was a man to watch. "The United States doesn't have so many capable and honest men in public life that it can afford to neglect any favorite son, particularly if he comes from Ohio. Lausche, like [Harold] Stassen on the other side of the fence seems to be a natural, despite his defeat [for Governor] in 1946."[1] Ten years later the Governor, now considered a favorite son candidate, joined a cast of previous Ohio convention contenders in the twentieth century, notably Democrats Judson Harmon in 1912, James M. Cox in 1920, Republicans Frank Willis in 1928, John W. Bricker in 1944 and Robert Taft in 1952.

When Lausche won back the governorship in 1948, the *New York Times* heralded the two-time governor as a presidential possibility. For several months the press badgered Lausche as to his intentions. He consistently answered in the negative. On one occasion he framed his answer so as to preclude every possibility that he was seeking the nomination. This ploy did not stop inquiries of the Governor about his political intentions.

President Truman announced on March 29, 1952, that he chose not to run for re-election. The President was eligible to run for a full four-year term in 1952. The newly passed Twenty-second Amendment prohibiting a President from serving more than two terms took effect with Truman's successor. Interestingly, several authors have written that in 1947 the President extended the Democratic presidential nomination to General Dwight Eisenhower for the 1948 election, and furthermore, Truman offered to run on the ticket as the general's vice president. Secretary of the Army Kenneth C. Royall presented this offer to Eisenhower. The general later made an off-the-record confirmation of this proposal to C. L. Sulzberger of *The New York Times*. In 1955 the now President Eisenhower told Lausche that Truman twice "personally asked me to run on the Democratic ticket for President with himself as the candidate for Vice-President. I told him no both times." Cabell Phillips reported Truman's offer in his 1966 book *The Truman Presidency*. Eisenhower declined to comment when Phillips asked him about this fact. Truman denied making this offer in a letter to Phillips. Royall insisted to Phillips that his account was "substantially correct."[2]

The president's announcement prompted political columnists to again question Lausche about his intentions regarding the Democratic nomination in 1952. On this occasion the Governor stated jocularly that he had given the inquiry deep thought. "The governor concluded that each morning at 8:30 a.m. he would walk approximately 150 steps leading to the dome of the capital, and would with a megaphone announce publicly in the procedure of a court bailiff, Hear Ye! Hear Ye! Hear Ye! Hear Ye! My position has not changed."[3] The following morning journalists came to the Governor's office and delivered a megaphone to him bearing the inscription *Lausche for President*. Reticent to project himself into the middle of a political fray, Lausche was not a major factor in the 1952 presidential election.

He supported Illinois Governor Adlai Stevenson for the Democratic nomination. His support was of little help, as Eisenhower easily routed Stevenson. The twenty-year reign of Democratic presidents ended. Lausche had kind words for the new President and maintained a warm relationship with him during his tenure.

Lausche friends intimated that during a critical period in U.S. foreign relations, Lausche wrote to the President stating that he knew of no one with greater ability to handle a national emergency, rally support of the citizens and unite the country. The President, in turn, made Lausche cognizant of his own respect for the Ohio Governor.[4] The wagging among the press increased when word leaked out at the state capitol that the Governor had joined President Eisenhower in a flight to Seattle to attend the National Governor's Conference in early August 1953. Speculation emerged as to whether the White House might exert pressure on Lausche regarding his senatorial appointment for the late Robert Taft.

This appointment was critical because of the narrow two-vote advantage for the Democrats in the Senate. No doubt Eisenhower would have appreciated a Republican replacement.[5] In actuality, Burke did not prove to be an anathema to either party during his two-year stay in the Senate. On the social side Eisenhower, an avid golfer, was known to have invited Lausche, a low handicap golfer, to play not only at Burning Tree Golf Club in Washington, DC, but also at Augusta National Golf Club, home of the Master's tournament.

One of Eisenhower's cabinet members was Ezra Taft Benson, new Secretary of Agriculture, from Salt Lake City. Benson proposed several reorganization changes in the United States Department of Agriculture. A storm of protests emanated from the opposition, mainly Democrats. One proposal recommended the elimination of seven regional offices of the Soil Conservation Service and the transfer of their responsibilities to various state offices of the Soil Conservation Service. In mid-November of 1953, Benson gave an address at a convention of Land Grant Colleges and Universities in Columbus. Who should show up for the address but Frank Lausche. When Benson finished his talk, he asked the Governor to make a few remarks. Lausche spoke of the loftiness of the principles Benson enunciated, the clarity of the recommendations, and the intense patriotism manifested by his statements. The Governor expressed respect for Benson's remarks. "As a public official—I know—there is nothing more difficult than the achievement of changes in government. The colors may be distinctly black and white, they may clearly demand a change, but when you attempt to introduce it, the cry is made that there is political motivation and that there is no soundness in the proposals made."[6] Lausche concluded his remarks by commending Benson on the excellence of his presentation. Coming from a Democratic Governor of an important Midwestern state, this praise was gratifying to the Secretary of Agriculture. Lausche's foray to the other side of the political fence reinforced his propensity for unorthodox political behavior.

Lausche continued to perplex Democratic moguls with his independent flair and his affinity for Eisenhower. In May of 1955 the now five-term governor refused to attend a meeting of Democratic Governors in Washington, DC to discuss political strategy (Lausche was now one of the senior governors). He demurred because he had just attended a White House conference of all governors to discuss domestic problems. The often-contrary Lausche exclaimed, "I cannot join a political meeting on ways and means of defeating a man [Mr. Eisenhower] who has just been my host."[7] This retort brought a sharp rejoinder from Democratic National Chairman Paul Butler. Lausche's actions did little to endear him to other Democratic governors.

⌒

DEMOCRATIC HOPES FOR THE 1956 ELECTION TOOK on a new look because of Eisenhower's heart attack in September 1955. There was concern whether the President had the stamina to run for a second term. The media speculated about possible Democratic candidates who might challenge the ailing President or his replacement. This list included a reticent Lausche. Prior to his victory in 1954, *Fortune Magazine* described the Democratic Party as lively and leaderless, and touted the Ohioan as a rising star in the party. Governor of Republican Ohio, "he is known as an excellent administrator and is well-liked. A Roman Catholic, he would be under that historical cap."[8] The issue of a Catholic successfully running for President had been tested in 1928 when Herbert Hoover had soundly defeated Al Smith, a devout Catholic from New York. Smith had even lost several states in the Democratic bastion of the *Solid South*. Democratic naysayers challenged the argument that Smith lost because he was Catholic, contending that, due to the prosperity of the twenties, Hoover would have won certain southern states no matter whom the Democrats had selected. This so-called inglorious spectacle of bigotry associated with the 1928 election dissipated thirty-two years later when John F. Kennedy, a Catholic, won the presidency in 1960. Lausche was not considered a strong Catholic, nor did he regularly attend Mass.

Regardless of his religious leanings, by 1955 Lausche was a hot item in the national political arena. His picture graced the covers of *Time* (Feb. 20, 1956) and *Newsweek* (May 21, 1956). Favorable articles about his political stature appeared in *Saturday Evening Post*, *The Reporter*, *Nation*, *American Mercury*, *Colliers*, and Robert Welch's extreme right-wing *One Man's Opinion*. Syndicated columnists touted his political acumen.

Raymond Moley, highly respected political columnist for *Newsweek*, speculated about Lausche's chance as a viable candidate in 1956. A native of Berea, Ohio, he taught political science at Western Reserve University during World War I. Moley moved to New York where he continued teaching at Columbia University's Barnard College. In 1933, the professor became an important member of President

Roosevelt's *Brain Trust* and one of the architects of the New Deal. In 1936 he departed from the President's group of advisors, reevaluated his political philosophy and drifted to a more conservative viewpoint, not unlike Lausche's position.

Moley understood Ohio politics and knew about Lausche's accomplishments and political philosophy. He remembered that the Governor's philosophy on domestic affairs came from Thomas Jefferson, "...a wise and frugal government, which shall restrain men from restraining one another, shall leave them otherwise free to regulate their own pursuits of industry and improvements, and shall not take from the mouth of labor the bread it has earned...is the sum of good government."[9] After the dust settled from the midterm election of 1954, Moley included Lausche among five prime Democrats to be touted for the 1956 Democratic candidacy. The political analyst believed that, in spite of Lausche's amazing capacity to garner votes in Ohio, he suffered from handicaps that would impair his national image. Conservative voters wished fervently that Lausche were a Republican. Radical Democratic leaders and labor bosses would vigorously oppose him. Being a Roman Catholic would not help. Lack of national exposure and difficulty in pronouncing his name posed as additional liabilities.

> "I cannot join a political meeting on ways and means of defeating a man [Mr. Eisenhower] who has just been my host."

On the positive side, Moley argued that the Ohio Governor was personally more colorful and attractive than Adlai E. Stevenson or Estes Kefauver. Like Stevenson, he was no spinner of rhetoric, nor was he a special pleader like Kefauver but, "He gets his special effects by his sense of timing and his art of dramatizing his indubitable handsome self. Since he is a strong believer in state's rights and responsibilities and is not indebted to city machines or labor, he might draw the support of southern leaders who must realize that there is little chance to nominate one of their own. His nomination would bring back to the party thousands of conservative Democrats and he would have the support of businessmen nationally just as he has commanded in Ohio."[10]

A highly reputable Cleveland businessman echoed Moley's words. The anonymous individual insisted that, if a Democrat were to be elected to the White House, Lausche would be the only one for whom he would vote. David Lawrence, respected political analyst for the conservative *U.S. News and World Report*, gave accolades to the Ohio Governor.[11] Fulton Lewis, Jr., a syndicated and popular *Rush Limbaugh* of his era, spoke well of Lausche, citing only the drawback of his being a Catholic.[12] For all the adulation from the national media, Lausche fared much poorer within the Democratic hierarchy. In a December 1955 United Press poll, among twenty-five Democratic governors and forty-four Democratic state chairmen, only two respondents selected the Ohio Governor as their first choice.[13] It was no secret that Lausche had burned bridges with several of his hard-nosed colleagues, some of whom were also presidential aspirants. Lausche's independent bent did not set well with old-line party faithful. As one political pundit explained, "Despite [Lausche's] baseball background, he doesn't have the record of a team player in politics."[14]

Lausche's conservatism proved not to be the primary point of agitation between him and the Democratic Party organization. The Governor's constant crossing of party lines to support Republican candidates and his refusal to back the Democratic Party organization in statewide campaigns irritated party leadership. Lausche played the political scene like that of a chess player, always thinking three moves ahead and weighing the political consequences for his actions.[15]

By mid-1955 candidates began to vie for position in 1956 Democratic presidential nomination. The acknowledged leading candidates included Governor Adlai Stevenson, Senator Estes Kefauver, and Averill Harriman, the wealthy railroad magnate and Governor of New York. Although a bit out of character, Lausche gave his opinion of the candidates. Lausche regarded Stevenson as the strongest candidate. He held the other leading candidates in high regard, questioning whether Kefauver and Harriman possessed enough experience to cope with the push and pull from pressure groups. The Governor considered Governor G. Mennen Williams from Michigan too controversial to be considered a serious candidate. As to his own chances, Lausche said others would have to answer that question because, "Frankly, I do not think that I have a chance.... The flurry of discussions... are not motivated and catalyzed by me. I wish they would come to an end."[16]

Although Lausche downplayed his presidential potential, others were not so sure. Political analyst Chesly Manly called the Governor Ohio's Taft Democrat and a dark horse candidate who might beat Eisenhower. A fellow Ohio Democrat, Wayne Hays the irascible U.S. representative, called Lausche "a gutless wonder full of promises and short on performance." On the other side of the aisle, Republican representatives categorized him as "an authentic political genius."[17] To reporters at the state capitol, he was a man of great personal charm, a ham, sincere and honest and a political paranoid.

The Lausche *boomlet* gained strong support from eleven states representing the Deep South. The Brown vs. Board of Education Supreme Court decision in 1954 declared segregated schools unconstitutional. The liberal element of the Democratic Party, mainly in the north, continued to exert pressure for equality for all American citizens. The south was reticent to move so quickly. Governor Lausche maintained an ambivalent position on the issue. He declared that the "Supreme Court's decision must be accepted as law," and added "the Court itself has said the transition could not be made overnight."[18]

From the point of view of northern liberals, Lausche owned an unassailable civil rights record. While Governor he had urged the adoption of a fair employment practice act. In 1956 he recommended legislation to withhold state aid from school districts practicing segregation. Conversely, during his years as governor, a segregated school operated in Hillsboro, a tiny rural community in southern Ohio, without state interference. The school remained segregated until exposed by the Cleveland *Press*. Court orders finally ended the segregation. For the record, no Federal Employment Practices Committee (FEPC) bill was passed during the Lausche regime, with the governor blaming the Ohio legislature for their inaction on this issue. In calling attention to his civil rights record in Ohio, Lausche invariably remarked that, "states rights must be maintained."[19] Southerners took this comment to mean that the Ohioan would not favor a federal employment practices act.

Conservative southern Democrats (They *were* Democrats in the *solid South* of the 1950s) felt boxed in with no viable presidential candidate to support. Although Stevenson was acceptable to several southern leaders, Kefauver and Harriman were considered liberal extremists in their zeal to push a civil rights agenda. Waging an uphill battle against the incumbent Eisenhower, the Democratic Party did not want to provoke another Dixiecrat rebellion like those in 1948 (loss of four states and 39 electoral votes) and 1952 (loss of four states and 57 electoral votes). The eleven southern states wrestled with how to get the most out of their numerical strength. Could Frank Lausche be the answer?

On December 9, 1955, Senator Richard Russell of Georgia and Governor Allan Shivers of Texas warmly endorsed Lausche for the country's top political position. Earlier Governor Robert Kennon of Louisiana told United Press the Ohio governor would make a good candidate. Senator John L. McClellan of Arkansas described Lausche as a formidable opponent to have as a candidate.[20] Soon thereafter, in succession, words of praise came from Governors George N. Craig (Indiana), Theodore McKellin (Maryland), and Arthur B. Langlie (Washington), all Republicans. Controversial J. Bracken Lee of Utah lent his support. Political analysts agreed that Lausche might poll more Republican votes than would any of the other potential Democratic candidates.

The South knew that little possibility existed to elect one of their own. Possibly their influence could be most beneficial to Lausche, who stood farthest right of all Democratic candidates. If the eleven southern states cast their convention votes in a solid bloc, their combined strength would total 290 votes. With the addition of Ohio's 58 votes and a smattering of votes from other delegates, the Ohioan could have conceivably counted on over half of the necessary 686 ½ votes needed to win a nomination.

Lausche continued to play his the-man-who-walks-alone role. *Fortune Magazine* sent out a questionnaire to seven leading Democratic candidates to ascertain their position on thirty-four questions regarding economic policy. The Governor, one of the candidates solicited, declined to respond because "to answer...would quickly be construed as an effort on my part to project myself in the national scene as a candidate.... I am not a candidate."[21] The *Fortune* editors researched Lausche's record as Governor and the content of his speeches. Like all of the other candidates, the Governor believed in an economy stimulated both by private initiative and by government action. The editors concluded that the enigmatic Lausche stood far to the right of the other six candidates, as well as President Eisenhower.

Unbeknownst to Lausche, the President's office was discussing Lausche's political credentials. On January 28, 1955, the re-elected Governor paid a visit to the President. Jim Hagerty, Eisenhower's press secretary noted in his diary, "When he [Lausche] told the President that the people of the country, particularly the people of the state of Ohio, supported him, the President was visibly affected and thanked Lausche...."[22] The President added that he had been reading stories in the paper to the effect that Lausche might be a Democratic candidate for President. Lausche acknowledged that he had heard these rumors, but insisted the President was the best-qualified man to guide the United States through difficult times.

The President appreciated the Governor's accolade, and then asked him about his golf game. Lausche responded that he played a little in Ohio even in the cold weather. Eisenhower, an avid golfer, slapped Lausche on the back and said, "I'll tell you what we'll do, Governor. When I go to Augusta in April would you come down and play golf with me a few days if I asked you?" Lausche responded that he would be delighted. The President laughed and added, "Let's do it. We'll confound all the political experts. They'll think we're trying to make up a combination ticket. O.K.?"[23]

Late in the summer of 1955 while recuperating from a heart attack, Eisenhower conjectured with Hagerty on Lausche's attraction as a possible Democratic presidential nominee, "Look, Jim, Lausche would be a natural. In 1952 many Democrats voted for me because they didn't like Stevenson and the Truman Fair Deal-New Deal boys.... Despite all we have done in four years, I'm the only Republican that the young folks will support. With me out of the picture, they will support a Democrat. Lausche would appeal to the youth, and hundreds of thousands of Democrats who left their party to vote for me would go back to their party, I am convinced, to vote for Lausche."[24]

The President discussed his unusual idea with Leonard Hall, Republican National Chairman. Eisenhower was intrigued with the idea and reminded Hall that labor hated Lausche. "Labor leaders don't like *you*," Hall countered, "but the laboring people vote for him and vote for you...[moreover], the Republicans seldom do something different; here you break the bugaboo of a Catholic [running for the presidency]."[25] Hall reminded the President that even Ohio Republicans told him that Lausche was an able man. Eisenhower continued, "It would just knock the props out of the [opposition], "Lausche for my money..., you could not improve on him...he is a great patriot." "A shocker," Hall agreed. "I'd love to run with a Catholic," Ike thoughtfully speculated, "if only to test it out."[26] Hall believed that if the Republicans didn't run a Catholic this time, the Democrats would next time. And he specifically mentioned the young and attractive John F. Kennedy.[27]

Eisenhower suggested that Hall take a public poll to determine whom the voters wanted for President. Because of the sensitivity of this issue, Hall avoided well-known opinion samplers and instead went to a detective agency, obtaining results written out in longhand. The poll proved that only one name on the ballot counted—Eisenhower's—but that in the number two spot, Lausche would run as well as anybody else.

Then Eisenhower considered the possibility of Lausche running on the Republican ticket as a vice presidential candidate. Hall mistakenly believed it would be easy to persuade Vice President Richard M. Nixon to drop out of the picture and accept another high-level government position. The President was more wary, but gave his approval, advising Hall to "see [Nixon] and talk to him. But be very, very gentle."[28] Hall took Bob Humphreys, former journalist and the closest man to Nixon at this time, with him and approached Nixon with the proposal. Hall recalled, "I never saw a scowl come so fast over a man's face. But beyond that, we got no response at all. He was so uptight when he heard the suggestion, he just stared at the ceiling."[29] This far-fetched proposal was dropped like a hot potato.

The high mark in Lausche's unsolicited role as a possible presidential candidate occurred in late 1955 and early 1956. The reclusive-like Governor, whether intentionally or otherwise, found himself the subject of increasing attention from the press. On December 9, 1955, David Lawrence wrote a column entitled "Why Not Governor Lausche?" The columnist made a case for Lausche's candidacy, asserting that he was the best vote-getter among Democratic candidates. He listed the reasons why the Ohio Governor would be an excellent candidate and why he had the potential to poll more Republican votes than any other Democratic candidate. Lawrence insisted that the Democratic Party must not allow themselves to be affected by the alleged potency of an outworn religious issue.[30]

With a presidential election year approaching, Lausche continued to impress the national media. On January 8, 1956, he traveled to Washington, DC to debut on national television with an interview on the highly acclaimed *Meet The Press* program. The panel included the well-known moderator Lawrence Spivak and panelists Jack Bell of *Associated Press*, Mae Craig of the Portland (ME) *Press-Herald* and Clyde Mann of the Akron *Beacon Journal*. This interview struck the politically *blasé* capitol like a thunderbolt. From among those who saw the show came such exclamations as "tremendous, what a personality, what sincerity, what honesty—from a politician." After viewing the program, one GOP Senator commented, "I'd be awfully afraid of that man if the Democrats nominate him."[31] Lausche's words came across as direct as his gaze. He obviously made a hit with the audience when he explained that he was running in Ohio's primary only "with the purpose of preventing political bosses of Ohio from gaining control of the Ohio delegation and then using it as a pawn or a mess of pottage to trade for spoils and patronage at the national convention."[32]

In answer to specific domestic issues such as tax cuts vs. debt reduction, Lausche responded that, in view of the country's huge debt, "Before we cut taxes...we ought to get our house in order and see that the debt is cut."[33] When asked about his view on the Taft-Hartley Act, Lausche didn't specifically say whether he favored repealing or amending the Act, but insisted on the rights of the American worker to work regardless of their association with a labor union, a fraternal association, or a religious creed. He did not believe in secondary boycotts or jurisdictional disputes. To Lausche, the Act was intended to give protection to all workers, and that was the spirit in which our government should run.[34]

On the farm issue Lausche understood the U.S. government had $7 billion dollars worth of surplus products in storage bins. The government paid a million dollars a day to store surplus farm produce. He believed rigid farm supports contributed to this buildup. The Governor did not view strict federal support as the answer, but preferred the possibility of a soil bank.[35]

Although Lausche hoped Mae Craig would not ask him if his religion was a liability to his candidacy, he added that it was a proper question. The Governor wanted citizens to judge him in the same light that Thomas Jefferson asked to be judged on this issue (Jefferson was not a Catholic.). Jefferson, in a letter to John Adams remarked, "My religion with my God belongs to him and me. It is a matter of private concern. Do not judge me by my religion, judge me by my deeds and my conduct, and if you think that they have indicated a devotion to my community, my state and my nation, then the religion by which it has been guided undoubtedly must be good."[36]

Lausche affirmed his conviction in a two-party system (He opposed third parties or the creation of splinter parties.) When Craig asked if the Governor—as implied by certain Democrats—was not even a fifty-percent Democrat, Lausche adroitly evaded answering directly and responded with a bit of Lincolnesque oratory, "I believe in government of the people, by the people, and for the people. I believe in according to the individual the full enjoyment of his native rights. I believe that every individual should have the right to exercise the creative capacity by mind and by hand. I believe that I have espoused legislation in my legislature of a nature that indicates a liberality commensurate with the times and capable of fulfillment within reason."[37]

The Governor answered several other questions and deferred to a question as to which Democratic candidate he favored. Lausche concluded that, all factors being equal, he would support a Democrat, then added, "I want to say...that in my judgment President Eisenhower has brought unity of thought to the nation. I think he has honestly and sincerely tried to evolve programs that would help the social, economic, and governmental structure of my country."[38] Further, Lausche hoped the President fully recovered his health and would again be the Republican candidate for the office of President.

PRIOR TO THIS NATIONWIDE INTERVIEW, LAUSCHE'S POLITICAL philosophy was not well known to most politicians and pundits. They had only a general impression that he was conservative in his outlook, eccentric in his behavior, and unbeatable in Ohio elections. There was no longer any reason for ignorance about the political specifics of Frank Lausche. The Cleveland *Plain Dealer* responded to Lausche's impressive showing on the *Meet The Press* program. An editorial maintained that the Governor's greatest asset was a sense of the sincerity he conveyed to his audience. In that respect, the editor believed only President Eisenhower was his equal. The editorial continued, "Lausche...does not believe he has a chance to get the Democratic nomination. For the political bosses will be in the center of the convention and the labor bosses are powerful enough to exercise the veto over any prospective nominees. So we have a suggestion. If President Eisenhower does not run for re-election, let the Republicans nominate Lausche. They could never find another candidate so much like Ike."[39]

The Ohio Governor's star continued to rise. A lengthy article entitled "The Lonely One" appeared in *Time* Magazine (January 23, 1956) describing his meteoric rise in Ohio and national politics. The Governor was so impressed by *Time* correspondent Ed Darby's incessant questioning on a speaking circuit that he winced whenever the correspondent took out his notebook. Addressing the Dayton chapter of the B'nai B'rith one evening, Lausche spoke of his state's system of using penitentiary inmates who were awaiting parole as trusties for assorted tasks at the governor's mansion. He remarked that a trustie had chauffeured him from the Capitol to Dayton. Later in a restaurant, the wife of one of the B'nai B'rith officers leaned over to the Governor and with a sidelong glance at *Time* correspondent Darby and at David Chatfield, the Governor's law secretary, whispered, "Which one is the trusty?" The Governor laughed, and whenever Darby took out his notebook after that, he pointed at the correspondent and ordered, "Put that away or I'll lock you up again."[40]

Lausche continued to be queried about his political philosophy, especially in view of his independent bent. He placed himself in the category of a conservative liberal. Lausche believed in governmental assistance to those who, because of a disability and/or other debilities beyond their control, were incapable of helping themselves. He was against governmental handouts, even though on the surface they seemed to be temporarily of a beneficent nature, but which in truth destroyed the character of the citizenry. His antipathy toward boss-ridden labor unions was well known. Lausche railed, not only against the formidable power of these labor monopolies, but also against equally formidable combinations of finance capital— viz General Motors with greater power than many states and Texas oilmen with huge and ever-growing accretions from depletion allocations. Lausche had an opinion about the conflict between capital and labor. Instances that the Governor pointed out occurred altogether too frequently in which capital and labor, especially demonstrated by some of their fanatical and unreasonable leaders, wanted the cards of government stacked in their favor. These irresponsible and shortsighted leaders of labor made their demands upon the Democratic Party; conversely, industrial titans made appeals to the Republican Party.

Lausche believed that, because the United States government was in the banking business due to the Federal Reserve System, there was a governmental responsibility to make certain that sales and purchases made on the credit basis were reasonably sound. The Governor recalled his days as a judge in the 1930s when he observed the calamities and tragedies because of extravagant extension of credit. In a prophetic tone he had an abiding conviction that, if there were an economic downturn, it would be the result of policies by financial institutions to make loans far above the prospective borrowers' ability to pay. The multiplicity of savings and loans scandals in the 1980s and 1990s gave credence to Lausche's worst fears.[41]

The Governor came as close as he ever would to declaring himself a candidate for the presidency in April, 1956, when with his flair for Aristolean oratory he told reporters, "I have not arrogated to myself the ability and the courage that it requires to fill the post.... I am not seeking the post. I want to repeat what I have said in the past; that if by some miraculous chance the assignment should come to me, I will not flee the responsibility."[42] In a roundabout manner Lausche was really saying yes to his candidacy. To consolidate Ohio's 58 votes for the Democratic convention, by law, Lausche had to enter the state's presidential primary. This he did to keep the delegate votes from supporting an undesired candidate or to discourage out-of-state participation. He was therefore the favorite son candidate. Senator Estes Kefauver decided against entering the Ohio primary because he did not want to incite intra-party animosities.[43] In the state primary election Lausche lost four of his delegate votes, three from the Cleveland and Canton areas and one from out-of-state.

In early May Lausche's independent posture came under attack, and he was ready with a reply. Democratic National Chairman Paul Butler visited Ohio Wesleyan University, and in an informal chat with students, expressed dismay at the Governor's recent endorsement of the President's farm bill veto (which would have provided additional farm subsidies). Lausche's view, according to Butler, was shocking to Democrats and in conflict with the majority. He added, "There is no room for independents in our political system."[44] That remark caught Lausche's attention, "My strength has been that no one has been able to dictate to me— bankers on down to labor leaders, strip miners, truckers, the utilities, and the whole raft of them. I can tell them all to go to hell except the people whom I've tried to represent."[45]

The Democratic National Convention took place in Chicago in mid-August. Lausche, who had only attended the 1952 convention (he appeared for only two hours in 1948), put in an appearance in the Windy City. He had instructed Michael V. DiSalle, Democratic nominee for Ohio Governor in 1956, to place Lausche's name in nomination as a favorite son. The Governor asked the former Toledo Mayor to write a nominating speech. DiSalle composed a speech on the second sweltering day of the convention, emphasizing the Governor's good record in office and his great vote-getting ability. After submitting this speech to Lausche and his staff, DiSalle thought he saw frost forming on the walls. He had not been lavish enough in praise of the Governor's virtues. Lausche's administrative secretary and a former newspaperman, Ray White, suggested beginning the opening paragraph with these words, "God has blessed this nation by making available... a man of Governor Lausche's unparalleled values...."[46] In the Governor's presence DiSalle told White that whenever he heard a speaker at a political meeting call upon God, he moved away for fear that the Almighty in His anger might send down a bolt of lightning to destroy those who called on Him for partisan ends. A painful period elapsed before the Governor agreed that the proposed change would be in bad taste. The original speech, slightly altered, was distributed to the press in the early hours of the third day of the convention. The total effort was for naught. A few hours earlier former President Truman had thrown his support to Governor Averill Harriman. When the roll call began it became obvious that Adlai Stevenson would be re-nominated for a second time. As the call for Ohio's vote approached, Lausche requested that DiSalle not place his name in nomination. DiSalle acceded to Lausche's wish. The Ohio delegation threw their support to Stevenson. Lausche had his day in the limelight. Despite his retreat from presidential aspirations the governor would maintain strong voter appeal. He was never again to reach this pinnacle as a *bona fide* presidential hopeful.

⁀

Lausche returned to Columbus. He now had the dual responsibility of completing his tenure as Governor and campaigning for a seat in the United States Senate. His opponent, George H. Bender, a fellow Clevelander, had fought the political wars for thirty years. Not particularly sophisticated, he took a page from another George, Sinclair Lewis' George in his novel *Babbitt*. Bender represented, according to a leading Ohio Republican, "the old-style, ward-heeler type of politician" that Ohio GOP had attempted to curb.[47]

Bender served in the Ohio senate from 1920 to 1930. He worked his way up the political ladder not unlike Lausche, and served as chairman of the Republican Central Committee of Cuyahoga County from 1936–1954. Bender won election to the U.S. House of Representatives in 1938 after four unsuccessful attempts and remained in office until 1948 when Stephen Young defeated him. After Ohio's congressional redistricting in 1951, he was again re-elected to Congress, this time from the 23rd district.

Bender narrowly defeated Thomas A. Burke for the remainder of the late Robert Taft's senatorial term.[48] He controlled Republican affairs in Cuyahoga County during the early fifties. A zealous campaigner, the rotund Bender gained considerable notoriety at the 1952 Republican convention in Chicago. Supporting Taft for the presidency, he reached the podium and became a cheerleader. He rang a cowbell and sang songs to lead the Ohio delegation. Fellow Republican William Saxbe remembered, "He made an ass of himself and led the Taft faction to defeat."[49] The Congressman acquired the image of a bell-ringing buffoon. (Bender later said that Senator Taft told him to be a cheerleader on the floor, even naming the songs to be sung.) Saxbe was so upset he challenged Bender in the 1954 primary election for the Taft Senate seat. The Bender political machine was too strong, and he defeated Saxbe by 65,000 votes. In spite of Bender's support of Taft in 1952, he later threw his support behind the Eisenhower presidency.

Bender had announced early in 1955 that he would seek re-election to the Senate. Several influential Republicans wanted a stronger candidate. No one stepped forward to be a sacrificial lamb in opposition to Lausche's candidacy. Bender did not believe in Lausche's invincibility. "Everybody who's ever run against Lausche has played dead for him...he's picked the wrong slot this time."[50] The race for a U.S. Senate seat was under way. With each candidate unopposed in the May primary, Lausche garnered 426,631 votes, and Bender received 509,682 votes.

Bender campaigned diligently, and at the Republican National Convention, campaign leaders and Ohio Republican chairman Ray Bliss took stock of Bender's chances. This Ohio Senate seat proved critical. The Democrats held a one-seat margin. If the Republicans retained this seat and party lines held on voting, Republican Vice President Richard Nixon would cast the deciding vote.

Bender, called a political hack by some members of his own party, was well known in the state. He had paid his dues and expected party support. Bliss was not a particular friend and, in reality, did not like Bender. Bender held the trump card because he was the darling of big money in Cleveland. He did exactly what the power brokers advised him to do. The corpulent party man had ties to unsavory elements of the Teamster's Unions in Cleveland. One of his big supporters included George Humphrey, Treasury secretary in President Eisenhower's cabinet. Humphrey was very important to the GOP and to Bliss as state party chairman.[51] In fact Eisenhower at one time believed Humphrey was presidential timber.

During the Republican convention, moguls gathered to determine how to give Bender's campaign a shot in the arm. His image was not the best, and delegates emphasized the need to dignify their candidate. Bliss warned the Ohio delegation, "The first person who hands a bell to George Bender will have to answer to me."[52] The dirty campaign waged by Bender in the 1954 election against Thomas Burke left delegates less than enthusiastic about this candidate.

Bender struggled to raise necessary money to make inroads against the popular

Lausche. Several leading businessmen donated money to Lausche's campaign (he took very little campaign money) that normally would have gone to the Republican standard-bearer. This support was badly needed by Bender. He had previously been the subject of criticism for the way he spent campaign funds. A special finance committee attempted to raise $500,000 for him, but succeeded in raising only $150,000. Republicans complained about contributing to a special fund. Bender suffered from a dearth of press support. He worked diligently to convince voters that he, while not a Robert Taft, was a hard working representative for the state of Ohio

With the conclusion of the Democratic National Convention in August, Lausche campaigned for the Senate as he had always campaigned before—ignoring his opponent and taking his campaign to the average voter. Once he started, the Governor worked long and hard. He wore his five-year-old suit and a haircut almost as old. Paying his own entrance fee, Lausche attended thirty of Ohio's 44 county fairs. He declined to make any speeches, wandered around the fairgrounds, shaking hands and admiring babies. At the Hardin County Fair in late September the Governor declined to sit on the officials' platform, turned down an opportunity to award a trophy and shook his head modestly when asked if he would like to make a few remarks at a livestock show.

Several weeks later in Middletown, the senatorial candidate turned down a chance to speak before an estimated crowd of 1,200 people. The occasion was a concert performance by Mahalia Jackson, concert singer of spirituals. The Governor declined overtures for him to give a political speech, insisting that a speech at such an affair would be sacrilegious. The Governor told Jackson, "We are better for having listened to you because there are many of us in politics who need our souls scrubbed."[53] After the concert newsmen questioned him about what they called his few speaking appearances during the current campaign. "Too many speeches are being made right now," Lausche said, "Let Bender do the talking. Every time he opens his mouth, he loses more votes."[54]

⌒

THE GOVERNOR CAMPAIGNED WITH LITTLE organized support. Labor disdained him. The CIO did not endorse either candidate. The AFL resoundingly backed Bender. Democrats had little choice but to vote for Lausche, but they disliked his open and heretofore successful wooing of Republican voters. Speaking at the Ohio Democratic convention in Columbus in September, Lausche was interrupted by a heckler who asked if he was a Democrat or a Republican. Lausche's emotional, spontaneous reply provided a synoptic statement of his principles, "All my life in public service, I have endeavored to do everything possible to give greater freedom to the individual and to improve his welfare. I have tried to do this within the Constitution of the United States. I do not believe that any one segment of our society should be given preferential treatment by government. Within the context of this statement, I am a Democrat."[55] This folksy style contributed to Lausche's great vote-getting ability in the Buckeye state. On another occasion the Governor declared, "When a public official does that which he believes is right, though for a moment there may be a prejudicial reaction, eventually the great bulk of the American public will subscribe to the man that does that which is decent and courageous."[56]

When President Eisenhower dismissed the possibility of Lausche running on the Republican ticket with him, the irony of politics placed the President in a compromising position. Because of the closeness of the make-up of the Senate and at the urging of George Humphrey, Eisenhower ended up crusading against Lausche and for the bumptious Bender. Bender was 100 percent loyal to the Republican cause. He was the same person who, long after Joe McCarthy's downfall, could still mindlessly conduct a tipsy Christmas crowd of Republican reactionaries in a bellowing chorus of "McCarthy is my leader, I shall not be moved."[57]

In late September, Eisenhower was discussing with his advisors local candidates in states where he was about to make speeches. In several instances the President lacked enthusiasm in supporting a dull and less than congenial fellow Republican, in spite of the individual's support for his legislative programs. Bender was such an example. Prior to a trip to Ohio, the President lamented, "What can I say about Bender in Cleveland? He has no more philosophy than this telephone. But he votes for my program one hundred percent. On the other hand Lausche is an old friend."[58] Bender, desperately attempting to ride on the coattails of the deceased Senator Taft, needed all the help possible. The support he received from the President and his backer George Humphrey were critical to his success. Throughout the last weeks of the campaign, he rallied voters with the slogan, "Ike needs Bender," and "Give Ike a Republican Congress."[59]

Lausche continued his low-key campaign on limited supporting funds. He frustrated Bender by declining to discuss issues or to partake of debates. Lausche appeared on television, not talking about issues; instead, he extolled the virtues of Johnny Appleseed, a legendary Ohio hero. Referred to as the artful dodger, the Governor played the coy game of not engaging in unnecessary dialogue about his political stance. "The people of Ohio know me, know my principles and know what I stand for."[60]

The basic issue between Bender and Lausche focused primarily on what kind of Democrat the governor professed to be. To many political pundits, he wasn't a very good capital "D" Democrat, but a very good Democrat with a lower case "d." "Of course I believe in the two-party system," Lausche confided to Seltzer while enjoying dinner, "I believe it is essential to our democracy. That...does not mean that I must blindly follow either people or policies I do not believe. It does not require me to take my thinking from political bosses who are in politics for profit, instead of patriotism. If I were...elected to the United States Senate, I would cross the aisle from one party to the other whenever the interests of the country seemed to require or justify it—regardless."[61]

In mid-October the outgoing Governor reiterated his party line to a group of black businessmen in Columbus. Unbeknownst to Lausche, Bender was in attendance at the gathering. In front of the audience, Bender questioned the Governor how he would vote, if victorious, to organize the Senate. Caught off guard by the question, Lausche quickly recovered, "I am," he replied, "a Democrat second and an American first. I will never hesitate to cross party lines when I think it will serve my country best."[62]

After declining over thirty invitations for joint appearances, Lausche finally agreed to debate Bender at the prestigious City Club of Cleveland. This forum provided an opportunity for members to discuss social, economic, and political issues on the local and national scenes. The forum provided an excellent venue for these two Clevelanders to challenge each other prior to the election. Those in attendance were not disappointed in the emotionally charged confrontation. Bender claimed Lausche was a fence-straddler, the darling of the Dixiecrats and the greatest myth in Ohio politics. Not prone to mudslinging, the Governor called Bender a rubberstamp politician who voted blindly for Eisenhower

Referred to as the artful dodger, the governor played the coy game of not engaging in unnecessary dialogue about his political stance.

legislation. Lausche then shocked the audience with a political bombshell. He gave a warm endorsement to Stevenson's candidacy, and then confided that if elected, "I would cast my vote in the manner which I believe the best for my country."[63]

By implication Lausche left the door open to vote with the Republican senators to assist them in gaining control of Senate machinery, should Eisenhower be re-elected. The Governor was ostensibly attempting to strengthen his foothold in Republican territory, at the expense of losing some regular Democrats. Although Bender—as well as the Democratic leadership—was outraged, the press expressed glee in hypothesizing on this comment as journalists had done in the 1950 incident when Lausche voted for Senator Taft.[64]

The presidential polls showed Eisenhower with an overwhelming advantage as Election Day approached. Would the President's vote-getting ability be enough to sweep Bender back into the Senate? Bender gained ground in the waning days of the campaign. But his efforts and those of the President in support of him fell short. On November 6, 1956, a cold damp Election Day, Ohio political leaders were shocked at the large turnout. A new record of 3,702,265 presidential ballots was cast. Once again, Lausche proved the truth of the local axiom that nobody likes him but the people. The senator-elect became the first Ohio Democrat to be elected to the Senate in 22 years. (Democrat James W. Huffman was appointed to replace the newly selected Supreme Court Justice Harold H. Burton in 1945.) Lausche carried the state by a plurality of 203,679 votes or a majority of 52.8 percent.

Geographically, the Governor captured only 34 of the 88 counties. He won in every metropolitan county except Hamilton (Cincinnati). Although Lausche carried more counties than he did in the 1954 gubernatorial race, the final tallies marked his lowest victory margin in six statewide elections. He did poorly in predominately rural areas, perhaps because during the campaign Lausche came out strongly against farm subsidies. In contrast, Eisenhower's margin of victory over Stevenson soared to 820,000, which exceeded his margin of victory over Stevenson in 1952 by 300,000 votes. Republican C. William O'Neill finally wrested the governorship from the Democrats, defeating Michael DiSalle by 400,000 votes. Amazingly, Lausche won in spite of swimming against the huge Republican political tide in his native state.

Lausche benefited from good press support, general prosperity, and prior publicity given to his presidential chances, and diminished attention to a senatorial race during a presidential election year. In contrast, Bender complained about the bad press he received. His cause was not helped when in Cleveland a strike halted the publications of all newspapers for the entire week preceding Election Day. The ultimate effect of these factors suggests the electorate voted their predispositions: that is to say, Bender failed to dispel the Lausche myth.[65] Lausche's legacy of being a vote-getter, leaving office with a balanced budget, parsimonious spending of the taxpayer's money, and few if any noteworthy scandals was too much for Bender to overcome in a short period of time. The fact that Lausche only spent $27,000 dollars for his campaign strengthened support of his followers.

Several other issues contributed to the fallout from the election and portend changes in the political landscape of the Buckeye state. The general consequence of nationwide prosperity brought a rapid expansion of Ohio's industry. Coupled with this expansion came a migration of Negroes and poor whites from a predominately-Democratic heritage. Estimates for 1956 showed that 30,000 black citizens registered for the first time. For the present, in spite of Republican efforts, these voters tended to gravitate to Lausche and the Democratic camp, particularly with Lausche's flair for emphasizing his humble beginnings.

Another factor became obvious. Ohio politics once controlled by city bosses was becoming a thing of the past. The organizations that passed for political machines in the 1950s went through the motions without much hope of making a meaningful voter impact. Ralph Miller, Lausche's long-time nemesis, served as an example of this demise of boss-ridden politics. In 1953 Miller organized a group known as the Northern Ohio Democratic chairmen to counter Lausche's independence. This organization included Democratic chairmen from twenty counties, which cast sixty-five percent of the Democratic votes in the state. Dissatisfied with Lausche, these members planned to "return the Democratic Party to the control of the Democrats."[66] Their influence was negligible, which no doubt pleased boss-resistant Lausche.

On the negative side, from the standpoint of a staunch Democratic Party loyalist, Lausche's detachment from the so-called inner circle of the party was of little help to DiSalle's efforts to win the governorship. Appointed federal czar of the office of Price Stabilization by President Truman in 1950, DiSalle had a strong 20-year record in the political arena. Running against an equally strong Republican candidate, DiSalle lost overwhelmingly. Although supported by Lausche, DiSalle suffered from efforts to bring cohesion to the Democratic Party, which had been frayed by Lausche's independence. Under Eugene Hanhart, Lausche's handpicked state chairman, the permanent staff at Democratic state headquarters consisted of only three people: an assistant to the chairman, a secretary, and a receptionist.[67] DiSalle gained state party support two years later and turned the tables in the 1958 gubernatorial race, defeating O'Neill by 455,000 votes.

Shortly after his election, Lausche received reliable information that U.S. Secretary of Treasury George Humphrey had solicited funds for the Bender campaign. He was indignant about this issue. Reporters heard Lausche comment, "If a tax commissioner in Ohio had done that, he would have been fired on the spot."[68] Republican Senators privately conceded that Humphrey's action was inexcusable, and they were fighting off attacks by Democratic senators. Lausche was in a good position to demand a thorough investigation by the Senate Ethics Committee concerning Humphrey's conduct. As a newly elected member of the Senate he dropped the issue. The departing Governor glorified in his independence of both parties and let it be known that he despised the shenanigans of *Big Business*, as well as those of *Big Labor*.

Meanwhile, Lausche and his wife prepared for their trip to Washington DC. He was about to join one of the most prestigious clubs in the world. A provocative, even contradictory individual in political life, the soon-to-be junior Senator from Ohio violated and defied every rule in the political primer. On his first day in the Senate chambers, he would continue to mystify the political world.

Frank and Jane Lausche
(Courtesy of Sally Jones)

ten

Jane Lausche—The Lady
Behind the Politician
(Or at the Side of)

BALLAD OF JANIE LAUSCHE

Born in Cleveland of Lake Erie
The fairest state in this Land of the Free
Studies the arts to a high degree
Was destined for great things all could see
Janie, Janie Lausche, First Lady we revere

Home in Ohio with her family
Came one to woo her, Frank Lausche
Loved her charm and repartee
Ended in a ceremony—
Janie, Janie Lausche, First Lady we revere

Life for them went ridin' a long
Years as happy as singin' a song
Knew the right cause and was never wrong
Frankie, Frankie Lausche, Champion of the Free

When votes were counted he'd win hands down
Over and over in this Columbus town
Helped in this office of high renown
By the sweetest Lady that could be found
Janie, Janie Lausche, First Lady we revere[1]

Board members sang this ditty to the tune of *The Ballad of Davy Crockett* at a meeting of the Martha Kinney Cooper Ohioana Library Association in Columbus. The date June 30, 1955, marked a celebration of Jane Lausche's 52nd birthday. Jane received the association's career medal, which is presented each year to an outstanding Ohioan. Her husband received this same career award in November 1981 a few days before Jane died.

Martha Kinney Cooper founded this organization. Myers Y. Cooper, her husband, served as Governor from 1929–1931. The book collection of the Ohioana Library Association contained over 11,000 volumes in 1955 and included books by Ohio authors and of Ohio history. This collection now exceeds 40,000 volumes and is currently located in the state library in Columbus.

The award and ballad recognized the respect and adulation Jane Lausche earned for her many years of public service. She was a perfect fit for a politician's way of life. Her distinctive qualities and temperament eventually contributed to 53 years of constructive, comforting, and happily married life. Graceful, nervous, and energetic, Jane's personality contrasted sharply with that of her husband. Being so, they were attracted to each other. Lausche was always certain to give his wife much of the credit for his political success.

Jane Lausche was born on June 30, 1903, in Cleveland of Scottish, Irish, and English descent. She was an only child born to Robert Erwin Sheal and Lillian Orem Sheal. The Orem family had settled in Cleveland where Jane's mother met her future husband. Lillian did not particularly relate well to children and never really nourished a close relationship with her daughter.

Jane's paternal grandfather, John Erwin Sheal, born in Liverpool, England, was a hunter and fur trader. An outstanding marksman, Sheal traded with the Sioux and Blackfoot tribes in the Upper Midwest in the mid-1800s. Sheal was captured by the Sioux in the 1850s, but was later released. He sold his furs to the John Jacob Astor Fur Company in St. Paul and in Manitoba, Canada. Sheal later settled in Steubenville, and there founded the Raney and Sheal Company. These two entrepreneurs established extensive grain and mill trading in the upper Ohio Valley. Sheal's son, Robert Erwin (Jane's father), was born March 23, 1871 in Steubenville. Growing up in the river town and demonstrating academic acumen Sheal graduated in civil engineering from Rensselaer Polytechnic Institute in Troy, New York, in 1894. Early in his professional career he worked for the C. Brown Hoist Company and Pittsburgh-Conneaut Dock Company in Cleveland. In his position as an engineering consultant, Robert became known for his design of heavy equipment.

An innovative professional, Sheal co-designed and co-developed the Hulett ore unloading machinery that was used for many years in major Great Lakes harbors. He also designed and patented a rack-drive used extensively in the operation of ore-loading machinery in the lake ports of Conneaut, Toledo, Cleveland and

Ashtabula. Robert and Lillian Sheal divorced in the 1940s. Despite their divorce, both parents moved with the Lausches to the governor's mansion. They took up separate quarters and were known to glower at each other at dinnertime. The father, now using a wheelchair, traveled to Washington, DC in January 1958 when Frank took over his senatorial duties. Three months later Jane's father suffered a stroke on March 19 and passed away in the Medical Center Hospital in Washington, DC on April 8. He was 87 years of age.[2]

Although not spoiled as an only child, Jane had the advantages that could be given to her by well-to-do parents. She attended Laurel Institute, a private school for girls in Cleveland, founded by Jennie Warren Prentiss in 1896. The school was moved to East 97th St. near Euclid Avenue in 1909, and there Jane received a college preparatory education.[3] Following graduation with a strong background in English and languages, she matriculated to Flora Stone Mather College for girls, an excellent school located on the Western Reserve University campus (now known as Case-Western Reserve University). Jane later attended Glen Eden finishing school in Philadelphia. With a bent for art she

"As a joke I sometimes illustrated letters with off-hand drawings. Occasionally these drawings took the form of a Mickey Mouse…so he began calling me Mick and Mick I've remained."

returned to Cleveland and completed classes at the Cleveland Art School. The young graduate, with financial assistance from her parents, began a promising career in commercial art. She ran a highly successful studio on Huron Road for four years. Specializing in interior decorating and commercial design of parchment shades and coverings for wrought iron fixtures, Jane began selling lampshades at the fashionable Sterling and Welch Department store in downtown Cleveland. A talented artist, Jane designed lighting fixtures for local restaurants, theaters, and public buildings. She fashioned several individual light fixtures, which were sold on a commission basis to art studios and enhanced her income. The attractive and slender, brown-eyed brunette stood five feet seven inches, and looked toward a career in commercial art design. Then Frank J. Lausche entered her life.

During their long engagement, Jane gained the nickname of Mick from her suitor. "In courtship days, Frank and I corresponded when we were separated," Jane recalled, "As a joke I sometimes illustrated letters with off-hand drawings. Occasionally these drawings took the form of a Mickey Mouse…so he began calling me Mick and Mick I've remained."[4]

After a long courtship the couple joined hands in marriage May 18, 1928, in a small wedding in Painsville. Neither wished to be involved in a large church wedding in Cleveland, which was so prevalent among Slovenian Catholics. Ironically, all of Lausche's five siblings chose to be married in small weddings as well. Lausche sent tongues wagging with his announcement that he not only planned to marry a Methodist, but also that the person he planned to marry was not of Slovenian background. Jane chose not to alter her religious affiliation, so each spouse attended his or her own church (when in Cleveland, Frank visited St. Vitus, his childhood church). Home of many Slovenian cultural and fraternal organizations, St. Vitus became the first Catholic Church in Cleveland designated for Slovenians.[5] The Lausche's mixed marriage caused gossip among Lausche's old-line Catholic friends. One must remember the restraints for mixed religious marriages were much more stringent in the 1920s than in the twenty-first century. In spite of different religious backgrounds between the two newlyweds, this issue never became a detrimental factor in their marriage.

The Lausches went to their respective churches in an irregular sort of way, but did not make a big thing of it. Because they were so amiable and clever, the couple managed to avoid most of the criticism that came from bigots. When the Lausches became better known, all the cosmopolitan families among whom they circulated in Cleveland loved Jane. She readily gained acceptance into the close-knit Lausche clan. Modestly the gracious Jane remarked, "Behind every successful man is a woman, and in Frank's case it is his mother." She recalled fond memories of the politician's mother, to whom she referred to as Ma Lausche. "Frank's mother taught [Frank] appreciation of and respect for all kinds of people," and Jane added, "She was the loving, dominant person in the family. Before her death every Sunday night was set aside for a family sing and get-together. I remember how happy I was the first time Ma Lausche sprinkled a few Slovenian words in our conversation—it meant I was completely one of the family."[6] Jane enjoyed the Lausche family musical get-togethers

After a short honeymoon to Washington, DC, the couple moved in with Jane's parents in their large home located at 2101 East 100th Street, just south of Carnegie Avenue. No in-law troubles clouded the horizon of the newlyweds. In a few weeks in an effort to go it on their own, the Lausches decided they should move into an apartment. After four months in this apartment near the Sheal's residence, Jane found her husband leaving home unaccountably early in the morning and eating practically no breakfast. She finally discovered the reason why he did not lose weight. He was stopping at Jane's family home to eat breakfast and engage in arguments with her father who was a dyed-in-the wool Republican. At the time Sheal was head of a firm of consulting engineers. Lausche missed the Sheals so much that he and Jane moved back into the big house where they lived for the next sixteen years.

Jane continued to work with her commercial art for several years. An attack of lead poisoning forced her to give up her profession. She devoted more time to homemaking and charitable causes. During the 1930s when her husband served on the judicial bench for nine years, Jane spent a total of exactly 15 minutes in the courtroom during that time period. She kept a file of all of Frank's cases and became knowledgeable answering questions on many of his legal decisions.

JANE'S LIFE CHANGED DRAMATICALLY IN 1941 when she became the First Lady of Cleveland and in 1945 assumed the same role for the State of Ohio. Jane never really wanted to be a first lady. She acclimated herself to this new responsibility in admirable fashion. The first lady was a far cry from the old-style politicians' concept of the little woman obscured behind an apron and plying a darning needle. She continued her involvement with several welfare and charitable organizations. One organization was the YMCA, where Jane served as chairperson of the international institute of this organization, helping new American citizens adjust to life in a large city. She held many roles with the city's American Red Cross unit. The Mayor's wife, who had no children, gave considerable time and service to the Adoption Service Bureau. "You don't know how grand it is to see those proud couples with the babies they've adopted," she confessed.[7] Shortly after her husband took the reins as Mayor of Cleveland, she was elected to the board of the Child Health Association.

During World War II Jane encouraged Clevelanders to buy U.S. savings bonds. Lausche's wife, who disliked being in the public eye, kept busy taking care of her father's large home. The residence became a Mecca for politicians, numerous friends, and people seeking favors from the Mayor. In 1942 Jane received Mr. and Mrs. Henry J. Morganthau during their visit to the city. Morganthau served as an important member of Franklin D. Roosevelt's cabinet (Secretary of the Treasury). Jane was a strong asset to her husband and tackled any task when asked. She may have been requested to serve with the Civilian Service Corps or been observed breading fish for 1,200 people in the kitchen of the Cleveland City hospital. On other occasions she could be found directing a bedraggled soldier's wife and baby for food and rest at the Cleveland Terminal's USO. Jane's habit of pitching in extended to home duties as well. Jokingly, when her husband won his first election to the governor's office, she quipped, "I suppose I'll wind up firing the furnace in the governor's mansion."[8] She was reflective about taking her turn stoking the coal burner at her father's 80 year-old home.

One of Jane's main responsibilities was to take care of her absent-minded husband. She had a penchant for orderliness, not one of Frank's strengths. Jane contrived a home filing system for Frank's many law cases and papers from his mayoral office. "Frank can remember all about a law case, including the page and volume where it can be found, but for some reason he forgets anything that isn't attached to him," she related. "I always wire an extra set of car keys under the hood because he has a habit of locking himself out of his car."[9] Jane loved maps and charts and any fact that could be pinned down with a figure or statistic. When she and her husband Frankie, as she called him, traveled, Jane acted as navigator. If there was a debate over travel or financial issues, she drew up little statistical tables to prove her point.

On the eve of the newly elected Governor's first inauguration, Jane reluctantly agreed to an interview for the Columbus press, who knew little about the first lady. She acquitted herself quite well. *Better than Mrs. Roosevelt* was the response by one newspaperwoman. Jane had become somewhat better known in the state prior to the 1944 election. She occasionally substituted for her husband on the campaign trail. One notable example occurred when Frank made an emergency return from the stump to Cleveland in October 1944 to oversee the tragic aftermath of the East Ohio Gas Fire in his childhood environs.

Jane Lausche spent most of her life in Cleveland, and she hated to leave her hometown for Columbus. At the same time she looked forward to learning more about the state's capitol and managing the governor's mansion. Naively, she anticipated only a few simple changes in the 13-room mansion. Jane found that many alterations were necessary in what one journalist described as a gubernatorial barn and the "most unhome-like place you can imagine."[10] One thing was for sure, there was little adjustment necessary for the eating habits of the two occupants. The food was the plain and simple kind. "For Frank, you've got to be a short-order cook because you never know when he'll be there. You know, chops and what I think used to be called steaks."[11] She added that her husband was easy to cook for because he preferred basic meals rather than specially prepared cuisine.

Immediately following Lausche's first inauguration, the couple resided in the Neil House on High Street, directly across from the state capitol for a few days until the executive mansion was made ready for occupancy. Jane faced a major challenge in refurbishing this 40-year-old residence on a limited budget. The solid brick home with primitive Georgian simplicity was built in 1905. Ten of Ohio's first families had resided in the mansion until the Lausches moved out in January of 1957. The first governor to inhabit the mansion was the James Cox family in the early 1920s during his second term in office. The house was built by Charles H. Lindenberg, son of a German refugee, who became one of Columbus' leading citizens. The building designed by Frank Packard possessed an unusual architectural style.[12] Journalist Erma Kruse suspected an amateur Sherlock Holmes must have drawn up the plans for the mansion because of the architect's mania for hiding electric light switches in the most unsuspecting places. Making it confusing for a new tenant, the light switch in the breakfast room was in the Governor's study hidden behind a bookshelf.

A week after the new Governor moved into the mansion, the Lausches received unexpected guests late at night. Jane discovered that the beds in the guest room were unmade. Being Jane she refused to disturb the mansion staff and chose to make the beds herself. She looked furiously, searched closets, and finally found double sheets when she was looking for single sheets. "Then, what do you know... they had holes in them just like home," she recalled.[13]

The less than imposing brick structure located at the corner of East Broad

Street and Governor's place housed thirteen rooms at the living end, with modest quarters for mansion help, except for the center hall and accompanying broad stairways at the foot of the room where official affairs took place. Descending a spacious stairway to the reception hall, the Lausches entered a breakfast sunroom where they usually dined. The more formal dining room located off the reception hall featured heavy mahogany beams and panels. The Lausche's accommodated 12–14 dinner guests in this dining area. The under support of the old-fashioned mahogany tables showed scuff marks from the feet of distinguished visitors, lending a homey air to a room otherwise somber from heavy, dark woodwork. Moderately spacious lawns and gardens surrounded the two and one-half acre residence.

The Governor's wife inherited the mansion's furnishings. Some of the furniture was beautiful, such as the French bedroom furniture given by the Myers Y. Coopers during their occupancy. Other furniture and rooms took on a drab, worn look in need of a face-lift. In 1945 the state allowed only $600 yearly for interior replacements, repairs, and upkeep of the mansion. This figure stretched thin when Jane discovered that the dry cleaning bill for one room's draperies ran over this fund's monthly breakdown of $50. Those hangings required almost weekly cleaning: Columbus encountered its share of pollution. Jane substituted nylon curtains that could be washed easily and re-hung without ironing. Windows were numerous: in one room alone, 34 panel curtains were required. Nylon proved to be the answer, giving crisp window trim. Chairs and sofas were in dire need of new coverings. A worn spot on a carpet called for a scatter rug. Jane went shopping into basement stores, watching sales for markdowns. Like any thrifty homemaker, she came home chortling over her bargain finds. Jane's five years of experience as an interior decorator proved invaluable in her efforts to give the mansion a new look.[14] As for the Governor, he remained oblivious to household improvements, clothes, what he ate and even the weather.

In 1949 the meticulous and efficient Mrs. Lausche received an allowance of $2,400 for food for servants. Cook Carrie Barnett and upstairs maid Margaret McCullough had been with the mansion staff for nearly twenty years. Four or five other white and colored servants and yardmen were paroled life inmates or trusties from the Ohio Penitentiary. An armed guard transported the trusties to and from the mansion daily. Supervising these men did not bother Jane a bit. She believed each man was attempting to lead a new life.[15] Most of the men were due for commutation. Jane said she was never afraid. She knew they would protect her from any harm.

One to collect humorous anecdotes wherever she went, Mrs. Lausche amassed many stories from her ten-year stay at the mansion. On one occasion—perhaps there was a shortage of murderers at the time—a mere robber was assigned to the mansion, and he took advantage of the opportunity by escaping. Word was received that the escaped trustie had been captured. A regularly assigned first degree murderer-servant breathed a sigh of satisfaction upon hearing the news and told the Governor's wife, "I'm sure glad they got him, Mrs. Lausche. I always said you just can't trust them criminals."[16]

On one particular day Jane left the mansion for a fund-raiser rally and returned to learn of a fire at the State Institute for the Feeble Minded (name given to state mental institutions in the 1940s). She knew Frank would want to be at the scene of the fire, not far from the state capitol. She telephoned the state highway patrol, who located Lausche and had him at the site of the fire in a matter of minutes. Fortunately no one was hurt. Concurrently, Jane smelled smoke in the mansion. One of the servants had carelessly emptied an ashtray into the kitchen wastebasket and started a blaze.

A typical day for Jane found her attending a community fund rally, answering several of over 3,000 letters received yearly, in addition to holding organizational meetings at the mansion. Community and state organizations continually requested to hold their meetings at the Lausche's home. She was unable to accommodate all of the waiting list of some 900 requests.

Jane maintained her office on the second floor of the mansion. There she balanced the mansion household accounts as required quarterly by state auditors, and answered innumerable letters before retiring, often working into the early hours of morning.[17] During the week Jane sometimes carried her own basket to market, mended her own clothes and answered her many phone calls personally. An excellent seamstress, Jane fashioned and made her own attractive hats and many of her dresses.

The first lady encountered frustrating problems almost daily: receiving complaints over garbage collection and road repairs; communication regarding old-age pension problems; providing handmade items for church bazaars; requests for out-of-the-ordinary social reforms; and intervention for scheduled criminal executions. Requests for personal charitable contributions, many worthy, were numerous. In 1949 Jane studied this matter in desperation and found, that if she and the Governor replied favorably to all such requests for the month, they would use up to nine times the Governor's salary, which amounted to $13,000 that year. As a respite from their hectic schedules, the Lausches turned to music for relaxation and spent many evenings playing the violin and piano.

The mansion budget would become a source of agitation throughout Jane's stay in Columbus. She was a perfectionist and worked diligently to remodel an older structure so that the mansion would be presentable for the many scheduled events. A steady stream of guests visited the Lausches. Jane complained to her parsimonious husband that the budget did not allow her one penny for clothing or spending money. The first lady spent hundreds of dollars of her own money. In March of 1945 (the Governor's first term), Jane could take it no longer. At midnight after several verbal tiffs with her husband, she wrote him a note with attached budgetary figures, "Your arguments based on total ignorance of facts are still disturbing me to the point where I cannot sleep. Please give these figures a moment's attention. They represent some—not all—of expenses during January and February."[18] Needless to say the Governor persuaded Helen Hergenberger of the state finance department to adjust the budget upward.

Jane took to raising chickens at the mansion when World War II ended. Food remained relatively scarce and was still rationed. In September 1945 she purchased 50 two-week old Leghorn chicks from Erlay Hatchery in nearby Delaware. A month later the enterprising first lady purchased fifty more chicks, plus 300 pounds of starter mash. The total cost amounted to $49.40. By late November, the 74 surviving chickens weighed approximately three and one-half pounds each. These survivors eventually served as a main meat entrée for guests at the mansion.[19]

Jane anticipated purchasing more furniture and carpets for the mansion in 1946. Fortunately or unfortunately, her acquisitions were purchased not for the mansion but for her new residence, an apartment on 1900 East 30th St. in Cleveland. The governor had lost his bid for re-election in the fall of 1946. Maintenance of the mansion became the responsibility of new tenant, Governor Thomas J. Herbert. He was alone in the mansion for several months (Jeanette Judson, his first wife died in December 1945) until he married Mildred Helen Stevenson in 1948.

THE LAUSCHES RETURNED TO THE MANSION IN January 1949 after Frank's re-election. Jane resumed her many first lady activities and reunited with many friends in Columbus. Likely she did not anticipate that her primary address would be at the mansion for the next eight years. The social whirl included occasional visits downtown to a movie, the theater, or musical events. Jane could plan on accompanying her husband to opening day baseball games in Cleveland and Cincinnati. The Governor enjoyed delivering the first pitch on these gala occasions. The Lausches frequently attended football games at Ohio State University, often in the company of the Gaylord (Pete) Stinchcombs, friends of the Lausches.

Beyond normal visitations of friends and relatives, Jane occasionally put out the red carpet for special guests. On October 12, 1946, the Louis Bromfields celebrated their 25th wedding anniversary with an overnight stay at the mansion. Jane found it strange that the Bromfields chose to spend their 25th anniversary alone with the Lausches. "Perhaps they sensed that we wanted nothing whatever of them in return and that sincere friendship was all we had to offer. So many people fawned on [Bromfields] because of their fame."[20] Earlier in the day author-farmer Bromfield had received a medal-at-large from the Ohioana Library Association. This award was in honor of his 21 books and specifically for writing *The Farm* and *Pleasant Valley* that featured Ohio landscape. His novel *Early Autumn* won a Pulitzer Prize in 1926. The Bromfields and Lausches had been social friends for several years. When Lausche elected to run for governor in 1944, Bromfield called Lausche a godsend to state Democrats and added that the party had been in need "of such a leader since the death of Newton D. Baker."[21]

The close friendship continued until Bromfield died on March 20, 1956. Two of the Bromfield children stayed with Jane Lausche just before their father's death. He died at the exact moment the Sunday evening radio program "Monitor" aired. This particular nationwide program featured Bromfield and his celebrated Malabar Farm, near Mansfield, Ohio. Jane intimated that the Bromfields were on the verge of bankruptcy at the time of his death. Over the years Bromfield instigated innovations for soil conservation. The constant entertainment at Malabar Farm of those interested in his agricultural theories, left the family financially drained. Jane reflected, "[Bromfield] lived like an emperor—and sage—and never had to see his empire crumble."[22] Years after Bromfield's death, Malabar Farm became a state park operated by the Department of Natural Resources.

The governor's mansion was abuzz with excitement that Margaret Truman, the President's daughter, planned to give a concert in Columbus on November 2, 1949, sponsored by the Columbus Women's Music Club. On April 5, 1949, Jane wrote a gracious letter to Miss Truman extending an invitation for her to stay at the Mansion and offered to assist in any other way possible during her brief visit to Columbus.[23] The President's daughter responded by asking the Lausches for permission to see them the afternoon prior to her concert performance. "That would give us a chance to really visit and I do so look forward to seeing you both where we aren't tearing through the country side on a campaign train," and added, "I have found it impossible to go to any parties and keep to a tough concert schedule."[24] Jane delayed her response to this request because she was called to Florida due to the serious illness and subsequent death of her aunt, Polly Sheal Gordon. "She was very near and dear to us as my husband and I had lived with her and my father for nearly twenty years."[25] On November 1, the Lausches entertained Margaret Truman privately at the mansion, discussing political issues and the stunning upset pulled off by her father the previous year against Thomas E. Dewey. Margaret's concert was well received by local music aficionados, although her professional singing career had begun to wane. President Truman, responding to a brief note from the governor, thanked the Lausches, "Of course, I am vitally interested in Margaret and her career. She told me that she had been highly entertained by you and Mrs. Lausche and I can't tell you how very much Mrs. Truman and I appreciate that courtesy."[26] Albeit they were members of the same party, President Truman and Lausche never shared much of a political affinity. During Lausche's senatorial tenure, the then former President expressed disdain for Lausche's ultra-conservative stance and reticence to support the Democratic Party *carte blanche.*

In the fall of 1955, Jane escorted another political dignitary, Eleanor Roosevelt, from the airport to downtown Columbus. The former first lady was scheduled to give a speech for United Nations Day at Memorial Hall. Jane had a chat with Mrs. Roosevelt (at her request) in a dressing room before her speech. They talked at some length about national politics. Roosevelt expressed her desire to see Adlai Stevenson elected president. She was not too happy with John Foster Dulles as Secretary of State. Jane asked Mrs. Roosevelt whom she would choose for that position. She answered that it would depend upon which were the crucial areas: if Asia, she believed Chester Bowles to be the best person; if Europe, Averill Harriman. Mrs. Roosevelt evidently did not consider Harriman a likely presidential candidate.[27] Jane commented that the famous first lady appeared to be very alert and interested in everything. She seemed to be neat but indifferent about her clothes, she rose above those types of considerations and was always kind, considerate, and gracious. Jane learned much more about national politics from the question and answer session after the speech (over 3,000 attended). Mrs. Roosevelt fielded controversial inquiries with gentle good humor and wisdom.

President Truman, responding to a brief note from the governor, thanked the Lausches, "Of course, I am vitally interested in Margaret and her career. She told me that she had been highly entertained by you and Mrs. Lausche and I can't tell you how very much Mrs. Truman and I appreciate that courtesy."

Jane's busy schedule included a trip to Cincinnati the next day for a long-planned Midwest Trade Conference and banquet for Latin-American nations to stimulate trade. Twelve ambassadors from Central and South America planned to attend. The day before the conference, Carlos Davila (President General of the group of involved countries) died, and the ambassadors could not attend the banquet as honored guests. Concurrently, Jane's husband was invited by native Ohioan General Curtis LeMay, Chief of Staff of the Air Force, to Omaha to be briefed at the Strategic Air Command headquarters. He arrived back in Cincinnati in time for the Midwest Trade Conference banquet.

Jane's whirlwind schedule continued the following day back in Columbus where she attended the annual Authors Award meeting sponsored by the Ohioana Library Association. The Governor's wife spoke briefly, and Frank Lausche presented the career medal to Ohioan Willard Kiplinger, a nationally renowned financial expert. Other awards were presented to Harry Barnard for his biography of Rutherford B. Hayes and to two young playwrights, Robert Edwin Lee and Jerome Lawrence, for their Broadway hit, *Inherit the Wind.* Lausche inadvertently addressed Lee as Robert Irwin.[28]

Following a day of guests and phone calls at the mansion, the Lausches flew to New York where he was to address the Ohio Society of New York. It was customary for the Ohio governor to make this address, but in previous years Lausche had consistently refused the invitations. He finally agreed, mostly to please Louis

Seltzer of the Cleveland *Press,* who accompanied the Lausches. The two other Cleveland dailies became suspicious that there was some political significance to the Governor's speech. Lausche emphasized repeatedly that the presentation would be non-partisan.

Lausche rewrote the speech three times, then read it to the gathering of distinguished guests, including Chairman Norman Vincent Peale. Jane's consensus suggested his talk came across as non-political, non-partisan, non-controversial, and non-interesting. She vowed not to say anything to Frank, but could not contain herself the next day. Jane told her husband he did a horrible job in delivery. She made this comment because so much of the publicity and comments after the presentation had been favorable. Jane was afraid her husband might believe the accolades. She injected her personal philosophy to her husband commenting that "a wife has to be ready to hand out the moon and the stars when it's a dark night—and good solid brown earth when they start walking on little false pink clouds."[29] The next day Governor Lausche had lunch with the publisher, manager, and editor of the *New York Times.* Later Jane noticed that one of the *New York Times* correspondents was the only man she knew, other than her husband, who could tie a bow tie with ends pointing north, south, east, and west.

> *"a wife has to be ready to hand out the moon and the stars when it's a dark night—and good solid brown earth when they start walking on little false pink clouds."*

The Lausche siblings occasionally gathered at the governor's mansion. By 1950, including Frank, six of the original ten siblings of the Lausche family remained alive. The three brothers and two sisters were married. All of the Lausche children had attended college, with the exception of Frank. (He attended law school directly after serving in the army.) The get-togethers featured libations of one sort or another, a hearty Slovenian meal, and a musical session as the family members gathered around the mansion piano. Reminiscences of gatherings when Ma Lausche was alive always became part of the conversation.

Three nieces and a nephew accompanied their parents to these festive gatherings. Sally Jones, daughter of Frances Uranker (her husband August was a dentist), recalled fond memories of her visits to the governor's mansion. *Aunt Jane* loved children, and Sally was a particular favorite. Sally also spent time with one or both of Jane's parents. "We all knew we should stay away from Grandma Sheal. She didn't particularly like children, she didn't like much of anyone," Sally sadly commented.[30] Grandfather Sheal was a wonderful person, loved by everyone. Sally enjoyed going up to his room in the mansion. The room was filled with copies of *National Geographic.* The elderly gentleman loved to tell Sally stories of his engineering experiences, particularly the building of bridges. Sally remembered one occasion at the mansion when Aunt Jane was holding her niece. A member of the family was attempting to take a picture of the pair. Sally, being young and innocent, was pulling Jane's dress bodice down in front. Sally was sobbing as the modest Jane tried frantically to pull her dress up as the picture was snapped.[31] Those days were filled with fun and frivolity when the Lausche family convened at the mansion.

Jane continued her many household duties at the mansion when her frenetic schedule permitted. After Frank took the oath for his second term in 1949 (in all of Lausche's inaugurations, he used a time-worn Bible donated by the Sheal family), the first lady splurged on herself. She purchased a fur jacket from Madisons, a fashionable ladies clothing store on North High Street in Columbus. The cost was $243. Clothes were not of great importance to the first lady. Her tastes ran to tailored suits, frocks, and hats that did not come down over her brow. Pulling an off-the-face hat with scalloped edge from its box she said, "See, here's what I mean. Whenever I get a new one, I just say, 'Make me another hat like this one.'"[32]

As her tenure at the mansion continued, Jane pursued one of her favorite hobbies, gardening and landscaping on cultivated plots of ground that surrounded the mansion. She became innovative at raising garden produce for the mansion at a minimal cost. With the help of staff members, she maintained a small garden at the rear of the mansion. Jane knew that fresh vegetables helped her stretch the food budget. Early in the summer, the garden yielded lettuce and green onions. When fall approached the Lausches enjoyed tomatoes, red beets, carrots, green and yellow wax beans, cabbage, mustard greens, and corn. Canning the vegetables was an annual fall ritual. One fall Jane and her staff put 55 quarts of green beans in the deep freeze. A novice at first, Jane gained her gardening knowledge from a variety of books and journals. She was an active member of the Franklin County Garden Club. In September 1953, Jane, an aficionado of flowers, appeared on the cover of *American Rose Magazine*.

⌒

JANE LAUSCHE'S MAIN CHARGE DURING HER TENURE at the mansion (she was the only first lady to leave and later return to the Ohio mansion as of 1956) was to adapt to an antiquated structure. At the beginning of each two-year term, auditors spent a week itemizing everything in the house. The first lady was held responsible for all items in this inventory. She could not dispose of a single item. Instead, she placed unusable articles in the garage. Auditors determined whether the articles could be repaired at state institutions or were to be destroyed. Rusty plumbing pipes deteriorated. An emergency fund was tapped to install all new plumbing and put in new ceilings downstairs. On another occasion, Jane's assiduous attention to her accounting figures may have averted a possible fire. When the electric bill suddenly tripled, she requested a complete check of wiring. New wiring was installed. The state paid for all utilities except long distance phone calls. Several cryptic entries were noted throughout her account book. At the top of one page Jane noted: *Green wedding hat, 1928 in closet #1*. She had saved this precious hat. "I can't keep track of where my things are if I don't write them down."[33]

Jane seldom talked about politics whenever giving talks to professional and service organizations. She worked on building a legacy for the state. In 1945 looking ahead to Ohio's sesquicentennial (1953), the first lady began to fill the mansion with as many Ohio-made products as possible. She researched what Ohio products she could purchase that were practical for the mansion. "When I go outside, I try to talk Ohio without being offensive," Jane explained with a rueful smile, "but it's an awful temptation. You find yourself wanting to top anything anyone says, and that's hard to do and still be ladylike."[34]

Some of the first items purchased were draperies. One of her primary challenges was to find appropriate treatments for the many big windows in the mansion, including the long row in the sun parlor. The first lady conquered the dilemma. She installed curtains made from glass by the Owens-Corning Fiberglass Corporation in Toledo. This company was a world-leader in production of this magical material. Jane continued her Ohio purchases with the installation of a twin range in her now modernized kitchen. The Estate Stove Company of Hamilton manufactured this range. Reputably the oldest stove company in the United States, this manufacturer began production in 1832 in Hanging Rock, a small village on the Ohio River near Ironton.[35] Jane renovated the kitchen, her pride and joy, with Youngstown cabinets. Storage space became a premium. These new units provided badly needed space for kitchenware. A steel double sink replaced the old-fashioned pedestal sink. Additional Ohio products installed in the kitchen included tile from Fremont, rubber mats from Akron, ventilators, light fixtures, and plastic containers from other Ohio companies, and yellow Versibond from Columbus to cover shelves and backing. Other Ohio products located throughout the mansion included a table mirror from Toledo, glassware from Newark, Bellaire, and Roseville, woven tablemats from Wilmington and samples of Ohio-made china for the dining room.

The resourceful first lady, with her interior decorating skills, found a way to overcome the construction and decorating problems of this now 50 year-old residence. Repainting the kitchen walls presented a challenge. After a bit of experimenting and a lot of investigating, she found the only paint that would satisfactorily do the job. It was a non-yellowing, white Marietta paint called Shieldcote. One coat of flat and one of enamel covered the walls and the refrigerator doors that would have cost too much to refinish.

The kitchen ceiling, with its many defects, looked new and fresh with two coats of Glidden's Satin Spred in a dull finish. The kitchen needed a suction fan. A carpenter told Jane it could not be done. Hence she had the flue chipped out and a ventilation fan installed into the chimney. There were always more problems.

When workmen removed a large black restaurant stove, they noted a major hole in the chimney. Instead of placing bricks in the hole, Jane made a show spot out of the orifice by installing backing and shelves with yellow coverings of Versibond. A yellow plastic condiment set and like-colored plastic pots with green vines brightened the shelves. To save money, old chairs and stools were repainted yellow and white. Green painted walls in the hallway and service dining room, in addition to white paint over dark pinewood, provided a light and cheery atmosphere.

The first lady enjoyed extolling the virtues of her native state. She never failed to let her listeners know that. "You just can't get through a whole day without bringing in Ohio."[36] On a nationwide broadcast the first lady used one of her favorite expressions—that the Buckeye state gave the world light and flight with Thomas Edison and the Wright Brothers. "...you can expand that to mean both actual light and spiritual light," she pointed out. "After all, with McGuffey, Spencer, and Ray—the progressive educators of their day—we gave the nation advancement in all three Rs."[37] William Holmes McGuffey assembled material for *McGuffey's Eclectic Readers* that stressed vocabulary, introduced students to selections from fine literature, and emphasized high moral and ethical standards. Platt Spencer developed Spencerian script, a style of handwriting widely taught at a time when clear, attractive penmanship was prized. Joseph Ray won fame for his arithmetic texts, which systematized instruction in the subject and introduced *thought problems*.[38]

When talking to high school students, Jane liked to tell her audience how Ohio dominated the national political scene in 1881. When President James Garfield (Cuyahoga County) took the oath of office, outgoing President Rutherford B. Hayes (Fremont) flanked him, as well as the Chief Justice of the Supreme Court Morrison Waite (Toledo), retiring Secretary of Treasury John Sherman (Mansfield), and two leading military men William Tecumseh Sherman (Lancaster) and Philip Sheridan (Somerset in Perry County).[39]

Jane carried her cause for learning more about Ohio to one of her husband's favorite haunts, the Ohio State Fair. This city girl received several pointers at the swine-judging arena, "Poland swine should have five points...feet and nose. Their ears droop. The Hampshires, of course, have ears that stand up straight."[40] Mrs. Lausche noted a sheaf of papers she carried describing the cattle on display at the largest fair in the country. These pages gave brief histories of the best-known breeds. She believed similar descriptions of other livestock included in a loose-leaf notebook would provide children with a wonderful educational resource. Jane laughed at her own enthusiasm. "I've never left the 'why mother, why' stage."[41]

She proposed that one of the existing buildings on the fairgrounds or one of the New World Leadership Buildings be designated for dissemination of real information about farm animals—and their own state. "Children—and adults too—could learn a lot about Ohio. Go any place in the country and you'll find Ohio glass. We lead in pressed glass. More Bibles are published in Ohio than any place in the world...more playing cards. The first dental school started in Ohio. Why couldn't we have an exhibit showing the first instruments used and those [used] now?"[42] Her world of Ohio firsts seemed endless.

Although the Lausches were not prone to accept gifts during their tenure, Jane gladly made one exception. G.G. Nuss, vice president of White Sewing Machine Corporation, an old-line company in Cleveland, learned through a mutual friend that an antiquated foot treadle sewing machine served sewing needs in the mansion. Officials from the company (later known as White Consolidated Industries) shipped a new White sewing machine with an American walnut finish to the Governor's mansion. The first lady, who loved to sew, was overjoyed. She responded to Mr. Nuss exclaiming, "You have no idea how thrilled I am with that wonderful...machine. The mansion already has eight new sets of curtains.... What a change from the old treadle model! I felt as if I should have flight training at first, but it didn't take me long to solo expertly—I'm particularly intrigued with the little lever that told me to sew backwards—I've always hated to stop and tie threads at the end of a seam. No more knot stops now."[43]

Jane's excitement about her new sewing machine was matched by her fascination with trailer-coaches and camping trailers. During World War II the First Lady inquired about these portable homes as an alternative to the housing shortage. Jane visited numerous trailer camps in Columbus, "Frank will shoot me—but I take every trailer magazine published. You know—I used to cook in a kitchen no bigger than a trailer kitchen...the trailer kitchen is such a marvelous job of engineering space."[44] *Trailer Topics* magazine discovered Jane's interest in trailers and requested permission to publish an article about her views regarding these highway vehicles. She complied, sent a glossy photo and a rewritten article assembled from newspaper articles that appeared in the June 1950 issue of *Trailer Topics*.[45] Unfortunately, Jane never had the opportunity to spend any time traveling in a camper trailer.

To some degree Jane satisfied one of her other passions: the relatively new avocation of flying. She gained her pilot's license in the 1940s and was qualified to fly small planes like a Cessna, Piper Cub, or Beechcraft. Often when Frank made short trips around the Buckeye state, Jane and the Governor's pilot combined skills to transport their important passenger from the nearby Columbus airport to his destination. The first lady became an excellent pilot and never missed an opportunity to whet her flying skills. Prior to moving to Washington, DC, Jane donated her trusted gyroscope to the Ohio Historical Society.

A major reason the first lady could not take to the road or fly more was due to her many responsibilities at the mansion. The schedule was filled nearly every day of the week with a luncheon, tea, or dinner. When an occasional visitor from a foreign country arrived at the mansion, Jane researched vital statistics about the guest's country so as to be more conversant with her visitor(s). Jane imposed a self-made rule that she would serve as official hostess only for those organizations with which she was personally acquainted. On one particular occasion five subversive groups posing under perfectly innocent names asked the Governor's wife to sponsor functions in her home. She checked first with army intelligence to ascertain their true identity before denying the requests of the imposters.[46]

Whatever her duties at the mansion, Jane acquitted herself in a magnanimous manner. Frank Lausche's number one asset was his thoroughly likeable wife. He often spoke of her responsibilities at the mansion. She worked silently and diligently behind the scenes to assist her husband in his political responsibilities. Jane's husband, reflecting on her management of receptions, attended ordinarily by about 150 guests and on occasion by as many as a thousand people, commented. "My wife...with the aid of personal women friends and trusted prisoners, managed these receptions without a blemish in the ten years I was governor."[47] Her husband went on to praise Jane's ability to oversee the mansion. Practically all the help in the operation consisted of trusted prisoners from the Ohio Penitentiary. These inmates served as mansion gardeners, chauffeurs, waiters, and repairmen. For Jane, "It was no easy task to keep control over these trusted servants, but surprisingly and satisfyingly the task was lightened by the trusty's expectations of being released by the governor from their prison term as a reward for their good behavior."[48] Lausche added, "It brought my wife and I closer together. She was a great help to me in the management of the Mansion."[49]

"It was no easy task to keep control over these trusted servants, but surprisingly and satisfyingly the task was lightened by the trusty's expectations of being released by the governor from their prison term as a reward for their good behavior."

☞

IN SERVING AS A HOSTESS, THE FIRST LADY earned additional important political points for her husband. She had an amazing capacity for remembering names and faces (Frank also was above average with this attribute). When a newly elected state legislature convened in January, the Lausches held a reception at the mansion for 150 or so legislators. Nearly half were new to Columbus, and as they filed out at the close of the reception, Jane recalled every one by name without prompting or committing an error. An associate declared the first lady could remember by name five years later a person she had met previously in a receiving line.[50] In politics such a talent was more precious than rubies.

Bishop A. Edward Pevec, former pastor at St. Vitus Catholic Church and close friend of the Lausches, extolled the first lady's tenderness, gentleness, charm, and love. She projected no selfish ambition, no faulty motivation, and no pretentious air. The bishop remembered the hectic days of the governorship and how Jane responded to inevitable crises. Even if she was taken aback when Frank told her, "We're going to a dinner party for 150 people this weekend," or "We have to go to this formal reception in a couple hours," or "St. Vitus is having a birthday party for me and we should be there,"[51] the always gracious Jane handled these urgent requests with patience and aplomb.

Occasionally Jane substituted for her husband to give a talk when he encountered a scheduling conflict with governmental business. One example occurred in April 1953 when the First Lady was asked to speak at a meeting of leading women civic leaders in Cleveland. The powerful Louis Seltzer was in attendance. He wrote a letter to the Governor immediately upon returning to his office: "Had you enveloped in an invisible cloak and listened and watched...you would have been prouder of [Jane] than at any time in your life. It was a difficult spot. This particular meeting had become something of a tradition in town. The outstanding women—and a good many men—have been in its audience for some years.... Many excellent speakers have been scheduled.... Jane topped them all. It was a superb job, natural, unaffected, tied together effectively, and expressed in such beauty of feeling and prose that I count it, as others of our office present did, as one of the finest we have ever heard.... That's it Your Excellency, I had my say, for whatever my two cents worth comes up to."[52]

Porter of the Cleveland *Plain Dealer*, although laudatory, wrote of Jane with a bit of a twist of the pen. He claimed Lausche's charming wife Jane served the Governor with radiance and grace. She was, according to Porter, a thoroughly likeable woman who gave the impression of being a non-political, simple-minded soul, whose mission in life was to take care of her preoccupied, absent-minded husband. Jane was always amiable, always amused, always well-groomed—qualities that endeared her to Republican women. "They figured that Jane was a martyr to Frank's idiosyncrasies and that she hated public life. The opposite [was] probably true. She enjoyed it and the innocent-lamb role she played was as effective as Frank's mystique."[53]

Early in 1956 Mrs. Sheal was hospitalized at St. Anthony's Hospital in Columbus. She was later transferred to a nursing home and died a few days later on February 11, 1956. Jane deplored the lack of care for the chronically ill. Only St. Anthony's hospital in Columbus took such patients. A German Franciscan Order founded by Mother Frances Scherier ran this hospital.

Jane's overall personal enthusiasm was tempered in 1956 by release of news that the first lady had suffered from lead arsenic poisoning since 1925. It was an ailment similar to that suffered by Clare Booth Luce, Ambassador to Italy in the 1950s. In the 1920s Jane had worked with paints in her business of making lampshades and lighting fixtures. When the malady was finally detected, medical results showed Jane was filled with lead and arsenic. Shortly after the Lausche's marriage in 1928 an undetermined illness forced the new bride to spend six months as a virtual invalid. She did not know what was wrong. After many tests, doctors treated her for tuberculosis. "I kept telling [the doctors] the excruciating gastro-pains started when I had my studio...

doctors must have thought I only dabbled with a brush." She continued, "I didn't know the chemical analyses of paints when I worked with them. I mixed them with my hands, wiped the paint on my smock and ate food without cleaning my hands well. I worked 14 hours a day and was too busy to eat... I had a thriving business."[54]

In 1933 tests conclusively proved the presence of lead and arsenic in her body tissues. Jane received treatment with calcium glutinate intravenously. Evidence indicated that lead poisoning developed primarily because Jane licked the end of her paint brushes to make the bristles more pointed and more effective for the intricate painting she applied on lampshades. Lay people and internal medicine physicians knew little about the deleterious effects of such action upon the gastro-intestinal system.[55] In a letter to her cousin Mary Wilcox, Jane wrote that she did not like heavy clothing because, "it makes me miserable

"I am better...but after you have lead poisoning, you never completely recover.... I have continuously suffered from terrible fatigue."

as I get over-heated easily. I do think we have to recognize the fact that I had a near fatal illness—lead poisoning—and that I'm really able to be amazingly active in view of my past medical problems."[56] There was conjecture among friends that the lead poisoning prevented Jane from having children. Doctors placed her on a high protein, high caloric diet in which she ate no uncooked food. "I am better...but after you have lead poisoning, you never completely recover.... I have continuously suffered from terrible fatigue."[57] This illness stimulated her interest in industrial diseases. "Every medical school should have a chair of industrial medicine," the first lady advocated, "Since World War II dozens of new chemicals have been introduced into industry with little or no tests and no control for workers' benefits."[58] Jane had difficulty adding weight to her slender body. Unfortunately, Jane suffered more serious health debilities in the 1960s during her husband's senatorial years.

Jane was called on for even more political speeches in the 1956 senatorial race. She gave speeches throughout the state in support of her husband's candidacy against Bender. By 1956, television had become a more important medium in political campaigning, Frank used television occasionally while Jane made her in-person speeches. Telephone strikes and a newspaper walkout in Cleveland obviated efforts of campaigners to spread their message. The travel-weary barnstormers reunited on the weekend prior to the election at the Carter Hotel, campaign headquarters in downtown Cleveland. Jane remarked, "In some ways it's rather restful and pleasant—don't have to see our opponent's latest attack on us, or his huge ads. What a fortune he's spending!"[59] A newspaper reporter came to the Lausche retreat—two modest rooms at the hotel—looked around and wanted to know the whereabouts of the Lausche headquarters. "This is it," replied one of Lausche's nieces, Joanne, who was working for the Lausche campaign at the hotel. "No, I mean your regular *state* headquarters," the reporter insisted. Again Joanne said he was looking at it. "But where are your branch offices—in what cities?" "We haven't any." "How much staff do you have?" "Just the two of us here," replied Joanne. "Good Lord!" said the inquiring reporter, "Do you realize your opponent has 76 on his payroll in Columbus alone?"[60] In spite of the tremendous tide for the Republicans and Eisenhower in the 1956 election, Lausche prevailed with a majority of 201,000 votes. Jane expressed happiness over the margin of victory for a special reason. Eugene Hanhart, former chairman of the State Democratic Executive Committee, normally a very modest, temperate, non-gambler had taken some large bets that the outgoing Governor would win by more than 150,000 votes.[61] Regardless of the margin of victory, Jane and her husband were headed for the nation's capitol. Jane regretted leaving Columbus. "I love Columbus, I love the size of it, the people, the house." She added, "Nothing will ever take Ohio's place. My roots...are deep and hard to pull up. Ohio is very special."[62]

Lausche's election to a senate seat confounded his niece, Sally, then nine years old. She overheard Aunt Jane tell a friend that, in the event of Lausche's election as a senator, she supposed they would buy a home in Cleveland and live in an apartment in Washington, DC. Sally, who had never known her aunt and uncle to live in any home other than the Governor's mansion, asked in a horrified voice, "Do you mean that if Uncle Frank becomes a senator, you'll then be just regular people?"[63] There isn't a record of Jane's retort.

⌒

ONE COULD BE SURE THAT THE WILLIAM O'NEILL family, new tenants of the governor's mansion, would find a beautifully decorated and immaculately kept residence. After ten years in the mansion, Jane would now encounter major adjustments in her new surroundings in Washington, DC. She had visited the nation's capitol several times on short jaunts with her husband. After a brief visit in December, she located a small four-room apartment on Massachusetts Avenue, a far cry from the governor's mansion. Accustomed to living with a staff of eleven servants, Jane now managed her apartment with only the assistance of a part-time maid. Cautiously moving into the social whirl, Jane soon adjusted to her new lifestyle. She had considerable help from wives of other senators, particularly Harriet Bricker, wife of senior Ohio Senator John W. Bricker and Emily Taft Douglas, wife of Illinois Senator Paul Douglas.

The Lausches did not particularly enjoy apartment life. After several months of looking for a home, Jane was horribly shocked by real estate prices in the suburbs of Washington, DC. In September 1958, she finally bit the bullet and purchased a new home northwest of the capitol in Kenwood Park, Bethesda, Maryland. It became the first and only home the Lausches owned. Jane's husband never saw the home before moving in, and Jane took care of all the details. Frank's disinterest was just his way except when he saw the small home, he exclaimed, "My God,

Jane, You mean that's our life savings?"[64] The one-story brick rambler home cost $41,000 and carried a mortgage of $21,000.

The newly constructed home, although not extravagant, fit the Lausche needs quite well. The four-bedroom structure included a large kitchen (Jane's favorite part of the home), dining room and large living room, plus two baths. A den located off the dining room provided space for Frank to peruse his many senatorial documents and correspondence. The basement contained a family room, bedroom, bath and entrance to a backyard patio. A carport provided space for the Lausche's 1953 Chevrolet.

A reporter expressed amazement that Lausche had not been curious enough to take a brief ride into the suburbs to look at his new home. The couple was content in their new home. Jane had a yard large enough to plant some of her favorite vegetables and flowers. As for Frank, she remarked, "There is nothing he is fussy about—the food he eats or the place he lives in—so long as it is simple."[65]

By her very nature and as a wife of a politician, Jane felt a need to enmesh herself with organizations supported by the wives of the U.S. Senators. A family friend confided that Jane was one of the more active wives, without directly interfering with her husband's senatorial duties.[66] Two organizations affiliated with the U.S. Senate took a portion of her time. She became active in the U.S. Senate Wives Red Cross Unit and especially the International Neighbors organization. The latter organization devoted time and energy to promoting better relations with women and children in other countries, particularly in Latin and South America.

Jane spent time in the Senate gallery when she knew that Frank was scheduled to make a speech or when he was to be involved in a debate over a given issue. After due time on any given visit, she might leave the hard seats of the gallery and tour the capitol building. Jane researched the record of William Allen, whose statue stands in Statuary Hall as one of Ohio's two contributions to capitol décor. (A veteran political warhorse, Allen served in the U.S. House of Representatives in the 1860s. The septuagenarian was elected Governor of Ohio in 1873. After one term, fellow Ohioan Rutherford B. Hayes defeated him in a close election.) The other is a statue of James A. Garfield, 20th President of the United States.

Although the Lausches occasionally expressed their loneliness for Ohio, they soon adjusted to their new life in the nation's capitol. Jane was happy to have more time with her husband. Periodically they had a date where they went to a movie theater—they both liked Cinerama and saw films, such as the animated film, *Fantasia*. On another occasion the couple enjoyed one of Shakespeare's plays staged by England's famed Old Vic Company. When they moved into their new home in Bethesda, they were less prone to drive into Washington, DC. Lausche was a homebody who went to bed early and arose at the crack of daylight each day. Jane stayed home much of the time to assist Frank with his paperwork. The couple liked to take an occasional drive around Washington, DC to see the sights.

Jane recalled an odd experience on one trip. "I drove down a block in Georgetown and it seemed just like being home—everyone was waving and I smiled and waved back. Because our Ohio license plates were still on the car, I thought perhaps I'd come upon a colony of Ohioans. Then I discovered I was going the wrong way on a one-way street."[67]

The charming Jane Lausche made a personal commitment that she would not comment on any political issues while her husband was in the senate. This stance was consistent with her role when serving as the Governor's wife. She heeded her husband's advice that "he could get into a lot of trouble without [her] help."[68] Jane took this political stance partly because of an incident in the White House soon after the Lausches arrived in Washington, DC. President Eisenhower had chided Secretary of Defense Charles E. Wilson for making critical remarks about the national guard. In Eisenhower's view, Wilson's remarks were unwise. Mrs. Wilson jumped into the fray publicly stating the President was unfair to her husband. "I would have kept quiet," Jane commented, but added.... It is up to the individual."[69] One way Jane did assist her husband on the political front was to read the major newspapers. She underlined the important stories and placed them in his office, "If there's something he absolutely had to see," she commented, "I cut it out and put it on his [bathroom] mirror."[70] "We don't go to cocktail parties," she related, "My husband thinks they are such a waste of time. He spends his evenings studying documents, some of which I have condensed for him during the day."[71]

Jane's life took a turn for the worse in the 1960s when she suffered several setbacks. The Senator's wife seemed accident-prone. On September 6, 1962, while visiting in Columbus and riding with Mrs. Anna J. Stinchcomb, their car was struck at an intersection of Long Street. Jane suffered an injured spine and neck, nose fracture, and multiple bruises, particularly on her face. She recovered from this accident after several months. Jane filed a $153,000 damage suit from which she received financial compensation. The injuries required prolonged plastic surgery and left her with permanent dizziness from an inner-ear problem. On October 29, 1966, the beleaguered Jane fell and suffered fractures of the left hip and left forearm. She endured considerable discomfort and received physiotherapy. A plate and a pin were placed in her hip and Jane's arm remained in a cast for several weeks. Eventually she moved about in a wheelchair and later walked with crutches.

In early 1968 the unlucky Mrs. Lausche was involved in another serious auto accident. Again she was confined to a wheelchair for several weeks. Slowly her frail body responded to physical therapy. She spent a good portion of her time recuperating in Cleveland. It was an election year for the Lausches. She helped her husband's campaign by answering the phone and preparing campaign flyers. "I spend about eight hours a day sorting clippings, reading and condensing reports for my husband," she confided, "It would be impossible for a senator to read carefully every document that crosses his desk. I could do this for him even when I was confined to a wheelchair and I like doing it."[72] Her injured body eventually recovered, but considerable pain remained.

After Frank left the Senate, the twosome spent Jane's last ten years bereft of the hustle and bustle of the political arena. The couple grew even closer and enjoyed their retirement years, splitting their time between Bethesda and Cleveland. Jane's impaired body gave out, and she died in her sleep on November 24, 1981. She was 78 years of age, and the couple had been married 53 years.

Jane Lausche was one of Ohio's most charming and devoted daughters. She was a brilliant person, modest in her demeanor and highly sensitive to the problems of all with whom she came in contact. In spite of her modesty and self-effacement, she vigorously defended her husband against what she perceived to be unfair attacks.[73] In the harsh world of politics where everyone is fair game, no one on either side of the aisle ever spoke of Jane Lausche but in most admiring and affectionate terms.

The Lausches had been an extraordinarily compatible couple. They demonstrated the sort of mutual admiration and respect that greatly enriches a marriage. The couple always had a sense of humor about themselves, and there was never any stuffiness in their demeanor. Jane liked to tell stories about Frank, and he enjoyed the repartee. Occasionally he shook his head in a kind of perpetual amazement as she captured in words his personality so well.

Lausche enjoys a laugh with Frank J. Kern (left) and prominent Slovenian sculptor, France Gorse (right) at the unveiling of Slovenian poet and composer Ivan Zorman's monument in the Slovenian (Yugoslav) Cultural Gardens, Rockefeller Park in Cleveland, 1959. (Courtesy of Dr. Rudolph Susel)

eleven

The Senator Swims
against the Tide

LYNDON B. JOHNSON LIKELY NEVER EXPECTED that his political fortunes would be dramatically affected by the actions of a newcomer from Ohio to the United States Senate. This newcomer, Frank J. Lausche, along with the irascible Senator Wayne Morse (OR), held strong playing cards in determining the political clout of the hard-driving and manipulative Johnson. He was initially and indirectly involved in Johnson's political career in the Senate in 1953. When Lausche appointed Democrat Thomas Burke to succeed Robert Taft in late 1953, senate Democrats edged into a 48 to 47 majority over Republicans. Concurrently, Oregon Senator Wayne Morse, the gravel-voiced, self-proclaimed Independent Party of one, declined to end his feud with Johnson. Morse continually voted in support of Republican organization of the Senate, and with Vice President Nixon's tie-breaking vote, prevented Johnson from becoming majority leader. The Republicans chose the extreme right wing Senator William Knowland (CA) as their majority leader in 1954.[1]

The California Senator's majority leadership role proved to be short-lived, and again Morse became a key player. After the mid-term elections in 1954, he declared himself an independent Republican and soon thereafter joined the Democratic party. Morse, with a bit of Johnson's persuasion, tipped the scales in favor of the Democrats by voting for Johnson to serve as majority leader. The Texan became the youngest majority leader (at age 46) in the history of the U.S. Senate. In exchange for Morse's vote, Johnson appointed the Oregonian to the much sought after Foreign Relations Committee. In addition, he appointed him to the Banking and Currency Committee.[2]

Fast forward to early January 1957. Enter Frank Lausche again. "I don't know if I'll be the majority or minority leader," Johnson told his colleagues.[3] Why? Newly elected Senator Lausche had encouraged rumors that he would vote with the Republicans to organize the senate. This scenario evolved after Lausche's victory in the 1956 election. Because of Lausche's admiration for President Eisenhower, he had intimated that it was important for the President to have support for his legislative agenda. The Senator planned to help the President, even if it meant crossing the senate aisle. Lausche reaffirmed his plans to complete his gubernatorial term, which expired on January 14, 1957. Such action would preclude the junior Senator's attendance at the Senate organizational meetings. Over the Christmas holidays, Lausche changed his mind and resigned the governorship on January 3. His early departure set off a bizarre footnote to Ohio political history.

Republican Lieutenant Governor John W. Brown of Medina was sworn in as interim Governor for eleven days, as stipulated by the Ohio Constitution. Newly elected Governor C. William O'Neill could not take office until January 14. Brown moved into the Governor's mansion and Lausche's vacated office. He replaced portraits of Democratic governors with portraits of Republican governors. Midway through his brief tenure "Governor" Brown called a session of the general assembly and delivered a State of the State address.

Brown infuriated O'Neill, still Attorney-General for the state, by asking for Governor's pay instead of a Lieutenant Governor's salary for the short duration of his governorship. Reluctantly, O'Neill complied and issued an official opinion that Brown could be paid at a rate of $25,000 a year instead of $6,000.[4]

On New Year's Day, two Ohio insiders called Washington, DC and notified Republican Senators Knowland and Styles Bridges (NH) that Lausche planned to vote with the Republicans at the Senate organizational meeting. Knowland anticipated the possibility of regaining his majority leadership position.[5] Lausche failed to show up for the Democratic caucus on January 3. Democrats questioned the new Senator's intent. Johnson knew Lausche would have no political clout in either party if he joined the Republicans. He ignored the freshman Senator.[6] (After the November election, Lausche repeatedly refused to accept phone calls from Johnson, who had wanted to congratulate him on his victory).[7] When the Senate met to organize later in the day, the script might well have followed that of a Hollywood cliffhanger. The vote was going to be close. Tension was high, much like a face-off between a sheriff and a villain.

Both sides mustered support. Democrat Matthew Neely (WV) left his sickbed to attend the session. Jacob Javits, newly elected Republican senator (NY) awaited a call while hidden away in an office beneath the capitol dome near the Senate chamber. He wanted to retain his position as New York's Attorney-General until the New York Senate Legislature met. The New York GOP-controlled legislature then planned to pick a Republican to succeed Javits. If he resigned before the legislature convened, Democratic Governor Averill Harriman most certainly would have appointed a Democrat.

When the session began, Lausche—described by one journalist as a wide-faced, slow-thinking and slow-talking reactionary Democrat[8]—entered the Senate chamber. Sporting a sober black suit with a red carnation, he sat in the back, silent and inscrutable. Robert Oliver, aide to Senator Johnson, recalled the setting, "I was up in the gallery...seated next to the press gallery. I leaned over to whoever was with me and I said, 'Lausche is going to vote with the Democrats.' How did I know that? I said Johnson was the only man on the floor who knew it. Johnson was relaxed and I could always tell when Johnson was working energetically to put together a vote or he had what he wanted."[9]

The test arrived when Democrats and Republicans introduced motions to elect Johnson or Knowland as majority leader. The air crackled with electricity when the roll call on the Knowland motion began. The Senate clerk took eighteen minutes to reach Lausche's name. The balloting stood 27–27. Tension tightened, and the gallery crowd stood to watch Lausche. The Ohio Senator made no immediate reply, and loud murmuring arose on the floor and in the galleries. Finally Lausche shouted a slow "No." Johnson had retained his position as majority leader for the 85th Senate. Knowland fumed with resentment. Regular Democrats sprang from their chairs to congratulate their new colleague. Southern Democrats were disappointed. As though the *Prodigal Son* had returned home, Johnson rose from his chair to shake hands with Lausche, both exchanging knowing smiles.[10]

George Reedy, one of Johnson's closest aides, described this occasion, "You know, Lausche had made a lifetime career of being only [superficially] on the Democratic side of the ballot. Johnson thought at that time quite possibly Lausche was holding out to ask for something in return for his vote and by the way, if Lausche had voted for the Republicans to organize the Senate, I think there might have been a dicey situation. I'll never forget that Johnson absolutely refused to talk to [Lausche] or send an emissary or deal with him in any way.... I can still remember the picture of his [Lausche] sitting—he was sitting in the last desk, last row, with his head buried in his hands, quite a perfect picture of a man who was caught in a very-deep-seated dilemma, I think hoping he would get a last minute offer from Johnson. He didn't."[11]

Two sidebars emanated from Lausche's climatic vote. One observer noted that

Lausche's admiration for President Eisenhower gave rise to his desire to vote with the GOP, if his action would prove beneficial to the President. Eisenhower was aware of Lausche's sentiments. The Ohio Senator was shrewd enough to know not to vote with the Republicans, unless he received word from the President that he needed Lausche's support. The unpredictable Senator never heard from Eisenhower. The President fervently desired control of the Senate. He wanted this control only if it were based on a more solid foundation than the political apostasy of one Senator.[12]

Reedy claimed Johnson handled the Lausche issue in a proper manner. The majority leader realized how much pressure Lausche would have placed upon himself if he shunned his own party.[13] Lausche had dodged the bullet of incrimination he would have suffered with a vote of support for a Republican cause. A number of Democrats had expressed their displeasure with Lausche's hesitancy to declare his party preference. To Ohio voters long accustomed to Lausche's maverick political behavior, his indecisiveness was not surprising. Nor had he established a precedent with a threat to bolt his party. Senator Glen Taylor, the Democratic singing cowboy from Idaho, doubled as vice presidential candidate for Henry Wallace's ill-fated Progressive Party in 1948. Senator Strom Thurmond (SC) accepted the Dixiecrat nomination for President in 1948, garnering 39 electoral votes. Following President Truman's surprising victory over Thomas E. Dewey, Thurmond (who still called himself a Democrat) eventually voted with his party to organize the Senate in January 1949. Senator Wayne Morse (OR) bailed out of the Republican Party at the beginning of the 1953 congressional session. He declared himself an Independent. Morris did vote with the Republicans to organize the Senate. Morse was elected a Republican and believed he owed it to his party and to President Eisenhower.[14]

James B. L. Rush, editor of the Winston-Salem *Journal*, asked Lausche why he voted with the Democratic Party. The editor questioned whether the Senator realized that his party, many of whom were as conservative as Lausche, would give better support than a Republican Senate led by Knowland.[15] Adroit at responding to critics and allies alike, Lausche reasoned that the electorate preferred a Congress controlled by Democrats in opposition to Eisenhower. The Ohio Senator believed a Democratic House of Representatives and a Republican-dominated Senate was imprudent. "Based on the President's favorable experience with the Democratic control of the 84th Congress, which often gave him greater support than members of his own party," Lausche mused, "there was substantial reason to conclude that such treatment of the President's program by the Democrats, when sound, would continue."[16]

Lausche no doubt realized that bolting to the Republican side was impractical. He would be reduced to a position at the bottom of the almighty seniority list. Lausche may have agreed to trade his organization vote for choice committee assignments. He immediately received appointment to the coveted commerce and banking committees. Two years later, Lausche was appointed to the highly prestigious foreign relation's committee.

THE SENATOR SOON SETTLED INTO A DAILY ROUTINE. The transition from governor to senator did not bother him. "The problems confronting me are not new and my range of experience is a great help. There never has been a job to which I haven't adapted myself and found contentment in doing."[17] Lausche would change his mind by the time he left the Senate in 1968.

Lausche supported the Democratic agenda on certain issues—particularly foreign aid. For the most part, he maintained a conservative posture. His conservatism meshed with the Senator's personal frugality, and was deeply rooted in his own childhood. He remembered his parents buying a wagonload of cabbage to make kraut for their large family and the boarders. "Bushels of potatoes would fill the bin, whole hogs would be bought, and not even the ears were wasted.... Economy was practiced everywhere. Any man or nation that does not practice economy cannot help but get into trouble."[18]

The Senator spoke about thrift on February 4, 1957, making his first presentation in the senate chambers before only ten senators. The issue at hand was a bill to provide former Presidents with a $25,000 yearly allowance. Lausche expressed deep respect for the two surviving former Presidents (Herbert Hoover and Harry Truman), but could not support this bill. "There is a principle involved and that principle deals with the constant increase in the cost of government. If we urge economy in government, the practice of economy ought to be at the highest level."[19] The bill passed in spite of Lausche's dissent.

On another occasion, Lausche became irritated when he learned his conservative colleague, Senator John Williams, Republican from Delaware, had difficulty returning his unexpended stationery allowance to the Treasury Department. During his first three months in office, the Ohio Senator used only $40 of his allotted yearly budget of $7,900 for telegrams. He was chagrined to think unused senatorial funds could not be returned to the treasury department. Eventually, the two Senators persuaded Treasury Secretary George Humphrey to allow them to return unused funds. "We cannot expect economy in the lower echelons unless we who are in charge practice it in those quarters where we set the example and have control."[20]

Lausche used whatever leverage a freshman Senator could impart as a member of the commerce committee. He spoke up against subsidies for urban public transportation systems, funds for the Merchant Marine, railroads and for construction of municipal airports. In the Farm Bill of 1957, he unsuccessfully attempted to remove the acreage reserve program. In like manner, Lausche opposed appropriations for a monument and library in memory of James Madison. Nor did he support construction of a United States pavilion at the New York World's Fair. The Senator resisted pork barrel funds for his own state. In 1957, he scuttled a proposal for a $5 million appropriation to help build a stadium for the Pan

American Games scheduled in Cleveland in 1959. "I cannot support for Ohio what I would oppose for another state."[21]

The broad-shouldered lone wolf stood up for tax relief for small businesses. Imploring both sides of the aisle to support this tax break, he urged that "we must understand that there is a moral obligation...to provide aid for the small business man."[22] As was true for so many of Lausche's efforts, his plea went for naught.

During Lausche's senatorial tenure, his diatribe on economic frugality in the federal government became part of the *Congressional Record* day by day and page by page. As a rule, he merely sat in the senate chambers listening to arguments, observing the charges and counter charges. One could almost hear the wheels turning as Lausche compared the pros and cons before reaching a conclusion. The Senator remained silent only so long, then he expounded with a principle pertaining to the constant increase in government expenditures. Congress and the President needed to set an example. "I cannot help thinking of the proverbial camel, the back of which was broken by placing upon it one lone straw. The accumulation of many straws finally broke the camel's back...it is the accumulation of these small weights and their addition to the burden, which, in finality, is making the cost of government so great."[23]

Frugality in government spending wasn't Lausche's only cross to bear in the Senate. He continued his crusade against union bosses and unionism in general. After months of investigation, the Special Rackets Committee, headed by Senator John McClellan (AR), documented in 1958 sensational revelations about union corruption. After days of debate, Lausche upset the Democratic moguls in the Senate. Minority leader William Knowland attempted to attach a series of amendments to the Taft-Hartley law. One amendment would allow the rank and file members to check off the excesses of labor bosses. Under the leadership of Majority Leader Johnson, the Democrats voted solidly against the Knowland amendment.

Lausche cast the lone democratic vote for the amendment, charging, "Unless we act now, time will run out and prevent this session from taking any action to reform the evils and abuses disclosed...."[24] The Ohio Senator worried that the McClellan Committee investigation, which cost $1 million, would likely be in vain. Lausche lamented, "a meaningless, ineffective bill is likely to come to the Senate—wholly insufficient to save for the workers his [sic] liberties, for the employer his rights and for the government its sovereignty."[25] A watered-down labor bill sponsored by Senator John Kennedy (MA) and Republican Irving Ives (NY) passed the Senate with little labor reform. The venerable columnist Raymond Moley noted that Kennedy's strategic committee membership, his importance to the Democratic party, his relationship to McClellan meant there would be legislation to his liking or none at all. The discouraged Moley wrote, "the great crusade lies low, pierced with arrows of political expediency."[26] Lausche embraced his fellow Clevelander's words.

During Johnson's tenure as majority leader (1955–1960), the Senate could no longer call itself the greatest deliberative body in the world. Johnson's methodology—aided and abetted by acquiescent Republicans—saw backstage arm-twisting replace senate debate. Major bills did not reach the senate floor until *votes* were counted and victory apparently assured. Promise of support for legislation important to reticent senators brought them in line. Limited debate became the rule. Senators accepted unanimous consent agreements cutting off extended discussion and speeding final vote passage. This form of arm-twisting was not Lausche's style, and for the most part, he did not buy into it. In regards to this legislative chicanery, Lausche felt that "on the surface I may be losing good results from refusing to join the mob. I feel frustrated...but I'm not going to give up the battle or seek favors by voting against my conviction."[27]

The Senator did not see the legislative process as a kind of political game involving tactics and techniques to achieve the best possible outcome, as opposed to a series of moral crises in which one is true or false to himself. He resented any attempt to influence his vote or decision. Efforts to line up his vote became a rarity for fear he might vote just the opposite. Lausche did not fit into any particular political classification. Ironically, the Senator's voting stance turned out to be less conservative than that of John Bricker, his Senate colleague for two years. Politically, Lausche aligned more closely with Everett Dirksen (Rep-IL), John Williams (Rep-DE), Roman Hruska (Rep-NE), Richard Russell (Dem-GA) and James Eastland (Dem-MS).

Lausche would receive scant political support from several new liberal-minded senators elected in 1958. Notables included Frank Church (Dem-ID), Thomas Dodd (Dem-CN), Edmund Muskie (Dem-ME), Philip Hart (Dem-MI), Eugene McCarthy (Dem-MN), and Stephen Young, Ohio's other Senator.

After the election results were tabulated in 1958, Democrats scored their largest political gains in Ohio, as well as nationwide in twenty years,. These Ohio victories came with minimal assistance from Lausche. Lest his constituency should forget him, the Senator made his biannual trek to selected county fairs. Nor did he forget his friends on St. Clair Avenue. Lausche gave but cursory support to what would be a victorious campaign for governor-elect Michael V. DiSalle. The Senator's political charm did not extend to newly elected Young. He made major election news by upsetting the venerable Bricker, Lausche's close friend, for Ohio's second senate seat. This victory marked the first time since 1935 that two Democratic Senators represented the Buckeye state simultaneously. Young had dabbled in politics much of his life. The feisty Clevelander had defeated George H. Bender for a seat in the House of Representatives in 1936. Bender's political career ended twenty years later when Lausche defeated him in the 1956 senatorial race.

Young—cantankerous, outspoken, crafty and neither particularly effective nor beloved—was as liberal as Lausche was conservative. The junior Senator immediately created a stir in the senate. Breaking tradition, he refused to allow Lausche to escort him to the front of the Senate chambers for induction ceremonies. The bouncy junior Senator chose Johnson to escort him down the aisle, to the hearty applause of former President Harry Truman. At the same time, Johnson escorted Ralph Yarborough, his new senate colleague from Texas down the aisle. Veteran senate aides and Harry Truman could recall this break in protocol occurring only one other time. Hiram Johnson (CA) would not let his colleague Sheridan Downey escort him down the aisle in 1940. Smarting from the fact that Lausche had not campaigned for him, Young commented that 1,650,000 voters attested to his worthiness for the senate office. Jabbing his fellow Clevelander, Young affirmed that "Apparently I did not need Senator Lausche's support then, nor do I now."[28] (Young carefully refrained from mentioning that Jane Lausche publicly announced she would vote for him). Demonstrating that he felt no offense, Lausche walked over to Young's desk after the swearing in, shook his hand and congratulated him. Seemingly startled, Young was unable to get any words out before Lausche strolled into the Senate smoker.

During the next six years, the relationship between these senators mellowed somewhat. Politically they seldom agreed, although the two men worked together on pork barrel issues affecting the Buckeye state. In 1961, the two senators cancelled out each other's votes on 47 percent of the issues requiring a recorded vote. On 75 senate partisan roll calls that same year, Lausche voted in agreement with his party only 27 percent of the time, compared to 83 percent for Young.

In spite of their political differences, the two senators survived during Young's first term. They seldom agreed on appointments to federal positions. Lausche gave Young little if any campaign support in his bid for a second term. Young defeated Robert Taft, Jr. in the 1964 election. Now 76, the twice-elected Senator decided to let bygones be bygones, and walked down the center aisle with his Ohio colleague on January 4, 1965. This would be the last time either Senator would enjoy such an honor.

Lausche was assiduous throughout his political career in making sure no scandals were linked to his name. Journalists and the media were always anxious to uncover scurrilous information about politicians. Syndicated columnist Drew Pearson attempted to besmirch Lausche's name in the spring of 1959. This columnist had written about Senators' financial disclosures and the possibility of conflict of interest with lobbyists and the companies they represented. Pearson implied that Young, a millionaire, had fully disclosed his stock holdings. He questioned the accuracy of Lausche's and Bricker's financial reports.

Lausche reacted sharply, informing Pearson that his security holdings were inconsequential. His portfolio included $17,950 in government bonds; 396 shares of North American Bank stock that cost $4,545; twenty shares of Cincinnati *Enquirer* stock which cost $200; and nine shares of Bank of America stock purchases in 1956 for $315. The Senator had used a portion of his Series E government bonds worth $28,000 to make a down payment on his home in Bethesda. In 1959

Lausche's home mortgage balance amounted to $18,000.[29] This issue continued to fester, prompting Pearson to amend several critical remarks. He sent his comments to Bishop Wilbur Hammaker of the Methodist Church in Washington, DC (where Jane occasionally attended), and the columnist commented, "I have known [Lausche] for a long time, even from the days when he was mayor of Cleveland. Frank is a slow starter and has not been as active as a Senator as I had hoped, but I think he is developing into one of the real Senate leaders."[30]

Bishop Hammaker and Lausche were not entirely satisfied with Pearson's retort. In his original column, the columnist had implied that, as general counsel for the Federation of Railway Progress in 1947 and 1948, Lausche had earned $50,000 a year. Pearson erroneously added that Lausche put through a trucking tax indirectly favoring the railroads while Governor, putting him in a conflict of interest position, as far as the facts were concerned. Lausche vehemently challenged Pearson for a retraction of his accusation. Lausche was not governor during those years. The Senator informed the journalist that he had served as counsel for the Federation of Railway Progress for seventeen months. "My pay was $833 per month based on a yearly salary of $10,000. I had to provide the stenographic service...my total income...was about $14,500."[31] The press nearly always has the last say. Pearson responded, "I went out of my way to say that I did not believe the Senator was influenced by any law fees he received.... However, in a court of law the facts would have stood against him. It seems to me that rather than argue the case according to the legal merits, I should go all out to express my confidence in the Senator and my regret regarding the original story. This I did."[32]

This issue had no sooner faded from the scene when Pearson struck at Lausche again. The journalist questioned Lausche's vote in the highly controversial nomination of Lewis Strauss as Secretary of Commerce. Lausche, a member of the Interstate and Foreign Commerce Committee, voted yes on May 19, 1959, in a 9-8 vote recommending senate confirmation of Strauss. He believed the chief executive should have the widest latitude in choosing members of his cabinet. In a syndicated column two days later, Pearson inferred that George Humphrey, Secretary of Treasury from Cleveland, had brought pressure upon the senior Ohio Senator to vote for Strauss. Several days later Lausche vehemently responded to Pearson, commenting that "Humphrey neither directly nor indirectly in any manner whatsoever contacted me with regard to the Strauss nomination."[33] He reminded the Washington journalist about how strongly Humphrey had supported George Bender, Lausche's opponent in the 1956 senatorial election. Lausche was determined that his name not be smeared. He did not want to be a part of any exposé Pearson and fellow journalist Jack Anderson released to the public, such as their book, *The Case Against Congress, A Compelling Indictment of Corruption on Capital Hill* (1968). The authors had examined the abuses of power prevalent in the nation's capitol.

Strauss proved to be a controversial cabinet candidate. The brilliant former admiral had served as a member and later chairman of the Atomic Energy Commission in the late 1940s and 1950s. Many issues placed him under a cloud of controversy. Examples included the J. Robert Oppenheimer security problem, the Dixon-Yates power contract, the clean bomb, and shipping of isotopes to Europe. Additionally, an important issue was Strauss' conservative approach to the role of government, which did not set well with liberals in the senate, particularly with Western Democratic Senators who opposed him.

Longstanding feuds over these issues, differing philosophies of government and sharp personality conflicts complicated the protracted controversy. On June 19, the Senate rejected Strauss' confirmation by a 49-46 vote. The final vote adhered closely to party lines. Strauss became only the eighth cabinet nominee rejected by the senate. His rejection was the first since 1925 when the senate refused to confirm Charles B. Warren, Calvin Coolidge's nominee for Attorney General. He had been counsel for the Sugar Trust and had come under scrutiny for illegal activities.

Lausche, ever loyal to Eisenhower, voted for Strauss' confirmation. "The president is entitled to have his nomination confirmed, unless it was clearly shown that the nominee was lacking in ability, integrity or loyalty to the country. In one swoop, the Senate took from him (Strauss) a treasured and good reputation built through a lifetime of righteous living."[34] Referring to the value and meaning of a reputation, Lausche quoted Shakespeare, "Good name in man and woman, dear my Lord, Is the immediate jewel of their souls. Who steals my purse steals trash; tis something nothing 'Twas mine, tis his, and has been a slave to thousands; But he that filches from me my good name Robs me of that which not enriches him, and makes me poor indeed."[35]

Lausche found himself in a somewhat embarrassing situation concerning another of Eisenhower's nominees, namely Clare Booth Luce, nominated to serve as Ambassador to Brazil. A former Republican Congresswoman and Ambassador to Italy, she was the wife of Henry R. Luce, editor-in-chief of *Time, Life,* and *Fortune* magazines. Luce, a Catholic, received strong speeches of support from John Kennedy, Thomas Dodd, and Lausche, all three who were Catholic. Senator Fulbright, who was opposed to her ambassadorship, told Drew Pearson he could not defeat her appointment. "You know why." Pearson suggested. "It's a matter of religion." "Yes," replied Fulbright, "but I can't say that publicly."[36]

Luce's appointment seemed assured, although opposed by the voluble Senator Morse. Both Morse and Fulbright criticized Mrs. Luce for a 1944 campaign speech in which she charged that President Roosevelt had led the U.S. into war. Luce apologized for her language. She still believed Roosevelt should have candidly told the American people that the U.S. was going to fight the Nazis. After several rancorous remarks from upset senators, the senate overwhelmingly confirmed Luce's nomination on April 28.

That same day Luce provided ammunition for her own *coup de grâce*. She expressed appreciation for her confirmation and explained, "My difficulties...go back some years when Senator Wayne Morse was kicked in the head by a horse."[37] (He had suffered a broken jaw at a horse show in 1951). Senators reacted angrily to her remarks. Morse read Mrs. Luce's statement to the senate and commented, "This is part of an old pattern of instability on her part."[38] Lausche and Yarborough, who had voted to confirm Luce, later said that they regretted their votes. Three days later, under intense pressure, Luce resigned her ambassadorship. This case was closed.

"If I were...elected to the United States Senate, I would cross the aisle from one party to the other whenever the interests of the country seemed to require it or justify it—regardless."

Lausche marched to his own drumbeat in spite of senate party makeup. Although not categorized as one of Eisenhower's chief supporters, in 1957 Lausche voted 57 percent of the time for Eisenhower-initiated legislation. This figure increased dramatically over the next three years. On all the legislative issues that came before the senate in 1958, Lausche led all Democrats with a 69 percent vote for legislation proposed by the President.[39] In 1959, Lausche led all senate Democrats in most consistently voting against his party majority on legislative bills (83%). Lausche supported the President's position on 12 of 13 key issues.[40]

THE MOODY LAUSCHE WENT HIS OWN WAY, oblivious of Washington lobbyists, as well as most of his fellow senators. Lausche maintained he was for the two-party system and that this system was essential for a democracy. He told Louis Seltzer before his first election to the senate that such an arrangement did not mean he should blindly follow his party, nor should he be required to take directions from political bosses who were in politics for profit instead of patriotism. "If I were...elected to the United States Senate, I would cross the aisle from one party to the other whenever the interests of the country seemed to require it or justify it—regardless."[41] He was true to his word. Most of the time, the Senator went down in defeat when he proposed an amendment to a bill he opposed. Then, Lausche occasionally rose to deliver a speech that turned back the clock to the days when Daniel Webster, John C. Calhoun and Henry Clay bounced phrases off the walnut paneling of august senate chambers.

A heated presidential election took place in 1960. The presidential embers barely flickered for Lausche. Behind the scenes, Senator Majority Leader Lyndon Johnson aggressively pursued the office. In early August, newspapers reported that Eisenhower was asked about likely Democratic candidates. He mentioned Lausche first in addition to three southern senators. Johnson was incensed that the President had not mentioned his name. Johnson was not placated until the President apologized for any misunderstanding.[42]

Unexpected support for Lausche came from Ralph McGill, liberal editor of the Atlanta *Constitution*. The editor reasoned that the front-runners (Kennedy, Symington, Humphrey, and Johnson) might kill each other off. The kingmakers might conceivably reach out to Lausche, whose conservative record surpassed Richard Nixon, Republican presidential candidate. Lausche's nomination would capture a significant number of Republican votes.[43] The Cleveland *Plain Dealer* came to the same conclusion. Syndicated columnist Holmes Alexander said of Lausche, "he tries so hard to be like Lincoln that he'll never be satisfied until he's assassinated."[44]

Despite national-level accolades for Lausche, his power base in his native state began to erode. Governor DiSalle took a firm reign over the state Democratic organization. William Coleman, Democratic state chairman, took a more active role in rebuilding the state party organization and reaching out to county chairmen. There was no love lost between Lausche and the Governor, although Lausche did speak in support of DiSalle in the 1958 governor's election. The erstwhile Governor had begun to pull the Democratic party together, which Lausche had not previously chosen to do. Lausche was consulted less frequently on statewide Democratic strategy. The Senator countered by announcing early in 1960 that he might run a slate of delegates loyal to him as a favorite son in the May 3 primary. This slate would compete against the official party slate that pledged to support DiSalle, who in turn had pledged his support to John F. Kennedy. Later in the spring, citizens for Lausche opened a national campaign to nominate the eccentric Senator as a Democratic presidential candidate. Lausche denied knowledge of this movement. In reality, insiders knew he had contact with this group.

This turmoil became more confrontational due to efforts by Ray Miller. Serving as Cuyahoga County Democratic chairman, he enticed northeastern Ohio county chairmen to jump on the Kennedy bandwagon. On the day before the first Kennedy-Nixon debate, Kennedy made good on a longstanding promise by showing up at Miller's traditional Cuyahoga county steer roast. Over 100,000 Democrats attended this event. The day long outing reunited DiSalle and Miller dissidents who buried the hatchet. Observers noted that "one prominent Ohio Democrat who did not attend the festivities was Senator Frank Lausche, obviously because he considered Kennedy to be a [likely] loser."[45]

On the day after the first presidential debate, Kennedy returned to Painsville. He planned a day-long motorcade throughout northern Ohio. Early in the morning of the motorcade, Lausche arrived at Kennedy's motel. He inquired of Kennedy advance men whether he could join the motorcade with Kennedy and DiSalle. Observers wryly commented that "if we had any lingering doubts about Kennedy's success in the debate, Lausche removed them."[46] The motorcade began in Painsville and moved through Cleveland, Lorain, Elyria, Akron and Canton. Lausche, who rode in the procession, affirmed the crowds were the largest and noisiest of any since General Eisenhower had returned as conquering hero from his victory in Europe.[47]

During the campaign, the Kennedy brain trust committed a potentially damaging blunder. The press had neglected to mention that both Lausche and Democrat Thomas Dodd (CN) had not announced their support for Kennedy's candidacy. Both were Catholic. On September 5, the Washington *News* reported that when this *faux pas* was brought to the attention of Kennedy strategists, they admitted to an oversight in not asking Lausche to campaign for their ticket.[48]

This oversight reminds one of a similar occasion in the 1916 presidential election. While campaigning in California, Charles Evans Hughes, Republican presidential candidate, ignored California's powerful GOP Senator Hiram Johnson, himself a political maverick. In a close election, Hughes lost California and the election to President Woodrow Wilson. Kennedy mended fences with Lausche, and later the two men campaigned together in Ohio. Pollsters expected the race with Vice President Nixon to be close, and Ohio was a pivotal state with 25 electoral votes. Lausche (who respected Nixon) could not swing Ohio into the Kennedy camp. Nixon won the Buckeye state by a margin of 300,000 votes. Kennedy carried victory to the White House by a majority of a scant 118,000 popular votes. He fared better with the electoral college, defeating Nixon by 84 votes. This World War II hero became the youngest elected candidate at age 43 to ascend to the presidency. Theodore Roosevelt was a few months younger when he assumed the presidency due to William McKinley's assassination in September 1901. Kennedy was the first Roman Catholic to occupy the White House. Based on his prior voting record, Lausche cared little whether the President was Democrat or Republican.

"Lausche has played his old go-it-alone theme too long and too hard. The magic isn't there anymore...his erratic behavior has embarrassed some of his closest personal and political friends. No one waits breathlessly for Lausche to speak...when he does, no one pays much attention."

Seltzer, in a rare chastisement of Lausche, challenged his friend to change his political ways. The editor was critical of Lausche's decision not to attend the 1960 Democratic convention in Los Angeles. The Senator explained that he stayed away because the convention was rigged for Kennedy. Seltzer admonished Lausche, suggesting that "Lausche has played his old go-it-alone theme too long and too hard. The magic isn't there anymore...his erratic behavior has embarrassed some of his closest personal and political friends. No one waits breathlessly for Lausche to speak...when he does, no one pays much attention."[49] Seltzer questioned whether Lausche stayed away from the convention to attract more publicity than had he attended. Seltzer challenged Lausche not to make such a point of standing apart from the crowd. He maintained that Ohio's national political prestige was low and that Lausche must take some of the blame.[50]

The senior Ohio Senator ignored Seltzer's admonishment and politically went on his merry way. In 1960 Lausche recorded the highest percentage vote (70%) of any Democrat in opposition to his own party. He equaled Senator Byrd for the greatest Democratic percentage (69%) of votes aligned with Republican minority leader Everett Dirksen on issues coming up for a final vote. By the closing of the 86th Congressional session, Lausche began to experience unfavorable reviews from Ohio press. The Senator had been less than supportive during Kennedy's first year in office. The Toledo *Blade*, not always a friend to Lausche, wrote a critical editorial, "...when...are Ohioans of both parties going to wake up and stop throwing their votes to this venerable spellbinder who is more anxious to strike a phony pose than to represent either party."[51] Clevelander Charles Vanik of Czech heritage, and member of the House of Representatives for 26 years, asserted that his Senate friend was a modern-day advocate of small government. The Congressman added that Lausche would have fit in well with the ultra-conservative Republicans of the 1990s (Newt Gingrich and his ilk). He maintained the Senator's views would have been compatible with President Reagan's economic philosophy. In contrast, the liberal Vanik believed in big government. He pushed for appropriate taxation to provide adequate health care, prevention of environmental abuses and adequate support for education.[52]

Lausche was not deterred by these critical reviews. On 115 of 320 votes in the senate in 1961, only Strom Thurmond (SC), a drummer for the far right, and Lausche voted with the Republicans more than half of the time.[53] On 155 of 189 roll calls that presented a clear-cut support for legislation promoted by Kennedy in 1961, the only Democratic senators voting against Kennedy more than 55 percent of the time were Lausche and five southern senators. John Fenton, consultant to the Department of Finance for Ohio in the late 1950s, confirmed that on his voting record, Lausche was the second most conservative Democratic Senator (Thurmond was first) in 1961.[54]

Lausche's voting record caught the attention of Americans for Constitutional Action, a conservative organization located in the nation's capitol. The senior Ohio Senator received the organization's Distinguished Service Award for his "support of those legislative principles of the Constitution of the United States, as these were defined by the Founding Fathers of our Republic."[55]

Lausche faced an uphill battle to restrain government spending. For the most part, lobbyists carried too much weight for the Senate body to stand up and be counted. The Ohio Senator never wavered in his opposition to lobbyists. "Lobbyists have infested the halls of Congress. Bankers, lawyers, friends—they've all asked me to lay off...I am compelled by my judgment and my good conscience to oppose [them]."[56]

Lausche's constituents inquired about his personal political philosophy. He told his supporters that he wanted to ensure continual existence of the country's freedom and Democratic form of government. He resisted any legislation that might allow the United States to drift into a socialist state. The Senator favored sound fiscal practices and a guarantee that the tax load would neither be unbearable nor transferred to innocent future generations. Lausche believed in a balanced budget (deficit spending had occurred for 26 of the previous 33 years—1932–1965).[57]

The Senator's voting record found him rejecting new and unessential government projects. He dismissed the creation of new subsidies for farmers, federal aid to education, or literally any federal aid to government-sponsored programs. He occasionally voted for cuts in military appropriations.

⌒

DAVID HALBERSTAM, NOTED AUTHOR AND HARVARD GRADUATE, wrote a best seller entitled *The Fifties*. The Pulitzer Prize winner described numerous social and political entities of this rather bland decade. The American populace had settled into a peacetime atmosphere after President Eisenhower negotiated a merciful termination of the Korean War in 1953. The 1960s became a different story, developing into one of the most contentious decades in American history. The counter-culture movement led by young hippies burst into full bloom. This post-World War II generation spent much energy protesting military action in the Vietnam malaise. Political and military leaders struggled about how best to combat an enemy in a guerilla war many miles away from the American mainland. Society agonized over the assassination of three major American political and religious figures. President John F. Kennedy met death at the hand of Lee Harvey Oswald on November 22, 1963. The country had hardly recovered from this devastating tragedy when, on April 4, 1968, a sniper murdered Martin Luther King, Jr. in Memphis. Two months later to the day—June 4—Robert Kennedy was shot in Los Angeles while campaigning for the Democratic presidential nomination. The late President's brother died one day later. Racial hatred was fueled by demagogic actions of men like George Wallace, Governor of Alabama and third-party candidate in 1968. The social fabric of American society unraveled. Citizens began to ask, What is happening to our country? Lausche could not easily accept this upheaval.

Amidst these unsettling times, Lausche left little doubt he would run for a second term in the senate. On February 24, 1961, Ohio's all-time vote-getter announced his candidacy. His statement ended speculation that Lausche might run for the governorship of Ohio.[58] The Senator had confided with close friends that he was not particularly enamored with the life of a Senator. He accepted the challenges from morning until night. "The United States Senate opens up vistas that are not available in any other pursuit. There are in the Senate excellent minds with which one is in combat...if one has any dynamism at all, he becomes sharpened in this exchange of thoughts and wits."[59]

Organized labor in Ohio did not take kindly to Lausche's decision to seek a second term. The Senator's reticence to support labor legislation did not set well in the Buckeye state. Rumors circulated that, at the urging of state labor leaders, erstwhile Ohio Governor Michael DiSalle considered a run against Lausche. "Let's put it to rest now," DiSalle told newsmen, "I mean no, no. I'm not going to run against Lausche. I could not be drafted to run against Lausche. My statement is apodictic," the Governor concluded as he cited from a dictionary that apodictic means capable of clear and certain demonstration.[60] Labor leaders valiantly searched for a worthy opponent. Lieutenant Governor John W. Donahey, a well-known name in Ohio Democratic politics flatly refused. State Representative Michael A. Sweeney, another popular political name in Cleveland, also declined. Two unknowns—Raymond W. Beringer, a Toledo gasoline station operator, and Albert T. Ball, a business consultant—ran against Lausche in the primary election. Both were swept aside by the Senator, who did not bother to campaign.

In the Republican primary, John Marshall Briley, a lawyer and industrialist from Perrysburg (south of Toledo) gained victory over three political hacks. Briley confronted an attitude expressed by Republicans that, "The trouble is...we have to start with everyone saying Senator Lausche is a sure winner."[61] The challenger possessed excellent credentials. Briley—a large man, slightly bald, deliberate of speech with an engaging smile—was the most erudite Ohioan to run for the Senate since the days of the sage Theodore E. Burton, member of the House of Representatives and U.S. Senate in the early 1900s.

An orphan originally from Monmouth, Illinois, Briley's work ethic allowed the young man to graduate from Monmouth College on commencement day with $3,000 saved. While in college one summer, Briley worked for Cleveland entrepreneur Mantis J. Van Sweringen. An outstanding student at Harvard Law School, the young graduate obtained employment with Sherman and Sterling, one of the largest law firms in New York City. Ten years later, Briley served as lawyer for the largest bank in the world, National City Bank in the Gotham city. He had responsibility for consummating bank transactions in Europe. A career change brought Briley to Owens Corning Fiberglass in Toledo. This company retained him as chief legal counsel. After several years, the astute lawyer received a promotion to general manager. Owens Corning flourished under Briley's leadership. He was especially adept at developing good employee relations where several unions were involved. He promoted cohesion between the company's executive and staff personnel, which included grooming a potential successor.

Briley raised over a million dollars for his campaign, the greatest Republican largess collected in an off-year election in Ohio. The challenger looked for openings in which to attack his opponent. The prospects looked bleak. Lausche's political record was difficult to renounce. During the 1962 Congressional session, Lausche voted against half of Kennedy's legislative proposals and in opposition to more than 50 percent of the President's spending recommendations. He followed closely the voting record of conservative Senator Harry F. Byrd (Dem-VA).

Briley's attacks on Lausche's political stance were much like a pugilist who constantly bobs and weaves in the ring. Lausche's image was that of an intelligent conservative who resisted welfare statism. After careful research, the challenger came up with a scorecard showing that Lausche managed to remain independent by voting on both sides of the spectrum. During three roll calls in May 1962, Lausche voted to give the President authority to fix tariffs in the cotton classification. Kennedy had promised the Southern states support for a higher tariff on cotton in return for support of a free trade bill. A fortnight later, Lausche voted to raise the President's public works pot from $600 million to $750 million. On July 17, the Ohio Senator cast a significant vote to save a Medicare bill from being labeled a failure. He voted against a Republican amendment to a trade bill that would give Congress veto power over any tariff treaty set up by the President, thereby helping to save the bill for Kennedy. Lausche helped a Cleveland congressman with a proposal for a new $40-60 million federal building in Cleveland (later to be named after Lausche).

Conversely, Lausche voted against numerous spending bills. He called for a halt to the frightening growth of a giant federal government. "The trend is growing greater all the time to abandon services in the local community and let the government perform them."[62] Briley made a valiant effort to cut into Lausche's advantage by claiming the Senator could not disassociate himself from the rampant spending that had resulted in a $300 billion national debt. "My opponent tries very hard to avoid responsibility for this debt by pointing to some of his votes against specific items of spending. The spending partly gave him committee assignments," Briley continued, "and put him where his votes in committees could not block the wishes of the Democratic leadership."[63] Lausche ignored Briley and continued his time-worn pattern of campaigning. He made few political speeches, visited county fairs, and actively campaigned only ten days. He restricted his campaign schedule partly because Jane had been hospitalized due to a serious automobile accident.

In the only public debate held by the two candidates, Briley twitted the Senator for concealing or forgetting how he voted on a free trade bill in the 87th Congress. With outraged dignity worthy of former Ohio politicians Theodore Burton or Joseph B. Foraker, Lausche questioned how this fledging could attack the duplicity of a statesman who had been elected six times by Ohio voters. He asked how a senator, who had voted more than 450 times, could be expected to remember every vote he cast. Briley had run a negative campaign, commenting during the campaign trail that the 66-year-old Lausche seemed "a little old and tottery and can't remember what happened just four and a half weeks ago."[64]

A week before the election Lausche entered Bethesda hospital suffering from exhaustion and recurring chest pains. Briley demanded to know the Senator's condition, citing rumors of a heart attack. The attending physician issued a public statement that Lausche was merely bothered by stress and fatigue.

Briley's somewhat subtle efforts to parlay Lausche's illness into an upset victory proved futile. The election returns gave the incumbent a majority of 692,000 votes. Lausche carried 77 of 88 counties, losing only in staunch Republican strongholds in rural northwest and southeastern counties. Lausche emerged as the lone Democrat to win in statewide elections. The Cleveland *Plain Dealer*, reacting to Lausche's one-sided victory, determined that, in the history of Ohio politics, there was no parallel to Lausche's magnetic influence over voters of all persuasions. Lausche's vote-getting ability was simple and confounded some of his critics who had stamped the Senator with such opprobrious terms as fence straddler. "To every question [put] before him, Lausche applies an extraordinary sensitive conscience. He struggles to get the right decision. His devotion to the country to which his parents came is so compelling as to approximate an obsession. He wants to be right regardless of the consequences. And the people intuitively sense this, and sensing this, trust him."[65]

Unfortunately for Ohio Democrats, Michael DiSalle, Lausche's once-removed successor as Governor, fell to defeat to Republican James Rhodes. Rhodes would win the governorship three more four-year terms for a total of sixteen years in office. There had been a paucity of taxes thrust upon Ohio citizens for fourteen years prior to DiSalle's term in office, including during Lausche's long tenure. The state desperately needed additional appropriations to renovate Ohio's aging facilities and to grow the state. The voters didn't agree and rejected not only a proposed new sales tax, but also turned DiSalle out of office.

⌒

WHEN LAUSCHE RETURNED TO WASHINGTON, DC, most of his small staff were already at work. In the Senator's absence, whether it be due to illness or otherwise, the staff knew what to do to keep the Senator caught up with a myriad of paperwork. To constituents and fellow senators, Lausche's management of his office was reminiscent of the Renaissance Age. The Senator's office was located in the northeast corner of the New Senate Building, adjacent to Hubert Humphrey's office (until Humphrey became vice president in 1965). This office, located on the first floor, contained four rooms. Lausche's office was nicely appointed with a carpeted floor. He had a private exit (convenient for escaping to Burning Tree Country Club). Celie M. Jirsa, Lausche's secretary and receptionist, occupied the reception area where she served in both capacities. Jirsa determined who must see the Senator, and Lausche was careful to receive visitors from his home state. One visitor in 1964 was Gabe Paul, President and General Manager of the Cleveland Indians. He had threatened to move his team elsewhere, but eventually opted to keep the Tribe in Cleveland.

The remaining offices were decorated with tiled floors and were Spartan in appearance. The middle office housed staff members who carried out day-to-day activities. The adjacent third room found staff members conducting research and fulfilling constituency duties. Across the hall, the fourth room served as a typing and filing center for the Senator's many legislative papers. A large portion of the

17-member staff (five less than Senator Young employed) had followed Lausche from the Ohio statehouse to Washington, DC. One individual was the spritely Marie King, who served as office manager. She had been with the Senator since early in his gubernatorial years. King was well acquainted with the Senator's philosophy, and more importantly, with his idiosyncrasies. She took responsibility for seeing that office work was finished on time. Her salary in 1965 was $8,816.

Ray White took on the duties of Lausche's primary administrative assistant. Earning $18,320 in 1965, White literally emulated the Senator in responsibilities except to be able to enter the Senate chambers and vote. A former member of the Ohio House of Representatives, White believed his most valuable asset to Lausche was his experience as editor of *Holmes County Hub*, a small-town newspaper in Millersburg. He often made decisions that could not wait for Lausche's personal attention.

Joseph Scanlon from Cincinnati held the position of legislative assistant, and Stanley Andrews supervised legislative research. Lausche hired 29-year-old Scott Shotwell to assist the Senator with his responsibilities on the commerce committee. He handled technical casework pertaining to social security and workmen's compensation. The remaining staff members served as receptionists, clerk assistants and office boys who attended nearby colleges.

The staff consisted of insiders (those who came from Columbus) and outsiders (from the Washington DC area). The locals often bounced from one senator to another, and did not build strong loyalty to any one senator. Lausche did little to bridge the gap between insiders and outsiders. The office remained lily-white in a city where the black population was predominant. The Senator returned yearly approximately 75 percent of his telegraph allocation and one-half of his telephone allocation to the government contingency fund. White and other staff members seldom took their yearly government-financed trip. Lausche did not maintain a home office or staff in Ohio. The Senator did not endear himself to his staff in 1963-64. Congress passed a measure increasing general staff wages. Lausche had raised eyebrows by not accepting his own pay increase. He hesitated to give his staff an increase after setting a precedent by not taking his own financial raise. Eventually Lausche gave in to pressure and approved staff raises.

The Senator did not receive any accolades from his fellow senators when he consistently spoke out against proposed salary raises for Congressmen, cabinet members, and federal judges. Lausche began his second term earning $30,000 yearly. A proposal before Congress in 1964 would have raised salaries to $32,000. The Senator informed his constituency of the fringe benefits for a senator: $3,000 of their salary was tax deductible, each senator was reimbursed annually for two round trips to their home state, and received a yearly stationery account of $1,800. A senator could claim any unused portion at the end of the year. Each senator received an allowance of $1,200 per year for office rental in their home state. The Senator's retirement pay was fixed as a rate of 2 ½ percent for each year in office.[66]

In 1969, one year after Lausche departed, the senators raised their annual salaries from $30,000 to $42,500. Senator Young also consistently opposed congressional pay hikes. (Young was a millionaire). Several reporters suggested this ploy against salary increases played well with the voters. Several years earlier, Ohio Congressman Wayne Hays proposed a sliding pay scale, with each senator determining his worth, the limit established at $35,000. "If my amendment passes and either Ohio senator says he is worth more than $5,000, he should be tried for perjury." Reminded of Hays' remarks, Lausche responded, "Aw, you know how Wayne is."[67]

A Washington correspondent recalled visiting the Senator's office four days after Christmas in 1967. A blanket of snow had covered the capitol. The snow turned to sleet. The scene was reminiscent of a Cleveland winter. In the halls of the new Senate building, there was not a miniskirt in sight. Doors to the offices of most senators were shut tight for the holidays. The female employees with the well-displayed gams who usually graced the hallways and offices were not present. The females of Lausche's staff did not wear miniskirts. The Senator frowned upon hiked hemlines. On this snowy day, his female employees were at the office. And there, too, with Congress in recess, was Senator Lausche.[68]

⌒

LAUSCHE NOT ONLY TENDED TO BE A SOCIAL LONER, he was also a political loner. Ross Baker, long-time United States Senate staff member and historian, commented that political loners avoid becoming part of any particular bloc in the Senate. The political loner is often an anomalous senator. A northern solon may not behave like other northern Democrats, or a southern Democrat may be markedly more liberal than his fellow southerners of the same party. Sometimes senators like Wayne Morse or Frank Lausche were simply independent-minded. Morse, often unpredictable in his political actions, was in no sense a social loner. Only on rare occasions could the same be said about Lausche. The Senator's participation in the Senate Prayer Breakfast was an exception. He was a pillar in this organization.

An outgrowth of the National Prayer Breakfast, this gathering began in the 1950s with the blessings of President Eisenhower. This breakfast became an important social event in the upper chambers. A cursory review of regular attendees indicated the group reflected a conservative bent, with certain notable exceptions. At its inception, the guiding spirits behind this group—besides Lausche—included Frank Carlson (Rep-KS), Homer Ferguson (Rep-MI), A. Willis Robertson (Dem-VA), Alexander Wiley (Rep-WI), and John Stennis (Dem-MS). The breakfast was open to senators of all faiths. One of a small group of Catholics, Lausche attended regularly and helped to make this occasion spiritually worthwhile.

The breakfast took place in the Vandenberg room on the first floor of the

Capitol Building across from the senate restaurant. The senators met at 7:30 a.m. and had breakfast prior to a ten to fifteen minute presentation about a philosophical, moral, or religious topic thought to be important to the country at large. When the leader finished with his oration, he would ask for comments, and Senators each spoke their piece or passed. The breakfast ended at 9:00 a.m. with a short prayer.[69] Senator Clifford P. Hansen of Wyoming was one of several senators who recognized Lausche's leadership at the Senate Prayer Breakfast. "Your activities with the...Senate Prayer Breakfast...[meant] a great deal and all of us who participated were made better by your activities."[70]

Lausche's attendance at the Senate Prayer Breakfast was exemplary. The same could not be said about the Senator's attendance in the Senate chambers. Lausche was less than candid about his whereabouts during many senate sessions. Golf was the reason. A low handicap player, Lausche joined Burning Tree Country Club in suburban Bethesda soon after arriving in Washington, DC. Membership cost $14,000 in the late 1950s. The manner in which the Senator camouflaged his absence from senate chambers became well known to certain fellow senators.

Jerry Brady, a member of Senator Frank Church's staff in the 1960s and Democratic candidate for Governor in Idaho in 2002, recalled one incident. He had difficulty tracking down senators, including Lausche in 1963 to form a quorum for passage of a civil rights bill. Lausche was one of those senators whom Brady emphasized "really wanted to be on the golf course instead of defending a civil rights bill."[71] Few people, including his constituents, knew Lausche played golf in Washington, DC almost every day. The Senator had a famous older black caddy by the name of Dooley who told Tom Vail of the *Plain Dealer* how often Lausche played at Burning Tree Country Club.[72] This figure is a deep, dark secret. Harold E. Sherman, administrative assistant to Senators Paul Douglas (IL) and William Proxmire (WI) explained how Lausche committed his *larceny*. "Lausche would come to the floor at noon and invariably he would ask a lot of questions to prove he was there. Then he left and played golf many afternoons. But the [*Congressional*] *Record* always showed he was there, taking part in debates, asking questions, putting stuff in the *Record*.... Not many people knew about it, but it was true."[73]

With a mirthful look on his face, Ernest "Fritz" Hollings, long-time Democratic Senator from South Carolina, verified how Lausche, after finishing his round of golf, returned to the senate halls. He made sure he was noticed and ready if necessary to cast a vote.[74] Lausche was known to have played golf with President Eisenhower and Vice-President Richard Nixon. Senators who often joined Lausche at Burning Tree included Edmund Muskie, Eugene McCarthy, Milton Young, Leverett Saltonstall, Prescott Bush and Alexander Smith. Lausche occasionally teamed up with Fulbright and Scott Lucas (IL), even though Lucas was no longer a member of the senate.

The Ohio AFL-CIO began to research Lausche's Senate attendance. In January

1968, the union publication *Focus* reported Senator Lausche absent 26 percent of all roll calls taken on Mondays and Fridays during the first session of the 90th Congress.[75] Lausche may have been ahead of his time. Journalist Bob Schieffer, writing in his best seller *This Just In*, related how from the 1970s onward, Congress and the Senate began to meet only Tuesday through Thursday. This arrangement allowed more and closer contact with voters back home.[76] Not one to stay at his office any longer than necessary, Lausche likely would have embraced this trend.

A senator's most important decision is to decide what issues take precedence in an ill-defined occupation. He must determine what legislation most affects his constituency, how to allocate his resources, and where to concentrate his energy. A senator is incapable of satisfying expectations of all his constituents. One must strive for support and respect in those social and political circles he considers most vital.[77] For Lausche, the rural populace became an important voter base. The fairgoers in many of Ohio's 88 counties generally agreed with Lausche's conservative fiscal philosophy and his incessant attacks upon Communist-led countries. Although the Senator was sensitive to his voters' needs, he had to balance those needs with his own inclinations, values and sense of what mattered.

An example of significance to Lausche concerned the distribution of pornographic materials. He praised Postmaster General Arthur Summerfield for his efforts to eliminate the distribution of obscene materials through the mails. He decried the availability of books and magazines at news stores and in airports that appealed to the sensual qualities of men. The Senator deplored a supreme court ruling, which due to the court's interpretation of the right of free speech, allowed the distribution of films that previously would have been prohibited unless offensive parts were removed. The Senator continued his fight for adequate constitutional legislation to "curb this evil influence which is ruining our youth."[78] Lausche believed Rudyard Kipling's introductory to *Land and Sea Tales* addressed this issue, "Nations have passed away and left no traces and history gives the naked cause of it—one single, simple reason in all cases, they fell because their people were not fit."[79]

⌒

LAUSCHE OFTEN TOOK UP THE CAUSE OF THE UNDERDOG, in one case attempting to defend the Amish, a small segment of the populace in Ohio, approximately 35,000 individuals who lived mostly in Defiance, Geauga, Holmes, Stark, Tuscarawas and Wayne counties. At issue was an Amish request for exemption from paying social security taxes. This request emanated from their religious tenets, which dictated that the Amish take full responsibility for their families, the poor, and aged without government assistance. This issue became inflamed when the Internal Revenue Service seized a New Wilmington, Pennsylvania Amish farmer's horses for his refusal to pay social security taxes. The federal law stated that social security taxes must be paid regardless of whether one ever takes money from the government. Lausche fought a losing battle declaring the government's position wrong on this issue. He contended that the law as written was diametrically in conflict with Amish religious edicts. The Senator argued that an exemption had been granted physicians. He pleaded that these religious groups were not guilty of providing spurious and artificial excuses for not complying with a federal law. The Senator and his Amish supporters bowed to defeat when the Senate voted against an exemption from the social security system for the Amish.[80]

Lausche took a leading role as an underdog in another matter close to his heart, that being the ravages of strip mining. His efforts were directed towards restoration of land in twenty-seven counties in southeastern Ohio and numerous counties in neighboring states. He had fought this battle as Governor without much success. Coal company lobbyists had too much clout with the Ohio legislature.

Recognized as a pioneer in land restoration, Lausche attempted to push favorable legislation through the senate. In 1962, he introduced Senate Bill 3304; in 1963, Senate Bill 1013; and Senate Bill 368 in 1965. Hugh Scott (Rep-PA) and Vance Hartke (Dem-IN) co-sponsored this last bill. The earlier bills did not pass committee review. Senate Bill 368 elicited more interest and support.[81] Major portions of this bill were incorporated into the Appalachia Bill. Unfortunately, this bill did not properly address this issue. As directed by this bill, Secretary of Interior Stewart Udall made an interim report to Congress in 1966, stating that federal government had a responsibility to cooperate with state governments to reclaim the strip mine lands.

Lausche did not give up. He received approval to place an important article in the *Congressional Record*. This essay, entitled "A Visit to Strip Mining Country: The Ohio Bad Lands," was written by Grace Goulder Izant, longtime columnist for the Cleveland *Plain Dealer*. Photographs accompanied her treatise and depicted soil damage caused by coal mining companies. One caption described a new strip mine shovel, "The Silver Spade rises almost to the height of a ten-story building; weighs 70,000 tons and has a boom 200 feet long. It cost $8 million and is about to turn Ohio earth upside down." Lausche added, "the shovel...will...lift practically 170 tons—in one bite...the massive shovel will dig into the tender soil, destroy the grass cover and legumes, the flowers and the trees, drive out the birds, lower the water table, and finally after the coal has been removed, bequeath the land to posterity."[82]

> "The Silver Spade rises almost to the height of a ten-story building; weighs 70,000 tons and has a boom 200 feet long. It cost $8 million and is about to turn Ohio earth upside down."

Lausche continued his crusade into his last year in the senate. He came back in 1968 with Senate Bill 217 to plead for funds to reclaim lands and water damaged by coal mining operations. The coal mining lobby struck back with all their force to scuttle the passage of, in their judgment, adverse legislation. Lausche lost this battle throughout his senatorial tenure. The war was finally won on August 3, 1977. The 95th Congress passed Public Law 95-87, known as the Reclamation Act of 1977. This act provided for reclamation of rural lands and the acquisition and reclamation of damaged lands. The now retired Senator could take satisfaction that his prolonged efforts finally consummated in appropriate land reclamation.[83]

Except for selected issues during the sixties, Lausche primarily fought defensive political battles. He challenged the excessive expenditures of federal funds, the radical actions of the counter culture movement and the demands of labor bosses and lobbyists. Proposed subsidies submitted by Kennedy continually drew the ire of Lausche, particularly if monies were scheduled for Communist-dominated countries. The Senator fought Kennedy's attempt to establish a Domestic Peace Corps. "Such a program would be just another step in the direction of centralizing power in the plethora of bureaus already existing in Washington."[84]

Lausche continued his resistance to Kennedy's New Frontier program until that fateful day November 22, 1963. Government operations came to a standstill as the country suffered shock and disbelief over the loss of their leader. Closing ranks, Senator Lausche delivered a touching eulogy in the senate chambers. He received a warm note of appreciation from Edward Kennedy, the late President's brother.[85]

Lausche had worked with Kennedy and Lyndon Johnson, the new President, in the Senate chambers during the late 1950s. The Ohio Senator knew that the hard-driving Johnson would be a force to be reckoned with in the coming years as he promoted his Great Society agenda. Johnson was determined to carry out legislation proposed by the late President. One major item was an $11 billion tax cut. The President had coerced Senator Harry Byrd (Dem-VA) to support his proposed budget and tax cuts. But not Lausche. The Senator was adamant that an income tax cut would be "an experiment which if it proves wrong, will be catastrophic in its damaging impact upon the strength of our country." Lausche's plea fell on deaf ears. The tax cut gained approval by an overwhelming 77 to 21 votes.[86]

As the 1964 election approached, Johnson easily captured the Democratic nomination at Atlantic City. Lausche surprised Ohio Democrats by attending the convention and spending time with the Buckeye delegation. He left the convention before the scheduled first session. Lausche had displayed coolness toward Johnson in the early days of his presidency. In part, the Senator was upset that he had been thwarted in attempts to meet with the President. He wanted to plead his case for several pork barrel projects in Ohio.

Lausche continued his aloofness toward Johnson as the Fall election approached. He did not accompany the President to Cleveland on October 8 where Johnson addressed a $100 a plate dinner. Jane, more active on the political trail, accompanied Johnson's wife Ladybird to Columbus for a political rally. A few days earlier, Jane had commented that she didn't know who her husband would support in the general election. On October 23, after weeks of soul searching, the Senator made a short statement saying, "I favor Lyndon Johnson and shall vote for him. I will have nothing more of any character whatsoever to say about the present campaign."[87] Johnson would be the last Democrat Lausche would vote for in a presidential election. Lausche's reticent behavior had little effect upon election results. Johnson swept into office in a landslide over Barry Goldwater (AZ) with a mandate to push forward with his *Great Society* program. He returned to the White House on his own merits. The President's overwhelming victory meant little to Lausche, who would continue to be a thorn in the President's side where domestic issues were concerned.

Steven Young returned to the Senate for a second term. He narrowly defeated Robert Taft, Jr., son of the late Senator Robert Taft. The assertive redhead John J. Gilligan gained a seat in the House of Representatives, defeating Republican Carl W. Rich of Cincinnati.[88] It was a name Lausche would reckon with in four years.

Lausche finally met with Johnson in the Oval Office. The Senator made a plea to have a new Health, Education, and Welfare (HEW) Environmental Facility located at the Robert A. Taft Sanitary Engineering Center in Cincinnati. Lausche wanted to know if the President was making decisions on pork barrel projects without any consultation with the House of Representatives or Senators affected by these decisions. This dialogue followed:

Senator Lausche: Jack Valenti [a presidential assistant] told me that you had decided where the HEW Environmental Health Center would be located.

President Johnson: I didn't decide this morning. Frank, I told him the other day I can't be determining where hospitals, post offices should go and still do what I'm trying to do. I can't do it all myself. Up all night two nights ago working on Cypress and Viet Nam issues and half of last night. If I start seeing the Congressmen and Senators on these local patronage allocations (sic). I have ten assistants: I have asked any one of them to see the Congressmen. They said you expected to see me and then the papers write why I'm not there. I was away on other things. I can't physically do it.

Senator Lausche: Well, now I understand.

President Johnson: If you want to see me on anything else, I'll see you. I've got Bob Byrd coming in, Irwin coming in, Jordan coming in, Lester Hill coming in, God knows.

Senator Lausche: I agree with that. I said I would write you a letter. There are other matters I want to talk to you about.

President Johnson: I'll see you any time you want to see me. I'm just the paper courier. If Senator X saw me about Building Y, then Senators ABCDEF immediately think they've got to do it to protect their constituency. And you have no idea of the run I have.

Senator Lausche: Alright, we'll have an understanding. You're going away tomorrow. How long will you be gone?

President Johnson: Most of this week. I'll be in Florida tomorrow, Canada Wednesday and California Thursday and back here on the weekend.

Senator Lausche: Can I say I spoke to you and that I'd like to see you when you return?

President Johnson: Sure, sure, sure.

Senator Lausche: I'm not disturbed about this. What the hell, if you see me, you've got to see the others.

President Johnson: That's right. I have Congressmen who want to see me about the same things. The other calls.

Senator Lausche: Okay. That's okay with me.
President Johnson: Goodbye.[89]

The Senator left the White House still convinced that he must fight against Great Society legislation. The 89th Congress of 1965 rivaled the New Deal Era's 73rd Congress in the enormous quantity of social and economic legislation enacted. In the first session, President Johnson submitted 87 measures of which 84 were passed. The second session saw 112 proposals sent to Congress from the White House, of which 87 were approved.[90]

Lausche attempted to help Everett Dirksen (IL) stonewall Johnson's Great Society legislation. The Senator had a special affection for Dirksen, Republican Minority Leader during the 1960s. Both shared similar views on much of proposed Senate legislation. Dirksen had become minority leader in 1959. During Dirksen's first session with the 86th Congress, Lausche voted with him on 69 of 89 legislative issues. This pattern of Lausche's approximating Dirksen's vote record continued throughout the sixties. The two men worked together on several senate commit-tees. These solons fought to reduce subsidies, whether to the airlines, railroads or urban transit systems. Two aspects of the Great Society disturbed both Lausche and Dirksen. The first concerned the rapid growth of the federal bureau-cracy, while simultaneously increasing government centralization. Secondly, this governmental growth led to unbalanced budgets, inflation and higher taxes. By 1966, Lausche's voting record was the most conservative of any northern Democrat (Senator Harry Byrd, previously the most conservative northern Democrat, had resigned on November 10, 1965 for health reasons).

⌒

LAUSCHE'S FISCAL PHILOSOPHY ADVOCATED THAT subsidies for maintenance and growth primarily belonged to state and local governments. He could not abide a democratic government taking on entities which could more readily be managed by private enterprise, except when non-governmental businesses demonstrated reticence to take on a project.

Lausche did embrace certain exceptions. Long an advocate for the reduction or elimination of pollution, Lausche believed the federal government must appropriate funds to fight pollution in the Great Lakes. He took his cause to the senate floor. "While the estimated cost will be enormous [approximately $100 billion]," Lausche asserted, "each year it is delayed will add substantially more to the ultimate costs." He rallied fifteen senators representing states adjacent to the Great Lakes. He pleaded that, "at the pace we are moving, it will take a century to clean up our rivers and lakes and that will be too late.... Ports and cities will have suffered irreparable economic blight. Industry, so dependent on water, will have moved elsewhere."[91] Several years later, Lausche took satisfaction that the Great Lakes region, including Cleveland's much maligned Cuyahoga River, had made significant strides in ridding the Great Lakes and adjacent rivers of pollution.

In the larger picture of economics and government spending, Lausche continued his opposition to the President's Great Society program and his war on poverty. The Senator's caveat that the stability of U.S. economy was being seriously undermined fell upon deaf ears with the exception of a small cadre of conservative senators. He presented a speech on the senate floor describing how the lure of federal monies halted Cleveland's willingness to proceed with their own plans to build an extension of the transit system from downtown Cleveland to Hopkins Airport. "Did the founding fathers contemplate this policy of largess and gifts by our government? Were they cringing persons who depended upon gifts, or were they courageous individualists who believed in the free enterprise system and that our Nation would triumph, and that the welfare of our people would be promoted? Everyone is trying to get his hand in the till."[92] A devotee of Ralph Waldo Emerson, Lausche referred to his *Essays on Compensation*, insisting that the law of action and reaction was catching up with the administration. The sage of Concord wrote, "Every secret is told, every crime is punished, every wrong redressed, in silence and certainty. What we call retribution is the Universal necessity."[93]

Lausche's voting record supported his political philosophy. In 44 significant votes on anti-poverty legislation from 1957 through 1966, the Senator voted 11 percent of the time with the moderate to liberal Democratic bloc of the Senate, 79 percent with the conservative and Southern Democratic bloc. He was absent 10 percent of the time. In 30 other key votes over the same time period, Lausche voted approximately 16 percent of the time with the moderate to liberal bloc and 84 percent of the time with the conservative Southern bloc. He demonstrated a pattern of almost total opposition to federal aid to education in any form.[94]

On the issue of housing, 26 percent of the time Lausche found himself allied with the moderate to liberal bloc. In 74 percent of the housing votes, he was aligned with the conservative and Southern Democratic bloc. The truth of the matter is the fact that, in spite of Lausche's tacit support for Johnson in the 1964 election, he told friends privately that he detested Johnson. He found the President to be mean-hearted. Conversely, Johnson could not often count on Lausche to support domestic issues. On August 28, 1967, the Senate rejected an amendment by the Ohio Senator to cut in half rent supplemental aid to poor families. Consequently, Johnson knew quite well how to fight a political game. Shortly thereafter, on orders from Johnson, Mike Mantos and other presidential aides were asked to have a hardnosed count of senators who will vote to support a move to restore rent supplements to a supplemental appropriations bill. Mantos told his fellow aides, "I would *not* alert the following senators who will [vote against] rent supplements in the hope they might be out of town."[95] The list included fifteen southern senators and Lausche.

Time after time he voted against favorable labor legislation. He was adamant that the Taft-Hartley Law not be revamped. In 48 significant votes in the field of labor legislation, he voted 77 percent of the time with the conservative Southern bloc.[96]

Lausche did support several of Johnson's Great Society programs. Notably, he voted for a Medicare bill in 1965. The Senator's voting record on civil rights was considerably more liberal than in other areas of legislation. Of 57 significant votes in the field of civil rights legislation between the 85th and the 89th Congresses (1957–1966), Lausche voted 68 percent of the time with the moderate to liberal Democratic bloc of the senate. He voted 32 percent of the time with the conservative and Southern bloc of the senate. He voted for all of the major big name civil rights legislation (including the Civil Rights Act of 1960, Civil Rights Act of 1964 and the important Voting Rights Act of 1965). He was less likely to vote for measures designed to promote the assertion of individual civil rights.[97]

Lausche was most disturbed by the outbreak of riots that occurred in part as a protest to Martin Luther King's assassination. In early 1968, Lausche and Strom Thurmond (SC) sponsored an anti-riot amendment, which readily passed in the Senate. Lausche could not tolerate mob appeal and incitement from the likes of Stokely Carmichael, chairman of Student Nonviolent Coordinating Committee (SNCC). He regarded Carmichael as the architect of *Black Power* and his actions little short of treason. He took his stand with FBI Director J.

Edgar Hoover. Such behavior by what Lausche called an arrogant protagonist of anarchy must be thwarted with tighter Internal Security laws. Responding to the riots in Washington, DC and other metropolitan cities, Lausche charged, "Instead of moving toward unification...of all people on an equal basis, the rioting...has created...greater disunity."[98]

Lausche fought the good battle on most legislative issues. His ultra-conservative stance on domestic issues meant he usually supported a losing cause. His actions, although respected by his Senate colleagues, did not make him very popular with the mainliners in the Democratic Party.

A classic example of Lausche's rigidity and stubbornness occurred in June 1967. Democratic Senator Thomas Dodd (CN) faced censure by the Senate for alleged double billing for his airplane tickets. During debate on the Dodd issue, Lausche responded to an article in the Washington *Daily News*. The paper accused him of being a straight man for Senator Russell Long (Dem-LA), Dodd's chief defender against censure.[99] Gesturing to the press gallery above, Lausche accused reporters of trying to browbeat him into voting against Dodd on the censure motion. "I will do my duty first and surrender to them, never." The Senator shouted to the surprised reporters, "At the risk of being condemned, they can all go to hell."[100] Lausche also attacked the press in the Senate gallery for their audible chorus of "oh, no" when Thurmond rose to speak in defense of Dodd. "There is a black mark, a black stain in our proceedings when a man asks...to speak and the gallery yells, 'No.' Are we in a Roman gladiator's pit [where] they sit above dictating what we should do?"[101] Lausche voted against censure, and Dodd was exonerated of the charges against him.

The overall rejection of Lausche's political philosophy caused him much anguish. Edward Gobetz, editor of *Frank J. Lausche: Life History of Ohio's Lincoln*, may have said it best: "Lausche was not in tune with the turbulent sixties—or vice versa, the turbulent sixties were not in tune with Frank J. Lausche, a gray-haired son of immigrants who emphasized thriftiness, fiscal responsibility, the spirit of the American Constitution, service and sacrifice, long-range goals and an all-pervasive American patriotism."[102]

Lausche was approaching his 72nd birthday as his second term in the Senate concluded in 1968. His twelve years in the senate had taken their toll, but the Senator still appeared to be in excellent health. He had fought battles to maintain fiscal responsibility in government operations. Though not many bills Lausche had initiated were passed into law, he gave support to those bills that fit into his political philosophy. Lausche did not excel as a pro-active Senator on the domestic scene. He played a more significant role in the country's foreign policy, particularly in regard to the dilemma in Vietnam. Lausche's contribution to foreign affairs began in 1959 when Johnson appointed him to the foreign relations committee. The sixties were marked as a period many Senators were categorized as hawks or as doves. Lausche left little doubt that he would join league with the hawks.

Lausche enjoying his favorite avocation at Burning Tree Country Club in Bethesda, Maryland on October, 1984. (Photo courtesy of Sally Jones).

twelve

Communism, the Rooskins
and the Vietnam War

BETHINE CHURCH, WIDOW OF THE LATE SENATOR FRANK Church (Dem-ID), was asked what she remembered about Frank Lausche during his Senate years. Bethine replied that, although she seldom had occasion to visit him, when she did encounter Senator Lausche, "He nearly always made reference in an unflattering manner his disdain for the *'rooskins'* and communism in general."[1] Lausche's response would not have surprised anyone who knew him well. He left little doubt where he stood in dealing with the Soviet Union and other Communists countries and in denouncing Communism. Lausche's animosity toward Communism was exacerbated by the fact that the Soviet Union's sphere of influence included much of central and eastern Europe, including Slovenia, his family's homeland. "We [the United States] are paying the price for the grievous mistakes that were made by allied leaders yielding to Stalin's demand that the sphere of communist domination be extended to cover the eastern and middle-eastern Europe nations, including Yugoslavia."[2] Lausche's hard-line opposition to Communism did not waver during his twelve-year tenure in the senate.

While still governor, Lausche's political stance gained attention of the ultra-right and strongly anti-communist John Birch Society. Prior to Lausche's election to the senate in 1956, Robert Welch, editor of the society's publication, *One Man's Opinion* (title changed to *American Opinion* in the 1960s) wrote an article entitled "On the Right Side," which depicted Lausche's political leanings. Welch wrote, "His pro-American instincts are too sound and deep-rooted for him to remain very long or go very far in any of the doubtful company that may welcome him in Washington. He is nobody's fool and he *is* a patriot."[3] Lausche clearly amplified his views on patriotism in response to an Ohio high school student. Lamenting the lack of patriotism in the country, the Senator quoted from an article in *Reader's Digest* about what students were not learning, "There were two things we didn't teach them. One was that many of the inhabitants of this big, bad-tempered, battling planet hate our American insides. The other was to believe and live Stephen Decatur's great toast: 'Our Country! In her intercourse with Foreign Nations May She Always Be in the Right: But Our Country, Right or Wrong.'" He went on to write that schools had been so busy educating for life adjustment that the country had forgotten to educate for survival. As Lausche was prone to do, he quoted in his letter the concluding statement of the Declaration of Independence, "...and for the support of this Declaration, with a firm reliance of the protection of Divine Providence, we mutually pledge to each other our lives, our fortunes, and our sacred honor."[4]

In 1959, two years after becoming a member of the Senate, Lausche was appointed to the prestigious Senate Foreign Relations Committee (SFRC). He had lobbied vigorously for this assignment, even to the point of offering to give up his assignment on the Interstate and Foreign Commerce Committee. Senate majority leader Lyndon Johnson had bulldozed this new appointment through his advisory board, much to the satisfaction of Lausche. He had every intention of making his voice heard as a hawk on foreign issues. He likely did not anticipate the difficult issues the SFRC would encounter in the 1960s.

During his first term, Lausche continued his support and subsequent friendship with strongly anti-communist Vice President Richard Nixon. The vice president toured South American in May 1958. He encountered serious verbal attacks (and several near physical attacks) from Communist blocs in many of those countries. In an act completely out of character for Lausche, he was one of 15,000 supporters who went to the airport on May 29 to greet the vice president and Mrs. Nixon. He explained that his presence was for no other purpose than to swell the crowd. In spite of certain political differences, Lausche maintained that, with respect to the integrity and honor of the United States, the two politicians stood as one. He believed Nixon had conducted himself nobly. Nixon acknowledged Lausche's presence commenting that "the trip had its difficult moments, but...any personal discomfort we may have experienced was completely forgotten when we saw so many of our friends...at the airport."[5]

When Anastas Mikoyan visited Washington, DC in 1959, Lausche was among the small group who had lunch with the Soviet Union deputy premier. Because Lausche understood some Russian, he was able interpret Mikoyan's asides to his interpreter. Lausche spoke briefly to Mikoyan and later told Jane that Mikoyan was a very shrewd, clever operator, and was not to be taken lightly. Jane wrote her sister-in-law Ruth Lausche that the *Meet the Press* panel was no match for Mikoyan on the weekly Sunday night program. She "hoped people are not taken in too much by him. Russia may vary the tune a bit but the song is still the old one."[6]

One important and wealthy Clevelander who tried to soften Lausche's rigid attitude toward the Soviet Union was the indomitable Cyrus S. Eaton. A millionaire many times over, Eaton transformed his boyhood home in Pugwash, Nova Scotia into a thinker's lodge. He cultivated friendships with Soviet leaders, and urged the United States and the Soviet Union to develop amiable relations. In 1957 he organized the first Pugwash Conference of Nuclear Scientists from around the world to discuss international issues. Eaton received the Lenin Peace Prize in 1960 for his efforts to promote international peace and understanding.[7]

The entrepreneurial Eaton encountered little success in persuading Lausche to give support to his own efforts to bridge the ideological gap between the U.S. and the Soviet Union. In a memorandum to the Senator December 29, 1957, Eaton shared a letter he had received from Nikita S. Khrushchev, Chairman of the Council of Ministers of the USSR. The Soviet leader had read with interest and satisfaction the documents of the Pugwash Conference of Scientists. Khrushchev gave a warm endorsement to the Pugwash movement for better international understanding.[8]

There is no record of a response by Lausche to Eaton's entreaty until November 10, 1960. Eaton had forwarded a note to Lausche containing an editorial taken from the London *Daily Express* urging that Red China be admitted to the United Nations. Lausche responded with a four-page letter detailing why he vigorously opposed the admission of Red China into the United Nations and/or diplomatic recognition by the United States government. Lausche laid out point-by-point his reasons for resisting any diplomatic interchange with Communist governments. To Eaton specifically, Lausche emphasized, "With your views about Khrushchev and Castro, Communists China and Russia, I am in total disagreement. These Communists Governments and individuals are our enemies—not by our action but by their choice. They are intent upon destroying us; to give them aid and comfort is wrong." The Ohio Senator ended his letter with a reminder striking at the heart of Eaton's economic efforts, "Whatever you are in importance you achieved under our system of government. Unless you abjectly gave up your properties and personal liberties, in Communist Russia, China, and Cuba, you would be stamped as an enemy of the people. Khrushchev, Castro, and Mao Tse-Tung are using you as a decoy. You have painfully fallen victim to their communist subversive techniques and blandishments."[9]

Obviously Eaton, as strong-minded as Lausche, expressed his disappointment in a reply to the Senator. "For the sake of my 13 grandchildren...I am going to go on fighting the good fight for honorable peace, even if it causes old friends like you to vilify me...you are one of an exceedingly small number of Americans in official positions who may tip the balance between war and peace."[10] In a note to I.F. Stone, editor and publisher of *I.F. Stone's Weekly*, a leftist publication, Eaton suggested, "In one of your pungent paragraphs, you can effectively expose Senator Lausche for the pious humbug that he is."[11]

Several years later noted literary critic Tristram Coffin wrote to Eaton that he had lunch with Mike Kirwin, longtime outspoken Democratic member of the House of Representatives from Youngstown. He told Coffin, "Cyrus Eaton has more brains and sense in his little finger than all the God-damned State Department. He's a great man and we're proud of him in Ohio."[12] To say that Kirwin and Lausche did not see eye to eye would be an understatement. Kirwin's pet peeve was Lausche. "I told Lausche the last time he came up to me with his hand out, 'If you ever try to speak to me again, you phony SOB [sic], I'll expose you.'"[13] Coffin informed Eaton that Senator William J. Fulbright (Dem-AR) told him a couple days earlier that the only time he lost his temper in the SFRC was at Lausche.

Lausche had little concern about what his contemporaries thought of him. He was determined not to be a participant in putting a halo of honesty and decency upon the head of Khrushchev or any other Communist leader, and a badge of shame upon his own country. William Safire, syndicated political columnist and member of Nixon's White House staff, has written a political dictionary. He defined *hard line* as demonstrating strong support of the containment of Communism. In his definition, Safire included a quote from the *Wall Street Journal*, "Such hard-liners as Sens. Bourke Hickenlooper [Rep-IA] and Frank Lausche can't shake the fear that the various national Communist parties around the world still want to seize political and social control everywhere, that they still have the common goal of toppling capitalism. Former ambassador [to the Soviet Union] [George] Kennan, a hard-liner himself during Stalin's day, contended this economical goal [capitalism] is becoming increasingly theoretical. Eastern Europe policy shapers may continue to make mischief for the West, but for reasons that are uniquely Russian or Polish or Rumanian, and not because they are Communist."[14] The wisdom of the hard-line came under increasing attack in the United States and abroad with the escalation of the Vietnam War.

In many respects American history, particularly in the twentieth century, was a continuation of human struggles prevalent in earlier European history. This was true for Lausche and his immigrant parents who came from a unique district of pre-World War I Yugoslavia. This area—Gottscheer Kočevje—was home to approximately 700,000 Gottscheer in what is now Slovenia. Between Nazi and partisan warfare, most of the Gottscheer disappeared or were exterminated in

World War II. This series of events influenced Lausche's consistent and determined opposition to anything in U.S. foreign policy that favored Titoist Communist Yugoslavia. The Senator held this view despite U.S. policies that delineated among various types of Communism in order to serve U.S. purposes.[15] Lausche held a special antipathy for Marshal Tito, titular head of Communist Yugoslavia for many years (1945–1980). Slovenia was one of several constituent republics located within the borders of this Communist country. The Senator resisted the blandishments and standing invitation of the Yugoslavia government to visit that country.

Not all Slovenians in Cleveland were sympathetic to Lausche's hard-line stand against Yugoslavia. Many progressive, radical socialists, who were opposed to home-land clerics, believed the country was better off under Tito's rule. These Slovenians had migrated to the United States after World War II. They had been closer to the Yugoslavian scene than had Lausche. This younger generation of Slovenes observed material improvements, better economic times and a different type of freedom in their native land. The monasteries were not censored, clergy were on social security, and the Communist-led country did not impose organized opposition to the church. These young Turk Slovenians held resentment toward the pre-World War II clerics. They realized these clerics had kept the masses ignorant and had laid guilt on the parishioners if they did not tithe enough for the church. As a result many of the common people already struggling to make a living remained poor. The new Slovenian immigrants questioned whether Lausche favored the wealthy class at the expense of the less fortunate.[16] This whole issue could be debated, depending upon whom one questions.

Lausche took every opportunity to speak out for the freedom of mid-European countries under the yoke of Soviet Communism. He believed that by continually urging these countries to seek the opportunity of self-determination, they would eventually rebel against totalitarian domination by the Communists. "Let us not ascribe to those...people of middle European absence of common sense. They possess it.... I might speak of my mother, who had three years of education but was gifted with common sense beyond the recognition of those who frequently spend unlimited years in achieving it."[17]

Lausche made efforts to help over 20,000 Hungarians gain legalized residence in the United States after fleeing from their embattled homeland in the 1950s. "If we do not do something to help them, we shall have a black stain upon the fulfillment of our responsibility to people who believe in our cause."[18] For his efforts Lausche received the Abraham Lincoln Award presented by the American Hungarian Foundation on June 11, 1975 in Washington, DC. The Senator championed the liberation of Communist-enslaved countries, and the press called him the most consistent promoter [in the senate] of rights of nations to self-determination.[19]

Lausche used the senate floor to eulogize past leaders of Balkan countries who promoted the cause of freedom and democracy. On March 7, 1960 Lausche praised the great Czechoslovakian patriot Thomas G. Masaryk in honor of his 110th birthday (he was born on March 7,1850). Masaryk was founder and first President of Czechoslovakia (1918–1935). These patriotic accolades are printed in the *Congressional Record*. Ray White, Lausche's administrative assistant, made certain press releases of these tributes were carried in Cleveland papers. Many ethnic groups observed Lausche in his finest hour.

☞

WITHIN THE REALM OF FOREIGN AFFAIRS, LAUSCHE FOUND that the SFRC demanded a large portion of his time. J. William Fulbright chaired the seventeen-member Senatorial committee (later 19 members). A large number of the members lined up—in Safire's lexicon—as doves or hawks. During Lausche's tenure on this committee the hawks generally favored aggressive administrative policies on issues such as the Cuban crisis, relations with the Soviet Union, and Vietnam strategies. The chief agitator of administrative policies proposed by Presidents Kennedy and Johnson was Fulbright. In the early 1960s, the doves besides Fulbright included Democrats Wayne Morse (OR), Frank Church (ID), Albert Gore (TN), Joseph Clark (PA), and to a lesser extent, Claiborne Pell (RI) and Mike Mansfield (MT). Among Republican members, only George Aiken (VT) favored de-escalation of the Vietnam conflict. Frank Carlson (KS) and Clifford Case (NJ) either went along with the administration or said little that could be construed as unfriendly or antagonistic to the White House. In 1964 Eugene McCarthy (MN) became an influential Democratic dove on the committee.

Democratic hawks included Thomas Dodd (MA), Lausche, Russell Long (LA), soon to be replaced by Gale McGee (WY), John Sparkman (AL) and Stuart Symington (MO), as well as Republicans Bourke Hickenlooper (IA) and Karl Mundt (ND). Carl Marcy, chief of staff, was effective in carrying out the behind-the-scenes research requested by committee members. Marcy, an important aide to Fulbright and a committed dove, was associated with the committee in the 1950s when Tom Connally (Dem-TX) and Arthur Vandenberg (Rep-MI) were members. Most of these members were influential in different kinds of ways. The chairman and members of the staff realized that they all had significant input. Marcy inferred that some Senators would participate, but their input never seemed to have much effect. Speaking about Lausche, the chief of staff commented that the Ohio Senator was "loveable, but I doubt that you see his imprint in anything that the Committee might have done."[20] Legislatively, there were very few instances in which a Lausche amendment was introduced, adopted and passed by the senate.

This powerful committee played much more of a key role in foreign policy during the 1960s. The public tended to think the committee members spent their time flying from world capitol to world capitol, thus forgetting their domestic constituency. This inference was certainly not true of Lausche. He took only one overseas sojourn in his entire twelve-year tenure as senator. In spite of his reticence to travel overseas, Lausche's anti-communist stance was well known beyond the borders of the United States, particularly in Cuba.

As a member of the SFRC, Lausche became immersed in the politically charged crisis in Cuba. Following Fidel Castro's ascendancy to power in Cuba in 1959, relations between the United States and Cuba deteriorated rapidly. Perhaps U.S. policies played a compelling part in driving Castro, a grassroots Communist, toward the Soviet Union. Interestingly, for several months after Castro's takeover, trade with the United States escalated sharply. Castro used much of this money garnered from the lucrative export of Cuban raw materials to buy U.S. machinery for military purposes. Exiled Cuban leaders thought they were being deceived when U.S. dollar sales and exports bolstered the Castro regime. Conservative columnist Victor Riesel's report did not conform to figures Carl Marcy gave Lausche.[21] Marcy reported that in 1960 seventy percent of Cuban exports to the United States were eliminated. Trade with Cuba amounted to $32 million in imports and $14 million in exports. Tobacco accounted for ninety percent of Cuban exports. Objections to a sudden embargo came from industries in Florida whose employment would be affected. Cuba continued to earn sorely needed hard currency to purchase military weapons.[22]

The Cuban situation was compromised even more when Lausche's senatorial colleague from Ohio, Stephen M. Young, sent out a letter to his constituents, maintaining that the Castro-Communist threat to the United States was exaggerated. Dr. Manuel A. de Varona, exiled chairman of Foreign Relations in Cuba, vigorously challenged Young's assertion and sent a copy to Lausche.[23] The two senators were diametrically opposed in their views about how to treat this Communist threat. The issue was exacerbated by President John Kennedy's approval of the doomed Bay of Pigs invasion. U.S.-supported Cuban exiles were repulsed by the invasion attempt in mid-April 1961 to the utter embarrassment of the Kennedy administration. Lausche considered this episode a grave and unpardonable error by the U.S. government. "Our government trained the invaders, it promised them air and sea protection...in the last moments before the invasion those promises were withdrawn, they were revoked at a time far too close to the actual deed to have been able to reverse the initial program."[24] Because of the Bay of Pigs debacle, Lausche insisted that the U.S. close its ports to all ships (mainly Soviet) carrying arms to Cuba and to deny United States government cargoes (mainly wheat) to any foreign flag fleets whose owners had any ships engaged in Cuban trade.[25] In time, the United States adopted these proposals as implored by Lausche.

The Cuban underground knew of Lausche's outspoken view against Communism. He was one of the few senators the dissidents could trust. At great risk, members of the Cuban resistance movement periodically delivered important information to Lausche's home in Bethesda regarding subversive Soviet-led activities in their native land. These informants came to the Lausche home in the middle of the night and slipped vital documents through the mail slot on his front door.[26] Lausche perused the documents and then forwarded them to President Kennedy (with whom he was not particularly close) and to Fulbright. In late 1962, Lausche sent Fulbright several pieces of information he had received concerning the seriousness of the Cuban missile crisis. He asked Fulbright to call a meeting of the SFRC. To Lausche's chagrin, Fulbright was leaving Washington, DC for a NATO parliamentarian conference in Paris. For a myriad of reasons, Lausche's requests to Fulbright were put aside, to the Senator's disappointment.[27]

Concurrently, Lausche won his second term to the senate. Shortly after the election, he was admitted to Naval Hospital for what was described as exhaustion. This setback restricted his effort to exert pressure on Fulbright. "It is essential that we know what is happening [in Cuba], what agreement was made with Russia, to what extent is it being fulfilled, and what, if any, are the potential menaces to our country as a consequence of what has happened."[28]

Fortunately in a showdown with Khrushchev, President Kennedy forced the Soviet Union to remove their missiles from Cuban soil in October 1962. Lausche continued to call for a committee inquiry into the exact nature of this agreement. In the Senator's view, key questions were left unanswered. The press praised Lausche for pressuring the Kennedy administration to provide answers to resolve the missile agreement.

Lausche criticized the Kennedy Administration's efforts to provide financial support to foreign countries without SFRC approval. President Kennedy acted under the amended Foreign Assistance Act of 1961 to provide aid to the Dominican Republic, India, Laos, Pakistan, Tunisia, and Mali. In correspondence with Fulbright, Lausche believed these foreign aid grants ought not to be dealt with superficially and warranted a hearing by SFRC.[29]

Kennedy's foreign aid program came under incessant scrutiny in 1963. Senators Wayne Morse and Lausche raised critical questions about the size and scope of the U.S. foreign aid program. Secretary of State Dean Rusk defended the administration's $4.5 billion request. Lausche told Rusk his confidence in the aid program had been weakened by U.S. experiences with countries in Europe. Rusk countered that the lesson to be learned was that small countries had shown remarkable stubbornness in protecting their independence. Rusk added, "Aid is not a means of buying another country, and that this is something we have to take into account when we extend aid." The Ohio Senator countered, "Isn't the lesson that foreign aid philosophically does not achieve what is expected of it by its supporters?" Rusk replied that it depends on the objectives, "Our aim is to assist countries in becoming economically pliable and independent."[30] Morse mentioned that the United States was aiding 79 countries and asked Rusk how he would choose if an amendment dictated reducing the amount of aid for a large segment of the countries or eliminating aid entirely to several countries. Senator Church suggested that rich countries (Belgium, the Netherlands, Norway, Great Britain, France, and West Germany) should have been dropped off the list long ago. Rusk defended Kennedy's decision to continue a broad aid program.

Lausche pushed his proposal for restricted foreign aid again in mid-1963. Speaking as chair of the President's Committee to Strengthen the Security of the Free World, General Lucius Clay strongly advocated to the SFRC that, "The United States should not aid a foreign government in projects establishing government-owned industries and commercial enterprises which compete with existing private endeavors."[31] Lausche enthusiastically endorsed this professed Clay Doctrine, which the Kennedy administration opposed. The Senator proposed specifically that no aid should be forwarded to Tito-run Yugoslavia, nor should any aid be extended to India's socialized steel plants. The Clay papers and Lausche's outspoken support set the stage for a proposed amendment by Lausche to Kennedy's foreign aid bill. He was hoping to restrict *carte blanche* dispensation of foreign aid in an effort to combat Communism and socialism and, thusly, to strengthen capitalism.

Lausche was not naïve enough to believe the United States could withdraw foreign aid completely. Following World War II, every President, secretary of state and secretary of defense (The secretary of war became the secretary of defense in 1947) supported foreign aid programs as a shield for U.S. national defense. Lausche was trying to make certain U.S. funds did not provide support for state-aid industries in Communist countries. The Mundt-Lausche amendment attached to the 1963 foreign aid proposed an elimination of any financial assistance for foreign government-assisted projects including manufacturing, merchandising, and processing enterprises. This amendment was defeated. In a losing cause, Lausche subsequently voted against the over-all foreign aid bill, which ultimately passed.

⌒

LAUSCHE INCREASED HIS DEFIANCE OF STATE DEPARTMENT policies with a scathing attack in 1964. In an article entitled "Dangerous Failing of Our State Department," which was published in the widely read *Reader's Digest*, Lausche lashed out at five chronic weaknesses of the state department. The Senator's sources were his experience on the SFRC and the vast amount of material on public record. Lausche accused the state department of glossing over critical issues until disaster struck. He believed the state department's hesitant behavior caused the country to forfeit its role as the free world's leader. He advocated courageous use of the country's military resources when deemed necessary. It was the Senator's opinion that the state department had not developed a consistent plan to thwart Communism's Cold War strategy. In the Senator's judgment, naiveté had filled the corridors and conference rooms of the state department for years.

Lausche pointed out specific examples of state department ineptitude. From

Panama to Cambodia to Ghana, and to Bolivia, the state department had backpedaled while being belittled and battered on the diplomatic front. "Our flag is trampled, our prestige and power are flouted. Our embassies are mobbed, our officials threatened or arrested at gunpoint. Respect for our strength dwindles,"[32] admonished the fervent anti-communist. Lausche noted that state department personnel were not disciplined enough to make tough decisions. He quoted Under Secretary of State William Crockett, who admitted to a congressional committee that a rigorous weeding-out process in the state department was a matter of highest priority. Often it was the wrong person who was dismissed. Ambassador Clare Timberlake, among those credited with saving the Congo from a Soviet-run takeover, was called home in 1961 because Rajeshwar Dayal, the Indian UN commander in the Congo, considered him too anti-communist. U.S. Ambassador to Panama Joseph S. McFarland, perhaps the one man who could have prevented the January 1964 crisis in Panama, was relieved of his duties the previous summer because the self-help techniques he used successfully among Panama's poor ran counter to state department policy of government-to-government aid. These decisions did not set well with the patriotically-minded Lausche. Additionally, he pointed out blunders made in Cuba, including acquiescence to Cuba's blatant training center for guerrillas and terrorists. The Senator cited Cuba's aggression against Venezuela in the form of financial aid and substantial arms shipments for guerrilla units.[33]

Lausche considered Dean Rusk a decent and humane secretary of state. What bothered Lausche were the vast state department organizations, which contained long-entrenched and frequently misguided men whose views too often accounted for unsuccessful policies. Randall Woods, author of an insightful biography about Fulbright, considered Rusk somewhat of an enigma. He was depicted as an impotent bureaucrat and naive Southern missionary in his early governmental years. By the time Rusk became secretary of state in the Kennedy administration (1961), he had shed the mantra of impotency. Rusk became a major force in escalating the United States' position in world affairs. This mission was intended to save the world from the scourge of Communism. On this premise Lausche was in complete agreement with Rusk.[34] Meanwhile, a clash between the SFRC and Rusk had shown evidence of fester for a long time. Observers questioned why liberal supporters of President Kennedy later became opponents of President Johnson's similar policies. A serious split had developed among members of the SFRC. Carl Marcy believed he had an obvious answer, "We have tried to force upon the rest of the world a righteous American point of view which we maintain is the consensus others must accept. Most of the tragedies of the world have come from such righteousness."[35] The chief purveyor of this American haughtiness, according to Marcy, was Dean Rusk. As a result, a serious chasm developed between the hawks and doves in the SFRC. Lausche remained a fervid hawk in future debates.

Congressional hawks supported Lausche's strong attack against the state department. A congressional colleague, ultra-conservative Samuel L. Devine, house representative from the Twelfth District in Ohio (Columbus and adjacent communities) sent Lausche a letter of commendation for his stand against the state department. Devine informed the Senator he had introduced House Bill 11070 to abolish the state department and to transfer its functions to an executive department. The new title would be the Department of Foreign Affairs, headed by a secretary appointed by the President with the consent of the Senate. This bill never moved out of committee review.[36]

Overall, Lausche supported Rusk on most foreign policy issues, but on occasion he challenged the secretary of state. One such occasion was when President Kennedy wished to obtain a unanimous favorable report from the SFRC concerning passage of the nuclear test ban treaty. When informed that this request would be difficult to accomplish, the President asked why. "There are two main obstacles," replied Senate Democratic leader Mike Mansfield, "Lausche and [Karl] Mundt [Rep-SD]. They have strong misgivings. Of the two, Lausche is the most critical. He has asked some very tough questions of administration witnesses."[37]

Illustrative of Senator Lausche's bare-knuckled grilling occurred when he gave Secretary Rusk a difficult time on the Soviet Union's long record of broken and betrayed international agreements. Lausche recited in detail Russia's past conduct in breaking treaties. He recalled February 1920, when Russia made separate peace treaties with Estonia, Latvia, and Lithuania, recognizing their independence and sovereignty, and then breaking every one of those treaties. "Now we come to the last agreement that the Soviet broke," continued Lausche. "I am referring to the commitment that we would have the right to inspect whether...missiles were removed from Cuba. That promise was not kept."[38] Rusk replied in the affirmative, stating Fidel Castro would not

"Our flag is trampled, our prestige and power are flouted. Our embassies are mobbed, our officials threatened or arrested at gunpoint. Respect for our strength dwindles,"

accede to the request. Lausche argued that a commitment had been made whereby neutral nations would be permitted to ascertain whether the missiles had been removed, and that commitment was not fulfilled. Again, Rusk agreed with Lausche. The Senator then asked the all-important question that, if the United States is to judge the Soviet Union in the future by what it had done in the past, what could the United States expect on the nuclear test ban treaty? Rusk responded, "I believe there would be no particular reason for them to enter into this treaty unless they had a present intention of living up to it.... We must ask ourselves whether the interests of the United States are adequately protected in the event of violation. I think the answer is *Yes*."[39] In spite of Lausche's reticence to enter into a nuclear test ban treaty with the Soviet Union, the senate ratified the treaty by an 80-19 margin on September 24, 1963, with Lausche voting in opposition.

After a hiatus of nine years in the senate, Lausche relented and agreed to embark on his first overseas venture in late November 1965. At the request of the Indian

Parliament, Vice President Hubert Humphrey asked seven senators to make this around-the-world trip, led by Wayne Morse. Lausche, as chairman of the SFRC subcommittee on Far Eastern affairs, thought he had an obligation to investigate conditions in Japan, India, Pakistan, Afghanistan, and Israel before spending a few days in Spain. A jet plane was not available, so the troupe settled for a Navy C-118 four-engine, prop-driven plane, which took 23 hours to reach Hawaii. Jane Lausche, who accompanied her husband, could have joined several other Senate wives who made the first leg of the trip by commercial jet, "But it never occurred to me not to be with Frank," she remarked.[40] The Navy plane traveled half the speed of a jet, but provided free transportation to the senators and their wives. Lausche shunned overseas junkets, partially because he frowned upon spending the taxpayer money. The Lausches returned to the states on December 23, 1965. Lausche expressed his observations in a report to the Senate, "...I had an opportunity to oversee the progress achieved in the welfare and social fields. My experience is inspiring and astounding. In many areas where the land had been sterile and dead, vegetation was in abundance. Hard work and resourcefulness had achieved this. The Greatest Republic, the United States of America and the small Republic, the state of Israel are both jewels shining in different parts of the world."[41] The Senator avoided travel to any Communist-affiliated countries, thus bypassing an opportunity to visit his ancestral Slovenian homeland. A month later Lausche entered Naval Hospital in Bethesda, Maryland, suffering from kidney and bladder infection and a hacking cough. Doctors determined his ailments were from the effects of an Asian bug he had contracted in New Delhi, India. Ten days later the Senator left the hospital fully recovered from his maladies.

The senator avoided travel to any Communist-affiliated countries, thus bypassing an opportunity to visit his ancestral Slovenian homeland.

THE DECADE OF THE SIXTIES WOULD BE FILLED WITH many foreign policy issues, but the deepening crisis in Vietnam commanded more and more time and deliberation by Lausche and the SFRC. It was a time of much acrimony between the hawks and the doves on the committee. The United States became increasingly polarized over what should be done in Vietnam. Also on the domestic scene, the country swirled in a cauldron of social unrest. African-Americans, incensed by the assassination of Martin Luther King, Jr., fomented major uprisings resulting in considerable property damage and loss of life in major cities. The blacks in the South joined hands to eliminate long-standing segregation policies. The hippie movement further alienated staid and conservative elements of society.

During this period of *détente* in Europe, the United Stares found itself on the verge of stepping into quicksand in Asia. The continuing menace of Red China, coupled with increased Communist activity in Southeast Asia, made Washington officials jittery. The struggle between the Viet Cong and a political coalition called the National Liberation Front in Vietnam was considered critical in putting to rest the much-publicized domino theory. Weeks before Kennedy's fateful trip to Dallas, the President attempted—with little success—to prop up the National Liberation Front and the corrupt regime of Ngo Dinh Diem. This was the situation in September 1963. In an effort to pressure Diem to reform his government, the Far East subcommittee led by Senator Frank Church threatened to introduce a resolution to end aid to South Vietnam. In a rare case of agreement with Church, fellow subcommittee member Lausche signaled similar displeasure with the course of events when he delivered a senate speech advocating a change of policy and a change of personnel in South Vietnam.[42] Within three months Diem and his brother Bien Phu Diem would be murdered in a military coup. On November 22, 1963, President John F. Kennedy was assassinated.

Now President, Lyndon B. Johnson's hopes for strengthening the Saigon government proved illusory. Haunted by the same political ghosts that bewitched Eisenhower and Kennedy and persuaded by Vietnam's importance to the U.S. national security, Johnson was not about to change the nation's course in Vietnam. Kennedy's failed crusade in Vietnam now belonged to Johnson. The daily expenditure of $1.5 million buttressed the more than 16 thousand troops stationed in South Vietnam when Kennedy died. Johnson escalated the war to the point that American ground forces climbed to 380,000 troops in December 1966 and to 450,000 by the following December.[43] This escalation came both with support and with dissent from members of the SFRC. Opposition to escalation of the war occasionally came from Lausche, normally a strong hawk in support of the war. On March 26, 1964, in an executive session of the SFRC with Secretary of Defense Robert McNamara and Chairman of the Joint Chiefs of Staff Maxwell Taylor in attendance, Hickenlooper and Lausche questioned McNamara closely. A strong advocate of Douglas MacArthur, the Ohio Senator reinforced the general's firm admonition not to repeat the mistakes of the Korean War by challenging China on the Asian mainland.[44] McNamara gave a major foreign policy speech on Vietnam policy, to which SFRC member Wayne Morse vociferously tagged Vietnam McNamara's War.

No action was taken by the foreign relations committee with respect to Johnson's decision to begin attacking North Vietnam. On February 9, 1964, the SFRC Far Eastern affairs committee, chaired by Lausche, met with McGeorge Bundy, presidential special assistant for National Security Affairs. He explained why it was necessary for U.S. troops to retaliate following North Vietnam attacks on Pleiku in South Vietnam. In Congress, the reaction to U.S. retaliatory raids was muted, with a general attitude that the President was right in striking back. Lausche wholeheartedly concurred.

In August 1965 an incident filled with intrigue became the basis for a change of U.S. strategy in Vietnam. Patrol boats, including a destroyer, the USS *Maddox*, were conducting intelligence raids within the 12-mile coastal limit (claimed to be the coastal limit by North Vietnam; the United States recognized only a 3-mile limit). Three North Vietnamese torpedo boats attacked the *Maddox*, reportedly thirty miles from their coast. No damage was inflicted. Further attacks from both sides occurred two days later, with nebulous results and subsequent reports. The U.S. patrols had embarked on an authentic intelligence-gathering mission. Subsequent evidence suggested these naval forays were almost certainly meant to be provocative. Information advanced by Edwin Moïse in his definitive study of these incidents entitled *Tonkin Gulf and the Escalation of the Vietnam War* confirmed that the aggressive actions of these naval patrols were coordinated with 34-A raids by South Vietnamese commandos. Johnson and his advisors reacted swiftly. Within hours, the President ordered American bombers to blast coastal bases and oil installations in North Vietnam.

Immediately, Johnson asked Congress for a resolution to support his policy in Vietnam and the nation's sacred honor. With the exception of Morse, the Senate moved forward to pass what was known as the Tonkin Resolution. Morse was vehement that the United States knew about the 34-A raids on North Vietnamese islands and insisted the United States should not have had ships anywhere in this area. Lausche challenged Morse, insisting, "our government had no knowledge" about the 34-A raids.[45] Morse proved to be right. Years later McNamara acknowledged, "Long before the August events in the Tonkin Gulf, many of us who knew about the 34-A operations had concluded they were essentially worthless."[46] As debate wound down Carl Marcy observed, "You almost had to be a Wayne Morse or a fool—and I never thought Wayne Morse was a fool—to have voted against the Tonkin Resolution.[47] On August 7, 1964, after ten hours of debate, the senate voted for the formal statement with only Morse and Ernest Gruening (Dem-AL) opposing the resolution. The house of representatives approved the resolution 416-0. As classified U.S. materials regarding the Tonkin Gulf attacks later became declassified, Lausche referred to an unpublished SFRC staff report and conceded that, "Every statement in this secret report tends to prove that we should not have done what we did.[48]

Lausche's judgment on this controversial issue was verified years later based on a plethora of newly-released information. Whatever provocation the renewed U.S. raids may have created, the weight of evidence is overwhelming that the unprovoked North Vietnamese attacks on the *Maddox* and a sister destroyer, the *Turner Joy* never took place. Instead reports of attacks appear to have been the result of a dark, stormy night, nervous crews, and a radar condition called *Tonkin Spook,* which formed in that area and which generated false images on radar screens. Six weeks after this incident President Johnson privately expressed his own doubts, telling McNamara in a telephone call, "When we got through with all the firing, we concluded maybe they hadn't fired after all."[49]

In the fall of 1964 Johnson won an overwhelming victory over hawkish Barry Goldwater (Rep-AZ). Johnson was now President on his own merits. The Texan determined he had received a mandate from the voters to insist on repulsion of the Viet Cong from South Vietnam. Johnson believed the SFRC hawks would support him and the need for increased military pressure on North Vietnam. Lausche insisted the course chosen by Johnson was not the President's choice, but had been forced upon him by the Communists of North Vietnam. The Senator maintained that Southeast Asia was the United States' first line of defense, and that an attack there was, in principle, an attack upon American soil. He reminded fellow Senators that in 1954 Indochina was broken into small nations. Pursuant to solemn promises made by the Communists, Laos gained its independence, and Vietnam was to be divided into North and South Vietnam. In Lausche's judgment, Communist China and Communist North Vietnam never kept their word in compliance with the Geneva Agreement (1954). The Senator argued, "If we yield to the Communists in their attack upon our country's honor, we definitely shall lose the respect of the people of the world who want to be with us, not with the Reds.... I am convinced the Congress will overwhelmingly stand by the President.... To do otherwise would be to manifest a will not to resist lawless, unwarranted and unjustified attack upon our sovereignty."[50]

The political and military situation in South Vietnam grew worse in 1965. Congress curtailed Johnson's Great Society programs against poverty, and the government published mounting lists of war casualties. More and more notable figures spoke out against the war. Disaffection increased among the doves on the SFRC and, in particular, by chairman Fulbright. The SFRC was consumed with the increasing criticism of America's involvement in Southeast Asia.

As if the Vietnam embargoes were not difficult enough for Johnson, the government became involved in a civil upheaval occurring in the Dominican Republic. This situation had festered for years, due to corruption, military takeovers, and the threat of Communists establishing another Castro-like Cuba. On April 28, 1965, Johnson dispatched 20,000 marines to the Central American country. Unlike Vietnam the crisis in the Dominican Republic did not last long before order was restored. U.S. officials and representatives of the Organization of American States (OAS) helped broker a deal between the two sides that ended the fighting and set a time frame for elections. In the June 1966 election, American-backed Joaquin Belaguer defeated former President Juan Bosch. Again, in defense of Johnson's foreign policy, Lausche spoke on the senate floor describing how various factions in the Dominican Republic were infiltrating and upsetting a weak government in an effort to bring about a successful coup. Lausche sent his statement to the *Plain Dealer*. He was dismayed to learn the Cleveland paper had not published his news release. He wrote a letter to Tom Vail, who had taken over the daily as publisher and editor in 1963. He complained that the readers were entitled to know their Senator's position on this matter. "Is it possible that you have censorship exercised by members of your staff determining what they feel ought or ought not to be carried by your newspaper?"[51] Lausche generally had good rapport with Cleveland newspapers and had reluctantly written to Vail. He believed failure to do so would have been a denigration of his own character. There is no evidence that Vail responded.

On another occasion, Lausche responded to an editorial written by Vail. The editor had urged allowing the Communists to take over the whole of Southeast Asia, and that the United States should remove themselves from military involvement. Lausche could not accept this position. He maintained Vail's position was completely contrary to advice given by Presidents Truman, Eisenhower, Kennedy, and Johnson. These administrations—and Senator Lausche—vigorously advocated the proposition that Southeast Asia must be the United States' first line of defense. "I [Lausche] expect that by prearrangements, the South Vietnamese will ask our country to pull out. We will do so by defying every argument made since 1952 about the need of keeping from our shores the devastation that will come from this initial international involvement." The Senator concluded his comments to Vail, "Your will, will be done. I hope that it proves right but must frankly say to you that I have a deep conviction it will prove wrong."[52]

⤨

PRESIDENT JOHNSON CAME UNDER INCREASING FIRE for his escalation of the Vietnam conflict. He faced constant pressure from Congressmen opposed to the war. In early 1966, Lausche responded to a talk given by Vail regarding Johnson's military stance. He reiterated his view that President Johnson was trying to do everything in his power to bring a slowdown in hostilities. The Senator considered Johnson to be an astute politician who was honestly attempting to serve the best interests of his country. Lausche again asked the all-important question, "If we pull out of South Vietnam conceding defeat, to what base do we move? Are we assured that by pulling out, our troubles will be ended? Will we or will we not be confronted with problems equally acute in Thailand, Burma, the Philippines, and even Australia? Tom, we are in a dilemma. Whether we pull out or stay in Vietnam, the cost of lives and property of the people of the United States will not be little. The battlefields on which we are defending the security and honor of the word of the United States are about 11,000 miles away. If we pull out, that line of battle will be persistently and constantly moved closer to the shores of California and especially of Hawaii."[53] In the final analysis, Lausche believed U.S. interests were best served by standing its ground in Vietnam.

As chairman of the subcommittee of Far Eastern Affairs, the Ohio Senator became one of the first senators to declare that the United States should not allow the North Vietnam Communists to have privileged sanctuary from attack. "I insist that if our men are to be required to stay there, we must stop the movement of troops from the North. I would not stand for one minute and watch equipment and troops coming in from the North moving down on our men and tell them: 'You stay there. We will not protect you.' In my judgement that is not the course to follow."[54]

In December 1965 McGeorge Bundy (national security advisor to Kennedy and Johnson), Undersecretary of State George Ball, McNamara, and Rusk urged Johnson to consider a Christmas bombing halt. On Christmas Eve 1965, the constant bombing of North Vietnam, which had been going on since May, suddenly stopped. From the beginning, Carl Marcy sensed that the bombing halt was a ploy by the administration to undercut and divide congressional opposition to the war. Pulitzer prize-winning journalist David Halberstam described the prevailing mood as the President, faced with growing skepticism and opposition in Congress and with the public, began to show his frustration, "The Senate was beginning to rise up...he knew why—it was that damn Fulbright. He knew what Fulbright was up to.... The deeper we were in [the Vietnam War] the more the outcry in the country, in the Senate, and in the press, the more Johnson hunkered down, isolated himself from reality...everything he had wanted for his domestic program, his offering to history, was slipping away and the knowledge of this made him angrier and touchier than ever."[55] A break between Fulbright and Johnson was imminent. Lausche stayed the course with Johnson.

Many years before and during Fulbright's chairmanship, the SFRC had assumed a quiet backwater of congressional influence on government policy. The committee met around a large table, under a crystal chandelier, in an ornate room on the first floor of the capitol. Most of their activity was closed to the press. A small, unified staff responded to all members, Republican and Democrat. This pattern changed in February 1966 with the advent of news-making public hearings. The SFRC had begun discussing the issue of public hearings on Vietnam on January 11, 1965 after Mansfield and Senator George Aiken (Rep-VT) reported on their trip to Saigon and other capitols. After an hour of discussion about Vietnam issues, Lausche praised the hearing as "the most constructive hearing we have had in the whole time I have been a member of this committee."[56]

A few days later the SFRC persuaded Rusk to testify on the need of a supplemental appropriations bill for Vietnam. Rusk found the foreign relations hearing room unusually full. The meeting was long and intense. The committee battered Rusk with questions, which were not about foreign aid funds for Vietnam, but rather about the subject of U.S. involvement in Vietnam. Rarely had virtually all nineteen members of the senate committee put a secretary of state through such a cross-examination. Woods described the scene, "Rusk squirmed; his eyes flashed. Frank Lausche tried to run interference. 'What gallant composure under fire Rusk was showing,' the Ohio Democrat interjected. Upon seeing the secretary's strained, beleaguered face on television the night before [Rusk had appeared on a network news program to discuss Vietnam], Lausche declared, 'I pretty nearly wept.' Rusk and Fulbright ignored him."[57] The SFRC eventually approved the supplemental appropriations bill for Vietnam. At the same time, Johnson consulted with the entire congressional leadership. Everett Dirksen, minority leader of the senate, Richard Russell (Dem-GA) John McCormack (Dem-MA), Hickenlooper, House Speaker Carl Albert (Dem-OK), and others urged the President to resume and even expand the bombing. Only Mansfield and Fulbright spoke out for a continuation of the bombing pause.[58] The bombing resumed on January 31, 1966.

As Johnson had feared, his party faced a bruising battle over Vietnam. Some like Russell, Stennis, Dodd, Long, McGee, Symington and Lausche favored an all-out military effort to achieve a quick and decisive victory. The number of U.S. troops in Vietnam had swelled to over two hundred thousand. The increasing ranks of open dissenters included the powerful Fulbright, Mansfield, and the dissident Morse. Other prominent Senators to cross over the line against the war were Eugene McCarthy and the young and bright, but sometimes outspoken, Frank Church. Often accused of being on cloud nine concerning foreign affairs, Lausche described Church as one of the wild Turks on the SFRC who damaged America's war effort and prolonged North Vietnam's Ho Chi Minh's will to resist. Several months later Lausche told Mike Mantos, administrative assistant to the President, "It's frightening to see Senator Church arrogate unto himself a wisdom which no man in history has ever had, including Socrates."[59] Mantos was sure the President would enjoy this gem.

"the wild Turks don't seem to understand that they are causing great damage to our efforts by their attitudes and that they are prolonging Ho Chi Minh's will to resist."

Neither Mansfield nor Fulbright anticipated the powerful reaction to the public hearings. It was not the newspapers but the television networks that whipped up public interest. Senators, war critics and government officials debated the wisdom of U.S. actions in Vietnam for the first time in high profile fashion. The SRFC proceedings began on February 4, 1966, and all three major television networks—ABC, CBS, NBC—covered the hearings live, gavel to gavel, preempting their entire weekday schedules. The televised testimony introduced doubts about the war to a broad spectrum of the American public, damaging the nearly complete dominance of the White House over mainstream information and opinion regarding the war. A steady stream of military and diplomatic personnel testified before the SFRC. An example of the biting exchange in these historic debates occurred between Senator Morse and General Maxwell Taylor, who at this time was a consultant to the President. Morse argued that there could be honest differences of opinion. He believed the American people would soon repudiate the war in Southeast Asia. Morse and Taylor bantered back and forth:

General Taylor: That, of course is good news to Hanoi, Senator.

Senator Morse: I know that is the smear artist—that you militarists give to those of us who have honest differences of opinion with you.... I don't intend to get down in the gutter with you and engage in that kind of debate...all I'm asking is if the people decide that this war should be stopped...are you going to take the position that is weakness on the home front in a democracy?

General Taylor: I would feel that our people were badly misguided and did not understand the consequences of such a disaster.

Senator Morse: Well, we agree on one thing that they can be badly misguided. You and the President...have been misguiding them for a long time in this war."[60]

After the hearing Taylor received a note from presidential aide Bill Moyers, "The President was very proud of you, and less importantly, so were all of us who believe we must carry forward the pursuit of our policy in Southeast Asia."[61] That same evening Mike Mantos forwarded a memo to the President, "When I finally caught up with Senator Lausche and told him how pleased you were with the support he has been giving your Vietnam posture he was really delighted. He asked me to tell you that General Taylor's testimony was truly *remarkable*."[62] Lausche expressed amazement that "the wild Turks don't seem to understand that they are causing great damage to our efforts by their attitudes and that they are prolonging Ho Chi Minh's will to resist."[63] In spite of a two week stay in the hospital (February, 1966), Lausche kept abreast of world affairs and the debates in the SFRC. Jane provided him with newspaper clippings and he kept up with his mail. After two weeks the senator was released and rejoined his colleges on the senate foreign relations committee.[64] The SFRC public hearings continued into spring of 1966 with no resolution as to how to end the war. The war lingered on month after month with more and more casualties. Fulbright and Johnson polarized in their views about why the war should or should not be escalated. Fulbright did not want to alienate himself from Johnson. He was fearful the war would undermine the Great Society at home and damage the country's standing abroad.

Frank Church, who aligned himself with Fulbright in opposing the war, believed Johnson knew he was in a different kind of fight once the hearings commenced. The President could try to disguise the fact, but he understood that the hearings presented a different kind of political challenge. Once the SFRC moved their discussion from behind closed doors, the committee became less of a prisoner of the White House and state department. Johnson knew and understood the senate.[65] Fulbright continued to argue his case against the war in early 1967 with the release of his newest book *Arrogance of Power*. This publication detailed Fulbright's stance as a leading spokesman advocating de-escalation. The Arkansas Senator outlined his program for achieving peace in Vietnam, as well as a general statement of his evolving views about American foreign policy.

☞

LAUSCHE CONTINUED TO GIVE HIS SUPPORT OF JOHNSON'S policies in Vietnam. The Senator found foreign relations a subject almost as close to his heart as fiscal conservatism. One issue that involved considerable debate in the SFRC was the controversial Consular Convention Treaty. This treaty provided for peaceful co-existence between the Soviet Union and the United States. Lausche had looked for some signs of reconciliation from Soviet Premier Alexi Kosygin to relax tensions between the two countries. He noted no signs by the Soviet Union of easing the stringent relations. "I would like to go along with the President [who favored the treaty]...if I can conscientiously and honestly bring myself to the belief that Russia has any purpose to actually—and by deed—to cultivate a state of peaceful coexistence."[66] Instead the Soviet leader labeled the U.S. as the aggressors in Vietnam and described how this country was trying to exploit by neocolonization various people of underdeveloped nations in Africa, South America, and Asia. Before the full Senate convened, Lausche voted against the treaty in the SFRC. Approval of the treaty passed by a bare two-thirds vote.

During the SFRC hearings Lausche often railed against Fulbright. He complained that the committee chairman conducted a slanted, one-sided hearing by not giving opposition senators their share of time for questions. Senator Morse, a dove like Fulbright, defended the chairman on this issue. Lausche took his complaint to the President's office. In a visit to the White House he went to great lengths to expound to Mike Mantos and Frank Valeo, Presidential administrative aides, his views on the seniority system, particularly as it applied to the Senate Foreign Relations Committee. The Senator indicated that Fulbright had abandoned the 10-minute rule on questioning of witnesses. Consequently, only the senior members asked questions—sometimes for 25 minutes—and then the witness left the room. "He [Lausche] told us (as well as Senator Spessards Holland (Dem-FL] who came in later) that Senator Fulbright is doing more damage to our cause than all the rest of the Senate put together. He was pleased for the first time today (September 14, 1966) to hear both Senator Fulbright and Senator Morse make public statements that they do not advocate (sic) withdrawing from Viet Nam."[67]

One statement Lausche made, which was forwarded to the President, bothered Mantos. The Senator indicated that he had the feeling that he was being held at arms length from the President. Mantos told Lausche that was not the case—that Johnson had told Mantos he would see any senator that wanted to see the President, when he could work it into his schedule. The Senator indicated he would like to stop by with a view of discussing Vietnam.[68] Lausche soon thereafter visited with the President about his concerns.

Lausche may have disliked the manner in which Fulbright conducted SFRC affairs, but the feeling between the two men was likely mutual. SFRC staff member Darrell St. Claire commented that the reason he liked Fulbright was the fact that he would suffer people like the Ohio Senator. "Lausche was never on time for a hearing, always came in midway in the hearing and asked questions that had already been asked, asked them in a loud voice, and ultimately ended up saying something about Red Rooskins."[69] Lausche was not the only Senator to display such behavior. Fulbright would lean back in his chair, pull on his hair, and allow the Senators to go on and on. He knew he had to let the record run down before he could ask for a vote. Staff members lauded Fulbright for his patience.

By 1967 the United States had reached a nationwide turning point on domestic issues and foreign policy in Vietnam. Discontent escalated rapidly in the nation. Racial violence heightened. The number of anti-war protesters increased significantly and became more vocal. Johnson, more haggard and worn-out day by day, looked for some way to extricate the U.S. from the malaise in Southeast Asia and do it with honor. The President was beginning to lose confidence in Defense Secretary Robert McNamara. The Defense Secretary began to question himself whether the Untied States could win this war. On March 27, 1967, General William Westmoreland, commander of U.S. forces in Vietnam, requested 210,000 more troops, which would have increased the military count to 665,000 men.

> "Lausche was never on time for a hearing, always came in midway in the hearing and asked questions that had already been asked, asked them in a loud voice, and ultimately ended up saying something about Red Rooskins."

In spite of support for this request from the Joint Chiefs of Staff, McNamara balked at sending such a large number. After months of debate President Johnson gave Westmoreland a total of 525,000 troops. McNamara had prevailed. However, his already frayed standing with the military hierarchy was damaged beyond repair. Johnson continued to suffer one setback after another.

Johnson began to lose significant support from his own party. In June 1967 Mansfield informed Johnson that 17 Democratic Senators expressed *confusion and deep concern* over the country's inability to find a way out of Vietnam. Johnson took personally much of the criticism of his policies.[70] The President privately referred to Fulbright as *Half-bright* and said that Senator George McGovern should be in jail for protesting the Vietnam War so vehemently.[71] A frustrated and angry Johnson increasingly formed alliances with friendly Republicans, a strategy that only worsened his alienation with many Democratic liberals.

Lausche considered North Vietnam the aggressor and questioned how the U.S. could stop bombing North Vietnam. Speaking to the Lima (Ohio) Area Chamber of Commerce, Lausche noted that three former Presidents had faced aggression in

Southeast Asia. "The U.S. must take a stand in Vietnam, because if we don't, the Communist aggressors will strike in Thailand or some other small nation in that area."[72]

In early July 1967 Lausche, who was now the sixth member of the SFRC in seniority, suddenly announced his support for unconditionally halting the bombing in North Vietnam for a protracted period. Pressure was building to somehow end what seemed to be a no-win war. The Senator hoped the bombing cessation would bring North Vietnam to the conference table, a condition the adversary had repeatedly requested. More importantly, Lausche counted on this executive directive to unite Americans into a common cause resulting in an honorable end of the war in South Vietnam.[73]

Later in the month when Fulbright went to the White House for a meeting of senate committee chairs, he was in no mood to offer Johnson soothing words. He told the President he detected an attitudinal shift about Vietnam amongst the senators. The Arkansasan mentioned that Lausche, a loyal supporter of Johnson's Vietnam policies, had changed his mind on the bombing issue. "The Vietnam War is a hopeless adventure," Fulbright reiterated. "Vietnam is ruining our domestic and foreign policy."[74]

Senator Lausche also spoke of the country being painfully divided on U.S. involvement in Vietnam and he believed this disagreement precluded military victory. SFRC members Fulbright and Morse reiterated this disunity repeatedly. The Cincinnati *Enquirer* challenged Lausche's change of heart about cessation of bombing, "Unless Senator Lausche knows something the rest of us don't, we fear he has picked a bad time to temporize with our war effort."[75] In a sense, Lausche played both ends against the middle. He carefully avoided any suggestion as to a future course of action. The decision to end the bombing would be in the nature of a *condition* placed over the head of Ho Chi Minh, the North Vietnam leader. Bombing in North Vietnam had been discontinued five times. Lausche conceded that to stop bombing again might be detrimental, but reasoned that possible over-riding good might result.[76] An underlying reason for Lausche's turnaround was his potential political vulnerability with a large segment of anti-war voters in Ohio. He, along with SFRC members Church, Fulbright, Morse, and Joseph Clark of Pennsylvania, faced re-election in 1968. On the committee, Lausche was described by a staff member as one of four dissenters to the Fulbright majority. The other three dissenters were Dodd, Symington, and Hickenlooper.

Skirmishes in the war zone often resulted in heavy fighting and more casualties, leaving U.S. citizens polarized on this debacle. Thousands of protesters spilled out into the streets. Congressmen in Washington, DC were cognizant of an increasing opposition to U.S. foreign policy in Vietnam. On August 28 Mansfield delivered a major speech in the Senate again proposing a meeting of all warring parties with the U.N. Security Council. He was supported on this proposal by a wide spectrum of senators, including Lausche.

BEGINNING IN LATE SEPTEMBER 1967, there was a barrage of congressional criticism and proposals for Congress to assert its power and end the war. The chasm between the President and Congress grew deeper and deeper. On September 26 Senator Clifford Case (Rep-NJ), a member of the SFRC, lashed out at the President. He insisted, as he had earlier, that Johnson's handling of the war had produced a crisis of confidence springing from a growing conviction in Congress that he was not telling the truth. Case chastised the President for his *perversion* of the Gulf of Tonkin Resolution. The Senator was convinced that Johnson had used this resolution to justify sending half a million U.S. forces to Vietnam, bombing the North and turning the war into a largely American war with no end in sight.[77]

Case, a well-informed, responsible Republican, had voted for the Gulf of Tonkin Resolution and had supported the war until 1967. His criticism of the President and the war produced a strong reaction. In a two-hour Senate debate following his speech, by pre-arrangement with the White House, Mansfield and Dirksen, as well as Long, Lausche, and McGee attacked Case. Long and Lausche charged Case with giving comfort to the enemy. In spite of Lausche's change of mind about a bombing cessation, he remained loyal to Johnson on this issue.[78]

More flare-ups between the SFRC and the President took place. In early November, the SFRC scheduled a meeting with Dean Rusk. The first question asked was whether Rusk needed to testify in public session (including television). This debate went on for days. Hickenlooper, ranking Republican on the SFRC said, "I see no reason to pillory him [Rusk] in a public session."[79] Mansfield agreed with Hickenlooper, as did Lausche and Symington. In spite of opposition from Fulbright and Senator Gore, Rusk eventually testified in an executive session of the SFRC.

On November 30, 1967, the Senate adopted the Mansfield Resolution by a vote of 82-0. The President was opposed to this resolution. He feared the U.S. would be asked to stop the bombing with nothing in return. Subsequent consultations by Arthur Goldberg, U.S. Ambassador to the U.N., failed to acknowledge any solid support among security council members for formal U.N. discussion of the Vietnam conflict. The Mansfield Resolution was not introduced to the United Nations.[80]

Late in the fall of 1967 Lausche defended President Johnson against his war critics in a speech on the senate floor. He believed the libel, slander, and abuse heaped upon the administration might lead North Vietnam to think the United States was so divided on the war issue that the country would pull out of Southeast Asia. The Senator worried that Ho Chi Minh was waiting for the 1968 presidential election and a possible repudiation of the Johnson policies. The Communists could win by default. Lausche continued to favor a halt in the bombing of North Vietnam. "A halt in the bombing would serve the purpose of solidifying our people and to tie the tongues of those slandering the United States." [81] The administration did not agree with this logic.

Lausche was distressed at civic leaders, professors, and ministers who sanctioned civil disobedience to plead their anti-war cause. "Law and order is being flaunted." [82] He could not understand the wisdom of draft card burners or peace demonstrators who failed to allow their country's leaders to speak. The Senator specifically referred to a visit by Secretary of State Rusk to the University of Indiana campus in Bloomington. Demonstrators would not let him speak. "This conduct is supposed to come under the heading of dissent...what right of free speech did they give Rusk? None. The Communist way is to create disorder and I regret to say they are succeeding in our country." [83]

Domestic and international crises continued to plague Johnson. Nineteen sixty-eight was an election year, and in January of that year, the President was confronted with two critical wartime incidents. On January 23, the North Koreans captured the *USS Pueblo*, an outdated coastal freighter, overhauled and outfitted with modern electronic gear, with 82 men aboard. This woefully ill-equipped ship was fulfilling its mission to intercept messages; however, it was hopelessly defenseless. Rabid hawks denounced the President for failing to retaliate. Author Trevor Armbrister reacted, "An ill-prepared nation sends an unfit ship with an inexperienced crew on an unsuccessful, perhaps unnecessary mission off the coast of an unfriendly nation." [84] The major significance of the *Pueblo* incident, Armbrister wrote, was that it "demonstrated—perhaps more shockingly and convincingly than any event in recent years—the real limitations of American power." [85] Critics of the Vietnam War—particularly Senators Fulbright, McCarthy, and Robert Kennedy—had forcefully said the same thing.

The President received another blow one week later. On January 30 during the traditional cease-fire period of Tet, the Vietnamese New Year, the Viet Cong and North Vietnamese troops staged well-coordinated attacks on 44 provincial capitols, 64 district capitols and five of the six major cities in South Vietnam. Within two weeks, the Americans and South Vietnamese regained the upper hand, at the cost of many casualties. Several days later, General William Westmoreland, commander of the U.S. troops, appealed for more troops to maintain the initiative. This request led to one of the liveliest senate debates about Vietnam in months. Fulbright demanded that the senate assume greater responsibility for decision-making in Vietnam. Not only did Fulbright's remarks generate a chorus of support, but they also received howls of protest from hawks like Stennis, Lausche, and Republican John Tower of Texas, who attempted to shut down the debate. In Congress, the ranks of those who opposed the war continued to swell, especially in the Senate. In an informal poll of the nineteen SFRC members in late 1967, eleven were opposed to the war (excluding Lausche).

Fulbright expressed satisfaction with the SFRC. To him, the committee had reached a new level of public service. The members had shown themselves to be fair and diverse in their interests before the staring eye of a television camera. Author Tristram Coffin noted Lausche was an exception, "A somewhat volatile individual with a wild shock of hair and excited manner, [he] interrupted [the hearings] several times. Lausche was one of Fulbright's *crosses*, wished on him by Lyndon Johnson. Once, after a particularly heavy day with the Committee, including Lausche, the Senator from Arkansas gloomily suggested to a reporter he might resign the chairmanship."[86]

The intensity of the SFRC hearings, particularly on the Vietnam issue, caused Lausche repeatedly to exchange words with the chairman. At the beginning of one committee meeting Lausche demanded to know if the committee was operating under the rule restricting each senator to a ten-minute-time limit to question a witness. Fulbright answered "no." Lausche quickly demanded, "Why not?" The chairman responded with a wry smile, "Call it *arrogance of power* if you want to."[87] Members of the committee chuckled. Senator Lausche did not.

Tempers flared and frustration dominated committee members as the war continued. Lausche showed his antipathy for Fulbright on March 7, 1968, during a major debate on the Vietnam issue. Fulbright introduced a resolution to do one of three things. 1) Repeal the Gulf of Tonkin Resolution; 2) if not that, adopt a resolution to accept the Gavin Enclave recommendation; or 3) if President Johnson did not want to do either of the first two, then to present a resolution to declare that the U.S. pull out of South Vietnam and raise the white flag of surrender.

One of the nation's distinguished military men, General James M. Gavin, had written an article published in *Harper's Magazine* (February 1966) about how Chief of Staff General Matthew B. Ridgway asked him to explore a landing in the Hanoi Delta. Gavin said this action would bring China into the war. Hanoi was the worst place for the U.S. to wage a war. Gavin recommended stopping the bombing, withdrawing to enclaves on the coast and seeking peace. This proposal became known as the Gavin Enclave. However, Johnson did not want to talk to Gavin.

Later that year in October 1966 Senator George Aiken—no friend of Johnson—proposed a similar enclave. He recommended the combination of redeployment of troops with cessation of bombing and a declaration of victory. This action would force the burden of further escalation on the enemy, and open the door to a resumption of political warfare that had properly characterized early U.S. involvement in Vietnam.

The Burlington (VT) *Free Press* quipped, "Senator Aiken must be joking." He wasn't, and his idea wasn't completely original. Lausche and numerous newspapers noted Aiken was essentially calling for a shift to the enclave strategy enunciated earlier in the year by General Gavin. The Senator added the novel addition of a *victory* statement to serve as a face-saving device for the President and the nation.[88]

Looking directly at Fulbright, the Ohio Senator implored "...let us quit talking.

Let us quit being divided. Let us reach a decision. The only way we can reach a decision, instead of talking, is for the Senator from Arkansas to present a resolution to the Senate so that we will not be discussing matters in the abstract, but will go right to the heart of the matter. Until he does, I suggest that he quit talking. I too am distressed with what is happening to the youth of the United States in South Vietnam but these acrimonious controversies will not lessen the losses."[89]

Regardless of Lausche's plea, in a meeting with Johnson and the chairmen of Senate committees, Senator Fulbright said, "Mr. President, what you really need to do is stop the war.... I think there is a change in attitude on the war. Senator Lausche changed his mind and said that he thought the bombing should be stopped in the North. The Vietnam war is a hopeless venture. Nobody likes it."[90]

☞

NO ONE SEEMED ABLE TO LIFT JOHNSON out of the entrapment of an ever-deepening abyss. On February 27, 1968, the proud Robert McNamara admitted defeat and amidst tears resigned, "We...simply have to end this thing. I...hope you [President Johnson] can get hold of it. It is out of control." Clark Clifford, a long-time political hack on the Washington scene and McNamara's successor, later wrote, "This proud intelligent and dedicated man was reaching the end of his strength on his last full day in office. He was leaving the Pentagon just in time."[91] A few months later McNamara accepted the presidency of the World Bank. Some years afterwards, he reevaluated his role in the tragedy of Vietnam, first in his memoirs entitled *In Retrospect, The Tragedy and Lessons of Vietnam* and in an excellent documentary film, *The Fog of War.*

Johnson's approval ratings on the Vietnam issue continued to plummet. Then the President received another setback. Walter Cronkite, CBS news anchor, publicly pronounced his opposition to America's continued role in Vietnam. Described as America's most trusted public figure, Cronkite, upon returning from Vietnam in February 1968, determined that the U.S. was neither close to victory nor to defeat. "To say that we are mired in a stalemate seems the only realistic, yet unsatisfactory conclusion. It is increasingly clear to this reporter that the only rational way out...will be to negotiate, not as victors, but as honorable people who lived up to their pledge to defend and did the best they could."[92] White House press secretary George Christian commented that when Cronkite released this statement, "the shock waves rolled through the government."[93] Lausche was not swayed by Cronkite's assessment of the war. He was convinced that Ho Chi Minh was insincere and that Communist expansion remained his only objective. The Senator believed the Tet offensive was evidence that North Vietnam was unwilling to negotiate a peace settlement and that he was correct in his assessment.[94]

The war continued to take its toll on Johnson. The President's health was not good. The Johnson family had a medical history of strokes. Doris Kearns Goodwin, author of a biography on Johnson and a confidante, wrote that the President had long struggled with paranoia.[95] When the war was in its early stages in 1965 and the President expected a quick victory, he parried with the opposition, including Fulbright. By 1968 when the war had become a catastrophe, Johnson delivered vitriolic attacks on his presumed enemies—the intellectuals, the big-city press, the television networks, the liberals and the Kennedys.[96] By late March the President had made a fateful decision, which he shared with the nation on March 31. Johnson announced he would not seek re-election for the presidency. Furthermore, he ordered the immediate cessation of bombing of North Vietnam, with exception of the area above the demilitarized zone (17th parallel).

Lausche was shocked by the President's decision. He believed the President's motive was to bring about more unification among the American people in their thinking about the war. Johnson placed himself in a position whereby he could now make wartime decisions without charges of political chicanery. Lausche believed that delegates at the Democratic National Convention would compel the President to change his mind about seeking another term.[97]

In his memoirs Johnson complained that the media devoted considerable attention to Fulbright's anti-war views on Vietnam, but virtually ignored the pro-administration position of Frank Lausche and Mike Mansfield.[98] (Mansfield, out of loyalty to the President, repeatedly wavered on what the U.S. should do in Vietnam). Johnson recalled that the principal issue was not where the precise line marking no bombing was drawn (20th or 10th parallel), but rather how Hanoi would react to the United States' self-imposed restriction. Lausche had raised the key question in Johnson's mind relative to the senate debate: "How can Ho Chi Minh give affirmative action when the senator from Arkansas and others attack the government before he can respond?" The President continued, "While Fulbright's allegations dominated the news stories and headlines, Lausche's pertinent question received scant attention. I saw it mentioned only once in the *New York Times* on April 3 [1968] and then only in the thirtieth and last paragraph on page 14. When the North Vietnamese hear what Fulbright said, I thought they will probably delay their answer—if they intended to react favorably."[99] Shortly thereafter Hanoi agreed to meet to discuss a possible termination of the war. This meeting did not come to fruition until January 27, 1972, when the Paris Accords to end the war and restore peace in Vietnam were finally signed by both parties.

As the war lingered on in 1968, Lausche was less than optimistic about prospects for a military victory. By 1969 Lausche specified where the blame for failure belonged. "We have lost this engagement, not because our cause was not right, but because we allowed ourselves to be divided by our own shortsighted leaders—primarily in the Senate. The pullout of troops under the present, disunited thinking of our people is necessary."[100]

Occasionally Lausche gave mixed signals with his viewpoints about the Vietnam conflagration. Overall, he remained a highflying hawk. Perhaps some of his utterances were calculated to convince the electorate back home that a vote for Lausche would be a vote for peace. Lausche seldom, if ever, deviated from his basic political philosophy (besides fiscal responsibility) that the U.S. must be a bulwark against Communist domination. The Ohio Senator embodied his beliefs with a strong dose of patriotism. To his opponents and several of his friends, Lausche's patriotism, like his conservatism, seemed old-fashioned. He challenged certain members of the senate, asking "How long [can a nation] endure if its leading citizens unjustly and falsely condemn that nation as being perpetrators of wrongs."[101] Lausche made a fetish of the proposition that Americans must demonstrate a unity of purpose in regards to the Vietnam War. The Senator dismissed the SFRC hearings as a service to the enemy. He railed at colleagues who snipped at the Johnson administration. "It is one thing to discuss things," Lausche remarked, "It is another to denounce our country as a liar, an exploiter, and a cheater."[102]

This kind of rhetoric had stood well for Lausche over the years. To the chagrin of Lausche, the texture of the country changed dramatically during the 1960s. An unpopular war had divided the country. Racial tensions had escalated to a dangerous point of open conflict. The counter-culture movement did not set well with old-timers like Lausche, who believed "demonstrations by long-haired, dirty-faced, so-called intellectuals are causing the death and injury of American fighting men in Vietnam."[103] Lausche wanted every man, woman, and child to present a solid front behind the nation's Vietnamese efforts. He believed to take any other course served the interests of Ho Chi Minh.

To the chagrin of Lausche, the texture of the country changed dramatically during the 1960s. An unpopular war had divided the country

The debate over Vietnam issues took much of Lausche's time. He was embroiled in a campaign for re-election in the Democratic primary in early May. His Democratic opponent was intellectual John J. Gilligan. He would prove to be a formidable opponent for the crusty 72-year-old political veteran, worn from many years on the campaign trail. The word had reached Washington, DC that the incumbent was in the political battle of his life. He sat one day in the senate room, smoking a Roi-Tan cigar when Alan Bible, his senatorial colleague from Nevada quipped, "Do you have an opponent who's on TV a lot? Gilligan's Island?" "Aw," retorted Lausche, "Why'd you go and ruin my appetite?"[104]

Lausche, the day after the 1968 primary, reading about his defeat to John Gilligan. Taken at his brother Charles' home in Gates Mills. (Courtesy of the Cleveland Plain Dealer. All rights reserved. Reprinted with permission.)

thirteen

The Great Upset

By 1968 Lausche's politically polarized philosophy resulted in two distinct and opposing camps. Mixed emotions were no longer prevalent concerning the aging, silver-curled senior Senator from Ohio. He was either revered or reviled. Supporters and friends depicted him as the Lincoln of Ohio. Lausche had become the archetype of the ethnic politician and the archenemy of the progressive ethnic in America. This long-time politician held on to Jeffersonian principles when it came to government affairs. "Frank Lausche is a myth" was the opinion of an opponent. "Frank Lausche is a very shrewd politician making the most of a good thing," retorted a friend of the Senator.[1]

State Democratic leaders wanted to dump Lausche, who had never been a party favorite or a party cooperative. The Senator, arguably the greatest vote getter in Ohio political history, was in an enviable position. He had everyone against him—party, labor, and such—everybody that is, except the voters.

There was an axiom in Ohio politics that went something like this: Run for anything as often as possible, but for goodness sake, keep out of the way of Frank J. Lausche. With the exception of two losses early in his political career, Lausche had been defeated only once (for governor in 1946) in his 34-year political career.

In early 1968 Howard Metzenbaum, influential Cleveland political gadfly and once Lausche's floor leader in the Ohio Senate, claimed his fellow Clevelander should seek re-election as a Republican. Metzenbaum demanded that Lausche offer his candidacy in a manner consistent with his voting record. "Senator Lausche must recognize, as a man of integrity, that his views are supported in only two places—among Republicans and Southern Democrats." The future U.S. Senator did not quarrel with Lausche's right to vote in opposition to his party label, "But he owes it to the people of Ohio to file as a Republican."[2]

Journalists began to nip at Lausche's heels in 1966. Richard Zimmerman, former Columbus columnist for the Dayton *Journal Herald* and author of *Call Me Mike*, a political biography of Michael V. Di Salle, wrote a scathing column about Lausche. The journalist suggested that it would be difficult to drum Lausche out of the Democratic Party because he was so hard to find. He questioned whether anyone could empirically prove that the Senator was really representing Ohio in Washington, DC. He queried, "Have you seen a flesh and blood Lausche lately? Has he spoken in your city? Has he walked your streets or been to your fair asking about your problems? Have you ever received a newsletter or opinion questionnaire from Lausche? Do you know if Lausche has an Ohio office in Columbus? Cleveland? Anywhere?"[3]

Zimmerman conceded that the Senator had appeared on television during his last campaign and during recent senatorial hearings on Vietnam. He concluded, "When we have been in Washington, we never get past Lausche's administrative assistant.... We've been told that the caddies at Burning Tree Golf Course...are experts on Lausche and can verify his existence.... Maybe one of the Cleveland newspapers should write an editorial titled "Yes, Virginia, There Is a Frank Lausche."[4]

Though there may have been a semblance of exaggeration in Zimmerman's rhetoric, ample evidence had accrued that Lausche's ultra-conservative voting record and absence from his senatorial office had begun to cut into his popularity. Many of Lausche's enemies were more and more directing venom toward him. At a reception held by one labor organization, the venerable Mike Kirwin referred to his fellow legislator as "a menace to mankind."[5] This animosity lasted another three years until Kirwin's death in 1970. The coolness between Lausche and Senator Young had shown no signs of diminishing.

Organized labor finally united to create a serious obstacle to Lausche's re-election. Lausche's falling-out and antagonism with organized labor had begun back in the 1940s. During his first term, the new Mayor of Cleveland had repeatedly opposed pay raises for city workers. In the midst of a nationwide coal workers strike in 1943, the mayor denounced the lawlessness of legendary labor leader John L. Lewis.[6] Some say Lausche's troubles with labor began with Eliot Ness. When Lausche took over the reins as mayor, Ness was safety director in charge of police and fire departments. Democratic leaders and labor insisted Ness, who had an anti-labor reputation, be replaced. Lausche failed to do so, and retained Ness in his administration until Ness self-destructed. Neither did Lausche endear himself to organized labor when he indirectly mentioned that he had voted for Robert Taft in 1950, one of the architects of the anti-labor Taft-Hartley Bill (1947). His anti-labor position continued in 1958. While a member of the U.S. Senate, he strongly urged Ohioans to vote for a constitutional right-to-work amendment initiated by a Republican-controlled Ohio legislature.

Although Lausche believed in collective bargaining, he was also of the opinion that the right to work should not be conditional upon membership in any type of business, labor, fraternal, or religious association. He held the view that the right to work was just as sacrosanct as the right to free speech, jury trial, freedom of assembly and all other rights delineated in the Declaration of Independence and vested to the citizenry by the Constitution of the United States. "I think the right to work...is just as sacred as the right to vote and the right to a jury trial. Don't join a labor union under the threat of losing your job or not getting it. I favor a situation which will allow the American worker to take a job whether he belongs to a union or not."[7]

Organized labor in Ohio joined hands to fight against passage of the right-to-work amendment. Under the leadership of Elmer Cope, Secretary-Treasurer of the Ohio AFL-CIO, various unions coordinated their political and campaign activities through the Committee on Political Education (COPE). By Labor Day 1958, the right-to-work campaign was losing momentum. Organized labor, now united in Ohio, picked up steam in opposition to the amendment. Spokesmen crisscrossed the state to plead their case. War chest funds increased, and a massive voter registration drive proved successful. In the waning weeks of the campaign, the Chamber of Commerce and other backers of the right-to-work amendment sought desperately to regain momentum. Ultra-conservative Senator John Bricker came out in support of the amendment. Governor C. William O'Neill added his endorsement. These endorsements made the amendment a partisan Republican issue. "Sheer stupidity," responded Vice President Richard Nixon when he learned of O'Neill's endorsement.[8] Bliss believed the Republicans had sealed their fate for failure at the polls. He was correct. When the votes were counted on November 4, Ohioans rejected the right-to-work amendment by a vote of two to one. Democrat Michael Di Salle replaced O'Neill as Governor. Perennial candidate Stephen Young replaced the popular Bricker in the U.S. Senate. For the

"Senator Lausche must recognize, as a man of integrity, that his views are supported in only two places—among Republicans and Southern Democrats."

first time in over a decade, Democrats sympathetic to labor controlled both houses of the Ohio General Assembly.

The voter's response was a message to Lausche that he was increasingly fomenting antipathy from organized labor. The Senator's continual denunciation of federal spending and opposition to pay-raises exacerbated the wrath of labor leaders. In 1966 labor legend I.W. Abel, President of the United Steelworkers of America, spoke at the Ohio AFL-CIO convention in Cleveland. The craggy Abel vehemently criticized Lausche's anti-labor votes and advocated that organized labor work to rid the senate of a man who had forgotten the people of Cleveland and the people of Ohio.[9] Lausche had developed a reputation as a Senator who tried to block passage of bills. "There are floor senators and there are committee senators," remarked Charles Vanik, longtime Democrat from Cleveland who was a committee Congressman. "Some senators prefer working through committees and others prefer working the senate floor. Frank was a floor senator. While he wasn't always very successful he had nothing to lose in openly criticizing others because he wouldn't participate in pork-barrel politics."[10]

THIS WAS THE SETTING AS THE **1968** election approached. Times were changing rapidly. The mood of the sixties was a sharp contrast to the placid fifties. Growing ranks of young voters demonstrated concern for, of all things, issues. In addition to the country's social upheaval in the sixties, which Lausche abhorred, he found his support among the blacks beginning to erode, particularly in Cleveland. While mayor of Cleveland during World War II, Lausche promoted good relations with the Negro population and encouraged the migration of blacks from the south to industrial Cleveland where good-paying jobs were available. This migration significantly changed the demographics of the Lakefront City; however, in spite of this influx from other states, the city population decreased by 104,000 to 810,000 citizens between 1945 and 1960.

The black population between 1950 and 1965 more than doubled from 147,000 to 297,000, an increase from 16.5 percent to 36.6 percent of the city's population.[11] Despite a certain amount of discrimination, Cleveland had acquired a reputation as a *good city* for the black populace. Many Cleveland blacks who migrated from the south reported "if you can't make it in Cleveland you can't make it anywhere in the North."[12] Cleveland's eastside where Lausche grew up changed rapidly between 1950 and 1960. The blacks settled in this area, creating autonomous neighborhoods with their own customs and traditions, not unlike the pattern established a century earlier by European immigrants. The enlarged black population and their shift into new areas of the city created opportunities for black politicians.

At this same time so-called Lausche clones, Thomas A. Burke (1945–1953),

Anthony J. Celebrezze (1953–1962), and Ralph Locher (1962–1967), mayors of Cleveland in the postwar era, were all men of great integrity. George E. Condon, Jr., Cleveland's humorist-journalist-historian described the men as "deadly because they were not innovators."[13] Although Condon may have excessively denigrated these mayors, they seemed not to think in large pictures and large concepts. The stark reality of black slums and attendant issues (housing, employment, education, and police brutality) became the catalysts for unrest of an explosive nature. By 1960 28.2 percent of all black-occupied housing was either substandard or dilapidated.[14] Suburban housing was off limits to middle-class blacks. Because black families were unable to move outside the city, these groups were squeezed into Cleveland's well-defined slum areas.

This was the situation Lausche encountered in 1967 in his hometown. Carl Stokes, a new political entity and a black, had arrived on the scene. Stokes worked his way up the political ladder. Then in 1958, Stokes, fresh out of Marshall Law School (where Lausche received his law degree), was appointed as an assistant police prosecutor in the law department for the city of Cleveland. After four productive years in this position he sought a seat in the Ohio legislature and twice won two-year terms. His heart lay elsewhere, specifically Cleveland's City Hall and the mayor's office. He was publicly criticized for his poor attendance in the state legislature.

Stokes resigned in 1964 to seek the mayoralty against the amiable Ralph Locher, Lausche's former administrative assistant in the governor's office. Locher became mayor in 1962 when as law director for the city of Cleveland he replaced Anthony Celebrezze. In March 1962 President Kennedy had appointed Celebrezze Secretary of a new cabinet office, Department of Health, Education, and Welfare. Stokes was swimming upstream amid McCarthy-like mud slinging during the campaign. In a four-way election, Stokes lost this election to *safe* Locher by less than 2,500 votes.

Stokes suddenly found himself famous. His near election excited the curiosity of black and white groups throughout the country, and he became deluged with speaking engagements. In 1966 Stokes ran for his third term in the state legislature and easily won. Stokes' political fortunes were about to dramatically change. He knew that to win the mayoral election in 1967 he would need to come face-to-face with as many white people as possible. If they had a chance to talk to him, there would be no need to whisper behind his back. He also needed a more professional staff and money for television appearances. Importantly, every Negro who was eligible to vote must be registered.

By the early 1960s, economic discrimination against the blacks had declined in Cleveland. A substantial number of Negroes had achieved an adequate standard of living and realized the benefits of a modern industrial society. While poverty was declining among many black households with male leadership, the gap between the have and have-nots was widening. Unemployment among blacks stood at 15 percent in 1966. Poverty was more visible among the have-nots—garbage was gathering in the streets and rats flaunted their own tenancy over that of human slum dwellers. Racial troubles finally boiled over in Cleveland. Only nine months after Locher's (the unifying candidate) re-election in July 1966, the city was torn apart by the Hough riots—four days and nights of terror and destruction that left Cleveland a bewildered and directionless city. Day and night in the streets of Hough, Carl Stokes appeared dodging bullets, bottles, and bricks along with the police and National Guard, until finally the nightmare was over. Stokes' popularity spread among the Cleveland populace and he gained endorsements from the local press. Tom Vail, publisher of the *Plain Dealer,* gave total support to Stokes in the primary election. He believed his approval of Stokes would unite the restive blacks and the business community and give the city a chance to move forward after the dismal years of Locher. Lausche gave tacit backing to Locher without trying to alienate himself from the black voters he would need in 1968. His endorsement made little difference. In a heated and often contentious primary, Stokes defeated Locher by 18,000 votes, preventing Locher from seeking his fourth term as mayor in the general election. An analysis of the voting results showed that the approximate number of whites voting for Stokes had been 18,000 or 14 percent—his margin of victory! Many more votes for Stokes came from the cosmo wards (wards inhabited primarily by foreign-born offspring) than had been expected.[15]

Lausche faced a dilemma concerning whom to support for mayor in the fall election, if anyone. The Senator knew he would need the cosmo votes in the 1968 primary. Lausche studied the results of the mayoral primary while in Washington, DC, and announced he would withhold any statement on which candidate he would support in the general election. He knew the Ohio AFL-CIO was ready to back any viable Democrat brave enough to challenge him in the primary in May. This person could well be the beneficiary of black votes throughout Ohio should Lausche fail to endorse Stokes.

Importantly Stokes received an unexpected boost when *Szabadsag* (meaning liberty), a Cleveland daily Hungarian newspaper printed in Hungarian and in English endorsed Stokes for Mayor. Page-length ads in Cleveland dailies carried the paper's editorial including the following excerpt: "Cleveland has had many firsts, especially in the political field.... This was the first major city to elect a man of ethnic background, Frank J. Lausche, the son of humble but proud immigrants, as its mayor. [The author had obviously overlooked Fiorella Laguardia's prior election to the mayor's office in New York City.] This city also gave the inspiration and impetus to Lausche to be the first man of ethnic background and of Catholic faith elected governor and later U.S. senator for the great state of Ohio. The citizens of Cleveland will have the opportunity to be the first again among the major cities by electing a Negro, Carl B. Stokes, as their mayor and thereby demonstrating to the free world...that they have none of the very prejudices that forced them or their parents to leave their native country and settle in our city."[16] This endorsement was ingenious in that the editorial emphasized what appeared to be an implicit agreement with everything the Senator believed. It was one of the few times in Lausche's political career that he had been outflanked.

Stokes' opponent in the general election was Seth Taft, wealthy Cleveland suburbanite. A close election was anticipated. Behind the scenes, pundits questioned whether Lausche would support another Taft as he had with Seth's uncle, Robert, in 1950. There was nothing, certainly not Democratic Party loyalty, to prevent him from endorsing a second Taft in 1967. Although Stokes naturally coveted Lausche's support, he did not openly seek it. He had become committed to no one in his race for mayor, and he was wary of Lausche. He considered Lausche a nominal Democrat who was as conservative as any Dixiecrat and as independent as a cat.[17]

The racial unease remained intense in Cleveland prior to the fall election. City leaders, including Louis Seltzer, had failed to quell violence. Lausche was unaware of these conditions. With his only office located in Washington, DC he was oblivious to the fact that his previous support among blacks in east Cleveland had begun to dissipate. Stokes had the endorsement of Democratic leaders at the top of the party, with the noticeable exception of Lausche. The Senator refused repeated requests to endorse Stokes' candidacy. Stokes did not need Lausche's support. In a close election Stokes emerged victorious over a less than aggressive Taft by 2,500 votes. He doubled the number of white votes from the primary election (18,000 to 35,000), which amounted to 20 percent of the total white votes. He became the first black mayor of a major American city. Stokes was elected to a second term in 1969. Not until after the first election did John P. Leacacos, Washington correspondent for the *Plain Dealer*, disclose why Lausche withheld support for Stokes. During the mayoral primary, he had been insulted by Stokes' assertion that the onus for Cleveland's problems had its origin with the former Cleveland mayor. Lausche reacted resolutely to this allegation. He had taken pride in his efforts to make Cleveland a sanctuary and a place of refuge for Negroes. When Lausche became mayor in 1941 the city was 91 percent white and 9 percent Negro. In 1967, the figures more nearly balanced with 61 percent white and 39 percent black inhabitants. Lausche explained further, "I took no part in the mayoralty campaign between Seth Taft and Carl Stokes. I did not do so because in the primary campaign Mr. Stokes, on the public platform, denounced me and asserted that when I was elected mayor in 1941 and served during the war, I so badly conducted the government of the city of Cleveland that its present ills had to be placed on my shoulders. I waited patiently to hear if Mr. Stokes would contact me and give me some explanation or apology for what he said: I received no word from him. I, too, have self-respect. To have participated in the campaign would have been giving confirmation to the unjust and wrongful argument he made against me."[18]

After this mayoral election took place, Lausche explained in more detail why he remained non-committed to supporting either candidate. Stokes raised Lausche's ire after the election. He was quoted as saying during the campaign that he would fire every member of outgoing Mayor Locher's cabinet. "The only question is which one goes first.... There's Harold Lausche (properties director). He's totally incompetent. The only reason he is there is because of that other man who started us on the down grade in 1941 —Frank Lausche."[19] Viewing this matter in the most charitable manner, Lausche found it impossible to understand how Stokes expected him to be supportive of his candidacy in the general election.

Lausche let the cat out of the bag. "I know Carl B. Stokes. He worked in my Liquor Department while I was governor.... He resigned voluntarily as far as the records show, but the truth is that his resignation was involuntary. In the different districts which he worked, proof was available that he used his office not in the objective maintenance of law and order but in the purpose of promoting himself financially...his conduct as a Liquor Agent showed he could not continue in that position. He had to either resign voluntarily or be fired. He resigned."[20] The former Mayor added that Stokes had made condemnations of occupants in city hall that could not be justified. He was sure that Stokes had made charges which were untrue and promises he would not be able to fulfill. Stokes' victory foreshadowed the difficulties Lausche faced in his bid for re-election.

⌒

OHIO LABOR LEADERS AND LIBERAL MEMBERS of the state Democratic organization had for several months privately discussed how to oust the venerable Lausche from his Senate seat. They could never agree on a unified strategy or candidate. Sources indicated that $80,000 had been raised and much more had been promised to support a candidate other than Lausche. Ohio Senate Minority Leader Frank King of Toledo led this coup. King, a statewide political power and one who came from a blue-collar city, seldom saw eye to eye with Lausche's anti-labor stance. Others anxious to see Lausche replaced included Kirwin and Young.

State party leaders offered tacit agreement to stay out of the way. These men included state Democratic Chairman Morton Neipp from Toledo; Albert Porter, Cuyahoga County Democratic Chairman; Jim Stanton, Cleveland City Councilman, a rising star on the political scene; and Robert W. Blakemore of Summit County.[21] Many Democratic leaders believed Lausche was invincible in the general election. There were other state leaders, less in awe of the legendary Lausche, who believed the Senator was more vulnerable in the Democratic Party primary election than in the general election. The reasoning of this latter view seemed logical. The name Frank Lausche had appeared with such regularity on the ballot that it had a ring of success to the voter playing sure shots. Republicans had found the Lausche philosophy of tight-fisted economy to be such a risk-free commodity that they adopted the high priest as one of their own. A Lausche defeat likely could come only at the hands of his own party in a primary election. The question was this: Who could the Democratic Party and labor organizations rally behind? "You always ended up with some boob on the ballot against Lausche in the primary and some nondescript Republican in November," commented Paul J. De Gradis, Jr., a vice-chairman of the Democratic organization and leader in the party's youth movement. "It couldn't have happened if he [Lausche] had faced one of the old-style politicians, a Bob Sweeney or a Mark McElroy or those guys who's (sic) always running for something statewide," commented another Democrat. "To beat Lausche you...have to [run] a man of substance."[22]

Organized labor was determined to play a more active role in unseating Lausche. The Ohio AFL and CIO joined forces in the late 1950s after Lausche left the state and began to demonstrate more influence in the Democratic Party. Frank W. King emerged as a major catalyst in placing organized labor in a more responsible role in Ohio's political arena. Born in 1912, King grew up in the Toledo area where he became an apprentice bricklayer at the age of sixteen. This labor leader was linked to the powerful building trade unions for thirty-six years. A 25-year veteran in the increasingly influential American Federation of Teachers, King turned to the state legislature to provide more political clout. The Toledoan won a seat in the Ohio House in 1949 and advanced to the state senate in 1954. As Senate majority leader of the Democratic controlled 103rd General Assembly King presided over the passage of the most favorable labor legislation in decades.[23] In 1964 King won presidency of the Ohio AFL-CIO. He was now the kingpin in the Ohio labor movement, which needed a more unified front.

In 1967 the executive board of the state AFL-CIO approved a new political strategy. Called *The Spirit of '67*, this program embodied three major components. Most importantly this strategy called for enjoining with emerging computer technology and data processing. Files of statewide union members were updated with pertinent registration and voting information. Second, using computerized lists, the state labor organization planned to provide each of the organization's 800,000 members with vital information about political candidates. The vehicle for these admittedly biased reports was a high quality monthly publication called *Focus*. The third part of The Spirit of '67 linked the state labor organization with city and county political leaders to bring about more unity. King and his cohorts determined they must be successful. They did not wish to see another failure that had occurred with the disappointing Blueprint for Victory effort to mobilize voters in 1962.

The state Democratic Party believed they had picked a man of substance to challenge Lausche. The individual in question was John Joyce Gilligan from Cincinnati, a Republican stronghold. Gilligan was one of several young, aspiring politicians who had been swept into Congress in 1964 on the tide of President Johnson's one-sided victory over Senator Barry Goldwater. Just as quickly, the rookie legislator relinquished his seat in Congress in 1966 as a result of a Republican backlash. He lost to Robert Taft, Jr., a name which commanded deep respect in the hard-core Republican-dominated Second Congressional District. In spite of his defeat in 1966, Gilligan caught the eye of intellectuals for his steadfast support of progressive ideals. The 47-year-old Gilligan was as liberal during the 89th Congressional session as Lausche was conservative.

Gilligan did not act like or look like a politician. Clean cut, his red hair neatly trimmed and his clothes well tailored, he looked more like an instructor in English literature. Gilligan was fourth generation of an Irish family who had settled in Cincinnati in the 1840s. John's mother, Jean, gave birth to two sets of twins, John and Jean in 1921 and Frank and Harry, Jr. in 1929. Harry Gilligan Sr., John's father, was of the old Irish school which set high expectations for their children in academic achievement, sports and work. John did not fail his father in this respect. He attended Summit Day School where he participated in sports and extracurricular activities. John graduated from Xavier High School, a small Jesuit school of 300 students. Gilligan continued his Catholic education at Notre Dame University where he pursued his interest in English Literature. After graduation, the young scholar joined the Navy in 1942. Gilligan, a gunnery officer, served with distinction both in the European and in the Pacific theaters, earning decorations, including a Silver Star for gallantry in Okinawa. After the war and now married to his childhood sweetheart Mary Kathryn Dixon, Gilligan reluctantly joined his father's funeral business. His mind and heart were set on college teaching. While helping with his father's business, the young instructor taught English at Xavier University from 1947 until 1952. He pursued a doctorate in English at the University of Cincinnati, but never completed that program.

In 1953 Gilligan won election to the Cincinnati City Council as a member of the reform-minded Charter Party (also included was Charles Taft, Lausche's 1952 gubernatorial opponent). This rising political star distinguished himself as an active and productive member of the council for nine years. His record helped catapult Gilligan into the U.S. Congress in 1964.[24] Gilligan built a reputation as an Adlai Stevenson-type liberal Democrat, which put him at odds with Lausche's conservatism.

Gilligan did not want to enter the 1968 Democratic primary unless he was assured of enough support to have a fighting chance against Lausche. Financial resources did not pose a problem. In an effort to convince Gilligan to run, the state AFL-CIO released a poll of Ohio Democrats taken in October 1967. The poll showed seven percent favored Gilligan, 55 percent favored Lausche, and 38 percent were undecided. These figures might have discouraged the average politician, but the urbane Gilligan reasoned that with 45 percent of the voters not committed to the man who had been respected by the voters for so long, he might indeed have a chance.[25] He was ready to risk the battle.

The groundwork was laid for Gilligan's uphill climb to win the nomination. Several state Democratic leaders took a leadership role to pave the way for Gilligan. In 1966 Frazier Reams, Toledo Democratic candidate for governor ten years earlier, selected fellow Toldeoan, successful attorney and businessman Morton Neipp as the new state party chairman. Neipp in turn appointed Cleveland political leader Peter O'Grady as executive director to run the Columbus office. Both men were determined to build a stronger and more united state party. Lausche's blatant undermining of the Democratic platform and candidates had thwarted the party's efforts to have a greater impact on elections. Neipp, an unsung hero, worked tirelessly behind the scenes to help modernize the state party. Once Neipp achieved a financial base for the party he renewed a strategy that would best strengthen the Democrats—forming a closer relationship with organized labor. The principal unions in Ohio were the United Steelworkers and United Auto Workers, both affiliated with the AFL-CIO. Neipp met with labor leaders in Washington, DC, which led to a decision by AFL-CIO President George Meany to make Lausche's defeat a national labor priority. Frank King and various state labor leaders used the national AFL-CIO Committee on Political Education (COPE) to solidify plans for the primary election. Under the aegis of campaign slogan The Spirit of '67, the Ohio AFL-CIO employed 34 female students from Columbus' Bishop Ready High School. Working every day after school and on Saturdays these students compiled information about prospective voters to be keypunched on data processing cards. The teenagers collected information on about 70 percent of the state's union membership. This knowledge was both revealing and distressing: six out of ten unionists in Ohio were not registered to vote. The leaders of the Ohio AFL-CIO and the city and county central organizations contacted these union members. The massive drive registered 85,000 new voters.[26]

To provide state party leaders solid evidence that Lausche could be beaten, Gilligan and Neipp persuaded the state labor organization to commission a private public opinion poll. The poll provided Gilligan with anticipated evidence. Lausche's greatest voter strength came from older voters. The Senator did not realize until it was too late that the mood of younger voters was changing. The country was experiencing a cultural revolution. These voting newcomers looked for liberal political stances on contemporary issues, such as the war in Vietnam, crime, poverty, civil rights, women's rights and taxes. Gilligan was more in touch with younger voters on these issues than was Lausche.

A further analysis determined that Lausche's opponent could not win on these issues alone. Many of the elders, veterans groups, rural folks (mostly Republican) and less liberal in general, respected Lausche's flag-waving style. These voters responded to his loud shouts for less government spending, and identified with his self-engineered rise from the old ghetto. The Americans for Constitutional Action, a group dedicated to promoting conservatism, reported that Lausche voted 76 percent of the time for money-saving measures. He was surpassed only by 15 Republicans (mostly southern) and one other Democrat, Harry F. Byrd, Jr. of Virginia. Lausche's record was 3 percent more conservative than that of Senate Republican leader Everett M. Dirksen of Illinois.[27] Gilligan planned to emphasize Lausche's weaknesses: his fence sitting, his lack of loyalty to the Democratic Party, his antipathy to organized labor, his opposition to the Kennedy and Johnson domestic programs, and his advancing age.

On the last day of 1967, Lausche's campaign received unexpected support. Representative Wayne L. Hays (Dem., 18th District) released a statement that the state party moguls would be stupid to oppose Lausche. He gave two reasons: Lausche could beat any Republican around, and the Senator would be valuable to the party ticket at a time when prospects suggested that the Democrats would need to cash in all assets at hand.[28] Lausche conceded that he was delighted and surprised by Hays' endorsement. In the past, Lausche and Hays had shown about the same mutual admiration as draft-card burners and Lt. General Lewis B. Hershey, Director of the Selective Service program. Other Ohio politicians came to Lausche's defense and called for an end to intra-party feuding. Former Congressman Robert E. Sweeney claimed that Lausche was the all-time top vote getter in Ohio history and emphasized that "The Ohio Democratic Party needs Frank to head its ticket in 1968. Many congressional seats, state legislative posts and county level posts could be lost without the pull of Lausche's name."[29]

Lausche received more good news. G.O.P. Congressman Robert Taft, Jr. from Cincinnati chose not to oppose Lausche in the senatorial race. Instead Taft chose to seek re-election to the House of Representatives. Reflecting that he and Taft saw eye to eye in their basic governmental beliefs, Lausche commented that Taft's decision "makes me hopefully happy and fortified in the conviction that the course I have followed in the performance of my duties...is substantially sound."[30] One week later Ohio Attorney General William B. Saxbe from Mechanicsburg announced that he would seek the Republican nomination to oppose the Democratic candidate in November. Popular in Ohio political circles, Saxbe was considered a moderate Republican and a good choice to unseat the Democratic incumbent. Taft's withdrawal prompted a journalistic *faux pas* not unlike the famous headline the night of the 1948 presidential election when the Chicago *Tribune* declared Thomas E. Dewey the victor over President Harry Truman. The Cleveland *Press* printed a headline that read "SAXBE TO OPPOSE LAUSCHE."[31]

Charles Sawyer provided additional support when he endorsed Lausche for re-election. The Cincinnati attorney was Secretary of Commerce under President Truman in 1948, and also former ambassador to Belgium. "What does an American voter want in a public official?" Sawyer asked. "Honesty, courage, intelligence, high ideals and experience. Frank Lausche has them all."[32] His prepared statement intimated that Lausche would win easily if anyone were foolish enough to oppose him in the primary. As might be expected, Lausche received support from other old-time political cohorts. Former U.S. Senator Thomas A. Burke claimed that Lausche had been an outstanding public servant. "A wrong would be perpetrated on the people of Ohio to deny them his continued fearless, honest and constructive service."[33]

The day before the State Democratic Committee caucus, Lausche issued a statement to the effect that, out of self-respect, the Senator could not call upon individuals to press his cause at the meeting. "If those in attendance believe that the Democratic Party, acting in conformity with its true purposes, represents the rich and the poor, the strong and the weak and is not a slave to any powerful economic group—they will help me and not help any possible opponent."[34]

But the State Democratic Party cast the die against Lausche. In an unprecedented and historic move on January 11, 1968, the Ohio Democratic Party State Central Committee in a closed session, broke tradition and lined up behind Gilligan. After more than an hour of heated debate, the roll call vote was 45-14 to throw their support behind the former Cincinnati Congressman. This action may have marked the first time in U.S. political history that a state party endorsed the rival of its own incumbent Senator. Most of the key party leaders chose to line up behind Gilligan. Two of these state leaders opposing Lausche included Albert Porter from Cuyahoga County and Frazier Reams, Jr., the state party's titular leader. Delegates from every urban area except Youngstown voted for Gilligan. Lausche's main support came from rural areas. Gilligan had made it clear to party leaders that he would challenge Lausche only if the party gave him strong support.

The fourteen votes opposed to Gilligan were not united for Lausche. Six of the voters favored withholding endorsement from both candidates. Angry shouts of opposition came from several delegates, notably Frank Vanelli, chairman from Belmont County. His voice carried through the closed doors of the Ulysses S. Grant Room of the Hotel Sheraton-Columbus. Vanelli shouted. "We are finally at a point where we can win an election. Why are we going to have a primary fight and tear our party apart? I'll produce a slate of Democratic winners if Lausche heads our ticket."[35]

During the daylong meeting Gilligan had lunch with three colleagues from southwest Ohio. After lunch Gilligan went back to his hotel room and took a nap. Later in the afternoon, Edward J. Waynes, who served as legislative assistant during Gilligan's one term in Congress, walked into the bedroom, woke Gilligan, and said, "You son-of-a-bitch, you did it!"[36] The next day Gilligan held a press conference to announce he would be a candidate for the U.S. Senate.

The afternoon of the Democratic Party meeting Lausche released a statement from his Senate office on the action of the delegates, "I am neither pleased or distressed through the action taken by the majority of those in attendance.... The action will hurt the cause of the Democratic Party in Ohio more than it will hurt me; it does not reflect the true thinking of genuine Democrats nor the general voters of Ohio. The forces which promoted the rejection of my candidacy…would have been glad to support me if I had allowed my thinking and voting to be dictated by them. These forces have unsuccessfully opposed me in every political contest in which I have been since 1943."[37]

Two weeks later Lausche confidently predicted he would win the primary by a tremendous number of votes. "No gang of 45 men is going to drive me out of this fight." The Senator commented that his campaign would be brief and no major organization would promote his campaign. "I've never had an organization in my contests and I'm not going to have one this time."[38] A small group of about ten people would run his campaign.

To add insult to injury Lausche suffered further embarrassment from the Democratic Executive Committee. The committee voted Stephen M. Young, Lausche's counterpart in the Senate, as the state's favorite son for the 1968 presidential convention. Frazier Reams declined to say whether Young would campaign for Gilligan, but emphasized, "I can promise you he will not endorse or campaign for Lausche."[39] A sample of the political polarization between the two Ohio Senators was released in January 1968. Young and Lausche scored highest (45 percent) of all senators in disagreement on roll call votes in 1967. The two Senators marked the highest disagreement record for the fifth straight year.[40] This tugging of the rope in opposite directions was not helpful for gaining approval of pork barrel projects in Ohio. The Gilligan forces realized that defeating Senator Lausche in the May 7 primary would be a difficult task. "Since the death of Bob Taft he [Lausche] is the biggest political name in Ohio," Gilligan commented in an interview shortly after accepting the challenge, "Senator Lausche has been able to win Republican support with his conservative record and get the Democratic votes by default."[41]

⌒

LAUSCHE BELIEVED THAT THE DEMOCRATIC Party's actions were a political breakthrough for him. He commented that rebuttal of his candidacy removed the final obstacle to his re-election.[42] The younger voters in metropolitan areas did not agree with Lausche. Several weeks before Gilligan's entrance into the primary race, a group of youthful Cleveland Democrats announced the formation of *Citizens for Gilligan* campaign. Defining Gilligan as among a new breed of politicians who emerged under President Kennedy, the young leaders called Lausche an anachronism. Stephen Kovacic, a name well known within the Slovenian community, contended that the Senator had ignored important issues and "has not made a single legislative contribution"[43] during eleven years in the Senate.

Editorials from the press early in the primary campaign suggested that Lausche did not have too much to worry about in quest of his third senatorial term. A journalist with the Youngstown *Vindicator* wrote that, although the veteran Senator did not wear the liberal stripe many Democrats prefer, the daily did not consider him an archconservative on all issues. His financial conservatism was quite appealing as the national debt skyrocketed far beyond $300 billion.[44] The Columbus *Dispatch* printed an editorial cartoon showing the Democratic Party leaders and labor bosses holding a hoop and whip telling Gilligan "We're endorsing you because Lausche wouldn't jump through the hoop when we told him to!"[45] In spite of being located in Gilligan's home lair, the Cincinnati *Enquirer* reminded readers that Lausche characteristically did not beseech the Democratic Executive Committee to support him. The editorial questioned whether an attempt to purge Lausche when he garnered 62 percent of the vote in his last election was appropriate. "No one can argue, in light of his popularity, that Senator Lausche has acted without the approval of the people of Ohio, although in the course of doing so, he obviously has run afoul of various elements which make up the party leadership."[46] There was little disagreement that Lausche was a magical name in Ohio politics. Several party members admitted that, if Lausche won by a large margin, it would have the effect of making future candidates question the value of party support and thus possibly adopt Lausche's successful independent approach.

Lausche gave the outward impression that whatever actions the State Democratic Party took, he was not hurt. This impression was not true. In an interview in late January, his voice quivered, his eyes became moist, and he thumped his fist angrily on his cluttered desk. "Mercenaries! They're all mercenaries, that's all. Trying to hurt me because I wouldn't jump through their hoops." He took off his heavy glasses and continued, "You'd have to be made of stone not to feel this deeply." He became restless. He puffed on a cigar, snubbed it out a few minutes later, and lit another cigar. He looked like a Senator should look, knew it, and decided to make a speech. "All my life," he said, "I've tried to follow a course to help the country. Now this gang has made a decision to hurt me.... The impact of the repudiation vote has strengthened my resolve to go to the people. We'll let them decide this cause."[47]

The campaign began with a divergence of political ideologies and evolved into a contest of contrasting styles. One commentator observed that the race pitted Lausche, the inveterate hand-shaker, stumping the state in his 1940s fashion, against Gilligan, the reluctant pitchman, hoping to capture most of the electorate on television.[48] Before groups who considered themselves independent thinkers and voters (clubs like Kiwanis or Rotary), the veteran campaigner received standing ovations. Lausche's audiences in the ethnic neighborhoods were still charmed by his capacity to converse in several languages. The rebuke by the Democratic Executive Committee produced a deluge of communications containing statements of encouragement, inspiration, and promises of unlimited and unconditional support. Small-town newspapers came to his defense. In response to a supportive column written by Jack Ripley, editor of the Leetonia *Courier* (several miles south of Youngstown), the Senator confessed that "Mrs. Lausche, when she read what you [wrote] about the happenings in the last two weeks with respect to myself, found her cheeks covered with tears of pride and joy..."[49]

John (Jack) Gilligan was just as outgoing and congenial as Lausche, but he lacked the sense of timing of his opponent. On a tour of Cleveland's Hough section, the scene of rioting in 1966, the challenger disappointed his backers by neglecting to mingle with local residents, preferring instead to confine his conversations to area leaders. Lausche would never have missed this opportunity. Gilligan tried to speak before small citizen groups, but he found it nearly impossible to change the opinions of long-time Lausche supporters. Even with his Silver Star from World War II, he encountered difficulty getting across to veterans groups that the Senator voted against the Cold War GI Bill, against the 1959 Veterans Readjustment Act, and against the 1960 Veteran Life Insurance Act.[50] Gilligan's backers decided to concentrate on new voters and disenchanted Democrats with a continual outpouring of television pronouncements. This was not Lausche's style.

The senior Senator complained of the massive organization built up to oppose him. He planned to run his campaign with a limited committee.

Organized labor quickly swung into action to solicit votes for Gilligan. Local unions conducted extensive voter registration drives. At the conclusion of the registration campaign, labor leaders estimated the percent of union membership registered, including immediate family members, increased from 40 percent to 70 percent. In several of the larger counties, labor unions set up telephone banks and recruited workers for distribution of campaign literature. The national AFL-CIO verbally committed over $100,000 to help Gilligan's campaign.[51] The Committee on Political Action stepped up its efforts. When 400 members of COPE met on February 21, 1968, they abstained from endorsing any specific candidate, and instead, directed their undivided resources behind Gilligan. The State Democratic Party nearly drained its treasury to fund the campaign. A large portion of these funds paid for extensive television advertising. None of the state's large newspapers endorsed Gilligan. To counter this setback, the AFL-CIO public relation's department utilized the updated national and state computerized lists to mail special regional issues of *Focus*. Additionally, they sent a twenty-four-page pamphlet to unionists throughout the state comparing the political stances of Lausche and Gilligan.[52] "For the first time," said a press release by COPE, "the working people of Ohio will go to the polls fully informed on the real issues of this contest."[53]

⌒

FROM THE OUTSET OF THE PRIMARY ELECTION challenge, the Gilligan forces maneuvered Lausche into a defensive position. The Senator made a stereotyped attack on a "small band of party-bosses dictating to the ranks and file people of Ohio.... I am criticized for failing to comply with the directions given by the top persons of my party. These chiefs of the Democratic Party are of the opinion that all members of Congress who hear that label must follow their commands even before the arguments in favor or against a proposal are known."[54] The senior Senator complained of the massive organization built up to oppose him. He planned to run his campaign with a limited committee. A lone secretary managed his small campaign headquarters in the Carter Hotel in Cleveland. Lausche's complacency was predicated on the premise that his history of strong voter strength would not desert him in this election.

Gilligan traveled the state declaring of Lausche, "He talks like a Republican, votes like a Dixiecrat and never misses an opportunity to undercut the Democratic Party, its candidates and its philosophy."[55] Lausche merely stiffened his anti-labor stances, "That labor has decided my concept of government does not fit into its ideas of how government should be run leaves me with no sorrow or distress," he reiterated in a campaign speech.[56]

The alienation between Lausche and the AFL-CIO COPE intensified in mid-February. The union invited the Senator to appear before committee members for an interview. The incumbent Senator interpreted this invitation as a clever gesture to give the committee's already hostile action toward him a front of decency. "I will not join in the promotion of this deception."[57] Lausche said the press of Senate business prevented him from attending the screening session. He would not have attended even if he could have cleared his schedule. The Senator was certain that the AFL-CIO had already made up its mind about whom they would support. He was likely correct on this issue. The next day, February 21, COPE endorsed Gilligan for the contested Senate seat. Key members of the union and the media and press received a synopsis setting forth the voting record of the two candidates.

The labor organization scheduled dinners in the state's six largest cities in April. The cost was $10 per plate, and Gilligan was present to build up voter enthusiasm and give the challenger an opportunity to extol his campaign agenda. On March 6 the Ohio AFL-CIO released under Frank King's signature a letter to all segments of the media asking for support and an endorsement of Gilligan. King quoted a January 24, 1968, editorial in the Toledo *Blade*, "While posing as a Democratic senator representing a large industrial state beset with urban problems, he [Lausche] was in Washington voting against the model cities' effort to eradicate slums, working to cut poverty funds, aid to education, and chances for Ohio ports to compete for commerce."[58] King suggested that Lausche would conduct his campaign as he had in the past. He would refuse to discuss his record and instead looked for a whipping boy as a divergence. The union questioned whether the newspaper lords had the guts to tell the Ohio public the true facts about Lausche as the AFL-CIO interpreted them. The union was determined the working people would go to the polls fully informed. Billboards supporting Gilligan appeared throughout the state saying, *Vote for a REAL Democrat.*

While the challenger and his supporters moved forward aggressively on the campaign trail, Lausche continued his homespun method of campaigning. In late January 1968, Jonas R. Troyer, an Amish farmer in Sugar Creek (Tuscarawas County) invited Lausche to have dinner with his family and some friends. They sat on benches and ate family-style as Lausche and his hosts exchanged reminiscences. "There wasn't a word of politics spoken," commented Mennonite preacher William H. Stauffer. "We talked about soil and water conservation and things strip miners leave behind...."[59] After dinner an overflow crowd of 300 persons, about one-third of them Amish, gathered at the Sugar Creek community hall. "He had them eating out of his hand," recalled Rev. Stauffer.[60]

Lausche basked in the limelight with members of the press. Walter Trohan, syndicated columnist for the Chicago *Tribune*, questioned why state party moguls repudiated Lausche for re-election because of his age (72). The liberal wing of the state party didn't find junior Senator Stephen M. Young's age (75) objectionable when he was elected in 1964. Trohan wrote words that the Senator and his supporters cherished, "Lausche is a phenomenon in American politics, a thoroughly honest man. He is certainly one of the most honorable, courageous and independent men ever to serve in public life. He is devoted to his country and is convinced the greatest service to the country is morality in politics...."[61]

The issues during the campaign reduced themselves to Gilligan's liberalism versus Lausche's conservatism. Gilligan argued that the senior Senator was insensitive to the plight of the cities due to his fear of the danger inherent in federal subsidies. "If I had one consuming interest," Gilligan proclaimed, "it is to get through to the people...that the federal government is our government, not an alien force."[62] To Lausche's proposal to give money instead to rural America (sounded almost Jeffersonian) making life there more attractive, and thereby drawing the *city cloggers* to the open spaces, the challenger answered, "That's a marvelous attitude. What Senator Lausche is saying is that we would make things so miserable in the cities, the people will find their way back to the farms and eat grasshoppers or something."[63] Lausche retorted that as mayor he "made Cleveland a haven for the oppressed and exploited people. They knew," he boasted, "they would get a square deal in Cleveland and they came there."[64]

Early in the race Gilligan decided to confine his campaign against the Senator to domestic issues. This was not possible. The Vietnam War was too controversial as a political issue. Public opinion had moved closer to Gilligan's views, "We had better start making some limits and reduce the situation to reality, ending our Holy War against communism," Gilligan declared. "The question this nation must ask itself is whether it intends to be a police force for the world. If we decide that's what we want, it will be expensive. It will mean bringing our boys home in boxes for a long time to come."[65] Senator Lausche talked about a nation where every man, woman, and child was united behind the government's Vietnam policy. "Lausche's simplistic views of foreign policy are frightening," Gilligan commented in a private interview with *The Nation*, "but he knows such views go down well at home. In Cleveland's ethnic neighborhoods, he still talks about liberating the satellite nations of Eastern Europe. The man is not talking about the real world. This is irresponsible claptrap."[66]

⌒

As mentioned in chapter 12, on March 31, 1968, President Johnson delivered two shocking announcements. He ordered a bombing cessation in Vietnam. The President further announced that he would not seek re-nomination for the presidency in 1968. These decisions were not helpful to Lausche's election chances. Had Johnson not withdrawn from the presidential race, he might eventually have given his endorsement in the primary to Lausche. Johnson had been in dire need of friends in the Senate, and certainly Lausche had been supportive of the President's foreign policy. Gilligan was not in Johnson's camp on the Vietnam issue. In the back of his mind Lausche believed Johnson would change his mind about running or the convention delegates would draft him. Johnson's double-barreled decision gave impetus to the dovish Gilligan campaign. Gilligan publicly favored a bombing halt in Vietnam. A poll taken a few days after the President's announcements saw Gilligan's voter support increasing to 21.5 percent, Lausche's plummeting to 37.2 percent, and a massive 41.3 percent of the voters remaining uncommitted.[67]

Lausche actively began to campaign in early April. The Senator continued to believe he would emerge victorious. "Never before in my life has the evidence been so encouraging," he commented in reference to 2,000 letters and wires he received after the Ohio Democratic Executive Committee endorsed Gilligan. "Much of [my] support is coming from the Republicans."[68] The State Republican Party was confident that Lausche would be victorious. Republican nominee William B. Saxbe knew Lausche well. He told a gathering prior to the primary election that he would consent to debate Lausche "only if he agreed not to cry."[69]

The incumbent struck a nerve in the Gilligan camp when he accused the challenger and his labor cohorts of attempting to buy the Senate seat. He charged that a million dollars was being spent to elect Gilligan with much of the money pouring into the campaign from union treasuries in other parts of the country. Lausche compared this situation to organized labor's massive effort in 1950 to defeat the late Senator Robert Taft—whose Senate seat Lausche occupied.[70]

Gilligan did not take kindly to Lausche's accusation. "This is the type of slanderous allegation which [Lausche] has frequently resorted to during [his] political career...and may be in part responsible for [his] reputation as the master politician of the age."[71] Gilligan asked for a retraction, but none was forthcoming. The Cincinnati native followed up with a complaint to the fair campaign practice's committee in Washington, DC. After an exchange of letters Lausche admitted he had made the statement about the approximately $1 million contribution by labor organizations. He added that the accusation stated originally came from Gilligan and his supporters. To Lausche these facts justified his conclusion. This issue made good copy for the newspapers and media, but amounted to little else as the election drew closer. Lausche's antics did not surprise Gilligan. The challenger had learned from previous experiences that the major obstacle to getting anything done in the Democratic Party was Frank J. Lausche. "He wasn't even neutral. He'd just chop your head off to protect his base. Anyone crazy enough to challenge him went *goofy*. He made sure no one cut him off." Gilligan continued, "Lausche had a great personality, was a marvelous speaker and had the so-called common touch. He was not a philosophical orator, but he knew how to talk to people. Lausche could reduce any crowd to tears in ten minutes. The crafty politician played on his ethnic background, the influence of his mother. His ethnic base never left Lausche—it was a working man's base and Democratic. As Lausche drifted more and more to the center of the political spectrum, he took these people with him and kept his political power."[72]

In late March, Morton Neipp, chairman of the State Democratic Executive Committee, sent out another plea for grassroots support to overturn Lausche. "We have a real Democrat...running for the Untied States Senate, against Frank J. Lausche, who has been, since he went to the Senate in 1957 more of a Republican than a Democrat."[73] The Democratic Party pulled out all stops in a feverish attempt to derail the one-man Lausche juggernaut. Weekly polls indicated Gilligan was gaining. The Vietnam War continued to be a major issue in the campaign. The citizenry began to note significant political differences between the candidates.

Lausche continued to campaign throughout April. He drove around the state, visiting old friends and stopping at newspaper offices. His schedule was sparse, a shadow of the rigorous kind of crusade he had carried on in past campaigns. The practical, but shrewd campaigner followed a timeworn plan of soliciting votes. He visited Rotary and Kiwanis Clubs' luncheons and Chamber of Commerce dinners. The Senator never passed up Future Farmers of America gatherings or an American Legion post. Lausche was the old pal coming back for a visit. He was genial with husky handclasps to go with his wide crinkly smile. The veteran politician refused to mention his opponent's name. He declined to debate issues or to appear on the same platform with Gilligan. "I'm not going to make a crowd for him," Lausche exclaimed.[74]

State Senator Frank King, President of the Ohio AFL-CIO, fanned the flames of this political rejection by Lausche, proclaiming, "The year is 1968 not 1868. The era of the covered wagon has ended. Lausche represents that era. He is out of touch with the people in this state."[75] Lausche retaliated with his old cry of bossism. "The forces which prompted the rejection of my candidacy would have been glad to support me if I had allowed my thinking and voting to be dictated by them. Past experience has demonstrated the correctness of the views, which I have promoted. The future...will give added support to my views."[76]

By THE TIME LAUSCHE BEGAN TO CAMPAIGN seriously day-by-day, Gilligan had visited 29 of the 88 counties, given 180 speeches, held six major press conferences, and visited the editors of every major newspaper in the state. Gilligan felt confident he could win. He portrayed Lausche as an arrogant maverick who espouses "a type of government that went out with President [William] McKinley while displaying a calculated contempt for not just the Democratic Party but anyone who believes in the two-party system."[77] This caricature of Lausche was similar to that expressed by James V. Stanton, long-time Cleveland politician and U.S. Congressman (1970–1977). He characterized Lausche as self-centered and anxious not to make any enemies, but not interested in helping other Democratic candidates.[78]

During the last month of the campaign Gilligan advisors recommended that he produce a 30-minute film for release during the final ten days of the campaign. Charles Guggenheim, a nationally known film director, created a biographical vignette emphasizing Gilligan's background, his stand on issues and his political activities. His intent was to give the laboring community a better insight into what Gilligan really represented. This documentary entitled *Against All Odds*, increased Gilligan's campaign expenses to nearly $300,000, a sharp contrast to Lausche's expenditure of $45,000. The Senator used television sparingly, sprinkling 35-second promotional spots across the state and seeking free television time whenever possible. Lausche was never known to spend much of his own money on a campaign. Significant financial resources were unnecessary until this election. A correspondent interviewed Lausche in the ornate Senate dining room in the last weeks of the campaign. He graciously offered to pick up the tab—$3.67 for his own hamburger and the Senator's fruit salad. "Sure," said Lausche handing the bill across the table without a second thought. "If the election is going to be determined on the amount of money spent I have to yield.... Ohio has never sold an election to the highest bidder."[79]

Lausche reacted to the pressure of a tight race shortly before the election. On April 26 the incumbent spoke to the Lancaster Rotarians and Kiwanians. Following his speech Columbus correspondent Steve Delaney asked the Senator if he might have a show of hands of the number of registered Democrats in attendance. Lausche, realizing the implication of this question (many were Republicans), refused this request and what he considered to be an improper question. The audience supported Lausche, and several in the audience berated Delaney and asked for an apology. He refused and maintained the question was proper.[80] Two days later, after giving a speech to the Delaware County Democrats, Lausche exploded before reporters could ask him a single question. Abe Zaidan of the Akron *Beacon-Journal* wanted to ask the Senator a question related to his comments about Vietnam. Lausche lifted his arm and brushed the reporter aside charging, "You heard my speech—no more questions."[81] A confrontation erupted when Orly Bosworth, a reporter for a Columbus-based statewide radio and television news service approached Lausche with microphone and tape recorder in hand. Lausche refused to talk to Bosworth who asked, "You mean you don't want to answer questions for radio and television?" Lausche put his hand over the top of the microphone and wrenched it away, saying "I made my talk—please don't disturb me!"[82] After some milling around during which time it became clear that most onlookers were siding with Lausche, the reporters left satisfied with their story. The tension of a close election was apparent.

Lausche continued to aggravate the Gilligan camp by insisting that labor was buying the senate seat for the challenger from Cincinnati. The Senator forwarded a statement of his accusation to Samuel J. Archibald, Executive Director of the Fair Campaign Practices Committee in Washington, DC. This letter was sent only six days before the election. Gilligan denied the charges, and this last ditch effort by Lausche to castigate his opponent paled into insignificance as Election Day approached.

President Johnson, his nerves frayed from the Vietnam fiasco, hesitated to endorse either candidate. Lausche had supported Johnson's foreign policy, particularly the Vietnam engagement. Conversely, the Senator seldom provided support for Johnson's Great Society programs. The specter of the administration was thrust into the conflict only once—to the advantage of Gilligan. On a visit to Columbus in March, George W.P. Weaver, an assistant U.S. Secretary of Labor was quoted, "Lausche is the man you imposed on us [administration].... I can say the administration will do anything it can to help Gilligan win the Democratic nomination...."[83] In a fluster of embarrassment, Weaver insisted the next day he had been misquoted. The administration quickly asserted its neutrality.

Lausche garnered support from an important political source, newspapers from five of Ohio's six largest cities. Not one of these dailies endorsed Gilligan. The Toledo *Blade*, considered a Gilligan ally, refrained as a matter of policy from endorsing either candidate in a primary election. The opinion expressed by editors across the state suggested that Gilligan could not win. The Cleveland *Press*, generally in Lausche's corner, wrote, "The *Press* has not always agreed with [Lausche's] financial views, but it believes a challenging voice like his is necessary when it comes to dispensing tax money...Lausche is not a slave to the party line. He relishes a good fight with the power structure, be it of political party, government agency, labor, or whatever. Therein lies much of his election appeal—he is a strong independent source."[84]

On the other side of the coin Gilligan, who said he wouldn't run unless labor put up a million-dollar kitty, reportedly settled for somewhere around $300,000.[85] Approximately 30 of the state's 88 Democratic organizations, including heavily populated Lucas, Hamilton, Montgomery, Mahoning, and Stark counties endorsed Gilligan. Franklin, Cuyahoga, and Summit counties abstained from an endorsement. Four small counties endorsed Lausche.[86] Lausche literally cut off all avenues for party support at the state and national levels. Two weeks before the election, the embattled Senator turned down a public endorsement from Democratic National Chairman John M. Bailey. In spite of Lausche's unpredictable Senate voting record, the national Democratic Party was anxious to retain his seat for Senate control.[87]

⁀

VOTERS WERE GREETED WITH COOL AND CLOUDY spring weather on primary Election Day (May 7). By the time the polls closed, nearly one million voters had marked their ballots. Early returns indicated an upset was in the making. Gilligan gained majority votes in precincts which had previously been sure winners for Lausche. In Cuyahoga county, cornerstone of Lausche's political fortress, 57 percent of the Democrats voted for Gilligan. Ward after ward in ethnic neighborhoods recorded final tallies that gave Lausche only a marginal plurality. African-Americans turned against the man, who as governor appointed the state's first black judge. Black voters emerged in massive numbers from political dormancy to overwhelm Lausche. Precinct 13-V in east Cleveland registered 223 votes for Gilligan and 34 votes for Lausche.

Downstate in the conservative domain of farm-oriented voters, few had ever held a tighter grip on election outcomes than the senior Senator. In seven previous statewide elections, Lausche carried downstate Ohio with 65 to 80 percent of the votes. The Senator barely held his own in this election. He won 51 small counties by margins as narrow as 11 votes. Lausche's downfall occurred in the densely populated areas. Gilligan captured large majorities in ten of 12 major population centers. The challenger won nine of the ten largest counties contributing 60 percent to his final count. Gilligan received 544,814 votes, 55 percent of the total and Lausche tallied 438,588 votes or 45 percent of the total. This upset was a sharp turnaround from the 1962 senatorial election when Lausche won by 692,640 votes.[88] The Cleveland *Press* asked a question on everyone's mind the day after the election, "How does a man win an office one term by 600,000 and lose it the next term so decisively? Especially a man named Lausche—Cleveland judge, Cleveland mayor, Ohio governor, U.S. Senator?"[89]

Several reasons stand out in explaining this major upset. Despite warning signs, Lausche did not take his opponent—the strongest he had ever faced—seriously and ran a frugal, low-key campaign until the final days. Gilligan's campaign staff judged the documentary film, extolling Gilligan's attributes throughout the state as a major factor in the monumental victory. Saxbe offered a simplistic answer. "Lausche would go to a [Senate] session and get up and make some wild statement and leave to play golf at Burning Tree Country Club. That is why he lost."[90] Saxbe was correct about Lausche's propensity to visit the golf course too often during working hours, but it is probably a stretch to blame the defeat on this issue. An interesting sidebar to Gilligan's victory came to light some years later. Saxbe,

Gilligan's Republican opponent in the general election, surmised that, when he ran for the Senate seat supposedly against Lausche, he would take his beating. Saxbe would then have a clear shot to win the governor's election two years later. Gilligan, the giant killer who in reality wanted to be governor, however, was persuaded to run for Lausche's senate seat. Gilligan lost to Saxbe in the general election for the Senate seat and two years later won the governorship.[91] Saxbe was appointed as U.S. Attorney General in 1974, replacing Elliot Richardson who had resigned in protest during Watergate. Saxbe would never serve in the Governor's office.

Lausche believed firmly that labor's efforts in the primary brought about his downfall. "For twenty-five years, labor leaders fought," Lausche complained, "...they beat me. They flooded Ohio with money from the unions throughout the country. I wasn't conscious of what was going on. I was late recognizing it and the turn against me occurred in the very last part of the campaign. By then, it was too late."[92]

James J. Kilpatrick, syndicated columnist, concurred with Lausche's analysis. It was not his age. Many senators have functioned quite well long past their 72nd birthday. To Kilpatrick's way of thinking—aside from Lausche's stubbornness—Gilligan benefited from one of those great efforts that labor can mount, in this case in Ohio. During Gilligan's single term in the U.S. house of representatives (1965–66), the Cincinnatian rated a near 100 percent on the AFL-CIO scorecard. His rating with the conservative Americans for Constitutional Action was a feeble seven percent.[93] For Democratic candidates, traditionally less well heeled than their Republican counterparts in congressional races, the difference between lukewarm and fervid union support can swing the election into the win column.

Two other factors were important in the final outcome. Lausche's once strong base of support from the black population had dissipated. Lausche was supporting his *clones* in the 1950s and 1960s, at a time when *Black Power* was on the rise. At the same time that he abhorred rioting and civil disobedience, the Senator favored civil rights legislation. Lausche didn't appear to have the ability to grasp the emergence of black power at the ballot box. Furthermore, Stokes' victory as mayor over a Lausche clone did not help the Senator's cause. Politicians tend to place more importance on the endorsement of persons in high places than do voters. Albert Porter, Cuyahoga County Democratic Chairman, whose strong endorsement for Stokes—combined with that of other local Democratic brass—was more meaningful to Stokes' election than was support from President Johnson, Hubert Humphrey, or Frank Lausche.[94]

Formerly the darling of ethnic voters, Lausche lost the political edge he once held in his home county. Ethnic solidarity blurred the *cosmo* voter's eyes to Lausche's action and inaction. Lausche rejected what the cosmo favored: unions, better pay, and strong federal government services. The deposed Senator's political stance was diabolically opposite to Congressman Charles Vanik, a fellow Clevelander of Czech ethnic background. Vanik strongly believed that taxes were necessary and that the government had an obligation to provide public services where needed.[95] Vanik defeated Republican Frances Bolton, 29-year congressional veteran from Cleveland's 22nd district, in the 1968 election.

Lausche's generation of immigrant offspring had grown up to become parents and grandparents. Second- and third-generation progeny outnumbered him and his generation. The new generations did not speak the ancestral language. They had lost touch with the Old Country customs and nationalism, which Lausche's generation cherished. The old ethnic neighborhoods began to break up, due in part to steady income, social progress, and late model automobiles. Old peasant tools were put away. Ethnics in their new affluence put down new roots in an expanding economy. They no longer winced when taxes were needed for better public services.[96]

Gilligan understood these social and demographic changes. The candidates faced a new generation of laboring people who were looking for solutions. Gilligan met this challenge and reached out to the younger voters with his proposals for a better society. He provided statistics about the tons of pollution per square mile falling on the east side of Cleveland. The challenger toured the ghettos offering possible answers as to how government could improve urban life. These younger voters respected fresh new positions on Vietnam, crime, poverty, and civil rights. In the spirit of Bobby Kennedy and Eugene McCarthy, these Democrats demonstrated a heightened interest in politics and decided their candidate preference on the basis of issues. Lausche, in his timeworn style of campaigning, avoided specific issues. He discussed the fallacies of Charles de Gaulle, the necessity to stem inflation, and the need to end inner city riots. Young voters who registered Democrat were inevitably drawn to the 47-year-old liberal, not to the 72-year-old conservative. The old style of politicking had changed. Samuel L. Abrams, public relations consultant for Lausche, made this point succinctly, "We're in new era of politics, we thought Lausche was so well entrenched...some of the early polls showed him winning two to one—that it created a feeling that Lausche didn't have to do anything different than he always has."[97] Lausche was caught up in a political trend to remove older solons and elect new and younger aspirants.

The day following the primary election, Lausche told the newsmen gathered at his brother Charles' home in Gates Mills where he usually stayed when in Cleveland, "I am going to treat this like any other day," he commented, "There aren't going to be any post-mortems. It was wonderful, but it has ended, and now I am looking forward to coming back to Cleveland and resuming the practice of law." The following day he added, "Neither Jane nor I feel any distress. You could nearly say I'm happy. I feel free—liberated.... I am grateful to the people of Ohio for their loyalty in the past."[98]

Three weeks after the startling upset, Lausche's staff was still in a state of shock. "I couldn't believe it election night when they said we were in trouble," commented Ray M. White, the Senator's 66-year old administrative assistant, "and I still don't believe it." "I had a Cleveland station on," Celie M. Jirsa, Lausche's personal secretary since his mayoral days, remarked, "As the returns came in the station kept fading. I turned the radio sideways and upside down, but [the election returns] came out the same way."[99] White, Jirsa, and Marie A. King, office manager, all accustomed to Lausche winning, pondered their futures. For now, they planned to help the Senator complete his term. The remainder of the twelve-person staff rejoined the Senator in the capitol. A shorter association with Lausche tempered their reaction. Business continued as usual in Suite 1327 of the New Senate Office Building. Incoming mail was normal, and included many sympathy notes. The biggest change noted in office decorum was a significant decrease in the number of constituents who dropped by the Senator's office. Racial tension had caused a decrease in travel to the capitol. "Have any senators been around to offer condolences?" White was asked. "Not a one," he replied.[100]

Throughout his remarkable career, Lausche built a reputation as a dyed-in-the-wool independent. His vote could seldom be predicted in advance, often to the consternation of his Democratic senate colleagues. The Ohio Senator displayed aloofness from partisan politics. "You ask as many people in Ohio as you want how Frank Lausche has voted in the Senate," said one Lausche crony, "They don't know. But if you ask them why they vote for Frank Lausche and they'll tell you its because he's independent."[101]

The turbulent sixties brought about radical social and political upheavals. Lausche had difficulty accepting these societal changes. His political ideologies, style of campaigning and personal image were throwbacks from the forties and fifties. The Senator's emphasis on fiscal responsibility, his all-pervasive spirit of patriotism encountered resistance with a country many believed was in a mode of self-destruction. His political philosophy clashed with the mood of the sixties. The invincible Lausche had met his Waterloo. His political career would end in a few months. The lame-duck Senator planned to pursue meaningful projects before closing the book on his public career.

Frank J. Lausche speaking at the dedication of the Frank J. Lausche State Office Building, October 28, 1978. (Used with permission of the Columbus Dispatch)

fourteen

The Twilight Years

HISTORY HAS RECORDED MANY ACCOUNTS whereby an underdog emerged victorious in a competitive encounter. The media often asked the vanquished loser about the reasons for his defeat. Transposing this question to Gilligan's victory, the downtrodden Lausche found it difficult to respond. In the 1940s the Senator asserted that defeat could be a victory if one is rebuffed by those who are only thinking of immediate gains for themselves. Lausche believed that he had scored a moral—if not a political—victory in the 1968 primary. "If this [election defeat] had happened to me 15 years ago, I'd be heavily distraught.... But I take it philosophically.... My deepest feeling of satisfaction resides in the fact that I never allowed anyone to get control of me in any way. I remained a free person."[1]

Several months later Lausche again expounded on his feelings about his surprising defeat, "I have not yielded to pressure groups...that are only thinking of the immediate gains and advantages that can come to them...." He noted that Gilligan "pledged himself to carry into effect the demands of special pressure groups in return for their promises to provide him with a superfluity of money to carry on the campaign against me." Lausche added that victory or defeat resides in the state of conscience of a participant, "I feel certain that I won and my opponent lost because of the practices in which he indulged...to gain more votes...."[2]

Lausche continued to be rankled about how labor organizations had so heavily financed Gilligan's campaign. On June 30, 1969, Lausche's former colleague Senator Carl Curtis (Rep-NE) addressed this issue in Congress and asked for a senatorial investigation. The unions in Ohio and at the national level contributed $218,000 to Gilligan's cause. Curtis quoted the Federal Corrupt Practices Act that forbade campaign contributions by corporations, banks or labor organizations.[3] Efforts were made to tighten abuse of this act, often with little success. The consequences of contributions meant little to Lausche as he prepared to abdicate his senate seat.

After 35 years in the public limelight, Lausche's unexpected exit from the political arena brought a sense of relief to the Senator and his wife. He and Jane prepared to return to the nation's Capitol. Lausche paused to reflect on his political career. He still supported the shock of white hair atop his head. His voice was still theatrical, rich and full. "Of all the offices I have held, the most soothing and satisfying was the judgeship. That position was free of slander." He continued, "The governorship produced the greatest acclaim. And the senatorship in these chaotic times is the most chaotic. The evidence on issues of import is not clear. Never can you be sure you have been absolutely right." Lausche concluded, "Over my desk...has hung the advice that Polonius gave to Laertes, 'To thine own self be true and it must follow as night follows day thou canst not be false to any man.'"[4]

With those words to fortify them, Lausche and Jane wasted no time moping and flew back to Washington, DC. He dropped Jane off at their home in Bethesda and headed for Burning Tree Country Club. Lausche played well. He shot a 79 on the par 72 course. Sand traps looked benign after recovering from his shocking defeat.[5] The next day Lausche went to his office and checked the mail that had accumulated during his absence.

The fallout from Lausche's defeat continued for several weeks. AFL-CIO officials were gleeful over his exit from the Senate, suggesting that the union's money and manpower had crushed Ohio's greatest vote-getter. A top aide of Vice President Hubert Humphrey asserted, "Lausche was just not relevant to modern America."[6] An acquaintance of the Senator's blamed Lausche's defeat on his refusal to adapt his philosophy to present-day realities. He quoted the White House as having said, "Hell, we've been trying to get him to change for the last five years."[7]

Possibly Tom Vail, publisher and editor of the *Plain Dealer*, said it best, "The younger generation has the ballot box and will use it as never before."[8]

Two columnists gave contrasting views of the deposed Senator. Syndicated columnist James J. Kilpatrick described Lausche as a restless conservative with the air of a statesman who looked like a solo pianist or great conductor with his hands always in motion. "He is known as a pragmatist, a savvy campaigner, a competent middle-of-the-roader with broad appeal across the Republican spectrum." Anticipating a William Saxbe victory in the general election, Kilpatrick wrote, "He [Saxbe] won't bring to the Senate the color, the verve and the bare-knuckled spirit of Ohio's little giant. In the lovely hurly-burly of the Hill, Lausche has fought the good fight. It's a pity to see him knocked out."[9]

"Over my desk...has hung the advice that Polonius gave to Laertes, 'To thine own self be true and it must follow as night follows day thou canst not be false to any man.'"

Don Robertson, writing for the Cleveland *Press*, was considerably more acerbic in his evaluation of Lausche. Calling the Senator an obstructionist and reactionary, Robertson contended Lausche had outlived his time—if he ever really had one. "He was aloof. He was too old. He was too much the creature of the newspapers and the fat cats (most of them Republican). His Claghorn rhetoric had become anachronistic. The voters had become too sophisticated; they no longer accepted the old clichés about 'bosses' and 'independence' and all that jazz."[10] Robertson noted that Lausche had been on the ballot only once in the past twelve years. A new generation had come of age in this period of time. The Lausche magic had no meaning to this younger element.

Lausche trudged through the remaining months of his tenure. He seemed lonely and forlorn, retreating from the world. He kept up with his daily tasks, made an occasional speech and participated in senate debate until the November election. Those who knew him well said he was merely going through the motions. Away from the senate he remained in virtual seclusion. He stopped seeing long-time friends and was out of touch with newsmen he had known so well.

A telephone conversation between Lausche and a Washington newsman illuminated his state of mind. The newsman suggested they talk about the election year (1968), the Democratic Party's ticket and other political matters. Lausche responded that he would not speak out on political issues for the remainder of the year.[11] That statement was likely true with one exception. Lausche knew how to generate a news story. On October 15, the deposed Senator dispatched a press release stating that he would vote for Republican Richard Nixon for President. He believed Nixon was best equipped to handle the grave problems besetting the nation. The former Vice President would take a new and uncommitted look at the Vietnam issue, eliminate extravagant and unjustified spending and lead the country out of its quagmire. Defending his choice Lausche said, "I am first of all an American citizen. When my country faces a crisis involving its future life, I cease to be a political partisan. In this crisis there is neither a Republican nor Democratic side but only an American side."[12] The Senator's announcement came as no surprise to those who had followed his voting predilections. To the press, Lausche's reasoning behind his support for Nixon tortured the record, at best. He showed the same knack for stirring up the wrath of his own party members. At the same time, he gained support of the opposition party that had stood him in such good stead for more than 20 years. Lausche would cross party lines several more times in his retirement years.

It is doubtful that Lausche's unexpected removal from office was a major issue in his choice for President. Once Lausche had decided, in his mind, that Nixon was the best of the three presidential candidates (Nixon, Hubert Humphrey and George Wallace), he would in all probability have endorsed him regardless of his own political standing. That was the nature of this enigmatic individual. During his tenure in the senate, Lausche danced to his own tune, moving from one side of the aisle to the other as his conscience dictated. He assisted the Republicans in their right-to-work laws, thus enraging organized labor. His long-time friends at the Slovenian National Home took his pictures down from the walls. An avid anti-communist, he supported Lyndon Johnson's escalation of the war in Vietnam, but he had little use for the President's Great Society programs. Lausche had imperceptible sympathy for the social unrest of the sixties—flag burners and draft dodgers infuriated him—and had little understanding of the poor.[13]

The 90th Congress adjourned on October 19 due to the presidential election. Lausche and Republican Thurston Morton, his neighboring senator from Kentucky, cast their last official votes on matters foreign and domestic. In 1981 after Reagan defeated Carter for the presidency, Lausche reiterated his viewpoint about fiscal responsibility. "In the 12 years I spent in the Senate, I said at least 200 times that the time would come when an atonement would have to be made for the extravagant spending. That has been proven by the inflation we are suffering."[14] Lausche would be disappointed in the next eight years because, although Reagan's administration helped to bring about a moderate reduction in inflation, at the same time Reagan accrued one of the highest deficits in the country's history.

Lausche had come to view his senate tenure with a sense of regret. "Among the most miserable and painful days of my entire political life were spent in the U.S. Senate," he reminisced in an interview in 1985. "I was surrounded by 70 extravagant spendthrifts of the Democratic Party. Day after day I had to keep fighting against their spending, foretelling that the day would come when atonement would be demanded for their misdeeds. Day after day I was beaten, dreadfully. I was left totally unable to devote time to constructive new projects."[15]

PRIOR TO LEAVING HIS SENATE OFFICE, FRANK AND JANE had indicated they would move back to Cleveland. They found difficulty in cutting all of their ties in Washington, DC. The couple changed their minds and decided to stay in Bethesda and make frequent trips back to Cleveland, particularly to visit relatives and friends. Frank enjoyed playing golf at Burning Tree Country Club. After having lived in the nation's capitol for twelve years, Jane had many friends and enjoyed the social whirl that prevailed in Washington, DC. The Senator's wife intimated that after 35 years in politics, her husband and she were having a ball. After a few months the Lausches began to spend about equal time in the two cities.

Lausche opened a law office with the Frost and Tower firm in Washington, DC. This partnership represented James Lemon, owner of the Washington Senators baseball franchise in his sale of the team to Robert Short. In Cleveland he practiced law with his brother Charles, who was an attorney with an office in the Fidelity Building in downtown Cleveland. Unfortunately Charles lived for only a few more months, dying on July 25, 1969. The deposed Senator did not foresee that his legal responsibilities required him to register with Congress as a lobbyist. "I've never been idle and I don't want to go stale now. I want to keep occupied and in the midst of action."[16] The legal cases Lausche accepted were neither large nor overly remunerative. He soon found that the esteem in which he had been held as governor and senator meant little in the courtroom. One of Lausche's first clients was controversial Cyrus Eaton. At issue was a challenge by Eaton, a major stockholder in the Cleveland Trust Company. He objected to the bank's practice of voting blocks of its own stock held in trust for other interests when electing bank directors. Lausche became interested in the Eaton case after he had written a letter of protest to the Ohio Banker's Association. His personal views in opposition to bloc voting were consistent with his stand on this issue in the senate. "It is absolutely wrong to countenance conditions in the management of a bank where, through the bank's hold of stock in a trust capacity, bank officers are able to forever perpetuate themselves in office."[17]

"Among the most miserable and painful days of my entire political life were spent in the U.S. Senate," he reminisced in an interview in 1985. "I was surrounded by 70 extravagant spendthrifts of the Democratic Party.

Eaton won two early rounds in lower courts. In March 1970, the Ohio Supreme Court upheld the Cleveland Trust's policy. Eaton sold his stock. The U.S. Justice Department charged the bank with antitrust violations because it controlled stock in four competing machine tool companies and the bank's alleged role in the merger of the Cleveland Trust Drill Company and National Acme Company. The first case of its kind, the suit challenged a practice widespread in the banking industry of maintaining interlocking directorates and control over corporate stock. The suit was settled in 1975 when the Justice Department dismissed all but one issue. The bank agreed to refuse to hire any director who sat on the boards of two or more machine-tool companies.[18]

Now a private citizen, Lausche continued to speak out on issues of concern to him. In April 1969 he wrote a letter to Tom Vail of the *Plain Dealer* lauding the newspaper for printing a series of articles about how oil companies pay half-rate taxes. An analysis of 40 oil companies showed that these companies in 1967 paid federal income tax at an average rate of 8.2 percent. Several companies paid no taxes. The 1968 tax percentage paid by family and individual wage earners amounted to approximately 14 percent.

Lausche remembered how, when he entered the senate in 1957, Senator Paul Douglas (Dem-IL) and John Williams (Rep-DE) pointed out shameful inequities of oil firms enjoying huge incomes from their businesses, but paying no income tax. "For twelve years straight I joined with other senators...denouncing this special privilege—shameful and scandalous—granted by the Congress of the United States." Lausche pointed out that President Johnson, coming from an oil-producing state, never uttered a word in denunciation of these special privileges. He continued, "Senators Robert Kerr of Oklahoma and Russell Long of Louisiana, who both represented large oil producing states... were able through their high offices to stop any effort...to change the law." The law in 1969 provided a 27½% tax exemption to the oil companies. The former Senator added that, "The oil companies...with shameful unjustification, have been granted the privilege of saying that they should not be taxed because the oil which they had taken out of their lands constituted a depletion of their capital holdings."[19]

"As a boy in school, I learned about the Ten Commandments and about devotion to my country.... Now I find myself in the dismal position of hearing people say these teachings of my youth are meaningless and do not belong in the modern day. Well, I don't believe it."

To Lausche this logic was an insult and an affront to the intelligence of U.S. citizens. He rejoined, "The man who works in the factory depletes the strength of his body—after the age of 45 and 50 his ability to find employment is practically gone. No tax exemption has been granted to the worker on the assumption he had depleted and exhausted his capital structures."[20] The former Senator believed it was a crime that oil magnates—who garnered millions of dollars through the extraction of oil from the ground and due to an indefensible tax exemption law—had in many instances not paid a penny of income taxes. Again Lausche was on the losing side of improper and seemingly unfair malfeasance by Congress. In this particular case, instead of railing against organized labor, Lausche showed that he could attack industry and the rich boys, when he believed an injustice was being perpetrated.

In late 1969 rumors spread that Lausche might be tempted to run for a sixth term as governor the following year began to surface. This speculation was prompted by the fact that many county party leaders found neither Robert Sweeney of Cleveland nor John Gilligan politically attractive. Jane Lausche confirmed that her husband received much encouragement to return to the political scene. She insisted that she was not one of those encouraging him to run. Lausche left the door open with the anticipation of a groundswell of support for his candidacy. Lausche, in a letter to the Wall Street *Journal*, wrote that the plain, simple and ordinary citizens of Ohio who were extraordinarily potent in their influence were urging him to run for the governor's office. "Representing the Republican, the Democratic and the Independent sections of our political spectrum, I am giving neither encouragement or discouragement to the many letters which I am receiving from these several sectors of the electorate."[21] Whatever momentum developed for Lausche to run for governor soon faded. John Gilligan was selected by the Democrats to run for the office against state auditor Roger Cloud. It wasn't much of a contest as Gilligan easily defeated his Republican opponent. Gilligan lost the governorship in 1974 to James Rhodes in an extremely tight race (difference of 11,488 votes).

In the broader spectrum of political life in the nation's capitol, Lausche tended to live a quiet and undisturbed life. Gilligan could not recall many political figures of Lausche's stature who dropped off the political stage so dramatically.[22] Lausche's non-involvement in the Ohio Democratic Party made his exile much easier. He was thoroughly content to occupy his position as a retired public official. However, Lausche could not restrain himself on occasions to comment on the social and political upheaval present in the country, particularly evident in the polarization over the long-suffering Vietnam War. "My mind has not become clouded to the extent that I will allow it to succomb (sic) to the preachments of the demagogues now occupying high public office—and especially several of them in the Senate... who think more of their personal advancements than they think of the security of our nation."[23]

The veteran politician who had continuously countenanced friendship of the press was always ready to speak out on subjects of vital concern to him. He seldom failed to advocate economy, old-fashioned morality and American patriotism. Speaking at the 13th Annual Governor's Breakfast in Boston in 1973, Lausche told attendees the teachings of the *Bible* and devotion to one's country still had a place in modern society. "As a boy in school, I learned about the Ten Commandments and about devotion to my country.... Now I find myself in the dismal position of hearing people say these teachings of my youth are meaningless and do not belong in the modern day. Well, I don't believe it."[24]

Referring to societies that fell because of decadence and debauchery, the former governor emphasized, "Now in the 20th Century, we cannot accept the argument that patriotism is old-fashioned; that the flag is a rag and should be burned and that pornography does not give harm to youth and womanhood."[25] Lausche never wavered in his admonition of pornography in whatever form. He praised local citizens in Cleveland, who in the late 1960s picketed Broadway Theater for fourteen days in protest of showing an obscene film. This protest caused the theater and two adult bookstores to close, if only for a temporary period.

Lausche vowed that if he were still in the senate, "I would not vote for the approval of Mr. [Abe] Fortas as either justice or chief justice of the Supreme Court if he was my own brother."[26] He represented producers of prurient and pornographic films. As a judge, Fortas issued a ruling, which made conviction of purveyors of pornographic materials nearly impossible. Lausche maintained the distribution of x-rated materials would only increase so long as the Supreme Court turned its head on this issue. Reminiscing, Lausche proclaimed, "When I was a judge I sent men to the penitentiary for showing pornographic movies. Now that is all wrong."[27] Lausche was not prudish. He just believed that such lascivious materials were immoral, were of no redeeming value and contributed to deterioration of a society. Lausche would be appalled at what viewers in contemporary society see on television and at the movies. The well-meaning efforts of organizations such as the Media Research Center, led by ultra-conservative Brent Bozell III, cause a mere ripple in an endeavor to eradicate offensive materials from public view. Nationwide efforts to stem an avalanche of pornography for public consumption have brought strong protests from proponents of the First Amendment of the Constitution. This issue is never-ending and not soon to be resolved to the satisfaction of naysayers.

⁂

LAUSCHE WAS OFTEN GOOD FOR A QUOTE OR TWO regarding presidential elections. In 1972 he repudiated George McGovern (his party's candidate) and endorsed President Nixon for a second term. He believed the security and welfare of Americans would best be served by re-election of President Nixon. "The President has taken long steps in terms of bringing peace in the world. He has lessened the tension between our country and Russia and China...."[28] Lausche was particularly critical of McGovern, who stood for most issues Lausche opposed. He believed McGovern was indecisive and inconsistent on his policy statements.

Two years earlier in 1970, Lausche further alienated himself with the State Democratic Party. He had agreed to serve as co-chairman of the Ohio Citizens for Republican Bob Taft, Jr. for a U.S. senate seat. The retired Senator called Taft "an expert in congressional work" and declared his character as unimpeachable.[29] Lausche's support of Taft may have been a deciding factor in this election. Taft defeated James Rhodes in the primary election by 5,200 votes one day after the Kent State tragedy. Taft went on to defeat Howard Metzenbaum in the general election by 74,000 votes out of more than 3 million votes cast a difference of two percentage points.

Lausche continued his maverick ways in 1976. Democratic candidate Jimmy

Carter's ambivalent remarks did not set well with Lausche. While trying to build his campaign on the issue of morality, Carter gave an interview for *Playboy*, a magazine representing the antithesis of Lausche's values. At the 1976 Democratic convention Lausche described how Carter glowingly praised the services Lyndon Johnson had rendered as president. Conversely in Carter's interview with *Playboy*, he called Johnson a liar and a cheat. On another occasion in his home state of Georgia, Carter supported the worker's right to work without being required to join a union. When he became a candidate for president, Carter declared his opposition to the right-to-work principle. Lausche gave other examples where Carter took opposing positions on the same issue (a stance for which Lausche himself was often chastised). For these reasons Lausche wrote an open letter in support of Gerald Ford. The Democrats for Ford organization in several Midwestern states distributed this letter.[30]

Lausche believed Ford, who replaced the deposed Nixon, entered office under circumstances that would have overwhelmed a less courageous and firm personality. Lausche received a call from Ford ten days prior to the primary in Ohio asking for his public endorsement. Ford knew he needed to carry Ohio to offset an anticipated loss of California votes to challenger Ronald Reagan. Lausche gladly acceded to the President's request. His endorsement no doubt helped Ford easily secure the primary. Prior to the general election in October, Lausche accompanied Ford on Air Force One during one of his campaign trips for the presidency.

At a pre-election rally for Ford at the statehouse in Columbus, Lausche diehards were embarrassed by the Senator's rambling comments in response to an introduction by the President. He commandeered the microphone and rattled on interminably while Ford stood by laughing. The primarily young crowd's reaction indicated that most of them had no idea who Frank Lausche was.[31] Sadly, his efforts were for naught. Jimmy Carter carried Ohio by a narrow margin of 11,000 votes.

Lausche again supported Senator Robert Taft, Jr. for re-election to the U.S. senate in 1976. He appeared with the incumbent Republican during a campaign swing through Cleveland in late October. Taft's opponent was Howard Metzenbaum, the ebullient and wealthy attorney-businessman from Cleveland. As a true FDR-style liberal Metzenbaum's political philosophy clashed sharply with that of Lausche's. Taft's health became a factor in his bid for this senate seat. He had suffered a heart attack the previous year.

The Republican Party was still reeling from fallout as a result of the Watergate scandal. In late 1973 incumbent Senator William Saxbe was coerced by capitol Republicans to accept the U.S. Attorney General's position. This change in Nixon's cabinet occurred a few months before his resignation from the presidency, thus leaving Saxbe's senatorial seat vacant. Governor Gilligan appointed Metzenbaum to fill this vacancy effective January 1974. In the fall of that year, astronaut John Glenn denied Metzenbaum the Democratic nomination for a full term. Metzenbaum turned the tables in 1976 by upsetting Taft in the general election. Lausche's support for Taft was in vain. Metzenbaum had fallen to Taft by two percentage points in 1970. Metzenbaum's political colleagues affectionately referred to him as the Tiger of the Senate. Senator Ted Stevens (Rep-AK), in a less friendly tone, called the Ohioan a "pain in the ass." The innovative Metzenbaum, who in 1976 had aligned with Carter and his Vice Presidential candidate, Walter "Fritz" Mondale, distributed bumper stickers that might have better suited a delicatessen: Fritz, Grits, and Metz.[32]

Lausche did not forget his friends in Cleveland, continuously crossing party lines. He supported what is considered the last of the Lausche clones, Ralph Perk, a Czech and Republican for mayor of Cleveland in his three successful elections (1971–1977). Perk reciprocated by proclaiming, "[Lausche] is the George Washington of the nationality people of the United States. He paved the way for people like Czechs, Poles, and Bohemians to make their way in politics."[33] In 1977 Perk lost in a nonpartisan primary to Democrats Dennis Kucinich and Edward Feighan. Kucinich won the general election to become the youngest big city mayor (1978) in the country at that time. Elected to the U.S. house of representatives in 1996, Kucinich ran unsuccessfully as a presidential candidate in 2004.

In 1978 Lausche endorsed James Rhodes, his friend and former political adversary, for governor. The two political titans remained friends throughout their twilight years. The only Ohio governor to serve longer than Lausche's 10 years, Rhodes patterned himself after his Democratic friend, often straddling the political fence. In a speech given in Cleveland, Rhodes said no one had contributed more dignity, honesty and administrative savy to the governor's office than Lausche had. In this campaign Lausche turned his back on Democrat Richard Celeste, fellow Clevelander and Lieutenant Governor. Calling for leadership that would unite Ohioans Lausche said, "To create this unified action, Rhodes is far better equipped than Celeste."[34] He defended Rhode's action in calling out the Ohio National Guard, which tragically resulted in the Kent State deaths of May 1970. Lausche emphasized that had he been Governor, he would have responded in a like manner. Governor Rhodes narrowly defeated Celeste. In a comeback effort in the 1986 election Celeste soundly defeated Rhodes. In his final public statements on political candidates, Lausche announced his endorsement of Ronald Reagan in 1980 and 1984. He chastised Carter for "failing miserably to control domestic problems of inflation and unemployment."[35]

Lausche confessed no remorse over his record of endorsing Republicans. He added that if he were a young man starting out in politics today he probably would join the Republican Party. "On the basis of past experiences, the Republican Party has shown a greater purpose to be conservative and frugal with the taxpayers money. Parties change and times change. The Democratic Party is far from dead...it is beginning to realize it needs a more conservative approach."[36] Lausche was somewhat prophetic with his comments, but not in the way he would have anticipated. The Republican administrations became the big spenders, and the Democrats became more budget conscious. Reagan's record deficit surely rankled the conservative Lausche. Twelve years later Democratic President William Clinton departed from the presidency with a financial surplus, a first in many decades. In 2004 as Republican George W. Bush prepared for his second term, Clinton's surplus of $236 billion had plunged into a deficit of $422 billion.[37]

Outside the political arena Lausche embraced several projects he cherished. He and Jane had been determined to set up a memorial fund in honor of his mother Frances Lausche, and he arranged for the funds to be apportioned to needy and deserving students wishing to attend college. At a later date he expanded the memorial fund to include Jane and himself as part of a foundation. Still in existence, the foundation has grown significantly over the years under the direction of Jim and Madeline Debevec, family friends and publishers of *American Home*.

In 1972 Lausche supported and encouraged a movement to save Malabar Farm and to allow the state to preserve the 630-acre homestead as an historical conservation site. Lausche had visited the farm numerous times when his friends Louis Bromfield and his wife were alive. An early conservationist himself, Lausche remembered that, "...in the area of Louis Bromfield's Malabar farm...scientific farming was promoted more than anywhere else.... Bromfield, in his novels, public speaches (sic), newspaper columns and private discussions everywhere was supporting the conservation of our natural resources, far ahead of the present strident cries of latecomers promoting the program."[38] Under the leadership of Governor Gilligan and with donations from tobacco heiress Doris Duke and actor James Cagney, the property was saved from the auctioneer's gavel. The Samuel R. Noble Foundation of Ardmore, Oklahoma, agreed to purchase the entire farm from the Malabar Farm Foundation and donated the $1.5 million property to the state. The farm became a state park in 1976 operated by the Ohio Department of Natural Resources.[39]

> "[Lausche] is the George Washington of the nationality people of the United States. He paved the way for people like Czechs, Poles, and Bohemians to make their way in politics."

UPON HIS EXIT FROM THE SENATE, Lausche became more involved with Slovenian-related activities in the capitol. Four prominent Slovenian-Americans residing in Washington, DC befriended him. Dr. Cyril A. Zebot, prominent economics professor at Georgetown University, advised Lausche on issues related to Slovenia's political fortunes. The Mejac brothers, Cyril and Conrad, were both leaders in promoting Slovenian cultural and religious activities in the Capitol. A fourth

Slovenian-American, Stanley Sustersic, met Lausche in Cleveland before moving to Washington, DC. All four men and their families were helpful in making the Lausches feel welcomed in the local Slovenian community.

Many Slovenian-Americans in Washington, DC met Lausche for the first time in August 1971 when, after years of diligent effort and with Lausche's support, a Slovenian chapel was dedicated in the Basilica of the National Shrine of the Immaculate Conception. This national shrine is the largest and most prominent Catholic monument in the United States. Dedication of this chapel came twelve hundred years after Slovenes embraced Christianity and were reborn into a new cultural identity. Our Lady of Brezje was the Patroness of Slovenia, and this monument serves as a testament to Slovenian religious and cultural heritage. Lausche's remarks at the dedication banquet gave high praise to the most important traits of Slovenian national character.[40]

Slovenian-American population in metropolitan Washington, DC was small in number. The Washington branch of the Slovenian Women's Union sponsored programs of interest to which Lausche's presence was an inspiration. He and Jane were faithful in attending the yearly Slovenian heritage evening. The Senator assisted this group in formulating their charter in 1974.[41] Slovenian Vladimir Pregelj, who worked in the Library of Congress, was an early president of the heritage committee. He gained nationwide notoriety when he served as foreman of the Watergate grand jury.[42]

Lausche loved the music of his parents' homeland, seldom missing a performance by the Washington, DC Slovenian Choral Club or an occasional visit from the Slovenian Singing Society (Gallus) from Carinthia, Austria. Lausche conveyed his feelings about Slovenian songs, "When my soul becomes heavy and my mind is in distress, and heaviness surrounds me and I feel that the light will never shine again, if I have good fortune of going to the Slovenian concert...the darkness disappears, the heaviness is gone, the lightness is with me and the soul becomes frequently clean by the tears I shed as I hear the songs that I once heard at my mother's knee."[43] Lausche's love of Slovenia both in song and word had prompted him to pursue the beauty of poetry. He was especially fond of France Preseren, Slovenia's poet laureate and transplanted Clevelander Ivan Zorman's poetry, which captured his fervid love for Slovenia.

In spite of Lausche's love for his mother's country, he was adamant in his refusal to visit Slovenia. He turned down numerous invitations, including an opportunity to represent officially the United States government at the opening of an American library in Ljubljana. Slovenia was still under the aegis of Yugoslavia and Marshall Tito. Lausche refused to be involved in any situation where he was giving any credence or recognition to Communists, particularly to Marshall Tito. He refused an invitation from President Tito to visit Yugoslavia. Lausche's good friend Dr. Zebot had implored Lausche to consider sending a message of encouragement to the

Slovenian people. Yugoslavia was on the threshold of throwing aside the yoke of Communism. This country would break up into republics, Slovenia being one of that group. For whatever reason, Lausche rejected Zebot's plea for a message from the most prominent Slovenian-American in the United States. His stance brought back memories of his propensity to straddle the fence on political issues.

Lausche preferred to devote his energies to praise of personages who resisted Communism. One such person was General Draja Mihailovich, a Serbian leader during World War II. In an oversimplified interpretation of the General's leadership, Mihailovich and his Chetnik movement were accused of not standing up to the Germans in the way Tito's Communist Partisans had done. Historians of Tito's career had successfully documented this version of the truth in the postwar era. In some areas the Chetniks fought courageously in opposition both to the Nazis and the Partisans in a struggle against totalitarianism in the Balkans.

In 1946 while governor of Ohio, Lausche was a signator to a committee for a fair trial for Mihailovich. Among members of this committee were noted columnist Dorothy Thompson, former Undersecretary of State Sumner Welles, House Representative Mike Mansfield, Senator Robert Taft, philosopher John Dewey, and AFL President William Green. The committee's efforts were ignored. The martyred Mihailovich was considered an enemy of Tito's Communist Partisan Army. Ill with typhus, Mihailovich was captured in March 1946 and brought to trial on July 15, 1946, before a commission of inquiry in Belgrade. This trial was described as a mockery. The Serbian leader was sentenced to death, and on July 17 fell before a firing squad.

Twenty years later the Serbian leader's accomplishments were brought to the public's attention. Congressman Edward J. Derwinski (Rep-IL) released a citation signed by President Truman in March 1948 awarding the Legion of Merit posthumously to General Mihailovich. The citation commended the general for his outstanding leadership as commander-in-chief of the Yugoslavian army forces and later as minister of war. He had organized and led important resistance forces against the Nazis. Through the dauntless efforts of his troops, many U.S. airmen were rescued and returned to friendly allies. Although lacking adequate supplies and fighting under extreme hardships, Mihailovich and his forces contributed materially to the Allied cause.[44] Mihailovich had launched his national resistance movement on May 15, 1941, hard on the heels of German occupation of Yugoslavia.

Lausche joined several dignitaries on July 17, 1974, to speak on Capitol Hill in a memorial service honoring the Serbian patriot. The National Committee of Airmen rescued by General Mihailovich during World War II organized this event. Over 500 airmen had been rescued. More than 1,000 Serbs from the United States and Canada gathered to pay homage to their heroic resistance leader.

The following year the Serbian Democratic Forum, an appendage of the Serbian National Committee, published a somewhat biased monograph on General

Mihailovich and his wartime heroics. Lausche wrote the forward to this publication. He expressed disdain over allied foreign policy on this particular issue. "As an American, I bow my head in shame whenever I think of the terribly mistaken policy which led the Allied leaders in World War II to abandon General Draja Mihailovich and throw their support instead to the communist cohorts of Marshall Josip Bros Tito. It was an unbelievable aberration of policy and of justice perpetrated by the Allies."[45] Lausche pointed out that Mihailovich resisted the Nazis at a time when the Soviet Union and Communists were still collaborating with the Third Reich. His early resistance delayed the Nazi timetable and may have been partially responsible for preventing the fall of Moscow to the Nazis.[46]

Revisionist historians support Lausche's lament. British Prime Minister Winston Churchill received much of the blame for not providing more support to Mihailovich. In route to Turkey in January 1944, Churchill stopped in Cairo where he consulted with his former research assistants Captain William F. Deakin and Colonel C.M. (Bolo) Keble about the situation inside Yugoslavia. As a result of this meeting and classified reports, Churchill decided to open direct contacts through Deakin with the Communist resistance movement under Tito. This decision proved to be the first step whereby the British began to abandon General Mihailovich and his Chetniks in favor of Tito with momentous consequences for the postwar period.[47] Noted British historian John Charmley explained Churchill's reason for changing allegiance to resistance leaders in Yugoslavia, "Churchill [was not] worried about the implications of the support which he had given...Tito. Churchill would like to have told him that he was breaking off relations with Mihailovich, but the [British] Foreign Office was reluctant to do so, but he did tell Tito that he was ceasing to send any military aid to the Chetniks...that Yugoslavia would be under communist rule in the postwar world, appeared not to worry Churchill at all; his optimism about the Soviets blinded him to anything save the hope that backing Tito would be the best way to tie down German divisions."[48]

In the short run, Churchill's decision may have served the Allies well. Lausche did not agree. He preferred that history record the truth about one of the heroic figures of World War II. In Lausche's view Mihailovich's actions inspired the formation of resistance movements in other subjugated countries.

⌒

IN SPITE OF TITO'S IRONCLAD HOLD on Communist Yugoslavia after World War II, Lausche was instrumental in helping keep the spirit of freedom alive in Slovenia. The mode for inspiring this freedom was to broadcast to Slovenia via Radio Free Europe (RFE), which originated in the '40s. Financed by the U.S. government, these broadcasts were designed to provide propaganda information, particularly to countries behind the Iron Curtain. Prominent Americans—in and out of government—promoted these broadcasts in the face of Soviet Union's rapid postwar efforts to establish complete hegemony over Eastern Europe. Impositions of the Berlin blockade and Communist takeover in Czechoslovakia in 1948 were two of the more dramatic manifestations of Soviet aggression.

Massive Soviet military presence dominated Eastern Europe, and more than 100 million people were isolated from the outside world. The Iron Curtain was characterized by censorship, pervasive secret police, strict border controls, and monopoly of all means of public communication in Soviet-controlled territories. Nationalities living behind the Iron Curtain during the Cold War heard and read only Communist propaganda. They saw only Communist movies and learned about the outside world only from information slanted by the Communist-controlled news media.

Under the leadership of George Kennan, an important figure in the state department, and Joseph C. Grew, former Ambassador to Japan, RFE had become a reality. President Truman authorized these broadcasts by a bill signed on January 27, 1948 (United States Information and Education Act, Public Law 402, 80th Congress). Under the aegis of a national committee for a free Europe, RFE began broadcasting to satellite countries behind the Iron Curtain. Eventually these broadcasts would be aired in eleven languages. By 1972 RFE broadcasted on an average of 15 hours a day to five Eastern European countries—namely Bulgaria, Czechoslovakia, Hungary, Poland, and Romania.[49]

The program was not without its critics, both in Communist countries and within the United States. With only moderate success the Soviet Union attempted to jam the broadcasts. In May 1960, Cyrus Eaton told a news conference in Budapest that no propaganda or military force could change the structure of the Communist countries. "The United States must radically revise its foreign policy, future U.S. foreign policy should be based on respect for other forms of government and that all propaganda vehicles such as Radio Free Europe and the Voice of America (VOA) should be abolished."[50]

The most serious threat to the continuance of the European broadcasts was Senator J. William Fulbright whose opposition stemmed from financial concerns about his pet program, the Fulbright Exchange Program. The United States Information and Education Exchange Act of 1948 had authorized the state department to seek appropriations to supplement the Fulbright grants. His exchange agenda was suffering acutely from lack of funds for individual stipends and new and enlarged programs.

Consequently, from 1950 through 1954, the junior senator from Arkansas played the dangerous game of pushing student and faculty exchange while denigrating the activities of VOA and RFE. In the summer of 1950 Fulbright rose on the floor of the senate and denounced America's two overseas networks. "I think the Europeans have an instinctive resistance to official propaganda and that we are wasting our money," he wrote Senator Richard Russell (Dem-GA).[51] Later in the summer he and Senator William Benton (Dem-CN) introduced a resolution declaring America's overseas propaganda agencies deficient in every respect.[52]

Fulbright overplayed his hand. The house of representatives cut the information program, including Fulbright's cherished exchange program by $34 million. Baffled by what he called the perversity of the lower house, Fulbright led an internationalist counter attack against cuts in the information program he had previously denounced. In part as a result of Fulbright's efforts, the house-senate conference committee raised the appropriation from $63 million to $85 million.[53]

For Lausche, Zebot and their Slovenian colleagues, there was constant fear that the VOA would be discontinued in languages of a number of countries and/or republics, such as Albania, Slovenia, and Georgia (USSR). One year after Lausche entered the senate, Zebot wrote to President Eisenhower imploring him not to drop this program to the smaller Eastern European countries. "If this plan is put into effect, it will be in overt opposition to your repeated insistence on the essential equality of small nations." The Georgetown economist added, "Such a silencing of the Voice of America to small peoples would come to them as a shock and would unavoidably be interpreted by them as de facto declaration of no interest on the part of the United Sates."[54] Eisenhower yielded to their pleas and allowed these programs to continue.

> "The paltry $80,000 savings allegedly realized by the abolition of the VOA Slovene broadcasts should not continue to be used by the USIA (United States Information Agency) or as an excuse for non-compliance with such a mandate."

Along with legislative and non-legislative advocates, Lausche and Zebot kept the broadcasts alive through the 1960s and early 1970s. Noted correspondents provided favorable reviews. Reporter for the Los Angeles *Times* Robert S. Elegant wrote that it was unfortunate that these radio broadcasts were criticized by "men of good will who champion free exchange of ideas and want to end the Cold War."[55] David Halberstam gave glowing endorsement to the radio broadcasts. He had become acquainted with RFE broadcasts during a stint as correspondent for the *New York Times* in Warsaw. Halberstam countered arguments advanced by Fulbright on the validity of the broadcasts. Fulbright derided the broadcasts as propaganda tools. Halberstam suggested information released by RFE compared favorably to NBC, CBS, or the *Times* for performance and accountability in the Cold War era.[56]

Zebot's sustained efforts helped keep the daily half-hour broadcasts (VOA) afloat until 1975, at which time Congress decided to terminate these broadcasts. Lausche and Zebot went into action again to have this decision reversed. These two advocates appeared before the Foreign Relations Committee in late April and early May testifying for the reinstatement of, as Lausche described, "a measly one-half hour of radio broadcasts by the U.S. Information Agency to Slovenia, my parents' ancestral home."[57] Lausche maintained that Slovenia was important to Yugoslavia and that the constitution of Yugoslavia provided that there should be three national languages, one of which was Slovenia (the other two were Croatian and Serbian). Lausche further stated, "...yet our government tells these humble small number of Slovenes you are not worthy to be talked to.... It is psychological trauma upon the dignity and decency of these people."[58] Lausche knew an argument had been put forth asserting that the United States was already friendly with Slovenia. He continued, "I tried to induce Mr. [William] Rogers [Secretary of State] to install a consulate in Ljubljana... but he decided not to do so. He put in an information center instead. The information center has one United States staff man, three local Slovenes. That is a poor substitute for the one half hour a day broadcast to the Slovenes."[59]

Lausche left the hearing room, and in a rare moment of levity he thanked the committee, chaired by John Sparkman (Dem-AL) commenting, "This is a novel position for me...and I'm glad you men did not go after me with embarrassing questions." The committee laughed as Lausche added, "As I did sometimes when I was up there." Sparkman responded, "I have never seen anybody get you down."[60] Lausche followed his appearance at the senate committee hearings with a short letter to Sparkman. In support of his argument for reinstatement of the broadcasts, the usually budget conscious Lausche pleaded, "The paltry $80,000 savings allegedly realized by the abolition of the VOA Slovene broadcasts should not continue to be used by the USIA (United States Information Agency) or as an excuse for non-compliance with such a mandate."[61]

Although appreciative of Lausche's persuasive arguments, James Keough, Director of USIA, countered that Serbia-Croatia was the native language of three-fourths of the Yugoslav population, many of whom lived in geographically isolated areas. VOA broadcasts proved to be the only practical way to provide information about the United States to these outlying territories. The director pointed out that Slovenes represented less than eight percent of the Yugoslavian population. These inhabitants—because of their location near Austria and Italy—had relatively easy access to a variety of western European sources for information.[62]

VOA broadcasts to Slovenia were discontinued for the remainder of 1975. The perseverance of the Slovenian bloc continued. In January 1976 the 94th Congress specifically mandated (HR. Bill 11598) that the USIA, through the VOA, reinstate daily one-half hour broadcasts to Slovenia. After having been silent for nearly a year, these broadcasts resumed on February 29 in twice daily installments of fifteen minutes each. Irascible and powerful House Representative Wayne Hays (no relation to Wayne Woodrow Hayes, the former Ohio State University football coach) from Ohio's eastern Eighteenth Congressional District provided strong support for this legislation. Thanking Hays for his help on the Voice of America reinstatement, Lausche wrote, "I am receiving no compensation of any character...for the voluminous work my participation entailed. What I have done all comes under the title—work rendered for the good of the U.S.A."[63]

Lausche's work was not yet finished. Budgetary cuts under the Reagan administration in 1986 threatened discontinuation of Slovenian broadcasts. The elderly statesman appealed to Charles Z. Wick, Director of the United States Information Agency. He wrote letters of appeal to selected Senators, house representatives and Frank Carlucci, assistant to President Reagan for National Security Affairs.[64] Following a series of letter exchanges, the weekend broadcasts were again reinstated. This successful effort would be the 90-year-old politician's last hurrah. Continued presence of Communism in Eastern Europe began to dissipate. By the late 1980s the Soviets found the need for jamming radio broadcasts increasingly difficult to justify. This fact became particularly true when Premier Mikhail Gorbachev initiated his policy of *glasnost*. With neither warning nor fanfare, the Soviet Union stopped jamming foreign radio broadcasts in November 1988, including those of Radio Liberty. Gorbachev encountered stiff resistance from the KGB (Committee for State Security) and old guard members of the *Politburo*. The premier's arguments against censorship prevailed.[65] Lausche's efforts to protect his family's country from Communism were no longer needed. In 1991 Slovenia gained independence—at long last, a nation free from the encumbering shackles of Communist intervention. The Slovenian-Americans were satisfied and happy with this turn of events.

⌒

IN EXPRESSING HIS BASIC PHILOSOPHY ABOUT government and Democracy, Lausche declared himself a Jeffersonian Democrat. This term could be interpreted in several ways. To Lausche his philosophy "abides substantially with what is the true definition of a Democrat in our country. [He] insists this means giving people their constitutional rights, promoting their welfare and doing it without imposing fat tax bites." Lausche said, "It is one thing for demagoguery to appeal to the passions for the purposes of getting votes. It is another thing to promote fiscal responsibility in the handling of the taxpayers' money."[66]

Lausche was elated that evidence had been uncovered perhaps linking Jefferson's drafting of the Declaration of Independence with an early Democratic custom observed in Carinthia, a province located in what is known in contemporary times as Slovenia. In 1967 Joseph Felicijan, a member of the teaching staff at St. John College, a Sister's College in Cleveland, wrote a book entitled *The Genesis of the Contractual Theory and the Installation of the Dukes of Carinthia*. Felicijan explored the impact of Frenchman Jean Bodin's famous *Republic* published in 1576 upon Jefferson's writing of the Declaration of Independence. He discovered Jefferson had initialed two pages of that document. Bodin had defined and characterized a tyrant on one page. Phrases similar in concept appear in the Declaration of Independence. On the other initialed page was a description of a Slovenian ritual known as the installation of the Dukes of Carinthia. Felicijan hypothesized, "Jefferson evidently considered the ancient ritual...a common law precedent and the Contractual Theory upon which he based his claim for the American Independence."[67] Lausche hypothesized that this ritual might have contributed greatly in helping America's founding fathers establish a new government.

This long-lasting custom practiced by the Slovenian people of Carinthia reflected strong elements of democracy. The Slovenians believed that power to govern rested with the people who were to be governed, not with those who were doing the governing. They further believed that their rulers should be men of all the people, governing with competency and concern. Lausche hypothesized about this theory, whereby a contract existed between those who were to rule and those who were to be ruled. Each party had rights and obligations under this contract. The rulers had the solemn duty to the people to be righteous.[68]

Many objected to this theory, including several of the colonial leaders at the time of the American Revolution. Jefferson may have believed the same way at certain stages of his life. No advanced society had made a contract with those individuals who ruled. Possibly Bodin's descriptions of Slovenian rituals and customs impressed Jefferson in his thinking regarding the nature of democracy. Historians note that the Virginian was affected by writings of John Locke, Jacques Rousseau, and Samuel Pufendorf. To what extent Bodin's treatise influenced Jefferson in drafting the Declaration of Independence remains a mystery. None of Jefferson's noted biographers associate the third U.S. President's writings with Bodin and his *Republic*.

Lack of evidence did not deter Slovenians in Cleveland from acknowledging Bodin and his reputed Slovenian contributions to America's Democratic origin. In honor of America's Bicentennial on May 15, 1976, the Slovenian-American Heritage Foundation dedicated a plaque honoring Bodin's *Republic*. This plaque contained the synthesis of Lausche's comments about Bodin's interpretation of democracy given on the senate floor on November 28, 1967. Lausche's name is inscribed at the bottom of a large plaque located on a high stone at the northwest corner of the mall adjacent to the convention center in downtown Cleveland.

Frank Lausche became the recipient of many honors and awards during his retirement years. To the retired politician, each in its own way carried a special message. He received more than 15 honorary degrees, mostly from Ohio colleges and universities. In 1984 Lasuche received a well-deserved recognition by being selected to the Ohio Natural Resources Hall of Fame. He was remembered for initiating a tree-planting program throughout Ohio beginning in 1953. In 1966 the Ohio Natural Resources Hall of Fame was established by the Ohio Department of Natural Resources. One hundred thirty-two individuals have been named to the Hall of Fame. This honor acknowledged Lausche's lifetime dedication to the preservation, protection, wise management of Ohio's natural resources. Hall of Fame honorees include the legendary Johnny Appleseed, Ohio-born explorer John Wesley Powell, botanist Lucy Braun, and conservationist-novelist Louis Bromfield, and now

Frank J. Lausche. Furthermore, the former lawyer was named a lifetime member of Delta Theta Phi national law fraternity in recognition of his vast service and dedication to public life. One other award pleased Lausche. In 1968, shortly after his defeat in the Democratic primary, the longtime statesman received the Harold Hitz Burton Award for distinguished service in Washington, DC by a Clevelander. This award honors the memory of the former Mayor of Cleveland, U.S. Senator, and Associate Justice of the Supreme Court of the United States. Burton was the first recipient of this award. On accepting his plaque, Lausche spoke with his well known Lausche flair, "Have no sorrow for me. I will be active and asserting, whether in or out of office.... There is no distress in my heart or soul. I never yielded a single bit in my concepts of what was necessary to preserve our country."[69]

Senator Lausche was named a Knight of St. John of Malta by Pope John Paul II, the highest civilian honor that can be bestowed by the Catholic Church. The order had their origins in the tenth century during the Crusades. In 1978 Lausche received a cherished honor—the Slovenian of the year—awarded by the Greater Cleveland Federation of Slovenian Homes. (These social and cultural centers for local Slovenian-Americans serve as a venue for musical and dance performances, political rallies, polka festivals, lodge meetings and special events.) Each of the city's nine national Slovenian homes paid tribute to Lausche as the most prominent Slovenian in the world. In accepting this honor, Lausche commented, "There are one and a half-million Slovenes in the world. It is said they conquered not by the sword, but with a musical instrument. Besides churches and schools, [the Slovenians] wanted cultural centers," and he added, "...they became the halls we have...used to promote the social and economic welfare of our citizens."[70]

An even more significant honor was bestowed upon Lausche with the construction and dedication of the Lausche State Office Building in Cleveland completed in 1979.

Senator Lausche anticipated receiving another award, but the Catholic Knights of Lithuania decided not to present an award to the Senator for a somewhat antiquated reason. The Knights had chosen Lausche to receive an award medal in recognition of his loyalty and friendship toward the cause of Lithuania and her fight for freedom from Communist subjugation. Lausche happily accepted an invitation to receive this award in Cleveland. Several weeks later, Lausche received an apologetic letter informing him the Knights had rescinded their invitation to honor him. An in-depth investigation by this organization determined the excommunicated Senator was living an invalid Catholic marriage. (He was married to a Protestant). Lausche had rejected a number of requests to rectify the marriage with the Catholic Church. He refused to do so. His status as excommunicated member from the church precluded his receiving the award. There is no evidence that Lausche responded to this decision. He never changed his status relative to his marriage and the Catholic Church.[71]

Every five years following Lausche's retirement, friends gathered to honor him with a large birthday party. It was a time to renew acquaintances. On his 85th birthday Lausche spoke of the brevity of life, vanished triumphs and the comfort derived from a peaceful mind, "As each new year comes on, I begin to realize how short life really is. All the things that seemed important when I was young and strong are of no consequence now. When I became a judge, I had thought that was the acme of achievement and joy. As each new office came on, I felt how great I was...all that has vanished and the offices I once held are...unimportant to me."[72]

Likely, one of two honors Lausche most cherished was the dedication of the Frank J. Lausche Youth Exhibits Building at the Ohio State Fair on September 2, 1965. Located at the north end of the fairgrounds, this $720,000 facility houses all youth exhibits except for livestock. The building reminded old-timers of how Lausche used county fairs and the Ohio State Fair as important venues for his many political campaigns. He received a special honor at the 1983 Ohio State Fair. The Ohio Exposition Commission designated August 17 Frank J. Lausche Day. Then 87, Lausche attended this occasion that featured a luncheon and other ceremonies in honor of the great fairgoer.[73]

An even more significant honor was bestowed upon Lausche with the construction and dedication of the Lausche State Office Building in Cleveland completed in 1979. This $23 million, thirteen-story building is located at Superior Avenue and Huron Road at the northwest corner of the Cleveland Union Terminal (now known as Tower City Center). An interesting aspect of this 425,000-square-foot office building is that it sits on a platform built above the railroad tracks leading into Tower City Center (old Terminal Tower Building). Clevelanders and others riding rapid transit downtown from the westside or going to Hopkins Airport travel right under the Lausche Building. A large number of state agencies are housed in this building; a branch of the Ohio Historical Society is an important tenant there. Exhibits and materials featuring ethnic groups in Cleveland are a valuable resource for local residents. Dedication of the Lausche Building, a tribute to one of Cleveland's favorite sons, brought forth considerable pride to Lausche's family and his many friends.

⌒

THE FEISTY LAUSCHE CONTINUED TO COME out of the bullpen and give 'em hell, much in the mold of Harry Truman. Slower of step and with hair turning whiter each year, Lausche once again turned on labor and unions. In 1947 the Ferguson Act, passed by the Ohio General Assembly, had forbade strikes by public employees. Democrats and labor unions attempted to enact a collective bargaining act (Senate Bill 70) in 1975. Lausche spoke out against this bill, reiterating his well-known rhetorical stance, "By permitting strikes against the government and allowing unions to force government workers to join or pay tribute to a union is in sharp conflict with principles old unionism enunciated...by such good friends of labor as Samuel Gompers, Presidents [Franklin] Roosevelt and Kennedy, and Arthur Goldberg, former member of the U.S. Supreme Court and former Secretary of Labor and AFL-CIO general counsel."[74]

State senator Anthony Celebrezze, Jr. countered that Lausche, his father's one-time ally and former Mayor of Cleveland, might have been putting words in the mouths of those former politicians. Senate Bill 70 passed both houses, Governor James Rhodes vetoed the bill quoting Franklin Roosevelt, who said strikes by public employees would be "unthinkable and intolerable."[75] The Ohio senate overrode Rhode's veto, but the House fell four votes short of an override.

This labor issue came up for a vote in 1977 under the aegis of Senate Bill 222. In a statement sent to state newspapers, Lausche challenged passage of this bill, which would "destroy the existing prohibition against forced unionization of public sector workers. Unions would be empowered to exact monthly agency shop fees from employees who refuse to join and don't want to be represented by the [union]."[76] Lausche's comments prompted a response from Curtis Mathews, clerk for the Ohio Department of Industrial Relations. He questioned whether Lausche, whom he called a fence-straddler, read the bill thoroughly. "Does it not seem strange that some of our lawmakers, when they join their exclusive clubs, are well aware of a strict policy that states Members Only. Would it be fair to Mr. Lausche for me to come to his club and enjoy his privileges, if I were eligible, while he paid the dues? Liken that to a labor union and see what kind of answer you come up with.... Mr. Lausche should look twice at how things are before he places his signature on the problems of today."[77]

State senator Harry Meshel, Democrat from Youngstown and sponsor of this collective bargaining bill, reacted to Lausche's attack philosophically, not angrily, "He has not been a Democrat philosophically, theoretically, or practically for a long time but it's still sad that people are taking advantage of his name for various conservative and right-to-work causes. It is an unfortunate use of an elder statesman."[78] The real tragedy was the fact that Lausche did not recognize that even if he were right about the bill, his opposition to this bill meant little in a legislature filled with politicians of a different generation. A collective bargaining bill for state employees was finally passed in 1983. Friends and journalists hoped the aging political icon would protect, rather than tarnish his good reputation.

With each passing day Lausche found time to answer his mail, practice a bit of law, play golf and have time to do a lot of reading. Quiet hours were spent enjoying Shakespeare, the poetry of John Keats, Percy Shelley, Robert Burns, and conservative stands of *The National Review*. He loved to read poetry and reread works of several poets he had studied, namely Thomas More, Samuel Coleridge, Oliver Goldsmith, and Alexander Pope. He enjoyed intensely studying the composition of their words and the beauty of their imagination and experience.

Most importantly, he was able to spend more time with Jane. "With each day of my life, she is an increasing joy to me. We've been married...53 years and the bond is stronger than it has ever been before."[79] He expressed these heartfelt words about his wife on November 3, 1981. Three weeks later on November 24, Jane died quietly in her sleep at their home in Bethesda. She was 78 years of age. Lausche's friend Cyril Zebot captured in words the loss Lausche suffered, "When one finds a worthy wife, her value is far beyond pearls. Her husband, entrusting his heart to her, has an unfailing prize. She brings him good, and not evil, all the days of her life."[80] The grief-stricken Lausche took his beloved wife back to Cleveland for burial. Having converted to the Catholic faith several years earlier, Jane was buried at Calvary Cemetery on the southeast side of Cleveland.

> "He has not been a Democrat philosophically, theoretically, or practically for a long time but it's still sad that people are taking advantage of his name for various conservative and right-to-work causes. It is an unfortunate use of an elder statesman."

Some years later as Lausche discussed Jane's funeral with the Mejac brothers and Stanley Sustercic in Washington, DC, the widower commented to Sustercic that his wife had made the then Father Edward Pevec, of Slovenian parentage and good friend of the Lausches, a bishop. Sustersic asked, "How?" Lausche answered, "When Father Pevec officiated as a celebrant at Jane's funeral, he was so magnificent, the Bishop [Anthony Pilla] saw him as the best candidate to serve as an auxiliary bishop in Cleveland."[81] He was appointed an auxiliary bishop one year later in 1982. There isn't any verification of this story, and this author hesitated to ask Bishop Pevec for his opinion about this appointment. The story may well have been accurate.

Lausche was truly a lonely man following Jane's death. Of his immediate family only his sister, Josephine Welf and brother Harold, a former director of Cleveland parks and city properties, remained. His friend John Lokar, former campaign manager and executive secretary, still resided in Cleveland. Within the next four years, two of his closest friends died—Cleveland lawyer John E. Elder and Zoltan Gombos, publisher of the Hungarian language newspaper *Szabadsag*. His loyal Italian-American friend Joe Gambatese lived in Washington, DC, and they met frequently at Burning Tree Country Club for a game of golf and camaraderie.

With a heavy heart, the widower Lausche returned to Bethesda. Friends wondered why he did not move back to Cleveland. Lausche reasoned that so many of his friends and relatives in Cleveland had passed away, and certainly, the ties to his hometown he once enjoyed were no longer there. At his age Lausche did not wish to confront the inconvenience and anxiety of moving from the Old Line state. He had resided in his home in Bethesda since 1957. Lausche was saddened at the poor reputation and publicity Cleveland had received in the post-Vietnam era. The city had become the butt of derogatory comments and jokes by news media and TV comedians. He made a valid prophecy about the Forest City, "Cleveland...occupies a low position as a city. Tragically it has developed a bad reputation...this will vanish and Cleveland will be restored to the high position that it occupied among the cities of the nation in the past."[82] As prophesized by Lausche, by the beginning of the twenty-first century, the formerly so-called mistake by the lake was characterized as a rejuvenated city with a bright future.

☙

LAUSCHE MADE AN EFFORT TO RETURN TO CLEVELAND once a month to see his sister Josephine Welf (Josephine was the longest living of the Lausche siblings, passing away in December 1990 at the age of 96.). While there, he would also visit his sisters-in-law Antonia (following his brother Harold's death in 1986) and Frances, wife of Charles. He lamented how time blurred the memory of Cleveland locals. On one occasion he was walking down Superior Avenue when a pedestrian approached him and called out Lausche's name. Lausche embraced the stranger and gave him a hug. He felt so happy to be acknowledged. On another occasion as he sat at a table in a cafeteria of the Cleveland Clinic, he commented, "There must have been 400 people that paid for their food and saw me sitting there and there wasn't a damn one that recognized me. The moral of the story is this: Famous for the day, soon forgotten with the passing of that day."[83]

Stanley Ertzen was one of Lausche's closest friends in Cleveland. He visited with Ertzen nearly every time he returned to his hometown. Lausche had met Ertzen, a Slovenian, through his youngest brother Harold. Harold and Ertzen had worked together as night cashiers in an eastside Cleveland liquor store after prohibition had been rescinded. Ertzen had become involved in political activities, helping Lausche in whatever way possible. He played softball with the Lausche brothers and remained a friend of the family throughout his life.

Lausche would go to Ertzen's home (Ertzen's wife had died) for a home-cooked meal. After a drink or two and good conversation, Ertzen remembered, "Lausche liked to eat Slovenian meals, particularly goulash. We also prepared potatoes, polenta made of corn meal, which went well with the goulash. At other times we prepared smoked sausage and sauerkraut. We also ate roast chicken and Slovenian dumplings."[84] The two friends began their meals with chicken soup made of ground chicken, garlic and onions. While in Bethesda, Lausche corresponded frequently with Ertzen about current events, and Ertzen noticed Lausche's failing handwriting as it became weaker and weaker over time. Lausche continued to write bitterly about Communism. He was not convinced that Mikhail Gorbachov's efforts to change the political structure of the Soviet Union would be successful. *Glasnost* and *perestroika* had little meaning to this political patriarch.

After his brief visits to his hometown, Lausche returned to what he called "that lonely house in Maryland." Glen Metzdorff, former Senate aide for Lausche, took care of many of the Senator's household duties. Unkempt to the point of living in a slovenly manner, Lausche left clothes and personal items strewn about his home. Lausche liked to smoke cigars, and he would occasionally doze off, resulting in cigar burns on his chairs, clothes, or the carpet. Friends feared he might cause a serious fire. Occasionally Metzdorff cooked dinner for his elderly friend. He and Lausche had learned about cooking from Freddy May Jones, Lausche's African-American maid. After an occasional drink of Old Crow with a chaser, Lausche enjoyed a hearty dish of hash. Increasingly a loner, the Senator was reticent to trust too many individuals. He feared he might get hurt along the way or that a friendship might result in using him for political leverage. Lausche was adamant about anyone coming to his home without prior approval. It probably made no difference because he frequently left the front door unlocked or lost his house keys.

In his discussions with Metzdorff, Lausche believed one must support America, right or wrong. He maintained a fundamental faith in representative government, that free enterprise was good, state ownership bad. Metzdorff believed Lausche had not created a personal political agenda that would work, but rather he was a product of a legislative program that he eventually supported.[85] As Lausche approached his 90th birthday (1985), he was troubled over the nation's future. He commented, "the world has been turned upside down," and he angrily deplored what he viewed as a deterioration of his nation's moral fiber.[86]

Following Jane's death, Virginia Wells, daughter of Ralph Locher, handled Lausche's financial affairs and payment of monthly bills. Extremely competent, Virginia lived in Alexandra near the nation's capitol. She worked closely with Jim and Madeline Debevic, who served as administrators of the Frances and Jane Lausche memorial fund. In spite of Lausche's advanced age, he continued to drive until he was 94. Accusations that he was a poor driver seemed overstated. Friends and neighbors assumed this to be the case because Lausche always raced the engine of his pre-owned 1968 Chevrolet before starting to drive. In reality his vehicle was in reasonably good shape. Wells persuaded him to buy a new Chevrolet, which he reluctantly agreed to do after Jane's death.

Practically every Wednesday morning, Lausche drove himself to the Senate prayer breakfast. When he left the breakfast to go to his car, the Senators possibly prayed, "God help the pedestrians." He drove because he was so fiercely independent in his personal ways. Senator David Durenberger (Rep-MN) remembered that Lawton Chiles (Dem-FL) sometimes supervised the prayer breakfast. "He gave Lausche the name Jeremiah. When we gathered in fellowship on these mornings, whenever we wanted to hear the voice of a prophet setting us straight on the mores of the times, we would turn to...Lausche...."[87] Lausche looked forward to his golf games at Burning Tree Country Club during the summer months. He often played three or four times a week with fellow retired senators. A good golfer, who on earlier occasions had shot par golf, he became frustrated as his handicap climbed higher. He was known to have shot 81 on his 81ˢᵗ birthday. In the summer of 1987 Virginia was at Lausche's residence when he came home from a round of golf. He was angry and disappointed at his game and threw his clubs into the corner of the living room. Virginia asked him what was wrong, to which he responded, "If you can't shoot your age, you shouldn't be on the golf course."[88] The 91-year-old Lausche never played golf again. He had played with Ben Hogan woods and irons and a Spaulding Deadline putter. The now former golfer gave some of his clubs to Stanley Ertzen, and the remaining clubs were sent to the Ohio Historical Society in Columbus. Late in 1989 Lausche summed up his feelings about his life, "I'm retired, I'm alone, and time gets heavy on my hands, doing my own cooking, my own depressive contemplation and meditation."[89] In an interview on one of his earlier trips to Cleveland, he wondered whether he had chosen the right profession. "In these later, dear days of my life, I find great comfort in reading matters that are not of a political nature, but basically related to a truly decent and good life. I find comfort in reading poetry. I am awakened...with the longing that I could have studied literature or languages, or other sophisticated subjects which would have been...highly more esteemable than the political profession which I followed."[90]

FRIENDS IN WASHINGTON, DC EXPRESSED concern that now in his 90s Lausche might suffer a debilitating injury or illness necessitating hospitalization. His mind was still keen, and he was stubborn when advised to do something he didn't think was necessary. The Lausche home—new when he and Jane moved to Bethesda in 1957—had not been kept up and was in need of major repairs. The political patriarch had been hospitalized several times for ailments associated with his advancing years.

In early January 1990, Lausche entered Bethesda Hospital suffering chest pains. Following his discharge, he contracted pneumonia from which he never fully recovered. Local friends persuaded him to return to Cleveland. He was flown back to his hometown and faced a waiting list at the Slovenian Home for the Aged on the east side of the city. Friends exercised a bit of political pressure to have Lausche admitted to the home on February 20, 1990. Slovenian Home employees took good care of the political war-horse. He was happy to be back near his birthplace and his Slovenian heritage. He continued to spend his time reading poetry and the Bible. Day by day Lausche's health declined precipitately. He died of congestive heart failure on April 20, 1990 at the age of 94.

Tributes poured into Cleveland from all over the country, most notably from newspapers and political figures in Ohio and Washington, DC. Eulogies were given by Senators John Glenn (Dem-OH), David Durenburger (Rep-MN), Strom Thurmond (Rep-SC), and Representative Michael DeWine (Rep-OH). All of these eulogies are printed in the *Congressional Record*.

For his funeral mass in St. Vitus Church Lausche was dressed in a black tuxedo, which was surrounded by a white cape—the finery of a papal honorary order, the Knights of Holy Sepulcher of Malta. He wore the order's amulet around his neck, and a rosary rested in his hand. Bishop A. Edward Pevec delivered the homily. This affable bishop had known Lausche for nearly 40 years. "I remember fondly the thrilling moment when I met [Frank Lausche] on my first mass at St. Vitus. The Governor of...Ohio was not too busy to be...in his parish church...and I felt humbled in the presence of such greatness. There were many occasions when he was being honored or someone else was being honored...that his words were greeted with the loudest applause. He would completely charm a crowd of Slovenians by stopping in the middle of a sentence and saying with a sigh, '*Morem kar po slovensku*' 'I just had to say this in Slovenian.' And the response would be deafening." Pevec noted that, "The Senator could recall vividly the old wooden St. Vitus Church on Norwood Road, the three-storied wooden building next to the church, the old rectory on Glass Avenue [now named Lausche Avenue]. Not many could say they knew personally all six pastors of the 97-year-old parish.... The places, these people were his own."[91]

> *"Lausche was an eloquent voice for his state and country—a dedicated patriot who could bring tears to young and old.... Frank J. Lausche was the most significant political figure in post-World War II Ohio."*

James A. Rhodes, longtime friend and former political adversary, spoke of Lausche's ability to assume and voice concerns of ordinary people with sincerity. The former Governor joked that he and other politicians were so influenced by Lausche's power of speechmaking that, "We actually stole word-by-word from his speeches.[92] Rhodes' political idol was a man of immense intellect, of unquestioned integrity and steadfast devotion to the highest principles of public service. Clevelander Richard F. Celeste, then Democratic Governor of Ohio, recalled as a youth listening to Lausche's speeches and added, "Lausche was an eloquent voice for his state and country—a dedicated patriot who could bring tears to young and old.... Frank J. Lausche was the most significant political figure in post-World War II Ohio."[93] Political analysts and Republicans might challenge Celeste's assertion.

Lausche was buried in Calvary Cemetery not far from Route 77. Honorary pallbearers included Rhodes and Celeste, joined by former Cleveland Mayors Ralph S. Locher, Michael R. White, Dennis Kucinich, Anthony J. Celebrezze, and Ralph J. Perk. Research by the author verified that Lausche's headstone is incorrectly inscribed with his year of birth as November 14, 1898 rather than accurately as November 14, 1895. In 2001, a beautiful flower garden with a statue (Our Lady, Queen of Heaven) was dedicated at the main entry of Calvary Cemetery. An appropriate plaque located in the garden states that the Frances and Jane Lausche Foundation in part financed this tribute to the Lausche family and those who in any way had been a part of their lives.

Propriety suggests that Lausche's meteor-like rise to political eminence (victor in 11 out of 14 elections) had few parallels in Ohio political history. One may ask why. Simply stated, because to many this political dinosaur often took a stance that seemed to find Lausche swimming against the tide. The fiercely independent veteran politician was never in the hip pocket of any particular political entity. The consummate statesman, Lausche was a man of unwavering integrity, strong beliefs and tender feelings. The sight of the American flag and the sound of the national anthem made him vibrate. He was thrilled to read the proud history of his country. He extolled John Hancock, Thomas Jefferson and Benjamin Franklin.

Rudolph Susel, editor of *American Home* remembered that "Frank Lausche was never one...to defend himself by pleading as former President Richard Nixon did on one pathetic occasion: 'I am not a crook'."[94] One may disagree politically with Lausche. However, in good conscience, it was difficult to question his ethics or basic honesty. To paraphrase a tune made popular by another Frank (Sinatra), Lausche did it his way. The press and other critics often accused him of straddling the fence on tough political issues. True or otherwise, Lausche had the propensity to incur the wrath of Democrats and finally lose the support of his alleged party. He was the rarest of political animals; one who believed his ultimate allegiance was not to his party, rather to his nation.

Epilogue

HISTORIAN AND NATIVE OHIOAN ANDREW R. L. CAYTON wrote in his excellent cultural history of Ohio that his home state had become synonymous with American normalcy. To paraphrase, Cayton attested that Ohio—like the rest of the Midwest—has become bland and predictable. The seventeenth state is no longer noted as a land of limitless possibilities. Ohio is a nice place to live, promoted by the state's bureau of tourism as being located in the heart of it all. Like all states, Ohio faces complex responsibilities in the twenty-first century. A population that overwhelmingly embraces traditional American values must constantly address these challenges.

Frank Joseph Lausche grew up at the turn of the twentieth century in an environment of limitless opportunities. He learned well from his parents, particularly from Ma Lausche, to appreciate the wonders of his homeland, to practice frugality, to live by the law, to promote those values inherent in a responsible citizen and to pursue opportunities for professional growth. Large numbers of immigrants, particularly those from southern and eastern Europe, migrated to the midwestern states including Ohio to seek a new life. The state of Ohio—known along with Virginia as a state of Presidents—had become an important political entity. Similar to Fiorella La Guardia of New York, Lausche rose like a phoenix to a political career encompassing three distinct levels: municipal, state and federal. In spite of his ethnic background, his foreign-sounding name, and his Catholic upbringing, Lausche was copacetic with Ohio voters. After thirty-five years, these same electors retired Lausche to the sidelines in one of the Buckeye State's greatest political upsets.

Political biographers face the daunting challenge of accurately portraying their subject's achievements within a particular political spectrum. Lausche was definitely not an exception. Politically unorthodox, a loner and extremely independent, he joined the ranks of those politicians who defy being pigeonholed. Names such as Wayne Morse, Strom Thurmond and John Anderson come to mind when looking for others with whom to compare Lausche. Frank J. Lausche confounded both major political parties. He was an enigma and a maverick.

Political analysts are sometimes queried about what would happen if a politician should come along and disregard all rules of the game. Such a figure would break the rules of the game by avoiding the usual shams, stratagem and machinations. He would offer no flattery to the electorate, neither promises nor favors. He would simply offer his own thorough honesty and utter sincerity. Frank Lausche came close to meeting this description. In spite of his unorthodox campaign style, little doubt remains that Lausche's political success evolved because the voting public believed him to be truthful and without guile.

Select individuals like Lausche have exhibited honesty in the political arena. Within Lausche, this quality was palpable. To those who met him or heard him speak, Lausche's honesty was self evident. He emanated sincerity, a quality the observer could nearly physically see in the man. Citizens believed in him. "This man may have made mistakes, but he was a good man. He meant what he said. He would not cheat or lie or dissemble." Lausche passionately believed in his principles, and refused to betray them.

Traditionally, politics is the systematic pursuit of what is expedient. Sometimes what is expedient is not always morally right. The successful politician is popularly expected to scheme, connive, compromise, make allowances where he can, promise whatever he must to get votes, cater to special interest groups at the expense of the general public and to the detriment of what is just and proper. However, Frank J. Lausche emphatically and purposefully strove to avoid this seamy side of the political landscape. No one defends all of his political actions and beliefs, nor implies that he ought to be placed on a pedestal. He did not always act in the best interests of his constituency. He was chastised, and rightly so, for his reticence to campaign for or provide words of support for his fellow Ohio Democrats.

An anomaly, Lausche departed from the anticipated rule of behavior or political action. His unpredictability was predictable. Political hack writers shook their heads in attempting to understand this perplexing and seemingly inexplicable individual. Lausche was looked upon as a political chameleon. Few American politicians have been more independent or unorthodox.

The veteran solon had learned early in his career how to play the political game. Lausche's bushy mane was the Clevelander's trademark. He considered himself one of the common people who drove an old car, wore unpressed suits and often didn't bother to comb his hair. Lausche never had the slightest inclination to accumulate great wealth. During his ten-year reign as governor, he saved a meager amount of money, even for the fifties. The eccentric governor never submitted an expense account, ordered the safe removed from his office and even discarded the key to his desk.

Lausche carried on his perpetual campaign at county fairs and in small hamlets. He was a man of the people, fighting to save taxpayers' money and preserve noble American virtues. The savvy politico literally dismantled the effectiveness of the State Democratic Party during his gubernatorial reign. He chose not to be beholden to party leaders, union officials or to lobbyists. When campaigning, Lausche adopted a slogan made popular by Ray Bliss, Ohio Republican Party State Chairman—*Keep issues out of campaigns.* Lausche's plan of action was amazing, for he ran for office as a Democrat and expounded Republican principles. To his way of thinking, this tactic was the only way a descendent of Slovenian immigrants could have possibly persuaded rural voters and small town Protestants to believe he had their best interests at heart.

What was the nature of the voters Lausche encountered? Difficulty surfaces when speculating about Ohioans and their political philosophy. They have been known to work themselves into a lather about issues and then do nothing about the issues. At considerable expense, political parties had held a convention in Columbus in 1873. Following arduous debate, legislators drew up a sorely needed new charter for Ohio. Voters defeated the proposal by a two-to-one margin. In 1958 Republicans attempted to pass a right-to-work amendment. The amendment lost by a two-to-one tally. In the same election, Governor C. William O'Neill was unceremoniously replaced by Mike DiSalle.

Precious few Ohio politicians have distinguished themselves in office. With the possible exception of William Howard Taft, none of the seven Ohioan presidents receives high marks. Until the repeated elections of James A. Rhodes, only one state administration could be considered dynamic. Democrat James M. Cox from Dayton, in his first term as governor (1913–15), pushed through reform legislation, a part of the Progressive movement.

Ohio voters seldom stray too far from the center of the political spectrum. Since 1892 the winning President has carried Ohio in every election with the exception of 1944 and 1960. So much for the timeworn cliché—*As Maine goes, so goes the nation*. Other than Cox, only two liberals in the twentieth century—Michael DiSalle and John Gilligan—resided in the governor's mansion, and then for only one term each.

Politically, Ohio has remained the "great Middle-class state." Job-oriented politics, combined with a resolute belief in the virtues of hard work and political conservatism, have dominated daily affairs. With rare exceptions, the caution with which state politicians have demonstrated in pursuing economic and social issues have reflected strong overtones of Jeffersonian traditionalism. Self-reliance and independence have prevailed. The ethnic hodgepodge in the state is legendary. The political impact of ethnic groups began to dissipate near the conclusion of Lausche's career. The state had retained a balance within the citizenry relative to interests and concerns. Whether it be business interests, labor unions or farm organizations, no single entity seemed to have an upper hand. Unlike Indiana, Illinois and Michigan, Ohio is not dominated by one large, metropolitan city. The Buckeye State's political base is spread among several cities with populations ranging between 150,000 and 500,000, thus diffusing political domination by any one metropolis.

Over the years, Ohioans have not perpetuated coherent schools of thought in reference to the state's political direction and attendant objectives. With the exception of a minority of intellectuals, the Ohio populace has demonstrated a general ignorance and indifference to state government and to political issues. Voters have seemed hesitant to associate their economic self-interests and statewide problems with their decisions at the ballot box. Voters have elected their candidates based more on personality, and ignored important social and economic concerns. This voting trend had been most advantageous to the charismatic Lausche, who downplayed specific issues and spoke in generalities. The conservatism of Ohio's elected officials and government has evolved out of the issueless character of the state's politics. Parties have failed to provide voters with meaningful policy alternatives in elections.

In the absence of significant issues, citizens have tended to distrust their legislators. Voters have expressed concern that legislative decisions would result in perquisites for particular entities at the expense of the general populace. Prior to the Rhodes era, voters kept state legislators on a short rope. Examples included a ten-mill tax limitation, a ban on state debt except through a constitutional amendment, a double hurdle for home rule charters, laws making it difficult for cities to annex adjoining communities and the retention of a preponderance of smaller school districts. This type of legislation pleased the conservative Lausche and lessened the likelihood the former Governor would have to clash with the nominally Republican assemblies in the statehouse.

The political makeup in the U.S. Senate presented different challenges for Lausche. As he became more and more conservative, his philosophy clashed dramatically with the Kennedy and Johnson administrations and to a lesser extent with that of Eisenhower's. Both Democratic presidents in the 1960s had advocated social programs under the banners of *The New Frontier* and *The Great Society*. These programs required approval of large sums of money and eventually plummeted the country further and further into debt. Lausche was constantly swimming upstream in an effort to restrict government spending, which he believed would plunge the country into the debit side. The Ohio Senator proposed amendment after amendment to curtail spending, and was repeatedly rejected by a Democratic-dominated senate.

Lausche's name appears on few significant pieces of legislation during his twelve-year tenure in the senate. When Democrat Harry Byrd of Virginia died in 1966, Lausche assumed the mantle as the Senate's most conservative member, Democrat or Republican. It is little wonder that Lausche found his senate years the least rewarding in his political career.

Concerning foreign relations, Lausche was more in sync with the three administrations under which he served. A confirmed hawk and adversary of Communism, the Senator agonized over the Vietnam debacle. Occasionally Lausche took a dove-like position in anticipation that the protracted conflict might be resolved. A member of the important U.S. Senate Foreign Relations Committee for nine years, Lausche gave more time and effort to this committee than to any other of his senatorial responsibilities. When Lausche left the senate in 1968, he was a beaten man who had fought the good fight to support the United States in Vietnam and to thwart excessive government spending.

Like those of most politicians, Lausche's tangible accomplishments present a mixed bag. Loyalists venerated his frugal management of state funds when serving as governor. He was proud of a $60 million surplus in the state coffers (part of which former Governor Bricker had stashed away). Lausche's highway program provided many badly needed miles of construction, including the Ohio Turnpike. Operators of heavy trucks paid their fair share of maintenance taxes. Lausche became a trailblazer in developing a progressive program of conservation and restoration of natural resources. His *Plant Ohio Today for Tomorrow* program for replenishing the state's tree supply gained nationwide recognition. Lausche valiantly attempted to have strip-mining lands restored to their original state. Strong mining lobbies defeated him at every turn. His efforts finally came to fruition in the United States Senate, although new laws requiring land reclamation did not take effect until 1976–77.

On the distaff side, public employees in education, welfare and finance, along with working newspapermen, claimed Lausche was one of the poorest governors in the history of the state. Often chastised for sitting on the fence, Lausche was accused of not having enough courage to ask the state legislature for additional tax monies to meet increased costs of the state government. He balanced income and expenditures through extensive debt financing. Consequently, with the combination of Bricker's six years of extremely parsimonious management of the governor's office and Lausche's ten years of rigid spending, Ohio fell to the lower echelons of the 48 states in support of publicly financed programs.

The lack of unity among the state's labor unions and the weak support of the Democratic Party exacerbated efforts to reverse a long-standing trend of minimal support for these state programs, especially for education. During his sixteen years in office, Rhodes took advantage of this political malaise and of deplorable state-wide conditions and engineered a major building drive in higher education and highways, and upgraded under-funded programs and facilities for welfare, prisons and mental health.

With a less than flattering legislative record in the statehouse and in the senate, one questions how Lausche became the greatest vote-getter in Ohio history. The answer rests on the premise that the Ohio populace trusted Lausche, and that they approved of what he stood for—patriotism and American traditions. Here was a man who made his way from the proverbial wrong side of Cleveland's tracks to the pinnacle of American politics. Like Rhodes, he rose from a blue-collar background (in contrast to John Bricker and Robert Taft). Lausche remained in office because voters accepted his value system and his dedication to the timeworn American adage, *Mom, apple pie and the American way*. He possessed a certain mystique—his awkward phraseology that defied simple English definition. His serious mien and air of preoccupation suggested Lausche knew things that ordinary men did not, akin to the prophets of old. He possessed that rare ability to stir emotion with his splendid voice and oratorical phrases, often quoting from the literary classics he so dearly loved. Lausche possessed all the qualifications of an actor—a deep, resonant voice, well-timed delivery, appropriate and effective gestures, and an unerring sense of the dramatic (often compared to the likes of Abraham Lincoln).

And so Lausche's legacy rests more on his personal character than on tangible legislative achievements. Much like Ronald Reagan, Lausche was the *Great Communicator*. A humble man, he never hesitated to make himself the brunt of a joke to set others at ease. Despite what seemed to many as an extremely conservative stance, Lausche served his state and country with dignity and integrity. Here was a public servant who did not compromise his principles. In a political climate where graft and corruption have seemed so widely to pollute the political air of congressmen, Lausche projected a refreshing contrast. Politicians raise obscene amounts of money to support their campaigns for election. Lausche campaigned on a miniscule amount of funds. Politicians are vulnerable and often capitulate to pressure of lobbyists. Lausche disdained the rhetoric and appeal of lobbyists. Politicians vote themselves questionable pay increases. Lausche voiced strenuous opposition to these salary increases and rejected his own pay raises. Lausche was well known for his determination to avoid promoting nepotism while in office. He resisted hiring anyone who may have been recommended to him for fear of charges of favoritism. Without success, opponents searched desperately for scandals involving Lausche.

James Neff wrote *Mobbed Up*, an account of the infamous Jackie Presser and his father, Bill, and their sleazy and illicit actions within Cleveland's local unions of the International Brotherhood of Teamsters. The Pressers' ties to local and national Mafia members have been well documented. Politicians at all levels bowed before the Pressers, currying favor and soliciting contributions and support at election time. According to Neff, politicians who catered to the Pressers included Governor Rhodes, Senator George Bender, a well-known lackey for the Teamsters Union, and three Lausche clones or near-clones. Neff makes absolutely no reference to Lausche or his friend Louis Seltzer having any affiliation to the Pressers.

In an unrelenting drive to achieve his goal of government parsimony, Lausche steadfastly renounced the Democratic Party's domestic programs and all of its public works and pomp, except for civil rights, for which he consistently voted. Lausche wanted a world in which every man saves, no matter what he spends. He desired a world where every man and nation pays cash, and nobody buys on credit, at least during good times. Lausche had preached this dogma most of his public life, despite John Maynard Keynes, the New Deal, the Fair Deal, the New Frontier and the Great Society. When the topics of frugality in government or resistance to Communism came to the forefront, Lausche was seldom a bundle of contradictions. His philosophy was rooted deeply in his boyhood on Cleveland's eastside.

Lausche established a remarkable connection with Ohio voters and his fellow politicians, even with those who disagreed with him on issues. In spite of Lausche's antipathy toward organized labor, he persuaded many blue-collar workers to vote for him. Republicans who crossed over at the polls were called *Lausche Republicans*.

In many ways Lausche was an impossible mystery. He was totally and unabashedly old fashioned, a true Renaissance man in the way he talked and in the way he carried himself. In retrospect, it is clear that this old fashioned public servant was attempting to bring America into the twenty-first century, embodying the principles that had served him so well in the early decades of the twentieth century.

Through all the ruckuses he caused, Lausche never lost his idealized outlook toward America or his ability to turn reality to match his optimistic views. His vision for America was a nation that pursues liberty and cares for its citizens. He disdained *playing* politics. Lausche believed in the ardor of individual responsibility and the spirit that made America great.

The flickering images of Senator Jefferson Smith, played by Jimmy Stewart in the classic 1939 film *Mr. Smith Goes to Washington*, come to mind when defining Lausche. Smith embodied enduring American ideals: fair play, honesty, patriotism and the courage to take a principled stand in the face of fierce opposition. Much like Smith, Lausche proceeded to Washington, DC, determined not to succumb to the same influences many of his colleagues had. His vote would neither be bought nor sold. He would hold back the reins of overspending the federal budget. Even the attire of his office staff would not fall to changing times. While in many ways, the aging solon is to be admired for his morals and ethics, most likely they ultimately became his political undoing.

Lausche was a statesman in the public life of Ohio and the United States who best represented the classic tragedy defined by Aristotle. He was destroyed—or his power and influence were—by his own strength and virtue. He would do nothing and would allow nothing to be done that might bring profit to himself or to other individuals. He would give no favor and accept none, except in the public interest. In the sense understood by all Americans, he was a man of conscience. Above all he was honest. That there is a higher honesty for government and its solons, he never comprehended. The Senator added his own postscript—he would never run with the pack.

The role of the politician is to ensure that government not become an obstacle and that those who govern understand that they are servants, not masters, and that public office is a public trust. To Lausche, the people supported the government—led it and left it unblemished. He believed that the futures of individuals and nations were imbued in what they did in the present. To Lausche's way of thinking, a man's measure ought to be ascribed in accordance to the totality of his actions. *As the days are, so shall thy strength be* was more than a slogan to Frank J. Lausche.

Bibliography

Books

Abell, Tyler, ed. *Drew Pearson Diaries, 1949–1959*. New York: Holt, Rinehart and Winston, 1974.

Abels, Jules. *Out of the Jaws of Victory*. New York: Henry Holt and Company, 1959.

Adamic, Louis. *Ellis Island: An Illustrated History of Immigrant Experience*. Ivan Chermayeff, et al, eds. New York: Macmillan, 1991.

Allen, Robert S. *Our Fair City*. New York: The Vanguard Press, 1947.

Armbrister, Trevor. *A Matter of Accountability*. New York: Coward-McCann, 1970.

Aronoff, Stanley and Vernal G. Riffe, Jr. *James A. Rhodes at Eighty*. Columbus: privately printed, 1989.

Ashby, LeRoy and Rod Gramer. *Fighting the Odds, the Life of Senator Frank Church*. Pullman, Washington: Washington State University Press, 1994.

Avery, Elroy McKendree. *A History of Cleveland and Its Environs*. Chicago: Lewis Publishing, 1918.

Baker, Ross. *Friend and Foe in the U.S. Senate*. New York: The Free Press, 1980.

Benderley, Jill and Evan Kraft. *Independent Slovenia, Origins, Movements, Prospects*. New York: St. Martin's Press, 1994.

Benson, Ezra Taft. *Cross Fire, The Eight Years with Eisenhower*. Garden City, New York: Doubleday and Company, Inc., 1962.

Benton, Elbert Jay. *Cleveland, Cultural Story of an American City*. pt. 2. Cleveland: Western Reserve Historical Society, 1948.

Bernstein, Irving. *Guns or Butter, The Presidency of Lyndon Johnson*. New York: Oxford University Press, 1966.

Binstein, Michael and Charles Bowder. *Trust Me*. New York: Random House, 1993.

Bittner, William C. *Frank J. Lausche, A Political Biography*. New York: Studio Slovenica, 1975.

Campbell, Thomas F. *Daniel E. Morgan, 1877–1948, The Good Citizen in Politics*. Cleveland: The Press of Western Reserve University, 1966.

Campbell, Thomas F. and Edward M. Miggins. *The Birth of Modern Cleveland, 1865–1930*. Cleveland: Western Reserve Historical Society, 1988.

Caro, Robert A. *The Years of Lyndon Johnson, Master of the Senate*. New York: Alfred A. Knopf, 2002.

Cayton, Andrew R. L. and Susan E. Gray, eds. *The American Midwest, Essays on Regional History*. Bloomington: Indiana University Press, 2001.

Cayton, Andrew R. L. *Ohio, The History of a People*. Columbus: The Ohio State University Press, 2002.

Chadwick, Bruce. *Baseball's Home Town Teams, The Story of the Minor Leagues*. New York: Abbeville Press, 1994.

Charmley, John. *Churchill, The End of Glory*. New York: Harcourt, Brace and Company, 1993.

Chudacoff, Howard P. and Judith Smith. *The Evolution of American Urban Society*. Englewood Cliffs, New Jersey: Prentice-Hall, 1975.

Coffin, Tristam. *Senator Fulbright, Portrait of a Public Philosopher*. New York: E.P. Dutton and Company, 1966.

Colakovic, Branko Nita. *Yugoslavia Migrations to America*. San Francisco: Rand E. Research Associates, 1973.

Condon, George E. *Cleveland, The Best Kept Secret*. Garden City, New York: Doubleday and Company, Inc., 1967.

Cramer, Clarence H. *Newton D. Baker, A Biography*. Cleveland: World Publishing Company, 1961.

Cronkite, Walter. *A Reporter's Life*. New York: Alfred A. Knopf, 1996.

Dalleck, Robert. *Lone Star Rising, Lyndon Johnson and His Times, 1908–1960*. New York: Oxford University Press, 1991.

David, Paul, Malcolm Moos, and Ralph Goldman. *Presidential Nominating Politics of 1953*. Volume IV. Baltimore: Johns Hopkins Press, 1983.

Davies, Richard O. *Defender of the Old Guard, John Bricker and American Politics*. Columbus: Ohio State University Press, 1993.

DeConde, Alexander. *Encyclopedia of American Foreign Policy*. second edition. New York: Charles Scribner's Sons, 2002

DiSalle, Michael V. *Second Choice*. New York: Hawthorn Books, Inc., 1966.

Divine, Robert A., et. al. *The American Story*. Volume Two. New York: Longman, 2002.

Donaldson, Gary A. *Truman Defeats Dewey*. Lexington: University Press of Kentucky, 1999.

Eisenhower, Dwight D. *The White House Years: Mandate for Change, 1953–1956*. Garden City, New York: Doubleday and Company, 1963.

Ewald, William Bragg, Jr. *Eisenhower The President, Crucial Days, 1951–1960*. Englewood Cliffs, New Jersey: Prentice-Hall, Inc., 1981.

Felicijan, Joseph. *The Genesis of the Contractual Theory and the Installation of the Dukes of Carinthia*. Klagenfurt, Austria: Druzba si Mohorja V. Celovcu, 1963.

Fenton, John H. *Midwest Politics*. New York: Holt, Rinehart and Winston, 1966.

Ferrell, Robert H., ed. *The Diary of James C. Hagerty, Eisenhower in Mid-Course, 1954–1955*. Bloomington: Indiana University Press, 1983.

Gibbons, William Conrad. *The U.S. Government and the Vietnam War.* Part III: January–July 1965. Princeton, New Jersey: Princeton University Press, 1989.

_____. *The U.S. Government and the Vietnam War, Executive and Legislative Roles and Relationships.* Part IV, July 1965–January 1968. Princeton, New Jersey: Princeton University Press, 1995.

Gleisser, Marcus. *The World of Cyrus Eaton.* New York: A.S. Barnes and Company, Inc., 1965.

Gobetz, Edward G., ed. *Ohio's Lincoln, Frank J. Lausche.* Willoughby Hills, Ohio: Slovenian Research Center of America, Inc., 1985.

_____. ed. *Slovenian Heritage.* Vol. I. Willoughby Hills, Ohio: Slovenian Research Center of America, Inc., 1981.

Gow, James and Cathie Carmichael. *Slovenia and the Slovenes.* London: Hurst and Company, 2000.

Grabowski, John, ed. *The People of Cleveland.* Cleveland: The Western Reserve Historical Society, 2001.

Grill, Vatroslav. *Med Duema suetovama.* Ljubljana, Slovenia: Mladinska Knjiga, 1979.

Gullan, Harold I. *The Upset That Wasn't, Harry Truman and the Crucial Election of 1948.* Chicago: Ivan R. Dee, 1998.

Gunther, John. *Inside U.S.A.* New York: Harper and Brothers, 1947.

Halberstam, David. *The Best and the Brightest.* New York: Random House, 1972.

_____. *The Fifties.* New York: Villard Books, 1993.

Hatcher, Harlan. *The Western Reserve: The Story of New Connecticut in Ohio.* Cleveland: The World Publishing Company, 1949.

Heimel, Paul W. *Eliot Ness.* Coudersport, Pennsylvania: Knox Books, 1997.

History of St. Vitus Church, 1893–1993. Cleveland: St. Vitus Church, 1992.

Howe, Frederick C. *Confessions of a Reformer.* New York: Charles Scribner's Sons, 1925.

Hurst, Louis. *The Sweetest Little Club in the World: The U.S. Senate.* Englewood Cliffs, N.J.: Prentice-Hall, Inc., 1980

Johnson, Lloyd. *The Minor League Register*, 1st edition. Durham, North Carolina: Baseball America, Inc., 1994.

Johnson, Lyndon Baines. *The Vantage Point: Perspectives of the Presidency, 1963–1969.* New York: Holt, Rinehart and Winston, 1971.

Johnson, Tom L. *My Story*, 2nd edition. Elizabeth Hauser, ed. Kent, Ohio: Kent State University Press, 1993.

Kearns, Doris. *Lyndon Johnson and the American Dream.* New York: Harper and Row, 1976.

Keating, W. Dennis, Norman Krumholz and David C. Perry. *Cleveland, A Metropolitan Reader.* Kent, Ohio: The Kent State University press, 1995.

Kessner, Thomas. *Fiorella LaGuardia and the Making of Modern New York.* New York: McGraw-Hill, 1989.

Key, Vladimer Orlando, Jr. *American State Politics*. New York: Alfred A. Knopf, Inc., 1956.

Klemenčič, Matjaz. *Slovenes of Cleveland and the Creation of a New Nation and a New World Slovenia*. Ljubljana, Slovenia: Triskarma, Novo Mesto, 1995.

Knepper, George W. *Ohio And Its People*. Kent, Ohio: Kent State University Press, 1989.

Lamis, Alexander P., ed. *Ohio Politics*. Kent, Ohio: Kent State University Press, 1994.

Larson, Arthur. *Eisenhower, The President Nobody Knew*. New York: Charles Scribner's Sons, 1968.

Leacasos, John P. *Fires in the In-Basket The ABCs of the State Department*. Cleveland: The World Publishing Company, 1968.

Levinson, David and Melvin Ember, eds. *American Immigrant Cultures*. Vol. 2. New York: Macmillan, 1997.

Lieberman, Carl, ed. *Government and Politics in Ohio*. Lanham, Maryland: University Press of America, Inc., 1984.

Little, Charles E., ed. *Louis Bromfield at Malabar—Writings in Farming and Country Life*. Baltimore, Maryland: Johns Hopkins University Press, 1988.

Mann, Robert. *A Grand Delusion, America's Descent into Vietnam*. New York: Basic Books, 2001.

Markham, Reuben Henry. *Tito's Imperial Communism*. Chapel Hill: The University of North Carolina Press, 1947.

Marshall, William. *Baseball's Pivotal Era, 1945–1951*. Lexington: The University of Kentucky Press, 1998.

McNamara, Robert S. *In Retrospect: The Tragedy and Lessons of Vietnam*. New York: Times, 1995.

Messick, Hank. *The Silent Syndicate*. New York: Macmillan, 1967.

Miller, Carol Poh and Robert Wheeler. *Cleveland, A Concise History, 1796–1996*, 2nd edition. Bloomington: Indiana University Press, 1996.

Montrie, Chad. *To Save the Land and People, A History of Opposition to Surface Coal Mining in Appalachia*. Chapel Hill: The University of North Carolina Press, 2003.

Moore, Leonard N. *Carl B. Stokes and the Rise of Black Political Power*. Urbana, Illinois: University of Illinois Press, 2002.

Neal, Steve. *Harry and Ike*. New York: Scribners, 2001.

Neff, James. *Mobbed Up*. New York: Atlantic Monthly Press, 1989.

Newman, Bernard. *Unknown Yugoslavia*. London: Jenkins Publishing Company, 1960.

Oberdorfer, Donald. *Senator Mansfield*. Washington, DC: Smithsonian Books, 2003.

O'Bryant, Michael, ed. *The Ohio Almanac*. Wilmington, Ohio: Orange Frazer Press, 1997.

O'Donnell, Kenneth P. and David F. Powers. *Johnny, We Hardly Knew Ye*. Boston: Little Brown and Company, 1970.

Patterson, James T. *Mr. Republican, A Biography of Robert A. Taft*. Boston: Houghton-Mifflin Company, 1972.

Pearson, Drew and Jack Anderson. *The Case Against Congress*. New York: Simon and Schuster, 1968.

Peirce, Neal R. and John Keefe. *The Great Lakes States of America*. New York: W.W. Norton, 1980.

Phillips, Cabell B. H. *The Truman Presidency: The History of a Triumphant Succession*. New York: The Macmillan Company, 1966.

Plut-Pregelj, Leopoldina and Carole Rogel. *Historical Dictionary of Slovenia*. Lanham, Maryland: Scarecrow Press, 1996.

Porter, Philip W. *Cleveland, Confused City on a Seesaw*. Columbus: Ohio State University Press, 1976.

Puddington, Arch. *Broadcasting Freedom: The Cold War Triumph of Radio Free Europe and Radio Liberty*. Lexington: The University of Kentucky Press, 2000.

Rader, Benjamin G. *Baseball: A History of America's Game*. Champaign: University of Illinois Press, 1994.

Rose, William Ganson. *Cleveland: The Making of a City*. Cleveland: The World Publishing Company, 1950.

St. Vitus Church, Cleveland, Ohio. South Hackensack New Jersey: Custombook, Inc., 1968.

Safire, William. *Safire's Political Dictionary*. New York: Random House, 1978.

Salsbury, Stephen. *No Way to Run a Railroad*. New York: McGraw-Hill, Inc., 1982.

Saxbe, William B. with Peter D. Franklin. *I've Seen the Elephant*. Kent, Ohio: Kent State University Press, 2000.

Schieffer, Bob. *This Just In*. New York: G.P. Putnam & Sons, 2003.

Schwab, Orrin. *Defending the Free World, John F. Kennedy, Lyndon Johnson and the Vietnam War, 1961–1965*. Westport, Connecticut: Praeger Publishing, 1998.

Schapsmeier, Edward L. and Frederick H. Schapsmeier. *Dirksen of Illinois, Senatorial Statesman*. Urbana, Illinois: University of Illinois, 1985.

Seltzer, Louis. *The Years Were Good*. Cleveland: World Publishing Company, 1956.

Shriver, Phillip R. and Clarence W. Wunderlin. *The Documentary Heritage of Ohio*. Athens, Ohio: Ohio University Press, 2000.

Smith, Page. *America Enters the World: A People's History of the Progressive Era and World War I*, Vol. VII. New York: McGraw-Hill, 1985.

Sobel, Robert. *Coolidge, An American Enigma*. Washington, DC: Regency Publishing Inc., 1998.

Steffens, Lincoln. *The Struggle for Self Government*. New York: McClure, Phillips, 1906.

Steinberg, Alfred. *Sam Johnson's Boy*. New York: The Macmillan Company, 1968.

Stokes, Carl B. *Promises of Power, A Political Autobiography*. New York: Simon and Schuster, 1973.

Steven Thernstrom, ed. *Harvard Encyclopedia of American Ethnic Groups*. Cambridge, Massachusetts: Harvard University Press, 1980.

Taylor, John M. *General Maxwell Taylor, The Sword and the Pen*. New York: Doubleday, 1989.

Truman, Harry S. *Years of Trial and Hope, Memoirs by Harry S. Truman*. Volume Two. Garden City, New York: Doubleday and Company, 1956.

Truman, Margaret. *Harry S. Truman*. New York: William Morrow and Company, 1973.

Van Tassel, David D. and John Grabowski, eds. *Cleveland, A Tradition of Reform*. Kent, Ohio: Kent State University Press, 1986.

_____. *The Encyclopedia of Cleveland History*. Bloomington: Indiana University Press, 1987.

Van Tine, Warren, C.J. Slanicka, Sandra Jordan and Michael Pierce. *In the Worker's Interest: A History of the Ohio AFL-CIO, 1958–1998*. Columbus: Center of Labor Research, The Ohio State University, 1998.

Vecoli, Rudolph J. *Gale Encyclopedia of Multicultural America*. Vol. 2. New York: Gale Research Inc., 1995.

Weinberg, Kenneth G. *Black Victory, Carl Stokes and the Winning of Cleveland*. Chicago: Quadrangle Books, 1968.

Williams, Cynthia, ed. *The Ohio Almanac*, 1972. Lorain, Ohio: Ohio Almanac, 1971.

Winegardner, Mark. *Crooked River Burning*. New York: Harcourt, 2001.

Woldman, Albert A. *The Governors of Ohio*. 2nd ed., Columbus: Ohio Historical Society, 1969.

Woods, Randall. *Fulbright, a Biography*. New York: Cambridge University Press, 1995.

Workers of the Writers' Program of the Work Projects Administration in the State of Ohio in 1942. *The Peoples of Ohio*. Cleveland: Western Reserve Historical Society, 2001.

Wunderlin, Clarence E., Jr., ed. *The Papers of Robert A. Taft, 1939–1944*. Volume 2, Kent, Ohio: The Kent State University Press, 2001.

Zannes, Estelle. *Checkmate in Cleveland*. Cleveland: The Press of Case Western Reserve University, 1972.

Zangrill, Israel. *The Melting Pot: Drama in Four Acts*. New York: McMillan Publishing Company, 1916.

Zimmerman, Richard G. *Call Me Mike, A Political Biography of Michael V. DiSalle*. Kent, Ohio: The Kent State University Press, 2003.

UNPUBLISHED STUDIES

Bindley, Joe Hoover. "An Analysis of Voting Behavior in Ohio." Ph.D. Dissertation, University of Pittsburgh, 1959.

Fordyce, Wellington G. "The Immigration Groups of Cleveland, Ohio." M.A. Thesis, Ohio State University, 1933.

Jauchius, Rollin Dean. "Gubernatorial Roles: An Assessment by Five Ohio Governors," Ph.D. Dissertation, The Ohio State University, 1971.

Kessel, John H. "Road to the Mansion: A Study of the 1956 Gubernatorial Campaign in Ohio." Ph.D. Dissertation, Columbia University, 1958.

Larson, David R. "Ohio's Fighting Liberal: A Political Biography of John J. Gilligan. Ph.D. Dissertation, The Ohio State University, 1982.

Van Tine, Warren R. *Institution of Senator Frank J. Lausche*, Unpublished Monograph, The Ohio State University, 1965.

Bonutti, Karl, Director, *The Cleveland Ethnic Heritage Studies Monograph Series*, 1975.

Cleveland Welfare Federation, *Central Area Study*, 1943 (on file at Cleveland Public Library).

National Associated Businessmen, *Economy Voting Record*, 1965–66.

Personal Transcript of NBC-TV program, "Meet the Press," with Frank J. Lausche, January 8, 1956.

Pevec, Bishop A. Edward, Personal Copy of Homily given at Jane Lausche's funeral, November 28, 1981.

Porterfield, John D., Director, *A Progress Report on Ohio's Mental Hygiene Program, 1945–46.*

Questionnaire to the Voters of Cleveland. (Distributed by Cuyahoga County Democratic Executive Committee, September, 1941).

Slovenian Chapel Dedication Booklet.

Vail, Thomas. *Notes and Memories* given to author, September 11, 2003.

ARTICLES

"Administration of State Affairs." *Everybody's Business*, May 1945, 3.

Alexander, Holmes. "The Clay Doctrine." The Charleston (S.C.) *News and Courier*, 18 July 1963.

Allen, Robert S. and Paul Scott. "JFK Masterminds Push for Approval of Treaty." Sarasota *Herald*, 3 September 1963.

Andrica, Theodore. "Senator Lausche To Speak at Dinner Marking Ukraine Independence." Cleveland *Press*, 15 January 1968.

Baker, John C. "Frank J. Lausche and Education." *Ohio's Lincoln, Frank J. Lausche.* in Edward Gobetz, ed., 116–117. Willoughby Hills, Ohio: Slovenian Research Center of America, Inc., 1985.

Beatty, Jerome. "Everybody's Mayor." *American Magazine*, March 1944, 38, 39, 139–142.

Boyle, Barbara E. "The East Ohio Gas Company Fire." *Timeline*, 12 (September–October 1955): 24, 36, 39.

Broder, David. "Ford Speaks Common Sense." The Idaho *Statesman*, 16 June 2000.

Burkholder, Ralph. "Frank J. Lausche—Hardworking Judge." The Cleveland *Press*, 26 October 1936.

"Cleveland Knew Lausche as a Miracle Man." Youngstown *Vindicator*, 7 January 1945.

Condo, Jerry. "Citizen Lausche." Cincinnati *Post*, 4 November 1981.

Condon, George E. "A Hit in Just About Any League." The *Plain Dealer*, 7 February 1977.

_____. "Down, Lausche A Sad Sight on the Political Scene." Cleveland *Plain Dealer*, 10 July 1977.

Davies, Richard O. "Whistle—Stopping Through Ohio." *Ohio History*, 71 (Spring 1962), 111–123.

Donaldson, Ralph J. "Lausche to Pit Ideals Against Ohio Intrigue." Cleveland *Plain Dealer*, 31 December 1944.

Dolgan, Robert. "The Spellbinder." *American Home*, 20 October 1978.

Douglas, Jean. "Lausche Takes 3rd Term Oath Without Frills." Toledo *Blade*, 8 January 1951.

_____. "Turnpike's Fate Peppered With 'Ifs'." Toledo *Blade*, 26 November 1950.

Doyle, C. J. "Columnist Says Governor Lausche Outwits Listless Opponent." The Oberlin *Times*, 12 September 1946.

Embrey, George. "Lausche's Opinion's Remain Firm." The Columbus *Dispatch*, 9 November 1979.

"Elect Lausche on Win-War Program Here." *Union Leader*, (Cleveland) 5 November 1943.

Feldkamp, Robert. "Lausche Can't Hide Hurt." Akron *Beacon Journal*, 21 January 1968.

_____."View From Washington." Akron *Beacon Journal*, 22 January 1967.

Feagler, Richard. "Lausche: It's Just Like Any Other Day." Cleveland *Press*, 13 May 1968.

Fenton, John H. "Ohio's Unpredictable Voters." *Harpers*, October 1962, 62.

Fordyce, Dr. Wellington G. "Governor Lausche's Election a Triumph for Democracy." *Everybody's Business*, March 1945.

Fritchey, Clayton. "Cleveland's New Mayor." *Common Ground*, Winter 1942, 13–18.

_____. "In Office One of High Achievement." Cleveland *Plain Dealer*, 15 November 1942.

Gerstle, Gary. "Theodore Roosevelt and the Divided Character of American Nationalism." *The Journal of American History*, 86 (December 1999): 1280–1307.

Gietschier, Steven P. "The 1951 Speaker's Rule at Ohio State." *Ohio History*, 87 (Summer 1978), 294–309.

Gibbons, Frank. "I'll Never Forget, Lausche Spurns Boxing Bid." The Cleveland *Press*, Date Unavailable.

Gorisek, Sue. "A Party of One." *Ohio Magazine*, August 1968, 66–67.

Goulder, Grace. "A Day With Jane Lausche, Ohio Scenes and Citizens." Cleveland *Plain Dealer Pictorial Magazine*, 11 December 1949, 11.

_____. "Ohio Scenes and Citizens." Cleveland *Plain Dealer Pictorial Magazine*, 20 January 1952.

"Governor Lausche Recalls Lake Logan History." Logan *News*, 20 July 1956.

Guthrie, Thomas R. "Lausche Takes To The Floor, Asks Pollution War Unity." Cleveland *Plain Dealer*, 3 February 1966.

Hamilton, Roulhac. "Governor's Strong Support of GOP Might Bring Strong Censure." The Columbus *Dispatch*, 29 July 1956.

Hess, David. "The Decline of Ohio." *The Nation*, 13 April 1970, 429–433.

Hessler, William H. "The Implacable Independence of Frank J. Lausche." *The Reporter*, 5 April 1956, 24–28.

Holli, Melvin G. "America's Best Mayor, Tom L. Johnson." *Timeline*, 19 (March–April 2002): 14–15.

Hoyt, Robert E. "Maverick Lausche Bucks for 'Mr. Economy' Tag." Akron *Beacon Journal*, 2 June 1957.

Jauchius, R. Dean. "Rugg is Praised by OSU Dean as Conference Ends." The Columbus *Dispatch*, 12 July 1951.

Joster, Margaret. "Ohio's First Lady is No Unbending Dignitary." Cincinnati *Enquirer*, 25 October 1951.

Kennon, Jack. "A Guiding Star Named Jane." Cleveland *Press*, 1954.

Keyerleber, Karl. "He Fields Ohio's Hot Ones." *The Nation*, 22 July 1944, 95–96.

Kilpatrick, James J. "A Sad Song on Lausche's Defeat." Cleveland *Plain Dealer*, 12 May 1968.

_____. "Lament For Lausche—A Virtuoso On The Hill." Washington *Star*, 12 May 1968.

Kolar, Michael. "The Young Frank J. Lausche." *American Home*, 20 October 1978.

Kruse, Erma. "A Day With Jane Lausche." Cleveland *Press*, 17 January 1945.

Kytle, C. "What Makes Lausche Run?" *Coronet*, April 1956.

Larkin, Brent. "Frank Lausche, A Legend in Ohio Politics." *The Plain Dealer Magazine*, 10 November 1985, 6–7, 18, 20–21, 25–27.

Larkin, Brent. "The Power Brokers, Glory Days of Political Bosses," *The Plain Dealer Magazine*, 3 May 1991.

Lausche, Frank J. "Dangerous Failings of Our State Department," *Reader's Digest*, June 1964, 54–60.

"Lausche Attacks Domestic Peace Corps." *Human Events* 19, 22 December 1962.

"Lausche Helped Many Slovenian Immigrants." *American Home*, 14 November 1975.

"Lausche Is Scored On U.S. Road Deal." Cleveland *Plain Dealer*, 7 March 1953.

"Lausche Run With GOP Is Suggested." Cleveland *Plain Dealer*, 12 January 1968.

"Lausche vs Lobbyists." Dayton *News*, 23 October 1946.

"Lausche's Conqueror: John Joyce Gilligan." *New York Times*, 9 May 1968.

Leacasos, John O. "Lausche's Crucial Decision in Vietnam." Cleveland *Plain Dealer*, 9 July 1967.

_____. "Lausche Ready to Battle." Cleveland *Plain Dealer*, 14 January 1968.

Lawrence, David. "Why Not Governor Lausche?" *U.S. News and World Report*, 9 December 1955.

Lewis, Fulton Jr. "Democrat Ohio Strong Man." Columbus *Citizen*, 4 January 1954.

"The Lonely One." *Time*, 20 February 1956, 20–23.

Lore, David. "Inside the Pen." The Columbus *Dispatch*, 28 October 1984.

Maeroff, Gene I. "Ohio: Politics After Johnson." *The Nation*, 22 April 1968, 538–540.

"Man of the Week: A Good and Fearless Judge." Cleveland *News*, 12 October 1940.

Maher, Richard L. "Hays Approval Delights Lausche." Cleveland *Plain Dealer*, 31 December 1967.

_____. "Political Paradox." *The Nation*, 4 October 1952, 299–300.

_____. "Sweeney Tells It To Ohio Dems: End Party Feuding, Aid Lausche." Cleveland *Plain Dealer*, 13 December 1967.

_____. " 'We're in Accord': Miller Says After Lausche Talk." The Cleveland *Press*, 24 July 1941.

Manly, Chesly. "Frank Lausche: Ohio's Taft Democrat." *Human Events*, 13 (31 March 1956).

Manning, Ralph. "Lausche Says Gag Rule Up to Trustees." Columbus *Citizen*, 15 October 1951.

Matson, Charles. "Frank J. Lausche New Municipal Judge." The Cleveland *Press*, 31 December 1932.

"Mayor Lausche of Cleveland." *New Republic*, 31 July 1944.

McCarry, Charles M. "Frank Lausche: Senator Without A Party." *True Magazine*, (October–November) 1958, 18–28, 112–116.

McCullough, David B. "Giving 'Em Hell in Ohio." *Timeline*, 24 (July–August 1995): 2, 3.

McDermott, William. "Mayor Breaks All Rules of Politics, Yet Honesty and Simplicity Win Him Governorship." Cleveland *Plain Dealer*, 9 November 1944.

McGarey, Mary. "Shocknessy: Official is Man of Words and Performance." The Columbus *Dispatch*, 20 August 1972.

_____. "The Governor's Lady—Ohio's Her Hobby." The Columbus *Sunday Dispatch Magazine*, 25 January 1953, 10.

"Mental Health Record." Cleveland *Plain Dealer*, 24 October 1946.

Mlachak, Norman. "Lausche was a Mayor for All." Cleveland *Plain Dealer*, 10 July 1977.

Mlachak, Norman. "Cleveland's Former Mayors." The Cleveland *Press*, 8 September 1980.

Moley, Raymond. "Phony Union Reform." *Newsweek*, 30 June 1958.

Morris, Joe Alex. "Who is Frank Lausche?" *The Saturday Evening Post*, 10 December 1955, 39, 114–117.

Naughton, James M. "Ohio: A Lesson in Changing Politics." *New York Times Magazine*, 5 May 1968, 33, 110, 114–120.

"New Governor Works Hard, Defies Politicians." Cincinnati *Enquirer*, 14 January 1945.

Norton-Taylor, Duncan. "The Leaderless, Lively Democrats." *Fortune Magazine*, January 1954.

O'Hara, Richard. "Popcorn or Not, Rhodes Still No Lausche." The Dayton *Daily News*, 25 August 1963.

"Ohio-Declaration of Independents." *Time*, 19 May 1956, 30.

"Ohio Democrats Dump Lausche." Cleveland *Plain Dealer*, 12 January 1968.

"Ohio Prosperity High Among Nation's States." The Columbus *Dispatch*, 28 August 1955.

"Ohio's Winning Governor Lausche—And the White House." *Newsweek*, 21 May 1956, 36.

"1,000 Sing Praises of Judge Lausche." Cleveland *Plain Dealer*, 24 February 1937.

"Pursuing the Artful Dodger." *Time*, 8 October 1956, 26.

Posvar, Vladimir. "Curb Remarriages! Lausche Tip on Divorce." Cleveland *News*, 29 December 1937.

"Progress Reported at Lausches." Columbus *Citizen*, 12 June 1945.

"The Question Of Federal Assistance For Urban Mass Transit Systems." *Congressional Digest*, January 1963, 19.

Reider, Robert W. "Reports From the State Capitol." Waverly *Watchman*, 24 March 1955.

Rich, Robert. "Ness, A Mr. Clean Cleveland Desperately Needed." Cleveland *Plain Dealer*, 16 June 1996.

Riesel, Victor. "Sales of Cuban Goods in U.S. Take Big Jump." Canton *Repository*, 25 December 1961.

Robertson, Don. "Confessions of An Old Man." Cleveland *Press*, 13 May 1968.

Rutherford, Roy. "Mother is a Guiding Influence in the Career of Frank Lausche." Cleveland *Plain Dealer*, 15 August 1948.

Schriftgiesser, Karl. "Lausche of Ohio, How to Survive a Landslide." *Colliers*, 28 March 1953, 74–80.

Shaffer, Samuel. "Ohio's Winning Governor Lausche and the White House." *Newsweek*, 21 May 1956, 35.

Seltzer, Louis. "For a Second Term—Gov. Frank Lausche." Cleveland *Press*, 15 October 1946.

_____. "The Magic Is Missing." Cleveland *Press*, 16 July 1960.

Silverman, Alvin. "Lausche Blasts Uncurbed Strikes." Cleveland *Plain Dealer*, 30 April 1943.

_____. "Jeer Lausche as Wage Veto is Overridden." Cleveland *Plain Dealer*, 1 April 1944.

_____. "Lausche Will Run; Blasts Bosses Rule." Cleveland *Plain Dealer*, 31 January 1948.

_____. "Truman Patches Lausche Wounds." Cleveland *Plain Dealer*, 27 October 1948.

_____. "Gov. Lausche Won't Accept Baseball Job." Cleveland *Plain Dealer*, 17 September 1951.

_____. "Lausche Backs O.S.U. Screening Order, Says It Is Fair, Is Not a 'Gag'." Cleveland *Plain Dealer*, 25 October 1951.

_____. "Honorable Curleytop Rides Again." Cleveland *Plain Dealer*, 17 October 1954.

_____. "Senator Lausche To Cast Vote For Johnson." Cleveland *Plain Dealer*, 23 October 1964.

Simm, Todd. "Ethnic Politics Fading Out." Cleveland *Plain Dealer*, 10 May 1968.

Small, Jack. "A New Governor—But the Work of Loyal John Lokar Made a Hope a Reality." The Cleveland *Press,* 10 November 1944.

Stacy, Harold A. "Dems Hope to Stay Clear of Ohio Battle." The Columbus *Dispatch*, 14 December 1947.

Susel, Rudolph. "A Great American, A Great Slovenian." *American Home*, 26 April 1990.

Tisdale, Frederick. "Strong Man of Columbus." *The Saturday Evening Post*, 7 July 1945, 17, 90–92.

Trohan, Walter. "Lausche Victory Premised On Independent Integrity." Chicago *Tribune*, 9 February 1968.

Vincent, Robert. "Key Man—John Lokar." Columbus *Citizen*, 24 January 1945.

Welch, Robert. "On the Right Side." *One Man's Opinion*,1 (July 1956), 1–10.

Woldman, Albert A. "Frank J. Lausche." *The Governors of Ohio*, 2nd ed., 189–94, Columbus: Ohio Historical Society, 1969.

"Won't Run Again, Lausche Eyes 'Quiet' Law Practice." Cleveland *Plain Dealer*, 14 December 1952.

Zimmerman, Richard. "Would You Believe There's A Lausche?" Dayton *Journal Herald*, 20 June 1966.

LIBRARIES

Cleveland Public Library.
Cleveland State University Library.
Columbus Public Library.
Everett Dirksen Library (Pekin, Illinois).
Dwight Eisenhower Presidential Library.
Lyndon B. Johnson Presidential Library.
John F. Kennedy Presidential Library.
Kent State University Press—*The Papers of Robert A. Taft*, Volumes 2 and 3.
Library of Congress.
    Branch Rickey Papers
    Congressional Record.
    Congressional Quarterly Almanac.
    Congressional Digest.
    Cyrus Zebot Papers.
    National Archives and Records Administration, Washington, DC. Records of the Committee on Foreign Relations.
    United States Senate Historical Office, U.S. Senate, Washington, DC
Mansfield (Ohio) Public Library.
    Louis Bromfield Papers.
Ohio Historical Society.
    Frank J. Lausche Papers.
    The Governors of Ohio.
The Ohio State University Library.
    Louis Bromfield Papers.
The Western Reserve Historical Society
    Thomas A. Burke Papers.
    Cleveland Mayoral Papers.
    Cyrus Eaton Papers.
    Ray T. Miller Papers.
    Eliot Ness Papers.

NEWSPAPERS—IN-STATE

American Home (Ameriška Domovina).
Akron *Beacon-Journal*.
Canton *Repository*.
Cincinnati *Enquirer*.
Cincinnati *Post*.
Cincinnati *Times-Star*.
Cleveland *Leader*.
Cleveland *Plain Dealer*.
Cleveland *Press*.
Columbus *Dispatch*
Dayton *Daily News*.
Dayton *Journal-Herald*.
Logan *News*.
Mansfield *News Journal*.
Ohio State *Journal*.
The Oberlin *Times*.
Toledo *Blade*.
Toledo *Times*.
Union Leader. (Cleveland).
Waverly *Watchman*.
Youngstown *Vindicator*.

NEWSPAPERS—OUT-OF-STATE

Chicago *Tribune*.
Los Angeles *Times*.
New York Times.
Sarasota *Herald*
The Idaho *Statesman*.
The *Sporting News*.
Washington *News*.
Washington *Post*.
Washington *Star*.
Winston Salem *Journal*.

JOURNALS

American Magazine
Atlantic Monthly
Colliers
Common Ground
Coronet
Everybody's Business
Fortune Magazine
Harpers
Human Events
Journal of American History
New Republic
New Yorker
Newsweek
Ohio History
One Man's Opinion
Reader's Digest
The Nation
The Reporter
The Saturday Evening Post
Time
Timeline
True Magazine
U.S. News and World Report

Personal Interviews

Bonutti, Dr. Karl: Cleveland, Ohio, 15 May 1997.

Brady, Jerry: Boise, Idaho, 10 October 2002.

Brown, Clarence, Jr.: Washington, DC., 26 June 1997.

Celebrezze, Anthony: Telephone interview, 17 June 1996.

Church, Bethine: Boise, Idaho, 6 December 1999.

Condon, George: Telephone interview, 20 June 1996.

Debevic, James and Madeline: Cleveland, Ohio, 14 May 1997.

Dolgan, Robert: Cleveland, Ohio, 14 May 1997.

Drobnick, Jean: Cleveland, Ohio, 20 May 1997.

Ertzen, Stanley: Cleveland, Ohio, 26 June 1995.

Gilligan, John J.: Cincinnati, Ohio, 24 June 1997 and 19 July 2004.

Herbstreit, Judy: Telephone interview, 30 July 2003.

Hollings, Senator Ernest 'Fritz': Washington, DC., 6 June 1997.

Jones, Sally: Puerto Gordo, Florida, 25 January 2000.

Larkin, Brent: Cleveland, Ohio, 21 July 2004.

Lausche, Antonia: Cleveland, Ohio, 20 May 1996.

Locher, Ralph: Cleveland, Ohio, 9 September 1996.

Mejac, Dr. Cyril and Conrad: Washington, DC, 29 June 1997.

Metzdorff, Glenn: Washington, DC, 28 June 1997.

Metzenbaum, Howard: Telephone interview, 20 May 1997.

Perk, Ralph: Cleveland, Ohio, 20 June 1997.

Pevec, Bishop Edward A.: Cleveland, Ohio, 9 June 1997.

Pryatel, August: Telephone interview, 22 May 1997.

Rado, Gloria: Parma, Ohio, 8 September 2001.

Rhodes, James: Telephone interview, 21 June 1996.

Ritchie, Dr. Donald: U.S. Senate Historical Office, Washington, DC, 28 June 1997.

Saxbe, William B.: Mechanicsburg, Ohio, 20 July 2004.

Stanton, James V.: Telephone interview, 15 November 2004.

Susel, Dr. Rudolph: Cleveland, Ohio, 20 May 1997 and 9 September 2001.

Sustersic, Dr. Stanley: Washington, DC, 29 June 1997.

Turkman, Josephine: Cleveland, Ohio 1 May, 1997.

Usher, Brian: Columbus, Ohio, 24 June 1995.

Vail, Thomas: Cleveland, Ohio, 15 September 2003.

Valencic, Joseph A. Cleveland, Ohio, 5 May 1997.

Van Tine, Dr. Warren: Columbus, Ohio, 25 June 1996.

Vanik, Charles: Telephone interview, 24 January 2000.

Wells, Virginia: Washington, DC, 27 June 1997 and 24 December 1999, 12 June 2004.

End Notes

CHAPTER ONE

1 *American Home*, April 26, 1990.

2 Robert Dolgan, "Lausche, 80, Parties With 400 Friends on Birthday," *The Plain Dealer*, November 10, 1975; speech given by Frank J. Lausche, undated (Frank J. Lausche Papers, Box 245), Ohio Historical Society

3 George E. Condon, Jr., *Cleveland, The Best Kept Secret.* (Garden City, New York: Doubleday and Company, Inc., 1967), 1.

4 David D. Van Tassel and John Grabowski, eds. *The Encyclopedia of Cleveland History.* (Bloomington: Indiana University Press, 1987), xvii and xviii.

5 Harlan Hatcher, *The Western Reserve: The Story of New Connecticut in Ohio.* (Cleveland: The World Publishing Company, 1949), 195–96.

6 Elbert Jay Benton, *Cleveland, Cultural Story of an American City*, pt. 2 "Under the Shadow of the Civil War and Reconstruction, 1850–1877," (Cleveland: Western Reserve Historical Society, 1948), 10–12; see also Carol A. Beal and Ronald R. Weiner, "The Sixth City: Cleveland in Three Stages of Urbanization," Thomas F. Campbell and Edward M. Miggins, *The Birth of Modern Cleveland, 1865–1930.* (Cleveland: Western Reserve Historical Society, 1988), 25–29.

7 Thomas F. Campbell and Edward M. Miggins, *The Birth of Modern Cleveland, 1865–1930,* 55–56.

8 David D. Van Tassel and John Gabrowski, eds. *The Encyclopedia of Cleveland History*, xxv.

9 W. Dennis Keating, Norman Krumholz and David C. Perry, *Cleveland, A Metropolitan Reader.* (Kent, Ohio: The Kent State University Press, 1995), 36.

10 David D. Van Tassel and John Grabowski, eds. *The Encyclopedia of Cleveland History*, 415.

11 William Ganson Rose, *Cleveland: The Making of a City.* (Cleveland: The World Publishing Company, 1950), 36; Elroy McKendree Avery, *A History of Cleveland and Its Environs.* (Chicago: Lewis Publishing, 1918), 1:307–8.

12 Thomas F. Campbell and Edward M. Miggins, *The Birth of Modern Cleveland, 1865–1930*, 104.

13 Ibid, 77.

14 Cleveland *Leader*, July 14, 1873 (taken from "Cleveland: The Making and Remaking of an American City, 1796–1993," by Carol Poh Miller and Robert A. Wheeler in *Cleveland, A Metropolitan Reader,* W. Dennis Keating, Norman Krumholz, and David C. Perry, eds.), 37.

15 Ibid.

16 Ibid.

17 Carol Poh Miller and Robert Wheeler, eds., *Cleveland, a Concise History*, 2nd edition. (Bloomington: Indiana University Press, 1996) 83; Thomas F. Campbell and Edward Miggins, *The Birth of Modern Cleveland, 1865–1930*, 105.

18   Thomas F. Campbell and Edward M. Miggins, *The Birth of Modern Cleveland, 1865–1930*, 104–105. The term Chicken Village was given to Slovenians who raised chickens in their backyard in the early years of settlement in East Cleveland.

19   Carol Poh Miller and Robert Wheeler, 2nd edition, *Cleveland, a Concise History*, 83; Thomas F. Campbell and Edward Miggins, *The Birth of Modern Cleveland, 1865–1930*, 105.

20   Thomas F. Campbell and Edward Miggins, *The Birth of Modern Cleveland, 1865–1930*, 106–108.

21   Carol Poh Miller and Robert Wheeler, *Cleveland, A Concise History*, 83.

22   Rudolph Susel, *Harvard Encyclopedia of American Ethnic Groups*, Steven Thernstrom, ed. (Cambridge, Massachusetts: Harvard University Press, 1980), 936–42; Edward Gobetz, "Slovenian Americans," in *American Immigrant Cultures*, Vol. 2, David Levinson and Melvin Ember, ed., (New York: Macmillan, 1997), 1258.

23   Rudolph Susel, *Harvard Encyclopedia of American Ethnic Groups*, 935–36; Edward Gobetz, "Slovenian Americans," in *American Immigrant Cultures*, Vol. 2, 1258.

24   *New York Times*, Travel Section, August, 2001.

25   Rudolph Susel, *Harvard Encyclopedia of American Ethnic Groups*, 936–42; Edward Gobetz, "Slovenian Americans," in *American Immigrant Cultures*, Vol. 2, 1259–60.

26   Jill Benderly and Evan Kraft, *Independent Slovenia, Origins, Movements, Prospects*. (New York: St. Martin's Press, 1994), 4–5.

27   Rudolph S. Susel, *Harvard Encyclopedia of American Ethnic Groups*, 934.

28   Jill Benderly and Evan Kraft, *Independent Slovenia, Origins, Movements, Prospects*, 5; Leopoldina Plut-Pregelj and Carole Rogel, *Historical Dictionary of Slovenia*. (Lanham, Maryland: Scarecrow Press, 1996), 2.

29   Jill Benderly and Evan Kraft, *Independent Slovenia, Origins, Movements, Prospects*, 7.

30   James Gow and Catkie Carmichael, *Slovenia and the Slovenes*. (London: Hurst and Company, 2000), 69.

31   Edward G. Gobetz, ed., *Frank J. Lausche: Life History of Ohio's Lincoln*. (Willoughby Hills, Ohio: Slovenian Research Center of America, Inc., 1985), 8; Bernard Newman, *Unknown Yugoslavia*. London; Jenkins Publishing Company, 1960), 198–99.

32   Edward G. Gobetz, ed., *Frank J. Lausche: Life History of Ohio's Lincoln,* Ibid; Reuben Henry Markham, *Tito's Imperial Communism*. (Chapel Hill, The University of North Carolina Press, 1947), 10–11.

33   Jill Benderly and Evan Kraft, *Independent Slovenia, Origins, Movements, Prospects*, 4.

34   Jill Benderly and Evan Kraft, *Independent Slovenia, Origins, Movements, Prospects*, 9–10; Rudolph Susel, *Harvard Encyclopedia of American Ethnic Groups*, 934.

35   Matjaz Klemenčič, *Slovenes of Cleveland and the Creation of a New Nation and a New World Slovenia*. (Ljubjana, Slovenia: Tiskarma, Novo Mesto, 1995), 16–17; Rudolph Susel, *Harvard Encyclopedia of American Ethnic Groups*, 934.

36   Jill Benderly and Evan Kraft, *Independent Slovenia, Origins, Movements, Prospects,* 9.

37   Rudolph Susel, *Harvard Encyclopedia of American Ethnic Groups*, 935.

38   Ibid.

39   Ibid.

40   Howard P. Chudacoff and Judith Smith, *The Evolution of American Urban Society*. (Englewood Cliffs, New Jersey: Prentice-Hall, 1975), 110.

41   Carol Poh Miller and Robert Wheeler, *Cleveland, a Concise History*, 77–78.

42   John Grabowski, ed., *The People of Cleveland*. (Cleveland: Western Reserve Historical Society, 2001), 83–84.

43   Louis Adamic, *Ellis Island: An Illustrated History of Immigrant Experience*, Ivan Chermayeff, et al, eds. (New York: Macmillan, 1991).

44   Page Smith, *America Enters the World: A People's History of the Progressive Era, and World War I,* Vol. VII. (New York: McGraw-Hill, 1985), 9–10.

45   Rudolph J. Vecoli, *Gale Encyclopedia of Multicultural America*, Vol. 2. (New York: Gale Research Inc., 1995), 820.

46   *History of St. Vitus Church, 1893–1993.* (Cleveland: St. Vitus Church, 1992), 32–34.

47   John Dyneley Prince, "The Gottschee Germans of Slovenia," *The Proceedings of the American Philosophical Society.* Vol. 20, No. 4, 1931, 391–93.

48   Ibid.

49   Letter from Frank J. Lausche to Theresa Herndon, Camden, Tennessee, June 24, 1968. (Frank J. Lausche Papers, Box 246), Ohio Historical Society.

50   Edward G. Gobetz, ed., *Frank J. Lauschc: Life History of Ohio's Lincoln*, 9.

51   Branko Nita Colakovic, *Yugoslavia Migrations to America.* (San Francisco: Rand E. Research Associates, 1973), 37.

52   Clayton Fritchey, "Cleveland's New Mayor," *Common Ground*, II, February, 1942, 13–18.

53   Rudolph Susel, editor *American Home*, interview by author in Cleveland on September 9, 2001.

54   "The Lonely One," *Time*, February 20, 1956, 21.

55   Ibid

56   Sigrid Arne, "Lausche's Parents Stirred Melting Pot," Cleveland *News*, October 21, 1957.

57   Interview between Edward G. Gobetz and Josephine Welf, Frank J. Lausche's sister, August 18, 1982, published in *Ohio's Lincoln, Frank J. Lausche*, 11.

58   Sigrid Arne, "Lausche's Parents Stirred Melting Pot," Cleveland *News*, October 21, 1957.

59   Interview between Edward G. Gobetz and Josephine Welf, Frank J. Lausche's sister, August 18, 1982, published in *Ohio's Lincoln, Frank J. Lausche*, 13.

60   C. Kytle, "What Makes Lausche Run?" *Coronet*, April 1956, 1025; "The Lonely One," *Time*, February 20, 1956, 22.

Chapter Two

1   William Ganson Rose, *Cleveland, The Making of a City*, 967.

2   W. Dennis Keating, Norman Krumholtz, and David C. Perry, eds., *Cleveland: A Metropolitan Reader*, 40.

3   Carol Poh Miller and Robert Wheeler, *Cleveland, A Concise History, 1796–1996*, 2nd ed., 100–01; W. Dennis Keating, Norman Krumholtz, and David C. Perry, *Cleveland: A Metropolitan Reader*, 40.

4   Cynthia Williams, ed., *The Ohio Almanac, 1972.* (Lorain, Ohio: Ohio Almanac, 1971), 28; William Ganson Rose, *Cleveland, The Making of a City*, 680.

5   Ibid.

6   Cynthia Williams, ed., *The Ohio Almanac, 1972*, 29; William Ganson Rose, *The Making of a City*, 702.

7   W. Dennis Keating, Norman Krumholtz, and David C. Perry, *Cleveland, A Metropolitan Reader* ,41.

8   Philip W. Porter, *Cleveland, Confused City on a Seesaw.* (Columbus: Ohio State University Press, 1976), 4.

9   Andrew R. L. Cayton and Susan E. Gray, eds., *The American Midwest*. (Bloomington: Indiana University Press, 2001), 20–21; Tom L. Johnson, *My Story*, 2nd ed., Elizabeth Hauser, ed., (Kent, Ohio: Kent State University Press, 1993), xi, xii.

10 Thomas F. Campbell, *Daniel E. Morgan, 1877–1948 The Good Citizen in Politics*. (Cleveland: The Press of Western Reserve University, 1966), 11.

11 Elroy McKendree Avery, *A History of Cleveland and Its Environs*. (Chicago: Lewis Publishing, 1918), 307–8.

12 David D. VanTassel and John J. Grabowski, *The Encyclopedia of Cleveland History*, xi.

13 Thomas F. Campbell, *Daniel E. Morgan*, 11.

14 Clarence H. Cramer, *Newton D. Baker, A. Biography*. (Cleveland: World Publishing Company, 1961), 34–44.

15 Frederick C. Howe, *Confessions of a Reformer*. (New York: Charles Scribner's Sons, 1925), 189–90.

16 George E. Condon, Jr., *Cleveland, The Best Kept Secret*, 167; David D. Van Tassel and John J. Grabowski, *The Encyclopedia of Cleveland History*, xii.

17 Melvin G. Holli, "America's Best Mayor, Tom L. Johnson," *Timeline*, March-April, 2002, 12–13.

18 George E. Condon, Jr., *Cleveland, The Best Kept Secret*,167; Carol Poh Miller and Robert Wheeler, *Cleveland, A Concise History*, 107.

19 George E. Condon, Jr., *Cleveland's Best Kept Secret*, 174–175; David D. VanTassel and John J. Grabowski, *Encyclopedia of Cleveland History*, 579; Melvin G. Holli, "America's Best Mayor, Tom L. Johnson," *Timeline*, March-April, 2002, 14–15; Carol Poh Miller and Robert A. Wheeler, *Cleveland, A Metropolitan Reader*, 40.

20 Ibid.

21 Ibid.

22 Lincoln Steffens, *The Struggle for Self Government*. (New York: McClure, Phillips, 1906), 161.

23 Carol Poh Miller and Robert Wheeler, *Cleveland, a Concise History, 1896 – 1996*, 103–105; Workers of the Writers' Program of the Work Projects Administration in the State of Ohio in 1942, *The Peoples of Ohio*. (Cleveland: Western Reserve Historical Society, 2001), 4–5.

24 Israel Zangrill, *The Melting Pot: Drama in Four Acts*. (New York: McMillan Publishing Company, 1916).

25 Israel Zangrill, *The Melting Pot*; Roosevelt to Israel Zangwill, October 15, 1908 in *Letters of Theodore Roosevelt*, Elting E. Morison, ed., 1288; Gary Gerstle, "Theodore Roosevelt and the Divided Character of American Nationalism," *The Journal of American History*, Vol. 86, No.3 (December, 1999) 1280–1307.

26 Thomas Kessner, *Fiorella LaGuardia and the Making of Modern New York*. (New York: McGraw-Hill, 1989), 12.

27 Ronald Weiner, "The New Industrial Metropolis; 1860–1929," in *The Encyclopedia of Cleveland History*, David P. VanTassel and John J. Grabowski, eds., xxxv.

28 Roy Rutherford, "Mother is a Guiding Influence in the Career of Frank Lausche," Cleveland *Plain Dealer*, August 15, 1948.

29 Joseph Zelle, "St. Vitus: Its People, Its History, and Its Faith," in *St. Vitus Church*. Cleveland, Ohio (South Hackensack, New Jersey: Custombook, Inc., 1968), 4.

30 "The Lonely One," *Time*, February 20, 1956, 21.

31 Edward G. Gobetz, "Men at the Top: Slovenian Chancellors of Germany and Austria and Senators of the United States and Australia" in Edward Gobetz, ed.; *Slovenian Heritage*, Vol. I. (Willoughby Hills, Ohio: The Slovenian Research Center of America, 1981), 213.

32 Karl Schriftgiesser, "How to Survive a Landslide," *Colliers*, March 28, 1953, 75.

33 Frederick S. Tisdale, "Strong Man of Columbus," *The Saturday Evening Post,* July 7, 1945, 90.

34 Letter from Frank J. Lausche to Scott Lucas (former senator from Illinois), undated (Frank J. Lausche Papers, Box 251) Ohio Historical Society.

35 Frederick Tisdale, "Strong Man of Columbus, "*Saturday Evening Post,* July 7, 1945, 90; *American Home*, October 20, 1978; Edward Gobetz, Ed., *Slovenian Heritage*, Vol. I, 211–222.

36 Edward Gobetz, ed., *Frank J. Lausche: Life History of Ohio's Lincoln,* 17.

37 Mike Kolar, "The Young Frank J. Lausche," *American Home*, October 20, 1978.

38 Bob Dolgan, "The Spellbinder," *American Home,* October 20, 1978.

39 John P. Nielsen, "The Aura of the Lausche Family," a vignette in *Frank J. Lausche: Life History of Ohio's Lincoln,* Edward G. Gobetz, ed., 97–99.

40 Karl Keyerleber, "He Fields Ohio's Hot Ones," *The Nation*, July 22, 1944, 96.

41 George E. Condon, Jr., "A Hit in Just About Any League," *The Plain Dealer*, Feb. 7, 1977.

42 Bruce Chadwick, *Baseball's Home Town Teams, The Story of the Minor Leagues.* (New York: Abbeville Press, 1944), 87.

43 Letter from Frank Lausche to Fritz Howell, sports columnist for the Associated Press, June 30, 1964 (Frank J. Lausche Papers, Box 251) Ohio Historical Society.

44 George E. Condon, Jr., "A Hit in Just About Any League," *The Plain Dealer*, Feb. 7, 1977.

45 Lloyd Johnson, *The Minor League Register*, 1st ed. (Durham, North Carolina: Baseball America, Inc., 1994), 173.

46 Frank Gibbons, "I'll Never Forget, Lausche Spurns Boxing Bid," Cleveland *Press*, date unavailable.

47 Letter from Frank Lausche to Fritz Howell, June 30, 1964, (Frank J. Lausche Papers, Box 251) Ohio Historical Society.

48 Frederick Tisdale, "The Strong Man of Columbus," *The Saturday Evening Post*, July 7, 1945, 90.

49 *Congressional Record*, Senate, April 15, 1964, 8039–40.

50 Clayton Fritchey, "Cleveland's New Mayor," *Common Ground*, II, February 1942, 13–18.

51 Letter from Frank J. Lausche to Jack Edchert, November 21, 1963 (Frank J. Lausche Papers, Box 255) Ohio Historical Society.

52 Frederick Tisdale, "The Strong Man of Columbus" July 7, 1945, 90.

53 "The Lonely One," *Time*, February 20, 1956, 22.

54 Carol Poh Miller and Robert Wheeler, *Cleveland, A Concise History, 1796–1996*, 11.

55 William Ganson Rose, *Cleveland, The Making of a City*, 781.

56 Carol Poh Miller and Robert Weaver, "The Making and Remaking of an American City, 1796–1993," in *Cleveland, A Metropolitan Reader*, 41.

57 David D. VanTassel and John J. Grabowski, *The Encyclopedia of Cleveland History*, xiii; Carol Poh Miller and Robert Wheeler, *Cleveland, A Concise History*, 116.

58 Carol Poh Miller and Robert Wheeler, *Cleveland, A Concise History, 1796–1996*, 2nd ed., 114–5.

59 Phillip W. Porter, *Cleveland, Confused City on a Seesaw*, 17–18.

60 Thomas F. Campbell and Edward M. Miggins, eds., *The Birth of Modern Cleveland, 1865–1930*, 320–21.

61 Ibid.

62 Wellington G. Fordyce, *The Immigration Groups of Cleveland, Ohio*, (M.A. Thesis, Ohio State University, 1933), 58.

63 Philip W. Porter, *Cleveland, Confused City on a Seesaw*, 8; Robert S. Allen, *Our Fair City*. (New York: The Vanguard Press, 1947), 131–32.

64 Carol Poh Miller and Robert A. Wheeler, *Cleveland, A Concise History, 1796–1996,* 120; Philip Porter, *Cleveland a City on a Seesaw*, 8; Robert S. Allen, *Our Fair City*, 132.

65 Philip Porter, *Cleveland, Confused City on a Seesaw*, 10; David D. VanTassel and John J. Grabowski, *The Encyclopedia of Cleveland History*, 185.

66 Philip Porter, *Cleveland, Confused City on a Seesaw*, 10–11; David D. Van Tassel and John J. Grabowski, *The Encyclopedia of Cleveland History*, 31, 208.

67 Chuck Matson, "Frank J. Lausche New Municipal Judge," The Cleveland *Press*, December 31, 1932; Jerome Beatty, "Everybody's Mayor," *American Magazine*, March 1944, 38.

68 Ray Rutherford, "Mother is a Guiding Influence in the Career of Frank Lausche," *Plain Dealer*, August 15, 1948.

69 David D. Van Tassel and John Grabowski, Eds. *The Encyclopedia of Cleveland History*, 758; Charles McCarry, "Frank Lausche: Senator Without A Party," *True Magazine*, Fall, 1958, 26, 28.

Chapter Three

1   Carol Poh Miller and Robert A. Wheeler, *Cleveland: A Concise History, 1796–1996*, 103.

2   David D. Van Tassel and John Grabowski, eds., *The Encyclopedia of Cleveland History*, 898.

3   Edward G. Gobetz, ed., *Frank J. Lausche: Life History of Ohio's Lincoln*, 328; Eleanor Prech, "City Heritage," Cleveland *Press*, December 9, 1976.

4   David D. Van Tassel and John Grabowski, eds., *The Encyclopedia of Cleveland History*, 452.

5   Frederick Tisdale, "Strong Man of Columbus," *Saturday Evening Post*, July 7, 1945, 92.

6   Clayton Fritchey, "Cleveland's New Mayor," *Common Ground*, II, February, 1942, 16.

7   Marvin R. Koller, "Lausche and Ethnic Humor," in Edward G. Gobetz, ed., *Frank J. Lausche: Life History of Ohio's Lincoln*, 137–138.

8   Clayton Fritchey, "Cleveland's New Mayor," *Common Ground*, II, 16.

9   Ralph J. Donaldson, "Lausche to Pit Ideals Against Ohio Intrigue," Cleveland *Plain Dealer*, December 31, 1944.

10 Excerpts from a summary of William J. Lausche's musical accomplishments prepared by his widow Alice in 1972 for Edward G. Gobetz, Director of the Slovenian Research Center of America, Inc. and published in *Frank J. Lausche: Life History of Ohio's Lincoln*, Edward Gobetz, ed., 143–45; David D. Van Tassel and John Grabowski, eds., *The Encyclopedia of Cleveland History*, 7. Dr. William Lausche died on July 8, 1967, in Cleveland.

11 Carol Poh Miller and Robert A. Wheeler, *Cleveland: A Concise History, 1796–1996*, 146.

12 Philip W. Porter, *Cleveland, Confused City on a Seesaw*, 53.

13 Thomas F. Campbell, *Daniel E. Morgan*. (Cleveland: The Press of Western Reserve University, 1966), 124.

14 Carol Poh Miller and Robert A. Wheeler, *Cleveland: A Concise History, 1796–1996*, 129–131.

15 Ohio State *Journal*, January 6, 1929.

16 Jean Drobnick, daughter of Frank Jaksic, important political figure in the 23rd Ward during 1920s and 1930s, interview by author in Cleveland, Ohio, on May 20, 1997; *American Home*, October 20, 1978.

17 Thomas F. Campbell, *Daniel E. Morgan*, 127.

18 Philip W. Porter, *Confused City on a Seesaw*, 65.

19 Philip Porter, *Confused City on a Seesaw*, 53; Louis Seltzer, *The Years Were Good*. (Cleveland: World Publishing Company, 1956), 22.

20 Cleveland *Plain Dealer*, January 6, 7, 11, 13, 1932.

21 Thomas F. Campbell, *Daniel E. Morgan*, 138.

22   Karl Schriftgiesser, "How to Survive a Slide," *Colliers*, March 28, 1953, 75.

23   Louis Seltzer, *The Years Were Good*, 228.

24   Clayton Fritchey, "Cleveland's New Mayor," *Common Ground*, II, February 1942, 13–18.

25   David D. Van Tassel and John Grabowski, eds., *The Encyclopedia of Cleveland History*, 897; Matjaz Klemenčič, *Slovenes of Cleveland*, 305–308; Vatroslav Grill, *Med duema suetovama.* (Ljubljana: Mladinska Knjiga, 1979),126–135.

27   "Lausche a Symbol of a Bygone Era," *The Plain Dealer*, May 8, 1969.

28   Matjaz Klemenčič, *Slovenes of Cleveland*, 320; "McGill to Get Appeals Court Job, Lausche Slated to Succeed Day," Cleveland *Press*, December 20, 1932; Louis B. Seltzer, *The Years Were Good*, 228.

29   Chuck Matson, "Frank J. Lausche–New Municipal Judge," The Cleveland *Press*, December 31, 1932, Ralph J. Donaldson, "McGill, Lausche Are Made Judges," Cleveland *Plain Dealer*, December 21, 1932.

30   William C. Bittner, Frank J. *Lausche, A Political Biography*. (New York: Studio Slovenica, 1975), 16.

31   Clayton Fritchey, "Cleveland's New Mayor," *Common Ground*, II, 16.

32   Jerome Beatty, "Everybody's Mayor," *American Magazine*, March 1944, 38.

33   "Rule Breaker," *Time*, November 7, 1955, 29.

34   Cleveland *Press*, July 16, 1935.

35   Ibid.

36   The Cleveland *Plain Dealer*, December 14, 1933.

37   The Cleveland *Press*, December 22, 1933.

38   John Gunther, *Inside U.S.A.* (New York: Harper and Brothers, 1947), 427.

39   Cleveland *Press*, July 5, 1934.

40   Ralph Burkholder, "Frank J. Lausche – Hardworking Judge," Cleveland *Press*, October 26, 1936.

41   Karl Schriftgiesser, "How to Survive a Landslide," *Colliers*, March 28, 1853, 76.

42   Edward G. Gobetz, *Frank J. Lausche: Life History of Ohio's Lincoln,* 21; John Gunther, *Inside U.S.A.,* 424.

43   George E. Condon, Jr., *Cleveland, The Best Kept Secret*, 108–109.

44   Louis B. Seltzer, *The Years Were Good*, 229.

45   Brent Larkin, "Frank Lausche, Ohio's Favorite Son," *The Plain Dealer Magazine*, November 10, 1985, 20.

46   Cleveland *Press*, February 13, 1936.

47   William Ganson Rose, Cleveland, *The Making of a City*, 780–91; Philip W. Porter, *Cleveland, Confused City on a Seesaw*, 72–73; David D. Van Tassel and John Grabowski, eds., *The Encyclopedia of Cleveland History*, 923.

48   Cleveland *Press*, September 29, 1936.

49   Cleveland *Press,* August 29, 1936.

50   Cleveland *Plain Dealer*, February 24, 1937.

51   Karl Schriftgiesser, "How to Survive," *Colliers*, March 28, 1953, 76.

52   Jerome Beatty, "Everybody's Mayor" *American Magazine*, March 1944, 38.

53   Frederick S. Tisdale, "Strong Man of Columbus, *The Saturday Evening Post,* July 7, 1945, 92.

54   Clayton Fritchey, "Cleveland's New Mayor," *Common Ground*, II, February 1942, 17.

55   Vladimir Posvar, "Curb Remarriages! Lausche Tip on Divorce," Cleveland *News,* December 29, 1937.

56   "Senate Chaplain Assails Divorce for Big Politicians," Washington *Star*, date unavailable.

57   Robert A. Divine, et. al., *The American Story*, Volume Two. (New York: Longman, 2002), 823.

[58] George Condon, Jr., *Cleveland, The Best Kept Secret*, 235; Paul W. Heimel, *Eliot Ness*. (Coudersport, Pennsylvania: Knox Books, 1997), 122.

[59] George E. Condon, Jr., *The Best Kept Secret*, 235.

[60] Carol Poh Miller and Robert A. Wheeler, *Cleveland: A Concise History, 1796–1996*, 142.

[61] Philip W. Porter, *Cleveland, Confused City on a Seesaw*, 96–97.

[62] Ibid, 97.

[63] Paul W. Heimel, *Eliot Ness*, 123.

[64] George E. Condon, Jr., *Cleveland, The Best Kept Secret*, 231.

[65] Cleveland *Plain Dealer*, December 12, 1935.

[66] Philip W. Porter, *Cleveland, Confused City on a Seesaw*, 99.

[67] Bob Rich, "Ness, a Mr. Clean Cleveland Desperately Needed," Cleveland *Plain Dealer*, June 16, 1996.

[68] Paul W. Heimel, *Eliot Ness*, 129.

[69] Brent Larkin, "Frank Lausche, A Legend in Ohio Politics," *The Plain Dealer Magazine*, November 10, 1985, 18.

[70] Karl Schriftgiesser, "How to Survive a Landslide," *Colliers*, March 28, 1953, 76.

[71] Ibid.

[72] Clayton Fritchey, "Cleveland's New Mayor," *Common Ground*, II, Winter 1942, 17–18; see also Clayton Fritchey, "A Worker Who Refused to be a Sucker," *The Reader's Digest*, June 1941, 63–66.

[73] Jerome Beatty, "Everybody's Mayor," *American Magazine*, March, 1944, 38.

[74] Paul W. Heimel, *Eliot Ness*, 130–131.

[75] Bob Rich, "Ness, a Mr. Clean Cleveland Desperately Needed," Cleveland *Plain Dealer*, June 16, 1996.

[76] Paul W. Heimel, *Eliot Ness*, 131; George E. Condon, Jr., *Cleveland, The Best Kept Secret*, 233–234; Philip W. Porter, *Cleveland, Confused City on a Seesaw*, 99.

[77] Paul W. Heimel, *Eliot Ness*, 132.

[78] Hank Messick, *The Silent Syndicate*. (New York: Macmillan, 1967), 139; Philip W. Porter, *Cleveland, Confused City on a Seesaw*, 100–102; George E. Condon Jr., *Cleveland, The Best Kept Secret*, 234–35; Paul W. Heimel, *Eliot Ness*, 133; Clayton Fritchey, *Common Ground*, II, Winter, 1942, 17–18.

[79] David D. Van Tassel and John Grabowski, eds., *The Encyclopedia of Cleveland History*, 491.

[80] George E. Condon, Jr., *Cleveland, The Best Kept Secret*, 243.

[81] "Man of the Week: A Good and Fearless Judge," Cleveland *News*, October 12, 1940.

[82] Cleveland *Press*, June 9, 1939.

[83] Clayton Fritchey, *Common Ground*, II, Winter, 1942, 17–18.

[84] Karl Schriftgiesser, "How to Survive a Landslide," *Colliers*, March 28, 1953, 77.

[85] "Powell Reelected as Court's Chief Justice," Cleveland *Press*, December 19, 1940.

[86] "Lausche Continues Criminal Court Wars on Rackets," Cleveland *Press,* December 20, 1940.

Chapter Four

[1] George E. Condon, Jr., *Cleveland, The Best Kept Secret*, 322.

[2] Andrew R. L. Cayton and Susan E. Gray, eds., *The American West, Essays on Regional History*. (Bloomington: Indiana University Press, 2001), 24–25.

[3] *Cleveland Press*, July 12, 1935; Louis B. Seltzer, *The Years Were Good*, 223–24.

[4] John Gunther, *Inside U.S.A.*, 425.

[5] Michael O'Bryant, ed., *The Ohio Almanac*. (Wilmington, Ohio: Orange Frazer Press, 1997), 145.

6   Richard L. Maher, "Declines Call to Enter Fight," Cleveland *Press*, July 17, 1935.

7   "1,000 Sing Praise of Judge Lausche," Cleveland *Plain Dealer*, February 24, 1937

8   Joseph Alex Morris, "Who Is Frank Lausche?" *The Saturday Evening Post*, December 10, 1955, 115.

9   "Cleveland Knew Lausche as a Miracle Man," *Youngstown Vindicator*, January 7, 1945.

10 Brent Larkin, "Frank Lausche, A Legend in Ohio Politics," *The Plain Dealer Magazine*, November 10, 1985, 20.

11 Philip Porter, *Cleveland, Confused City on a Seesaw*, 201–204.

12 Louis B. Seltzer, *The Years Were Good*, 225–226.

13 Karl Keyerleber, "He Fields Ohio's Hot Ones," *The Nation*, July 22, 1944, 95.

14 Ibid; Norman Mlachak, "Cleveland's Former Mayors," The Cleveland *Press*, September 8, 1980.

15 "Orthodox Political Procedure Disregarded by Governor-Elect," Columbus *Dispatch*, January 7, 1945; "Why I am for Miller," *The Bystander*, January 30, 1932, 13.

16 Frank J. Lausche, "We Americans" WHK Radio Program, Cleveland, Ohio, November 30, 1938.

17 Ralph Kelly, "Raps 'Mercenary Machine' Politics," Cleveland *Plain Dealer*, April 29, 1940; Clayton Fritchey, "Cleveland's New Mayor," *Common Ground*, II, Winter, 1942, 13.

18 Ralph Kelly, "Raps 'Mercenary Machine' Politics," Cleveland *Plain Dealer*, April 29, 1940.

19 Cleveland *Press*, March 28, 1941.

20 Karl Schriftgiesser, "How to Survive a Landslide," *Colliers*, March 28, 1953, 75; John Gunther, *Inside U.S.A.*, 425.

21 Richard L. Maher, "Dem Leaders' Aid Seen for Lausche," Cleveland *Press*, June 30, 1941.

22 John Gunther, *Inside U.S.A.*, 425.

23 Jerome Beatty, "Everybody's Mayor," *American Magazine*, March, 1944, 39.

24 Cuyahoga County Democratic Executive Committee, *Questionnaire to the Voters of Cleveland*, (no date of publication, but distributed in September, 1941).

25 Cleveland *Press*, September 4, 1941.

26 Cleveland *Press*, September 9, 1941.

27 Clayton Fritchey, "Cleveland's New Mayor," *Common Ground*, II, Winter, 1942, 13.

28 Cleveland *Plain Dealer*, November 5, 1941.

29 Richard L. Maher, "Huge Crowd Jams City Hall for Ceremony," Cleveland *Press*, November 10, 1941.

30 Letter from James A. Farley to Ray T. Miller, November 10, 1941 (Ray Miller Collection, Manuscript No. 3308,) Western Reserve Historical Society.

31 Richard L. Maher, "'We're in Accord,' Miller Says After Lausche Talk," Cleveland *Press*, July 24, 1941.

32 George E. Condon, Jr., *Cleveland, The Best Kept Secret,* 241.

33 Brent Larkin, "Frank Lausche, A Legend in Ohio Politics," *The Plain Dealer Magazine*, November 10, 1985, 18.

34 Letter from Ray T. Miller to Congressman Stephen Young, November 17, 1941 (Ray Miller Collection, Manuscript No. 3308), Western Reserve Historical Society.

35 Letter from James W. Shocknessy to Ray T. Miller, November 14, 1941 (Ray Miller Collection, Manuscript Collection, No. 3308), Western Reserve Historical Society.

36 "The Lonely One," *Time*, February 20, 1956, 22; Karl Schriftgiesser, "Lausche of Ohio, How to Survive a Landslide," *Colliers*, March 28, 1953, 77; Brent Larkin, "Frank Lausche, A Legend in Ohio Politics," *The Plain Dealer Magazine*, November 10, 1985, 20.

37 Carol Poh Miller and Robert A. Wheeler, "Cleveland: The Making and Remaking of an American City, 1796–1993," in *Cleveland, A Metropolitan Reader*, edited by W. Dennis Keating, Norman Krumholz, and David C. Perry, 43.

38 L.S. Robbins, *Decentralization: A Problem in Cleveland's Future.* (Cleveland: Cleveland Chamber of Commerce, 1941), 13.

39 Philip Porter, *Cleveland, Confused City on a Seesaw,* 126.

40 Letter from Elmer Fehlhaber, secretary, Cuyahoga County Communist Party to Mayor Frank J. Lausche, Dec. 8, 1941, (Thomas Burke Collection. Container No. 1, Folders 1–30), Western Reserve Historical Society.

41 Copy of statement issued by the American Communist Party, December 8, 1941 (in conjunction with a letter from Elmer Felhaber, Cuyahoga County Secretary of the Communist Party, (Cleveland Mayoral Papers), Western Reserve Historical Society.

42 Karl Schriftgiesser, "Lausche of Ohio, How to Survive a Landslide," *Colliers,* March 28, 1953, 77; Jerome Beatty, "Everybody's Mayor," *American Magazine,* March, 1944, 38.

43 Clayton Fritchey, "In Office One of High Achievement," Cleveland *Plain Dealer,* Nov. 15, 1942.

44 Jerome Beatty, *American Magazine,* March 1944, 38.

45 Clayton Fritchey, "In Office One of High Achievement," Cleveland *Plain Dealer,* Nov. 15, 1942.

46 Ibid.

47 Jerome Beatty, *American Magazine,* March, 1944, 38.

48 "The Home Front," Cleveland *Press,* April 24, 1943.

49 Letter from Mayor Frank J. Lausche to Nathan Loeser, National City Bank Building, May 3, 1943, (Cleveland Mayoral Papers, Folder 94), Western Reserve Historical Society.

50 (Cleveland Mayoral Papers, Folder 94), Western Reserve Historical Society.

51 Cleveland *News,* April 30, 1943; Alvin Silverman, "Lausche Blasts Uncurbed Strikes," Cleveland *Plain Dealer,* April 30, 1943.

52 Letter from Vernon Stouffer to Mayor Frank J. Lausche, April 30, 1943, (Cleveland Mayoral Papers), Western Reserve Historical Society.

53 Letter from Mayor Frank J. Lausche to City Council of Cleveland, June 24, 1943. (Cleveland Mayoral Papers, Folder 96), Western Reserve Historical Society; "Mayor Lausche of Cleveland," *New Republic,* July 31, 1944, 129–30.

54 Karl Schriftgiesser, "How to Survive a Landslide," *Colliers,* March 28, 1953, 77–78; Jerome Beatty, "Everybody's Mayor," *American Magazine,* March, 1944, 38.

55 Carol Poh Miller and Robert A. Wheeler, *Cleveland, A Concise History,* 150; David D. Van Tassel and John Grabowski, eds., *The Encyclopedia of Cleveland History,* xvii–xix.

56 Jerome Beatty, "Everybody's Mayor," *American Magazine,* March 1944, 38; Karl Keyerleber, "He Fields Ohio's Hot Ones," *The Nation,* July 22, 1944, 95.

57 Robert S. Allen, ed., *Our Fair City,* 142.

58 "Man to Watch," *Time,* November 15, 1943, 20.

59 Clayton Fritchey, "Cleveland's New Mayor," *Common Ground II,* Winter, 1942, 18.

60 Edwin A. Lahey, "Mayor Lausche of Cleveland," *The New Republic,* July 31, 1944, 129.

61 "Elect Lausche on Win-War Program Here," *Union Leader,* November 5, 1943.

62 Jerome Beatty, "Everybody's Mayor," *American Home,* March, 1944, 38.

63 David D. Van Tassel and John Grabowski, *The Encyclopedia of Cleveland History,* 948, 1073; Carol Poh Miller and Robert A. Wheeler, *Cleveland, A Concise History, 1796–1996,* 148–49.

64 *Cleveland, A Metropolitan Reader,* W. Dennis Keating, Norman Krumholz, and David C. Perry, eds., 127. Carol Poh Miller and Robert A. Wheeler, *Cleveland, A Concise History, 1796–1996,* 151–152.

65 Cleveland Welfare Federation, Central Area Study, 1943, 125, on file at Cleveland Public Library.

66 Christopher Wye, "At the Leading Edge: The Monument for Black Civil Rights in Cleveland, 1830–1969," in David D. Van Tassel and John J. Grabowski, eds., *Cleveland, A Tradition of Reform*. (Kent, Ohio: Kent State University Press, 1986), 129.

67 Carol Poh Miller and Robert A. Wheeler, *Cleveland, A Concise History, 1796–1996*, 151–152.

68 Letter from Mayor Frank J. Lausche to Honorable Harold J. Ickes, U.S. Secretary of Interior, July 21, 1944; letter from C.J. Potter, Deputy Administrator, Solid Fuels Administrator, United States Department of Interior, August 4, 1944; letter from Mayor Frank J. Lausche to C.J. Potter, Deputy, Solid Fuels Administrator, United States Department of Interior, August 9, 1944; letter from C.J. Potter, Deputy Administrator, Solid Fuels Administrator, United States Department of Interior, August 21, 1944; (Cleveland Mayoral Papers, Folder 71,) Western Reserve Historical Society.

69 Letters from C. J. Potter, Deputy Solid Fuels Administrator, United States Department of Interior, August 4, 1944; letter from Frank J. Lausche to C. J. Potter, Deputy Solid Fuels Administrator United States Department of the Interior, August 9, 1944. (Cleveland Mayoral Papers, Folder 71), The Western Reserve Historical Society.

70 Letter from Mayor Frank J. Lausche to William D. Guron, City Commissioner, January 13, 1944 (Cleveland Mayoral Papers, Folder 71), Western Reserve Historical Society.

71 Alvin Silverman, "Jeer Lausche As Wage Veto is Overridden," Cleveland *Plain Dealer*, April 1, 1944.

72 Letter to Council of the City of Cleveland from Mayor Frank J. Lausche, December 27, 1944 (Cleveland Mayoral Papers, Folder 7), Western Reserve Historical Society.

73 Louis B. Seltzer, *The Years Were Good*, 232–33.

74 Edwin A. Lahey, "Mayor Lausche of Cleveland," *The New Republic*, July 31, 1944, 128–29.

75 Barbara E. Boyle, "The East Ohio Gas Company Fire, The Lessons of Tragedy," *Timeline*, September–October, 1995, 24.

76 Cleveland *News*, October 21, 1944.

77 Cleveland *News*, October 21, 1944; Rosemary Kovacs, "It's Something We Want to Forget," *The Plain Dealer*, October 20, 1974.

78 The Cleveland *Press*, October 21, 1944; The Cleveland *News*, October 21, 1944; Barbara E. Boyle, "The East Ohio Gas Company Fire, The Lessons of Tragedy," *Timeline,* September–October, 1955, 29.

79 The Cleveland *Press*, October 21, 1944; Rosemary Kovacs, "It's Something We Want to Forget, *The Plain Dealer*, October 20, 1974.

80 Barbara E. Boyle, "The East Ohio Gas Company Fire, The Lessons of Tragedy," *Timeline*, September–October, 1995, 24; The Cleveland *Press*, October 21, 1944.

81 Ibid, 39; Barbara E. Boyle, "The East Ohio Gas Company Fire, The Lessons of Tragedy," *Timeline,* September–October, 1995, 36.

82 Minutes of Mayor's Committee on Disaster Meetings, October 28 and October 30, 1944 (Cleveland Mayoral Papers, Folder 71), Western Reserve Historical Society; investigative report from technical group of the Mayor's Board of Inquiry to Thomas A. Burke, Jr., Law Director, City of Cleveland, November 27, 1944. (Thomas A. Burke Papers, Folders 29–30), Western Reserve Historical Society.

83 Barbara E. Boyle, "The East Ohio Gas Company Fire, The Lessons of Tragedy," *Timeline*, September–October, 1995, 39.

CHAPTER FIVE

1   Cleveland *Plain Dealer*, February 1, 1944.

2   Jerome Beatty, "Everybody's Mayor," *American Home*, March 1944, Cleveland *Plain Dealer*, February 4, 1944.

3   William C. Bittner, *Frank J. Lausche, A Political Biography*, 21.

4   Karl Schriftgiesser, "Lausche of Ohio, How to Survive a Landslide," *Colliers*, March 28, 1953, 78.

5   Edwin A. Lahey, "Mayor Lausche of Cleveland," *The New Republic*, July 31, 1944, 129.

6   Cleveland *News*, February 1, 1944.

7   Cleveland *Plain Dealer*, February 28, 1944.

8   Cleveland *Plain Dealer*, April 10, 1944.

9   Cleveland *Plain Dealer*, April 13, 1944.

10 Cleveland *Plain Dealer*, April 29, 1944.

11 Cleveland *Plain Dealer* April 26, 1994.

12 Edwin A. Lahey, "Mayor Lausche of Cleveland," *The New Republic*, July 31, 1944.

13 Richard O. Davies, *Defender of the Old Guard, John Bricker and American Politics*. (Columbus: Ohio State University Press, 1993), 86.

14 Brent Larkin, "Frank Lausche, Ohio's Favorite Son," *The Plain Dealer Magazine*, November 10, 1985, 21.

15 Richard O. Davies, *Defender of the Old Guard, John Bricker and American Politics*, 93.

16 Jack Small, "A New Governor—but the Work of Loyal John Lokar Made A Hope A Reality," Cleveland *Press*, November 10, 1944.

17 Alexander P. Lamis, ed., *Ohio Politics*, 23.

18 Karl Schriftgiesser, "Lausche of Ohio, How to Survive a Landslide," *Colliers*, March 28, 1953, 78.

19 John Gunther, "Men and Politics in Ohio," in *Inside U.S.A.*, 426–27.

20 Ibid.

21 Ibid.

22 Louis B. Seltzer, *The Years Were Good*, 233.

23. Ralph J. Donaldson, "Lausche to Pit Ideals Against Ohio Intrigue," Cleveland *Plain Dealer*, December 31, 1944.

24 Frederick Tisdale, "Strong Man of Columbus," *Saturday Evening Post*, July 7, 1945, 92.

25 Springfield *News*, October 11, 1946.

26 Cleveland *Plain Dealer*, October 11, 1944.

27 William C. Bittner, *Frank J. Lausche, A Political Biography*, 22.

28 Edwin Lahey, "Mayor of Cleveland," *New Republic*, July 31, 1944, 129.

29 Youngstown *Vindicator*, October 11, 1944.

30 Cleveland *Plain Dealer*, October 17, 1944.

31 Cleveland *Plain Dealer*, November 4, 1944.

32 Alexander P. Lamis, ed., *Ohio Politics*, 23.

33 Roy Rutherford, "Mother Is a Guiding Influence in Career of Frank Lausche," Cleveland *Plain Dealer*, August 15, 1948.

34 Cleveland *Plain Dealer*, November 5, 1944.

35 Cleveland *Plain Dealer*, November 8, 1944.

36 Letter from Robert A. Taft to John W. Bricker, January 16, 1945; letter from John W. Bricker to Robert A. Taft, January 20, 1945. *The Papers of Robert A. Taft*, Volume 2, 1938–1944. Clarence E. Wunderlin, Jr., ed., (Kent, Ohio: The Kent State University Press, 2001), 7–8.

37   Letter from Robert A. Taft to John S. Knight, publisher of the Akron *Beacon Journal*, September 22, 1944, *The Papers of Robert A. Taft, Volume 2*, 1938–1944, Clarence E. Wunderlin, Jr. ed., 584.

38   Letter from Robert A. Taft to Captain David S. Ingalls, May 18, 1944, *The Papers of Robert A. Taft*, Volume 2, 1938–1944, Clarence E. Wunderlin, Jr., ed., 548–49.

39   William F. McDermott, "Mayor Breaks all Rules of Politics, Yet Honesty and Simplicity Win Him Governorship," Cleveland *Plain Dealer*, November 9, 1944.

40   Ibid.

41   John Gunther, *Inside U.S.A.*, 426.

42   Joe Alex Morris, "Who Is Frank Lausche?" *Saturday Evening Post*, December 10, 1955, 116; Frederick S. Tisdale, "Strong Man of Columbus," *Saturday Evening Post*, July 7, 1945, 16.

43   David Broder, "Ford Speaks Common Sense," *The Idaho Statesman*, June 16, 2000.

44   The Arizona *Republic*, March 3, 2003.

45   Dr. Wellington G. Fordyce, "Governor Lausche's Election A Triumph for Democracy," *Everybody's Business,* March, 1945.

46   John Gunther, *Inside U.S.A.*, 428.

47   Ralph T. Donaldson, "Lausche to Pit Ideals Against Ohio Intrigue," Cleveland *Plain Dealer*, December 31, 1944.

48   Frederick S. Tisdale, "Strong Man of Columbus," *The Saturday Evening Post*, July 7, 1945, 17.

49   John Gunther, *Inside U.S.A.*, 430; *New York Times,* December 19, 1945.

50   "Progress Reported at Lausches," Columbus *Citizen*, June 12, 1945.

51   Edward Gobetz ed., *Frank J. Lausche: Life History of Ohio's Lincoln,* 38.

52   Columbus *Dispatch,* January 13, 1945; Cincinnati *Enquirer*, January 14, 1945; Edward Gobetz, ed., *Frank J. Lausche: Life History of Ohio's Lincoln*, 43.

53   "Administration of State Affairs," *Everybody's Business*, May, 1945, 3.

54   Frederick Tisdale, "Strong Man of Columbus," *Saturday Evening Post*, July 7, 1945, 17.

55   John Gunther, *Inside U.S.A.*, 429.

56   Karl Schriftgiesser, "Lausche of Ohio, How to Survive a Landslide," *Colliers,* March 28, 1953, 78.

57   "New Governor Works Hard, Defies Politicians," Cincinnati *Enquirer*, January 14, 1945.

58   Robert Vincent, "Key Men—John Lokar," Columbus *Citizen*, January 24, 1945.

59   "For a Second Term—Governor Frank J. Lausche," Cleveland *Press*, October 15, 1946.

60   John Gunther, *Inside U.S.A.*, 430.

61   "Administration of State Affairs," *Everybody's Business*, May, 1945, 3.

62   "Lausche vs. the Lobbyists," Dayton *News*, October 23, 1946.

63   It is difficult in Ohio for Democrats to capture control of the legislature, because the districts are gerrymandered to favor the rural interests. Only one time in Lausche's five terms as Governor, did he have a Democratic controlled General Assembly (1948–1950). See Vladimer Orlando Key, Jr., *American State Politics.* (New York: Alfred A. Knopf, Inc., 1956), 187, and John H. Fenton, "Issues in Politics in Ohio," in *Government and Politics in Ohio*, Carl Lieberman, ed., 15–50.

64   C. Kytle, "What Makes Lausche Run?" *Coronet*, April 5, 1956, 101–105; *Newsweek*, January 15, 1945, 34.

65   "New Governor Works Hard, Defied Politicians," Cincinnati *Enquirer*, January 14, 1945.

66   Alexander P. Lamis, ed., *Ohio Politics*, 27.

67   Phillip R. Shriver and Clarence W. Wunderlin, *The Documentary Heritage of Ohio*. (Athens, Ohio: Ohio University Press, 2000), 387.

[68] Andrew R.L. Cayton, *Ohio, The History of a People*. Columbus: (The Ohio State University Press, 2002), 327, 329.

[69] Louis Bromfield, "Fifteen Years After" in Charles E. Little, ed., *Louis Bromfield at Malabar —Writings in Farming and Country Life*. (Baltimore: Johns Hopkins University Press, 1988), 222–23.

[70] The Akron *Beacon Journal,* October 15, 1946.

[71] The Cleveland *Press,* October 15, 1946.

[72] Ibid.

[73] Philip W. Porter, *Cleveland, Confused City on a Seesaw*, 127.

[74] *New York Times*, July 2, 1946.

[75] Cleveland *Press*, October 15, 1948.

[76] Ibid.

[77] John C. Baker, "Frank J. Lausche and Education," in Edward Gobetz, ed., *Frank J. Lausche: Life History of Ohio's Lincoln*, 116.

[78] Karl Schriftgiesser, "Lausche of Ohio, How to Survive a Landslide," *Colliers*, March 28, 1953, 78; Joseph H. Bindley, *An Analysis of Voting Behavior in Ohio,* Ph.D. dissertation (University of Pittsburgh*, 1959)*, 148.

[79] Karl Schriftgiesser, "Lausche of Ohio, How to Survive a Landslide," *Colliers*, March 28, 1953, 79.

[80] "The Lonely One," *Time*, February 20, 1956, 23.

[81] David D. Van Tassel and John J. Grabowski, eds., *The Encyclopedia of Cleveland History*, 499–500.

[82] Zanesville *News*, October 8, 1946.

[83] Joseph H. Bindley, *An Analysis of Voting Behavior in Ohio*, 159; *New York Times,* March 13, 1947, 32; "Herbert charged state highway department employees were requested to make cash contributions in unmarked envelopes." Cleveland *News*, October 17, 1946.

[84] Edward Gobetz, ed., *Frank J. Lausche: Life History of Ohio's Lincoln*, 46.

[85] Louis Seltzer, "For a Second Term—Gov. Frank Lausche," Cleveland *Press*, October 15, 1946.

[86] C.J. Doyle, "Columnist Says Governor Lausche Outwits Listless Opponent," The Oberlin *Times*, September 12, 1946. For a more detailed description of Lausche's accomplishments in the field of mental health—an overall increase of more than 25 percent in bed capacity of state institutions in less than two years—refer to "Mental Health Record," The Cleveland *Plain Dealer,* October 24, 1946.

[87] Cleveland *Plain Dealer*, October 11, 1946.

[88] "Lausche Legend Comes to An End," Cleveland *Press*, May 8, 1968.

[89] Karl Schriftgiesser, "Lausche of Ohio, How to Survive a Landslide," *Colliers*, March 28, 1953, 79.

[90] Alexander P. Lamis, ed., *Ohio Politics*, 30.

[91] Ibid, 25.

[92] Philip W. Porter, *Cleveland, Confused City on a Seesaw*, 127.

CHAPTER SIX

[1] William Ganson Rose, *Cleveland, The Making of a City*, 1023.

[2] Philip W. Porter, *Cleveland, Confused City on a Seesaw*, 133–34.

[3] Alexander P. Lamis, ed., *Ohio Politics*, 27.

[4] Carol Poh Miller and Robert A. Wheeler, *Cleveland, A Concise History*, 154.

[5] Ibid.

6   Memorandum from baseball owners meeting, April 25, 1945, (Branch Rickey Papers, Box 27) Library of Congress, Washington DC.

7   *The Sporting News*, February 19, 1945; John A. Bricker, former governor of Ohio, eliminated himself as a possible candidate for the commissioner's job. "I am not going into baseball. I am going to stay in Ohio and practice law"; William Marshall, *Baseball's Pivotal Era, 1945–1951*. (Lexington: The University of Kentucky Press, 1998), 19.

8   Memorandum from baseball owners meeting, April 25, 1945, (Branch Rickey Papers, Box 27), Library of Congress, Washington, DC, 11.

9   Memorandum from baseball owners meeting, April 25, 1945, (Branch Rickey Papers, Box 27), Library of Congress, Washington, DC, 13.

10   Benjamin G. Rader, *Baseball: A History of America's Game.* (Champaign: University of Illinois Press, 1994). 188.

11   *Columbus Dispatch*, February 10, 1951.

12   Ibid.

13   Ibid.

14   Lee Lowenfish, historian, letter to author, October 23, 2001.

15   Alvin "Bud" Silverman, "Gov. Lausche Won't Accept Baseball Job," Cleveland *Plain Dealer*, September 17, 1951.

16   Ibid.

17   Stephen Salsbury, *No Way to Run a Railroad.* (New York: McGraw-Hill, Inc. 1982), 79– 83.

18   Governor's message to Ohio General Assembly, January 13, 1953.

19   Malcom H. Galbraith, "Everyone Tried to Figure Why Reams Got Out," Columbus *Dispatch*, date unlisted, (Ray Miller Collection, Manuscript Collection No. 3308, Folder 6,), Western Reserve Historical Society.

20   Harold A. Stacy, "Dems Hope to Stay Clear of Ohio Battle," Columbus *Dispatch*, December 14, 1947, (Ray Miller Collection, Manuscript Collection 3308, Folder 6), Western Reserve Historical Society.

21   Alexander P. Lamis, ed., *Ohio Politics*, 30.

22   Cleveland *Press*, January 27, 1947; Cleveland *Plain Dealer,* January 28, 1947.

23   Comments by Ray Miller, (Ray Miller Collection, Manuscript Collection 3308, Folder 5), Western Reserve Historical Society.

24   Ibid.

25   Alvin Silverman, "Lausche Will Run; Blasts Bosses Rule," Cleveland *Plain Dealer*, January 31, 1948.

26   Cleveland *Plain Dealer*, October 19, 1948.

27   Ibid.

28   Cleveland *Plain Dealer*, October 28, 1948.

29   Editorial, Columbus *Citizen*, October 24, 1948; Cleveland *Plain Dealer,* July 8, 1948.

30   Cleveland *Plain Dealer*, October 31, 1948.

31   Harold I. Gullan, *The Upset That Wasn't, Harry Truman and the Crucial Election of 1948.* (Chicago: Ivan R. Dee, 1998), 3.

32   Joe Alex Morris, "Who is Frank Lausche?" *Saturday Evening Post*, December 10, 1955, 117.

33   David B. McCullough, "Giving 'Em Hell in Ohio," *Timeline*, July–August 1995, 2–3.

34   Ibid.

35   Ibid.

36   Margaret Truman, *Harry S. Truman.* (New York: William Morrow and Company, 1973), 29–30.

37   Ibid.

38 *New York Times*, October 21, 1948.

39 Brent Larkin, "Frank Lausche, A Legend in Ohio Politics," *The Plain Dealer Magazine*, November 10, 1985, 21; Alexander P. Lamis, ed., *Ohio Politics*, 30.

40 David McCullough, "Giving 'Em Hell in Ohio," *Timeline*, July–August, 1985, 10.

41 Richard O. Davies, "Whistle Stopping Through Ohio," October 12, 1948, *Ohio History*, Vol. 71, No. 2 July, 1962, 121.

42 William H. Hessler, "The Implacable Independence of Frank J. Lausche," *The Reporter*, April 5, 1956, 25.

43 Joe Alex Morris, "Who Is Frank Lausche?" *Saturday Evening Post*, December 10, 1955, 116.

44 Charles M. McCarry, "Frank Lausche: Senator Without a Party," *True Magazine*, Fall, 1958, 115.

45 Alvin Silverman, Cleveland *Plain Dealer*, October 27, 1948.

46 Charles M. McCarry, "Frank Lausche: Senator Without a Party," *True Magazine*, Fall, 1958, 20, 22.

47 Alvin Silverman, "Truman Patches Lausche Wounds," Cleveland *Plain Dealer*, October 27, 1948; Letter from Ray T. Miller to Cuyahoga County Precinct Committeemen, November 4, 1948 (Ray Miller Collection, 3308, Folder 5), Western Reserve Historical Society.

48 Alvin Silverman, "Truman Patches Lausche Wounds," Cleveland *Plain Dealer*, October 27, 1948; Letter from Ray T. Miller to Cuyahoga County Precinct Committeemen, November 4, 1948 (Ray Miller Collection, 3308, Folder 5), Western Reserve Historical Society.

49 Ibid.

50 Joe Hoover Bindley, *An Analysis of Voting Behavior in Ohio*, ix.

51 Paul David, Malcolm Moos, and Ralph Goldman, *Presidential Nominating Politics of 1953*. Volume 4, (Baltimore: John Hopkins Press, 1983), 9.

52 Joe Hoover Bindley, *An Analysis of Voting Behavior in Ohio*, ix.

53 Harry S. Truman, *Years of Trial and Hope, Memoirs by Harry S. Truman*. Volume Two, (Garden City, New York: Doubleday and Company, 1956), 221.

54 Richard O. Davies, "Whistle Stopping Through Ohio," *Ohio History*, July 1962, 114.

55 Ibid; Cincinnati *Times-Star*, October 12, 1948.

56 Gary A. Donaldson, *Truman Defeats Dewey*. (Lexington: University Press of Kentucky, 1999), 214.

57 Joe Hoover Bindley, *An Analysis of Voting Behavior in Ohio*, 166.

58 Jules Abels, *Out of the Jaws of Victory.* (New York: Henry Holt and Company, 1959), 295.

59 Ibid, 288.

60 Akron *Beacon Journal*, Sept. 7, 1953.

61 Brian Usher, "The Lausche Era, 1945–1957," in *Ohio Politics,* Alexander P. Lamis, ed., 32–33; Brent Larkin, "Frank Lausche: A Legend in Ohio Politics," *Plain Dealer Magazine*, November 10, 1985, 25.

62 Columbus *Dispatch*, May 11, 1949.

63 Alexander P. Lamis, ed., *Ohio Politics*, 31–32.

64 Columbus *Dispatch*, January 12, 1949.

65 Toledo *Blade*, February 8, 1949.

66 Ralph Locher, former Cleveland Mayor, interview by author in Shaker Heights, Cleveland, September 9, 1996.

67 Edwin C. Heinke, Cleveland *Press*, January 10, 1955.

68 Joe Alex Morris, "Who Is Frank Lausche?" *Saturday Evening Post*, December 10, 1955, 114.

69 Ibid.

70   Rollin Dean Jauchius, *Gubernatorial Roles: An Assessment by Five Ohio Governors,* PhD dissertation, (The Ohio State University, 1971), 34.

71   *New York Times*, November 20, 1949, Section IV: 6.

72   *New York Times*, July 3, 1949, 17.

73   *New York Times*, November 17, 1949, 33.

74   Ibid.

CHAPTER SEVEN

1   Robert Sobel, *Coolidge, An American Enigma.* (Washington, DC: Regency Publishing Inc., 1998), 156–57.

2   Karl Schriftgiesser, "Lausche of Ohio, How to Survive a Landslide," *Colliers*, March 28, 1953, 79.

3   "Outstanding Governor," The Cleveland *Press*, October 3, 1950.

4   Letter from Governor Lausche to Hulbert Taft, March 26, 1956; letter from Hulbert Taft to Governor Lausche, March 28, 1856, (Frank J. Lausche Papers) Ohio Historical Society.

5   Cleveland *Plain Dealer*, January 4, 1950.

6   Richard L Maher, "Political Paradox," *Nation*, October 4, 1952, 299.

7   Columbus *Dispatch*, February 12, 1950.

8   Canton *Repository*, July 7, 1950.

9   James T. Patterson, *Mr. Republican, A Biography of Robert A. Taft.* (Boston: Houghton-Mifflin Company, 1972), 456.

10   Cleveland *Plain Dealer*, October 27, 1950.

11   Ohio State *Journal*, June 20, 1950.

12   Joe Hoover Bindley, *An Analysis of Voting Behavior in Ohio*, 172.

13   Cincinnati *Enquirer*, June 21, 1950.

14   *New York Times*, June 22, 1950

15   Columbus *Citizen*, June 23, 1950.

16   Youngstown *Vindicator*, July 2, 1950.

17   *New York Times*, June 20, 1950.

18   Columbus *Citizen*, January 7, 1945.

19   Dayton *Journal-Herald*, April 17, 1950.

20   Speech given in Waverly, Ohio, and quoted in article by William Hessler entitled "The Implacable Independence of Frank Lausche," *Reporter*, April 5, 1956, 25–26.

21   William Porter, *Cleveland, Confused City on a Seesaw,"* 131.

22   Cleveland *Press*, September 25, 1950.

23   Ohio State *Journal*, June 24, 1950.

24   Joe Howard Bindley, *An Analysis of Voting Behavior in Ohio*, 174.

25   *New York Times*, October 27, 1952.

26   *New York Times*, November 8, 1950.

27   James T. Patterson, *Mr. Republican, A Biography of Robert A. Taft*, 469.

28   Charles McCarry, "Frank Lausche, Senator Without a Party," *True Magazine*, Fall, 1958, 115.

29   Personal transcript of NBC-TV show "Meet the Press Program," January 8, 1956.

30   Louis Seltzer, *The Years Were Good*, 234.

31   James T. Patterson, *Mr. Republican, A Biography of Robert A. Taft*, 469.

32   Jean Douglas, "Lausche Takes 3rd Term Oath Without Frills," Toledo *Blade*, January 8, 1951.

33   *New York Times*, August 3, 1951.

34   Ibid.
35   Frank J. Lausche, "Progress and Problems of the States," *State Government*, Vol. 24, No. 11, (November 1951), 288.
36   David Halberstam, *The Fifties*. (New York: Villard Books, 1993), x, xi.
37   Alexander P. Lamis, ed., *Ohio Politics*, 32.
38   Columbus *Dispatch*, March 1, 1951.
39   Columbus *Dispatch*, July 12, 1951.
40   Letter from William H. Brooks to Governor Frank J. Lausche, November 15, 1951. (Frank J. Lausche Papers), Ohio Historical Society.
41   Ohio State *Journal*, June 7, 1952.
42   Letter from Governor Frank J. Lausche to Colonel George Mingle, Superintendent, State Highway Patrol, June 11, 1952 (Frank J. Lausche Papers), Ohio Historical Society.
43   Letter from Ted J. Kauer, Director, Ohio Department of Highways, to Colonel George Mingle, Superintendent, Ohio State Highway Patrol, June 18, 1952 (Frank J. Lausche Papers), Ohio Historical Society.
44   Judy Herbstreit, Historian, Ohio Highway State Patrol, interview by author in Columbus, Ohio, on July 30, 2003.
45   Toledo *Times*, September 2, 1952; letter from Alex Brackenridge, Business Representative, United Brotherhood of Carpenters and Joiners of America, to Governor Lausche, September 4, 1952; (Frank J. Lausche Papers), Ohio Historical Society; Cincinnati *Post*, September 2, 1952.
46   Letter from Ralph S. Locher, Secretary to the Governor to Alex Brackenridge, United Brotherhood of Carpenters and Joiners of America Local No. 105, September 12, 1952 (Frank J. Lausche Papers) Ohio Historical Society; Cleveland *Press*, September 8, 1952; Cleveland *Plain Dealer*, September 8, 1952.
47   David Halberstam, *The Fifties*, 53.
48   Ohio State University, Board of Trustees, record of proceedings of the Board of Trustees of The Ohio State University, January 6, 1947, 275–76.
49   Steven P. Gietschier, "The 1951 Speaker's Rule at Ohio State," *Ohio History*, Volume 87, No. 3, (Summer, 1978), 295.
50   Akron *Beacon-Journal*, September 6, 1951.
51   Steven P. Gietschier, "The 1951 Speaker's Rule at Ohio State," *Ohio History*, 296.
52   R. Dean Jauchius, "Rugg is Praised by OSU Dean as Conference Ends," Columbus *Dispatch*, July 12, 1951; letter from Howard Bevis to Robert Black, July 23, 1951, Professor Harold Rugg, Official Correspondence, Box 45 (Howard Bevis Papers), Ohio State University Archives, Columbus, Ohio.
53   Akron *Beacon-Journal*, September 6, 1951.
54   Ibid.
55   Steven P. Gietschier, "The 1951 Speaker's Rule at Ohio State," *Ohio History*, 302.
56   Letter from Governor Lausche to Wilbur Sunday Lewis of the Institute for Public Education by Radio and Television. (Frank J. Lausche Papers), Ohio Historical Society.
57   The Columbus *Citizen,* November 11, 1951.
58   Letter from Carlton Dargusch to Governor Frank Lausche, October 11, 1951 (Frank J. Lausche Papers), Ohio Historical Society.
59   Statement of Board of Trustees of The Ohio State University, Wooster, Ohio, October 15, 1951 (Frank J. Lausche Papers), Ohio Historical Society.
60   Steven P. Gietschier, "The 1951 Speaker's Rule at Ohio State, *Ohio History*, 305.
61   *Ohio State Lantern*, October 16, 1951.

62   Ralph Manning, "Lausche Says Gag Rule Up to Trustees," Columbus *Citizen*, October 15, 1951.

63   Ibid.

64   Alvin Silverman, "Lausche Backs O.S.U. Screening Order, Says It is Fair, is Not a 'Gag'," Cleveland *Plain Dealer*, October 25, 1951.

65   Letter from Russell M. Chase to Governor Frank J. Lausche, October 26, 1951, (Frank J. Lausche Papers), Ohio Historical Society.

66   Steven P. Gietschier, "The 1951 Speaker's Rule at Ohio State," *Ohio History*, 309.

67   Alexander P. Lamis, ed., *Ohio Politics*, 35.

68   Columbus *Dispatch*, July 30, 1953; Alexander P. Lamis, ed., *Ohio Politics*, 36.

69   Governor's Veto Message, July 30, 1953 (Frank J. Lausche Papers), Ohio Historical Society.

70   Alexander P. Lamis, ed., *Ohio Politics*, 36.

71   Toledo *Blade*, July 26, 1950.

72   Mary McGarey, "Shocknessy: Official is Man of Words and Performance," Columbus *Dispatch*, August 20, 1972.

73   Ibid.

74   Jean Douglas, "Turnpike's Fate Peppered with 'Ifs,'" Toledo *Blade*, November 26, 1950.

75   Ibid.

76   Letter from Governor Lausche to B.W. Bowden, President, Bowden Oil Company, Hebron, Ohio, December 10, 1950, (in response to letter form B.W. Bowden dated December 4, 1950). (Frank J. Lausche Papers), Ohio Historical Society.

77   Letter from James Shocknessy, Ohio Turnpike Commission Chairman to Louis B. Seltzer, ed., Cleveland *Press*, November 10, 1952, (Frank J. Lausche Papers), Ohio Historical Society.

78   *New York Times*, August 3, 1951.

79   Columbus *Dispatch*, May 4, 1952.

80   James T., Patterson, *Mr. Republican, A Biography of Robert A. Taft*, 507–08.

81   Ibid, 122–129. Charles and Robert clashed in the 1920s over the structure of city government in Cincinnati. Graft and political inattention to city affairs by the Republican leadership led to a reform movement. This movement, led by Charterites, of which Charles was a key member, eventually gained control of city government. Robert Taft, having been sent to the State legislature three times by the regular party machine, out of loyalty refused to cross over to the Charterite platform. Robert and Charles eventually collided in their law office, resulting in a vehement argument over municipal politics and non-partisan versus party loyalty, particularly the strong support of a two-party system eschewed by Robert. The brothers remained law partners for ten more years, but difference in temperament and politics had strained their relationship, and probably only the ties of blood prevented a rupture of their partnership.

82   Ibid, 509; Akron *Beacon Journal*, January 5, 1953. In one speech Senator Taft had made in behalf of his brother, he referred to Lausche as "a nice fellow who hasn't done much."

83   Youngstown *Vindicator*, July 15, 1952.

84   Cincinnati *Times-Star*, March 7, 1952.

85   Richard A. Maher, "Political Paradox," *Nation*, October 4, 1952, 300.

86   Richard O. Davies, *Defender of the Old Guard, John Bricker and American Politics*, 150–51.

87   Cleveland Plain *Dealer*, August 5, 1952.

88   Ibid.

89   Cleveland speech reported in the Ohio State *Journal*, October 18, 1952.

90   *Time*, February 20, 1956, 23.

91   *New York Times*, August 5, 1952.

92   Ibid.

93   Cleveland *Press*, October 9, 1952.

94   Philip W. Porter, *Cleveland, Confused City on a Seesaw*, 128; Karl Schriftgeisser, "Lausche of Ohio, How to Survive a Landslide," *Colliers*, March 28, 1953, 80.

95   David Lore, "Inside the Pen," The Columbus *Dispatch*, October 28, 1984.

96   Ibid.

97   Alexander P. Lamis, ed., *Ohio Politics*, 54.

98   *New York Times*, November 1, 1962 and November 4, 1952.

99   George W. Knepper, *Ohio and Its People*. (Kent, Ohio: Kent State University Press, 1989), 392.

100   Joe Bindley, *An Analysis of Voting Behavior*, 185–186.

101   Cleveland *News*, November 5, 1952.

102   Columbus *Citizen*, November 5, 1952.

103   Cleveland *Plain Dealer*, November 6, 1952.

104   Dayton *Daily News*, November 6, 1952. This statement referred to charges made by Ferguson in 1950. He said that the ballot change had been carried out by Senator Taft to assist himself in winning re-election by making split-ticket voting easier. Conjecture suggests this ballot change may also have been one of the factors in the so-called "Lausche-Taft" ticket. In January 1953, Ferguson accused Taft and Lausche of a deal and insisted that his 1950 senatorial defeat carried over to his defeat for the auditor's race in 1952.

105   Akron *Beacon Journal*, January 5, 1953.

Chapter Eight

1   Raymond Moley, "Ohio, An Industrial Empire," *Newsweek*, April 30, 1956, 112.

2   William H. Hessler, "Big Boom Along the Ohio," *The Reporter*, September 19, 1957, 22–25.

3   Michael O'Bryant, ed., *The Ohio Almanac,1997–1998*, 8, 72.

4   Rollin Hart, "The Ohioans," *Atlantic Monthly*, 1899.

5   Jim Fain, ed., The Dayton *Daily News*, in a speech to the City Club in Cleveland, May 1964.

6   George W. Knepper, *Ohio and Its People*, 394.

7   Alvin Silverman, Cleveland *Plain Dealer*, October, 1954.

8   Alvin Silverman, "Honorable Curleytop Rides Again," Cleveland *Plain Dealer*, October 17, 1954.

9   "Won't Run Again, Lausche Eyes 'Quiet' Law Practice," Cleveland *Plain Dealer*, December 14, 1952.

10   Philip W. Porter, *Cleveland, Confused City on a Seesaw*, 129.

11   William B. Saxbe with Peter D. Franklin, *I've Seen the Elephant*. (Kent, Ohio: Kent State University Press, 2000), 45–46.

12   Ibid.

13   Brian Usher, "The Lausche Era," 1945–1957, in *Ohio Politics*, Alexander P. Lamis, ed., 34.

14   Governor's message to general assembly, January 13, 1953, (Frank J. Lausche Papers), Ohio Historical Society. Alexander P. Lamis, ed., *Ohio Politics*, 34.

15   Toledo *Blade*, January 23, 1953.

16   Letter to contractor, R.O. Perrott from Governor Frank J. Lausche, March 4, 1953, (Frank J. Lausche Papers), Ohio Historical Society.

17   "Lausche is Scored on U.S. Road Deal," Cleveland *Plain Dealer*, March 7, 1953; letter from Gordon Dean, Chairman, Atomic Energy Commission to Governor Frank Lausche, March 9, 1953; letter from Governor Frank Lausche to Congressman J. Harry McGregor, 17th District, March 15, 1953; letter from Samuel O. Linzell, Director, Department of Highways, State of Ohio, to Francis V. DuPont, Commissioner of Public Roads, Washington, DC, May 20, 1953, (Frank J. Lausche Papers), Ohio Historical Society.

18   Letter from Governor Frank J. Lausche to President Dwight Eisenhower, August 10, 1954; letter from Congressman Harry McGregor to Governor Frank Lausche, August 13, 1954; letter from Congressman Wayne L. Hays to Governor Frank Lausche, August 17, 1954, (Frank J. Lausche Papers), Ohio Historical Society.

19   Letter from Congressman Thomas A. Jenkins to Governor Frank J. Lausche, August 21, 1954, (Frank J. Lausche Papers), Ohio Historical Society.

20   William H. Hessler, "Big Boom Along the Ohio," in *The Documentary Heritage of Ohio*, Phillip R. Shriver and Clarence E. Wunderlin, Jr., eds. (Athens, Ohio: Ohio University Press, 2000), 394.

21   Letter from Governor Frank J. Lausche to Professor Francis R. Aumann, Department of Political Science, The Ohio State University, July 30, 1953, (Frank J. Lausche Papers), Ohio Historical Society.

22   Letter from Governor Frank J. Lausche to Senator Robert Taft, March 4, 1953, (Frank J. Lausche Papers), Ohio Historical Society.

23   Correspondence from A.W. Marion, Director Ohio Department of Natural Resources and Ray M. White, Secretary to Governor Frank Lausche, (Frank J. Lausche Papers), Ohio Historical Society.

24   *New York Times*, August 5, 1953; August 9, 1953.

25   Louis Seltzer, *The Years Were Good*, 235.

26   Ibid.

27   *New York Times*, October 10, 1953.

28   *New York Times*, October 13, 1953.

29   William B. Saxbe with Peter D. Franklin, *I've Seen the Elephant*, 53.

30   William H. Hessler, "The Implacable Independence of Frank J. Lausche," *Reporter*, April 5, 1956, 28.

31   Cleveland *Plain Dealer*, October 30, 1968.

32   Karl Schriftgiesser, "Lausche of Ohio, How to Survive a Landslide," *Colliers*, March 28, 1953, 74.

33   Toledo *Times*, May 15, 1953.

34   Columbus *Citizen*, June 23, 1953.

35   Letter from State Auditor James A. Rhodes to Governor Frank Lausche, September 23, 1953 (Frank J. Lausche Papers), Ohio Historical Society.

36   Alexander P. Lamis, ed., *Ohio Politics*, 60.

37   The Columbus *Dispatch*, March 5, 2001.

38   R. Dean Jauchuis, *Gubernatorial Roles: An Assessment by Five Ohio Governors*, Ph.D. dissertation, (The Ohio State University, 1971), 52.

39   Alexander P. Lamis, ed., *Ohio Politics*, 65.

40   Joe Alex Morris, "Who Is Frank Lausche?" *Saturday Evening Post*, December 10, 1955, 116.

41   Ohio State *Journal*, February 5, 1954.

42   Columbus *Dispatch*, February 28, 1954.

43   Columbus *Dispatch*, October 14, 1954.

44   Joe Alex Morris, "Who Is Frank Lausche?" *Saturday Evening Post*, December 10, 1955, 116.

45 William C. Bittner, *Frank J. Lausche, A Political Biography*, 36.

46 Akron *Beacon Journal*, August 5, 1954.

47 Letter from black activist Dan T. Moore to columnist Drew Pearson, September 7, 1954, (Frank J. Lausche Papers), Ohio Historical Society.

48 Toledo *Blade*, October 23, 1954.

49 Columbus *Dispatch*, November 1, 1954.

50 Alexander Lamis, ed., *Ohio Politics*, 37.

51 Columbus *Dispatch*, October 29, 1954.

52 Letter from Governor Frank J. Lausche to Reverend Raymond L. Butler, November 2, 1954, (Frank J. Lausche Papers), Ohio Historical Society.

53 Cleveland *News*, September 30, 1954.

54 Akron *Beacon Journal*, October 20, 1954.

55 Interview between Ray Bliss and Joe Bindley, April 30, 1955, quoted in Bindley's *An Analysis of Voting Behavior in Ohio*, 196.

56 Rollin Dean Jauchius, *Gubernatorial Roles: An Assessment by Five Ohio Governors*.

57 Stanley Aronoff and Vernal G. Riffe, Jr., *James A. Rhodes at Eighty*. (Columbus: privately printed, 1989), 25.

58 Samuel Shaffer, "Ohio's Winning Governor Lausche and the White House," *Newsweek*, May 21, 1956, 36.

59 Paul Nestor, employee at Scioto Country Club in the 1950s, interview by author on November 25, 1995.

60 James A. Rhodes, former Ohio governor, interview by author in Columbus, Ohio, June 21, 1996.

61 Ibid.

62 Richard G. Zimmerman, "Rhodes First Eight Years, 1963–1971," in *Ohio Politics*, Alexander P. Lamis, ed., 82–83.

63 Dick O'Hara, "Popcorn or Not, Rhodes Still No Lausche," The Dayton *Daily News*, August 25, 1963.

64 Letter from Barry Wood, President of NBC to Jane Lausche, November 10, 1954, (Frank J. Lausche Papers), Ohio Historical Society.

65 Letter from Jane Lausche to Barry Wood, November 25, 1954, (Frank J. Lausche Papers), Ohio Historical Society.

66 William E. Marsh, Attorney-at-Law, interview by author in Columbus, Ohio, June 21, 1995.

67 Toledo *Times*, December 2, 1954.

68 Letter from Charles H. Keating, Jr. to Frank Lausche, May 11, 1967, (Frank J. Lausche Papers), Ohio Historical Society; Arizona *Republic*, October 4, 1996.

69 Michael Binstein and Charles Bowder, *Trust Me*. (New York: Random House, 1993).

70 Ibid.

71 Cleveland *Press*, January 10, 1955.

72 Ibid.

73 Charles McCarry, "Frank Lausche: Senator Without a Party," *True Magazine*, Fall 1958, 23.

74 Michael O'Bryant, *The Ohio Almanac*, 1997–1998, 128.

75 "The Lonely One," *Time*, February 20, 1956, 23.

76 Brent Larkin, "Frank Lausche: A Legend in Politics," *Plain Dealer Magazine*, November 10, 1985, 21.

77 "The Lonely One," *Time*, February 20, 1956, 23.

78 "Governor Lausche Recalls Lake Logan History," Logan *News*, July 20, 1956, (Frank J. Lausche Papers), Ohio Historical Society.

79   George W. Knepper, *Ohio and Its People*, 434; Cleveland *Press*, June 6, 1955.

80   Haskell Short, "Lausche Proposes Ohio Eliminate 3 Big Boards," Youngstown *Vindicator*, January 2, 1957.

81   "The Lonely One," *Time*, February 20, 1956, 23.

82   "Ohio Prosperity High Among Nation's States," Columbus *Dispatch*, August 28, 1955.

83   John D. Porterfied, Director, *A Progress Report on Ohio's Mental Hygiene Program, 1945–1956*, Columbus, Ohio.

84   Phillip R. Shriver and Clarence E. Wunderlin, eds., *The Documentary Heritage of Ohio*, 396.

85   Robert W. Reider, "Reports from the State Capitol," Waverly *Watchman*, March 24, 1955.

86   Cleveland *Plain Dealer*, April 5, 1955.

87   Letter from James W. Shocknessy to Governor Frank J. Lausche, July 14, 1955, (Frank J. Lausche Papers), Ohio Historical Society.

88   Columbus *Citizen*, 1955.

89   Akron *Beacon Journal*, March 9, 1969; letter from Frank J. Lausche to James D. Hartshorne, March 18, 1969, (Frank J. Lausche Papers), Ohio Historical Society.

90   Neal R. Peirce and John Keefe, *The Great Lakes States of America*. (New York: W. W. Norton, 1980), 303.

91   John Gunther, *Inside U.S.A.*, 429.

92   John H. Fenton, *Midwest Politics*. (New York: Holt, Rinehart and Winston, 1966), 15.

93   Ibid.

94   Neal R. Peirce and John Keefe, *The Great Lakes States of America*, 315.

95   William Hessler, "The Implacable Independence of Frank J. Lausche," *The Reporter*, April 5, 1956, 26.

96   Ibid, 24.

97   Charles McCarry, "Frank Lausche: Senator Without A Party," *True Magazine*, Fall 1958, 116.

98   David Hess, "The Decline of Ohio," *The Nation*, April 13, 1970, 23.

99   Neal R. Peirce and John Keefe, *The Great Lakes States of America*, 305; William Hessler, "The Implacable Independence of Frank J. Lausche," *The Reporter*, April 5, 1956, 26.

100 John Fenton, *Midwest Politics*, 149.

101 Ibid, 148–49.

102 Rollin Dean Jauchius, *Gubernatorial Roles: An Assessment by Five Ohio Governors*, 35

103 Ibid.

104 Charles McCarry, "Frank Lausche: Senator Without A Party," *True Magazine*, Fall 1958, 116.

CHAPTER NINE

1   John Gunther, *Inside USA*, 430.

2   Steve Neal, *Harry and Ike*. (New York: Scribners, 2001), 111; Cabell B. H. Phillips, *The Truman Presidency: The History of a Triumphant Succession*. (New York: Macmillan, 1966).

3   Letter from Ralph S. Locher, Secretary to the Governor, to Barbara Olson, television representative, New York City, April 7, 1952, (Frank J. Lausche Papers), Ohio Historical Society.

4   Joe Alex Morris, "Who Is Frank Lausche? *Saturday Evening Post*, Dec. 10, 1955, 117.

5   Dwight D. Eisenhower, *The White House Years: Mandate for Change, 1953–1956*, (Garden City, New York: Doubleday, 1963), 298.

6   Ezra Taft Benson, *Cross Fire, The Eight Years with Eisenhower*, (Garden City, New York: Doubleday and Company, Inc., 1962), 155.

7   Joe Alex Morris, "Who Is Frank Lausche? *Saturday Evening Post*, Dec. 10, 1955, 117.

8   Duncan Norton-Taylor, "The Leaderless, Lively Democrats," *Fortune Magazine*, January 1954, 86.

9   Raymond Moley, *Newsweek*, November 8, 1954, 104.

10   Ibid.

11   David Lawrence, "Why Not Governor Lausche?" *U.S. News and World Report,* December 9, 1955.

12   Fulton Lewis, Jr., "Democrat Ohio Strong Man," Columbus *Citizen*, January 4, 1954.

13   "Ohio-Declaration of Independents," *Time*, May 19, 1956, 30.

14   "The Lonely One," *Time*, February 20, 1956, 23.

15   Richard L. Maher, Political ed., Cleveland *Press*, November 30, 1955, (Frank J. Lausche Papers), Ohio Historical Society.

16   Samuel Shaffer, "Ohio's Winning Governor Lausche—and the White House," *Newsweek*, May 21, 1956, 35.

17   Chesly Manly, "Frank Lausche: Ohio's Taft Democrat," *Human Events*, Vol. 13, No. 1, March 31, 1956.

18   Ibid.

19   *New York Times*, October 25, 1955.

20   "The Economics of Seven Democrats," *Fortune Magazine*, July 1956, 75.

21   Ibid.

22   Robert H. Ferrell, ed., *The Diary of James C. Hagerty, Eisenhower in Mid-Course, 1954–1955.* (Bloomington, Indiana: Indiana University Press, 1983), 177.

23   William Bragg Ewald, Jr., *Eisenhower The President, Crucial Days, 1951–1960.* (Englewood Cliffs, New Jersey: Prentice-Hall, Inc. 1981), 184.

24   Ibid, 185.

25   Ibid.

26   Ibid, 185–186.

27   Ibid.

28   Ibid.

29   Ibid, 187.

30   David Lawrence, "Why Not Governor Lausche?, *U.S. News and World Report*, December 9, 1955, 128.

31   *Human Events*, Vol. 13, No. 2, January 14, 1956.

32   *Time,* January 23, 1956.

33   Transcript of Governor Frank Lausche's *Meet The Press* interview, January 8, 1956, personal copy.

34   *Time*, January 23, 1956.

35   Ibid.

36   Transcript of Governor Frank Lausche's *Meet The Press* interview, January 8, 1956, personal copy.

37   Ibid.

38   Ibid.

39   "The People's Choice," The Cleveland *Plain Dealer*, January 10, 1956.

40   *Time*, January 23, 1956, 13.

41   Answers given at an informal gathering of newsmen and citizens, Date unknown, (Frank J. Lausche Papers), Ohio Historical Society.

42   *Time*, May 14, 1956.

43   *New York Times*, January 20, 1956.

44   Michael V. DiSalle, *Second Choice.* (New York: Hawthorn Books, Inc. 1966), 193.

45   Ibid.

46   *Time*, April 16, 1956.

47   William B. Saxbe, with Peter D. Franklin, *I've Seen the Elephant*, 54.

48   David D. Van Tassel and John J. Grabowski, *The Encyclopedia of Cleveland History*, 90.

49   William B. Saxbe with Peter D. Franklin, *I've Seen the Elephant*, 54.

50   "Pursuing the Artful Dodger," *Time*, October 8, 1956, 26.

51   Ibid; Bliss became National chairman of the Republican Party in 1965.

52   Joe Hoover Bindley, *An Analysis of Voting Behavior in Ohio*, 201.

53   Associated Press Clipping, October 1956, (Frank J. Lausche Papers), Ohio Historical Society.

54   Ibid.

55   "Ohio's Winning Gov. Lausche—And the White House," *Newsweek*, May 21, 1956, 36.

56   John Howard Kessel, *Road to the Mansion*, Ph.D. dissertation (Columbia University, 1957), 163.

57   William Bragg Ewald, Jr., *Eisenhower The President*, 188.

58   Arthur Larson, *Eisenhower, The President Nobody Knew.* (New York: Charles Scribner's Sons, 1968), 35.

59   Joe Hoover Bindley, "An Analysis of Voting Behavior in Ohio," 202.

60   "Pursuing the Artful Dodger," *Time*, October 8, 1956, 26.

61   Louis B. Seltzer, *The Years Were Good*, 236.

62   *Time*, October 22, 1956, 26.

63   New York *Times*, October 29, 1956, 26.

64   William C. Bittner, *Frank J. Lausche*, 44.

65   Ibid, 45.

66   John Howard Kessel, *Road to the Mansion*, 165.

67   Ibid.

68   *Human Events*, November 10, 1956.

CHAPTER TEN

1   Cincinnati *Enquirer*, July 1, 1955.

2   Vignette of Robert E. Sheal, Frank Lausche's father-in-law, (Frank J. Lausche Papers), Ohio Historical Society.

3   David D. Van Tassel and John J. Grabowski, *The Encyclopedia of Cleveland History*, 864.

4   Associated Press release by Cornelia E. Porea, November 18, 1944, (Frank J. Lausche Papers), Ohio Historical Society.

5   David D. Van Tassel and John J. Grabowski, *The Encyclopedia of Cleveland History*, 864.

6   Clayton Fritchey, "Cleveland's New Mayor," *Common Ground*, II, Winter, 1942.

7   Columbus *Dispatch*, January 8, 1945.

8   Cleveland *Plain Dealer*, January 8, 1945.

9   Cleveland *Press*, August 19, 1941.

10   Jack Kennon, "A Guiding Star Named Jane," Cleveland *Press*, 1954.

11   Columbus *Dispatch*, January 8, 1945.

12   Columbus *Dispatch*, November 25, 1973.

13   Erma Kruse, "A Day With Jane Lausche," Cleveland *Press*, January 17, 1945.

14   Grace Goulder, "A Day With Jane Lausche, Ohio Scenes and Citizens," Cleveland *Plain Dealer Pictorial Magazine*, December 11, 1949, 11.

15   Ibid.

16   Ray Dorsey, "Time Out," Cleveland *Plain Dealer*, date unlisted, (Frank J. Lausche Papers), Ohio Historical Society.

17   Grace Goulder, "A Day With Jane Lausche," Cleveland *Plain Dealer Pictorial Magazine*, December 11, 1949, 11.

18   Personal Papers of Jane Lausche, March 1945, (Frank J. Lausche Papers), Ohio Historical Society.

19   Personal Papers of Jane Lausche, September–November, 1945, (Frank J. Lausche Papers), Ohio Historical Society.

20   Correspondence from Jane Lausche to Mary Wilcox, a cousin from Palo Alto, California, March 22, 1956, (Frank J. Lausche Papers), Ohio Historical Society.

21   Mansfield *News Journal*, May 4, 1944.

22   Correspondence from Jane Lausche to Mary Wilcox, March 22, 1956, (Frank J. Lausche Papers), Ohio Historical Society.

23   Correspondence from Jane Lausche to Margaret Truman, April 15, 1949, (Frank J. Lausche Papers), Ohio Historical Society.

24   Correspondence from Margaret Truman to Jane Lausche, May 2, 1949, (Frank J. Lausche Papers), Ohio Historical Society.

25   Correspondence from Jane Lausche to Margaret Truman, May 10, 1949, (Frank J. Lausche Papers), Ohio Historical Society.

26   Correspondence from President Harry Truman to Governor Frank J. Lausche, November 9, 1949, (Frank J. Lausche Papers), Ohio Historical Society.

27   Correspondence from Jane Lausche to Mary Wilcox, October 30, 1955, (Frank J. Lausche Papers), Ohio Historical Society.

28   Ibid.

29   Ibid.

30   Sally Jones, niece of Frank and Jane Lausche, interview by author on January 25, 2000, Puerto Gordo, Florida.

31   Ibid.

32   Mary McGarey, "The Governor's Lady—Ohio's Her Hobby," The Columbus *Sunday Dispatch Magazine*, January 25, 1953.

33   Kathryn Sullivan, "First Lady Keeps House on Budget," The Columbus *Citizen*, June 7, 1953.

34   Mary McGarey, "The Governor's Lady—Ohio's Her Hobby," The Columbus *Sunday Dispatch Magazine*, January 25, 1953, 10.

35   Grace Goulder, "Ohio Scenes and Citizens," Cleveland *Plain Dealer Pictorial Magazine*, January 20, 1952.

36   Mary McGarey, "The Governor's Lady—Ohio's Her Hobby," The Columbus *Sunday Dispatch Magazine*, January 25, 1953, 10.

37   Ibid.

38   George W. Knepper, *Ohio and Its People*, 189.

39   Ibid.

40   Columbus *Citizen*, September 2, 1954.

41   Ibid.

42   Ibid.

43   Letter from Jane Lausche to G.G. Nuss, White Sewing Machine Corporation, January 20, 1951, (Frank J. Lausche Papers), Ohio Historical Society.

44   Dayton *News*, March 15, 1950.

45   Letters to Jane Lausche from *Trailer Topics Magazine*, March 29, 1950; April 5, 1950; Letter from Jane Lausche to *Trailer Topics Magazine*, April 6, 1950, (Frank J. Lausche Papers), Ohio Historical Society.

46 Margaret Joster, "Ohio's First Lady is No Unbending Dignitary," Cincinnati *Enquirer*, October 25, 1951.

47 Edward G. Gobetz, ed., *Frank J. Lausche: Life History of Ohio's Lincoln*, 207–208.

48 Ibid.

49 Collin Dean Jauchius, *Gubernatorial Roles: An Assessment by Five Ohio Governors*,34.

50 William Hessler, "The Implacable Independence of Frank J. Lausche," *Reporter*, April 5, 1956, 27–28.

51 Remarks expressed at Jane Lausche's Funeral by Reverend A. Edward Pevec, Auxiliary Bishop of the Catholic Diocese of Cleveland, November 28, 1981, copy given to the author at an interview with Bishop Pevec, June 9, 1997.

52 Letter from Louis Seltzer to Governor Frank Lausche, April 21, 1953, (Frank J. Lausche Papers), Ohio Historical Society.

53 Philip Porter, *Cleveland, Confused City on a Seesaw*, 131.

54 Cleveland *News*, July 20, 1956.

55 Virginia Wells, daughter of Ralph Locher, former mayor of Cleveland, interview by author in Phoenix, Arizona, on December 24, 1999.

56 Letter to Mary Wilcox from Jane Lausche, March 2, 1956, (Frank J. Lausche Papers), Ohio Historical Society.

57 Columbus *Dispatch*, July 20, 1956.

58 Cleveland *News*, July 20, 1956.

59 Letter to Mary Wilcox from Jane Lausche, November 2, 1956, (Frank J. Lausche Papers), Ohio Historical Society.

60 Ibid.

61 Ibid.

62 Columbus *Dispatch,* November 9, 1956; Dayton *Daily News,* February 4, 1957.

63 Peter Bellamy, "Lausches Go Regular," Cleveland *Press*, January 5, 1957.

64 Dayton *Daily News*, May 13, 1968.

65 Columbus *Citizen*, August 23, 1957; Los Angeles *Times*, September 22, 1957.

66 Virginia Wells, interview by author in Phoenix, Arizona, on December 24, 1999.

67 Cincinnati *Enquirer*, February 10, 1957.

68 Ibid.

69 Cincinnati *Times-Star*, February 9, 1957.

70 Dayton *Daily News*, May 11, 1961.

71 Cleveland *Press*, March 2, 1968.

72 Ibid.

73 Edward G. Gobetz, ed., *Frank J. Lausche: Life History of Ohio's Lincoln*, 207–08.

CHAPTER ELEVEN

1 Alfred Steinberg, *Sam Johnson's Boy.* (New York: The Macmillan Company, 1968), 353.

2 Robert A. Caro, *The Years of Lyndon Johnson, Master of the Senate.* (New York: Alfred A. Knopf, 2002), 557.

3 Robert Dalleck, *Lone Star Rising, Lyndon Johnson and His Times, 1908–1960.* (New York: Oxford University Press, 1991), 509.

4 Alexander P. Lamis, *Ohio Politics*, 38–39.

5 *Newsweek*, January 14, 1957, 30.

6 Robert Dalleck, *Lone Star Rising, Lyndon Johnson and His Times*, 509.

7 *Newsweek*, January 14, 1957, 30.

8   Alfred Steinberg, *Sam Johnson's Boy*, 448.

9   Robert Oliver, senatorial aide to Lyndon Johnson, interview by Michael I. Gillette on June 16, 1973, (Lyndon B. Johnson Papers), Lyndon B. Johnson Presidential Library, Austin, Texas.

10   Alfred Steinberg, *Sam Johnson's Boy*, 448.

11   George Reedy, senatorial aide to Lyndon Johnson, interview by Michael I. Gillette on October 13, 1983, Lyndon B. Johnson Papers (Lyndon B. Johnson Presidential Library), Austin, Texas.

12   *Newsweek*, January 14, 1957, 30.

13   George Reedy, senatorial aide to Lyndon Johnson, interview by Michael I. Gillette on October 13, 1983, Lyndon B. Johnson Papers (Lyndon B. Johnson Presidential Library), Austin, Texas.

14   Roulhac Hamilton, "Governor's Strong Support of GOP Might Bring Strong Censure," Columbus *Dispatch*, July 29, 1956.

15   "By the Grace of Lausche," Winston-Salem *Journal*, January 5, 1957, (Frank J. Lausche Papers), Ohio, Historical Society.

16   Letter from Frank J. Lausche to James B. L. Rush, Editorial ed., Winston-Salem *Journal*, January 9, 1957 (Frank J. Lausche Papers).

17   Cincinnati *Enquirer*, February 11, 1957.

18   James M. Naughton, "Ohio: A Lesson in Changing Politics," *The New York Times Magazine*, May 5, 1968, 117.

19   Akron *Beacon Journal*, June 2, 1957.

20   *Human Events*, Volume 14, No. 10, March 9, 1957.

21   Robert E. Hoyt, "Maverick Lausche Bucks for 'Mr. Economy' Tag," Akron *Beacon Journal*, June 2, 1957.

22   Ibid.

23   Ibid.

24   The Dayton *Daily News*, April 28, 1958.

25   Letters from Senator Lausche to Edwin H. Davis, May 14, 1958, (Frank J. Lausche Papers), Ohio Historical Society.

26   Raymond Moley, "Phony Union Reform," *Newsweek*, June 30, 1958.

27   Cincinnati *Enquirer*, October 23, 1958; Bureau of Unemployment Compensation, *Ohio Labor Market Information Report*, August 15, 1959 as reported in Alexander P. Lamis, ed., *Ohio Politics*, 50.

28   Alvin Silverman, "Lausche's Arm Opens in Vain for Young's," Cleveland *Plain Dealer*, January 8, 1959.

29   Letter from Senator Frank J. Lausche to Drew Pearson, April 21, 1959, (Frank J. Lausche Papers), Ohio Historical Society.

30   Letter from Drew Pearson to Bishop Wilbur Hammaker, May 2, 1959, (Frank J. Lausche Papers), Ohio Historical Society.

31   Letter from Bishop Wilbur Hammaker to Drew Pearson, May 7, 1959, (Frank J. Lausche Papers), Ohio Historical Society.

32   Letter from Drew Pearson to Bishop Wilbur Hammaker, May 12, 1950, (Frank J. Lausche Papers), Ohio Historical Society.

33   Letter from Senator Frank Lausche to Drew Pearson, May 27, 1959, (Frank J. Lausche Papers), Ohio Historical Society; Washington *Post*, May 21, 1959.

34   Letter from Senator Frank J. Lausche to Wilfred M. O'Keefe, June 23, 1958 (Frank J. Lausche Papers), Ohio Historical Society.

35   Ibid.

36   *Drew Pearson Diaries, 1949–1959*. Tyler Abell, ed. (New York: Holt, Rinehart and Winston, 1974), 518.

37   *1959 Congressional Quarterly Almanac*, Vol. 15, 1958, 670.

38   Ibid.

39   *Congressional Quarterly Almanac*, Vol. 14, 1958, 100.

40   *Congressional Quarterly Almanac*, Vol. 14, 1958, 127; *Congressional Quarterly*, Vol. 21, Part Two, 2176.

41   Louis B. Seltzer, *The Years Were Good*, 236.

42   Richard Dalleck, *Lone Star Rising*, 560; *Cleveland Plain Dealer*, July 29, 1960.

43   Omaha *World-Herald*, October 14, 1959.

44   Cleveland *Plain Dealer*, March 26, 1960.

45   Richard G. Zimmerman, *Call Me Mike, A Political Biography of Michael V. DiSalle*, 190.

46   Kenneth P. O'Donnell and David F. Powers, *Johnny, We Hardly Knew Ye.* (Boston: Little Brown and Company, 1970), 211–212.

47   Richard G. Zimmerman, *Call Me Mike, A Political Biography of Michael V. DiSalle*, 191.

48   Washington *News*, September, 1960.

49   Louis Seltzer, "The Magic Is Missing," The Cleveland *Press*, July 16, 1960.

50   Ibid.

51   Toledo *Blade*, December 27, 1961.

52   Charles Vanik, U.S. Congressman, interview by author in Florida on January 24, 2000.

53   *1950 Congressional Quarterly Almanac*, Vol. 6, 1950, 139.

54   John H. Fenton, "Ohio's Unpredictable Voters," *Harpers*, October, 1962, 62.

55   Letter from Americans for Constitutional Action to Senator Frank J. Lausche, April 21, 1961, (Frank J. Lausche Papers), Ohio Historical Society.

56   Letter from Senator Frank J. Lausche to Gary O. Chalupsky, July 19, 1965, (Frank J. Lausche Papers), Ohio Historical Society.

57   Cleveland *Plain Dealer*, February 25, 1961.

58   Toledo *Blade*, December 27, 1961.

59   Cleveland *Press*, July 19, 1961.

60   Columbus *Dispatch*, December 11, 1961.

61   Columbus *Dispatch*, June 7 and 8, 1962.

62   The *New York Times*, May 27, 1962.

63   Ibid.

64   Columbus *Dispatch*, April 11, 1962.

65   Cleveland *Plain Dealer*, October 30, 1962.

66   Warren R. VanTyne, *Institution of Senator Frank J. Lausche*, unpublished monograph. The Ohio State University, 28–30, 56–57, 86–87.

67   Ibid.

68   Cleveland *Plain Dealer*, December 31, 1967.

69   Ross Baker, *Friend and Foe in the U.S. Senate.* (New York: The Free Press, 1980), 98.

70   Letter from Senator Clifford P. Hansen to Frank J. Lausche, in honor of his 80th birthday, October 21, 1975 (personal copy).

71   LeRoy Ashby and Rod Gramer, *Fighting the Odds, the Life of Senator Frank Church.* (Pullman, Washington: Washington State University Press, 1994), 179; Jerry Brady, former aide for Senator Frank Church, interview by author in Boise, Idaho, on October 5, 2002. (Brady ran unsuccessfully on the Democratic ticket for governor of Idaho in the 2002 election).

72 Thomas Vail, publisher and editor, Cleveland *Plain Dealer*, notes and memories sent to author, September 11, 2003.

73 Donald Ritchie, Senate Historian, *Oral History interviews,* March 9, 1996 to April 15, 1996, Manuscript Division, Library of Congress, Washington, DC.

74 Senator Ernest "Fritz" Hollings, Democratic senator from South Carolina, interview by author at the Senate Dining Room, Washington, DC, June 29, 1997.

75 Ohio AFL-CIO *Focus*, January 1968.

76 Bob Schieffer, *This Just In.* (New York: G. P. Putnam & Sons, 2003), 323.

77 Doris Kearns, *Lyndon Johnson and the American Dream.* (New York: Harper and Row, 1976), 108–09.

78 Statement by Senator Frank J. Lausche on Postmaster General's drive to rid mail of obscenity, *Congressional Record,* Senate, May 22, 1959; letter to Postmaster General Arthur E. Summerfield, May 22, 1959, (Frank J. Lausche Papers), Ohio Historical Society.

79 Letter from Senator Frank J. Lausche to Jerry Will, October 17, 1958, (Frank J. Lausche Papers), Ohio Historical Society; Youngstown *Vindicator*, June 28, 1962.

80 Letter from Senator Frank J. Lausche to Mortimer M. Caplin, Commissioner of Internal Revenue, September 20, 1961, (Frank J. Lausche Papers), Ohio Historical Society.

81 *Congressional Record*, Senate, April 15, 1964, 8038–8040; January 25, 1965, 1596–1597; February 1, 1965, 1691–1962.

82 Grace Goulder, "A Visit to Strip Mining Country—The Ohio Badlands," Cleveland *Plain Dealer*, July 25, 1965.

83 "Lausche Attacks Domestic Peace Corps," *Human Events*, December 22, 1962.

84 Letter from Senator Edward Kennedy to Frank J. Lausche, December 12, 1963, (Frank J. Lausche Papers), Ohio Historical Society.

85 1977 *Congressional Quarterly Almanac*, Vol. 33, 1977, 617–626.

86 The Columbus *Dispatch*, February 4, 1964.

87 Alvin Silverman, "Senator Lausche to Cast Vote for Johnson," Cleveland *Plain Dealer*, October 23, 1964.

88 Alexander P. Lamis, ed., *Ohio Politics*, 205.

89 Tape of Senator Frank J. Lausche interview with President Lyndon Johnson, September 14, 1966, (Lyndon B. Johnson Papers), Lyndon B. Johnson Library, Austin, Texas.

90 The Voting Record of Senator Frank J. Lausche, (Ohio AFL-CIO Files, 1958–1968), Ohio Historical Society; *National Associated Businessmen Economy Voting Record, 1965–66.*

91 Thomas R. Guthrie, "Lausche Takes to the Floor, Asks Pollution War Unity," Cleveland *Plain Dealer*, February 3, 1966.

92 "The Question of Federal Assistance for Urban Mass Transit Systems," *Congressional Digest*, January 1963, 19.

93 Edward G. Gobetz, ed., *Frank J. Lausche: Life History of Ohio's Lincoln*, 73.

94 *The Voting Record of Senator Frank J. Lausche*, (Ohio AFL-CIO files, 1958–1968), Ohio Historical Society; *National Associated Businessmen Economy Voting Record*, 1965–1966; *Congressional Quarterly Almanac*, Vol. 22–24, 1966–1968.

95 Memo from Mike Mantos to presidential aides for President Lyndon Johnson, August 1967, (Lyndon B. Johnson Papers), Lyndon B. Johnson Presidential Library, Austin, Texas.

96 Ibid; memo from Mike Mantos to presidential aides for President Lyndon Johnson, August 1967, (Lyndon B. Johnson Papers), Lyndon B. Johnson Presidential Library, Austin, Texas.

97 Ibid.

98 Press release from Senate Office of Frank J. Lausche, April 8, 1968, (Frank J. Lausche Papers), Ohio Historical Society.

99   Cleveland Press, June 23, 1967.

100 Ibid.

101 Ibid.

102 Edward G. Gobetz, ed., *Frank J. Lausche: Life History of Ohio's Lincoln*, 78.

CHAPTER TWELVE

1   Bethine Church, widow of Senator Frank Church, interview by author in Boise, Idaho, on December 6, 1999.

2   Letter to Henry Lobe, Cleveland, January 20, 1959, (Frank J. Lausche Papers) Ohio Historical Society.

3   Robert Welch, "On the Right Side," *One Man's Opinion*, Vol. 1, No. 3, July, 1956, 9.

4   Letter to Carol Bobinchuck, Bedford, Ohio, November 1, 1961, (Frank J. Lausche Papers), Ohio Historical Society.

5   Letter from Vice President Richard Nixon to Frank Lausche, May 29, 1958, (Frank J. Lausche Papers), Ohio Historical Society.

6   Letter from Jane Lausche to sister-in-law Ruth Lausche, date unlisted, (Frank J. Lausche Papers), Ohio Historical Society.

7   David D. VanTassel and John J. Grabowski, eds., *The Encyclopedia of Cleveland History*, 360–61.

8   Letter from Nikita S. Khrushchev to Cyrus Eaton, December 24, 1959, (Frank J. Lausche Papers), Ohio Historical Society.

9   Letter from Frank J. Lausche to Cyrus Eaton, November 10, 1960, (Cyrus Eaton Papers), Western Reserve Historical Society.

10   Letter from Cyrus Eaton to Frank J. Lausche, November 13, 1960, (Cyrus Eaton Papers), Western Reserve Historical Society.

11   Letter from Cyrus Eaton to I.F. Stone, editor and publisher, *I.F. Stone Weekly*, November 16, 1960, (Cyrus Eaton Papers), Western Reserve Historical Society.

12   Letter from Tristram Coffin to Cyrus Eaton, March 26, 1964, (Cyrus Eaton Papers), Western Reserve Historical Society.

13   Ibid.

14   William Safire, *Safire's Political Dictionary*. (New York: Random House, 1978), 290–91.

15   John P. Leacasos, *Fires in the In-Basket The ABC's of the State Department*. (Cleveland: The World Publishing Company, 1968), 195.

16   Josephine Turkman, a post-World War II migrant from Slovenia, interview by author in Cleveland, Ohio on March 11, 1997.

17   *Congressional Record*, Senate, May 15, 1957, 6995.

18   *Congressional Record*, Senate, August 21, 1957, 15494.

19   Theodore Andrica, "Senator Lausche to Speak at Dinner Marking Ukraine Independence," Cleveland *Press*, January 15, 1968. Also see Gene L. Maeroff, "Ohio Politics after Johnson," *The Nation*, April 22, 1968, 539; Jose Melaher, "Lausche Helped Many Slovenian Immigrants," *American Home*, November 14, 1975.

20   United States Congress, Senate, Office of the Senate Historian, Oral History Interview with Carl Marcy, October 5, 1983, conducted by Donald Ritchie, 176–77.

21   Victor Riesel, "Sales of Cuban Goods in U.S. Take Big Jump," Canton *Repository*, December 25, 1961.

22   Memorandum from Carl Marcy, chief of staff, Senate Foreign Relations Committee to Frank J. Lausche, February 1, 1962 (Frank J. Lausche Papers) Ohio Historical Society.

23   Letter from Dr. Manuel A. de Varona, Chairman of Foreign Relations, Revolutionary Organization of Cuba. May 10, 1962, (Frank J. Lausche Papers) Ohio Historical Society.

24   Letter to Bob Crater, The Cincinnati *Post* and *Times-Star* from Frank J. Lausche, October 10, 1962 (Frank J. Lausche Papers) Ohio Historical Society.

25   Ibid.

26   Virginia Wells, daughter of Ralph Locher, interview by author in Washington, DC on May 12, 2004.

27   Correspondence between Senator Lausche and Senator J. William Fulbright, November 12, 1962; November 13, 1962, November 14, 1962, December 6, 1962. (Frank J. Lausche Papers) Ohio Historical Society.

28   Cleveland *Plain Dealer*, November 14, 1962.

29   Reports submitted by Carl Marcy, Chief of Staff, Senate Foreign Relations Committee, pursuant to provisions of the Foreign Assistance Act of 1961 as amended to members of the Foreign Relations Committee, January 28, 1963 (Frank J. Lausche Papers), Ohio Historical Society.

30   Washington *Evening Star*, June 17, 1963.

31   Holmes Alexander, "The Clay Doctrine," The Charleston (S.C.) *News and Courier*, July 18, 1963.

32   Frank J. Lausche, "Dangerous Failings of Our State Department," *Reader's Digest*, June, 1964, 54.

33   Ibid, 55–60.

34   Randall Woods, *Fulbright, a Biography.* (New York: Cambridge University Press, 1995), 397–99.

35   Ibid. (Taken from a briefing by Secretary Rusk in Executive Session, Senate Foreign Relations Committee, January 24, 1966 and letter from Carl Marcy to J. William Fulbright, August 17, 1965.) (Senatorial Papers of J. William Fulbright), Mullins Library, University of Arkansas, Fayetteville, Arkansas.

36   Letter from House Representative Samuel L. Devine to Senator Frank Lausche, June 4, 1964 (Frank J. Lausche Papers), Ohio Historical Society.

37   Robert S. Allen and Paul Scott, "JFK Masterminds Push for Approval of Treaty," Sarasota *Herald*, September 3, 1963.

38   Ibid.

39   Ibid.

40   Columbus *Citizen,* November 19, 1965.

41   *Congressional Record.* Senate, May 11, 1967, 12430.

42   Robert Mann, *A Grand Delusion, America's Descent into Vietnam.* (New York: Basic Books, 2001), 289.

43   Alexander DeConde, *Encyclopedia of American Foreign Policy,* second edition. (New York: Charles Scribner's Sons. 2002), 873–74.

44   Orrin Schwab, *Defending The Free World, John F. Kennedy, Lyndon Johnson and the Vietnam War, 1961–1965.* (Westport, Connecticut: Praeger Publishing, 1998), 94–95.

45   Robert Mann, *A Grand Delusion, America's Descent Into Vietnam*, 396.

46   Robert S. McNamara, *In Retrospect: The Tragedy and Lessons of Vietnam.* (New York: Times, 1995), 130.

47   United States Senate Historical Office, Oral History Papers #153, Washington, DC.

48   *Congressional Quarterly*, March, 1968, 714.

49   Donald Oberdorfer, *Senator Mansfield.* (Washington, DC: Smithsonian Books, 2003), 244–45.

50   *Congressional Record*, Volume 110, No. 151, August 5, 1964, p. 18084–18085.

51   Letter from Frank Lausche to Tom Vail, publisher and editor, Cleveland *Plain Dealer*, May 6, 1965. (Frank J. Lausche Papers) Ohio Historical Society.

52   Letter from Frank J. Lausche to Tom Vail, February 16, 1965 (Frank J. Lausche Papers) Ohio Historical Society.

53   Letter from Frank J. Lausche to Tom Vail, Cleveland *Plain Dealer*, January 24, 1966, (Frank J. Lausche Papers) Ohio Historical Society.

54   *New York Times*, April 27, 1964, 7; April 26, 1967, 1.

55   David Halberstam, *The Best and the Brightest*. (New York: Random House, 1972), 623–24.

56   Don Oberdorfer, *Senator Mansfield*, 303–04.

57   Randall Woods, *Fulbright, A Biography*, 397.

58   Ibid, 401.

59   Memo from Mike Mantos to President Johnson, February 17, 1966, National Security-Defense, Box 219, (Lyndon B. Johnson Papers) Lyndon B. Johnson Presidential Library, Austin, Texas.

60   William Conrad Gibbons, *The U.S. Government and the Vietnam War, Executive and Legislative Roles and Relationships,* Part IV, July 1965–January 1968. (Princeton, New Jersey: Princeton University Press, 1995), 243.

61   John M. Taylor, *General Maxwell Taylor, The Sword and the Pen*. (New York: Doubleday, 1989), 335.

62   Memo from Mike Mantos to President Johnson, February 17, 1966 (Presidential-Senatorial Papers). Lyndon B. Johnson Presidential Library Austin, Texas.

63   Ibid.

64   Cleveland *Press*, February 19, 1996.

65   Louis Hurst, *The Sweetest Little Club in the World: The U.S. Senate*. (Englewood Cliffs, N. J.: Prentice-Hall, Inc., 1980), 88.

66   Cleveland *Plain Dealer*, December 31, 1967.

67   Memo from Mike Mantos to President Johnson, September 14, 1966. (Lyndon B. Johnson Papers). Lyndon B. Johnson Presidential Library, Austin, Texas.

68   Ibid.

69   Darrell St. Claire, Assistant Secretary of the Senate, oral history interview conducted by Donald Ritchie, Senate Historical Office, December, 1976 to April 1978, Washington, DC.

70   Robert Mann, *A Grand Delusion, America's Descent Into Vietnam*, 518.

71   LeRoy Ashbey and Rod Gramer, *Fighting the Odds, The Life of Senator Frank Church*. (Pullman: Washington State University, 1994), 220.

72   The Lima *News,* May 5, 1967.

73   John O. Leacasos, "Lausche's Crucial Decision in Vietnam," Cleveland *Plain Dealer*, July 9, 1967.

74   Robert Mann, *A Grand Delusion, America's Descent Into Vietnam*, 548.

75   Cincinnati *Enquirer*, July 21, 1967.

76   Cincinnati *Enquirer*, July 23, 1967.

77   William Conrad Gibbons, *The U.S. Government and the Vietnam War*, Part IV, 824–25.

78   Ibid, 826.

79   Ibid, 910.

80   Ibid, 922.

81   *Congressional Record,* Senate, October 6, 1967, 28091–2.

82   Cleveland *Plain Dealer*, November 4, 1967.

83   Ibid.

84   Trevor Armbrister, *A Matter of Accountability.* (New York: Coward-McCann, 1970), 395.

85   Ibid.

86   Tristam, Coffin, *Senator Fulbright, Portrait of a Public Philosopher.* (New York: E. P. Dutton and Company, 1966), 278.

87   "Anecdote of the Week," author and date unavailable, (Frank J. Lausche Papers), Ohio Historical Society.

88   William Conrad Gibbons, *The U.S. Government and the Vietnam War*, Part IV, 448–9.

89   *Congressional Record*, March 7, 1968, S2378.

90   Robert Mann*, A Grand Delusion, America's Descent into Vietnam*, 548.

91   *Investor's Business Daily*, February 12, 2001.

92   Walter Cronkite, *A Reporter's Life.* (New York: Alfred A. Knopf, 1996), 258.

93   Ibid.

94   Gene I. Maeroff, "Ohio: Politics After Johnson," *The Nation*, April 22, 1968, 539.

95   Doris Kearns (Goodwin), *Lyndon Johnson and the American Dream.* (New York: Harper and Row Publishers, 1976), 314–17.

96   Irving Bernstein, *Guns or Butter, The Presidency of Lyndon Johnson.* (New York: Oxford University Press,1966), 354–58.

97   Press Release from Senator Frank J. Lausche, Senatorial Office, April 1, 1968 (Frank J. Lausche Papers) Ohio Historical Society.

98   Lyndon Baines Johnson, *The Vantage Point: Perspectives of the Presidency, 1963–1969.* New York: Holt, Rinehart and Winston, 1971, 495.

99   Ibid.

100   Letter from Frank J. Lausche to Janis Edwards, July 15, 1969, (Frank J. Lausche Papers) Ohio Historical Society.

101   Gene I. Maeroff, "Ohio: Politics After Johnson," *The Nation*, April 22, 1968, 539.

102   James M. Naughton, "Ohio, A Lesson in Changing Politics," New York *Times Magazine*, Section G., May 5, 1968, 112.

103   Gene I. Maeroff, "Ohio: Politics After Johnson," *The Nation*, April 22, 1968, 540.

104   James M. Naughton, "Ohio, A Lesson in Changing Politics," New York *Times Magazine*, Section G, May 5, 1968, 118.

Chapter Thirteen

1   James M. Naughton, "Ohio: A Lesson in Changing Politics," *New York Times Magazine*, May 5, 1968.

2   "Lausche Run With GOP Is Suggested," Cleveland *Plain Dealer*, January 12, 1968.

3   Richard Zimmerman, "Would You Believe There's A Lausche?" Dayton *Journal Herald*, June 20, 1966.

4   Ibid.

5   Robert Feldkamp, "View from Washington," Akron *Beacon Journal*, January 22, 1967.

6   Brent Larkin, "Frank Lausche, A Legend in Ohio Politics," *The Plain Dealer Magazine*, November 10, 1985, 20.

7   Letter from Frank J. Lausche to Chester H. Allen, October 20, 1958, (Frank J. Lausche Papers), Ohio Historical Society.

8   Warren Van Tine, C.J.. Slanicka, Sandra Jordan and Michael Pierce, *In the Workers' Interest— A History of the Ohio AFL-CIO, 1958–1998.* (Columbus: Center for Labor Research, The Ohio State University, 1998), 26.

9   Brent Larkin, "Frank Lausche, A Legend in Ohio Politics," *The Plain Dealer Magazine*, November 10, 1985, 25.

10   Ibid.

11   Leonard N. Moore, *Carl B. Stokes and the Rise of Black Political Power.* (Urbana, Illinois: University of Illinois Press, 2002), 20; Carol Poh Miller and Robert A. Wheeler, *Cleveland, A Concise History*, 170.

12   Estelle Zannes, *Checkmate in Cleveland.* (Cleveland: The Press of Case Western Reserve University, 1972), 8.

13   Ibid, 96–7.

14   Leonard N. Moore, *Carl B. Stokes and the Rise of Black Political Power*, 20.

15   Kenneth G. Weinberg, *Black Victory, Carl Stokes and the Winning of Cleveland*, (Chicago: Quadrangle Books, 1968), 119–120.

16   Ibid. 148–49.

17   Carl B. Stokes, *Promises of Power, A Political Autobiography.* (New York: Simon and Schuster, 1973), 48.

18   Cleveland *Plain Dealer*, January 14, 1968; Estelle Zannes, *Checkmate in Cleveland*, 109; statement released from Lausche's senate office, Washington, DC, January 10, 1968, (Frank J. Lausche Papers, Box 249), Ohio Historical Society.

19   Letter written by Frank Lausche, but not released to the media, December 20, 1967 (Frank J. Lausche Papers) Ohio Historical Society.

20   Ibid. (Harold Lausche quit on December 14, 1967. Stokes expressed his appreciation to Lausche for his service of ten years).

21   Robert Feldkamp, "View from Washington," Akron *Beacon Journal*, January 22, 1967.

22   Cleveland *Plain Dealer*, May 9, 1968.

23   Warren Van Tine, et al., *In the Worker's Interest: A History of the Ohio AFL-CIO, 1958–1998*, 71.

24   David R. Larson, *Ohio's Fighting Liberal: A Political Biography of John J. Gilligan*, Ph.D. dissertation, (Columbus: The Ohio State University, 1982), 4–31.

25   Ibid., 117.

26   Warren Van Tine, et al. *In the Worker's Interest: A History of the Ohio AFL-CIO, 1958–1998*, 93.

27   James M. Naughton, "Ohio: A Lesson in Changing Politics," *New York Times Magazine*, May 5, 1968.

28   Richard L. Maher, "Hays Approval Delights Lausche," Cleveland *Plain Dealer*, December 31, 1967.

29   Richard L. Maher, "Sweeney Tells It to Ohio Dems: End Party Feuding, Aid Lausche," Cleveland *Plain Dealer*, December 13, 1967.

30   Columbus *Dispatch*, January 3, 1968.

31   Cleveland *Press*, January 2, 1968.

32   Cincinnati *Enquirer-Post*, January 6, 1968.

33   Cleveland *Plain Dealer*, January 7, 1968.

34   Statement released by Frank J. Lausche, January 10, 1968. (Frank J. Lausche Papers), Ohio Historical Society.

35   "Ohio Democrats Dump Lausche," Cleveland *Plain Dealer*, January 12, 1968; Toledo *Blade*, January 12, 1968.

36   David R. Larson, *Ohio's Fighting Liberal: A Political Biography of John F. Gilligan*, 11.

37   Statement released by Frank J. Lausche from his Washington, DC. Office, January 11, 1968, (Frank J. Lausche Papers), Ohio Historical Society.

38   Cleveland *Plain Dealer*, January 15, 1968.

39   Toledo *Blade*, January 12, 1968.
40   *Congressional Quarterly* January 19, 1968, 92.
41   *New York Times*, January 12,1968.
42   Columbus *Citizen-Journal*, January 13, 1968.
43   Cleveland *Plain Dealer*, November 24, 1967.
44   Youngstown *Vindicator*, January 13, 1968.
45   Columbus *Dispatch*, January 14, 1968.
46   Cincinnati *Enquirer*, January 16, 1968.
47   Robert H. Feldkamp, "Lausche Can't Hide Hurt," Akron *Beacon-Journal*, January 21, 1968.
48   James Naughton, "Ohio, A Lesson in Changing Politics," *New York Times Magazine*, May 5, 1968, 114.
49   Letter from Frank J. Lausche to A.W. (Jack) Ripley, Jr., publisher and editor of The Leetonia *Courier*, January 22, 1968, (Frank J. Lausche Papers), Ohio Historical Society.
50   James Naughton, "Ohio, A Lesson in Changing Politics," *New York Times Magazine*, May 5, 1968, 119.
51   David R. Larson, *Ohio's Fighting Liberal: A Political Biography of John J. Gilligan*, 117.
52   Warren Van Tine, et al. *In The Worker's Interest: A History of the Ohio AFL-CIO, 1958—1998*, 93.
53   *New York Times*, May 8, 1968.
54   John P. Leacacos, "Lausche Ready to Battle," Cleveland *Plain Dealer*, January 14, 1968.
55   Brent Larkin, "Frank Lausche, A Legend in Ohio Politics," *The Plain Dealer Magazine*, November 10, 1985, 26.
56   Ibid.
57   Release of statement from Washington, DC in answer to COPE's request to attend a screening session for candidates, February 20, 1968. (Frank J. Lausche Papers, Box 219), Ohio Historical Society.
58   Letter sent by Frank King to Ohio Newspapers and Media, March 6, 1968, (Frank J. Lausche Papers, Box 249), Ohio Historical Society.
59   Cleveland *Press*, January 25, 1968.
60   Ibid.
61   Walter Trohan, "Lausche Victory Premised on Independent Integrity," Chicago *Tribune*, February 9, 1968.
62   "Lausche's Conqueror: John Joyce Gilligan," *New York Times*, May 9, 1968.
63   James M. Naughton, "Ohio: A Lesson in Changing Politics," *New York Times Magazine*, May 5, 1968, 114.
64   Ibid.
65   Gene I. Maeroff, "Ohio: Politics After Johnson," *The Nation*, April 22, 1968, 539.
66   Ibid, 538–39.
67   William C. Bittner, *Frank J. Lausche, A Political Biography*, 55.
68   Akron *Beacon-Journal*, January 21, 1968.
69   William B. Saxbe, interview by author in Mechanicsburg, Ohio, on July 20, 2004.
70   Toledo *Blade*, March 20, 1968.
71   John Gilligan, interview by author in Cincinnati, on June 21, 1997.
72   Ibid.
73   Letter from Morton Neipp, Chairman, Democratic Executive Committee to Democratic County Chairmen, Democratic state executive committe, Presidents of Young Democratic and Women Clubs and Democratic County Officials, March 28, 1968, (Frank J. Lausche Papers, Box 250), Ohio Historical Society.
74   The Ironton *Tribune*, May 5, 1968.

75 James M. Naughton, "Ohio: A Lesson in Changing Politics," *New York Times Magazine*, May 5, 1968, 110.

76 Ibid.

77 The Ironton *Tribune*, May 5, 1968.

78 James V. Stanton, former U.S. Democratic Congressman from Cleveland, interview by author in Washington, DC on August 5, 2004.

79 James M. Naughton, "Ohio: A Lesson in Changing Politics," *New York Times Magazine*, May 5, 1968, 115.

80 Cleveland *Plain Dealer*, April 27, 1968.

81 Cleveland *Plain Dealer*, April 29, 1968.

82 Ibid.

83 Gene I. Maeroff, "Ohio: Politics After Johnson," *The Nation*, April 22, 1968, 539.

84 Cleveland *Press*, April 24, 1968.

85 James M. Naughton, "Ohio: A Lesson in Changing Politics," *New York Times Magazine*, May 5, 1968, 113.

86 David R. Larson, *Ohio's Fighting Liberal: A Political Biography of John J. Gilligan*, 118–119.

87 Cleveland *Press*, April 23, 1968.

88 David R. Larson, *Ohio's Fighting Liberal: A Political Biography of John J. Gilligan*, 118–119.

89 Cleveland *Press*, May 8, 1968.

90 William B. Saxbe, interview by author in Mechanicsburg, Ohio, on July 20, 2004.

91 John Gilligan, interview by author in Cincinnati, Ohio on July 19, 2004.

92 Brent Larkin, "Frank Lausche, A Legend in Ohio Politics," *The Plain Dealer Magazine*, November 10, 1985, 26.

93 James J. Kilpatrick, "Lament for Lausche—A Virtuoso on the Hill," Washington *Star*, May 12, 1968.

94 Estelle Zannes, *Checkmate in Cleveland*, 109.

95 Charles Vanik, interview by author on January 24, 2000.

96 Todd Simm, "Ethnic Politics Fading Out," Cleveland *Plain Dealer*, May 10, 1968.

97 Cleveland *Plain Dealer*, May 9, 1968.

98 Cleveland *Press*, May 9, 1968.

99 Akron *Beacon-Journal*, May 26, 1968.

100 Ibid.

101 James V. Naughton, "Ohio: A Lesson in Changing Politics," *New York Times Magazine*, May 5, 1968, 118.

CHAPTER FOURTEEN

1 Dick Feagler, "Lausche: It's Just Like Any Other Day," The Cleveland *Press*, May 8, 1968.

2 Letter September 23, 1968, from Frank J. Lausche to Edward Gobetz, ed., in *Frank J. Lausche: Life History of Ohio's Lincoln,* 80.

3 91st Congressional Session, *Congressional Record,* Senate, June 30, 1969, 17748.

4 Dick Feagler, "Lausche: It's Just Like Any Other Day." The Cleveland *Press*, May 8, 1968.

5 Cleveland *Press*, May 9, 1968.

6 Cleveland *Plain Dealer*, May 9, 1968.

7 Ibid.

8 Cleveland *Plain Dealer*, May 8, 1968.

9 James J. Kilpatrick, "A Sad Song on Lausche's Defeat," Cleveland *Plain Dealer*, May 12, 1968.

10 Don Robertson "Confessions of an Old Man," Cleveland *Press*, May 13, 1968.

11   Akron *Beacon Journal*, September 8, 1968.

12   Press release from Senate Office of Frank J. Lausche, Washington, DC, October 15, 1968 (Frank J. Lausche Papers), Ohio Historical Society; *U.S. News and World Report*, November 4, 1968, 12.

13   Sue Gorisek, "A Party of One," *Ohio Magazine*, August, 1988, 66–67.

14   Jerry Condo, "Citizen Lausche," Cincinnati *Post*, November 4, 1981.

15   Brent Larkin, "Frank Lausche, A Legend in Ohio Politics," *The Plain Dealer Magazine*, November 10, 1985, 25.

16   Cleveland *Press*. February 1, 1969.

17   Cleveland *Plain Dealer*, April 5, 1969.

18   David D. Van Tassel and John J. Grabowski, eds., *The Encyclopedia of Cleveland History*, 32.

19   Letter from Frank J. Lausche to Thomas Vail, Publisher, Cleveland *Plain Dealer*, April 12, 1969. (Frank J. Lausche Papers), Ohio Historical Society.

20   Letter from Frank J. Lausche to Martha Rush, May 24, 1969, (Frank J. Lausche Papers), Ohio Historical Society.

21   Letter from Frank J. Lausche to Ronald G. Shafer, Wall Street *Journal*, September 2, 1969 (Frank J. Lausche Papers), Ohio Historical Society.

22   John Gilligan, interview by author in Cincinnati, Ohio, June 21, 1997.

23   Letter from Frank J. Lausche to Ronald G. Shafer, Wall Street *Journal*, September 2, 1969 (Frank J. Lausche Papers), Ohio Historical Society.

24   Boston *Evening Globe*, May 8, 1973.

25   Ibid.

26   Letter from Frank J. Lausche to M. Brandes, May 24, 1969 (Frank J. Lausche Papers), Ohio Historical Society.

27   Cleveland *Plain Dealer*, November 10, 1975.

28   Dayton *Daily News*, October 3, 1972; *U.S. News and World Report*, November 4, 1968, 12.

29   Columbus *Dispatch*, August 26, 1970.

30   "Democrats for Ford" Campaign Letter written by Frank J. Lausche, 1976 (Frank J. Lausche Papers), Ohio Historical Society.

31   George E. Condon, Jr., "Down, Lausche a Sad Sight on the Political Scene," Cleveland *Plain Dealer*, July 10, 1977.

32   Alexander P. Lamis, ed., *Ohio Politics*, 211.

33   Ralph Perk, former Mayor of Cleveland, interview by author in Cleveland, Ohio on June 20, 1997.

34   Columbus *Dispatch*, October 29, 1978.

35   Columbus *Dispatch*, date unavailable.

36   Brent Larkin, "Frank Lausche, A Legend in Ohio Politics," *The Plain Dealer Magazine*, November 19, 1985, 27.

37   *The New Yorker*, November 1, 2004, 38.

38   Letter from Frank J. Lausche to Mayor Robert Thomas, Mantua, Ohio, July 10, 1972 (Frank J. Lausche Papers), Ohio Historical Society.

39   Cleveland *Plain Dealer*, June 15, 1972.

40   Cyril Mejac, "Lausche and the Slovenian Community in Washington, DC," In *Ohio's Lincoln, Frank J. Lausche,* edited by Edward Gobetz, 153–154; *Slovenian Chapel Dedication* booklet, 20.

41   Letter from Frank J. Lausche to Cyril J. Mejac, February 12, 1974 (Frank J. Lausche Papers), Ohio Historical Society.

42   Vladimir Pregelj, interview by author at the Library of Congress, Washington, DC, June 25, 1997.

43   Cyril Mejac, "Lausche and the Slovenian Committee in Washington, DC," *Ohio's Lincoln, Frank J. Lausche,* edited by Edward Gobetz, 157.

44   *Serbian Democratic Forum*, Chicago: The Serbian National Committee, April 1975, 139.

45   Ibid, 5.

46   Ibid.

47   John Charmley, *Churchill, The End of Glory.* (New York: Harcourt, Brace and Company, 1993), 533.

48   Ibid, 558.

49   *Congressional Record*, Senate, March 6, 1972, 7057.

50   Marcus Gleisser, *The World of Cyrus.* (New York: A.S. Barnes and Company, Inc. 1965), 25.

51   Randall Bennett Woods, *Fulbright, A Biography*, 194–195.

52   Ibid.

53   Ibid.

54   Letter from Cyril Zebot to President Dwight D. Eisenhower, August 14, 1958 (Cyril Zebot Collection), Washington, DC.

55   Arch Puddington, *Broadcasting Freedom: The Cold War Triumph of Radio Free Europe and Radio Liberty.* (Lexington: The University of Kentucky, 2000), 205–206.

56   Ibid.

57   Hearings Before the Committee on Foreign Relations, United States Senate, Ninety-Fourth Congress, 1st Session, Washington, DC, April 29, May 1, May 5, 1975, 176–178; 200–202.

58   Ibid.

59   Ibid.

60   Ibid.

61   Hearings before the Committee on Foreign Relations, United States Senate, Ninety-Fourth Congress, 1st Session; letter from Frank J. Lausche to Senator John Sparkman, Committee on Foreign Relations, May 5, 2000.

62   Arch Puddington, *Broadcasting Freedom: The Cold War Triumph of Radio Free Europe and Radio Liberty*, 202.

63   Letter from Frank J. Lausche to Congressman Wayne L. Hays, April 6, 1976 (Cyril Zebot Collection), Washington, DC.

64   Letter from Frank J. Lasuche to Senator John C. Stennis (MS), Claiborne Pell (RI), John Glenn and Howard Metzenbaum (OH), Congressman Dante Fascell (Dem-FL), and Frank Carlucci, January 5, 1987 and April 15, 1987, (Cyril Zebot Papers), Washington, DC.

65   Arch Puddington, *Broadcasting Freedom: The Cold War Triumph of Radio Free Europe and Radio Liberty,* 223.

66   Dayton *Daily News*, January 28, 1968.

67   *Congressional Record*, Senate, November 28, 1967, 3398; Joseph Felicijan, *The Genesis of the Contractual Theory and the Installation of the Dukes of Carinthia.* (Klagenfurt, Austria: Druzba si Mohorja V. Celovcu, 1963), 47–48.

68   Ibid.

69   Edward Gobetz, ed., *Frank J. Lausche: Life History of Ohio's Lincoln,* 170.

70   "Slovenians Hail Lausche as Their Man of the Year," March 1978 (Frank J. Lausche Papers), Ohio Historical Society.

71   Letter from Knights of Lithuania to Senator Frank J. Lausche, June 6, 1961; letter from Frank J. Lausche to Knights of Lithuania, June 9, 1961; letter from Knights of Lithuania to Frank J. Lausche, July 12, 1961, (Frank J. Lausche Papers), Ohio Historical Society.

72   Cleveland *Press*, August, 1980.

73   The Columbus *Dispatch*, May 20, 1983.

74   "Lausche Speaks Out on Labor Bill," Columbus *Dispatch*, July 4, 1977.

75   Alexander P. Lamis, *Ohio Politics*, 112.

76   Columbus *Dispatch*, July 4, 1977.

77   "Lausche Rebutted," Columbus *Dispatch,* July 13, 1977.

78   Cleveland *Plain Dealer*, July 10, 1977.

79   Cincinnati *Post*, November 4, 1981.

80   Birthday message from Cyril A. Zebot to Frank J. Lausche on his 80th Birthday, November 1975 (adopted from a tribute to Jane Lausche by Senator Norman Brunsdale, North Dakota), (Cyril Zebot Papers), Washington, DC.

81   Cyril and Conrad Mejac and Stanley Sustersic, interview by author in Washington, DC, on June 29, 1997.

82   Norman Malachik, "Lausche Was a Mayor for All," Cleveland *Plain Dealer*, July 10, 1977.

83   Brent Larkin, "Frank Lausche, A Legend in Ohio Politics," *The Plain Dealer Magazine*, November 10, 1985, 18.

84   Stanley Ertzen, interview by author in Cleveland, on June 26, 1995.

85   Glenn Metzdorff, senatorial aide to Lausche, interview by author in Washington, DC, on June 28, 1997.

86   Brent Larkin, "Frank Lausche, A Legend in Ohio," *The Plain Dealer Magazine*, November 10, 1985, 27.

87   *Congressional Record*, Senate, April 26, 1990, S5035.

88   Virginia Wells, interview by author in Alexandria, Virginia, on June 12, 2004.

89   Brent Larkin, "Frank Lausche, A Legend in Ohio Politics," *The Plain Dealer Magazine,* November 10,1985, 27.

90   Cleveland *Plain Dealer,* April 21, 1990.

91   Copy of Frank J. Lausche's funeral homily given to the author by Bishop Edward Pevec, Cleveland, June 9, 1997.

92   Cleveland *Plain Dealer*, April 26, 1990.

93   Columbus *Dispatch*, April 22, 1990.

94   Rudolph Susel, "A Great American, A Great Slovenian," *American Home*, April 26, 1990.

Index

C

C. Brown Hoist Company, 256
Cabbage Patch, 28
Cagney, James, 377
Calhoun, John C., 289
Call & Post, 118
Call Me Mike (Zimmerman), 340
Calvary Cemetery, 393
Camp Gordon, Atlanta, GA, 56
canals
    construction of, 23
    demise of, 25
capitalism, development of, 31
Carinthia, 384–385
Carlson, Frank, 298
    member SFRC, 314
Carlucci, Frank, 384
Carmichael, Stokely, 307
Carniola, 33, 35
Carniolan sausage (*kranjske klobase*), 31
Carter Hotel, 273, 355
Carter, Jimmy, 374–375
Carter, Lorenzo, 23, 24
Case Against Congress, The, 287
Case, Clifford, 331
    member SFRC, 314
Case-Western Reserve University, See Western
    Reserve University
Case, William, 25
castles of Slovenia, 30
Castro, Fidel, 315
Catholic Church, Slovenes' allegiance to, 37
Catholic Knights of Lithuania, 386
Cayton, Andrew R. L., 397
Cedar Point Beach, 225
Celebrezze, Anthony J.
    future mayor of Cleveland, 108
    honorary pallbearer, 393
    Lausche clone, 105, 214, 343
Celebrezze, Anthony J., Jr., 388
Celebrezze, Frank, 88, 108, 122
Celeste, Richard, 222, 376
    honorary pallbearer, 393
Central Institute Preparatory School, 53, 54
Champlin, Marion Elizabeth, 99
Chandler, Albert "Happy," 155, 156
Charmley, John, 380
Charter Party, 348

Charterite movement, 197
Chase, Russell N., 191–192
Chatfield, David, 245
Chesapeake and Ohio Railroad, 157
Chicago lakefront, 85
Chicago *Tribune*, 356
Chicken Village, 28, 35
Child Health Association, 259
Chiles, Lawton, 391
Church, Bethine, 309
Church, Frank, 299, 309, 316–317, 327
    liberal senator, 285
    member SFRC, 314
    open dissenter, 326
    resolution to end aid to South Vietnam, 321
Churchill, Winston, 380
Cincinnati City Council, 348
Cincinnati *Enquirer*, 134, 141, 144, 219, 330
Cincinnati, orderly expansion of, 205
Cincinnati *Post and Times Star*, 134
cities, danger in taking federal subsidies, 356
Citizens for Decency Through Law, 222
Citizens for Decent Literature (CDL), 222
Citizens for Gilligan, 352
citizenship exam, 40
City Club of Cleveland, 251
    "Citadel of Free Speech," 62
city manager plan
    Cleveland, 60–61, 72, 73
    demise of, 73
city-states in Ohio, 206
civic rot, 45
civil defense, 111, 184
civil disobedience, 332
Civil Rights Act of 1960, 306
Civil Rights Act of 1964, 306
Civil War, Cleveland's part in, 24
Civilian Conservation Corps (CCC), 212
Civilian Service Corps, 259
Clark, Joseph, 330
    member SFRC, 314
Clay, General Lucius, 317
Clay, Henry, 289
"clear and present danger, a," 193
Cleaveland, Moses, 23
Clegg, William, 85

School Alumni Association, 79; emanated sincerity, 398; an enigma and a maverick, 397; entered mixed marriage, 258; and family responsibility, 51; and family values, 52; a great communicator, 402; as greatest Slovenian, 21; honesty, 171, 398; joviality, 172; known as "Curleytop," 208; lives with in-laws, 71; as a lonely man, 173; love of poetry, 128; as low-handicap golfer, 172; moody, 289; musical abilities of, 69; oration, 103; physical appearance, 78; played the violin, 223; preferred basic meals, 260; pride, 157; Renaissance man, 100; sense of duty, 41; skills as bowler and billiard player, 64; and Slovenian heritage, 22; and Slovenian principles, 12; smoked nickel cigars, 223; as "the man who walks alone," 16; third child of Slovenian parents, 11; trusted by Ohioans, 207, 401; violin playing, 69

considered for president: affinity for Eisenhower, 238; antipathy toward boss-ridden labor unions, 245; believer in state's rights, 239; categorized self as conservative liberal, 245; conservatism of, 240; considered as Eisenhower's running mate, 243; constant crossing of party lines, 240; conviction in a two-party system, 244; on covers of major magazines, 239; debt reduction, 244; declined to respond to inquiries to questionnaire, 241; endorsed president's veto of farm bill, 246; entered state's presidential primary, 246; against extravagant extension of credit, 246; favorite-son candidate for President, 236, 246; a great patriot, 242; Gunter said Lausche a man to watch, 236; handicaps in national image, 239; hoped Eisenhower would be Republican candidate, 244; independence of, 237; Lausche a rising star in the party, 238; not a factor in 1952 election, 236; not indebted to city machines or labor, 239; offered to run as Truman's vice president, 236; refusal to back Democratic Party organization, 240; religious issue, 243; running in Ohio's primary, 243; support for Benson's changes, 237; support of

conservative southern Democrats, 241; supported Adlai Stevenson, 237; surplus farm products, 244; Taft-Hartley Act, 244; urged fair employment practice act, 240; visits Eisenhower, 242; would support a Democrat, 244

early political years: first political break, 73; race for Ohio state senate seat, 63; race for the Ohio state assembly, 62–63; September 1928 meeting with Seltzer, 99; talent as orator, 62–63; turns down pleas to run for mayor in 1935, 1937, and 1939, 98; as ward leader, 75–76

early years: birth of, 15, 39; introduction to Jane Sheal, 64; marriage to Jane, 16, 64

education: Central Institute Preparatory School, 53; high school correspondence course, 53; law degree, 16; Madison Grammer School, 53; St. Vitus grade school, 53

employment: case against Harry Payer, 63–64; court interpreter, 54; lighting gas street lamps, 54; Locher, Green, and Woods, 58; Ohio state bar exam, 59; taught law class at John Marshall School of Law, 63, 79

fifth term as governor: $60 million surplus in state coffers, 401; agreed with *Brown* decision, 226; under attack for holding back highway monies, 228; avoided cronyism, 223; became friends with Rhodes, 220; became nation's senior governor, 221; capital improvements, 225; compassionate in clemency matters, 224; crackdown on Teamsters Unions, 230; elimination (proposed) of three state board, 225; failed to inaugurate needed capital investments, 230; fair employment practices laws, 230; film censorship law, constitutionality of, 222; fiscal responsibility, 229; frugal fiscal policies, 224; governorship produced the greatest acclaim, 368; highway improvement program, 401; improved statewide highways, 230; independence from the Democratic Party, 229; "Keep issues out of campaigns," 229; mixed bag review of his tenure, 228–229; no general tax increase,

224; opened Ohio Turnpike, 227; plan
to retire to law practice in 1952, 208;
"Plant Ohio" campaign, 224; plea for soil
conservation, 224; proposed north-south
highway, 227; record of parsimonious
honesty, 231; reputation for fairness, 229;
says he could have been elected to sixth
term, 232; showed honesty and integrity,
229; spent little on children's services,
231; stance against obscenity in literature
and movies, 222; state park system
flourished, 225; strengthened workmen's
compensation, 230; strip miners, 224;
support of Shocknessy, 227; took oath in
small ceremony, 223

fourth term as governor: advocates some
higher taxes, 209; agreement with
Federal Bureau of Public Lands, 210;
appointed Burke as Senator, 213; asked
Seltzer to take Senate appointment, 213;
attended Republican reception, 208–209;
conservation of natural resources, 212;
declined offer for District of Columbia
Circuit Court seat, 215; discusses fifth
term possibilities, 215; extensive debt
financing, 401; fiscal economy, 209;
improved statewide highways, 210;
launched *Plant Ohio* campaign, 212;
must appoint successor to Taft, 213;
Ohio Turnpike, 401; Ohio's favorite-
son candidate (1952), 184; opposition
to strip mining, 212; Plant Ohio Today
for Tomorrow, 401; planting of trees,
212; polarized feelings about him, 339;
politically erratic behavior, 209; possible
VP nominee, 184; praised Senator
Burke, 214; pressure felt on senatorial
appointment, 237; restoration of natural
resources, 401; takes oath of office, 209;
wanted strip-mining lands restored, 401;
wanted to be US senator, 213; wanted
to restrict government spending, 400;
wouldn't ask for additional tax monies,
401

as Governor: building of prisons, 201;
campaign for re-election, 147; disregard
for pressure groups, 144; distraught
over defeat, 150; efforts against strikers,

141; election, 16; failure to maintain
close ties with constituency, 150; fiscal
responsibility, 143; four basic tenets,
142; Inauguration Day, 140–141; labor's
disenchantment with Lausche, 150; loss in
re-election, 149–150; move to Columbus,
140; reforestation, 145; retention of
Republicans, 141; salary, 140; strip-
mining, restriction of, 145; success as
Governor, 145

gubernatorial run 1948: attack on Herbert,
160–161; campaigning in primary,
159; declared candidacy, 158; defeat of
Miller, 160; dislike of party bossism, 159;
general election campaign, 160–167; joins
Truman train, 163; position on Truman,
162; support for Truman, 164; wins
election, 166

health: admitted to Bethesda Naval
Hospital, 295, 316, 320, 327;
appendectomy operation, 81; contracted
Asian bug, 320; contracts pneumonia,
392; died of congestive heart failure, 392;
enters Bethesda Naval Hospital, 392;
enters Slovenian Home for the Aged, 392;
rumors of heart attack, 295

honorary celebration: 100th birthday
anniversary, 11

ideas, beliefs, opinions: admiration for
Abraham Lincoln, 207; adversary of
communism, 400; Communism, hatred
of, 17; concern for community, 12;
confirmed hawk, 400; as conservative,
22; as Democrat, 11, 63; dislike of party
bossism, 98; disregard for race or religion,
101; fight against discrimination, 115;
and free enterprise, 12; identification with
FDR, 114; independence of, 16, 71; as a
Jeffersonian Democrat, 100; left of center
views, 100; legacy of, 13; "Lincoln of
Ohio," 339; man of conscience, 403; as
man of the people, 17; not beholden to
party leaders, union officials or lobbyists,
398; and organized labor, 81; personal
political philosophy, 130; political
independence, 130; principles of, 17;
refusal of Miller's political offers, 74–75;
renounced Democrats domestic programs,

402; resists pressure to run for office, 97; stringent fiscal policies, 184; and support of Reagan, 12; voted for Taft, 182–183; voting for Republican presidential candidates, 17

as Judge: appointment to municipal court judge, 76; asked to serve second term, 91–92; cleaning up racketeering, 86; common pleas judge, 81; and corrupt labor unions, 91; Cuyahoga County Court of Common Pleas, 16; and divorce decrees, 82; and domestic relations court, 82; eradicated gambling and underworld activities, 97–98; fairness and caution in his decisions, 96; Fearless Frank, 16; and gambling, 16; and gambling clubs, 88; hope for appointment as federal judge, 208; judgeship most satisfying, 368; as municipal court judge, 16, 76–80; non-partisanship, 78; and organized gambling and crime, 83; race for common pleas court, 80–81; re-election (1993), 77; resignation from Common Pleas bench, 102; shutting down gambling clubs, 90–91

as lame duck: announced he would vote for Richard Nixon, 369–370; decided to stay in Bethesda, 371; says inflation caused by extravagant spending, 370

as Mayor: and 1932 mayoral campaign, 73–74; abolishment of pinball machines, 108; accepts Ness resignation, 108; animosity between unions and Lausche, 112–114, 120; avoided nepotism, 106; city planning, 109; East Ohio Gas Explosion, 12; editorial imploring him to seek office as mayor, 96; end of strikes during war, 110; "Everybody's Mayor," 128; increase in number of playgrounds, 111; Labor Management Committee, 112–114; labor unions, antagonism toward, 113; Mayor's War Production Committee, 110; problems of, 16; retains Ness as Safety Director, 106–107; run for second term, 115; showing political independence, 107; split with Miller, 107; and start of World War II, 108; strict law enforcement, 109; support of CIO, 115;

support of newspapers toward Ness, 107; suppression of political cronyism, 109; took oath of office 11/10/41, 105; veto of wage raise, 120; victory in '43 campaign, 115–116

out-of-office: accepted position as counsel for lobby, 157; return to Cleveland (1947), 153

political style: as a great actor, 178; similarities with Coolidge, 178

race for mayor: agreed to run for mayor, 102; believed buses answer future transportation needs, 103; concern for exodus of inhabitants from Cleveland, 104; disdain for large contributions, 104; dislike of party bossism, 101; independence from party influence, 103; and rehabilitation of youthful criminals, 101; support from newspapers in election, 105; support of local Democratic organization, 103

religious activities: attended St. Vitus when in Cleveland, 258; as Catholic, 127; first communion, 53

retirement: accompanied Ford on Air Force One, 375; appeared before SFRC, 382; became unkempt, 391; death of, 15; defended Rhode's calling out Ohio National Guard, 376; devotion to one's country had place in modern society, 373; dropped off the political stage, 373; drove until he was 94, 391; endorsed James Rhodes, 376; endorsed Richard Nixon, 374; endorsed Ronald Reagan, 376; established foundation, 377; established memorial fund in honor of Ma Lausche, 377; frequent trips to Cleveland, 371; golfed at Burning Tree, 389, 391; hated pornography, 373; a Jeffersonian Democrat, 384; large birthday parties, 387; Lausche State Office Building dedicated, 387; law office with Frost and Tower, 371; a lonely man after Jane's death, 389; name inscribed on plaque, 385; named Knight of St. John of Malta by Pope John Paul II, 386; named Slovenian of the year, 386; named to Delta Theta Phi, 386; quits golf at age 91, 392;

received 15 honorary degrees, 385; refusal to visit Slovenia, 378; served as chair of Ohio Citizens for Republican Bob Taft, Jr., 374; Slovenian-related activities, 377–378; spends more time with Jane, 389; supported Gerald Ford, 375; supported Robert Taft, Jr., 375; teaching of the Bible had place in modern society, 373; tempted to run for 6th term as governor, 372; visits sister once a month, 390; went to weekly Senate Prayer Breakfast, 391; would eat Slovenian food at Ertzens, 390; would not have voted for Abe Fortas, 374

run for fifth term: accused of paying off friends, 217; campaign techniques, 208; defends self against mudslinging, 218; endorsed St. Lawrence seaway, 217, 218; fifth term issue, 219; friend of the Negroes, 208; liquor scandal, 217; more funds for mental institutions, 218; picture taken with segregationist Talmadge, 218; proposes north-south turnpike, 218; received newspaper endorsements, 219; revision of the utility rate laws, 218; spoke on television, 218; victory for Lausche, 219

run for fourth term: advocated raising some taxes, 199; charisma and folksy campaign style, 202; endorsed Stevenson for president, 198; favorite-son candidate for President, 196; greeted Eisenhower, 200; inmate riot at Ohio Penitentiary, 200; loner and independent, 199; pressure from Taft, 198; put down commercial gambling, 199; ran unopposed in primary, 196; strip-mining, 200; support of newspapers, 199; supported DiSalle, 198; trust of people, 202; Turnpike behind schedule, 198; unprecedented (1952), 196; win because of split ticket voting, 201; wins election, 201

run for governor: bid for southern Ohio voters, 133–134; campaigning as Catholic, 133; campaigning in rural areas, 133; care for the mentally ill, 136; clean administration, 136; conservation of natural resources, 129; declared candidacy, 129; defense of FDR, 129–130; election

charges, 129; fight against bossism, 135–136; government frugality, 136; honesty in finances, 139; observation of strip mining, 131; and party bosses, 139; primary election campaigning, 129; race for Governor, 121; rehabilitation of state's welfare programs, 129; rejected campaign funds, 135; remission of wages while campaigning, 131, 133, 140; retention of natural resources, 136; skills as orator, 136; support of newspapers, 137; support of southern counties, 130; victory in primary, 131; warns against lobbyists, 158; wins election, 137

second campaign for Senate re-election: accused Gilligan of trying to buy senate seat, 357–358; age 72, 356; anti-labor position, 341; attack on party bosses, 354–355; avoided specific issues, 363; declined to debate, 358; downfall in densely populated areas, 361; favored civil rights legislation, 362; felt cities in danger from federal subsidies, 356; felt Stokes had denounced him, 345; had outlived his time, 369; hurt by state Democratic Party, 353; inveterate hand-shaker, 353; lost black support, 342, 362; lost ethnic voters, 362; low campaign costs, 359; no campaign organization, 352; not relevant to modern America, 368; older voters greatest strength, 349; and organized labor, 340–342; popularity waning, 340; reacted to pressure of tight race, 359–360; received press endorsements, 356; released statement, 351–352; right-to-work sacrosanct, 341; says labor buying senate seat, 360; sense of relief at loss, 368; support of newspapers, 360; tacit backing to Locher, 344; turned down endorsement from Democratic National Chairman, 361

as second term governor: administration, 168; budget woes, 169; capital improvements, 169; creation of Ohio State Department of Natural Resources, 171; creation of Ohio Turnpike Commission, 171; declared not a candidate for Senator (1949), 174; established precedent, 169; fought increase of teacher salaries, 169;

hard working governor, 171–172; lack of administrative skills, 171; penny pinching, 170; as a reactive politician, 170; shortfall in revenue, 169; social get-togethers, 173; sought favorable publicity, 170; strained relations with labor leaders, 171; urged Truman to seek re-election, 184; visit with Truman, 184

as Senator: absent 26% of Monday and Friday roll calls, 300; acreage reserve program, attempted to remove, 283; actively campaigned only 10 days, 295; admiration for Eisenhower, 280; always late for committee meetings, 329; announced candidacy for second term, 293; anti-communist stand, 148, 315; antipathy for Marshal Tito, 313; appointment to banking committee, 282; appointment to commerce committee, 282; appointment to foreign relations committee (SFRC), 282, 307; attack on State Department, 317–319; attacked Case, 331; attacks on communist-led countries, 300; attacks on distribution of pornography, 300; attended Atlantic City convention, 302; avoided travel to communist countries, 320; believed in balanced budget, 292; believed split precluded military victory, 330; campaigned with Kennedy in Ohio, 291; challenged counter culture movement, 302; challenged labor bosses, 302; challenged lobbyists, 302; challenges of, 17; for civil rights legislation, 306; on commerce committee, 283; communism, public denouncement of, 192; complete gubernatorial term, 280; conservative fiscal philosophy, 300; considered North Vietnam the aggressor, 329; critical of Kennedy's foreign aid program, 316; decided precedence of issues, 300; defended Johnson on senate floor, 331; Democratic primary re-election campaign, 336; detested Johnson, 306; devotion to the country, 296; did not attend 1960 Democratic Convention, 291; did not attend Cuyahoga County steer roast, 290; did not campaign in second Senate

primary, 294; did not maintain home office in Ohio, 297; disliked rapid growth of federal bureaucracy, 304; disturbed by rioting after King assassination, 306–307; encouraged rumors that he would vote Republican to organize Senate, 280; endorsed Clay Doctrine, 317; endorsed Johnson for President, 303; erosion of power base, 290; experienced unfavorable reviews in Ohio press, 292; faced re-election in 1968, 330; favored halt to bombing, 331; favored sound fiscal practices, 292; favorite-son candidate for President, 290; felt political vulnerability, 330; felt Southeast Asia US's first line of defense, 323; few political speeches, 295; financial standings, 286–287; foreign relations close to his heart, 328; forwarded Cuban information to Kennedy and Fulbright, 316; fought $11 billion tax cut, 302; fought against Great Society legislation, 304; fought establishment of Domestic Peace Corps, 302; fought excessive expenditures of federal funds, 302; fought for value of reputation, 288; fought increasing governmental centralization, 304; fought ravages of strip mining, 301–302; fought to reduce subsidies to companies, 304; friends with Nixon, 310; frugality in government spending, 284; gave touching Kennedy eulogy, 302; had 17-member staff, 297; had all-white office staff, 297; had lunch with Anastas Mikoyan, 311; hard-line opposition toward communism, 309; hated $300 billion national debt, 295; hated unbalanced budgets, inflation and higher taxes, 305; helped Hungarians, 313; image of intelligent conservative, 294; joined Democratic motorcade with Kennedy, 290; meeting with Johnson, 303–304; member SFRC, 400; modern-day advocate of small government, 292; nation must practice economy, 283; no aid to Tito-run Yugoslavia, 317; northern Harry Byrd, 17; office females did not wear miniskirts, 298; one of Fulbright's crosses, 333; opposition to federal aid to

pilot, 270; extolled the virtues of Ohio, 269–270; gained her pilot's license, 270; Methodist, 257; musical abilities of, 69; playing the piano, 262; praised by Louis Seltzer, 272

early years: artistic talents, 257; birth, 256; Cleveland Art School, 257; Flora Stone Mather College, 257; Glen Eden finishing school, 257; Laurel Institute, 257

Executive Mansion: all new plumbing, 267; auditors itemized household contents, 267; challenge in refurbishing, 260; on cover of *American Rose Magazine*, 267; daily frustrating problems, 262; entertained Margaret Truman, 264; experience as interior decorator, 261; filled mansion with Ohio-made products, 268; first resided in Neil House, 260; gardened and landscaped, 140, 267; "gubernatorial barn," 260; hidden light switches, 260; holding organizational meetings, 262; humorous anecdotes, 261; Lausche siblings gathered at mansion, 266; managing the governor's mansion, 260; mansion budget, 262–263; "most unhome-like place you can imagine," 260; musical session, 266; new electrical wiring, 267; office on the second floor, 262; purchased draperies, 268; raised chickens after WWII, 263; raised garden produce, 267; repainted the kitchen, 268; responsibilities at the mansion, 270; unusable article placed in garage, 267; upkeep of mansion, 261; used trusted prisoners, 271

family responsibilities: called to Florida, 264; father moved to Washington with the Lausches, 257; parents moved with the Lausches to governor's mansion, 257

as Frank's wife: acceptance into Lausche clan, 258; accused of being divorced, 138; apartment in Cleveland, 263; asset to Frank, 64, 116; attractive First Lady, 17; "better than Mrs. Roosevelt," 260; bought new fur coat, 105; commercial artist, 116; divorce of parents, 257; entered mixed marriage, 258; escorted Eleanor Roosevelt, 265; First Lady of Cleveland, 259; Frank

nicknamed her Mick, 257; his number one asset, 271; honeymoon in Washington, DC, 258; learned Slovenian cooking, 69; learned Slovenian language, 69; long engagement, 257; loved Ma Lausche, 258; marriage in a small wedding, 16, 64, 257; moved in with Jane's parents, 258; perfect fit for politician, 256; purchased a fur jacket, 267; received Mr. and Mrs. Henry J. Morganthau, 259; received note from Barry Wood, 221; return to mansion, 263; selected husband's wardrobe, 172; socializing, 263; substituted for husband on campaign trail, 260, 272, 273; urged to buy US Savings Bonds, 259; witnessed private oath taking, 183; worked as commercial artist, 258; worked in charitable organizations, 259; years of public service, 256

health: accidents, 276; diet, 273; fell, fractured left hip and left forearm, 276; hospitalized because of auto accident, 295; lead poisoning, 258, 272–273; received financial compensation for accident, 276

organizational abilities: contrived a home filing system, 259; kept a file on all of Frank's cases, 258; penchant for orderliness, 259; took care of absent-minded husband, 259

retirement: did not encourage Lausche to run for 6th term as governor, 373; died in her sleep, 1981, 277, 389; established memorial fund in honor of Ma Lausche, 377; spends more time with Frank, 389; split time between Bethesda and Cleveland, 277

Senate years: accidents, 276; accompanied husband overseas, 320; accompanied Ladybird Johnson to political rally, 302; announced she would vote for Young, 286; condensed newspaper articles for Frank, 276; condensed reports for Frank, 276; grew vegetables and flowers, 275; joined International Neighbors organization, 275; joined US Senate Wives Red Cross Unit, 275; lived in small apartment, 274; purchased new home in Bethesda, MD, 274; regretted leaving Columbus, 274;

said she didn't know who husband would vote for, 302; shocked by real estate prices, 274; would not comment on political issues, 276

Lausche, Josephine (Welf) (sister)
alive after Jane's death, 389
distinguished self, 39
musical abilities of, 70
recalls winery, 40
recording artist, 81
retirement: burial in Cleveland's Calvary Cemetery, 389
and string trio, 78
visited by Frank once a month, 390

Lausche, Louis Jr. (brother)
death of, 15, 40–41, 53
died at age 17, 39
musical abilities of, 69

Lausche, Louis Sr. (father)
death of, 40
Frank received practical experience from, 15
as interpreter, 39–40

Lausche Republicans, 403
Taft's efforts to win back, 198

Lausche, Ruth, 311

Lausche State Office Building, 387

Lausche, William (brother), 39
musical abilities of, 69, 70
and string trio, 78

Lavelle, Martin J., 85

Lawrence, David, 239, 243

Lawrence Jerome, 265

Lawrence, MA baseball team, 56

Lawrence, Wes, 85

Leacacos, John P., 345

League of Women Voters, 104

League Park, 60

Ledbetter, Eleanor E., 49–50

Lee, J. Bracken, 241

Lee, Robert Edwin, 265

Legislative Service Commission, 225

LeMay, General Curtis, 265

Lemon, James, 371

Lenin Peace Prize, 311

Leonard, Benny, 56

Lewis, Fulton Jr., 239

Lewis, John L., 114, 341

Lewis, Sinclair, 247

Life Magazine, 99, 288

Lincoln, Abraham, 116, 207, 402

Lincoln, Murray T., 178

Lincoln Savings and Loan Bank, 222

Lindenberg, Charles H., 260

Lithuania, 319

Little Bromo, See Seltzer, Louis B.

Little Italy, 28

Little Rock Central High School, 186, 226

Ljubljana, 30, 32, 37, 378, 383

lobbyists, Lausche warns against, 158

Locher, Cyrus W., 58–59, 62

Locher, Green, and Woods, 58, 64

Locher, John, 106

Locher, Ralph S.
appointed as Executive Secretary, 168
called Lausche a "working governor," 171
honorary pallbearer, 393
Lausche clone, 105, 343
served two terms as mayor, 214

Locke, John, 385

Lokar, John E., Jr.
liquor permit scandal, 159
president of Lausche Booster Club, 78
ran Lausche gubernatorial campaign, 129, 133
secretary for governor, 140
still alive after Jane's death, 389

London *Daily Express*, urged Red China be admitted to UN and be given diplomatic recognition, 311

"Lonely One, The," 245

Long, Russell
attacked Case, 331
member SFRC, 314
from oil-producing state, 372
wanted all-out military effort, 326

Looking Backward 2000-1888 (Bellamy), 99

Los Angeles *Times*, 382

Lovše, Charles, 38

Lovše, Frank, 37

Lovše, George, 38

Lovše, Jacob, 38

Lovše, Lojze (later Louis Lausche), 38

Lovše, Mary Jaklitsch, 37

loyalty oath on OSU, 188

Lucas, Scott, 52, 299

Z